RED RASCAL'S WAR

Recent Collections

Virtual Doonesbury
Planet Doonesbury
Buck Wild Doonesbury
Duke 2000: Whatever It Takes
The Revolt of the English Majors
Peace Out, Dawg!
Got War?
Talk to the Hand
Heckuva Job, Bushie!
Welcome to the Nerd Farm!
Tee Time in Berzerkistan

Anthologies

The Doonesbury Chronicles
Doonesbury's Greatest Hits
The People's Doonesbury
Doonesbury Dossier: The Reagan Years
Doonesbury Deluxe: Selected Glances Askance
Recycled Doonesbury: Second Thoughts on a Gilded Age
The Portable Doonesbury
The Bundled Doonesbury
40: A Doonesbury Retrospective

Special Collections

Action Figure!: The Life and Times of Doonesbury's Uncle Duke
Dude: The Big Book of Zonker
Flashbacks: Twenty-Five Years of Doonesbury
The Long Road Home: One Step at a Time
The War Within: One More Step at a Time
The Sandbox: Dispatches from Troops in Iraq and Afghanistan
The War in Quotes
Signature Wound: Rocking TBI
"My Shorts R Bunching. Thoughts?": The Tweets of Roland Hedley

RED RASCAL'S WAR

A DOONESBURY BOOK
by G. B. TRUDEAU

Andrews McMeel
Publishing, LLC
Kansas City • Sydney • London

DOONESBURY is distributed internationally by Universal Uclick.

Andrews McMeel Publishing, LLC
an Andrews McMeel Universal company
1130 Walnut Street, Kansas City, Missouri 64106
www.andrewsmcmeel.com

11 12 13 14 15 TEN 10 9 8 7 6 5 4 3 2 1

ISBN: 978-1-4494-0820-6

Library of Congress Control Number: 2011926187

DOONESBURY may be viewed on the Internet at
www.doonesbury.com and www.GoComics.com.

"War is God's way of teaching Americans geography."
—Ambrose Bierce

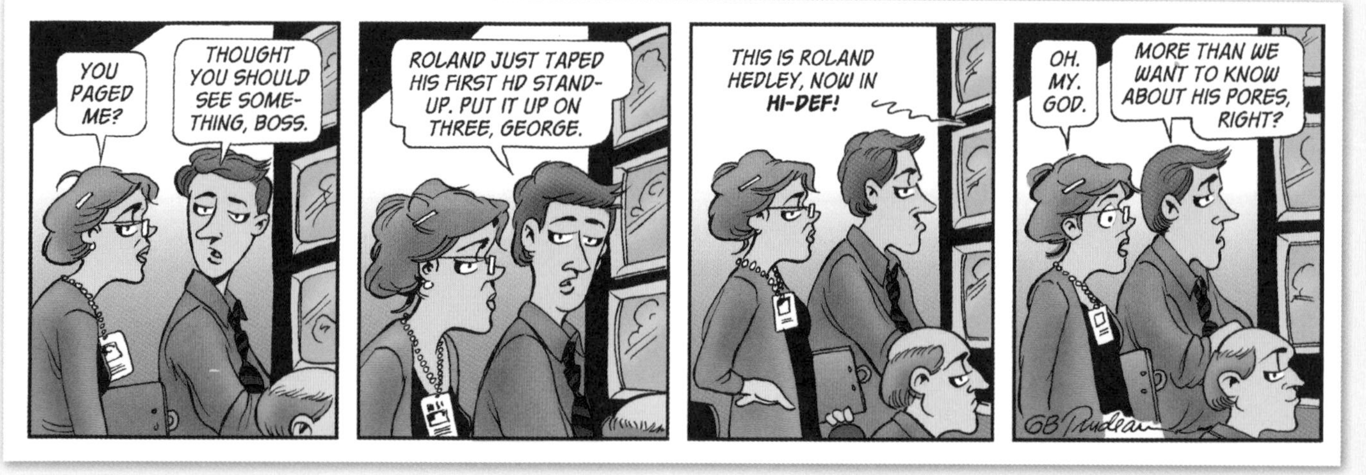
YOU PAGED ME?
THOUGHT YOU SHOULD SEE SOME-THING, BOSS.
ROLAND JUST TAPED HIS FIRST HD STAND-UP. PUT IT UP ON THREE, GEORGE.
THIS IS ROLAND HEDLEY, NOW IN **HI-DEF!**
OH. MY. GOD.
MORE THAN WE WANT TO KNOW ABOUT HIS PORES, RIGHT?
GB Trudeau

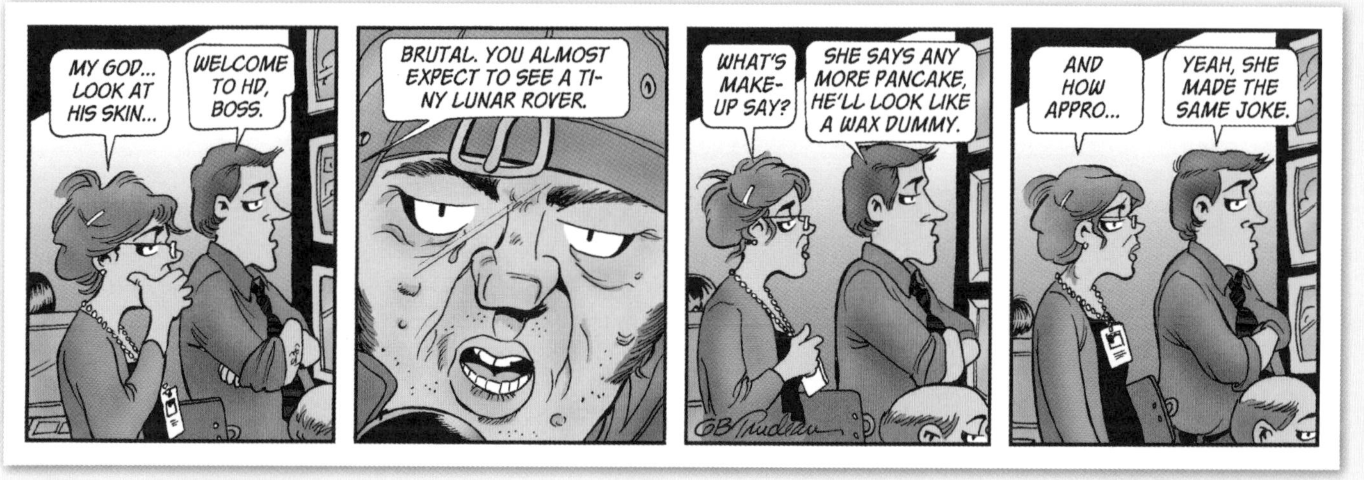
MY GOD... LOOK AT HIS SKIN...
WELCOME TO HD, BOSS.
BRUTAL. YOU ALMOST EXPECT TO SEE A TI-NY LUNAR ROVER.
WHAT'S MAKE-UP SAY?
SHE SAYS ANY MORE PANCAKE, HE'LL LOOK LIKE A WAX DUMMY.
GB Trudeau
AND HOW APPRO...
YEAH, SHE MADE THE SAME JOKE.

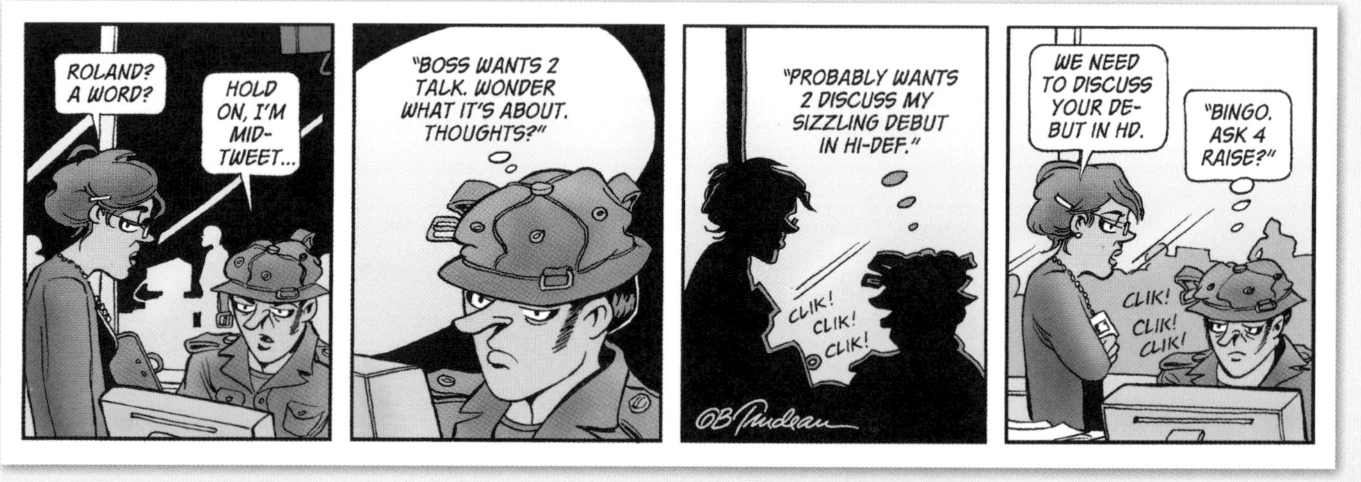
ROLAND? A WORD?
HOLD ON, I'M MID-TWEET...
"BOSS WANTS 2 TALK. WONDER WHAT IT'S ABOUT. THOUGHTS?"
"PROBABLY WANTS 2 DISCUSS MY SIZZLING DEBUT IN HI-DEF."
CLIK! CLIK! CLIK!
GB Trudeau
WE NEED TO DISCUSS YOUR DE-BUT IN HD.
"BINGO. ASK 4 RAISE?"
CLIK! CLIK! CLIK!

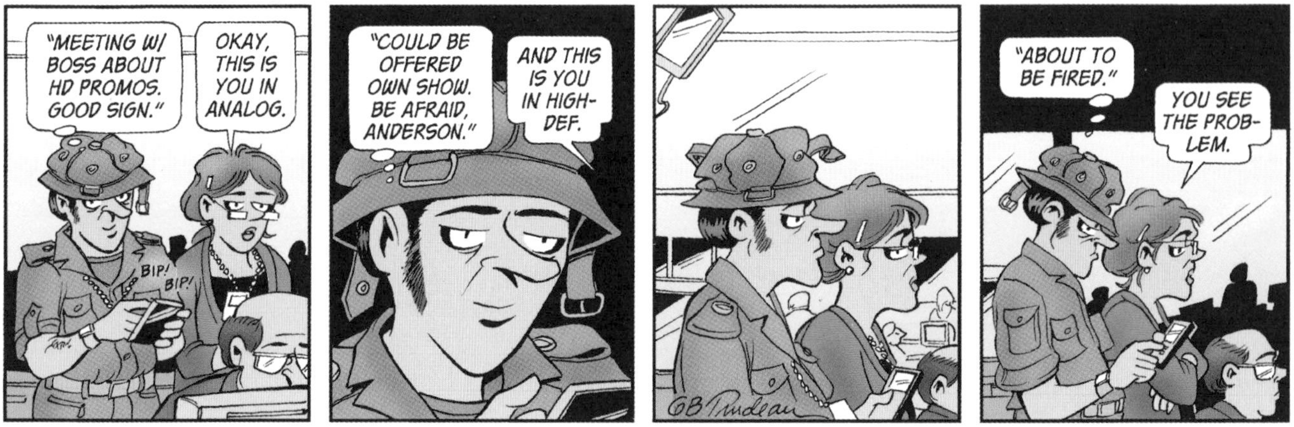
"MEETING W/ BOSS ABOUT HD PROMOS. GOOD SIGN."
OKAY, THIS IS YOU IN ANALOG.
BIP! BIP!
"COULD BE OFFERED OWN SHOW. BE AFRAID, ANDERSON."
AND THIS IS YOU IN HIGH-DEF.
"ABOUT TO BE FIRED."
YOU SEE THE PROBLEM.

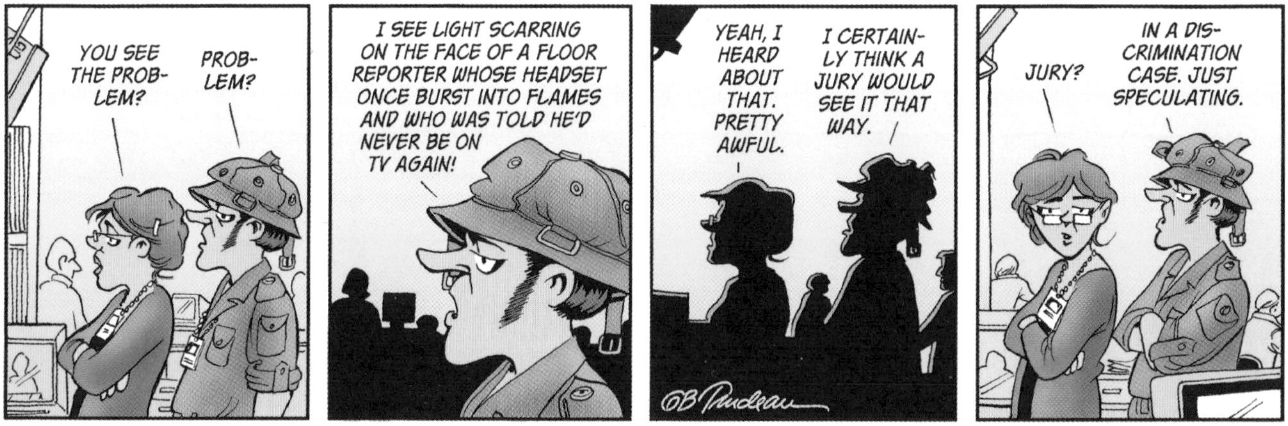
YOU SEE THE PROBLEM?
PROBLEM?
I SEE LIGHT SCARRING ON THE FACE OF A FLOOR REPORTER WHOSE HEADSET ONCE BURST INTO FLAMES AND WHO WAS TOLD HE'D NEVER BE ON TV AGAIN!
YEAH, I HEARD ABOUT THAT. PRETTY AWFUL.
I CERTAINLY THINK A JURY WOULD SEE IT THAT WAY.
JURY?
IN A DISCRIMINATION CASE. JUST SPECULATING.

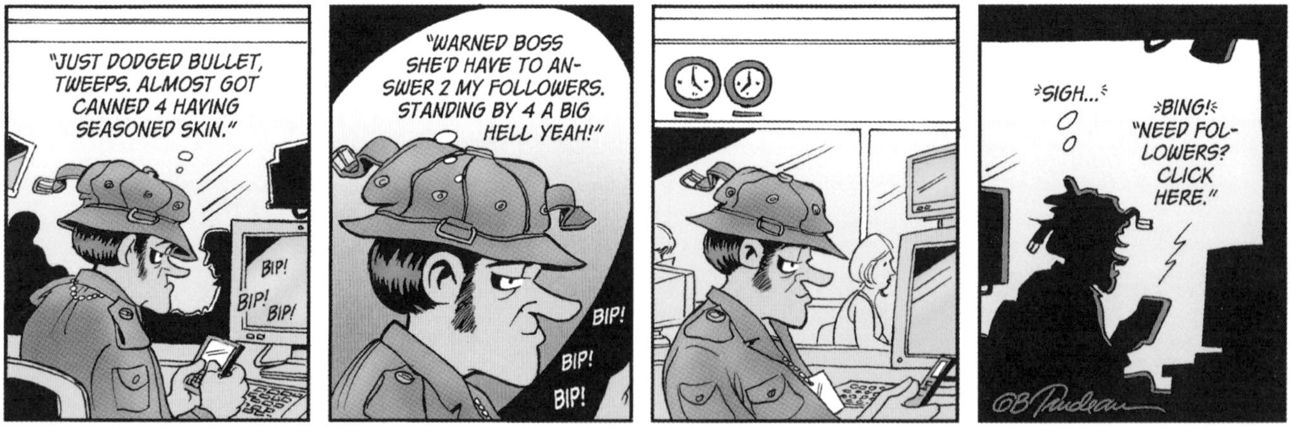
"JUST DODGED BULLET, TWEEPS. ALMOST GOT CANNED 4 HAVING SEASONED SKIN."
BIP! BIP! BIP!
"WARNED BOSS SHE'D HAVE TO ANSWER 2 MY FOLLOWERS. STANDING BY 4 A BIG HELL YEAH!"
BIP! BIP! BIP!
SIGH...
BING! "NEED FOLLOWERS? CLICK HERE."

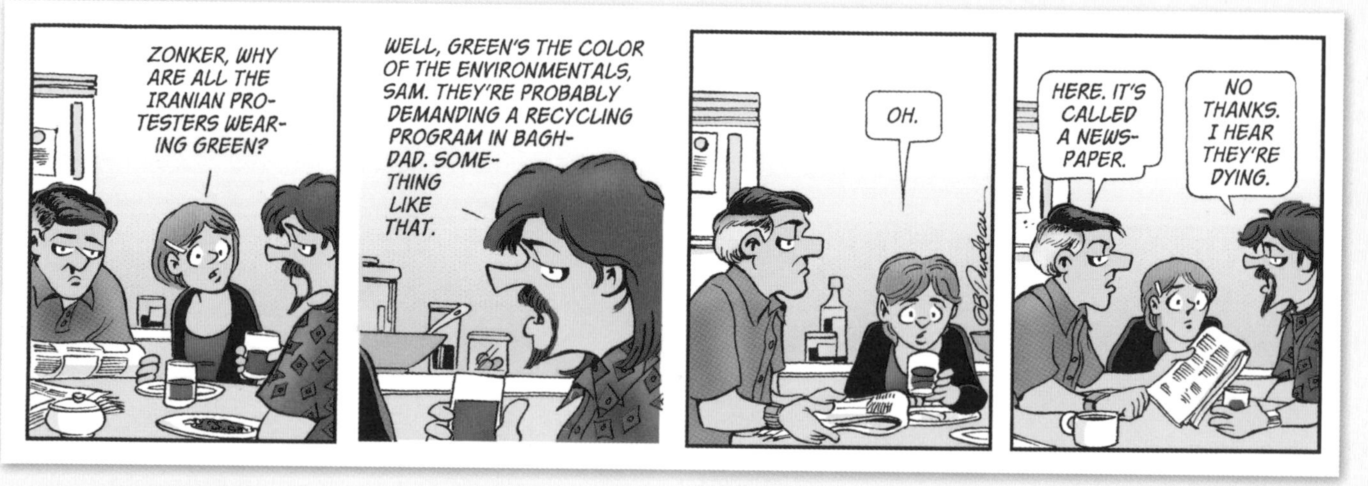
ZONKER, WHY ARE ALL THE IRANIAN PROTESTERS WEARING GREEN?
WELL, GREEN'S THE COLOR OF THE ENVIRONMENTALS, SAM. THEY'RE PROBABLY DEMANDING A RECYCLING PROGRAM IN BAGHDAD. SOMETHING LIKE THAT.
OH.
HERE. IT'S CALLED A NEWSPAPER.
NO THANKS. I HEAR THEY'RE DYING.

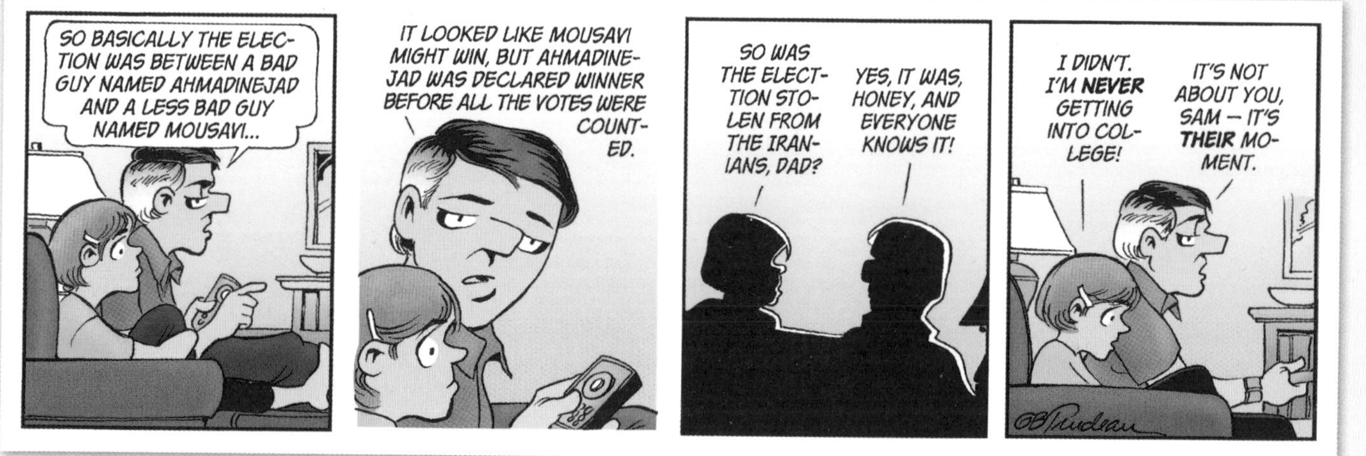
SO BASICALLY THE ELECTION WAS BETWEEN A BAD GUY NAMED AHMADINEJAD AND A LESS BAD GUY NAMED MOUSAVI...
IT LOOKED LIKE MOUSAVI MIGHT WIN, BUT AHMADINEJAD WAS DECLARED WINNER BEFORE ALL THE VOTES WERE COUNTED.
SO WAS THE ELECTION STOLEN FROM THE IRANIANS, DAD?
YES, IT WAS, HONEY, AND EVERYONE KNOWS IT!
I DIDN'T. I'M **NEVER** GETTING INTO COLLEGE!
IT'S NOT ABOUT YOU, SAM — IT'S **THEIR** MOMENT.

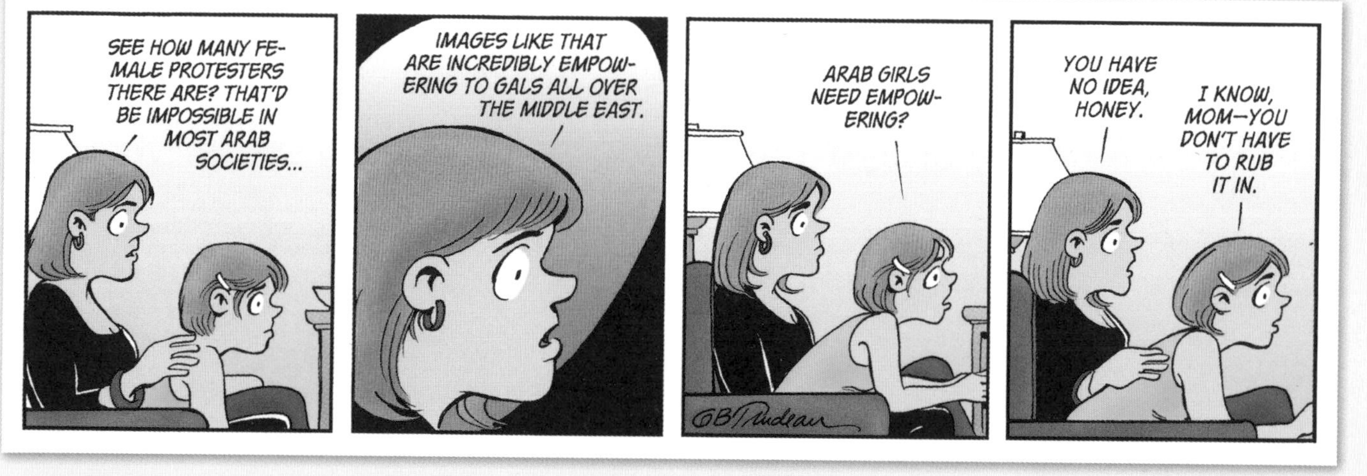
SEE HOW MANY FEMALE PROTESTERS THERE ARE? THAT'D BE IMPOSSIBLE IN MOST ARAB SOCIETIES...
IMAGES LIKE THAT ARE INCREDIBLY EMPOWERING TO GALS ALL OVER THE MIDDLE EAST.
ARAB GIRLS NEED EMPOWERING?
YOU HAVE NO IDEA, HONEY.
I KNOW, MOM—YOU DON'T HAVE TO RUB IT IN.

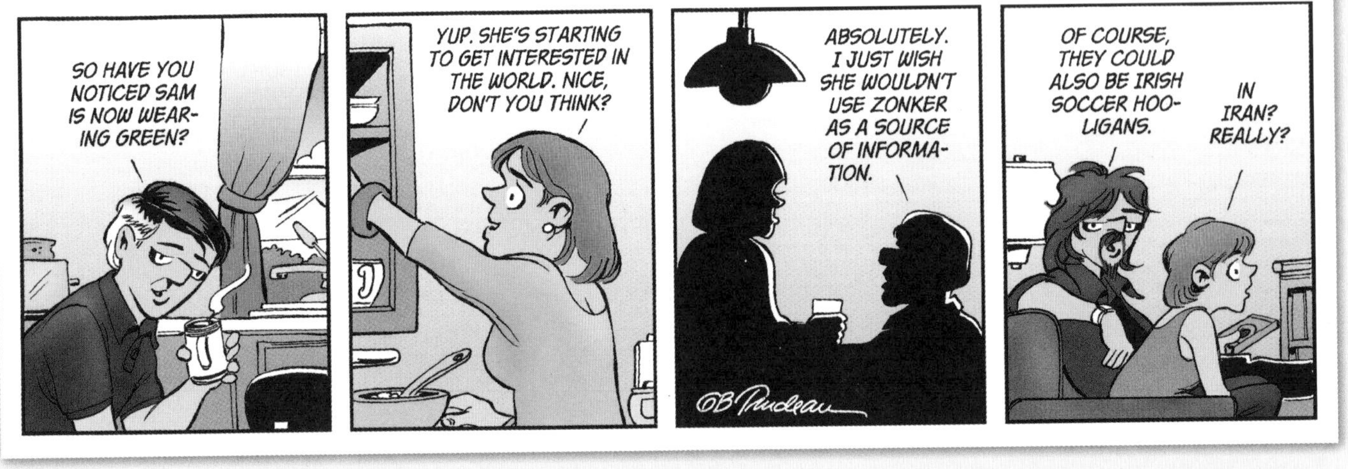
SO HAVE YOU NOTICED SAM IS NOW WEARING GREEN?
YUP. SHE'S STARTING TO GET INTERESTED IN THE WORLD. NICE, DON'T YOU THINK?
ABSOLUTELY. I JUST WISH SHE WOULDN'T USE ZONKER AS A SOURCE OF INFORMATION.
OF COURSE, THEY COULD ALSO BE IRISH SOCCER HOOLIGANS.
IN IRAN? REALLY?

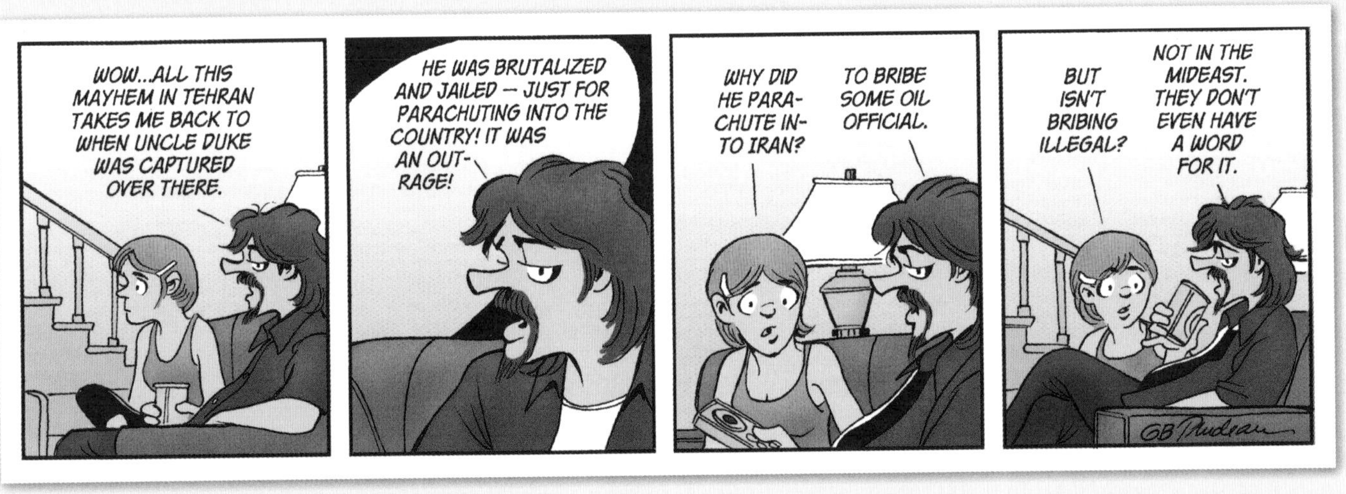
WOW...ALL THIS MAYHEM IN TEHRAN TAKES ME BACK TO WHEN UNCLE DUKE WAS CAPTURED OVER THERE.
HE WAS BRUTALIZED AND JAILED — JUST FOR PARACHUTING INTO THE COUNTRY! IT WAS AN OUTRAGE!
WHY DID HE PARACHUTE INTO IRAN?
TO BRIBE SOME OIL OFFICIAL.
BUT ISN'T BRIBING ILLEGAL?
NOT IN THE MIDEAST. THEY DON'T EVEN HAVE A WORD FOR IT.

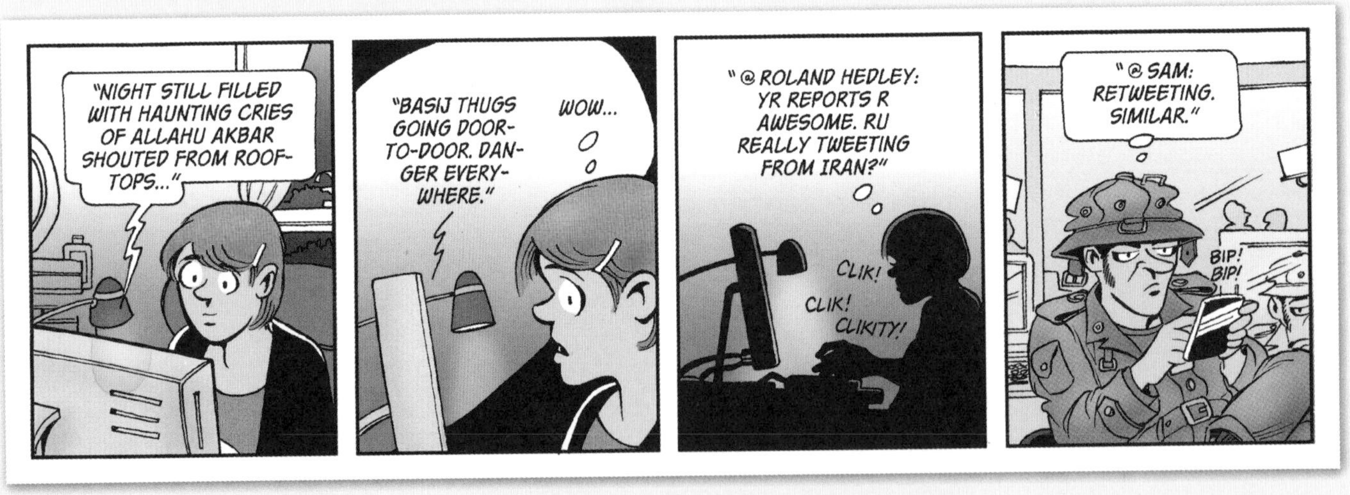
"NIGHT STILL FILLED WITH HAUNTING CRIES OF ALLAHU AKBAR SHOUTED FROM ROOFTOPS..."
"BASIJ THUGS GOING DOOR-TO-DOOR. DANGER EVERYWHERE."
WOW...
"@ROLAND HEDLEY: YR REPORTS R AWESOME. RU REALLY TWEETING FROM IRAN?"
CLIK!
CLIK!
CLIKITY!
"@SAM: RETWEETING. SIMILAR."
BIP! BIP!

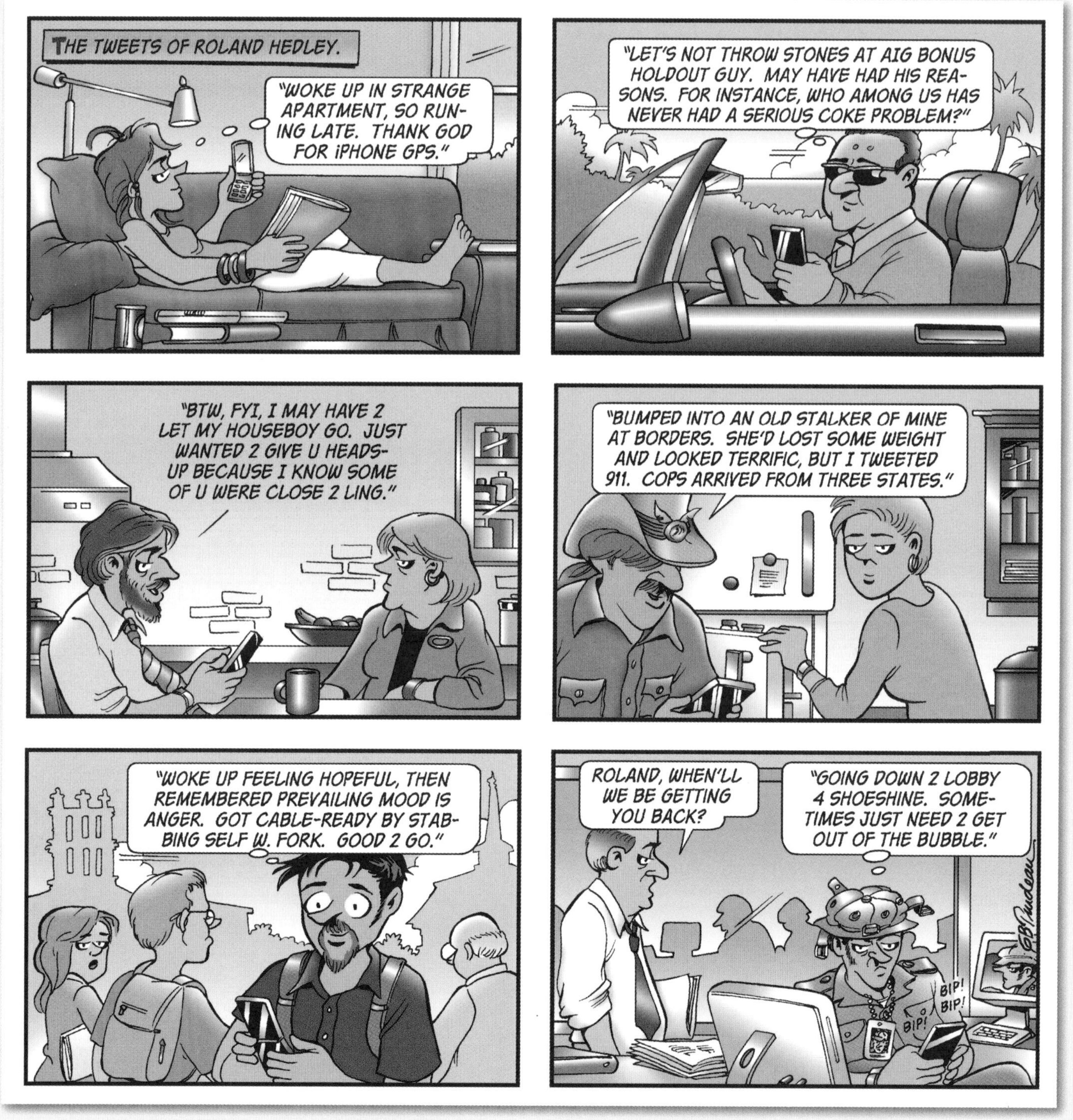
THE TWEETS OF ROLAND HEDLEY.
"WOKE UP IN STRANGE APARTMENT, SO RUNNING LATE. THANK GOD FOR iPHONE GPS."
"LET'S NOT THROW STONES AT AIG BONUS HOLDOUT GUY. MAY HAVE HAD HIS REASONS. FOR INSTANCE, WHO AMONG US HAS NEVER HAD A SERIOUS COKE PROBLEM?"
"BTW, FYI, I MAY HAVE 2 LET MY HOUSEBOY GO. JUST WANTED 2 GIVE U HEADS-UP BECAUSE I KNOW SOME OF U WERE CLOSE 2 LING."
"BUMPED INTO AN OLD STALKER OF MINE AT BORDERS. SHE'D LOST SOME WEIGHT AND LOOKED TERRIFIC, BUT I TWEETED 911. COPS ARRIVED FROM THREE STATES."
"WOKE UP FEELING HOPEFUL, THEN REMEMBERED PREVAILING MOOD IS ANGER. GOT CABLE-READY BY STABBING SELF W. FORK. GOOD 2 GO."
ROLAND, WHEN'LL WE BE GETTING YOU BACK?
"GOING DOWN 2 LOBBY 4 SHOESHINE. SOMETIMES JUST NEED 2 GET OUT OF THE BUBBLE."
BIP! BIP!
BIP!
GBTrudeau

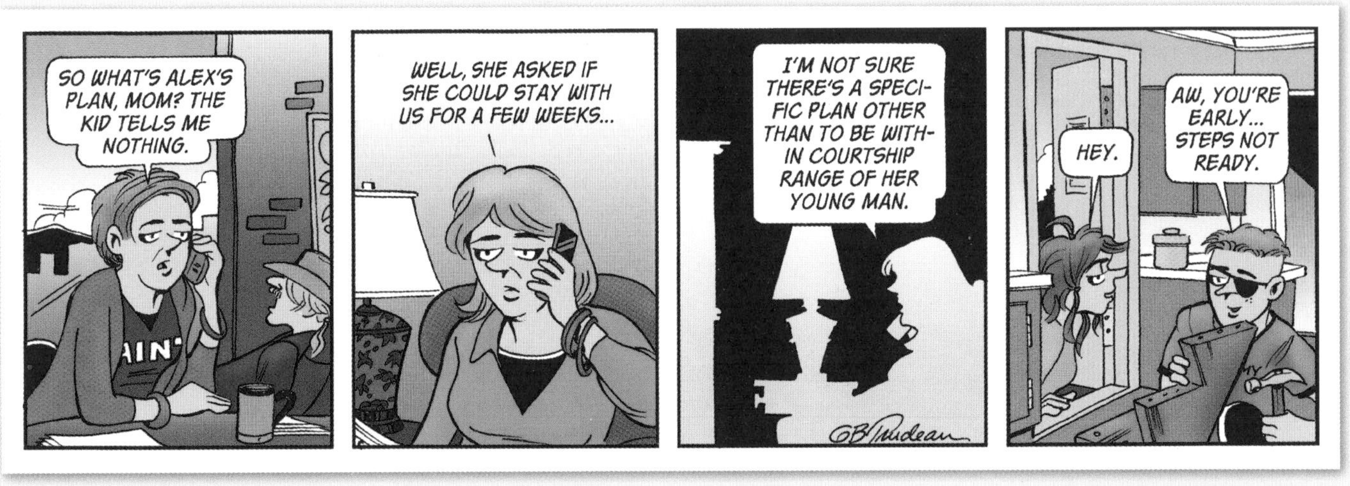
SO WHAT'S ALEX'S PLAN, MOM? THE KID TELLS ME NOTHING.
WELL, SHE ASKED IF SHE COULD STAY WITH US FOR A FEW WEEKS...
I'M NOT SURE THERE'S A SPECIFIC PLAN OTHER THAN TO BE WITHIN COURTSHIP RANGE OF HER YOUNG MAN.
HEY.
AW, YOU'RE EARLY... STEPS NOT READY.

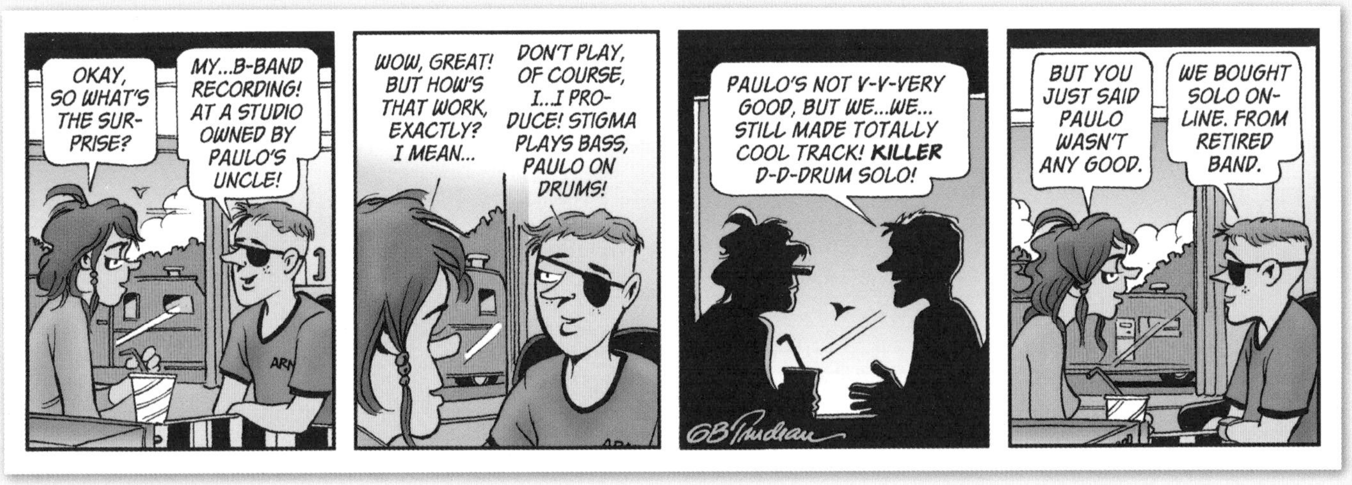
OKAY, SO WHAT'S THE SURPRISE?
MY...B-BAND RECORDING! AT A STUDIO OWNED BY PAULO'S UNCLE!
WOW, GREAT! BUT HOW'S THAT WORK, EXACTLY? I MEAN...
DON'T PLAY, OF COURSE, I...I PRODUCE! STIGMA PLAYS BASS, PAULO ON DRUMS!
PAULO'S NOT V-V-VERY GOOD, BUT WE...WE... STILL MADE TOTALLY COOL TRACK! **KILLER** D-D-DRUM SOLO!
BUT YOU JUST SAID PAULO WASN'T ANY GOOD.
WE BOUGHT SOLO ONLINE. FROM RETIRED BAND.

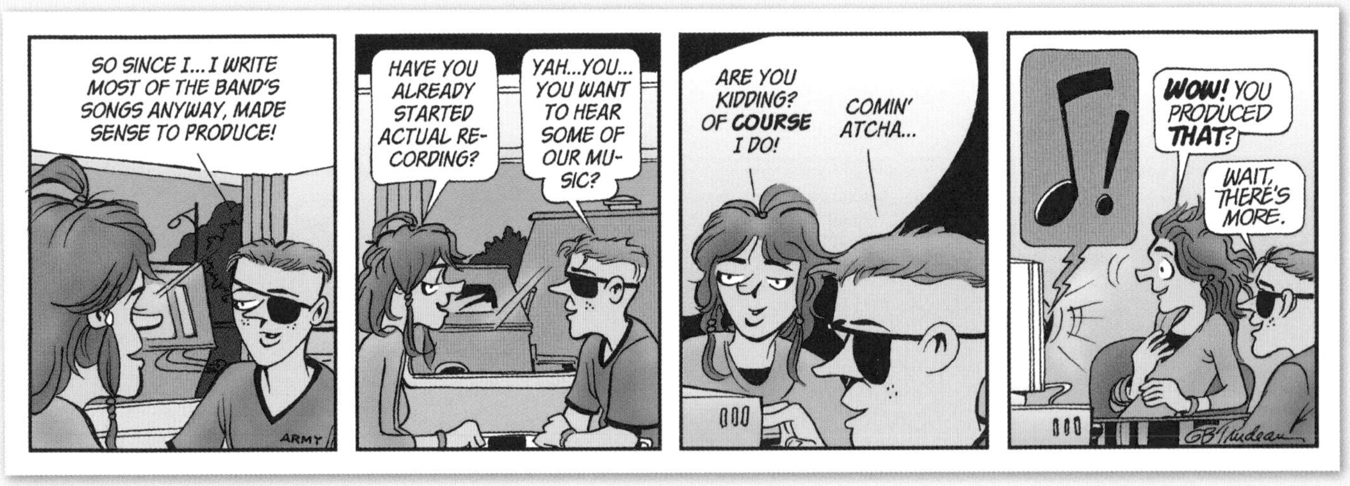
SO SINCE I...I WRITE MOST OF THE BAND'S SONGS ANYWAY, MADE SENSE TO PRODUCE!
HAVE YOU ALREADY STARTED ACTUAL RECORDING?
YAH...YOU... YOU WANT TO HEAR SOME OF OUR MUSIC?
ARE YOU KIDDING? OF **COURSE** I DO!
COMIN' ATCHA...
WOW! YOU PRODUCED **THAT**?
WAIT, THERE'S MORE.

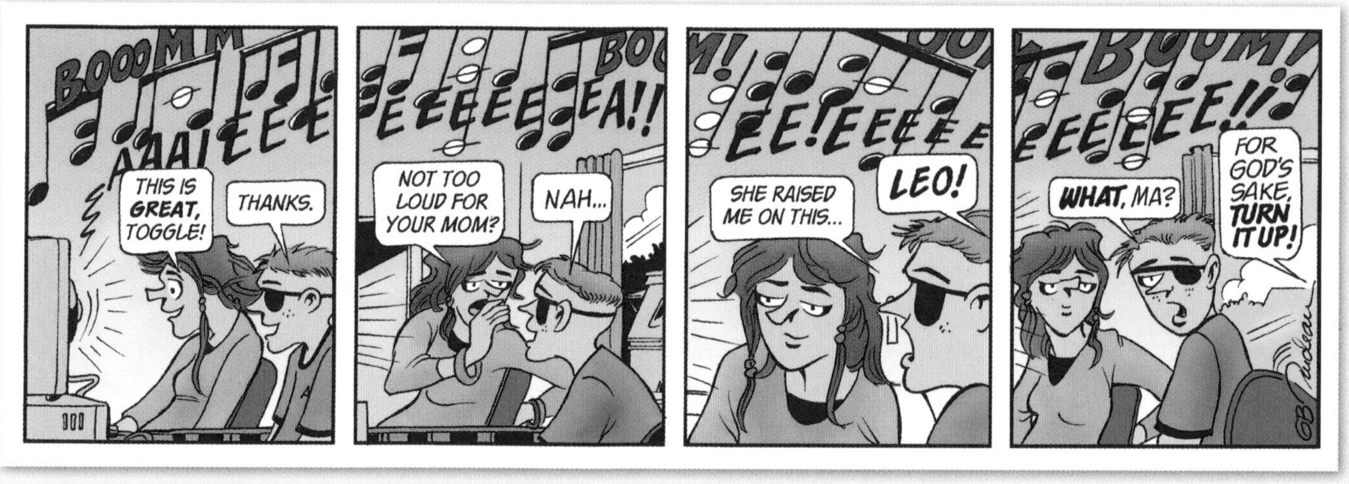
BOOOMM
AAAIEEE
THIS IS GREAT, TOGGLE!
THANKS.
EEEEEEEA!!
BOOM
NOT TOO LOUD FOR YOUR MOM?
NAH...
EE!EEEEE
SHE RAISED ME ON THIS...
LEO!
BOOM!
EEEEEEE!!
WHAT, MA?
FOR GOD'S SAKE, TURN IT UP!

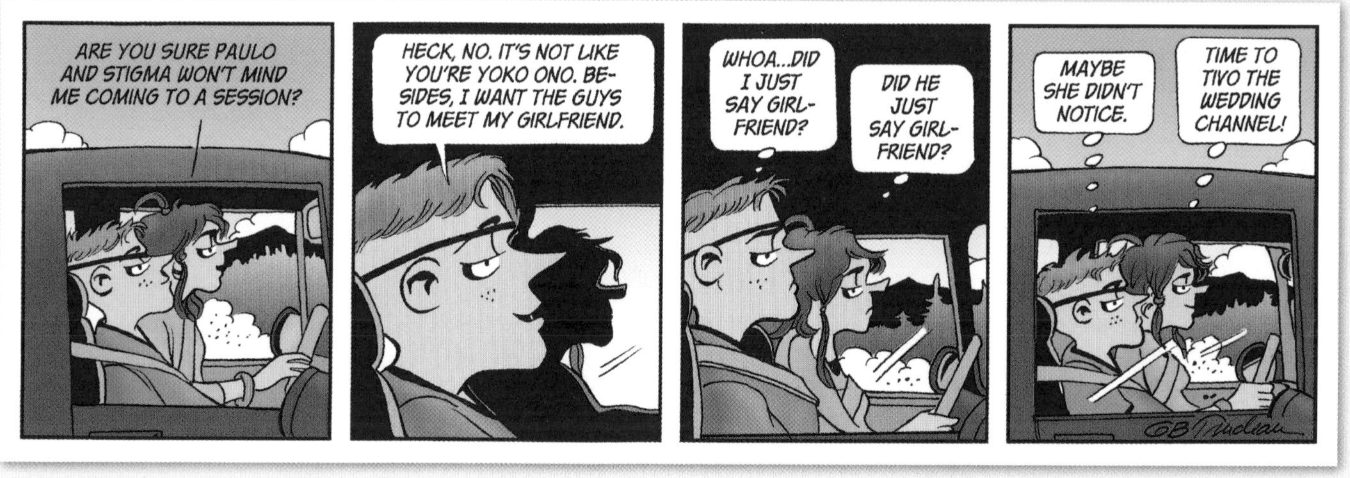
ARE YOU SURE PAULO AND STIGMA WON'T MIND ME COMING TO A SESSION?
HECK, NO. IT'S NOT LIKE YOU'RE YOKO ONO. BESIDES, I WANT THE GUYS TO MEET MY GIRLFRIEND.
WHOA...DID I JUST SAY GIRLFRIEND?
DID HE JUST SAY GIRLFRIEND?
MAYBE SHE DIDN'T NOTICE.
TIME TO TIVO THE WEDDING CHANNEL!

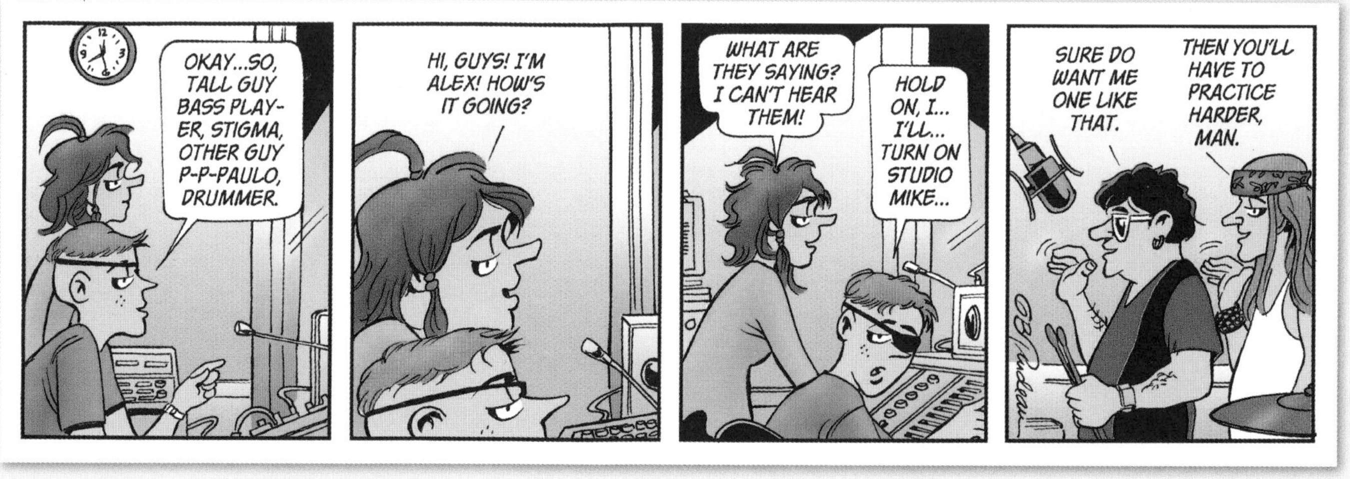
OKAY...SO, TALL GUY BASS PLAYER, STIGMA, OTHER GUY P-P-PAULO, DRUMMER.
HI, GUYS! I'M ALEX! HOW'S IT GOING?
WHAT ARE THEY SAYING? I CAN'T HEAR THEM!
HOLD ON, I... I'LL... TURN ON STUDIO MIKE...
SURE DO WANT ME ONE LIKE THAT.
THEN YOU'LL HAVE TO PRACTICE HARDER, MAN.

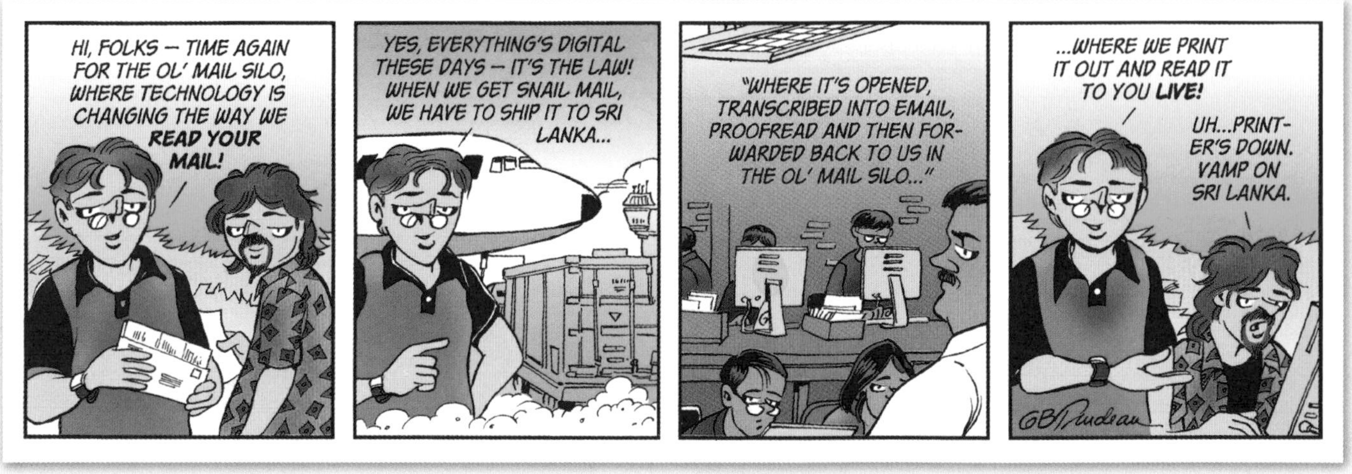
HI, FOLKS — TIME AGAIN FOR THE OL' MAIL SILO, WHERE TECHNOLOGY IS CHANGING THE WAY WE **READ YOUR MAIL!**
YES, EVERYTHING'S DIGITAL THESE DAYS — IT'S THE LAW! WHEN WE GET SNAIL MAIL, WE HAVE TO SHIP IT TO SRI LANKA...
"WHERE IT'S OPENED, TRANSCRIBED INTO EMAIL, PROOFREAD AND THEN FORWARDED BACK TO US IN THE OL' MAIL SILO..."
...WHERE WE PRINT IT OUT AND READ IT TO YOU **LIVE!**
UH...PRINTER'S DOWN. VAMP ON SRI LANKA.
GB Trudeau

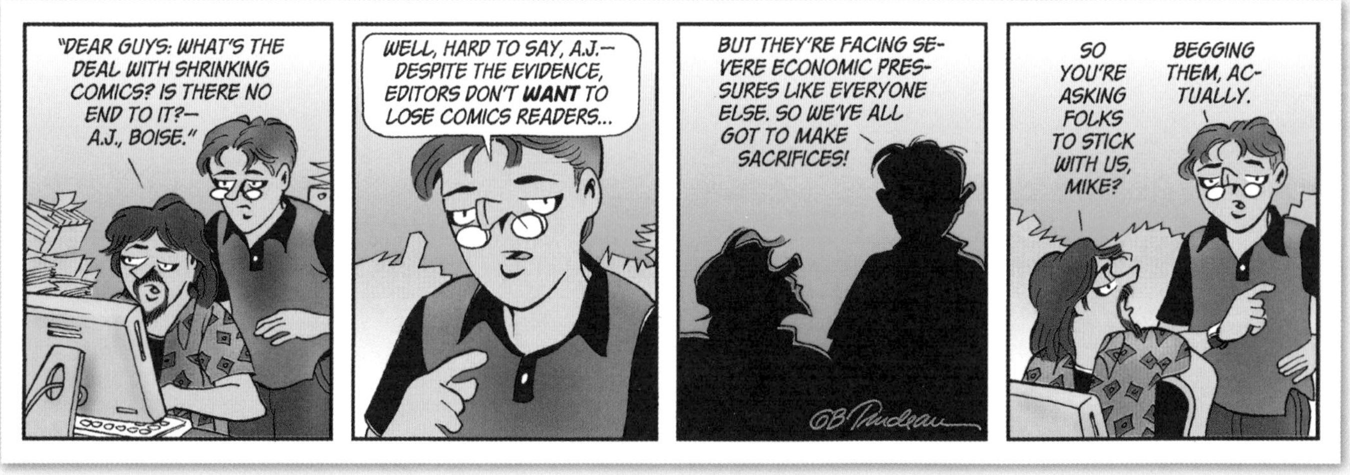
"DEAR GUYS: WHAT'S THE DEAL WITH SHRINKING COMICS? IS THERE NO END TO IT?— A.J., BOISE."
WELL, HARD TO SAY, A.J.— DESPITE THE EVIDENCE, EDITORS DON'T **WANT** TO LOSE COMICS READERS...
BUT THEY'RE FACING SEVERE ECONOMIC PRESSURES LIKE EVERYONE ELSE. SO WE'VE ALL GOT TO MAKE SACRIFICES!
GB Trudeau
SO YOU'RE ASKING FOLKS TO STICK WITH US, MIKE?
BEGGING THEM, ACTUALLY.

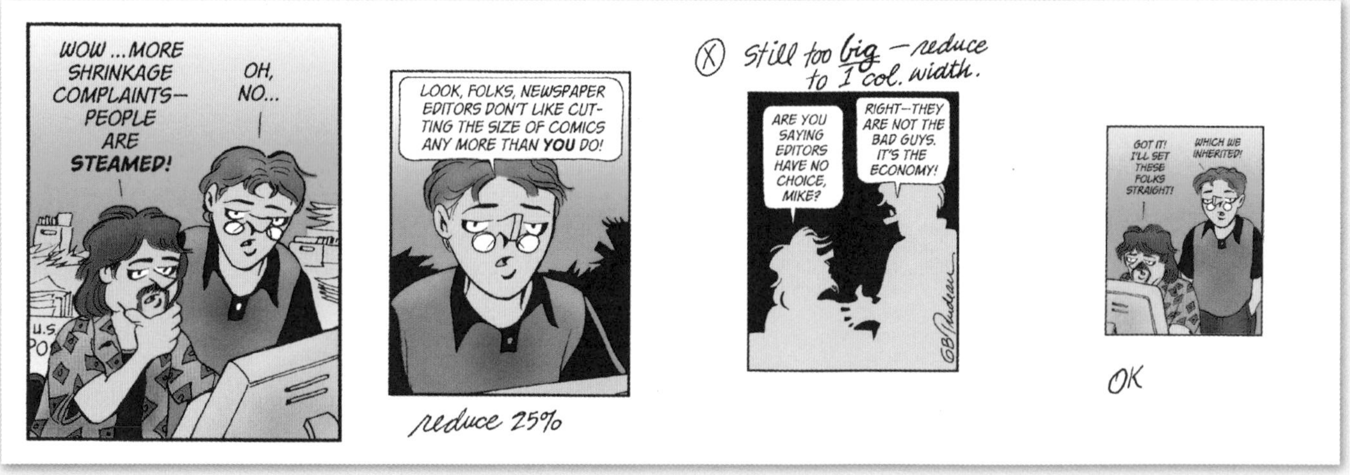
WOW ...MORE SHRINKAGE COMPLAINTS— PEOPLE ARE **STEAMED!**
OH, NO...
U.S. PO
LOOK, FOLKS, NEWSPAPER EDITORS DON'T LIKE CUTTING THE SIZE OF COMICS ANY MORE THAN **YOU** DO!
reduce 25%
Ⓧ still too big — reduce to 1 col. width.
ARE YOU SAYING EDITORS HAVE NO CHOICE, MIKE?
RIGHT--THEY ARE NOT THE BAD GUYS. IT'S THE ECONOMY!
GB Trudeau
GOT IT! I'LL SET THESE FOLKS STRAIGHT!
WHICH WE INHERITED!
OK

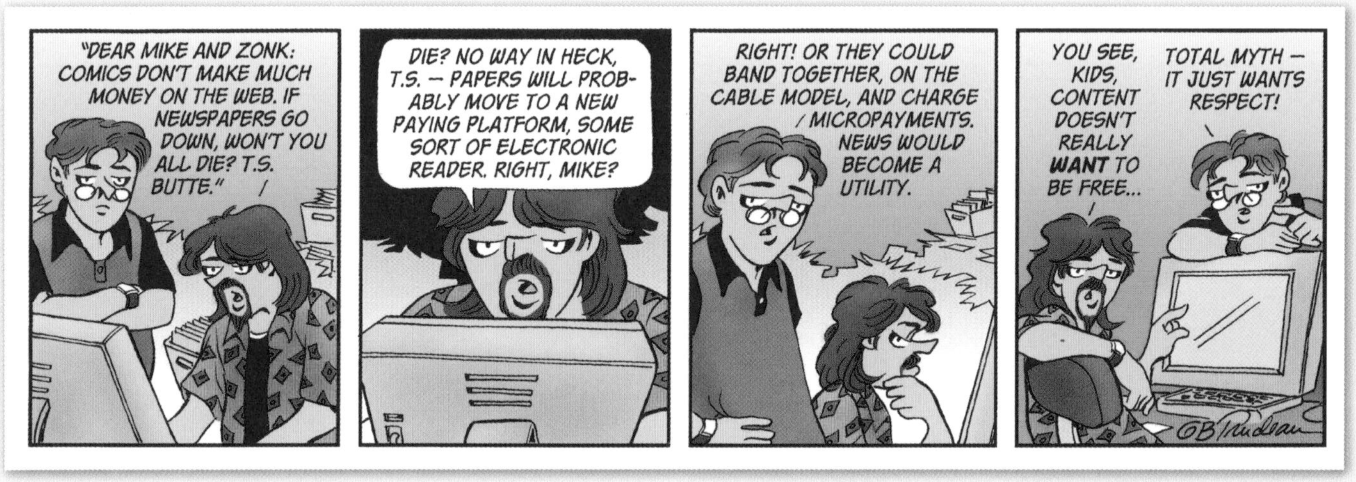
"DEAR MIKE AND ZONK: COMICS DON'T MAKE MUCH MONEY ON THE WEB. IF NEWSPAPERS GO DOWN, WON'T YOU ALL DIE? T.S. BUTTE."
DIE? NO WAY IN HECK, T.S. — PAPERS WILL PROBABLY MOVE TO A NEW PAYING PLATFORM, SOME SORT OF ELECTRONIC READER. RIGHT, MIKE?
RIGHT! OR THEY COULD BAND TOGETHER, ON THE CABLE MODEL, AND CHARGE MICROPAYMENTS. NEWS WOULD BECOME A UTILITY.
YOU SEE, KIDS, CONTENT DOESN'T REALLY **WANT** TO BE FREE...
TOTAL MYTH — IT JUST WANTS RESPECT!

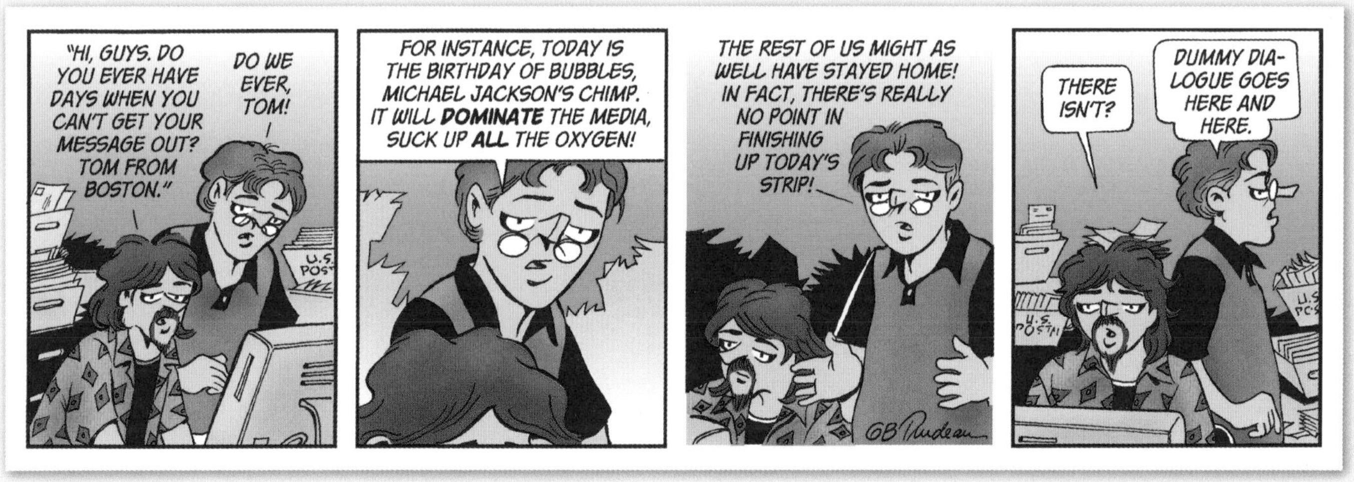
"HI, GUYS. DO YOU EVER HAVE DAYS WHEN YOU CAN'T GET YOUR MESSAGE OUT? TOM FROM BOSTON."
DO WE EVER, TOM!
FOR INSTANCE, TODAY IS THE BIRTHDAY OF BUBBLES, MICHAEL JACKSON'S CHIMP. IT WILL **DOMINATE** THE MEDIA, SUCK UP **ALL** THE OXYGEN!
THE REST OF US MIGHT AS WELL HAVE STAYED HOME! IN FACT, THERE'S REALLY NO POINT IN FINISHING UP TODAY'S STRIP!
THERE ISN'T?
DUMMY DIALOGUE GOES HERE AND HERE.

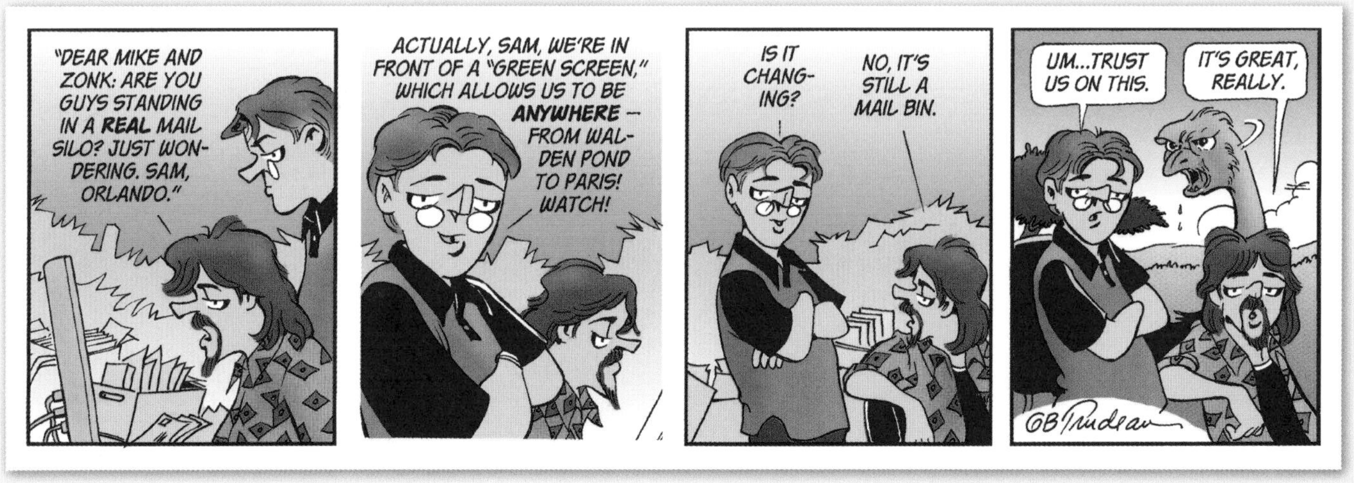
"DEAR MIKE AND ZONK: ARE YOU GUYS STANDING IN A **REAL** MAIL SILO? JUST WONDERING. SAM, ORLANDO."
ACTUALLY, SAM, WE'RE IN FRONT OF A "GREEN SCREEN," WHICH ALLOWS US TO BE **ANYWHERE** — FROM WALDEN POND TO PARIS! WATCH!
IS IT CHANGING?
NO, IT'S STILL A MAIL BIN.
UM...TRUST US ON THIS.
IT'S GREAT, REALLY.

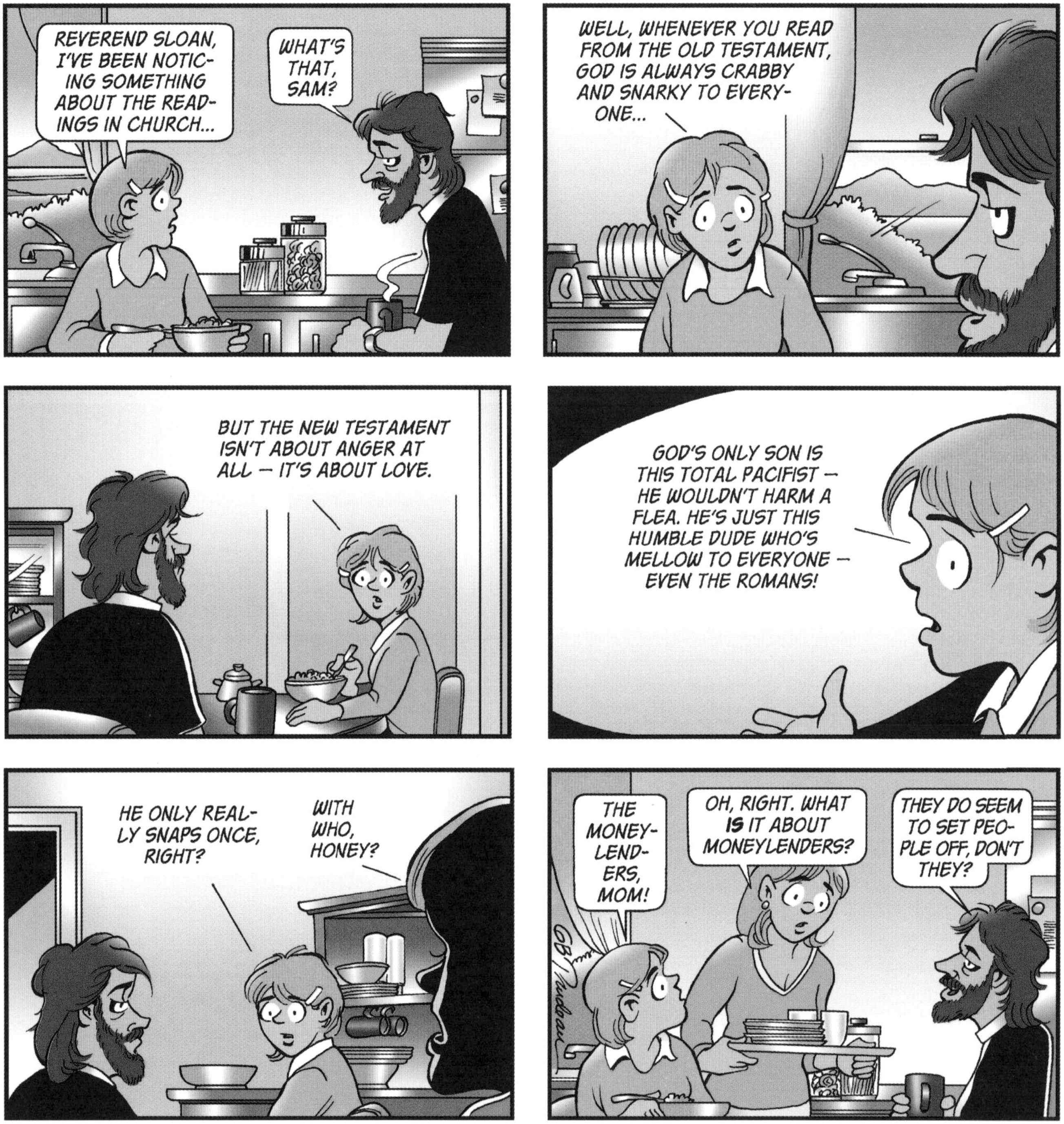
REVEREND SLOAN, I'VE BEEN NOTIC-ING SOMETHING ABOUT THE READ-INGS IN CHURCH...
WHAT'S THAT, SAM?
WELL, WHENEVER YOU READ FROM THE OLD TESTAMENT, GOD IS ALWAYS CRABBY AND SNARKY TO EVERY-ONE...
BUT THE NEW TESTAMENT ISN'T ABOUT ANGER AT ALL — IT'S ABOUT LOVE.
GOD'S ONLY SON IS THIS TOTAL PACIFIST — HE WOULDN'T HARM A FLEA. HE'S JUST THIS HUMBLE DUDE WHO'S MELLOW TO EVERYONE — EVEN THE ROMANS!
HE ONLY REAL-LY SNAPS ONCE, RIGHT?
WITH WHO, HONEY?
THE MONEY-LEND-ERS, MOM!
OH, RIGHT. WHAT **IS** IT ABOUT MONEYLENDERS?
THEY DO SEEM TO SET PEO-PLE OFF, DON'T THEY?

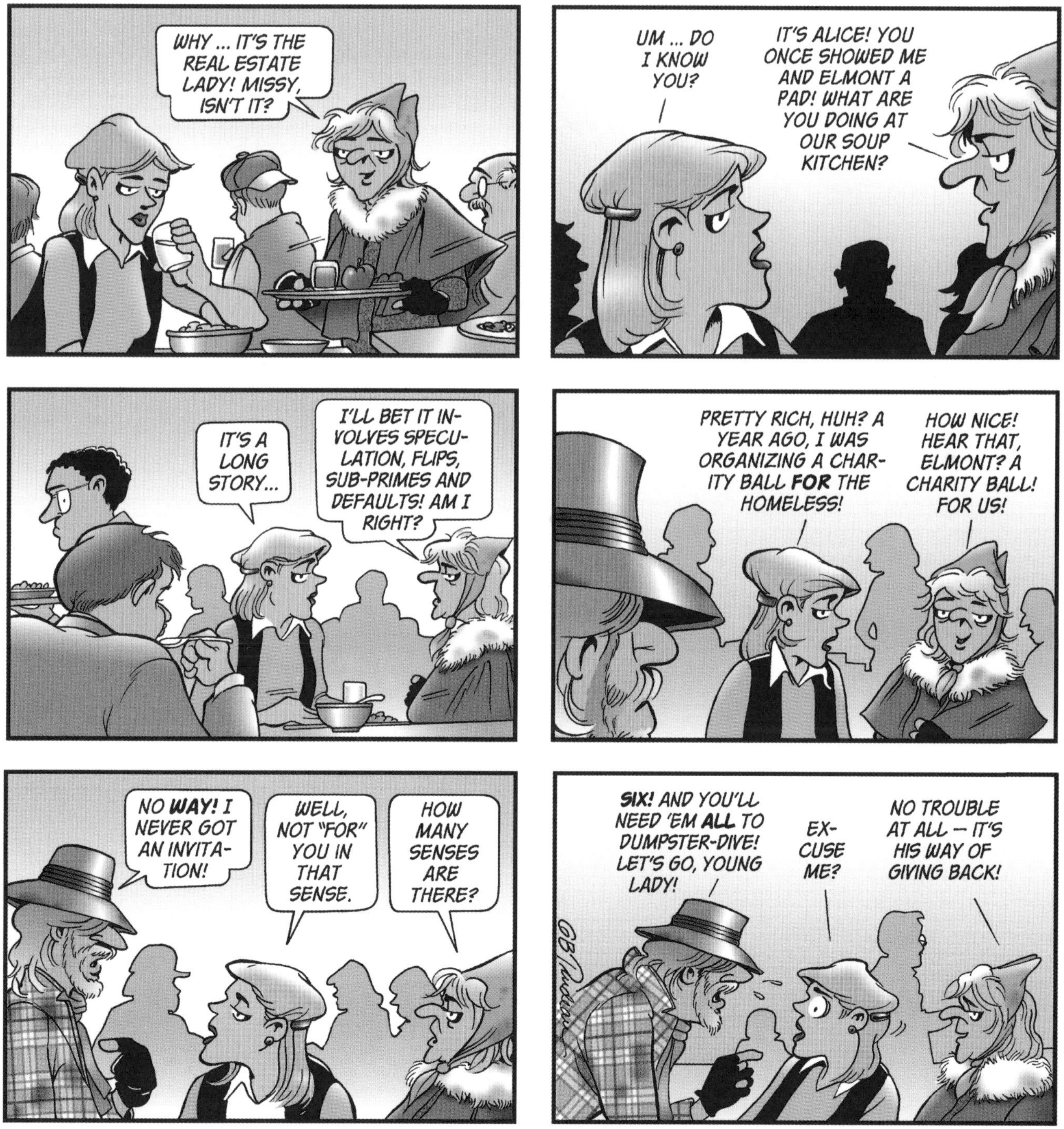
WHY ... IT'S THE REAL ESTATE LADY! MISSY, ISN'T IT?
UM ... DO I KNOW YOU?
IT'S ALICE! YOU ONCE SHOWED ME AND ELMONT A PAD! WHAT ARE YOU DOING AT OUR SOUP KITCHEN?
IT'S A LONG STORY...
I'LL BET IT INVOLVES SPECULATION, FLIPS, SUB-PRIMES AND DEFAULTS! AM I RIGHT?
PRETTY RICH, HUH? A YEAR AGO, I WAS ORGANIZING A CHARITY BALL FOR THE HOMELESS!
HOW NICE! HEAR THAT, ELMONT? A CHARITY BALL! FOR US!
NO WAY! I NEVER GOT AN INVITATION!
WELL, NOT "FOR" YOU IN THAT SENSE.
HOW MANY SENSES ARE THERE?
SIX! AND YOU'LL NEED 'EM ALL TO DUMPSTER-DIVE! LET'S GO, YOUNG LADY!
EX-CUSE ME?
NO TROUBLE AT ALL -- IT'S HIS WAY OF GIVING BACK!
GB Trudeau

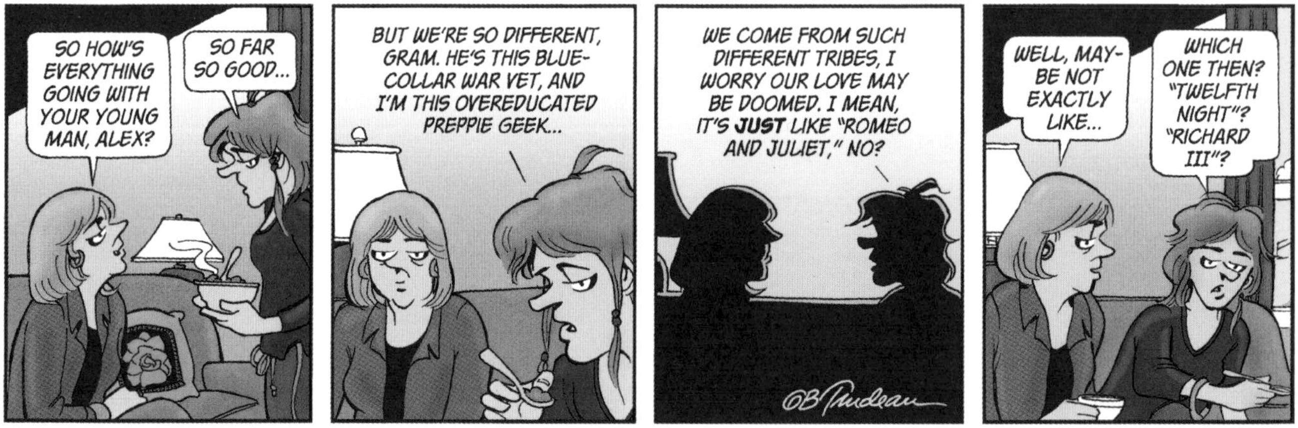
SO HOW'S EVERYTHING GOING WITH YOUR YOUNG MAN, ALEX?
SO FAR SO GOOD...
BUT WE'RE SO DIFFERENT, GRAM. HE'S THIS BLUE-COLLAR WAR VET, AND I'M THIS OVEREDUCATED PREPPIE GEEK...
WE COME FROM SUCH DIFFERENT TRIBES, I WORRY OUR LOVE MAY BE DOOMED. I MEAN, IT'S JUST LIKE "ROMEO AND JULIET," NO?
GB Trudeau
WELL, MAY-BE NOT EXACTLY LIKE...
WHICH ONE THEN? "TWELFTH NIGHT"? "RICHARD III"?

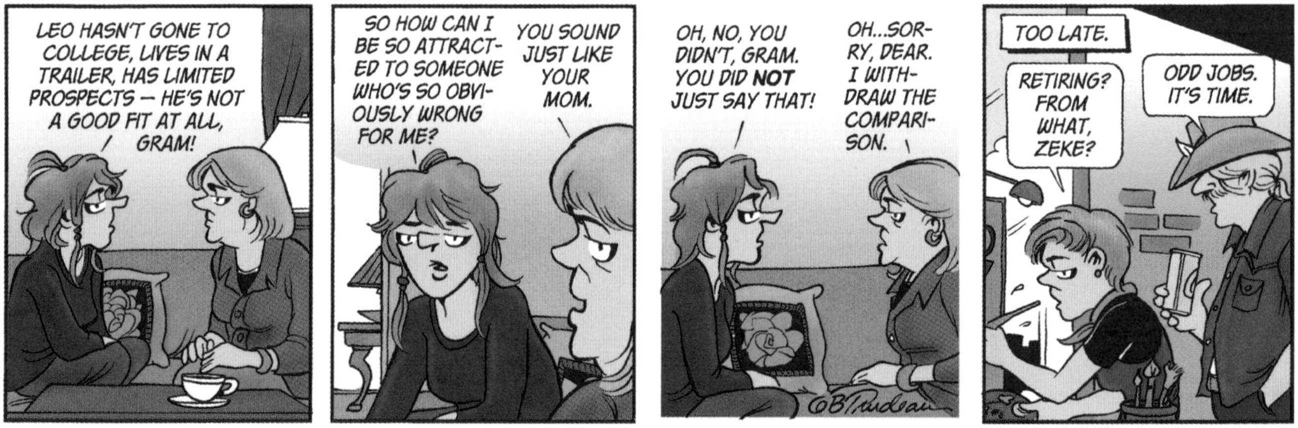
LEO HASN'T GONE TO COLLEGE, LIVES IN A TRAILER, HAS LIMITED PROSPECTS — HE'S NOT A GOOD FIT AT ALL, GRAM!
SO HOW CAN I BE SO ATTRACT-ED TO SOMEONE WHO'S SO OBVI-OUSLY WRONG FOR ME?
YOU SOUND JUST LIKE YOUR MOM.
OH, NO, YOU DIDN'T, GRAM. YOU DID NOT JUST SAY THAT!
OH...SOR-RY, DEAR. I WITH-DRAW THE COMPARI-SON.
GB Trudeau
TOO LATE.
RETIRING? FROM WHAT, ZEKE?
ODD JOBS. IT'S TIME.

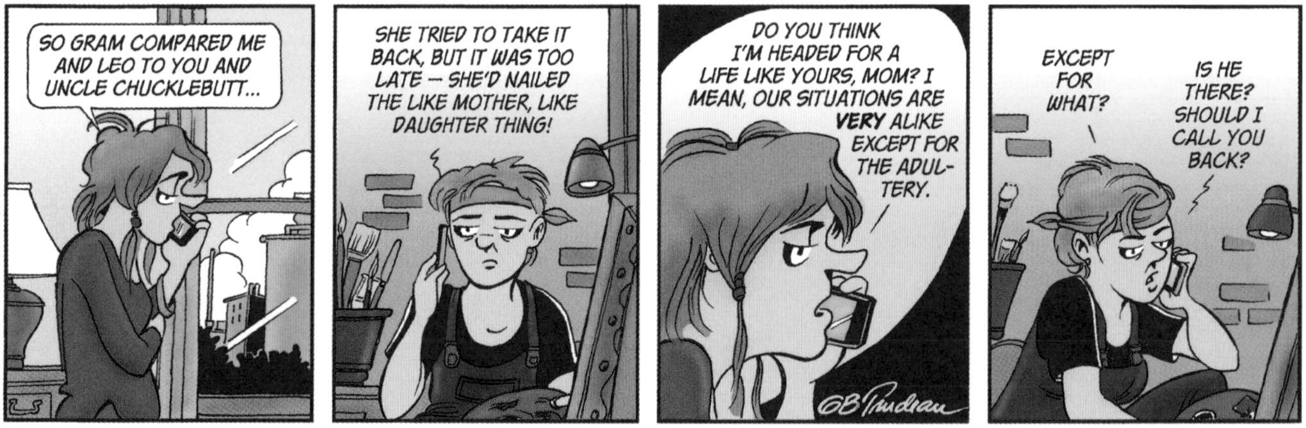
SO GRAM COMPARED ME AND LEO TO YOU AND UNCLE CHUCKLEBUTT...
SHE TRIED TO TAKE IT BACK, BUT IT WAS TOO LATE — SHE'D NAILED THE LIKE MOTHER, LIKE DAUGHTER THING!
DO YOU THINK I'M HEADED FOR A LIFE LIKE YOURS, MOM? I MEAN, OUR SITUATIONS ARE VERY ALIKE EXCEPT FOR THE ADUL-TERY.
GB Trudeau
EXCEPT FOR WHAT?
IS HE THERE? SHOULD I CALL YOU BACK?

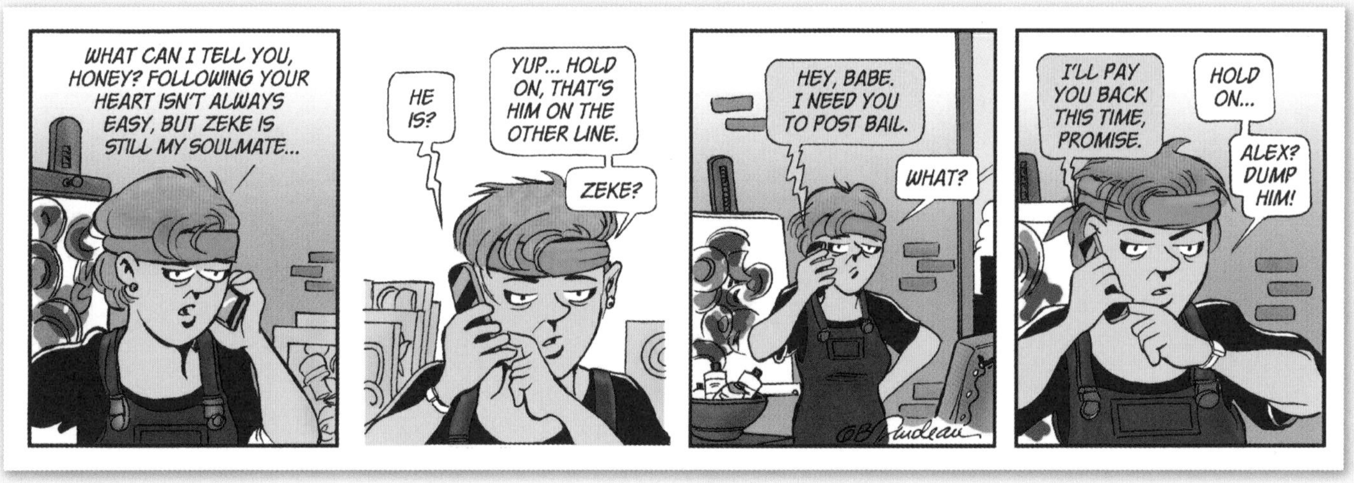
WHAT CAN I TELL YOU, HONEY? FOLLOWING YOUR HEART ISN'T ALWAYS EASY, BUT ZEKE IS STILL MY SOULMATE...
HE IS?
YUP... HOLD ON, THAT'S HIM ON THE OTHER LINE.
ZEKE?
HEY, BABE. I NEED YOU TO POST BAIL.
WHAT?
I'LL PAY YOU BACK THIS TIME, PROMISE.
HOLD ON...
ALEX? DUMP HIM!
©B Trudeau

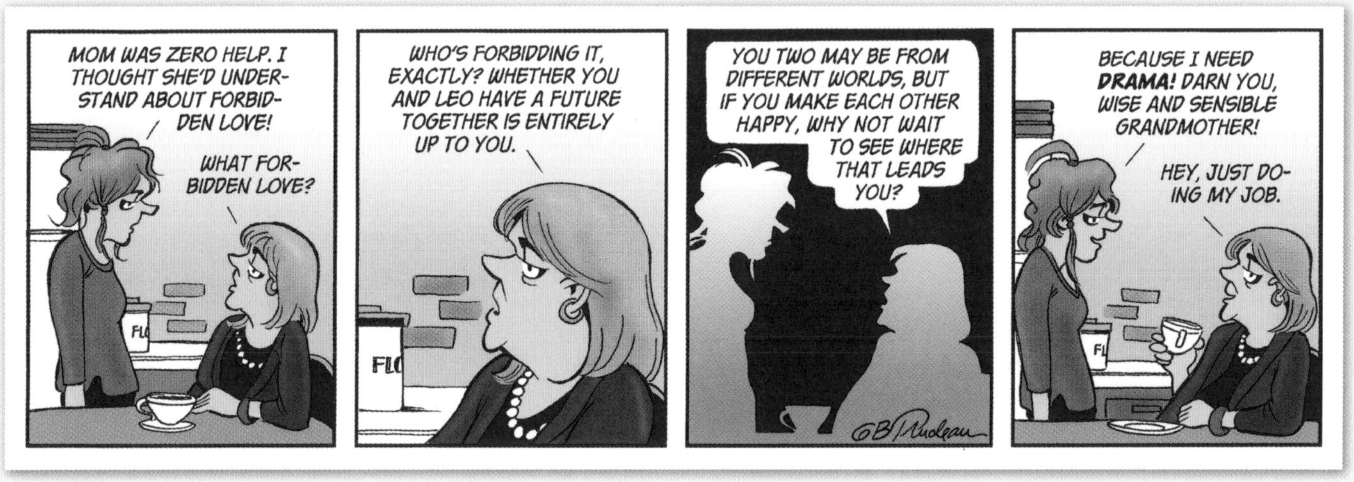
MOM WAS ZERO HELP. I THOUGHT SHE'D UNDERSTAND ABOUT FORBIDDEN LOVE!
WHAT FORBIDDEN LOVE?
WHO'S FORBIDDING IT, EXACTLY? WHETHER YOU AND LEO HAVE A FUTURE TOGETHER IS ENTIRELY UP TO YOU.
YOU TWO MAY BE FROM DIFFERENT WORLDS, BUT IF YOU MAKE EACH OTHER HAPPY, WHY NOT WAIT TO SEE WHERE THAT LEADS YOU?
BECAUSE I NEED **DRAMA!** DARN YOU, WISE AND SENSIBLE GRANDMOTHER!
HEY, JUST DOING MY JOB.
©B Trudeau

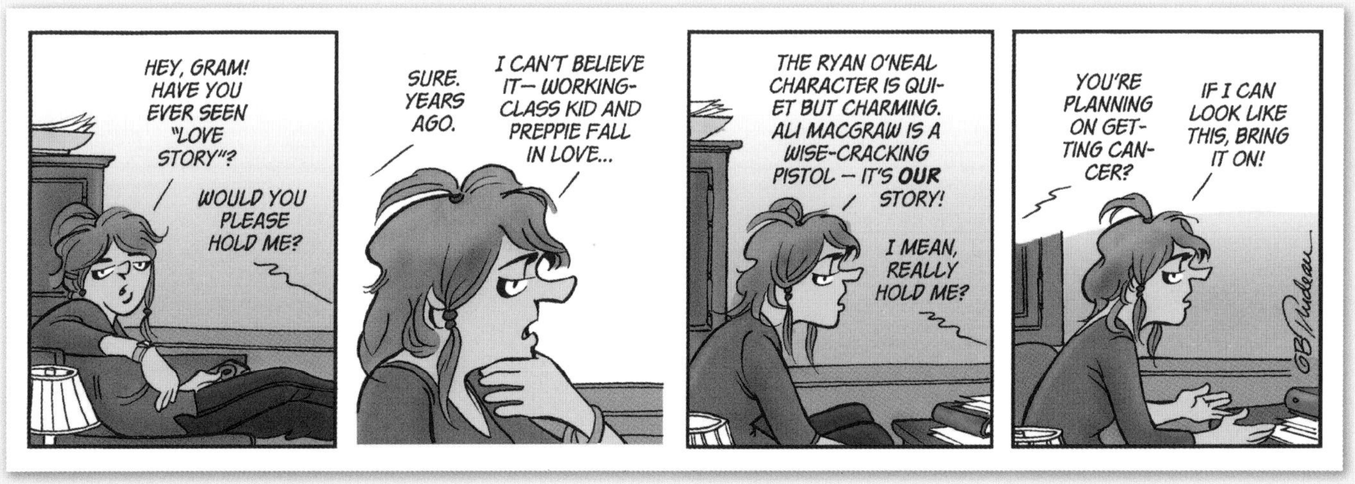
HEY, GRAM! HAVE YOU EVER SEEN "LOVE STORY"?
WOULD YOU PLEASE HOLD ME?
SURE. YEARS AGO.
I CAN'T BELIEVE IT— WORKING-CLASS KID AND PREPPIE FALL IN LOVE...
THE RYAN O'NEAL CHARACTER IS QUIET BUT CHARMING. ALI MACGRAW IS A WISE-CRACKING PISTOL – IT'S **OUR** STORY!
I MEAN, REALLY HOLD ME?
YOU'RE PLANNING ON GETTING CANCER?
IF I CAN LOOK LIKE THIS, BRING IT ON!
©B Trudeau

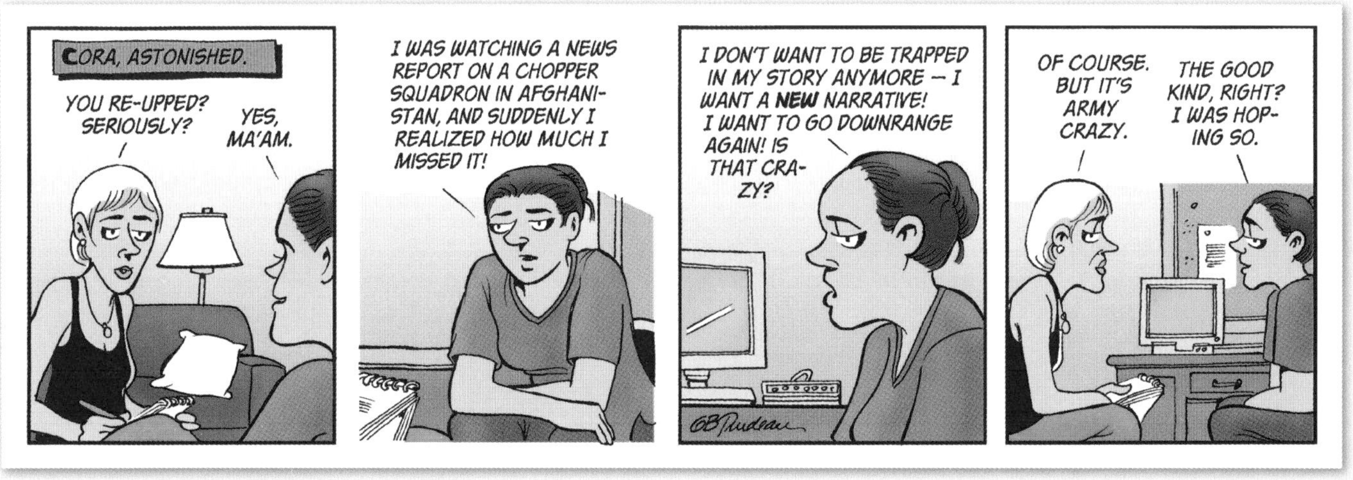
CORA, ASTONISHED.
YOU RE-UPPED? SERIOUSLY?
YES, MA'AM.
I WAS WATCHING A NEWS REPORT ON A CHOPPER SQUADRON IN AFGHANISTAN, AND SUDDENLY I REALIZED HOW MUCH I MISSED IT!
I DON'T WANT TO BE TRAPPED IN MY STORY ANYMORE — I WANT A **NEW** NARRATIVE! I WANT TO GO DOWNRANGE AGAIN! IS THAT CRAZY?
OF COURSE. BUT IT'S ARMY CRAZY.
THE GOOD KIND, RIGHT? I WAS HOPING SO.
GBTrudeau

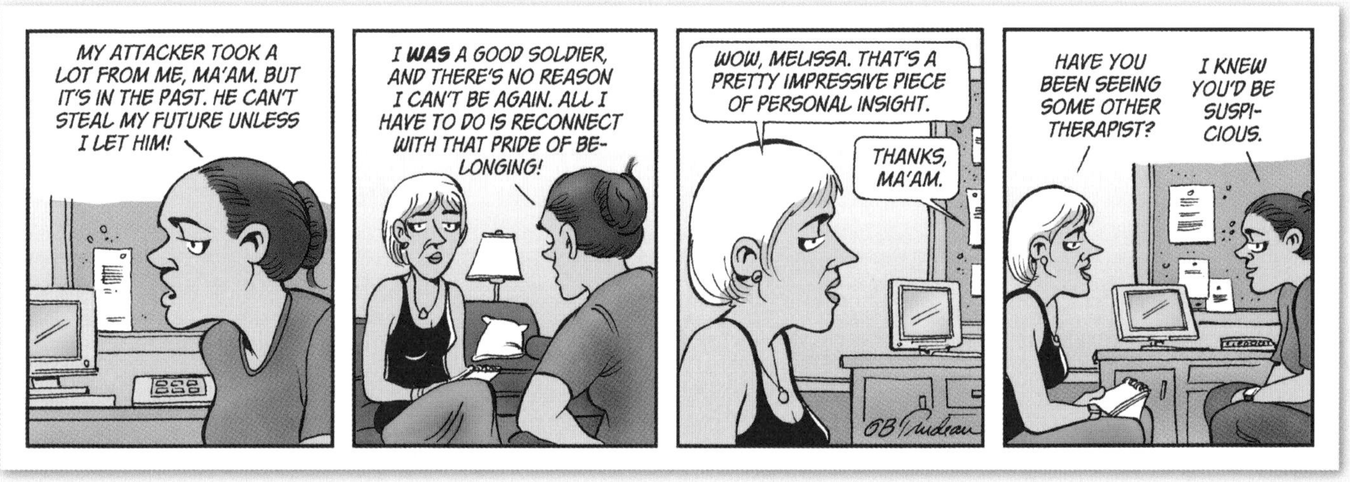
MY ATTACKER TOOK A LOT FROM ME, MA'AM. BUT IT'S IN THE PAST. HE CAN'T STEAL MY FUTURE UNLESS I LET HIM!
I **WAS** A GOOD SOLDIER, AND THERE'S NO REASON I CAN'T BE AGAIN. ALL I HAVE TO DO IS RECONNECT WITH THAT PRIDE OF BELONGING!
WOW, MELISSA. THAT'S A PRETTY IMPRESSIVE PIECE OF PERSONAL INSIGHT.
THANKS, MA'AM.
HAVE YOU BEEN SEEING SOME OTHER THERAPIST?
I KNEW YOU'D BE SUSPICIOUS.
GBTrudeau

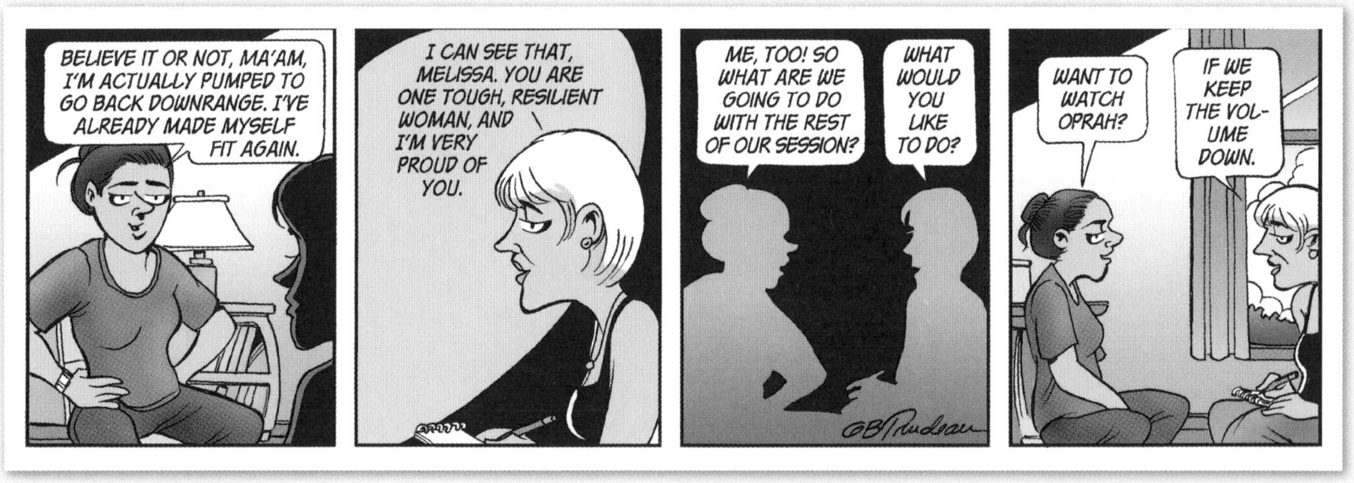
BELIEVE IT OR NOT, MA'AM, I'M ACTUALLY PUMPED TO GO BACK DOWNRANGE. I'VE ALREADY MADE MYSELF FIT AGAIN.
I CAN SEE THAT, MELISSA. YOU ARE ONE TOUGH, RESILIENT WOMAN, AND I'M VERY PROUD OF YOU.
ME, TOO! SO WHAT ARE WE GOING TO DO WITH THE REST OF OUR SESSION?
WHAT WOULD YOU LIKE TO DO?
WANT TO WATCH OPRAH?
IF WE KEEP THE VOLUME DOWN.
GBTrudeau

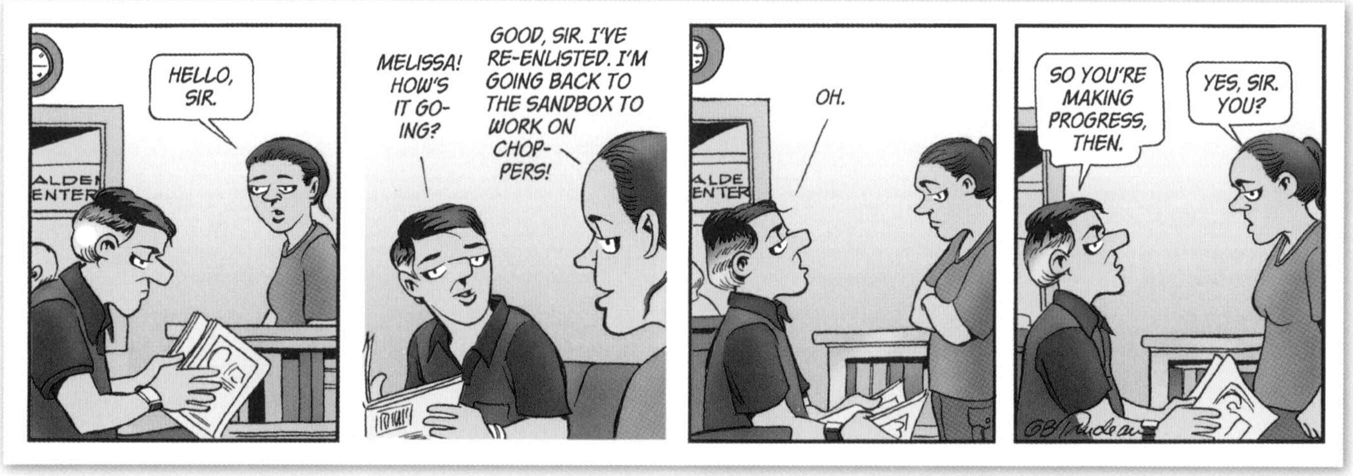
HELLO, SIR.
MELISSA! HOW'S IT GO-ING?
GOOD, SIR. I'VE RE-ENLISTED. I'M GOING BACK TO THE SANDBOX TO WORK ON CHOP-PERS!
OH.
SO YOU'RE MAKING PROGRESS, THEN.
YES, SIR. YOU?

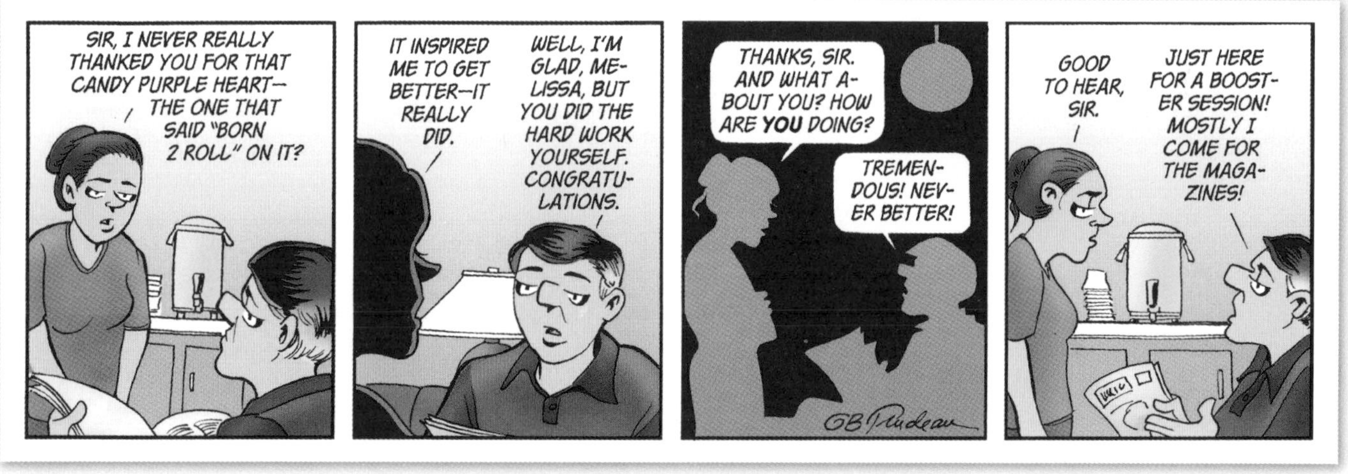
SIR, I NEVER REALLY THANKED YOU FOR THAT CANDY PURPLE HEART— THE ONE THAT SAID "BORN 2 ROLL" ON IT?
IT INSPIRED ME TO GET BETTER—IT REALLY DID.
WELL, I'M GLAD, ME-LISSA, BUT YOU DID THE HARD WORK YOURSELF. CONGRATU-LATIONS.
THANKS, SIR. AND WHAT A-BOUT YOU? HOW ARE **YOU** DOING?
TREMEN-DOUS! NEV-ER BETTER!
GOOD TO HEAR, SIR.
JUST HERE FOR A BOOST-ER SESSION! MOSTLY I COME FOR THE MAGA-ZINES!

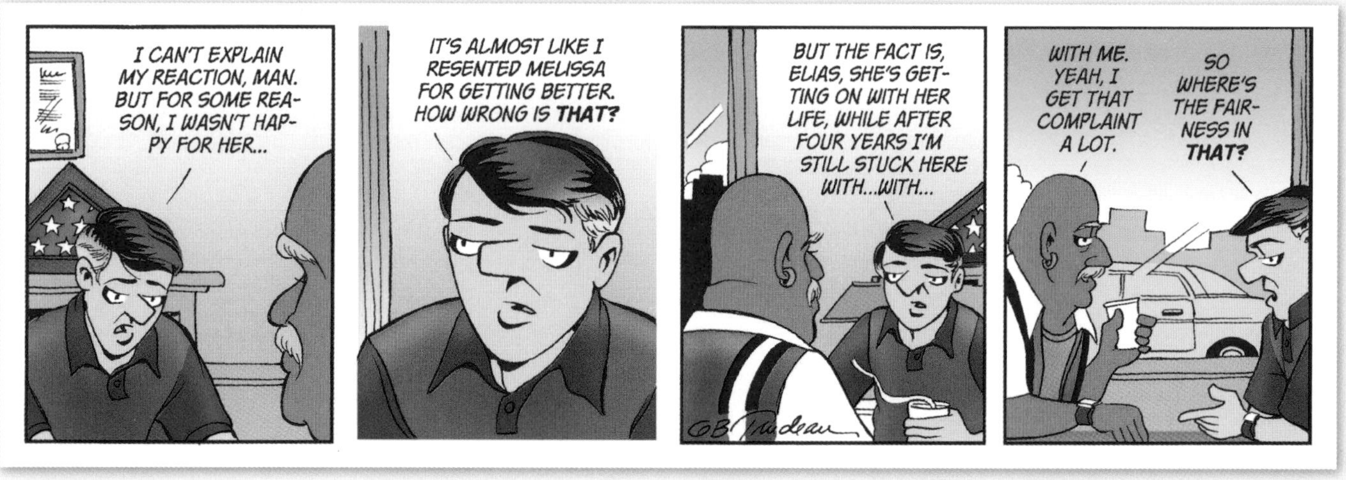
I CAN'T EXPLAIN MY REACTION, MAN. BUT FOR SOME REA-SON, I WASN'T HAP-PY FOR HER...
IT'S ALMOST LIKE I RESENTED MELISSA FOR GETTING BETTER. HOW WRONG IS **THAT?**
BUT THE FACT IS, ELIAS, SHE'S GET-TING ON WITH HER LIFE, WHILE AFTER FOUR YEARS I'M STILL STUCK HERE WITH...WITH...
WITH ME. YEAH, I GET THAT COMPLAINT A LOT.
SO WHERE'S THE FAIR-NESS IN **THAT?**

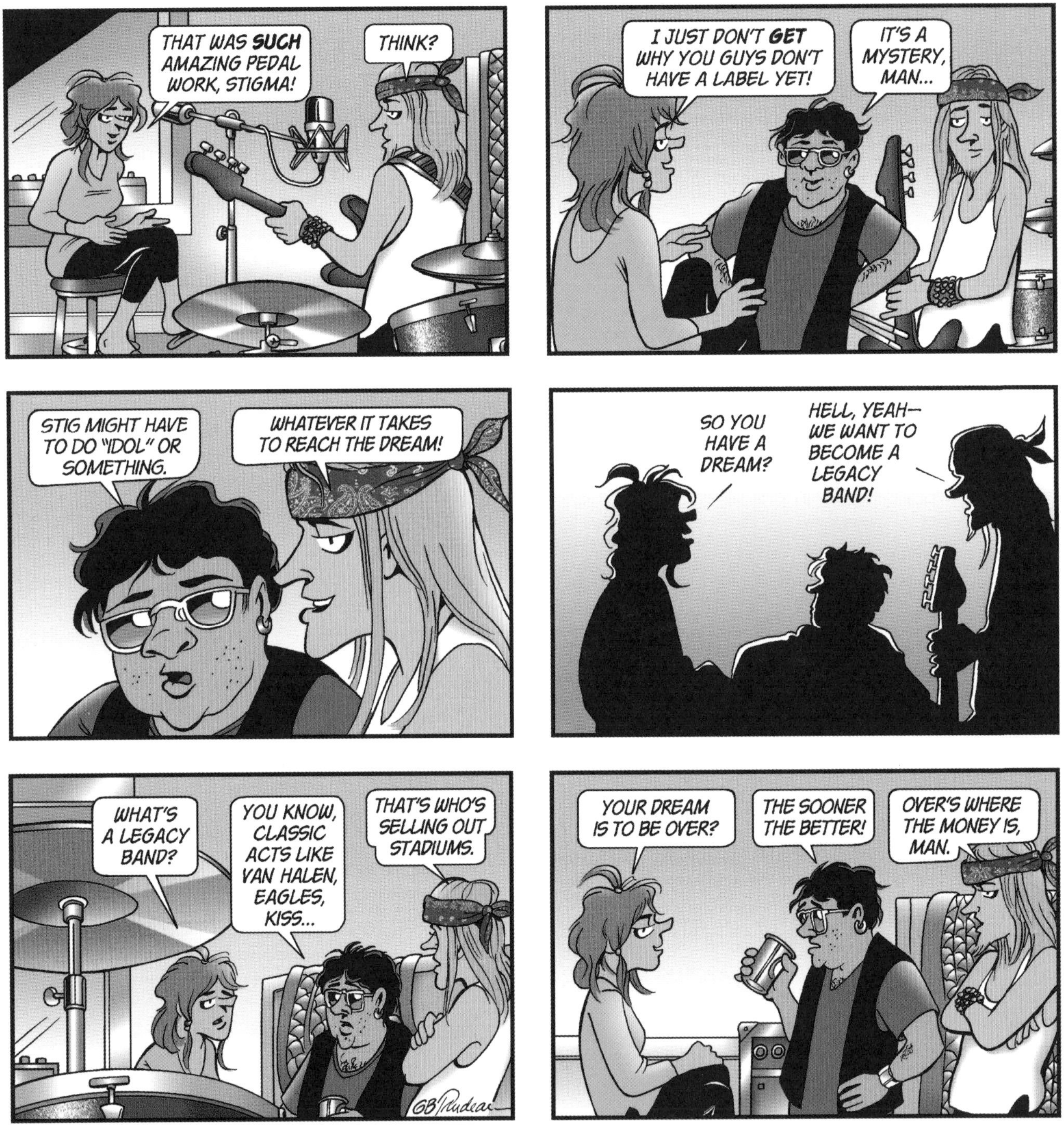
THAT WAS SUCH AMAZING PEDAL WORK, STIGMA!
THINK?
I JUST DON'T GET WHY YOU GUYS DON'T HAVE A LABEL YET!
IT'S A MYSTERY, MAN...
STIG MIGHT HAVE TO DO "IDOL" OR SOMETHING.
WHATEVER IT TAKES TO REACH THE DREAM!
SO YOU HAVE A DREAM?
HELL, YEAH— WE WANT TO BECOME A LEGACY BAND!
WHAT'S A LEGACY BAND?
YOU KNOW, CLASSIC ACTS LIKE VAN HALEN, EAGLES, KISS...
THAT'S WHO'S SELLING OUT STADIUMS.
GB Trudeau
YOUR DREAM IS TO BE OVER?
THE SOONER THE BETTER!
OVER'S WHERE THE MONEY IS, MAN.

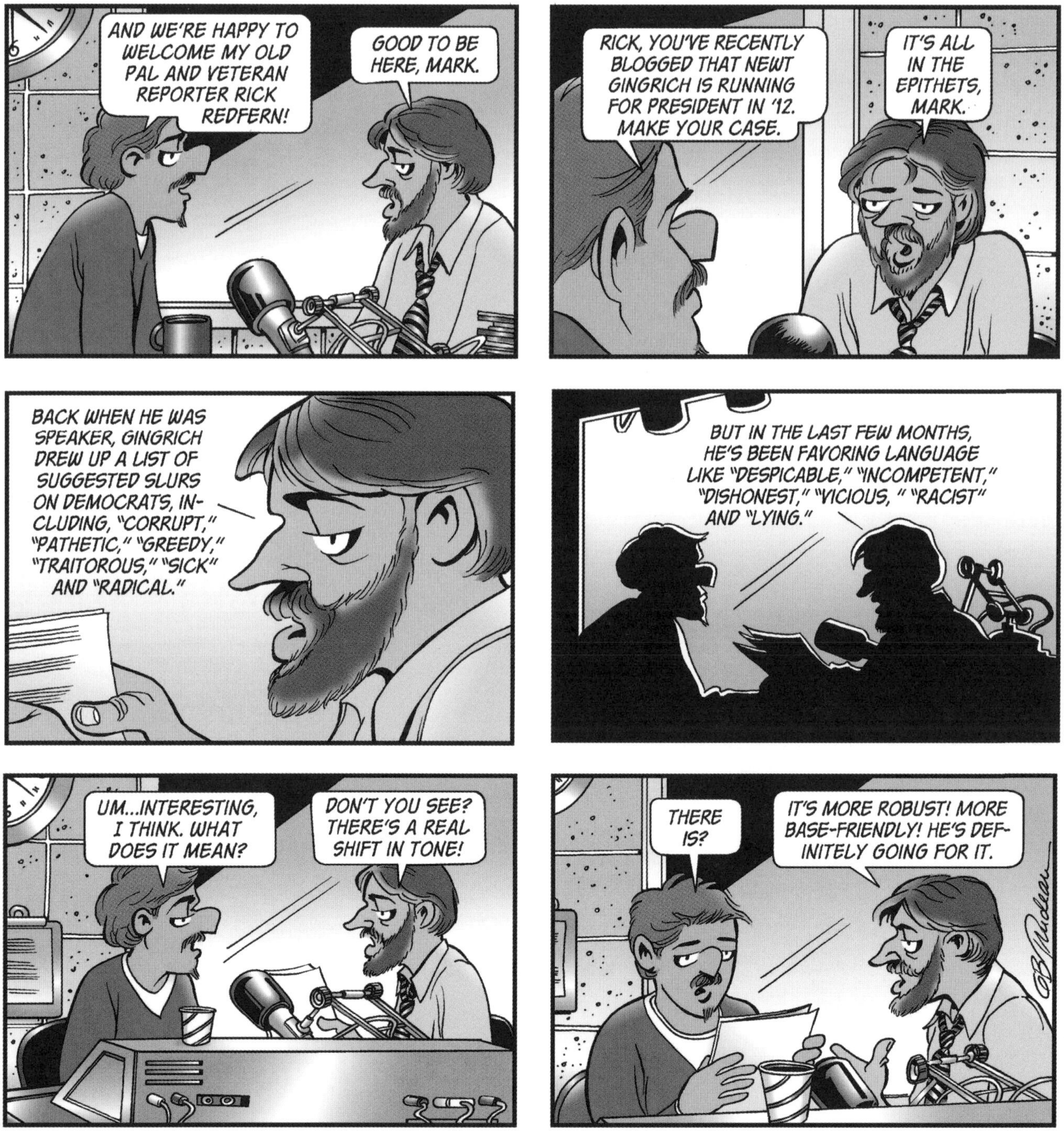
AND WE'RE HAPPY TO WELCOME MY OLD PAL AND VETERAN REPORTER RICK REDFERN!
GOOD TO BE HERE, MARK.
RICK, YOU'VE RECENTLY BLOGGED THAT NEWT GINGRICH IS RUNNING FOR PRESIDENT IN '12. MAKE YOUR CASE.
IT'S ALL IN THE EPITHETS, MARK.
BACK WHEN HE WAS SPEAKER, GINGRICH DREW UP A LIST OF SUGGESTED SLURS ON DEMOCRATS, INCLUDING, "CORRUPT," "PATHETIC," "GREEDY," "TRAITOROUS," "SICK" AND "RADICAL."
BUT IN THE LAST FEW MONTHS, HE'S BEEN FAVORING LANGUAGE LIKE "DESPICABLE," "INCOMPETENT," "DISHONEST," "VICIOUS," "RACIST" AND "LYING."
UM...INTERESTING, I THINK. WHAT DOES IT MEAN?
DON'T YOU SEE? THERE'S A REAL SHIFT IN TONE!
THERE IS?
IT'S MORE ROBUST! MORE BASE-FRIENDLY! HE'S DEFINITELY GOING FOR IT.
GBTrudeau

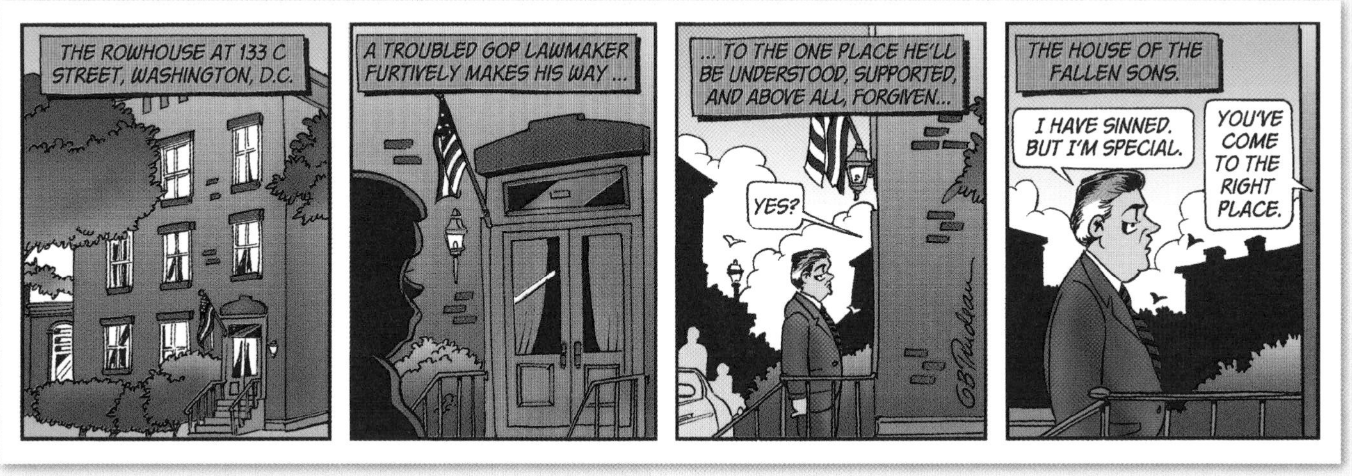
THE ROWHOUSE AT 133 C STREET, WASHINGTON, D.C.
A TROUBLED GOP LAWMAKER FURTIVELY MAKES HIS WAY ...
... TO THE ONE PLACE HE'LL BE UNDERSTOOD, SUPPORTED, AND ABOVE ALL, FORGIVEN...
YES?
THE HOUSE OF THE FALLEN SONS.
I HAVE SINNED. BUT I'M SPECIAL.
YOU'VE COME TO THE RIGHT PLACE.

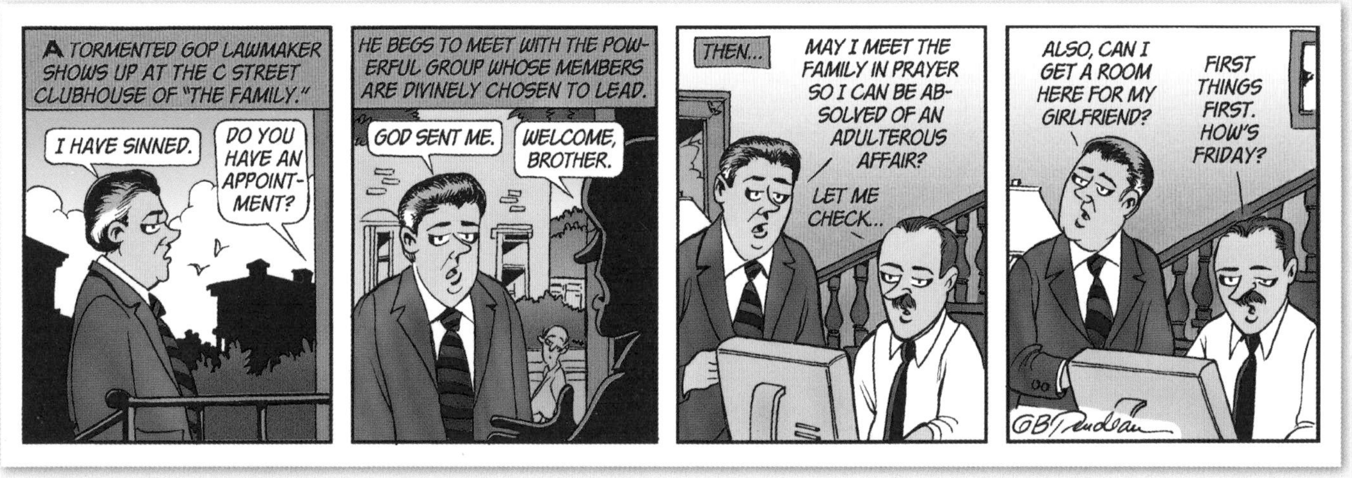
A TORMENTED GOP LAWMAKER SHOWS UP AT THE C STREET CLUBHOUSE OF "THE FAMILY."
I HAVE SINNED.
DO YOU HAVE AN APPOINT-MENT?
HE BEGS TO MEET WITH THE POW-ERFUL GROUP WHOSE MEMBERS ARE DIVINELY CHOSEN TO LEAD.
GOD SENT ME.
WELCOME, BROTHER.
THEN...
MAY I MEET THE FAMILY IN PRAYER SO I CAN BE AB-SOLVED OF AN ADULTEROUS AFFAIR?
LET ME CHECK...
ALSO, CAN I GET A ROOM HERE FOR MY GIRLFRIEND?
FIRST THINGS FIRST. HOW'S FRIDAY?

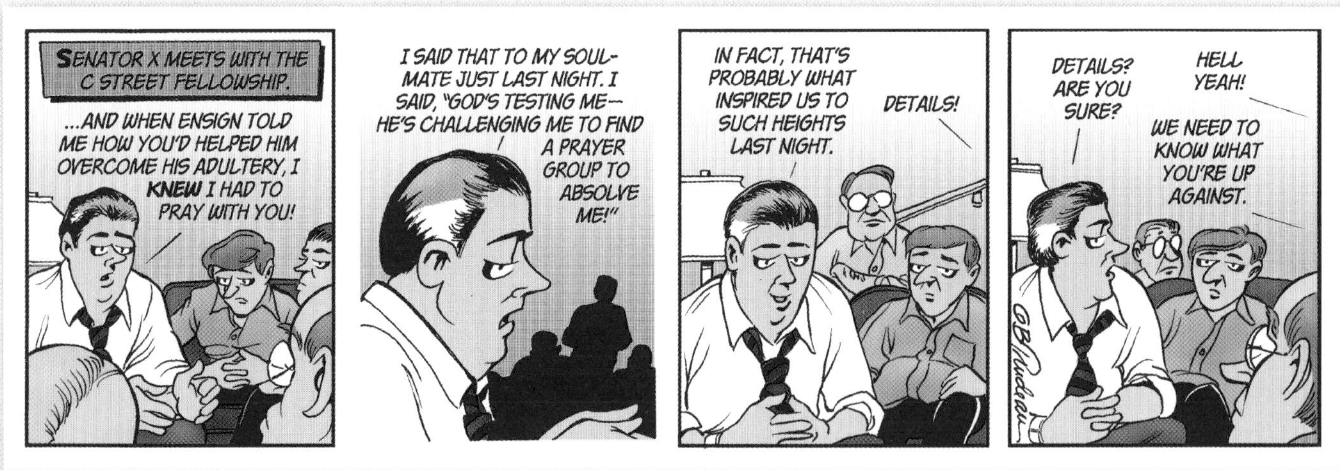
SENATOR X MEETS WITH THE C STREET FELLOWSHIP.
...AND WHEN ENSIGN TOLD ME HOW YOU'D HELPED HIM OVERCOME HIS ADULTERY, I **KNEW** I HAD TO PRAY WITH YOU!
I SAID THAT TO MY SOUL-MATE JUST LAST NIGHT. I SAID, "GOD'S TESTING ME— HE'S CHALLENGING ME TO FIND A PRAYER GROUP TO ABSOLVE ME!"
IN FACT, THAT'S PROBABLY WHAT INSPIRED US TO SUCH HEIGHTS LAST NIGHT.
DETAILS!
DETAILS? ARE YOU SURE?
HELL YEAH!
WE NEED TO KNOW WHAT YOU'RE UP AGAINST.

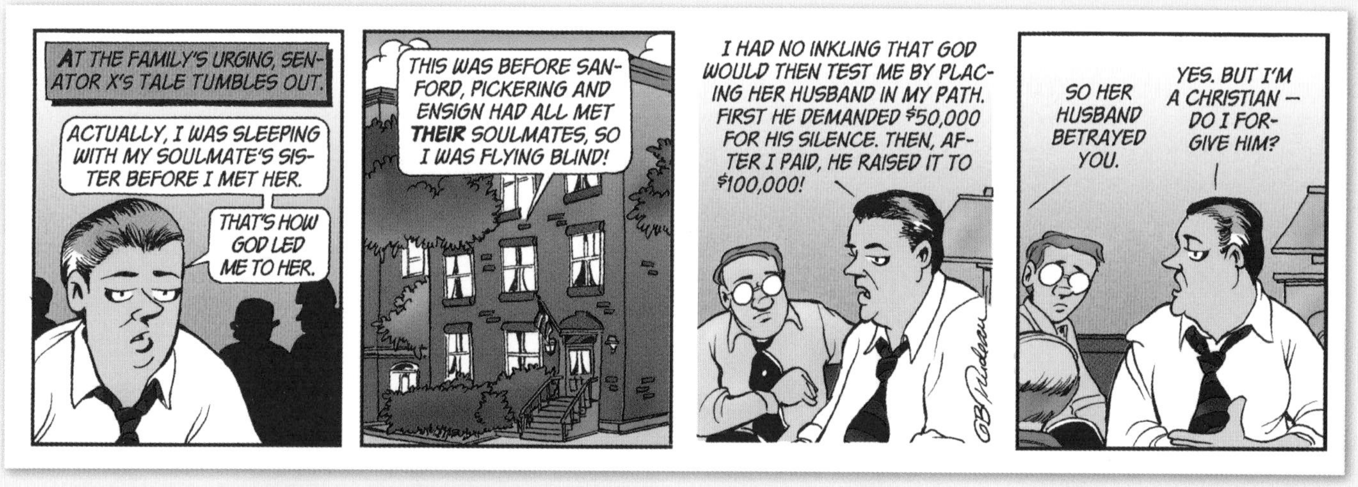
AT THE FAMILY'S URGING, SENATOR X'S TALE TUMBLES OUT.
ACTUALLY, I WAS SLEEPING WITH MY SOULMATE'S SISTER BEFORE I MET HER.
THAT'S HOW GOD LED ME TO HER.
THIS WAS BEFORE SANFORD, PICKERING AND ENSIGN HAD ALL MET **THEIR** SOULMATES, SO I WAS FLYING BLIND!
I HAD NO INKLING THAT GOD WOULD THEN TEST ME BY PLACING HER HUSBAND IN MY PATH. FIRST HE DEMANDED $50,000 FOR HIS SILENCE. THEN, AFTER I PAID, HE RAISED IT TO $100,000!
SO HER HUSBAND BETRAYED YOU.
YES. BUT I'M A CHRISTIAN — DO I FORGIVE HIM?
©B Trudeau

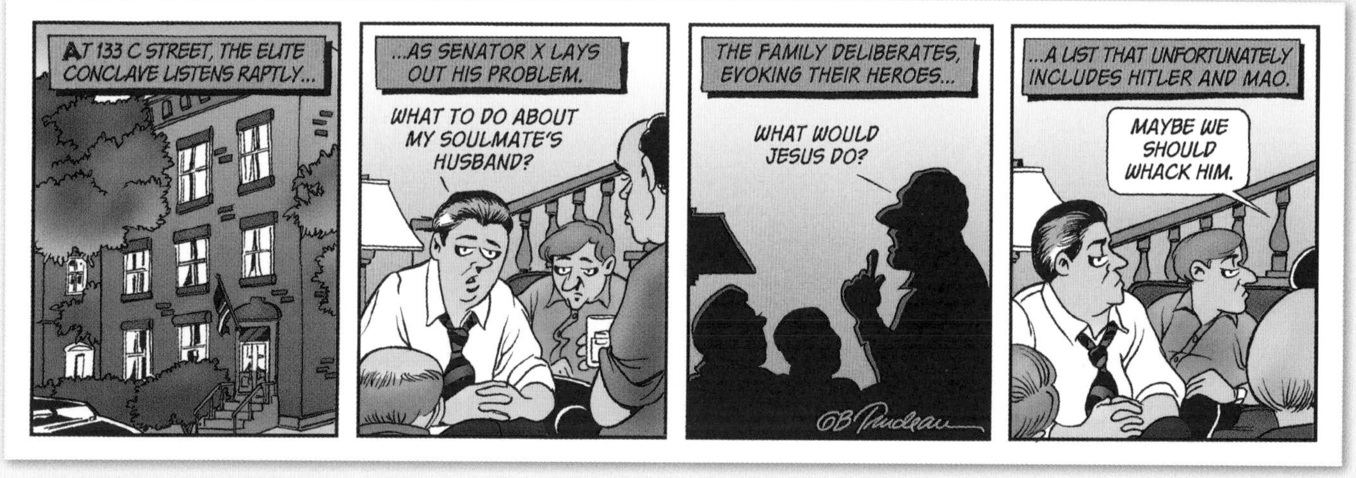
AT 133 C STREET, THE ELITE CONCLAVE LISTENS RAPTLY...
...AS SENATOR X LAYS OUT HIS PROBLEM.
WHAT TO DO ABOUT MY SOULMATE'S HUSBAND?
THE FAMILY DELIBERATES, EVOKING THEIR HEROES...
WHAT WOULD JESUS DO?
©B Trudeau
...A LIST THAT UNFORTUNATELY INCLUDES HITLER AND MAO.
MAYBE WE SHOULD WHACK HIM.

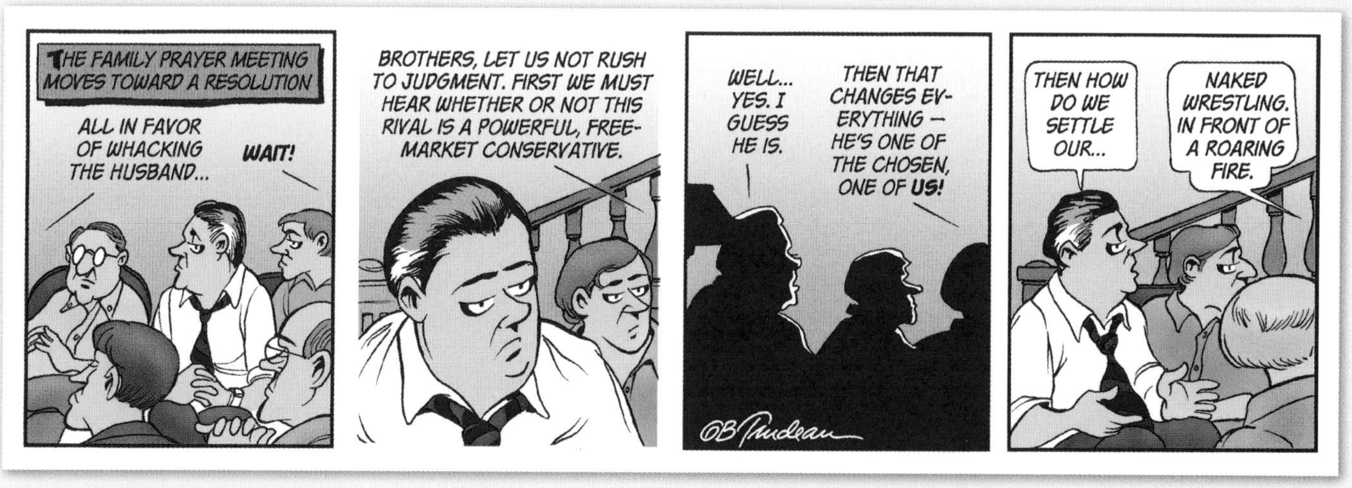
THE FAMILY PRAYER MEETING MOVES TOWARD A RESOLUTION
ALL IN FAVOR OF WHACKING THE HUSBAND...
WAIT!
BROTHERS, LET US NOT RUSH TO JUDGMENT. FIRST WE MUST HEAR WHETHER OR NOT THIS RIVAL IS A POWERFUL, FREE-MARKET CONSERVATIVE.
WELL... YES. I GUESS HE IS.
THEN THAT CHANGES EVERYTHING — HE'S ONE OF THE CHOSEN, ONE OF **US!**
©B Trudeau
THEN HOW DO WE SETTLE OUR...
NAKED WRESTLING. IN FRONT OF A ROARING FIRE.

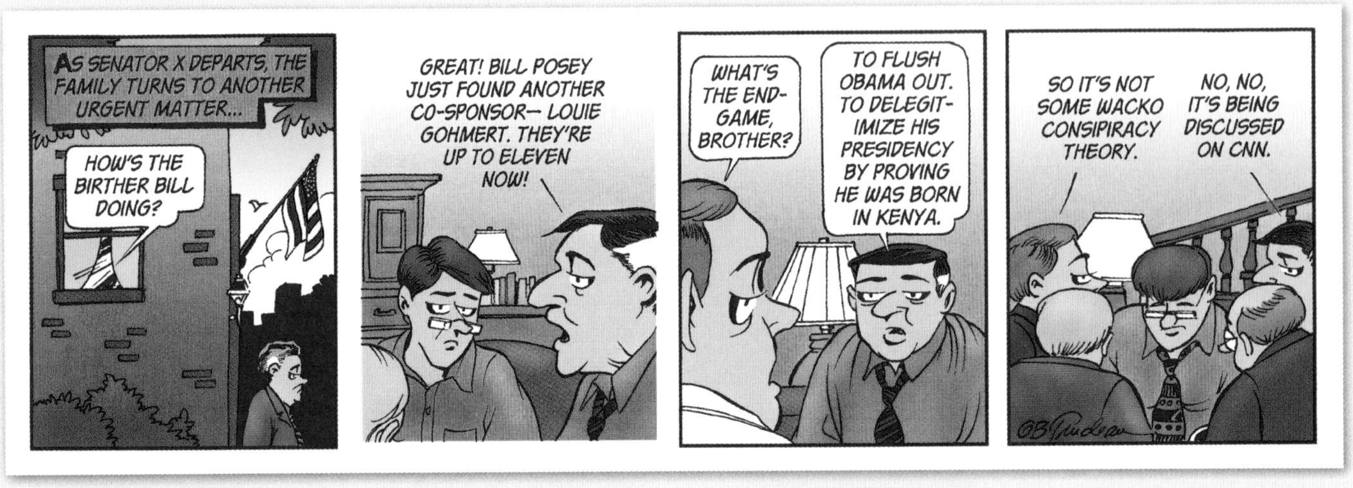
AS SENATOR X DEPARTS, THE FAMILY TURNS TO ANOTHER URGENT MATTER...
HOW'S THE BIRTHER BILL DOING?
GREAT! BILL POSEY JUST FOUND ANOTHER CO-SPONSOR— LOUIE GOHMERT. THEY'RE UP TO ELEVEN NOW!
WHAT'S THE END-GAME, BROTHER?
TO FLUSH OBAMA OUT. TO DELEGIT-IMIZE HIS PRESIDENCY BY PROVING HE WAS BORN IN KENYA.
SO IT'S NOT SOME WACKO CONSIPIRACY THEORY.
NO, NO, IT'S BEING DISCUSSED ON CNN.

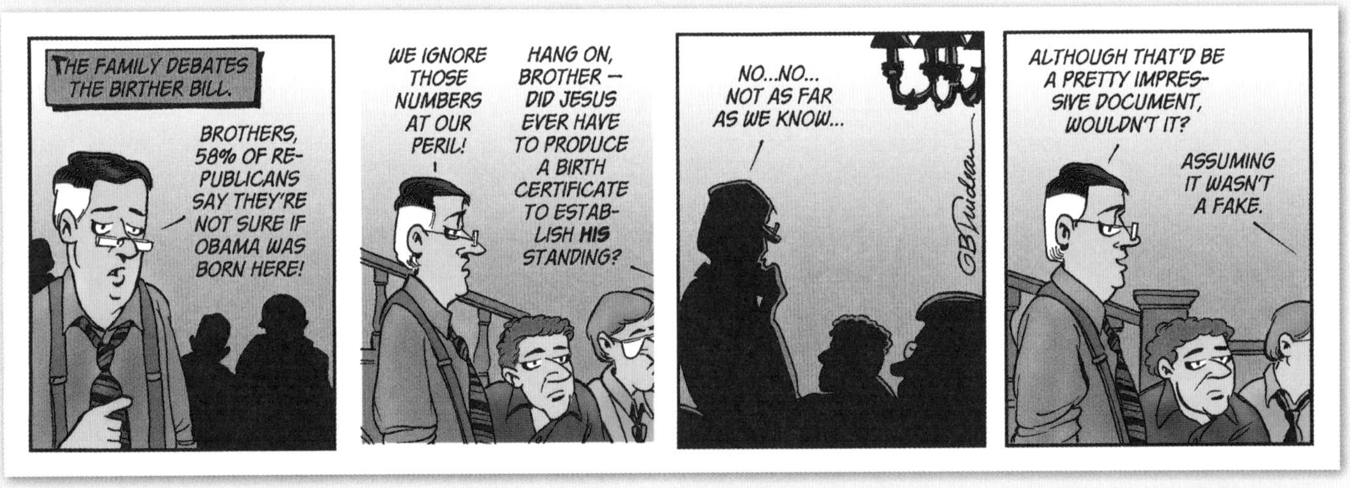
THE FAMILY DEBATES THE BIRTHER BILL.
BROTHERS, 58% OF RE-PUBLICANS SAY THEY'RE NOT SURE IF OBAMA WAS BORN HERE!
WE IGNORE THOSE NUMBERS AT OUR PERIL!
HANG ON, BROTHER — DID JESUS EVER HAVE TO PRODUCE A BIRTH CERTIFICATE TO ESTAB-LISH **HIS** STANDING?
NO...NO... NOT AS FAR AS WE KNOW...
ALTHOUGH THAT'D BE A PRETTY IMPRES-SIVE DOCUMENT, WOULDN'T IT?
ASSUMING IT WASN'T A FAKE.

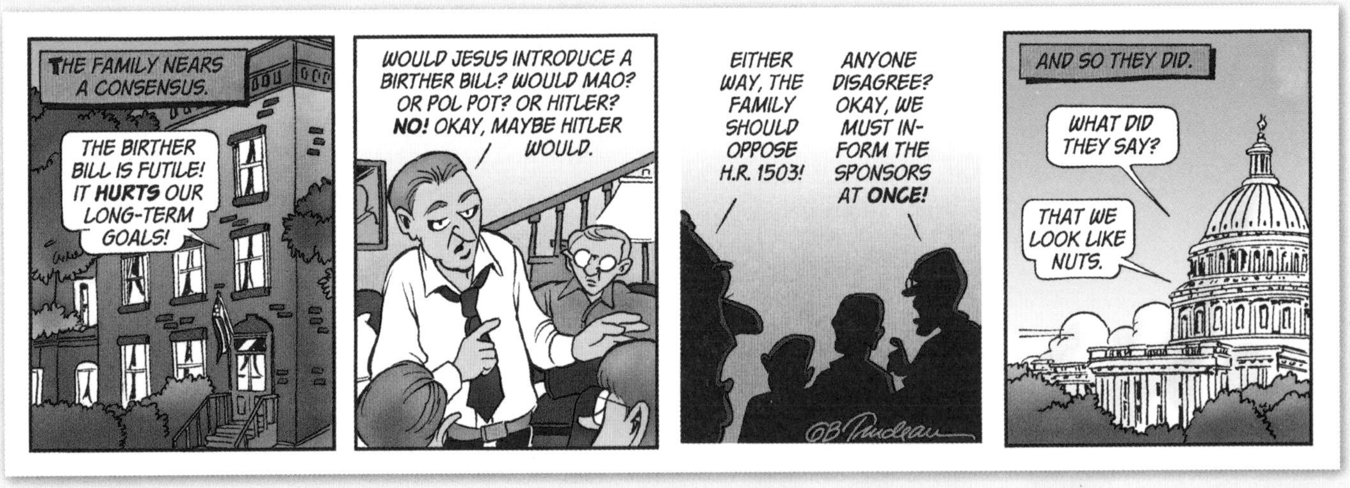
THE FAMILY NEARS A CONSENSUS.
THE BIRTHER BILL IS FUTILE! IT **HURTS** OUR LONG-TERM GOALS!
WOULD JESUS INTRODUCE A BIRTHER BILL? WOULD MAO? OR POL POT? OR HITLER? **NO!** OKAY, MAYBE HITLER WOULD.
EITHER WAY, THE FAMILY SHOULD OPPOSE H.R. 1503!
ANYONE DISAGREE? OKAY, WE MUST IN-FORM THE SPONSORS AT **ONCE!**
AND SO THEY DID.
WHAT DID THEY SAY?
THAT WE LOOK LIKE NUTS.

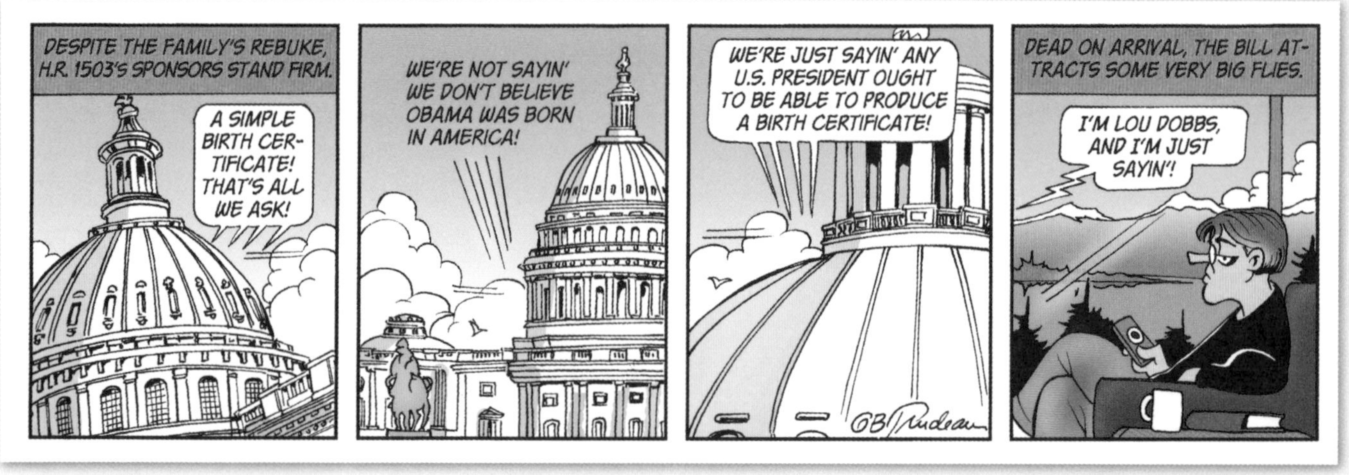
DESPITE THE FAMILY'S REBUKE, H.R. 1503'S SPONSORS STAND FIRM.
A SIMPLE BIRTH CERTIFICATE! THAT'S ALL WE ASK!
WE'RE NOT SAYIN' WE DON'T BELIEVE OBAMA WAS BORN IN AMERICA!
WE'RE JUST SAYIN' ANY U.S. PRESIDENT OUGHT TO BE ABLE TO PRODUCE A BIRTH CERTIFICATE!
DEAD ON ARRIVAL, THE BILL ATTRACTS SOME VERY BIG FLIES.
I'M LOU DOBBS, AND I'M JUST SAYIN'!
GB Trudeau

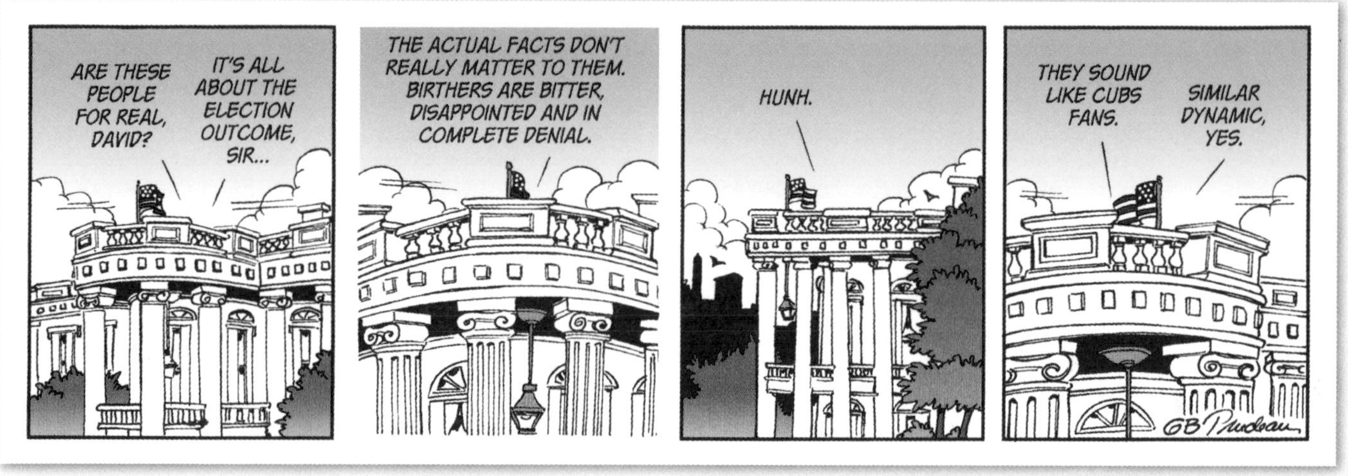
ARE THESE PEOPLE FOR REAL, DAVID?
IT'S ALL ABOUT THE ELECTION OUTCOME, SIR...
THE ACTUAL FACTS DON'T REALLY MATTER TO THEM. BIRTHERS ARE BITTER, DISAPPOINTED AND IN COMPLETE DENIAL.
HUNH.
THEY SOUND LIKE CUBS FANS.
SIMILAR DYNAMIC, YES.
GB Trudeau

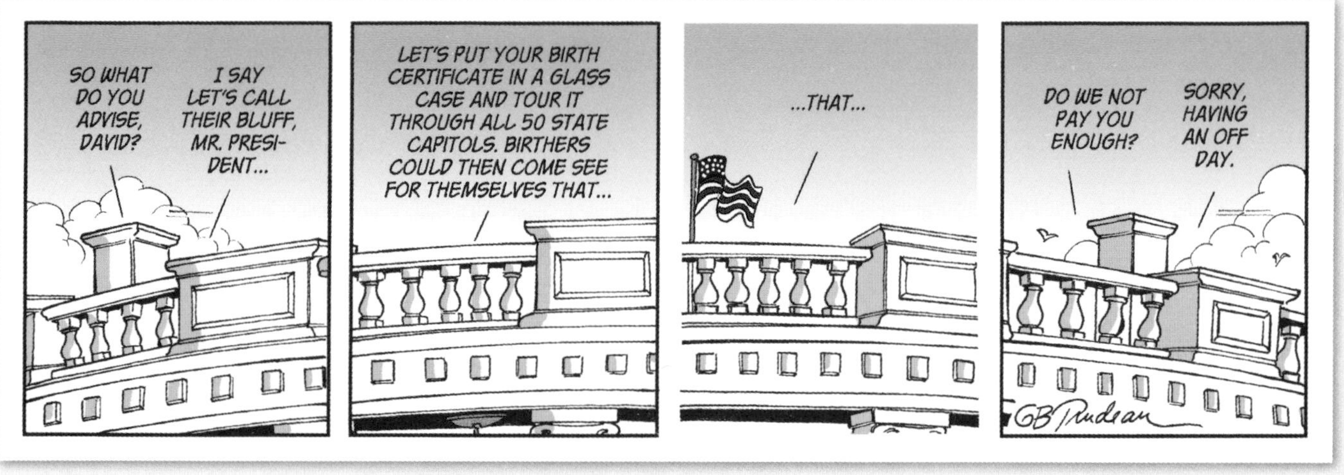
SO WHAT DO YOU ADVISE, DAVID?
I SAY LET'S CALL THEIR BLUFF, MR. PRESIDENT...
LET'S PUT YOUR BIRTH CERTIFICATE IN A GLASS CASE AND TOUR IT THROUGH ALL 50 STATE CAPITOLS. BIRTHERS COULD THEN COME SEE FOR THEMSELVES THAT...
...THAT...
DO WE NOT PAY YOU ENOUGH?
SORRY, HAVING AN OFF DAY.
GB Trudeau

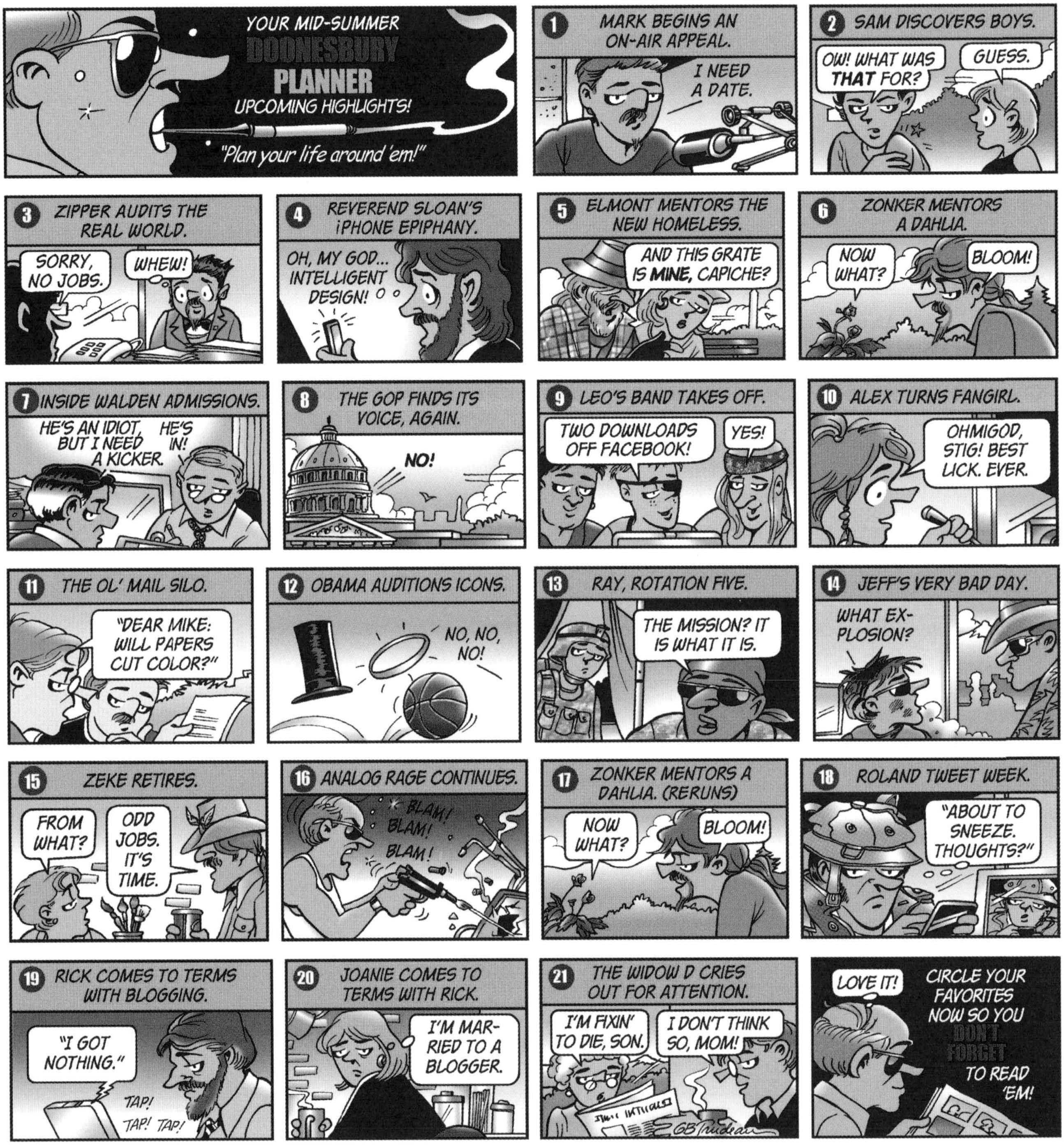
YOUR MID-SUMMER
DOONESBURY
PLANNER
UPCOMING HIGHLIGHTS!
"Plan your life around 'em!"
1 MARK BEGINS AN ON-AIR APPEAL.
I NEED A DATE.
2 SAM DISCOVERS BOYS.
OW! WHAT WAS THAT FOR?
GUESS.
3 ZIPPER AUDITS THE REAL WORLD.
SORRY, NO JOBS.
WHEW!
4 REVEREND SLOAN'S iPHONE EPIPHANY.
OH, MY GOD... INTELLIGENT DESIGN!
5 ELMONT MENTORS THE NEW HOMELESS.
AND THIS GRATE IS MINE, CAPICHE?
6 ZONKER MENTORS A DAHLIA.
NOW WHAT?
BLOOM!
7 INSIDE WALDEN ADMISSIONS.
HE'S AN IDIOT, BUT I NEED A KICKER.
HE'S IN!
8 THE GOP FINDS ITS VOICE, AGAIN.
NO!
9 LEO'S BAND TAKES OFF.
TWO DOWNLOADS OFF FACEBOOK!
YES!
10 ALEX TURNS FANGIRL.
OHMIGOD, STIG! BEST LICK. EVER.
11 THE OL' MAIL SILO.
"DEAR MIKE: WILL PAPERS CUT COLOR?"
12 OBAMA AUDITIONS ICONS.
NO, NO, NO!
13 RAY, ROTATION FIVE.
THE MISSION? IT IS WHAT IT IS.
14 JEFF'S VERY BAD DAY.
WHAT EX-PLOSION?
15 ZEKE RETIRES.
FROM WHAT?
ODD JOBS. IT'S TIME.
16 ANALOG RAGE CONTINUES.
BLAM! BLAM! BLAM!
17 ZONKER MENTORS A DAHLIA. (RERUNS)
NOW WHAT?
BLOOM!
18 ROLAND TWEET WEEK.
"ABOUT TO SNEEZE. THOUGHTS?"
19 RICK COMES TO TERMS WITH BLOGGING.
"I GOT NOTHING."
TAP! TAP! TAP!
20 JOANIE COMES TO TERMS WITH RICK.
I'M MAR-RIED TO A BLOGGER.
21 THE WIDOW D CRIES OUT FOR ATTENTION.
I'M FIXIN' TO DIE, SON.
I DON'T THINK SO, MOM!
GBTrudeau
LOVE IT!
CIRCLE YOUR FAVORITES NOW SO YOU DON'T FORGET TO READ 'EM!

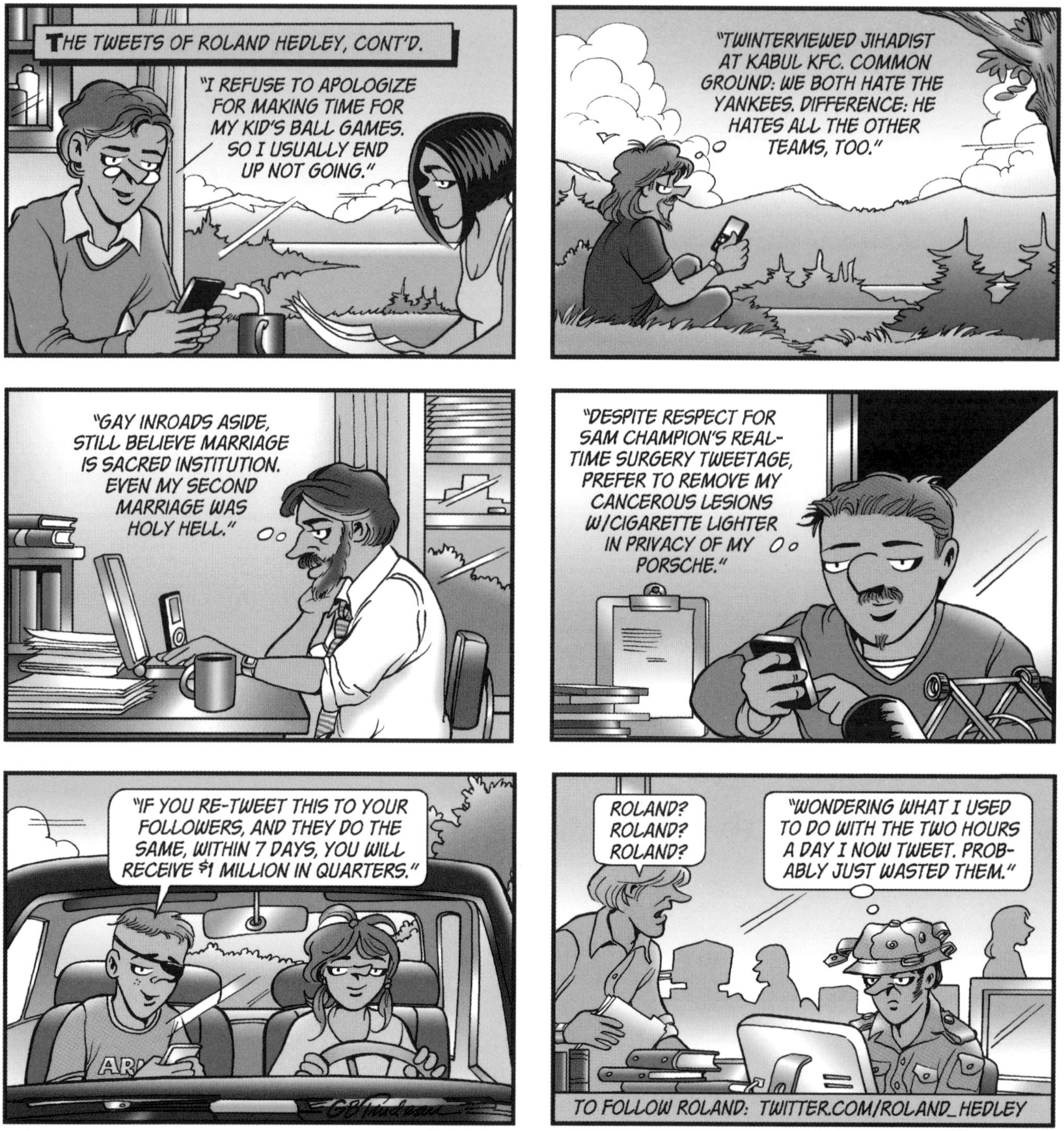
THE TWEETS OF ROLAND HEDLEY, CONT'D.
"I REFUSE TO APOLOGIZE FOR MAKING TIME FOR MY KID'S BALL GAMES. SO I USUALLY END UP NOT GOING."
"TWINTERVIEWED JIHADIST AT KABUL KFC. COMMON GROUND: WE BOTH HATE THE YANKEES. DIFFERENCE: HE HATES ALL THE OTHER TEAMS, TOO."
"GAY INROADS ASIDE, STILL BELIEVE MARRIAGE IS SACRED INSTITUTION. EVEN MY SECOND MARRIAGE WAS HOLY HELL."
"DESPITE RESPECT FOR SAM CHAMPION'S REAL-TIME SURGERY TWEETAGE, PREFER TO REMOVE MY CANCEROUS LESIONS W/CIGARETTE LIGHTER IN PRIVACY OF MY PORSCHE."
"IF YOU RE-TWEET THIS TO YOUR FOLLOWERS, AND THEY DO THE SAME, WITHIN 7 DAYS, YOU WILL RECEIVE $1 MILLION IN QUARTERS."
ROLAND? ROLAND? ROLAND?
"WONDERING WHAT I USED TO DO WITH THE TWO HOURS A DAY I NOW TWEET. PROBABLY JUST WASTED THEM."
TO FOLLOW ROLAND: TWITTER.COM/ROLAND_HEDLEY

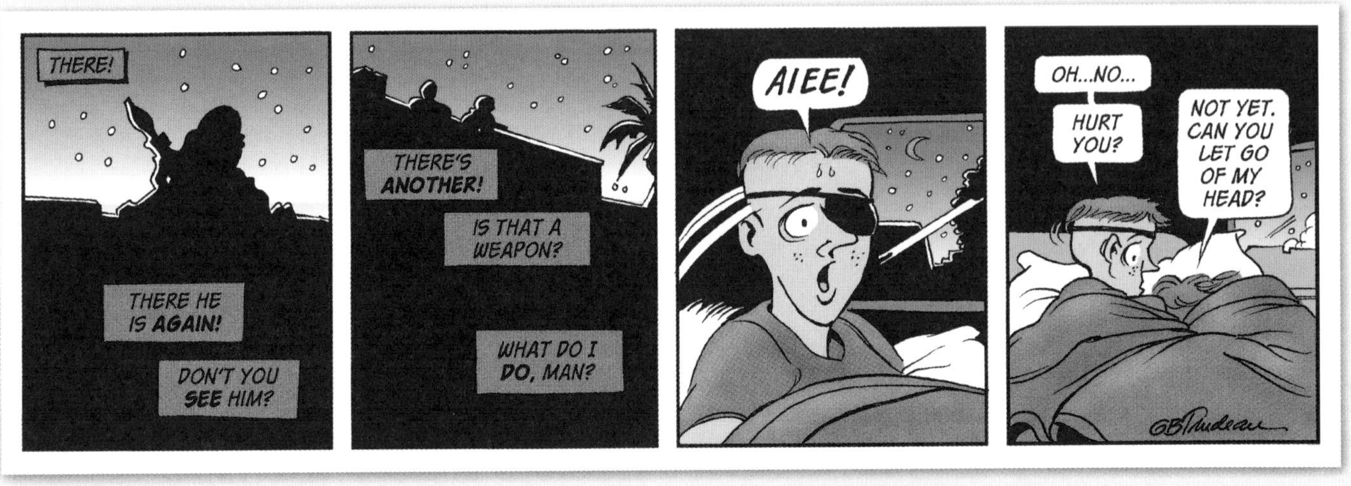
THERE!
THERE HE IS AGAIN!
DON'T YOU SEE HIM?
THERE'S ANOTHER!
IS THAT A WEAPON?
WHAT DO I DO, MAN?
AIEE!
OH...NO...
HURT YOU?
NOT YET. CAN YOU LET GO OF MY HEAD?
GB Trudeau

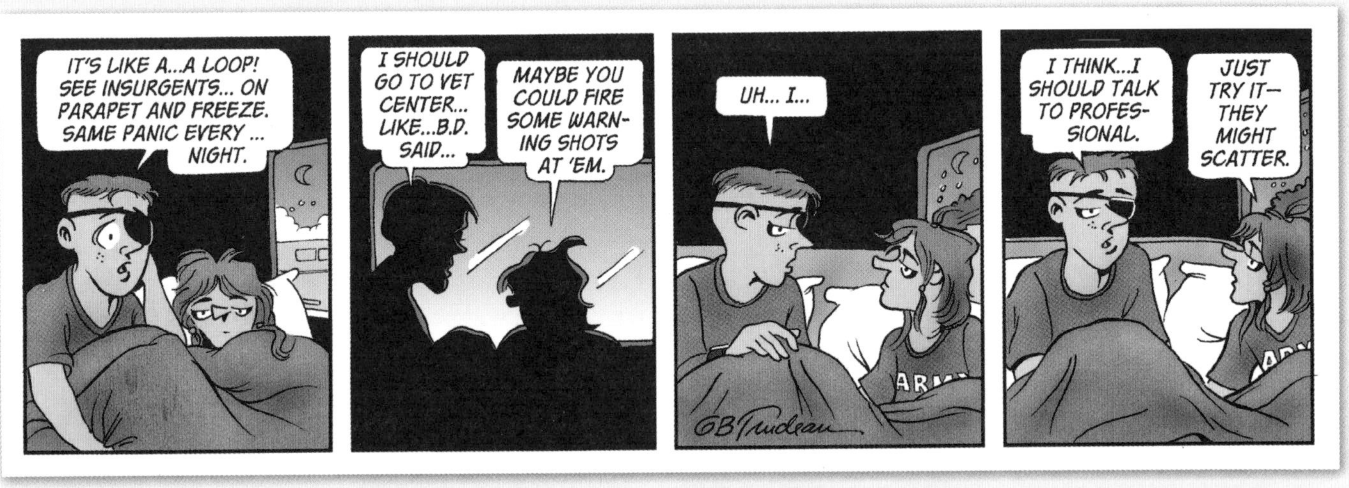
IT'S LIKE A...A LOOP! SEE INSURGENTS... ON PARAPET AND FREEZE. SAME PANIC EVERY ... NIGHT.
I SHOULD GO TO VET CENTER... LIKE...B.D. SAID...
MAYBE YOU COULD FIRE SOME WARNING SHOTS AT 'EM.
UH... I...
GB Trudeau
I THINK...I SHOULD TALK TO PROFESSIONAL.
JUST TRY IT— THEY MIGHT SCATTER.

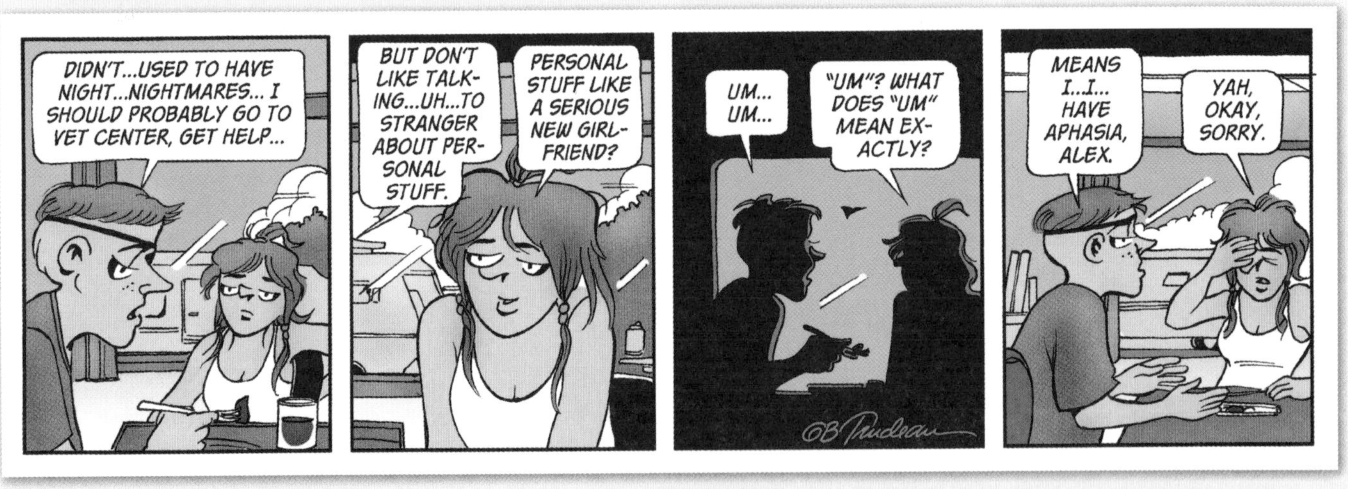
DIDN'T...USED TO HAVE NIGHT...NIGHTMARES... I SHOULD PROBABLY GO TO VET CENTER, GET HELP...
BUT DON'T LIKE TALKING...UH...TO STRANGER ABOUT PERSONAL STUFF.
PERSONAL STUFF LIKE A SERIOUS NEW GIRLFRIEND?
UM... UM...
"UM"? WHAT DOES "UM" MEAN EXACTLY?
GB Trudeau
MEANS I...I... HAVE APHASIA, ALEX.
YAH, OKAY, SORRY.

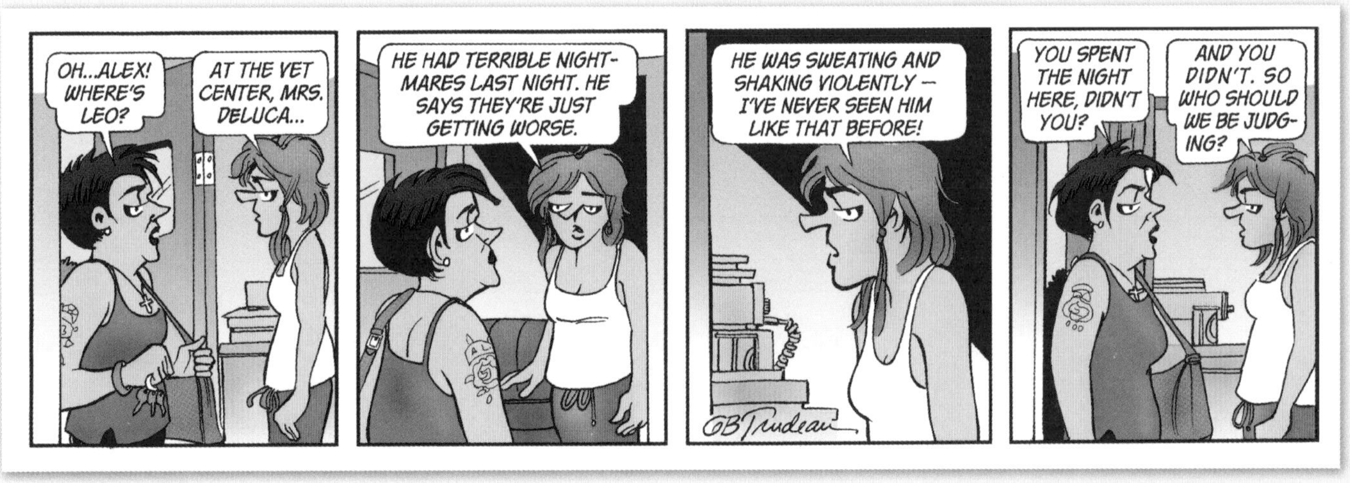
OH...ALEX! WHERE'S LEO?
AT THE VET CENTER, MRS. DELUCA...
HE HAD TERRIBLE NIGHTMARES LAST NIGHT. HE SAYS THEY'RE JUST GETTING WORSE.
HE WAS SWEATING AND SHAKING VIOLENTLY — I'VE NEVER SEEN HIM LIKE THAT BEFORE!
GB Trudeau
YOU SPENT THE NIGHT HERE, DIDN'T YOU?
AND YOU DIDN'T. SO WHO SHOULD WE BE JUDGING?

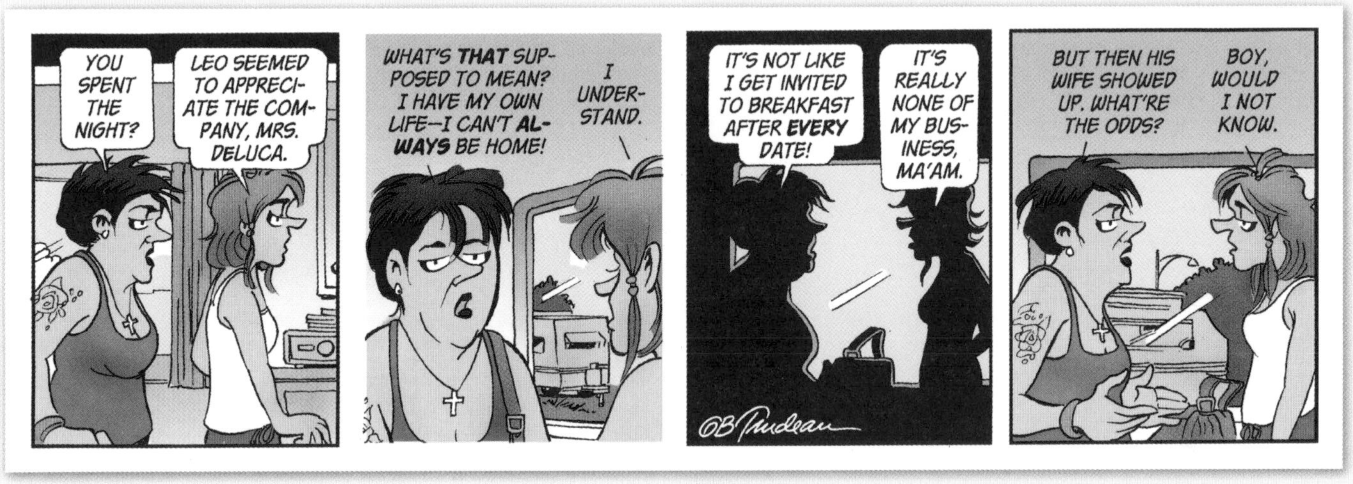
YOU SPENT THE NIGHT?
LEO SEEMED TO APPRECIATE THE COMPANY, MRS. DELUCA.
WHAT'S **THAT** SUPPOSED TO MEAN? I HAVE MY OWN LIFE--I CAN'T **ALWAYS** BE HOME!
I UNDERSTAND.
IT'S NOT LIKE I GET INVITED TO BREAKFAST AFTER **EVERY** DATE!
IT'S REALLY NONE OF MY BUSINESS, MA'AM.
GB Trudeau
BUT THEN HIS WIFE SHOWED UP. WHAT'RE THE ODDS?
BOY, WOULD I NOT KNOW.

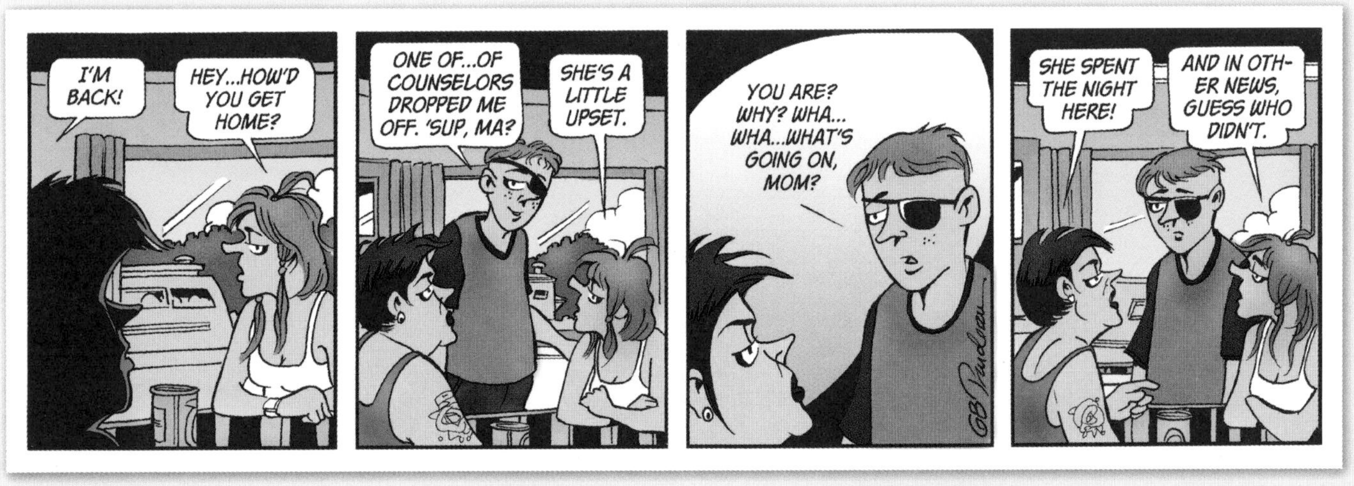
I'M BACK!
HEY...HOW'D YOU GET HOME?
ONE OF...OF COUNSELORS DROPPED ME OFF. 'SUP, MA?
SHE'S A LITTLE UPSET.
YOU ARE? WHY? WHA... WHA...WHAT'S GOING ON, MOM?
GB Trudeau
SHE SPENT THE NIGHT HERE!
AND IN OTHER NEWS, GUESS WHO DIDN'T.

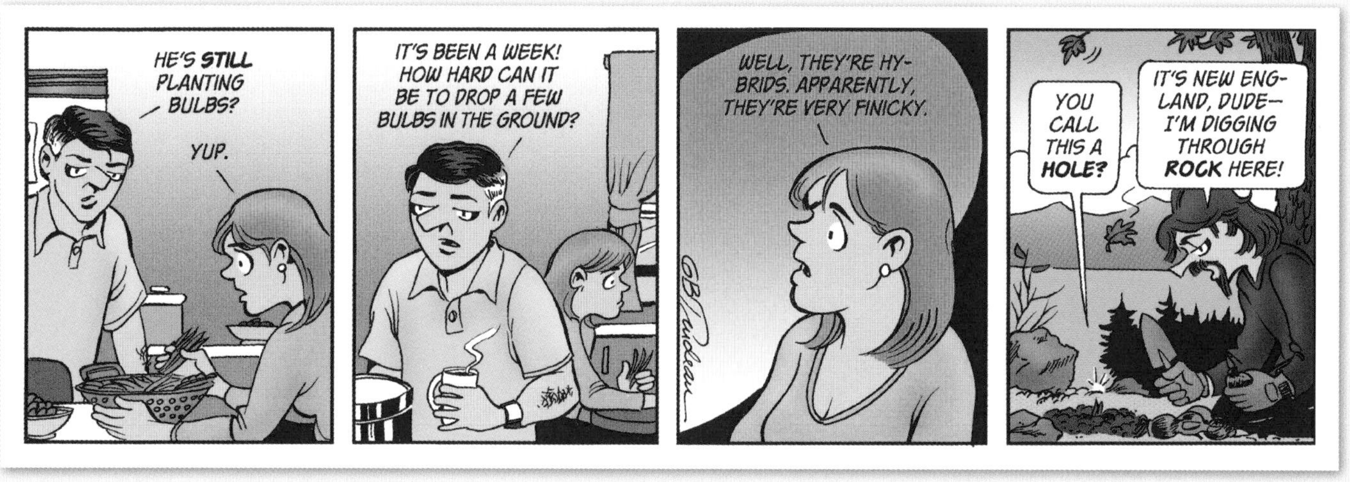
HE'S STILL PLANTING BULBS?
YUP.
IT'S BEEN A WEEK! HOW HARD CAN IT BE TO DROP A FEW BULBS IN THE GROUND?
WELL, THEY'RE HYBRIDS. APPARENTLY, THEY'RE VERY FINICKY.
YOU CALL THIS A HOLE?
IT'S NEW ENGLAND, DUDE— I'M DIGGING THROUGH ROCK HERE!

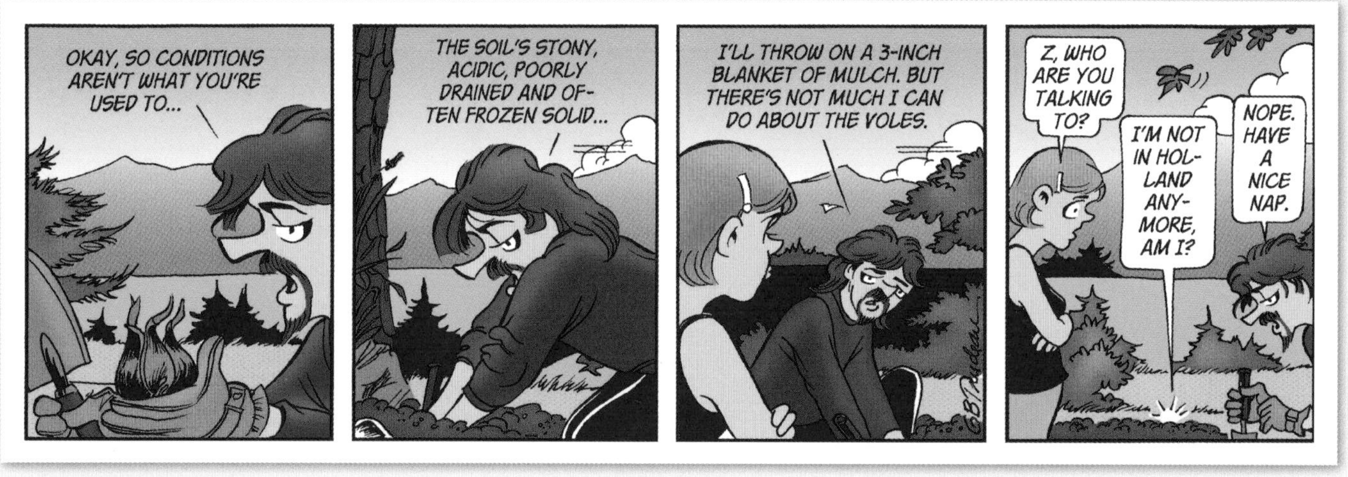
OKAY, SO CONDITIONS AREN'T WHAT YOU'RE USED TO...
THE SOIL'S STONY, ACIDIC, POORLY DRAINED AND OFTEN FROZEN SOLID...
I'LL THROW ON A 3-INCH BLANKET OF MULCH. BUT THERE'S NOT MUCH I CAN DO ABOUT THE VOLES.
Z, WHO ARE YOU TALKING TO?
I'M NOT IN HOLLAND ANYMORE, AM I?
NOPE. HAVE A NICE NAP.

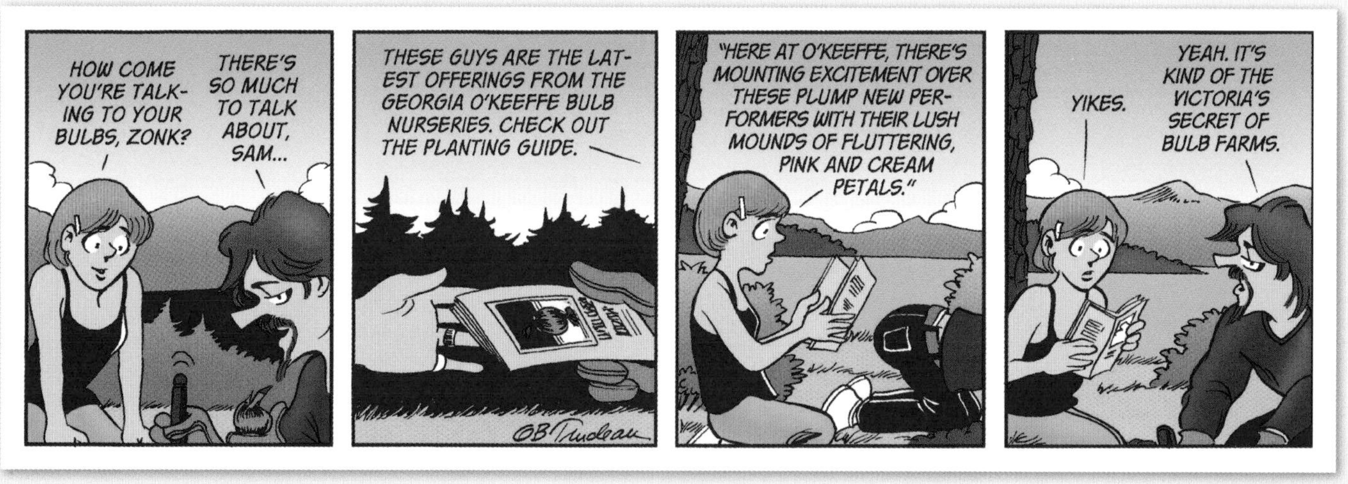
HOW COME YOU'RE TALKING TO YOUR BULBS, ZONK?
THERE'S SO MUCH TO TALK ABOUT, SAM...
THESE GUYS ARE THE LATEST OFFERINGS FROM THE GEORGIA O'KEEFFE BULB NURSERIES. CHECK OUT THE PLANTING GUIDE.
"HERE AT O'KEEFFE, THERE'S MOUNTING EXCITEMENT OVER THESE PLUMP NEW PERFORMERS WITH THEIR LUSH MOUNDS OF FLUTTERING, PINK AND CREAM PETALS."
YIKES.
YEAH. IT'S KIND OF THE VICTORIA'S SECRET OF BULB FARMS.

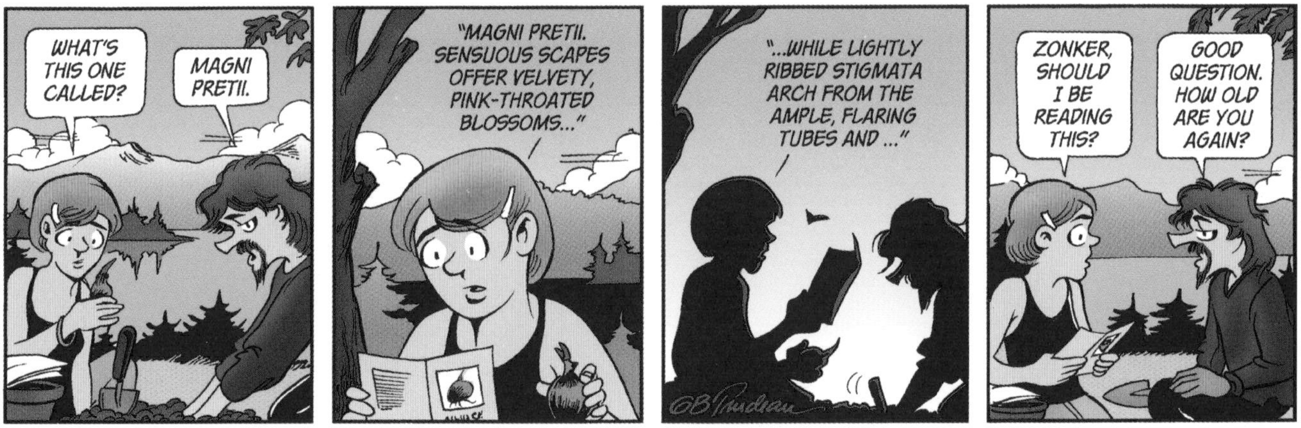
WHAT'S THIS ONE CALLED?
MAGNI PRETII.
"MAGNI PRETII. SENSUOUS SCAPES OFFER VELVETY, PINK-THROATED BLOSSOMS..."
"...WHILE LIGHTLY RIBBED STIGMATA ARCH FROM THE AMPLE, FLARING TUBES AND ..."
ZONKER, SHOULD I BE READING THIS?
GOOD QUESTION. HOW OLD ARE YOU AGAIN?

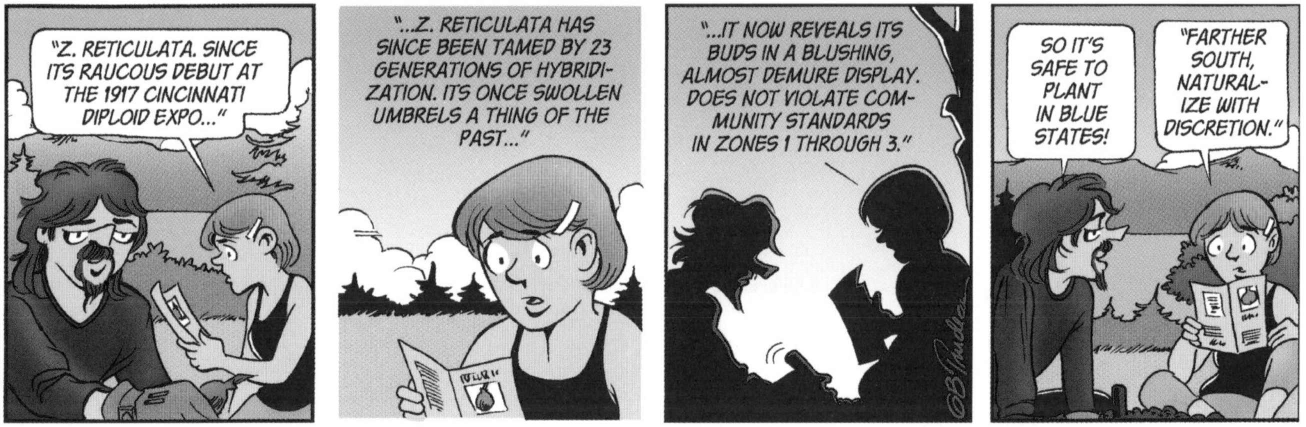
"Z. RETICULATA. SINCE ITS RAUCOUS DEBUT AT THE 1917 CINCINNATI DIPLOID EXPO..."
"...Z. RETICULATA HAS SINCE BEEN TAMED BY 23 GENERATIONS OF HYBRIDIZATION. ITS ONCE SWOLLEN UMBRELS A THING OF THE PAST..."
"...IT NOW REVEALS ITS BUDS IN A BLUSHING, ALMOST DEMURE DISPLAY. DOES NOT VIOLATE COMMUNITY STANDARDS IN ZONES 1 THROUGH 3."
SO IT'S SAFE TO PLANT IN BLUE STATES!
"FARTHER SOUTH, NATURALIZE WITH DISCRETION."

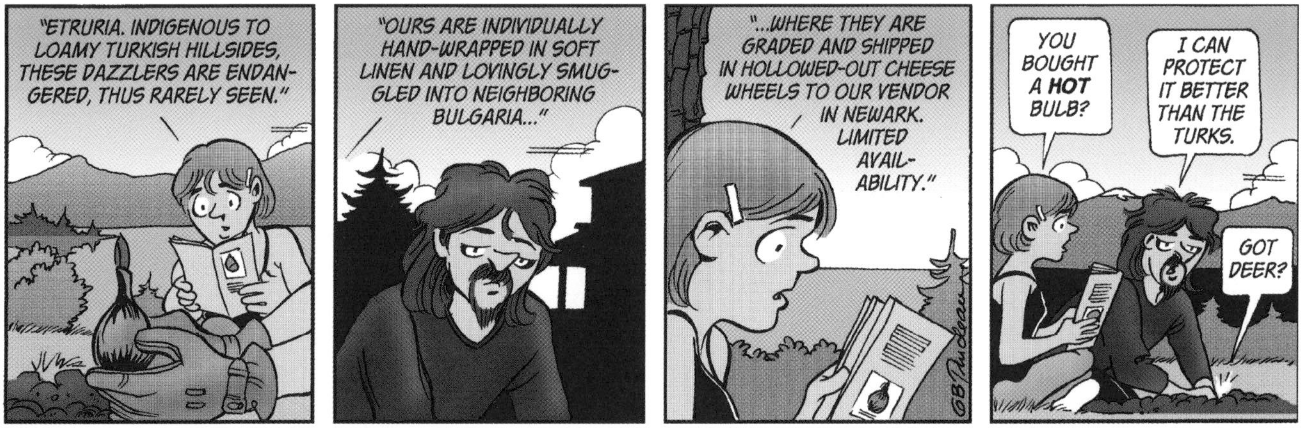
"ETRURIA. INDIGENOUS TO LOAMY TURKISH HILLSIDES, THESE DAZZLERS ARE ENDANGERED, THUS RARELY SEEN."
"OURS ARE INDIVIDUALLY HAND-WRAPPED IN SOFT LINEN AND LOVINGLY SMUGGLED INTO NEIGHBORING BULGARIA..."
"...WHERE THEY ARE GRADED AND SHIPPED IN HOLLOWED-OUT CHEESE WHEELS TO OUR VENDOR IN NEWARK. LIMITED AVAILABILITY."
YOU BOUGHT A **HOT** BULB?
I CAN PROTECT IT BETTER THAN THE TURKS.
GOT DEER?

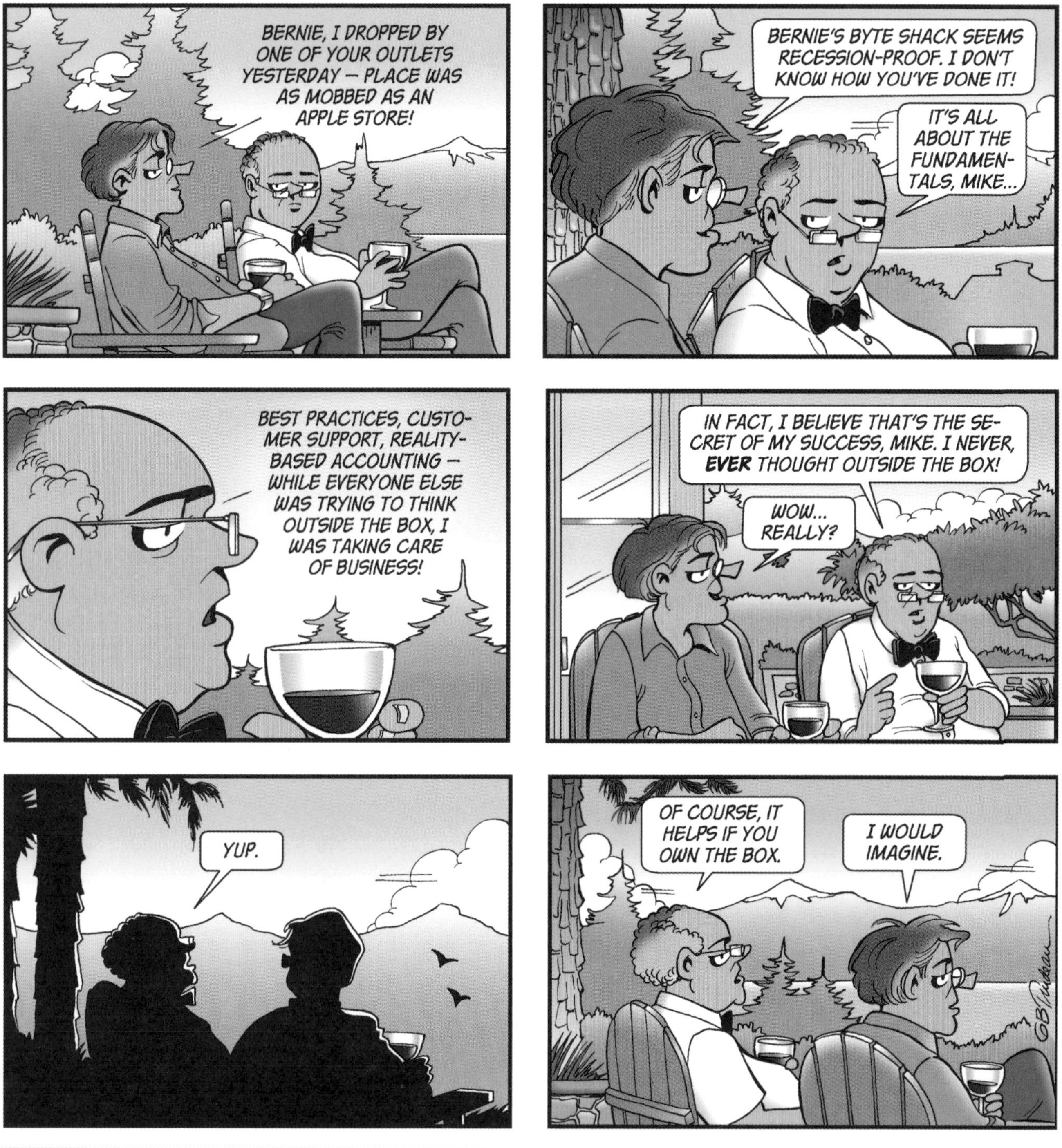
BERNIE, I DROPPED BY ONE OF YOUR OUTLETS YESTERDAY — PLACE WAS AS MOBBED AS AN APPLE STORE!
BERNIE'S BYTE SHACK SEEMS RECESSION-PROOF. I DON'T KNOW HOW YOU'VE DONE IT!
IT'S ALL ABOUT THE FUNDAMENTALS, MIKE...
BEST PRACTICES, CUSTOMER SUPPORT, REALITY-BASED ACCOUNTING — WHILE EVERYONE ELSE WAS TRYING TO THINK OUTSIDE THE BOX, I WAS TAKING CARE OF BUSINESS!
IN FACT, I BELIEVE THAT'S THE SECRET OF MY SUCCESS, MIKE. I NEVER, **EVER** THOUGHT OUTSIDE THE BOX!
WOW... REALLY?
YUP.
OF COURSE, IT HELPS IF YOU OWN THE BOX.
I WOULD IMAGINE.
GBTrudeau

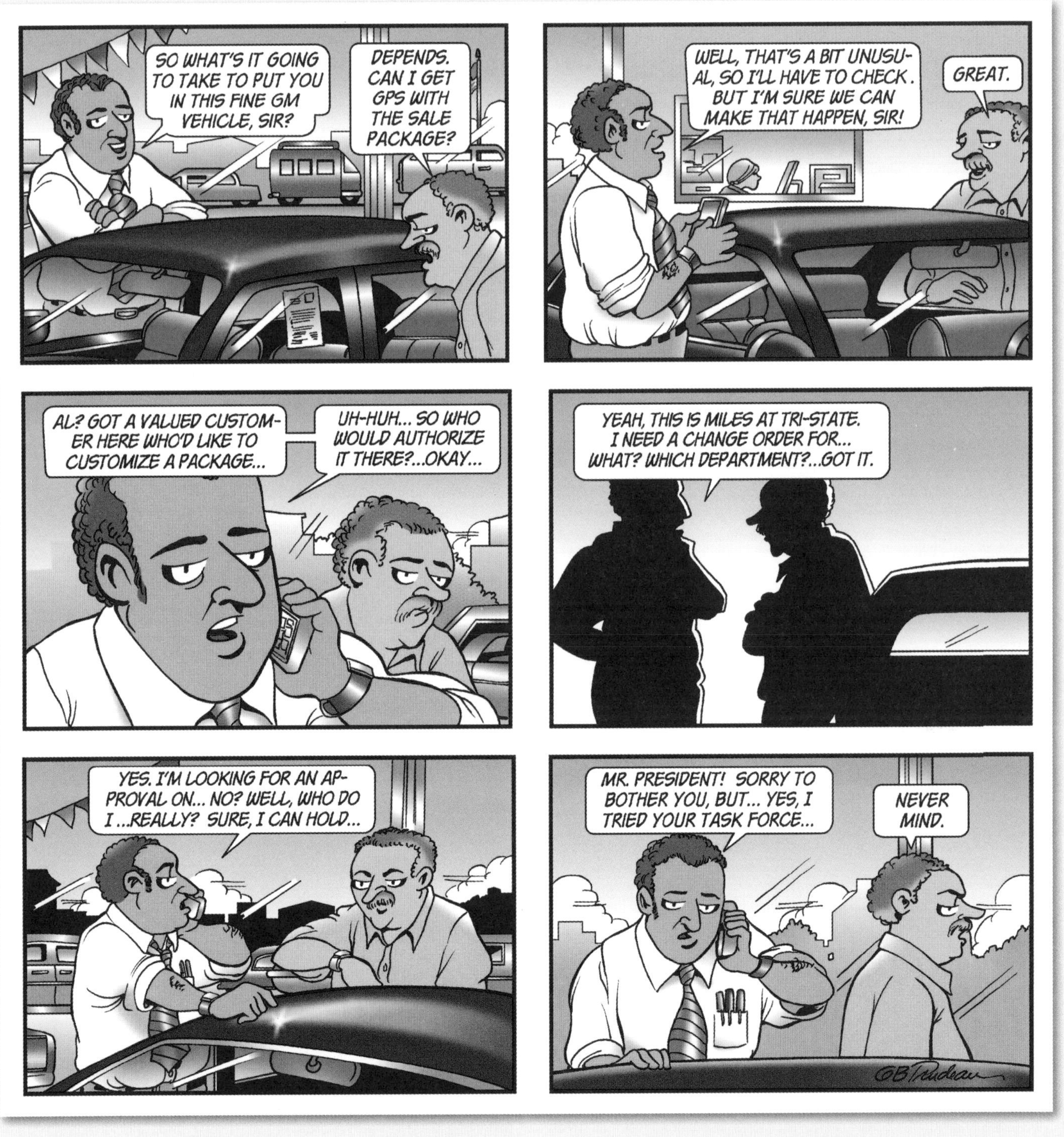
SO WHAT'S IT GOING TO TAKE TO PUT YOU IN THIS FINE GM VEHICLE, SIR?
DEPENDS. CAN I GET GPS WITH THE SALE PACKAGE?
WELL, THAT'S A BIT UNUSUAL, SO I'LL HAVE TO CHECK. BUT I'M SURE WE CAN MAKE THAT HAPPEN, SIR!
GREAT.
AL? GOT A VALUED CUSTOMER HERE WHO'D LIKE TO CUSTOMIZE A PACKAGE...
UH-HUH... SO WHO WOULD AUTHORIZE IT THERE?...OKAY...
YEAH, THIS IS MILES AT TRI-STATE. I NEED A CHANGE ORDER FOR... WHAT? WHICH DEPARTMENT?...GOT IT.
YES. I'M LOOKING FOR AN APPROVAL ON... NO? WELL, WHO DO I ...REALLY? SURE, I CAN HOLD...
MR. PRESIDENT! SORRY TO BOTHER YOU, BUT... YES, I TRIED YOUR TASK FORCE...
NEVER MIND.
GBTrudeau

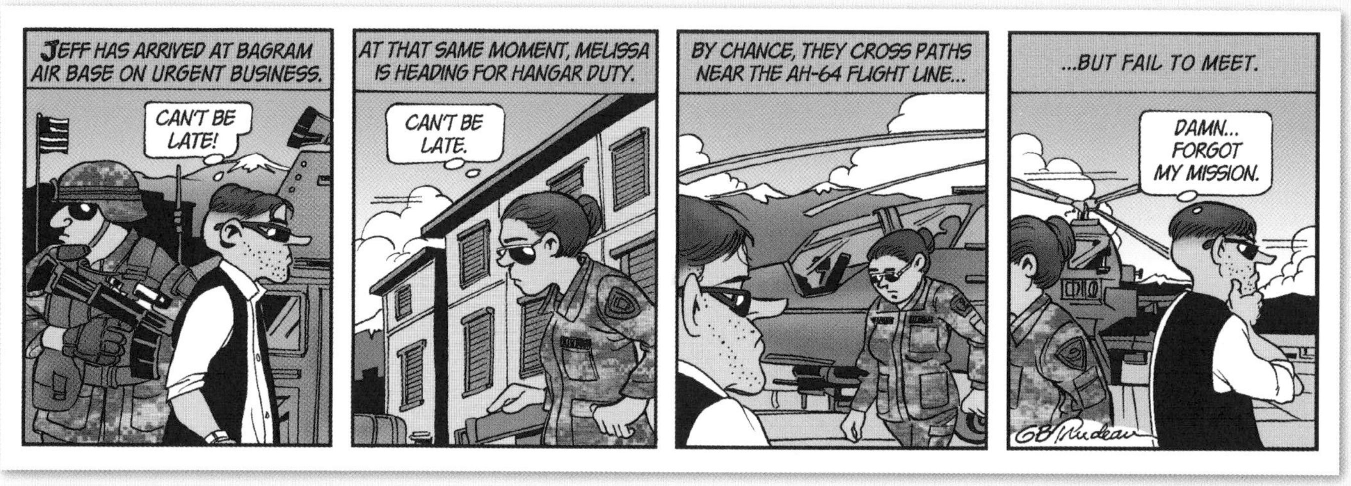
JEFF HAS ARRIVED AT BAGRAM AIR BASE ON URGENT BUSINESS.
CAN'T BE LATE!
AT THAT SAME MOMENT, MELISSA IS HEADING FOR HANGAR DUTY.
CAN'T BE LATE.
BY CHANCE, THEY CROSS PATHS NEAR THE AH-64 FLIGHT LINE...
...BUT FAIL TO MEET.
DAMN... FORGOT MY MISSION.

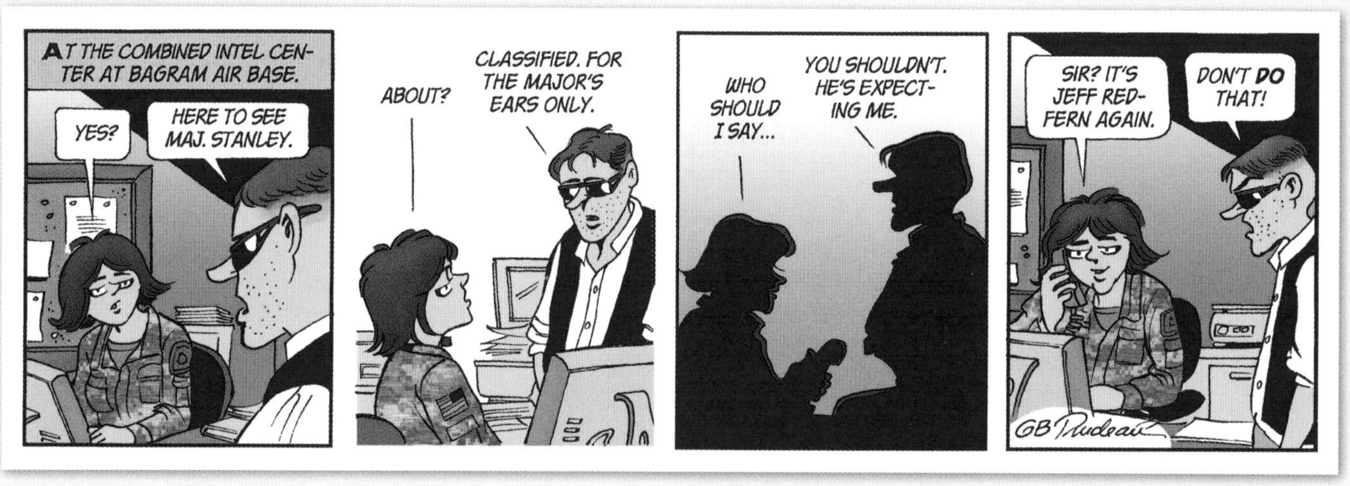
AT THE COMBINED INTEL CENTER AT BAGRAM AIR BASE.
YES?
HERE TO SEE MAJ. STANLEY.
ABOUT?
CLASSIFIED. FOR THE MAJOR'S EARS ONLY.
WHO SHOULD I SAY...
YOU SHOULDN'T. HE'S EXPECTING ME.
SIR? IT'S JEFF REDFERN AGAIN.
DON'T DO THAT!

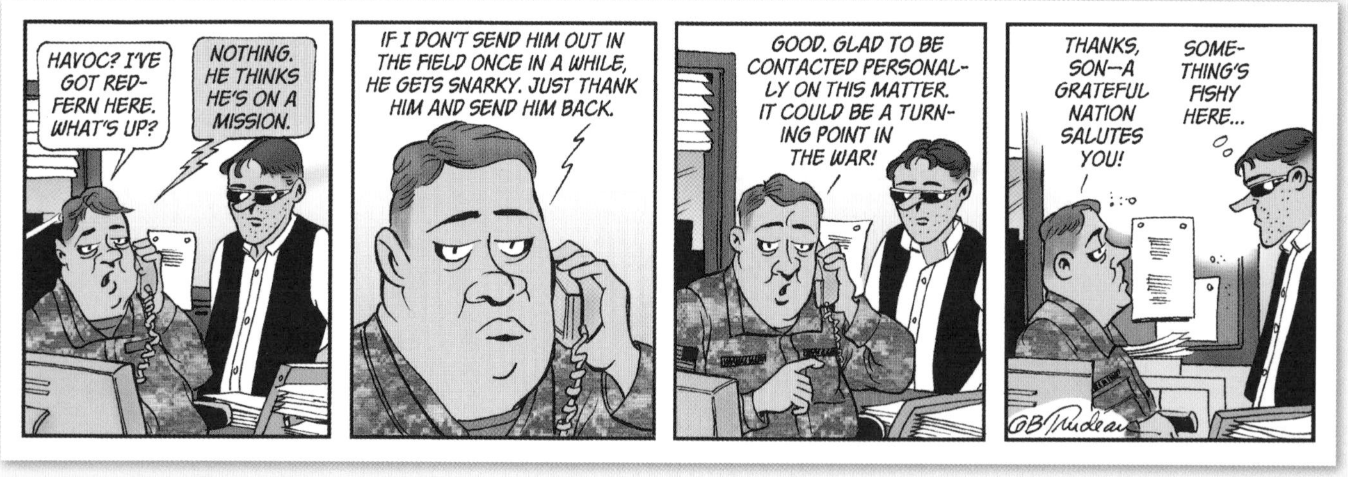
HAVOC? I'VE GOT REDFERN HERE. WHAT'S UP?
NOTHING. HE THINKS HE'S ON A MISSION.
IF I DON'T SEND HIM OUT IN THE FIELD ONCE IN A WHILE, HE GETS SNARKY. JUST THANK HIM AND SEND HIM BACK.
GOOD. GLAD TO BE CONTACTED PERSONALLY ON THIS MATTER. IT COULD BE A TURNING POINT IN THE WAR!
THANKS, SON—A GRATEFUL NATION SALUTES YOU!
SOMETHING'S FISHY HERE...

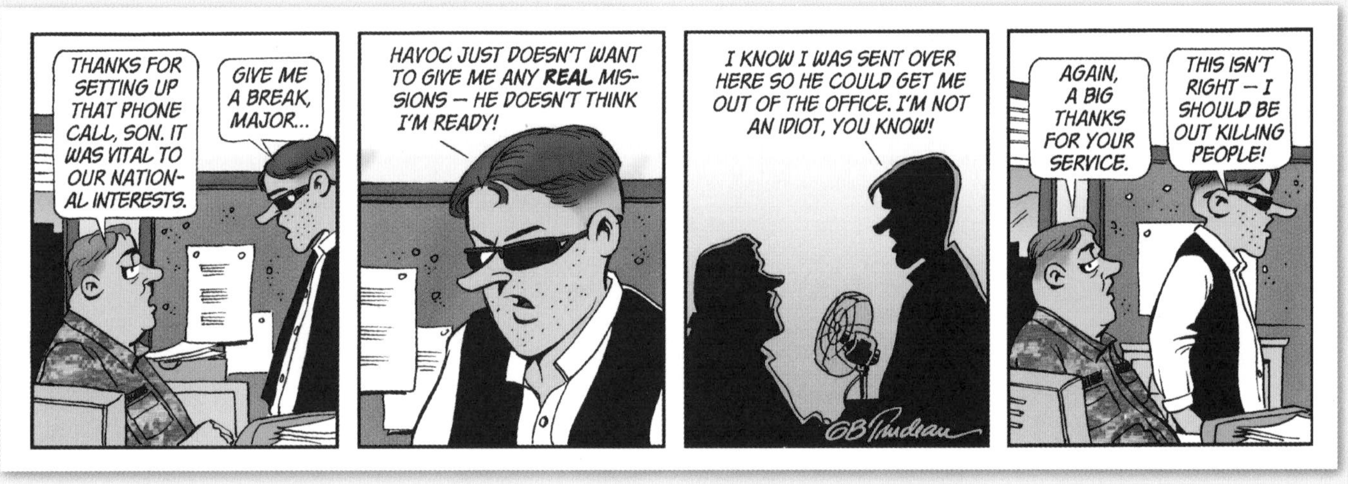
THANKS FOR SETTING UP THAT PHONE CALL, SON. IT WAS VITAL TO OUR NATIONAL INTERESTS.
GIVE ME A BREAK, MAJOR...
HAVOC JUST DOESN'T WANT TO GIVE ME ANY REAL MISSIONS — HE DOESN'T THINK I'M READY!
I KNOW I WAS SENT OVER HERE SO HE COULD GET ME OUT OF THE OFFICE. I'M NOT AN IDIOT, YOU KNOW!
AGAIN, A BIG THANKS FOR YOUR SERVICE.
THIS ISN'T RIGHT — I SHOULD BE OUT KILLING PEOPLE!

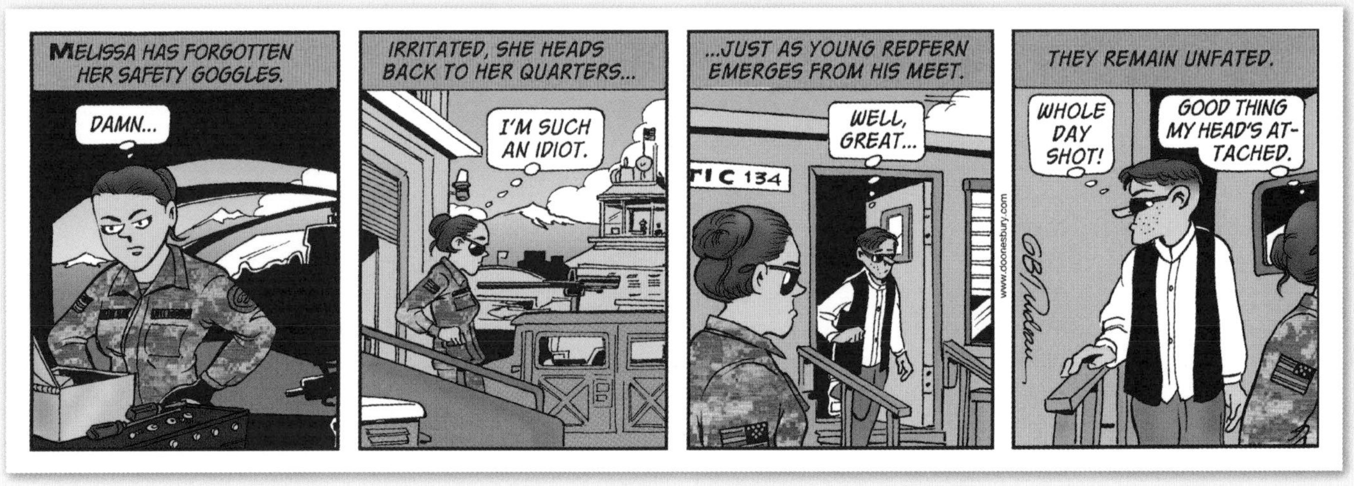
MELISSA HAS FORGOTTEN HER SAFETY GOGGLES.
DAMN...
IRRITATED, SHE HEADS BACK TO HER QUARTERS...
I'M SUCH AN IDIOT.
...JUST AS YOUNG REDFERN EMERGES FROM HIS MEET.
TIC 134
WELL, GREAT...
www.doonesbury.com
THEY REMAIN UNFATED.
WHOLE DAY SHOT!
GOOD THING MY HEAD'S ATTACHED.

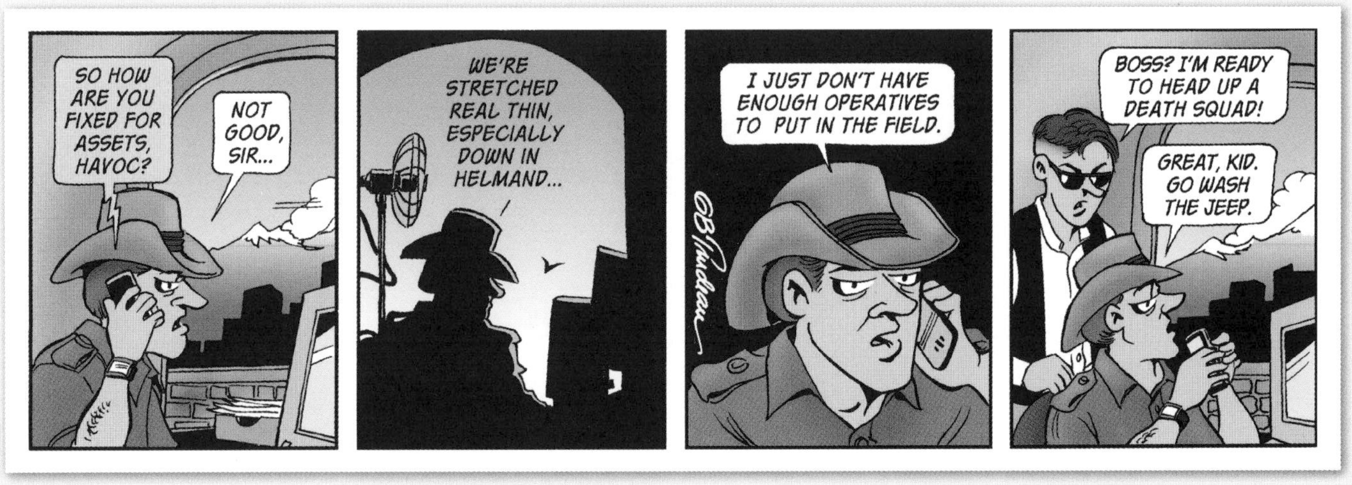
SO HOW ARE YOU FIXED FOR ASSETS, HAVOC?
NOT GOOD, SIR...
WE'RE STRETCHED REAL THIN, ESPECIALLY DOWN IN HELMAND...
I JUST DON'T HAVE ENOUGH OPERATIVES TO PUT IN THE FIELD.
BOSS? I'M READY TO HEAD UP A DEATH SQUAD!
GREAT, KID. GO WASH THE JEEP.

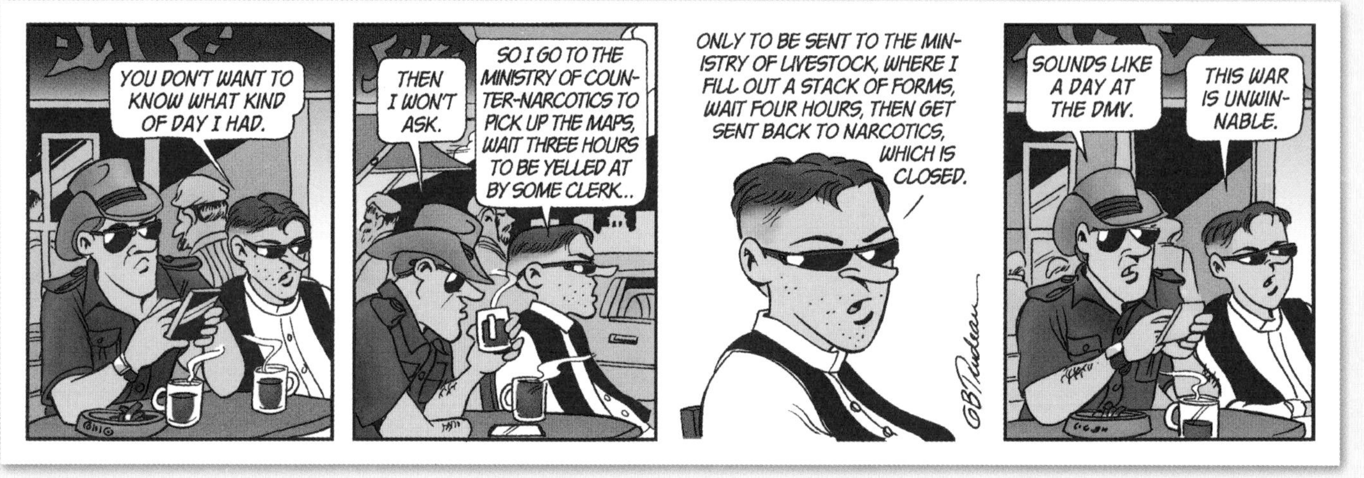
YOU DON'T WANT TO KNOW WHAT KIND OF DAY I HAD.
THEN I WON'T ASK.
SO I GO TO THE MINISTRY OF COUNTER-NARCOTICS TO PICK UP THE MAPS, WAIT THREE HOURS TO BE YELLED AT BY SOME CLERK...
ONLY TO BE SENT TO THE MINISTRY OF LIVESTOCK, WHERE I FILL OUT A STACK OF FORMS, WAIT FOUR HOURS, THEN GET SENT BACK TO NARCOTICS, WHICH IS CLOSED.
SOUNDS LIKE A DAY AT THE DMV.
THIS WAR IS UNWINNABLE.

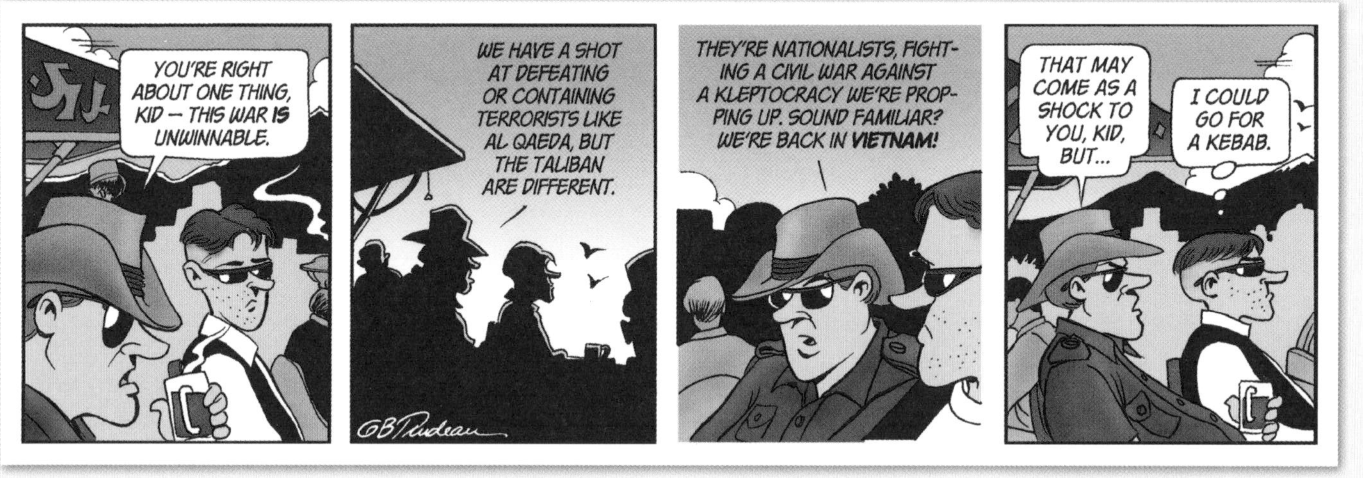
YOU'RE RIGHT ABOUT ONE THING, KID — THIS WAR **IS** UNWINNABLE.
WE HAVE A SHOT AT DEFEATING OR CONTAINING TERRORISTS LIKE AL QAEDA, BUT THE TALIBAN ARE DIFFERENT.
THEY'RE NATIONALISTS, FIGHTING A CIVIL WAR AGAINST A KLEPTOCRACY WE'RE PROPPING UP. SOUND FAMILIAR? WE'RE BACK IN **VIETNAM!**
THAT MAY COME AS A SHOCK TO YOU, KID, BUT...
I COULD GO FOR A KEBAB.

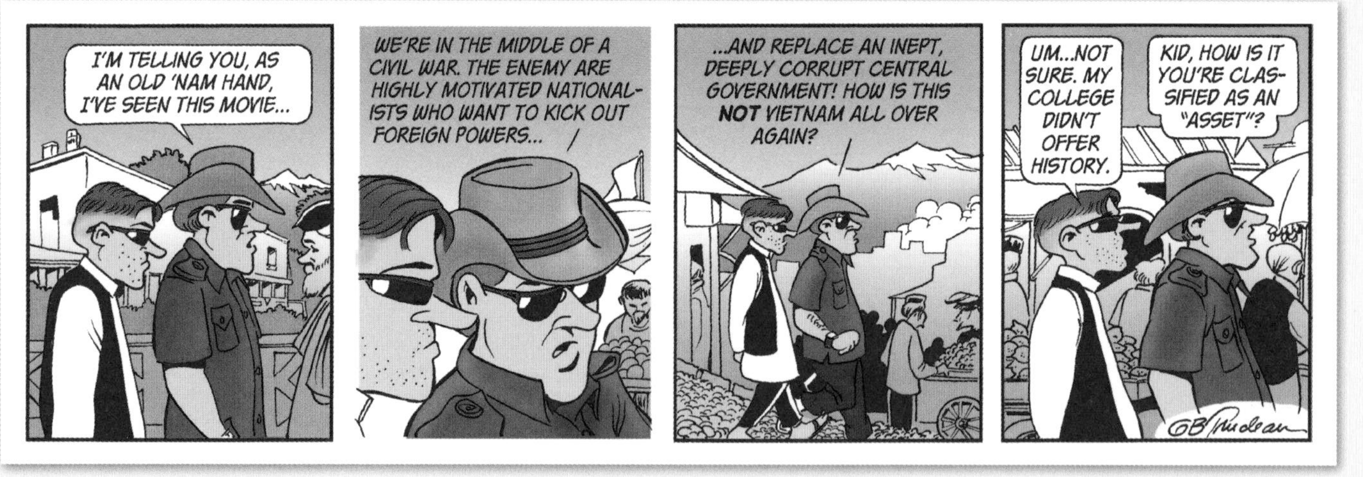
I'M TELLING YOU, AS AN OLD 'NAM HAND, I'VE SEEN THIS MOVIE...
WE'RE IN THE MIDDLE OF A CIVIL WAR. THE ENEMY ARE HIGHLY MOTIVATED NATIONALISTS WHO WANT TO KICK OUT FOREIGN POWERS...
...AND REPLACE AN INEPT, DEEPLY CORRUPT CENTRAL GOVERNMENT! HOW IS THIS **NOT** VIETNAM ALL OVER AGAIN?
UM...NOT SURE. MY COLLEGE DIDN'T OFFER HISTORY.
KID, HOW IS IT YOU'RE CLASSIFIED AS AN "ASSET"?

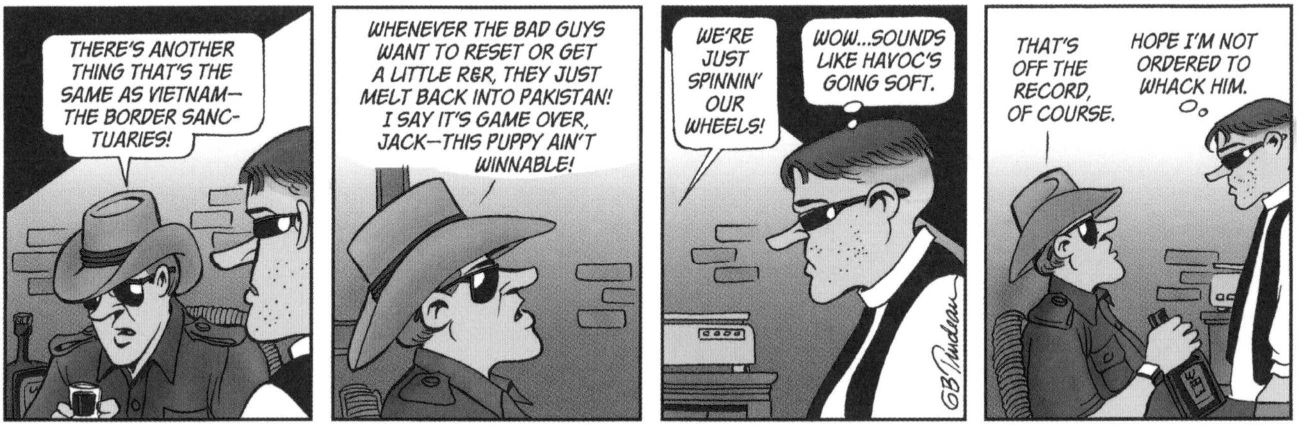
THERE'S ANOTHER THING THAT'S THE SAME AS VIETNAM— THE BORDER SANCTUARIES!
WHENEVER THE BAD GUYS WANT TO RESET OR GET A LITTLE R&R, THEY JUST MELT BACK INTO PAKISTAN! I SAY IT'S GAME OVER, JACK—THIS PUPPY AIN'T WINNABLE!
WE'RE JUST SPINNIN' OUR WHEELS!
WOW...SOUNDS LIKE HAVOC'S GOING SOFT.
THAT'S OFF THE RECORD, OF COURSE.
HOPE I'M NOT ORDERED TO WHACK HIM.

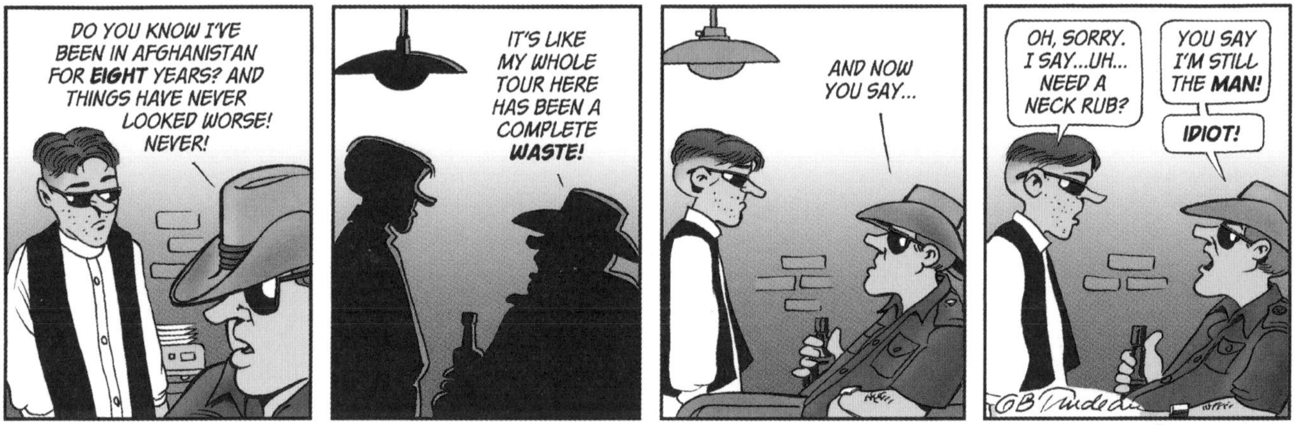
DO YOU KNOW I'VE BEEN IN AFGHANISTAN FOR **EIGHT** YEARS? AND THINGS HAVE NEVER LOOKED WORSE! NEVER!
IT'S LIKE MY WHOLE TOUR HERE HAS BEEN A COMPLETE **WASTE!**
AND NOW YOU SAY...
OH, SORRY. I SAY...UH... NEED A NECK RUB?
YOU SAY I'M STILL THE **MAN!**
IDIOT!

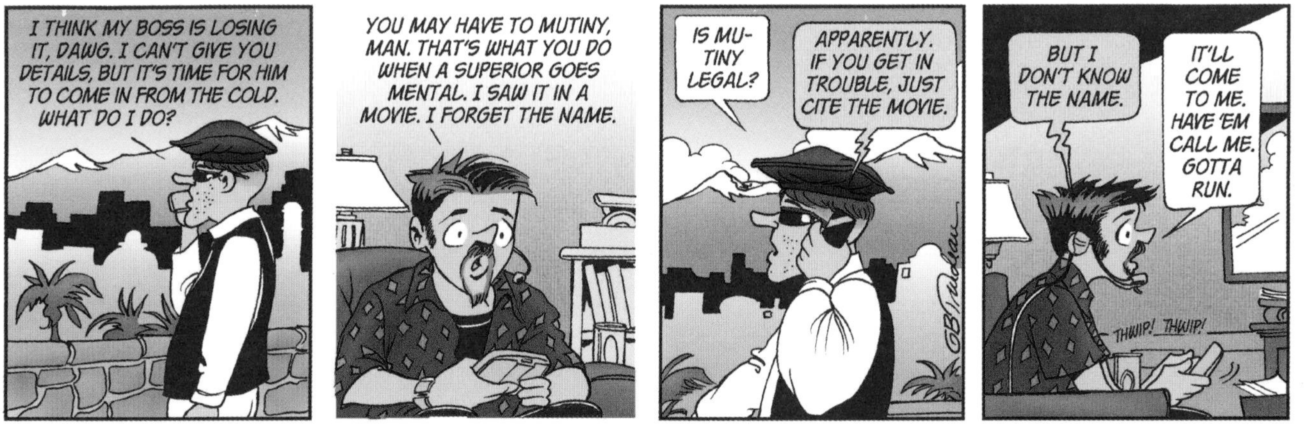
I THINK MY BOSS IS LOSING IT, DAWG. I CAN'T GIVE YOU DETAILS, BUT IT'S TIME FOR HIM TO COME IN FROM THE COLD. WHAT DO I DO?
YOU MAY HAVE TO MUTINY, MAN. THAT'S WHAT YOU DO WHEN A SUPERIOR GOES MENTAL. I SAW IT IN A MOVIE. I FORGET THE NAME.
IS MUTINY LEGAL?
APPARENTLY. IF YOU GET IN TROUBLE, JUST CITE THE MOVIE.
BUT I DON'T KNOW THE NAME.
IT'LL COME TO ME. HAVE 'EM CALL ME. GOTTA RUN.
THWIP! THWIP!

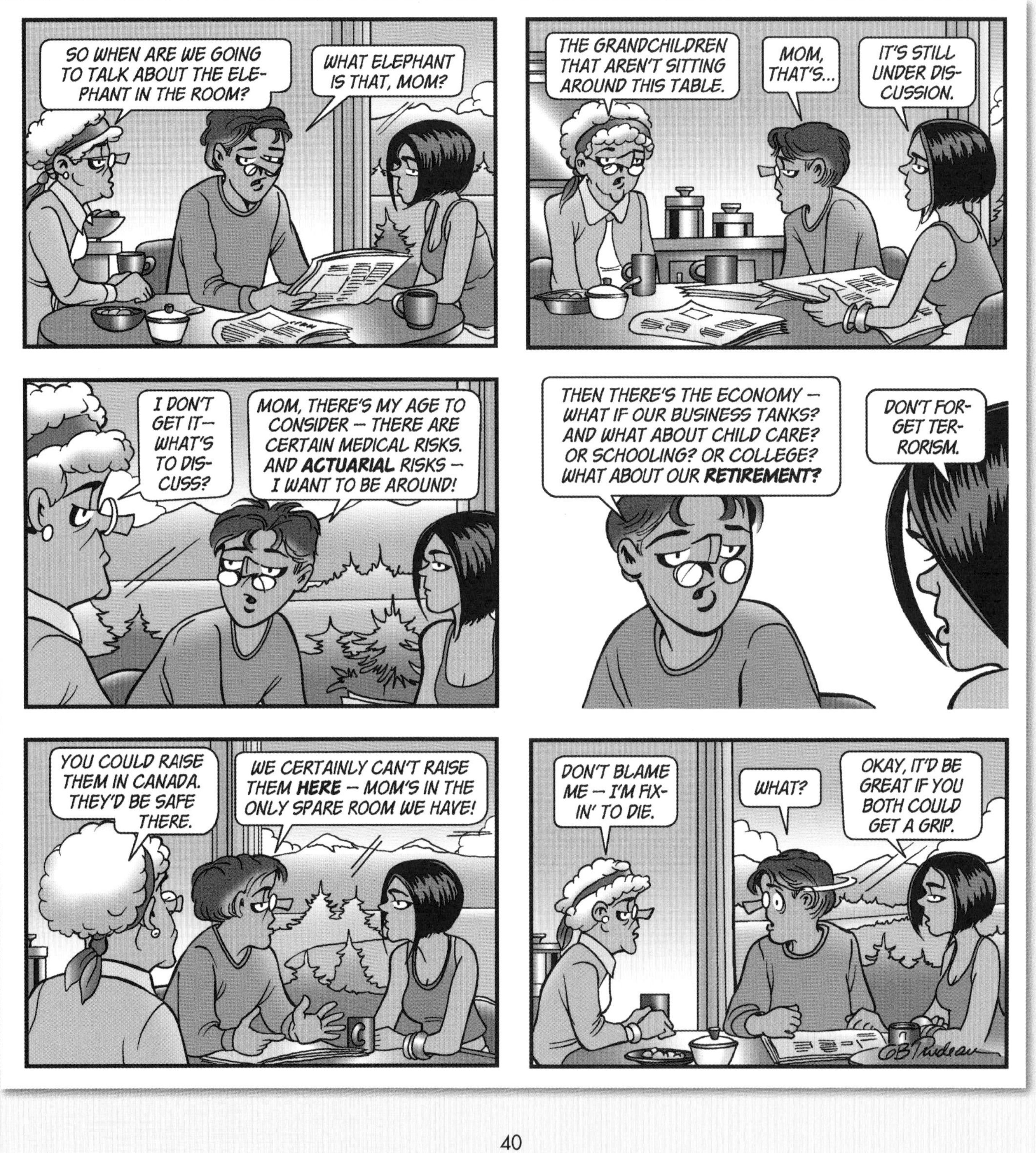
SO WHEN ARE WE GOING TO TALK ABOUT THE ELE-PHANT IN THE ROOM?
WHAT ELEPHANT IS THAT, MOM?
THE GRANDCHILDREN THAT AREN'T SITTING AROUND THIS TABLE.
MOM, THAT'S...
IT'S STILL UNDER DIS-CUSSION.
I DON'T GET IT— WHAT'S TO DIS-CUSS?
MOM, THERE'S MY AGE TO CONSIDER — THERE ARE CERTAIN MEDICAL RISKS. AND **ACTUARIAL** RISKS — I WANT TO BE AROUND!
THEN THERE'S THE ECONOMY — WHAT IF OUR BUSINESS TANKS? AND WHAT ABOUT CHILD CARE? OR SCHOOLING? OR COLLEGE? WHAT ABOUT OUR **RETIREMENT?**
DON'T FOR-GET TER-RORISM.
YOU COULD RAISE THEM IN CANADA. THEY'D BE SAFE THERE.
WE CERTAINLY CAN'T RAISE THEM **HERE** — MOM'S IN THE ONLY SPARE ROOM WE HAVE!
DON'T BLAME ME — I'M FIX-IN' TO DIE.
WHAT?
OKAY, IT'D BE GREAT IF YOU BOTH COULD GET A GRIP.
GBTrudeau

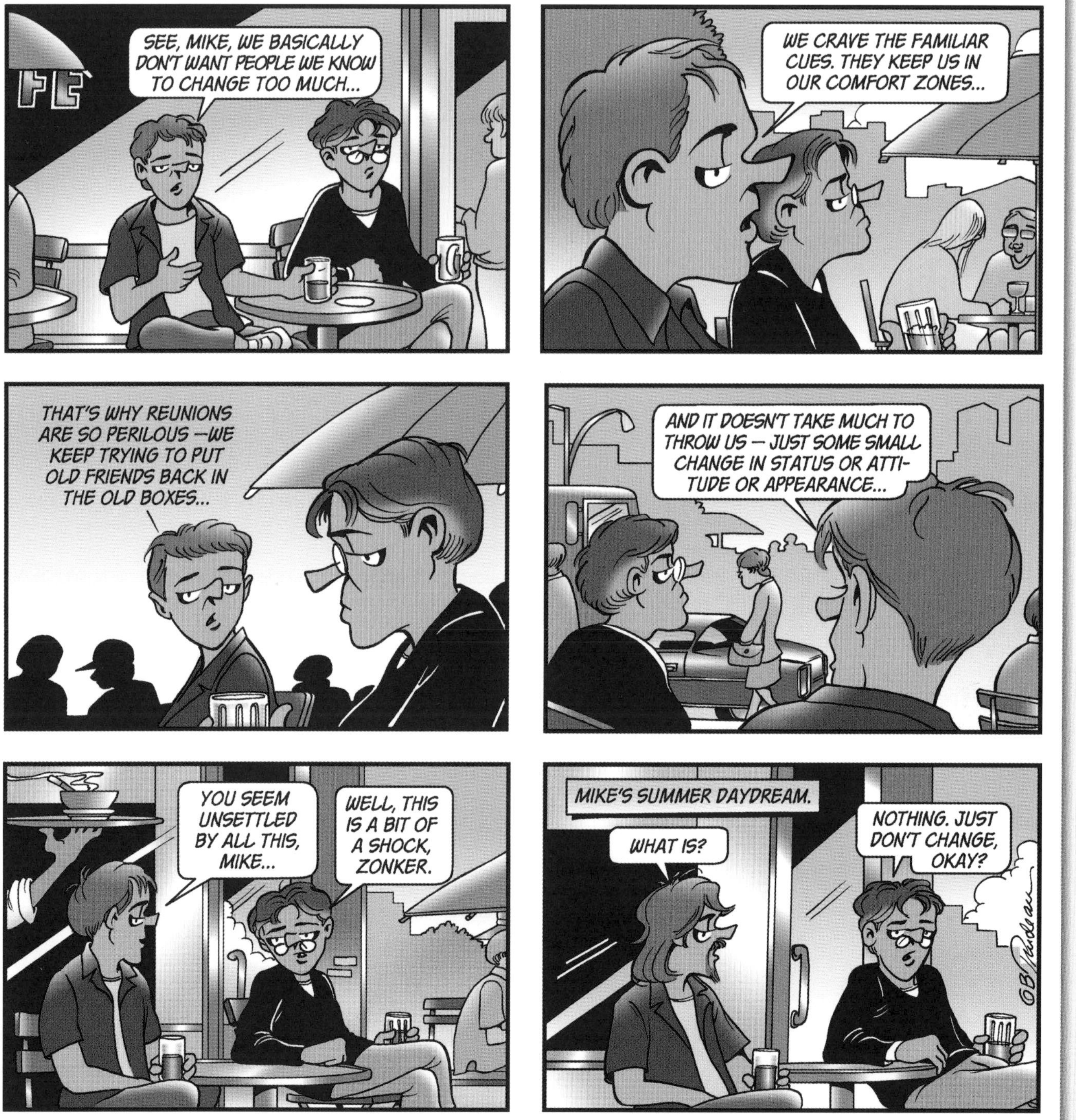
SEE, MIKE, WE BASICALLY DON'T WANT PEOPLE WE KNOW TO CHANGE TOO MUCH...
WE CRAVE THE FAMILIAR CUES. THEY KEEP US IN OUR COMFORT ZONES...
THAT'S WHY REUNIONS ARE SO PERILOUS —WE KEEP TRYING TO PUT OLD FRIENDS BACK IN THE OLD BOXES...
AND IT DOESN'T TAKE MUCH TO THROW US — JUST SOME SMALL CHANGE IN STATUS OR ATTI-TUDE OR APPEARANCE...
YOU SEEM UNSETTLED BY ALL THIS, MIKE...
WELL, THIS IS A BIT OF A SHOCK, ZONKER.
MIKE'S SUMMER DAYDREAM.
WHAT IS?
NOTHING. JUST DON'T CHANGE, OKAY?

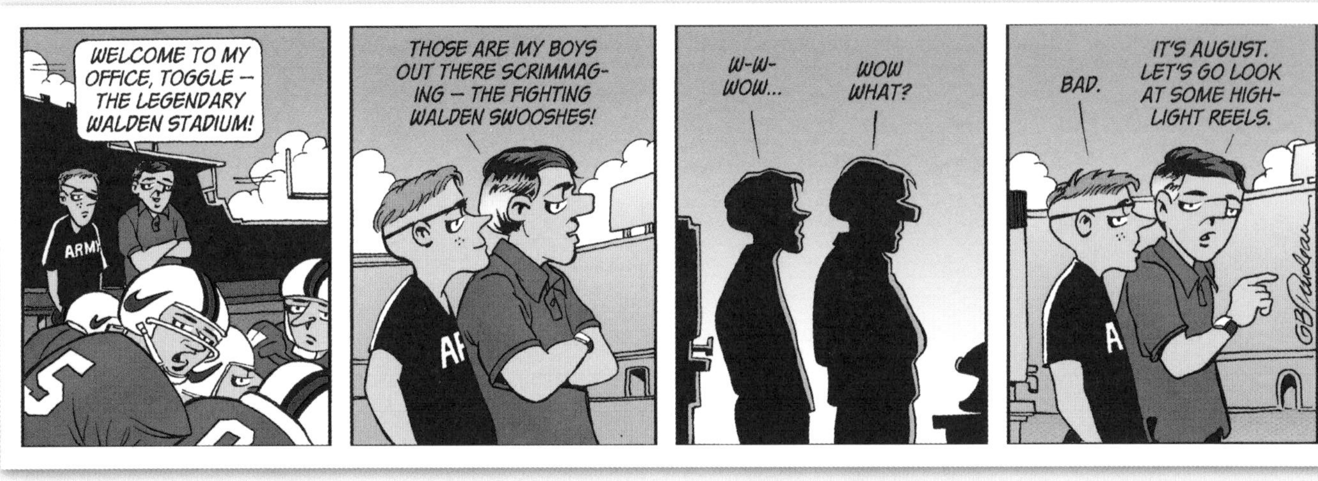
WELCOME TO MY OFFICE, TOGGLE — THE LEGENDARY WALDEN STADIUM!
ARMY
THOSE ARE MY BOYS OUT THERE SCRIMMAGING — THE FIGHTING WALDEN SWOOSHES!
W-W-WOW...
WOW WHAT?
BAD.
IT'S AUGUST. LET'S GO LOOK AT SOME HIGHLIGHT REELS.

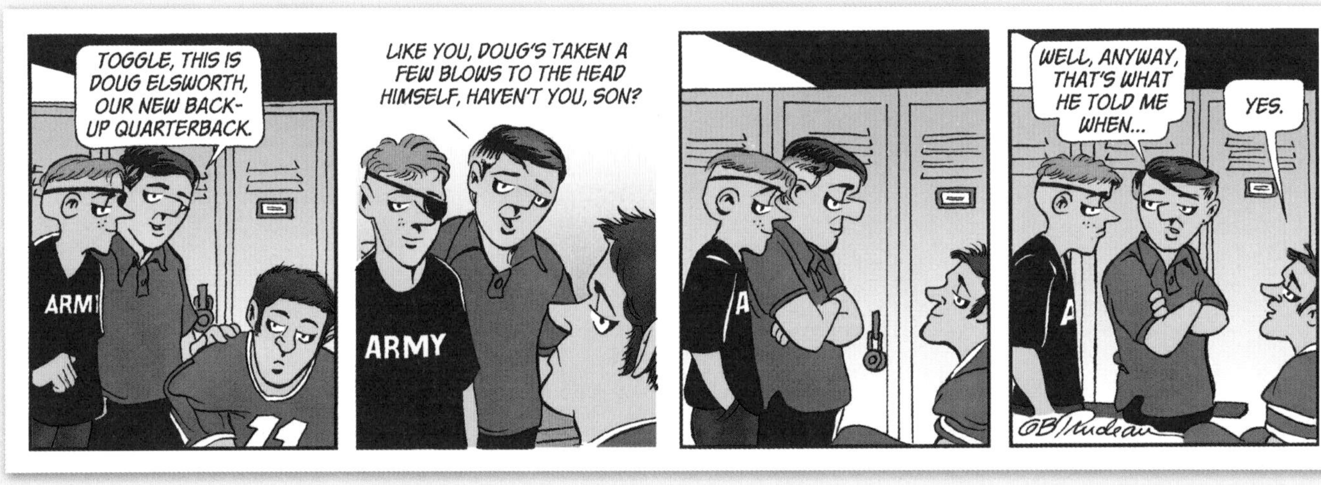
TOGGLE, THIS IS DOUG ELSWORTH, OUR NEW BACK-UP QUARTERBACK.
LIKE YOU, DOUG'S TAKEN A FEW BLOWS TO THE HEAD HIMSELF, HAVEN'T YOU, SON?
ARMY
WELL, ANYWAY, THAT'S WHAT HE TOLD ME WHEN...
YES.

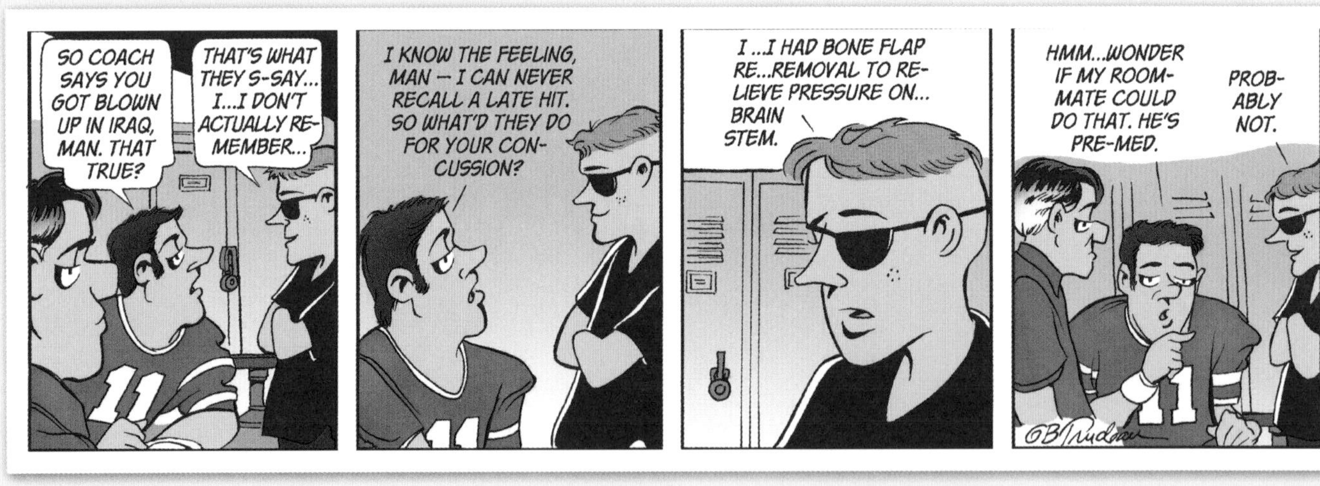
SO COACH SAYS YOU GOT BLOWN UP IN IRAQ, MAN. THAT TRUE?
THAT'S WHAT THEY S-SAY... I...I DON'T ACTUALLY REMEMBER...
I KNOW THE FEELING, MAN — I CAN NEVER RECALL A LATE HIT. SO WHAT'D THEY DO FOR YOUR CONCUSSION?
I ...I HAD BONE FLAP RE...REMOVAL TO RELIEVE PRESSURE ON... BRAIN STEM.
HMM...WONDER IF MY ROOMMATE COULD DO THAT. HE'S PRE-MED.
PROBABLY NOT.

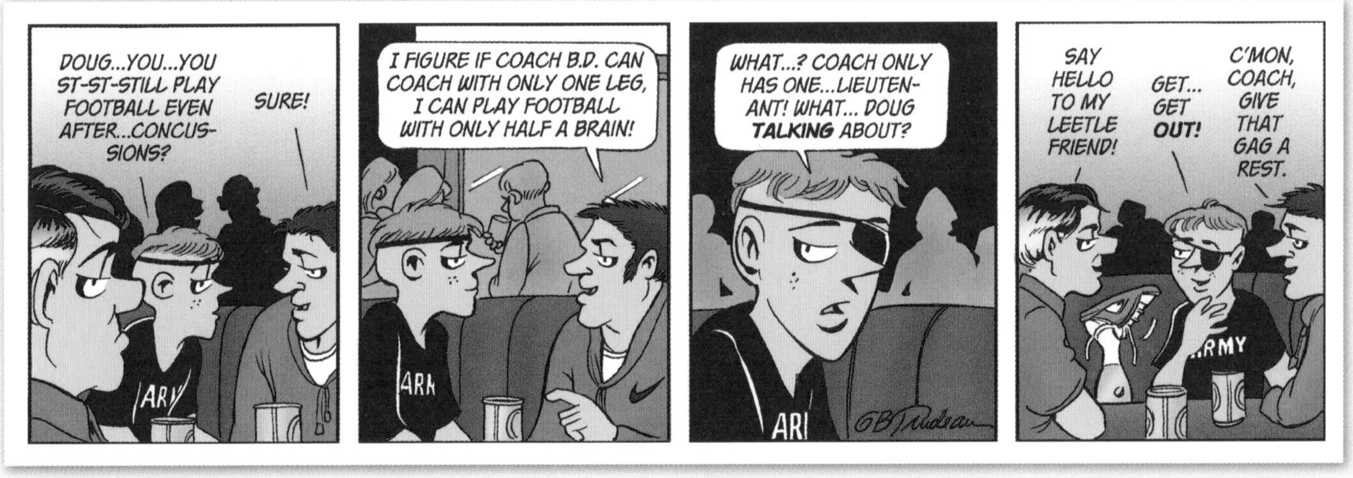
DOUG...YOU...YOU ST-ST-STILL PLAY FOOTBALL EVEN AFTER...CONCUSSIONS?
SURE!
I FIGURE IF COACH B.D. CAN COACH WITH ONLY ONE LEG, I CAN PLAY FOOTBALL WITH ONLY HALF A BRAIN!
WHAT...? COACH ONLY HAS ONE...LIEUTENANT! WHAT... DOUG **TALKING** ABOUT?
SAY HELLO TO MY LEETLE FRIEND!
GET... GET **OUT!**
C'MON, COACH, GIVE THAT GAG A REST.
GB Trudeau

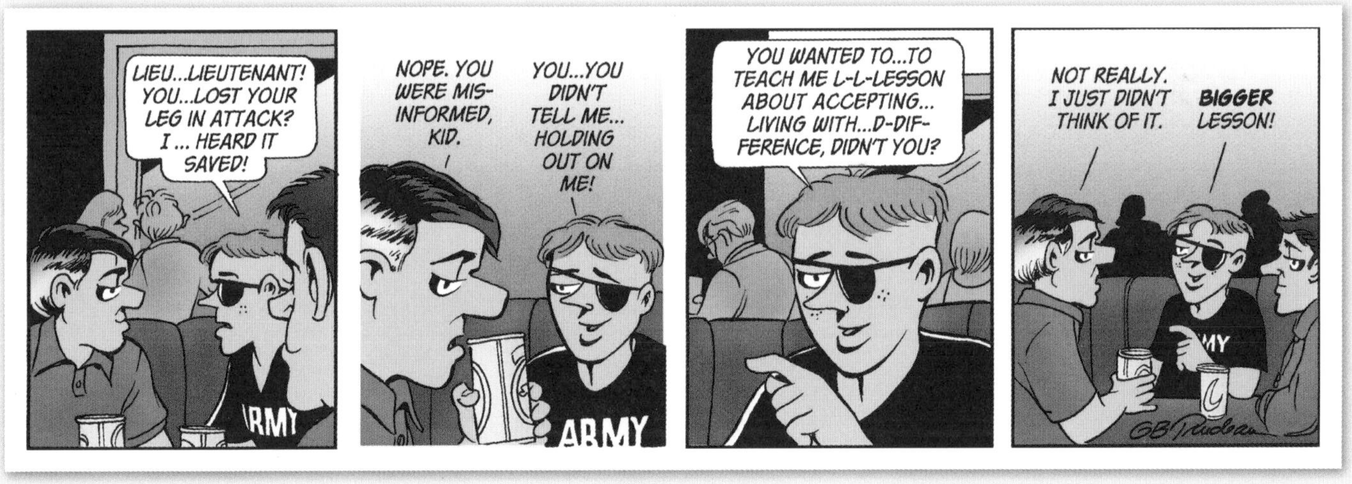
LIEU...LIEUTENANT! YOU...LOST YOUR LEG IN ATTACK? I ... HEARD IT SAVED!
NOPE. YOU WERE MISINFORMED, KID.
YOU...YOU DIDN'T TELL ME... HOLDING OUT ON ME!
YOU WANTED TO...TO TEACH ME L-L-LESSON ABOUT ACCEPTING... LIVING WITH...D-DIFFERENCE, DIDN'T YOU?
NOT REALLY. I JUST DIDN'T THINK OF IT.
BIGGER LESSON!
GB Trudeau

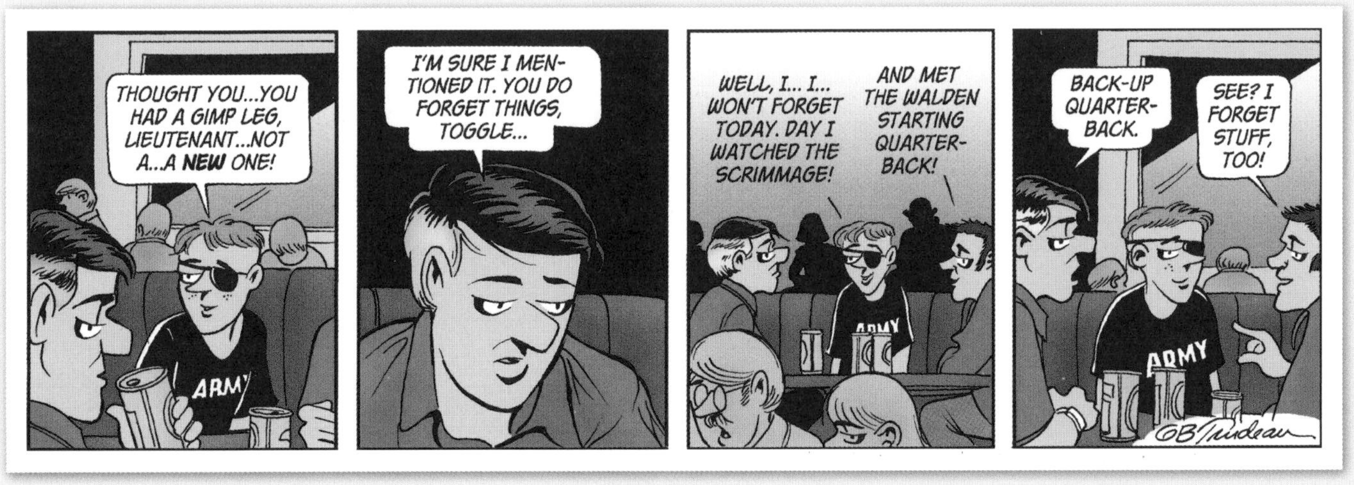
THOUGHT YOU...YOU HAD A GIMP LEG, LIEUTENANT...NOT A...A **NEW** ONE!
I'M SURE I MENTIONED IT. YOU DO FORGET THINGS, TOGGLE...
WELL, I... I... WON'T FORGET TODAY. DAY I WATCHED THE SCRIMMAGE!
AND MET THE WALDEN STARTING QUARTERBACK!
BACK-UP QUARTERBACK.
SEE? I FORGET STUFF, TOO!
GB Trudeau

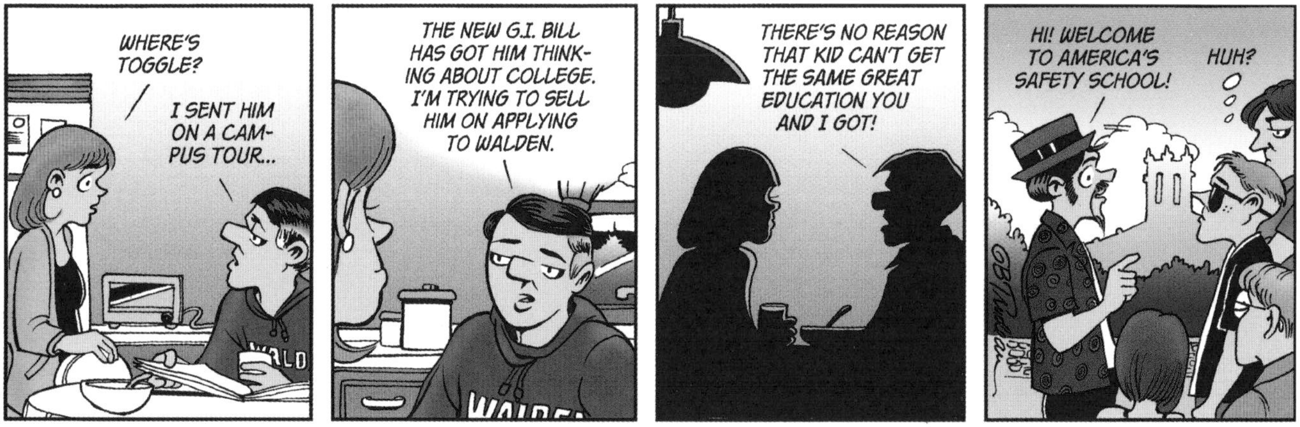
WHERE'S TOGGLE?
I SENT HIM ON A CAMPUS TOUR...
THE NEW G.I. BILL HAS GOT HIM THINKING ABOUT COLLEGE. I'M TRYING TO SELL HIM ON APPLYING TO WALDEN.
THERE'S NO REASON THAT KID CAN'T GET THE SAME GREAT EDUCATION YOU AND I GOT!
HI! WELCOME TO AMERICA'S SAFETY SCHOOL!
HUH?

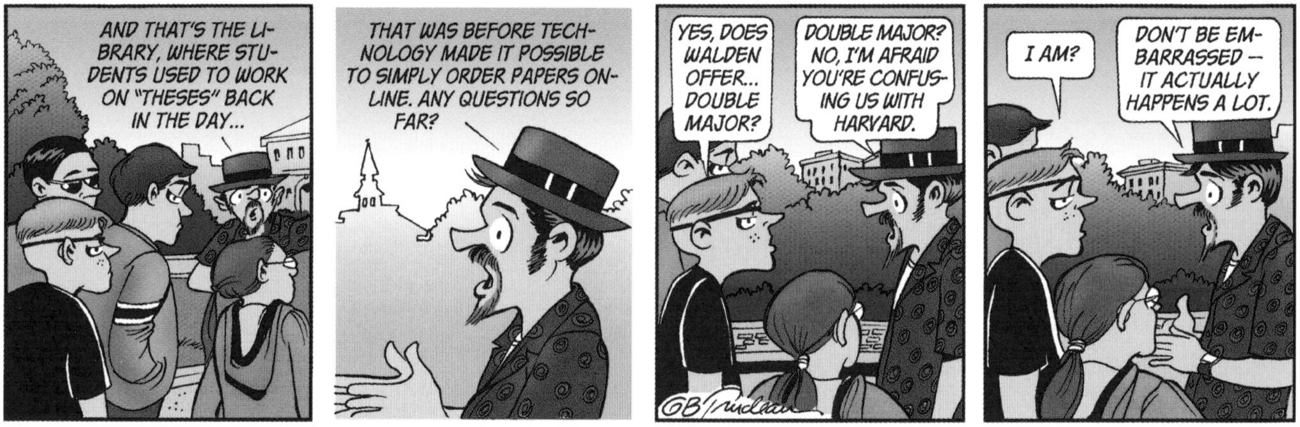
AND THAT'S THE LIBRARY, WHERE STUDENTS USED TO WORK ON "THESES" BACK IN THE DAY...
THAT WAS BEFORE TECHNOLOGY MADE IT POSSIBLE TO SIMPLY ORDER PAPERS ONLINE. ANY QUESTIONS SO FAR?
YES, DOES WALDEN OFFER... DOUBLE MAJOR?
DOUBLE MAJOR? NO, I'M AFRAID YOU'RE CONFUSING US WITH HARVARD.
I AM?
DON'T BE EMBARRASSED — IT ACTUALLY HAPPENS A LOT.

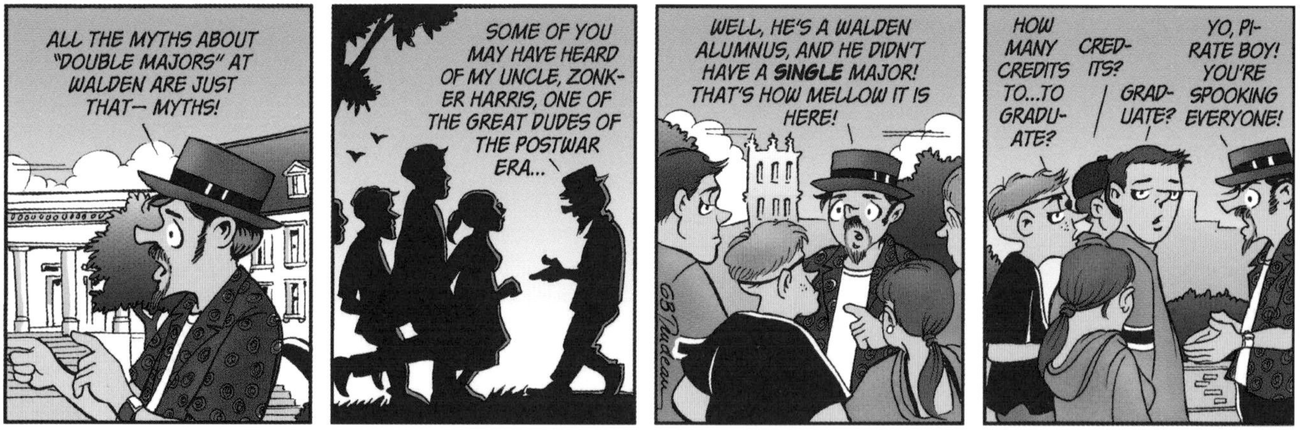
ALL THE MYTHS ABOUT "DOUBLE MAJORS" AT WALDEN ARE JUST THAT— MYTHS!
SOME OF YOU MAY HAVE HEARD OF MY UNCLE, ZONKER HARRIS, ONE OF THE GREAT DUDES OF THE POSTWAR ERA...
WELL, HE'S A WALDEN ALUMNUS, AND HE DIDN'T HAVE A **SINGLE** MAJOR! THAT'S HOW MELLOW IT IS HERE!
HOW MANY CREDITS TO...TO GRADUATE?
CREDITS?
GRADUATE?
YO, PIRATE BOY! YOU'RE SPOOKING EVERYONE!

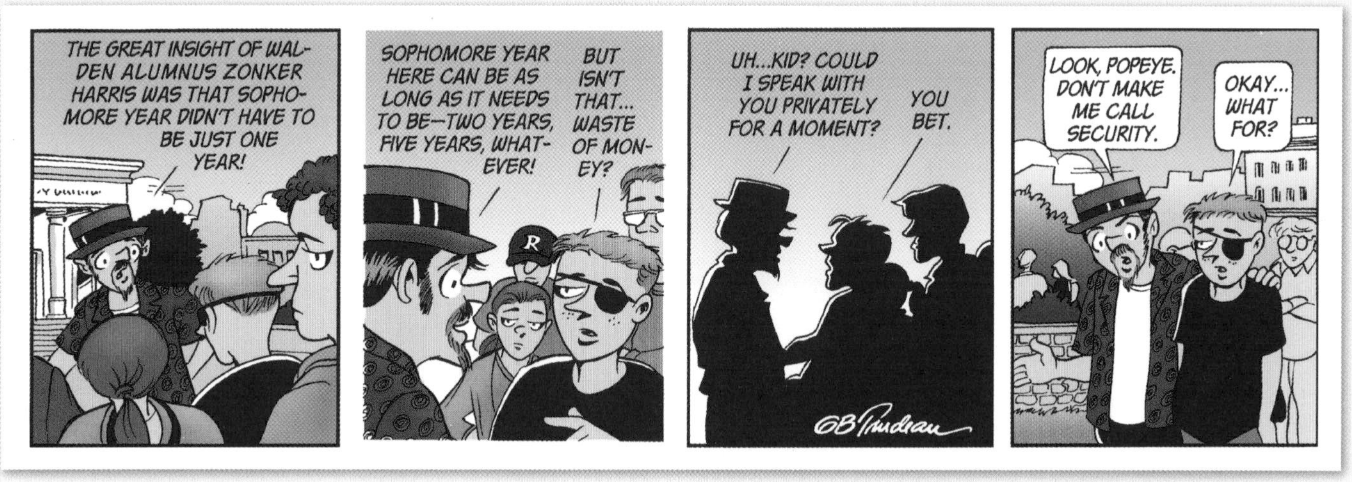
THE GREAT INSIGHT OF WALDEN ALUMNUS ZONKER HARRIS WAS THAT SOPHOMORE YEAR DIDN'T HAVE TO BE JUST ONE YEAR!
SOPHOMORE YEAR HERE CAN BE AS LONG AS IT NEEDS TO BE—TWO YEARS, FIVE YEARS, WHATEVER!
BUT ISN'T THAT... WASTE OF MONEY?
UH...KID? COULD I SPEAK WITH YOU PRIVATELY FOR A MOMENT?
YOU BET.
LOOK, POPEYE. DON'T MAKE ME CALL SECURITY.
OKAY... WHAT FOR?

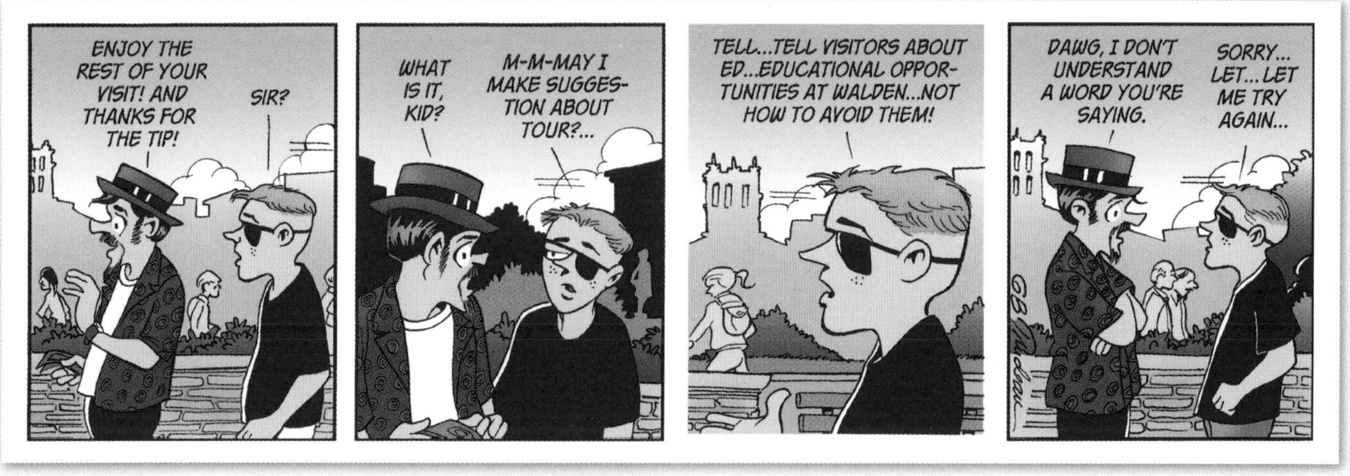
ENJOY THE REST OF YOUR VISIT! AND THANKS FOR THE TIP!
SIR?
WHAT IS IT, KID?
M-M-MAY I MAKE SUGGESTION ABOUT TOUR?...
TELL...TELL VISITORS ABOUT ED...EDUCATIONAL OPPORTUNITIES AT WALDEN...NOT HOW TO AVOID THEM!
DAWG, I DON'T UNDERSTAND A WORD YOU'RE SAYING.
SORRY... LET...LET ME TRY AGAIN...

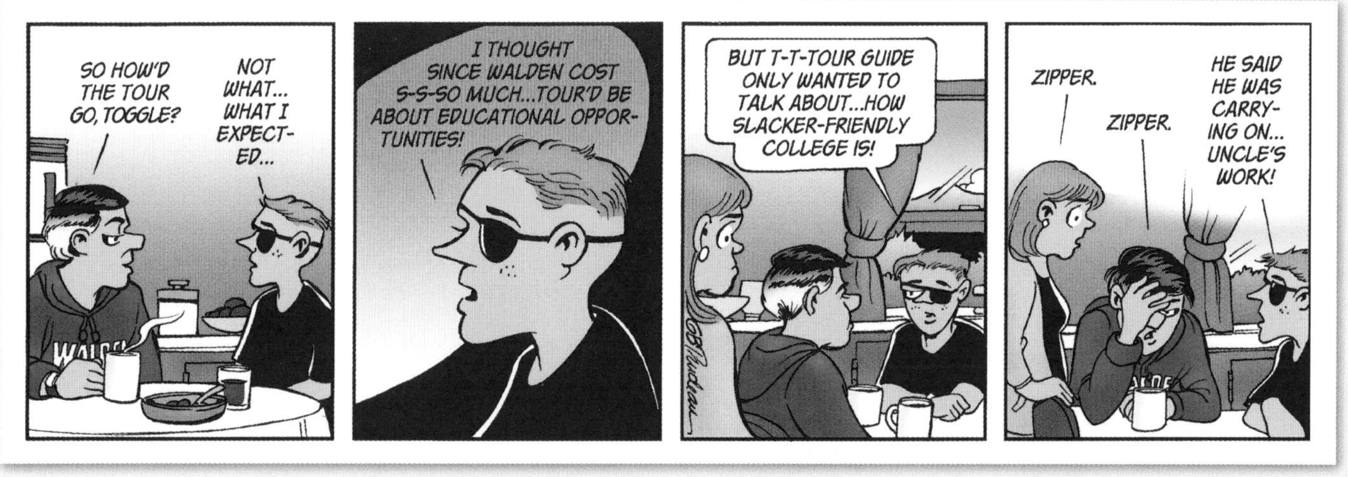
SO HOW'D THE TOUR GO, TOGGLE?
NOT WHAT... WHAT I EXPECTED...
I THOUGHT SINCE WALDEN COST S-S-SO MUCH...TOUR'D BE ABOUT EDUCATIONAL OPPORTUNITIES!
BUT T-T-TOUR GUIDE ONLY WANTED TO TALK ABOUT...HOW SLACKER-FRIENDLY COLLEGE IS!
ZIPPER.
ZIPPER.
HE SAID HE WAS CARRYING ON... UNCLE'S WORK!

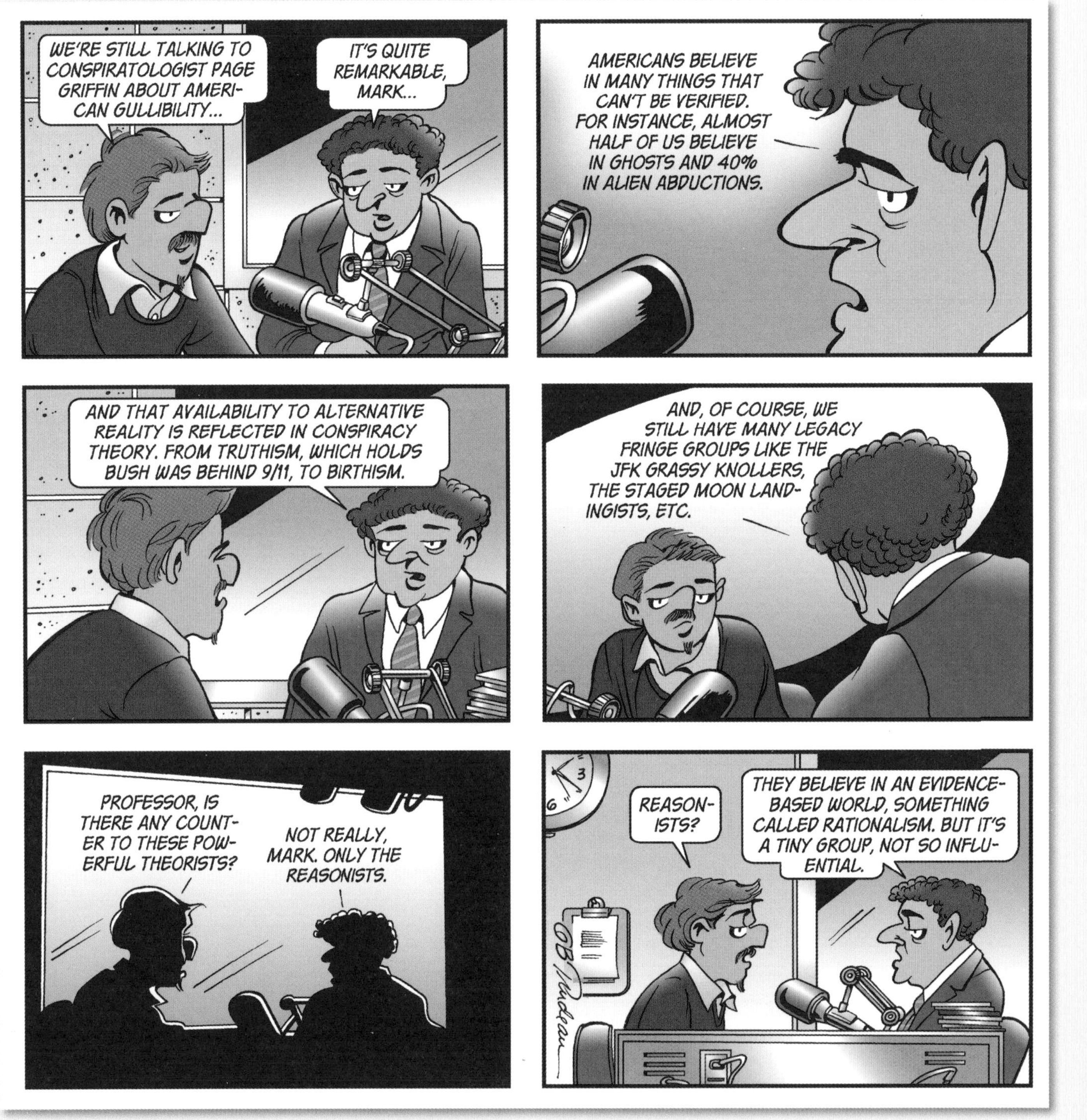
WE'RE STILL TALKING TO CONSPIRATOLOGIST PAGE GRIFFIN ABOUT AMERICAN GULLIBILITY...
IT'S QUITE REMARKABLE, MARK...
AMERICANS BELIEVE IN MANY THINGS THAT CAN'T BE VERIFIED. FOR INSTANCE, ALMOST HALF OF US BELIEVE IN GHOSTS AND 40% IN ALIEN ABDUCTIONS.
AND THAT AVAILABILITY TO ALTERNATIVE REALITY IS REFLECTED IN CONSPIRACY THEORY. FROM TRUTHISM, WHICH HOLDS BUSH WAS BEHIND 9/11, TO BIRTHISM.
AND, OF COURSE, WE STILL HAVE MANY LEGACY FRINGE GROUPS LIKE THE JFK GRASSY KNOLLERS, THE STAGED MOON LANDINGISTS, ETC.
PROFESSOR, IS THERE ANY COUNTER TO THESE POWERFUL THEORISTS?
NOT REALLY, MARK. ONLY THE REASONISTS.
REASONISTS?
THEY BELIEVE IN AN EVIDENCE-BASED WORLD, SOMETHING CALLED RATIONALISM. BUT IT'S A TINY GROUP, NOT SO INFLUENTIAL.

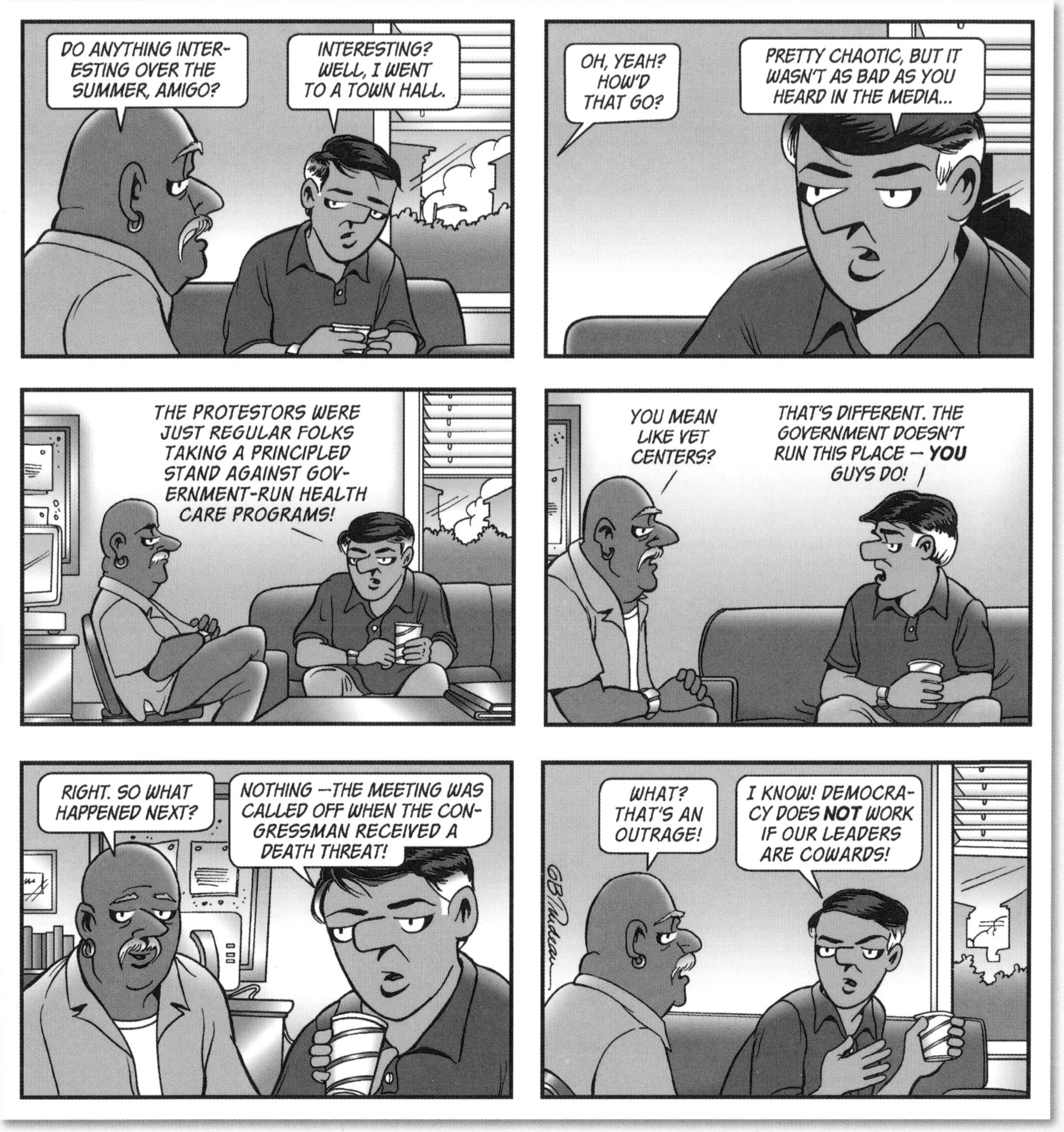
DO ANYTHING INTERESTING OVER THE SUMMER, AMIGO?
INTERESTING? WELL, I WENT TO A TOWN HALL.
OH, YEAH? HOW'D THAT GO?
PRETTY CHAOTIC, BUT IT WASN'T AS BAD AS YOU HEARD IN THE MEDIA...
THE PROTESTORS WERE JUST REGULAR FOLKS TAKING A PRINCIPLED STAND AGAINST GOVERNMENT-RUN HEALTH CARE PROGRAMS!
YOU MEAN LIKE VET CENTERS?
THAT'S DIFFERENT. THE GOVERNMENT DOESN'T RUN THIS PLACE — **YOU** GUYS DO!
RIGHT. SO WHAT HAPPENED NEXT?
NOTHING —THE MEETING WAS CALLED OFF WHEN THE CONGRESSMAN RECEIVED A DEATH THREAT!
WHAT? THAT'S AN OUTRAGE!
I KNOW! DEMOCRACY DOES **NOT** WORK IF OUR LEADERS ARE COWARDS!

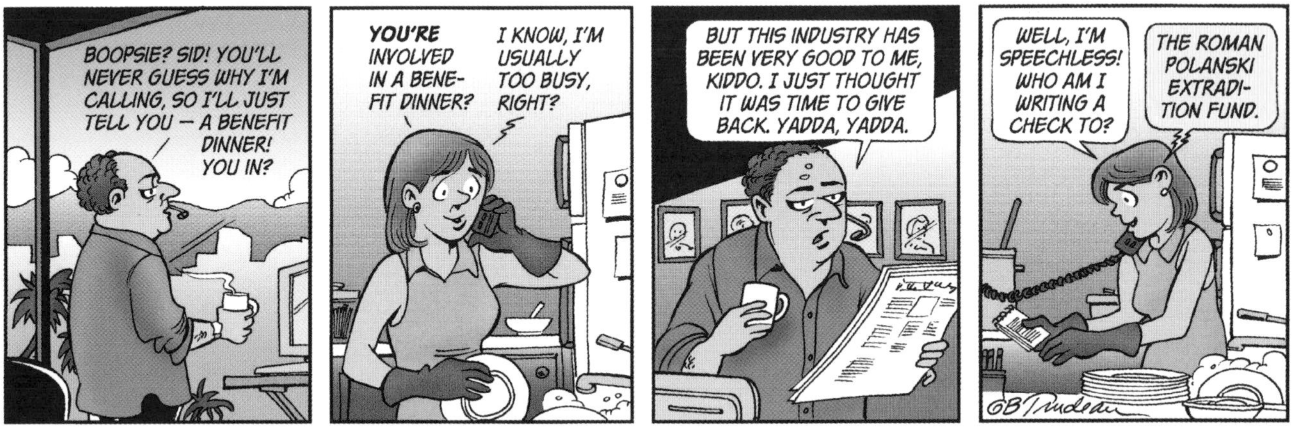
BOOPSIE? SID! YOU'LL NEVER GUESS WHY I'M CALLING, SO I'LL JUST TELL YOU — A BENEFIT DINNER! YOU IN?
YOU'RE INVOLVED IN A BENEFIT DINNER?
I KNOW, I'M USUALLY TOO BUSY, RIGHT?
BUT THIS INDUSTRY HAS BEEN VERY GOOD TO ME, KIDDO. I JUST THOUGHT IT WAS TIME TO GIVE BACK. YADDA, YADDA.
WELL, I'M SPEECHLESS! WHO AM I WRITING A CHECK TO?
THE ROMAN POLANSKI EXTRADITION FUND.
GBTrudeau

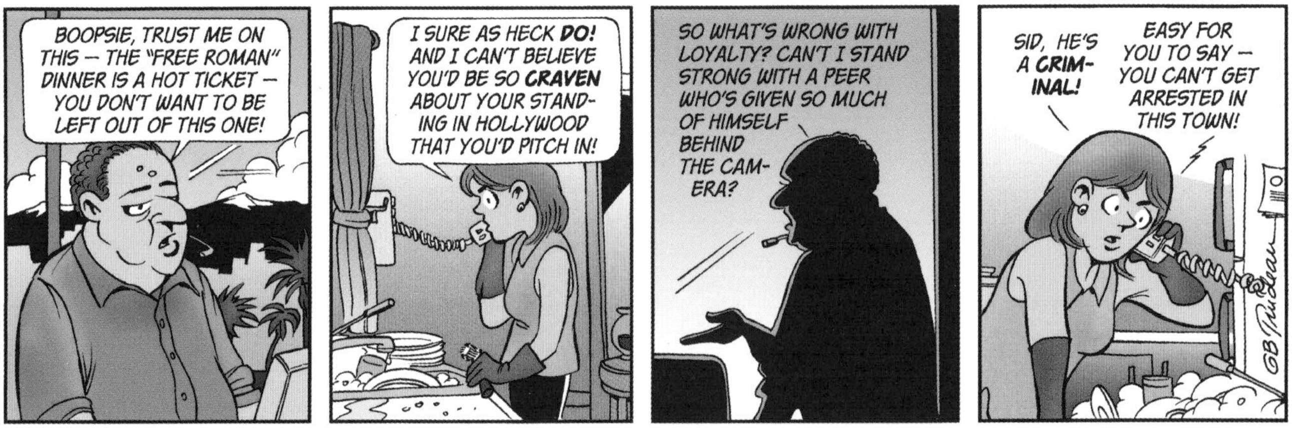
BOOPSIE, TRUST ME ON THIS — THE "FREE ROMAN" DINNER IS A HOT TICKET — YOU DON'T WANT TO BE LEFT OUT OF THIS ONE!
I SURE AS HECK DO! AND I CAN'T BELIEVE YOU'D BE SO CRAVEN ABOUT YOUR STANDING IN HOLLYWOOD THAT YOU'D PITCH IN!
SO WHAT'S WRONG WITH LOYALTY? CAN'T I STAND STRONG WITH A PEER WHO'S GIVEN SO MUCH OF HIMSELF BEHIND THE CAMERA?
SID, HE'S A CRIMINAL!
EASY FOR YOU TO SAY — YOU CAN'T GET ARRESTED IN THIS TOWN!
GBTrudeau

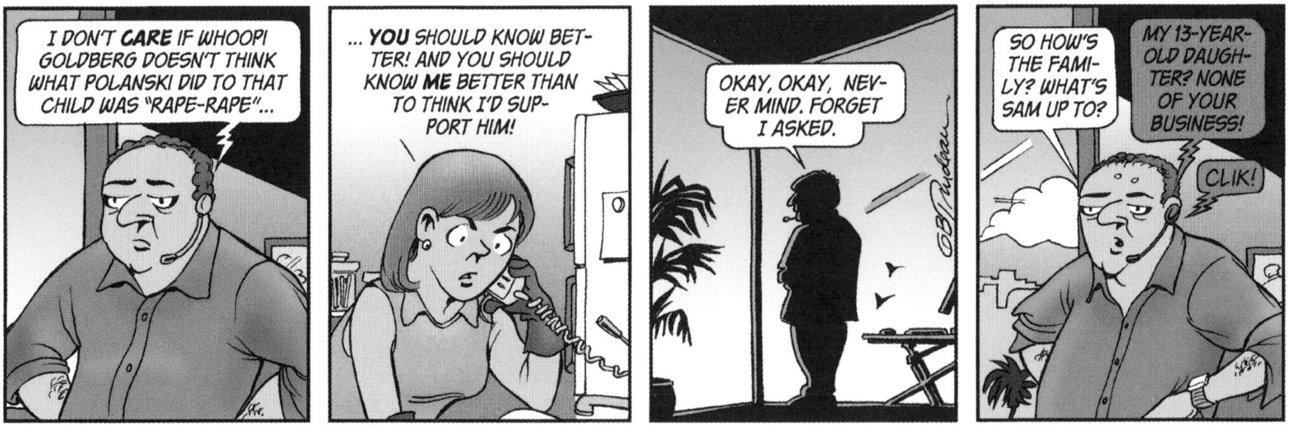
I DON'T CARE IF WHOOPI GOLDBERG DOESN'T THINK WHAT POLANSKI DID TO THAT CHILD WAS "RAPE-RAPE"...
... YOU SHOULD KNOW BETTER! AND YOU SHOULD KNOW ME BETTER THAN TO THINK I'D SUPPORT HIM!
OKAY, OKAY, NEVER MIND. FORGET I ASKED.
GBTrudeau
SO HOW'S THE FAMILY? WHAT'S SAM UP TO?
MY 13-YEAR-OLD DAUGHTER? NONE OF YOUR BUSINESS!
CLIK!

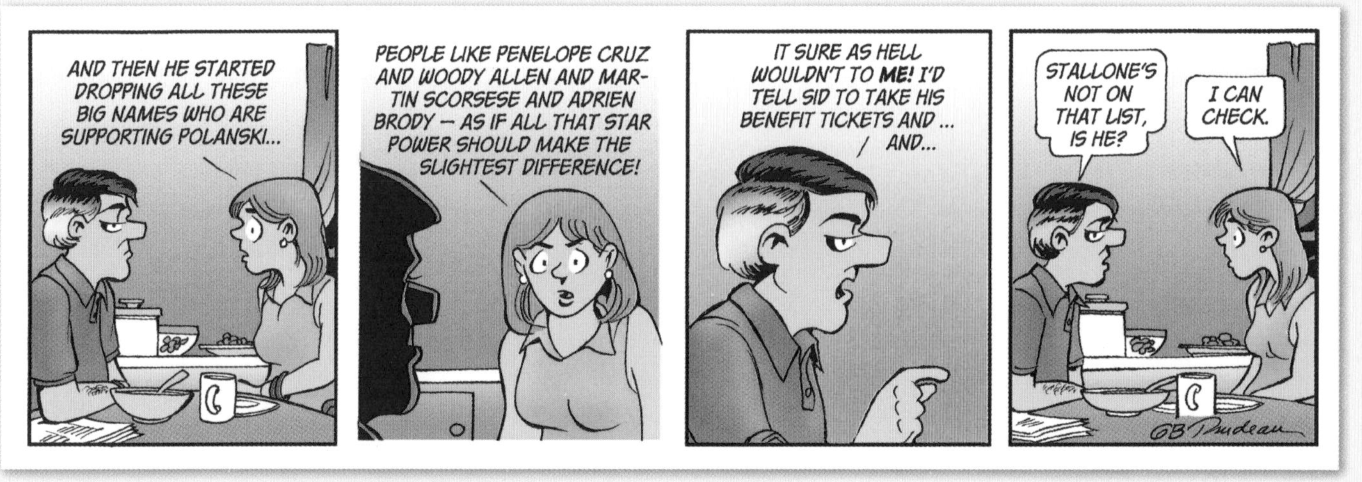
AND THEN HE STARTED DROPPING ALL THESE BIG NAMES WHO ARE SUPPORTING POLANSKI...
PEOPLE LIKE PENELOPE CRUZ AND WOODY ALLEN AND MARTIN SCORSESE AND ADRIEN BRODY — AS IF ALL THAT STAR POWER SHOULD MAKE THE SLIGHTEST DIFFERENCE!
IT SURE AS HELL WOULDN'T TO ME! I'D TELL SID TO TAKE HIS BENEFIT TICKETS AND ... AND...
STALLONE'S NOT ON THAT LIST, IS HE?
I CAN CHECK.
GB Trudeau

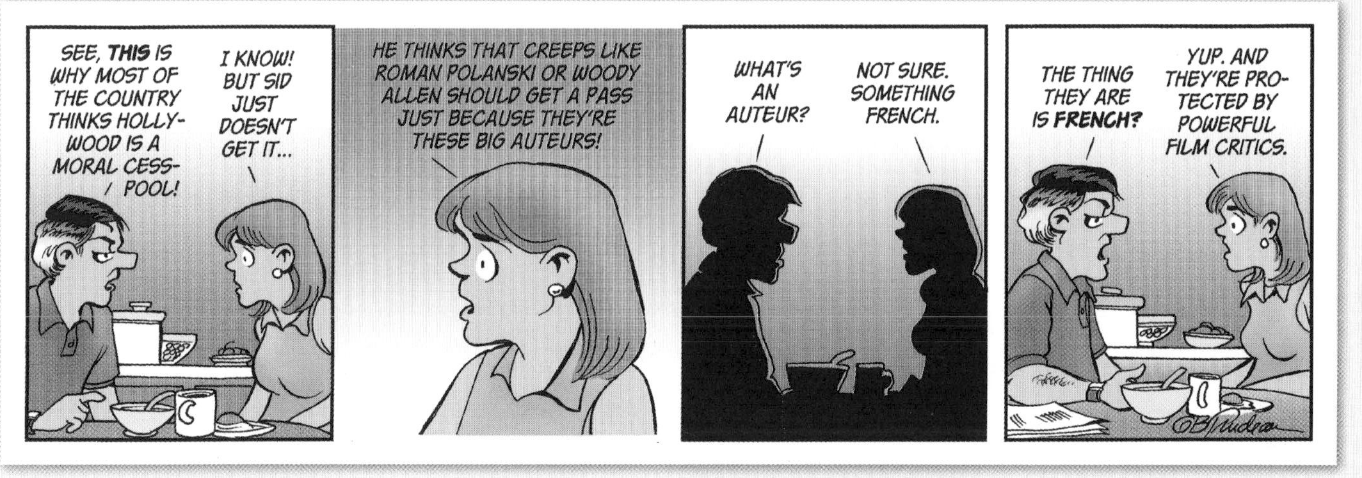
SEE, THIS IS WHY MOST OF THE COUNTRY THINKS HOLLYWOOD IS A MORAL CESSPOOL!
I KNOW! BUT SID JUST DOESN'T GET IT...
HE THINKS THAT CREEPS LIKE ROMAN POLANSKI OR WOODY ALLEN SHOULD GET A PASS JUST BECAUSE THEY'RE THESE BIG AUTEURS!
WHAT'S AN AUTEUR?
NOT SURE. SOMETHING FRENCH.
THE THING THEY ARE IS FRENCH?
YUP. AND THEY'RE PROTECTED BY POWERFUL FILM CRITICS.
GB Trudeau

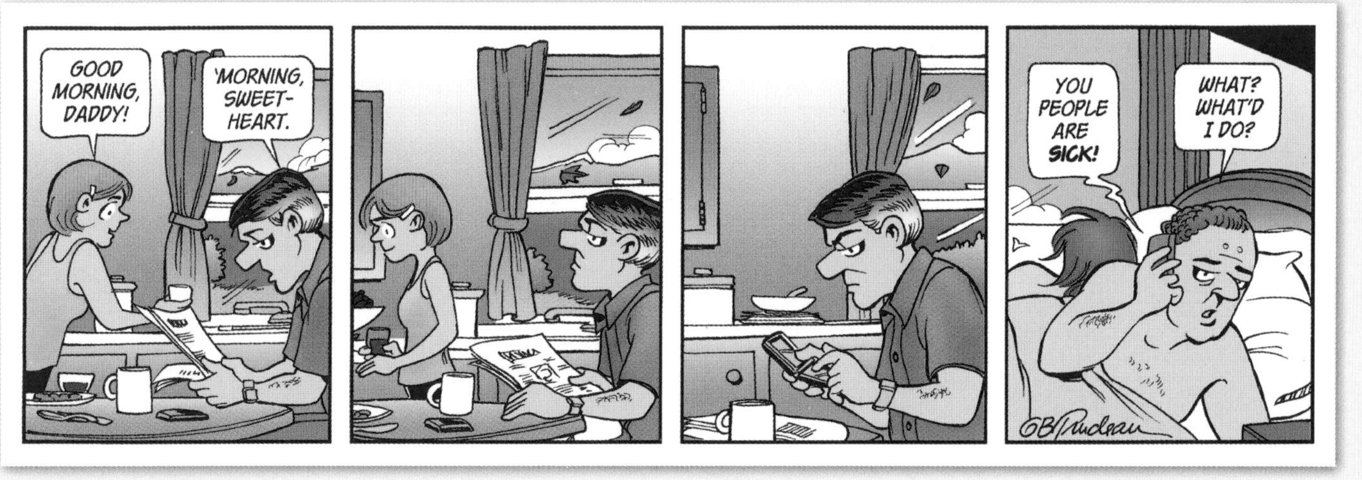
GOOD MORNING, DADDY!
'MORNING, SWEETHEART.
YOU PEOPLE ARE SICK!
WHAT? WHAT'D I DO?
GB Trudeau

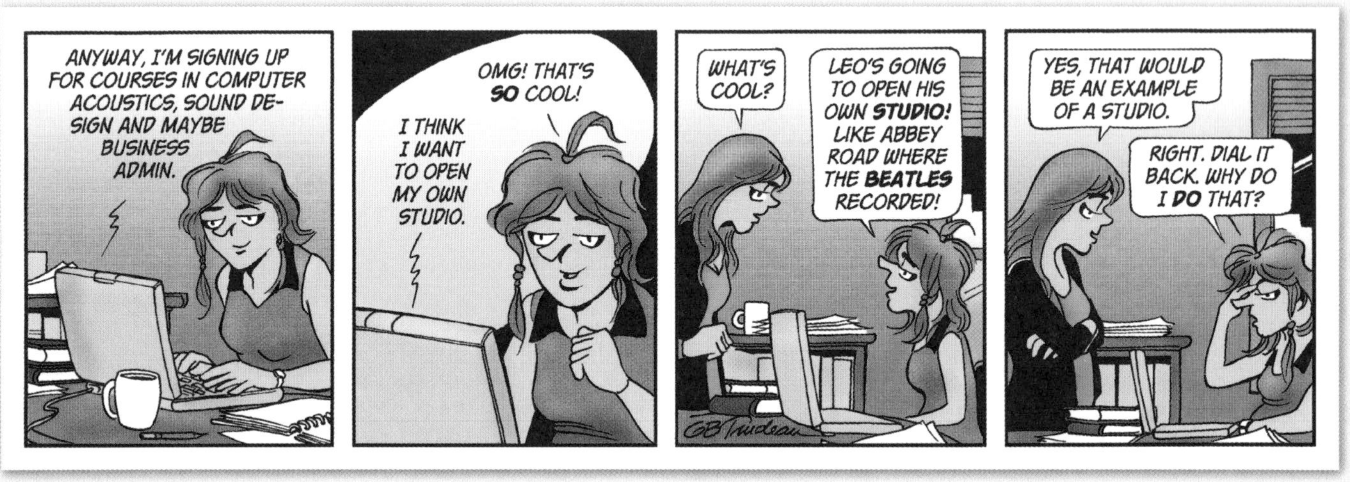
ANYWAY, I'M SIGNING UP FOR COURSES IN COMPUTER ACOUSTICS, SOUND DESIGN AND MAYBE BUSINESS ADMIN.
I THINK I WANT TO OPEN MY OWN STUDIO.
OMG! THAT'S **SO** COOL!
WHAT'S COOL?
LEO'S GOING TO OPEN HIS OWN **STUDIO!** LIKE ABBEY ROAD WHERE THE **BEATLES** RECORDED!
YES, THAT WOULD BE AN EXAMPLE OF A STUDIO.
RIGHT. DIAL IT BACK. WHY DO I **DO** THAT?
GB Trudeau

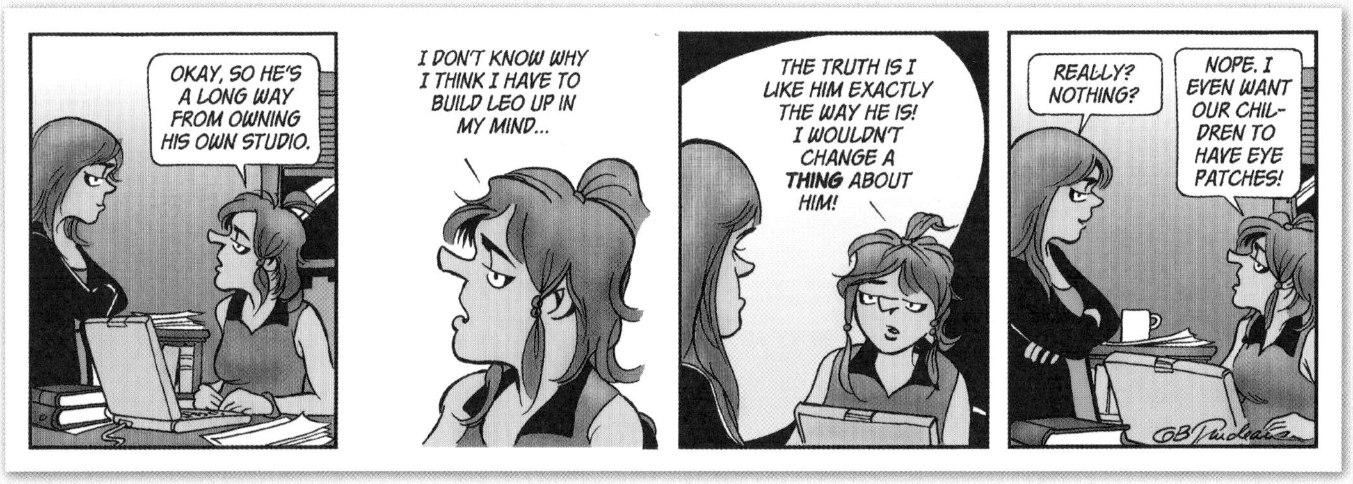
OKAY, SO HE'S A LONG WAY FROM OWNING HIS OWN STUDIO.
I DON'T KNOW WHY I THINK I HAVE TO BUILD LEO UP IN MY MIND...
THE TRUTH IS I LIKE HIM EXACTLY THE WAY HE IS! I WOULDN'T CHANGE A **THING** ABOUT HIM!
REALLY? NOTHING?
NOPE. I EVEN WANT OUR CHILDREN TO HAVE EYE PATCHES!
GB Trudeau

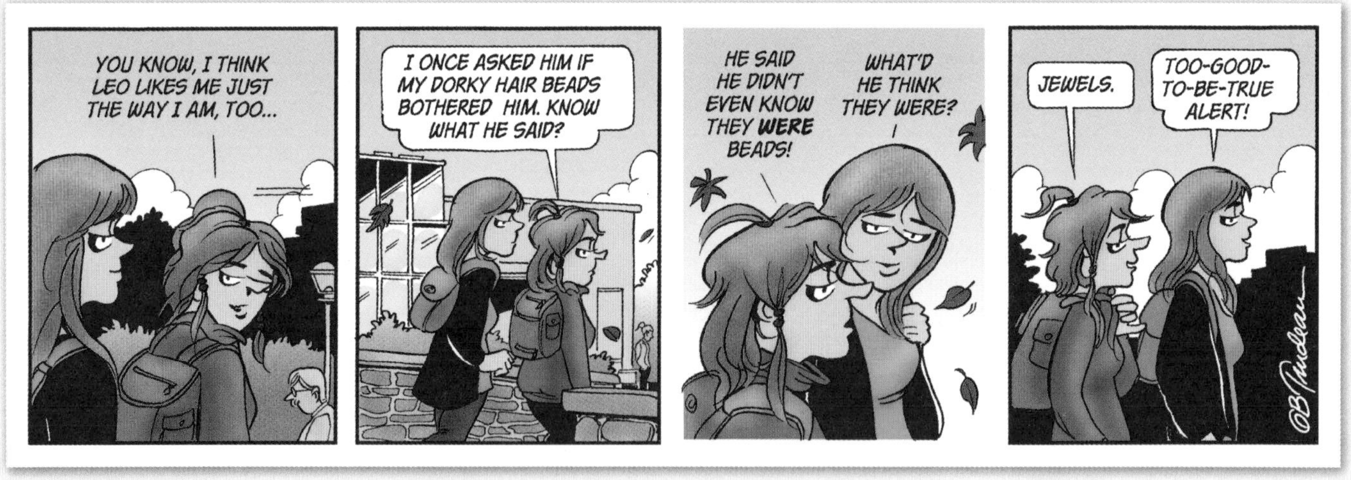
YOU KNOW, I THINK LEO LIKES ME JUST THE WAY I AM, TOO...
I ONCE ASKED HIM IF MY DORKY HAIR BEADS BOTHERED HIM. KNOW WHAT HE SAID?
HE SAID HE DIDN'T EVEN KNOW THEY **WERE** BEADS!
WHAT'D HE THINK THEY WERE?
JEWELS.
TOO-GOOD-TO-BE-TRUE ALERT!
GB Trudeau

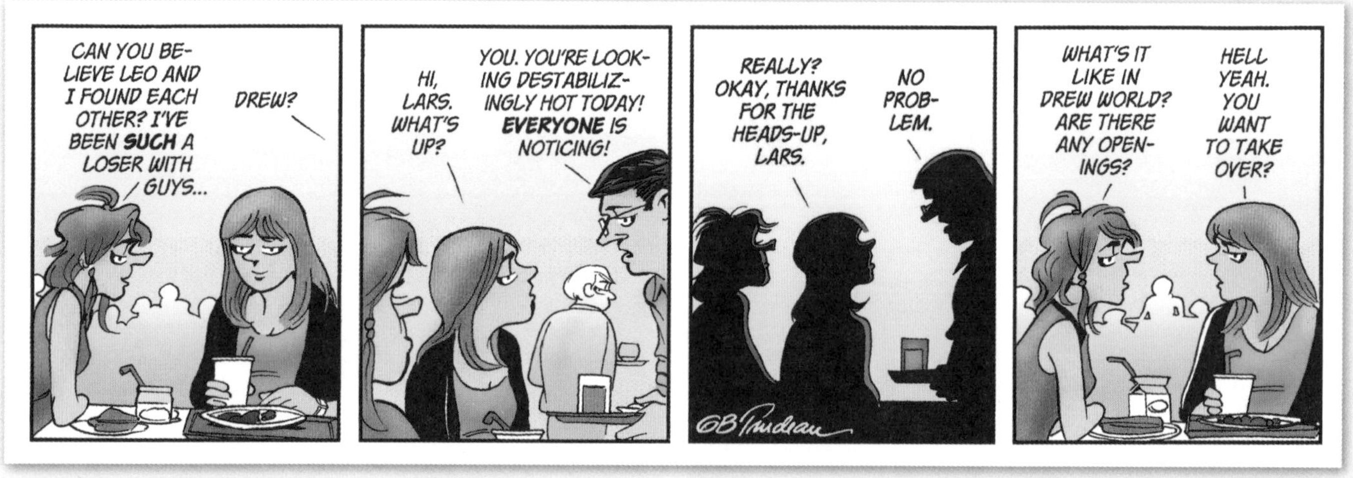
CAN YOU BE-LIEVE LEO AND I FOUND EACH OTHER? I'VE BEEN **SUCH** A LOSER WITH GUYS...
DREW?
HI, LARS. WHAT'S UP?
YOU. YOU'RE LOOK-ING DESTABILIZ-INGLY HOT TODAY! **EVERYONE** IS NOTICING!
REALLY? OKAY, THANKS FOR THE HEADS-UP, LARS.
NO PROB-LEM.
WHAT'S IT LIKE IN DREW WORLD? ARE THERE ANY OPEN-INGS?
HELL YEAH. YOU WANT TO TAKE OVER?

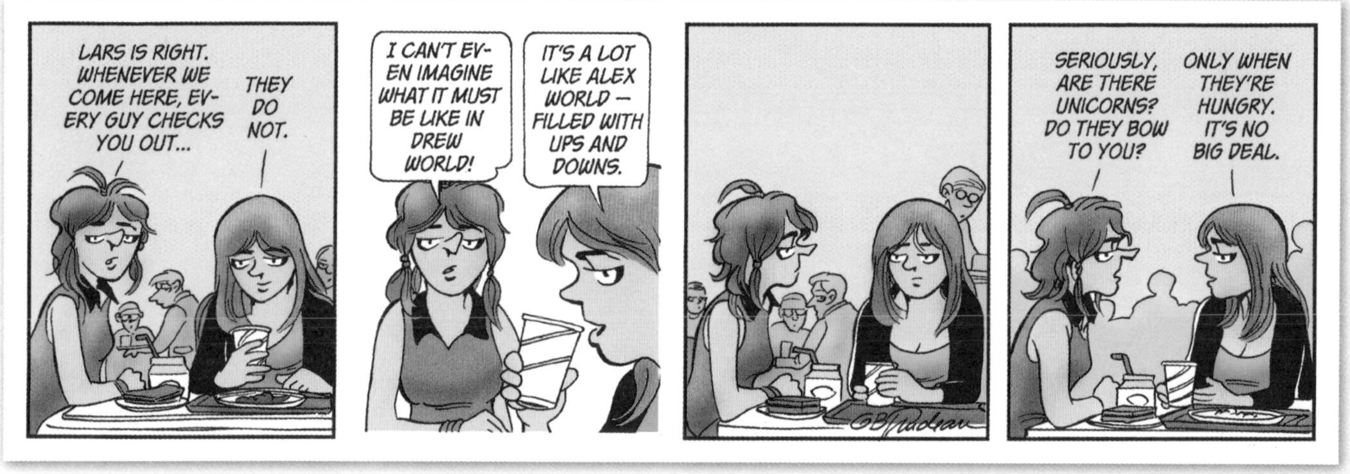
LARS IS RIGHT. WHENEVER WE COME HERE, EV-ERY GUY CHECKS YOU OUT...
THEY DO NOT.
I CAN'T EV-EN IMAGINE WHAT IT MUST BE LIKE IN DREW WORLD!
IT'S A LOT LIKE ALEX WORLD — FILLED WITH UPS AND DOWNS.
SERIOUSLY, ARE THERE UNICORNS? DO THEY BOW TO YOU?
ONLY WHEN THEY'RE HUNGRY. IT'S NO BIG DEAL.

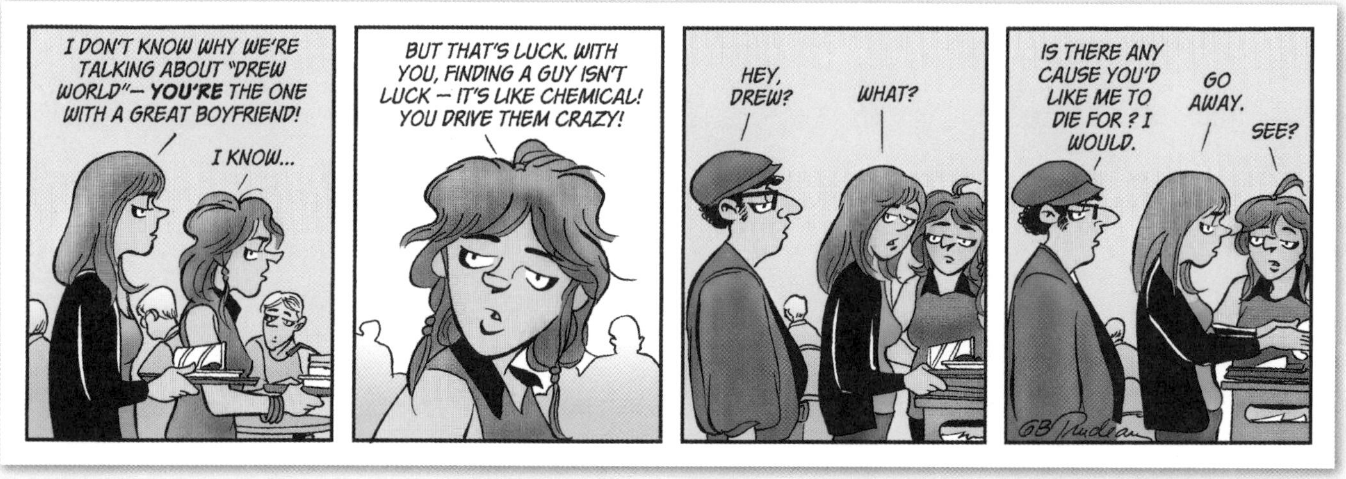
I DON'T KNOW WHY WE'RE TALKING ABOUT "DREW WORLD"— **YOU'RE** THE ONE WITH A GREAT BOYFRIEND!
I KNOW...
BUT THAT'S LUCK. WITH YOU, FINDING A GUY ISN'T LUCK — IT'S LIKE CHEMICAL! YOU DRIVE THEM CRAZY!
HEY, DREW?
WHAT?
IS THERE ANY CAUSE YOU'D LIKE ME TO DIE FOR ? I WOULD.
GO AWAY.
SEE?

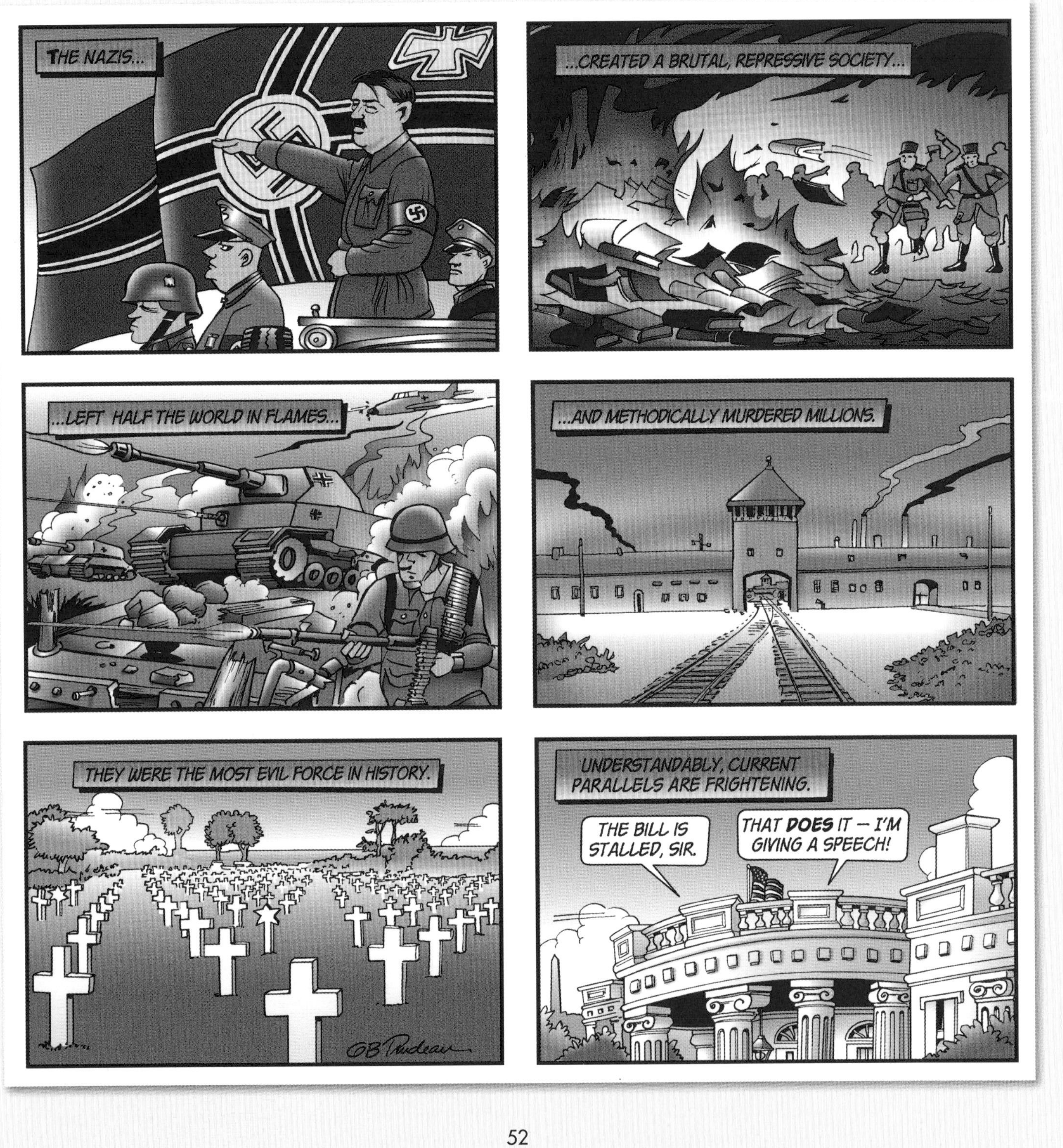
THE NAZIS...
...CREATED A BRUTAL, REPRESSIVE SOCIETY...
...LEFT HALF THE WORLD IN FLAMES...
...AND METHODICALLY MURDERED MILLIONS.
THEY WERE THE MOST EVIL FORCE IN HISTORY.
GB Trudeau
UNDERSTANDABLY, CURRENT PARALLELS ARE FRIGHTENING.
THE BILL IS STALLED, SIR.
THAT **DOES** IT — I'M GIVING A SPEECH!

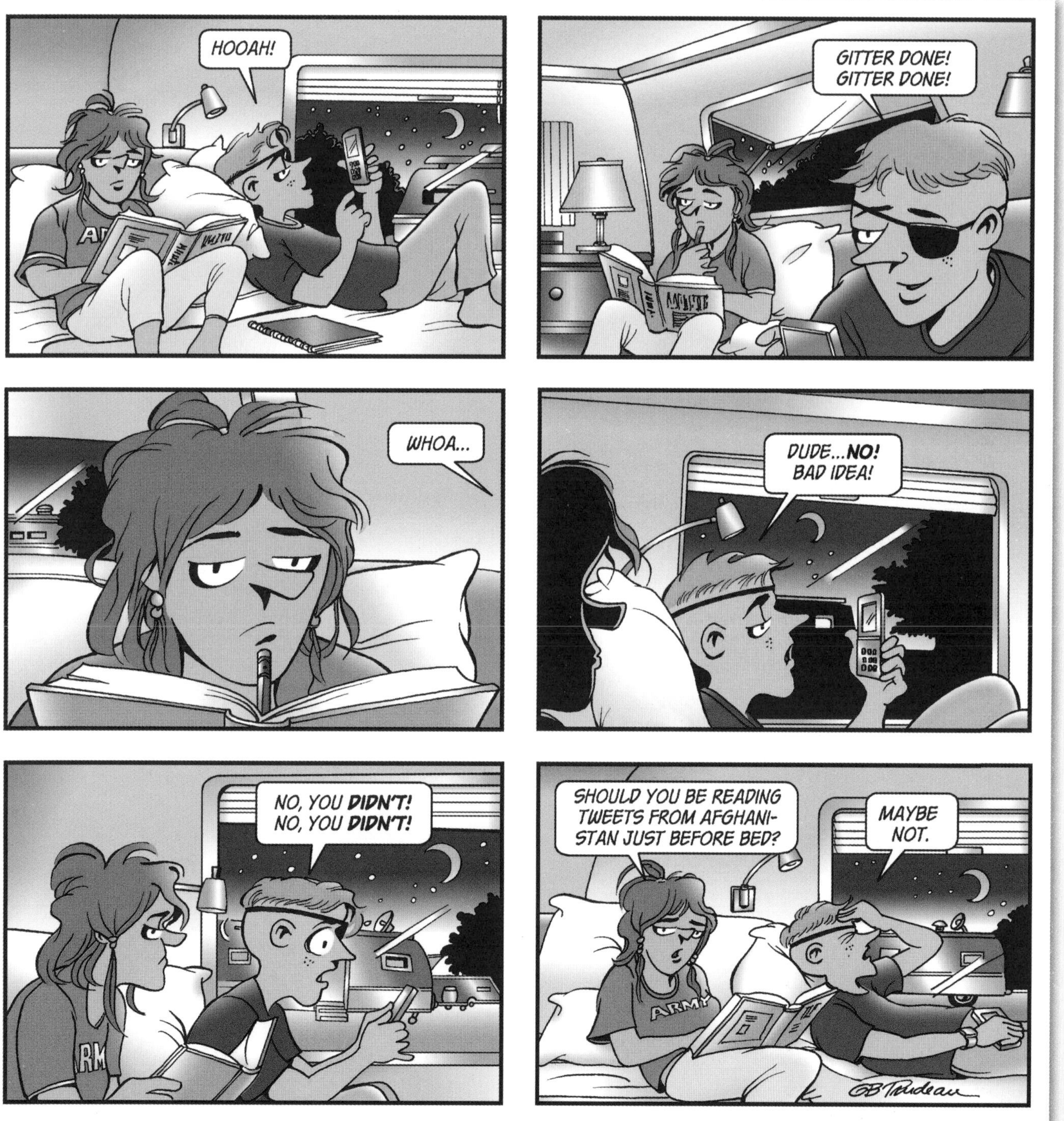

HOOAH!
GITTER DONE! GITTER DONE!
WHOA...
DUDE...**NO!** BAD IDEA!
NO, YOU **DIDN'T!** NO, YOU **DIDN'T!**
SHOULD YOU BE READING TWEETS FROM AFGHANI-STAN JUST BEFORE BED?
MAYBE NOT.
GB Trudeau

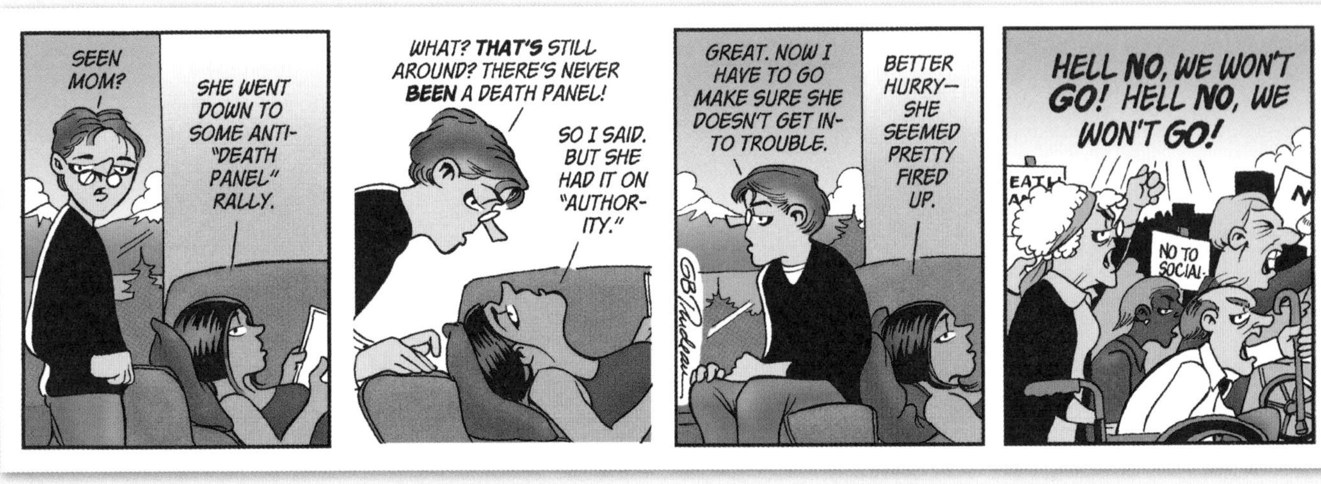
SEEN MOM?
SHE WENT DOWN TO SOME ANTI-"DEATH PANEL" RALLY.
WHAT? **THAT'S** STILL AROUND? THERE'S NEVER **BEEN** A DEATH PANEL!
SO I SAID. BUT SHE HAD IT ON "AUTHORITY."
GREAT. NOW I HAVE TO GO MAKE SURE SHE DOESN'T GET INTO TROUBLE.
BETTER HURRY— SHE SEEMED PRETTY FIRED UP.
HELL **NO**, WE WON'T **GO**! HELL **NO**, WE WON'T **GO**!

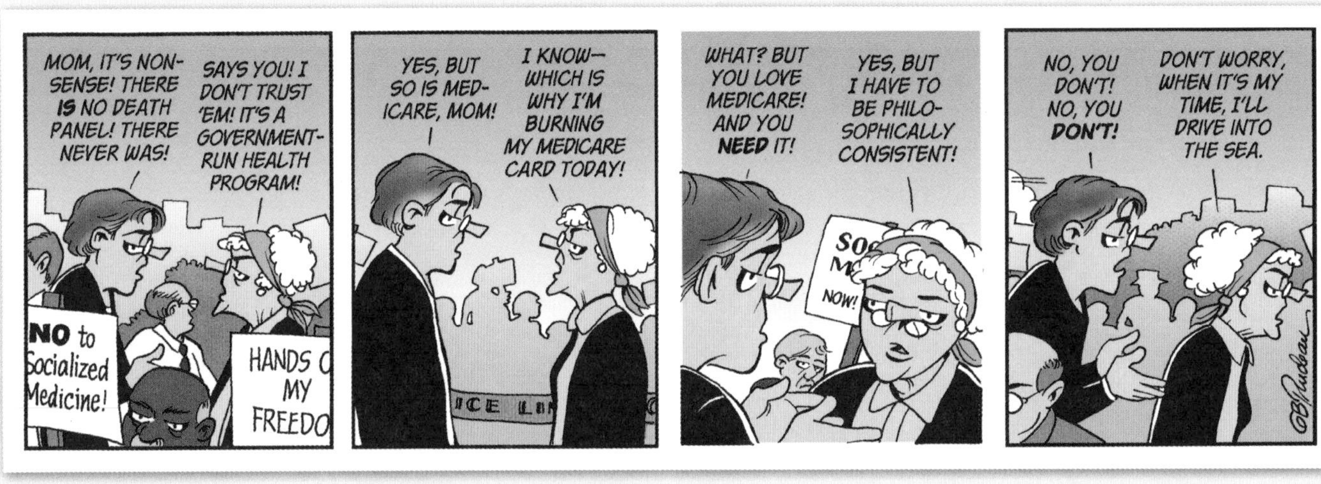
MOM, IT'S NONSENSE! THERE **IS** NO DEATH PANEL! THERE NEVER WAS!
SAYS YOU! I DON'T TRUST 'EM! IT'S A GOVERNMENT-RUN HEALTH PROGRAM!
NO to Socialized Medicine!
YES, BUT SO IS MEDICARE, MOM!
I KNOW— WHICH IS WHY I'M BURNING MY MEDICARE CARD TODAY!
WHAT? BUT YOU LOVE MEDICARE! AND YOU **NEED** IT!
YES, BUT I HAVE TO BE PHILOSOPHICALLY CONSISTENT!
NOW!
NO, YOU DON'T! NO, YOU **DON'T!**
DON'T WORRY, WHEN IT'S MY TIME, I'LL DRIVE INTO THE SEA.

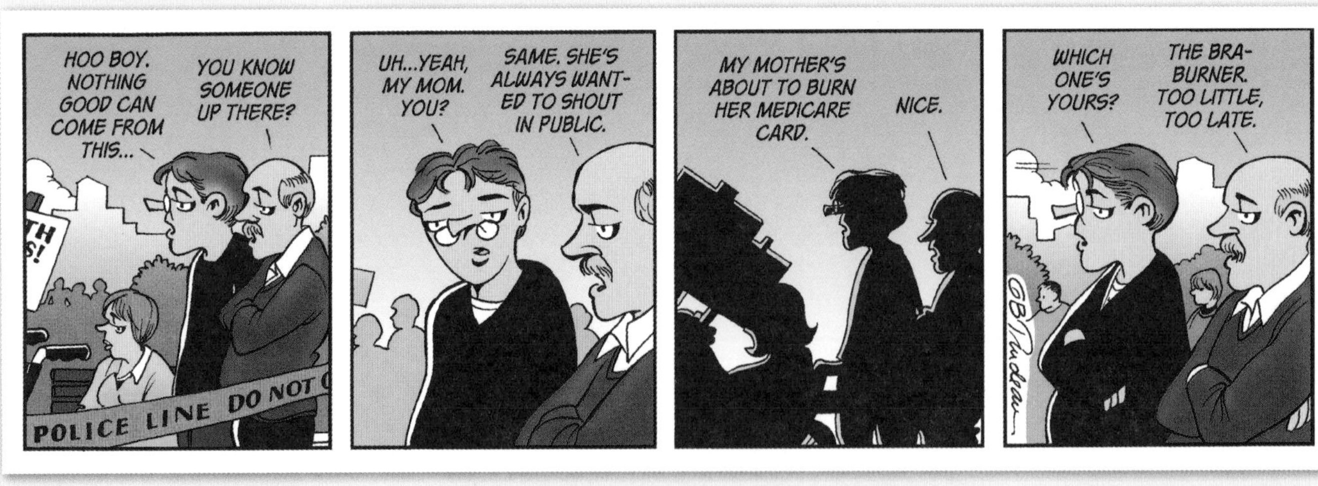
HOO BOY. NOTHING GOOD CAN COME FROM THIS...
YOU KNOW SOMEONE UP THERE?
POLICE LINE DO NOT
UH...YEAH, MY MOM. YOU?
SAME. SHE'S ALWAYS WANTED TO SHOUT IN PUBLIC.
MY MOTHER'S ABOUT TO BURN HER MEDICARE CARD.
NICE.
WHICH ONE'S YOURS?
THE BRA-BURNER. TOO LITTLE, TOO LATE.

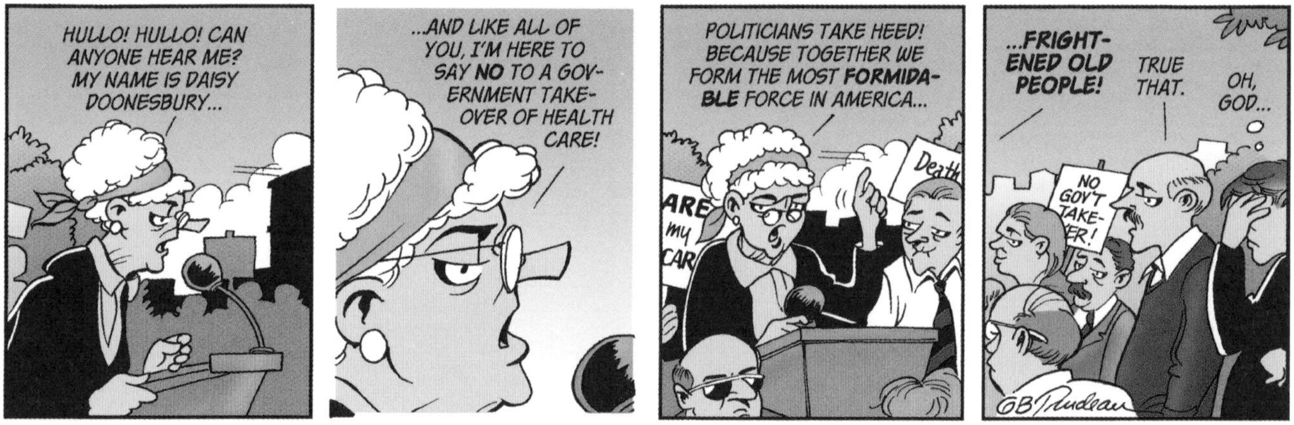
HULLO! HULLO! CAN ANYONE HEAR ME? MY NAME IS DAISY DOONESBURY...
...AND LIKE ALL OF YOU, I'M HERE TO SAY **NO** TO A GOVERNMENT TAKEOVER OF HEALTH CARE!
POLITICIANS TAKE HEED! BECAUSE TOGETHER WE FORM THE MOST **FORMIDABLE** FORCE IN AMERICA...
...FRIGHTENED OLD PEOPLE!
TRUE THAT.
OH, GOD...

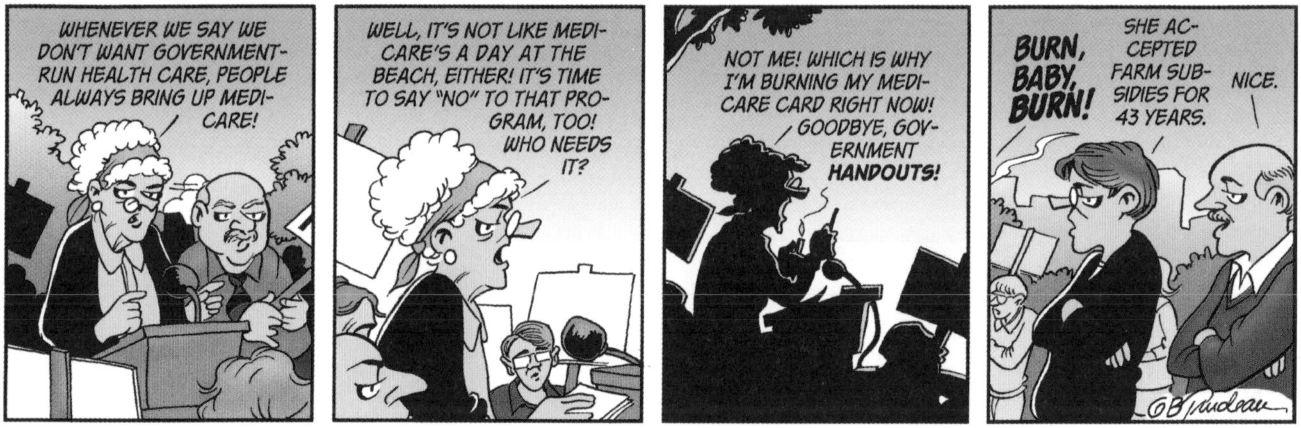
WHENEVER WE SAY WE DON'T WANT GOVERNMENT-RUN HEALTH CARE, PEOPLE ALWAYS BRING UP MEDICARE!
WELL, IT'S NOT LIKE MEDICARE'S A DAY AT THE BEACH, EITHER! IT'S TIME TO SAY "NO" TO THAT PROGRAM, TOO! WHO NEEDS IT?
NOT ME! WHICH IS WHY I'M BURNING MY MEDICARE CARD RIGHT NOW! GOODBYE, GOVERNMENT **HANDOUTS!**
BURN, BABY, BURN!
SHE ACCEPTED FARM SUBSIDIES FOR 43 YEARS.
NICE.

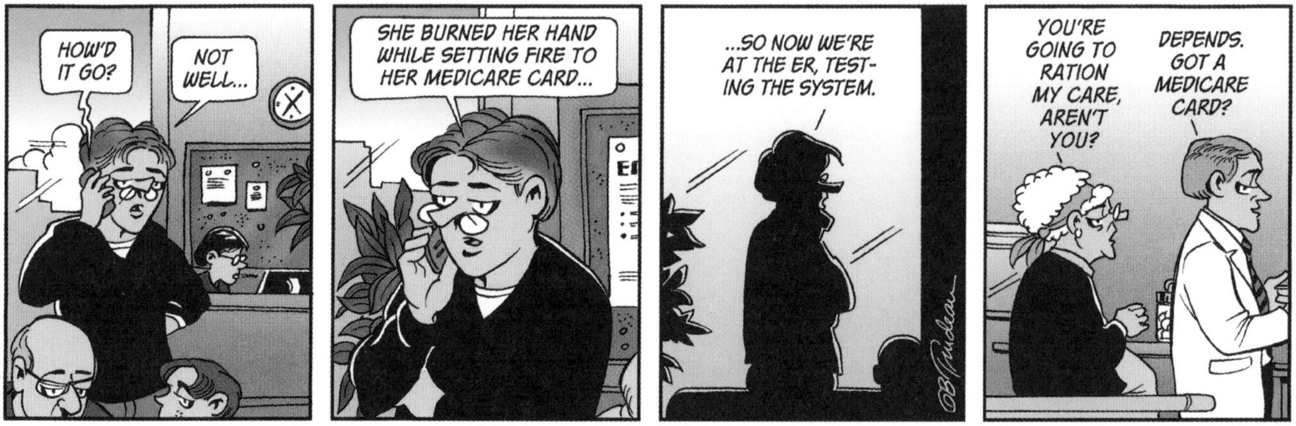
HOW'D IT GO?
NOT WELL...
SHE BURNED HER HAND WHILE SETTING FIRE TO HER MEDICARE CARD...
...SO NOW WE'RE AT THE ER, TESTING THE SYSTEM.
YOU'RE GOING TO RATION MY CARE, AREN'T YOU?
DEPENDS. GOT A MEDICARE CARD?

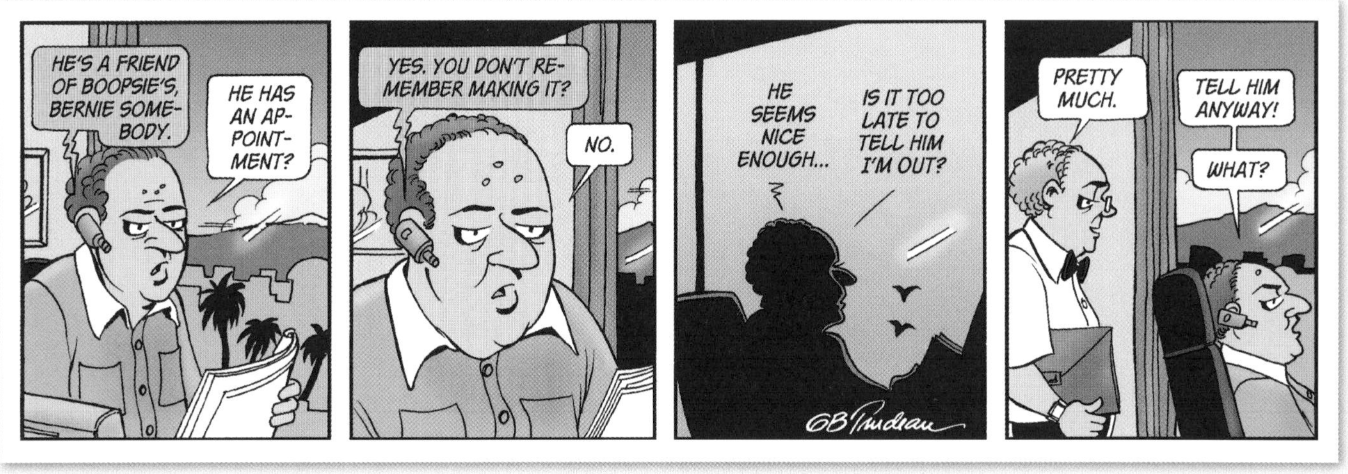
HE'S A FRIEND OF BOOPSIE'S, BERNIE SOME-BODY.
HE HAS AN AP-POINT-MENT?
YES. YOU DON'T RE-MEMBER MAKING IT?
NO.
HE SEEMS NICE ENOUGH...
IS IT TOO LATE TO TELL HIM I'M OUT?
PRETTY MUCH.
TELL HIM ANYWAY!
WHAT?

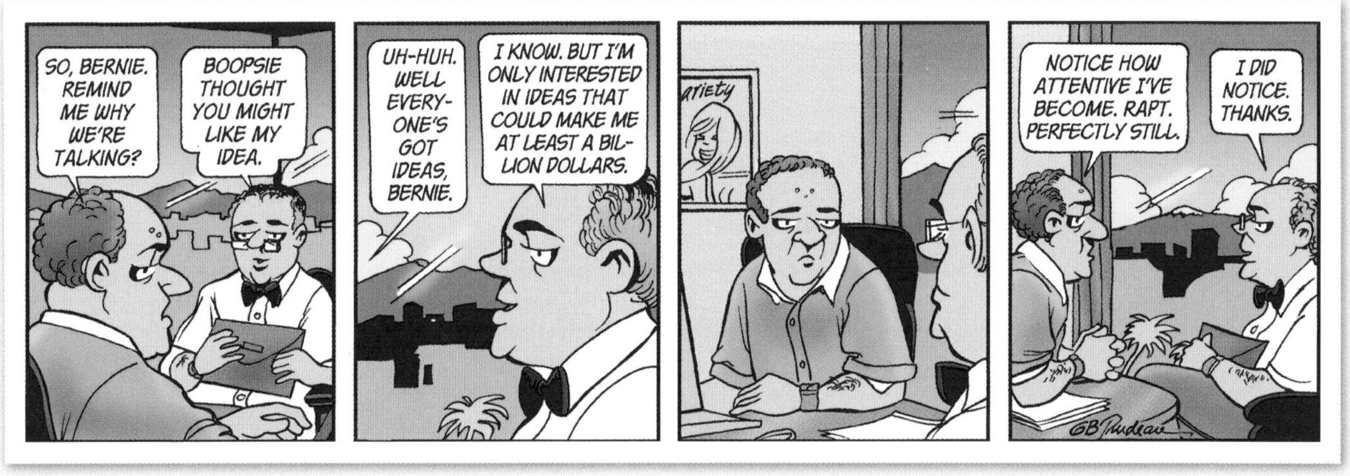
SO, BERNIE. REMIND ME WHY WE'RE TALKING?
BOOPSIE THOUGHT YOU MIGHT LIKE MY IDEA.
UH-HUH. WELL EVERY-ONE'S GOT IDEAS, BERNIE.
I KNOW. BUT I'M ONLY INTERESTED IN IDEAS THAT COULD MAKE ME AT LEAST A BIL-LION DOLLARS.
NOTICE HOW ATTENTIVE I'VE BECOME. RAPT. PERFECTLY STILL.
I DID NOTICE. THANKS.

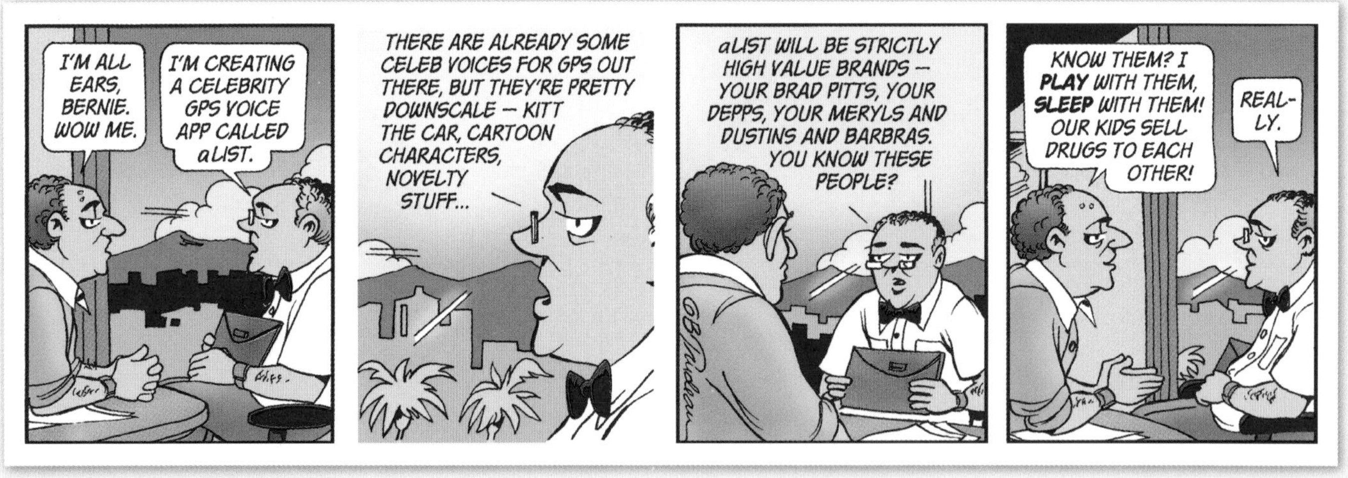
I'M ALL EARS, BERNIE. WOW ME.
I'M CREATING A CELEBRITY GPS VOICE APP CALLED aLIST.
THERE ARE ALREADY SOME CELEB VOICES FOR GPS OUT THERE, BUT THEY'RE PRETTY DOWNSCALE — KITT THE CAR, CARTOON CHARACTERS, NOVELTY STUFF...
aLIST WILL BE STRICTLY HIGH VALUE BRANDS — YOUR BRAD PITTS, YOUR DEPPS, YOUR MERYLS AND DUSTINS AND BARBRAS. YOU KNOW THESE PEOPLE?
KNOW THEM? I PLAY WITH THEM, SLEEP WITH THEM! OUR KIDS SELL DRUGS TO EACH OTHER!
REAL-LY.

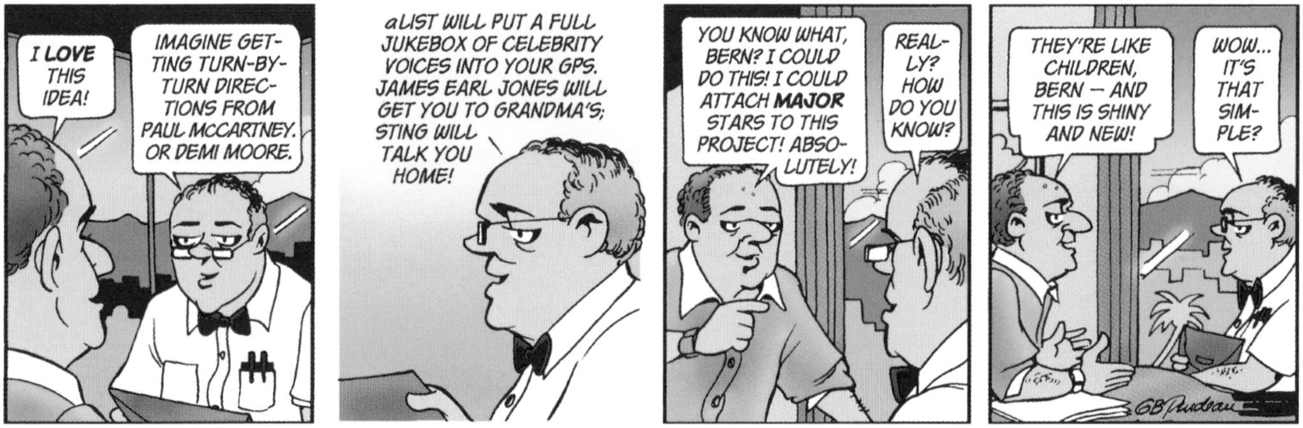
I LOVE THIS IDEA!
IMAGINE GETTING TURN-BY-TURN DIRECTIONS FROM PAUL McCARTNEY. OR DEMI MOORE.
aLIST WILL PUT A FULL JUKEBOX OF CELEBRITY VOICES INTO YOUR GPS. JAMES EARL JONES WILL GET YOU TO GRANDMA'S; STING WILL TALK YOU HOME!
YOU KNOW WHAT, BERN? I COULD DO THIS! I COULD ATTACH MAJOR STARS TO THIS PROJECT! ABSOLUTELY!
REALLY? HOW DO YOU KNOW?
THEY'RE LIKE CHILDREN, BERN — AND THIS IS SHINY AND NEW!
WOW... IT'S THAT SIMPLE?

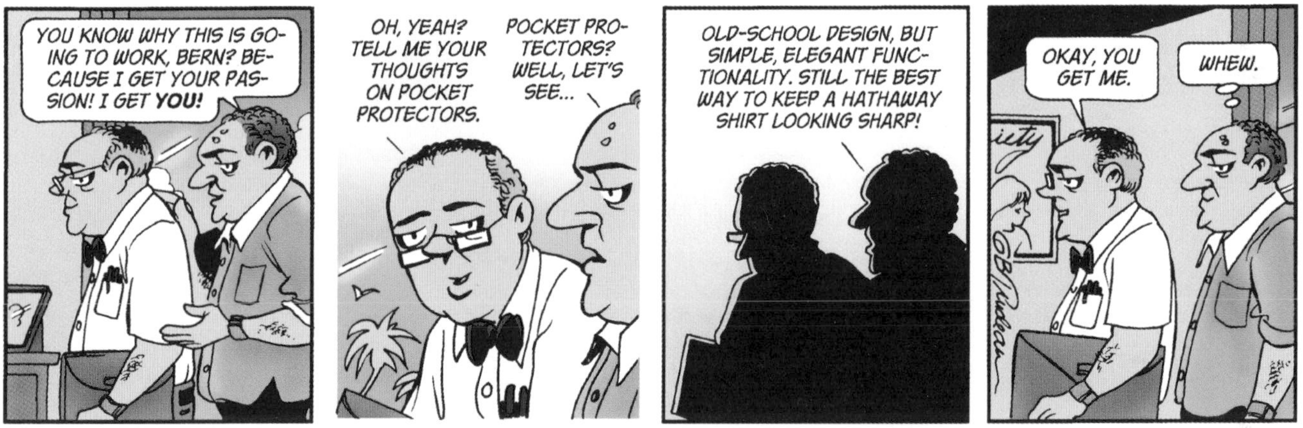
YOU KNOW WHY THIS IS GOING TO WORK, BERN? BECAUSE I GET YOUR PASSION! I GET YOU!
OH, YEAH? TELL ME YOUR THOUGHTS ON POCKET PROTECTORS.
POCKET PROTECTORS? WELL, LET'S SEE...
OLD-SCHOOL DESIGN, BUT SIMPLE, ELEGANT FUNCTIONALITY. STILL THE BEST WAY TO KEEP A HATHAWAY SHIRT LOOKING SHARP!
OKAY, YOU GET ME.
WHEW.

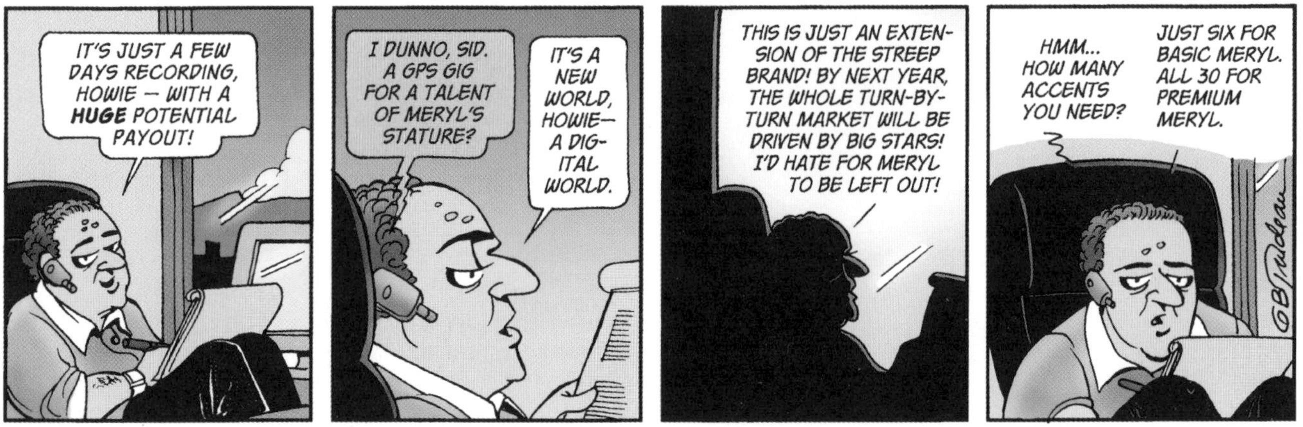
IT'S JUST A FEW DAYS RECORDING, HOWIE — WITH A HUGE POTENTIAL PAYOUT!
I DUNNO, SID. A GPS GIG FOR A TALENT OF MERYL'S STATURE?
IT'S A NEW WORLD, HOWIE— A DIGITAL WORLD.
THIS IS JUST AN EXTENSION OF THE STREEP BRAND! BY NEXT YEAR, THE WHOLE TURN-BY-TURN MARKET WILL BE DRIVEN BY BIG STARS! I'D HATE FOR MERYL TO BE LEFT OUT!
HMM... HOW MANY ACCENTS YOU NEED?
JUST SIX FOR BASIC MERYL. ALL 30 FOR PREMIUM MERYL.

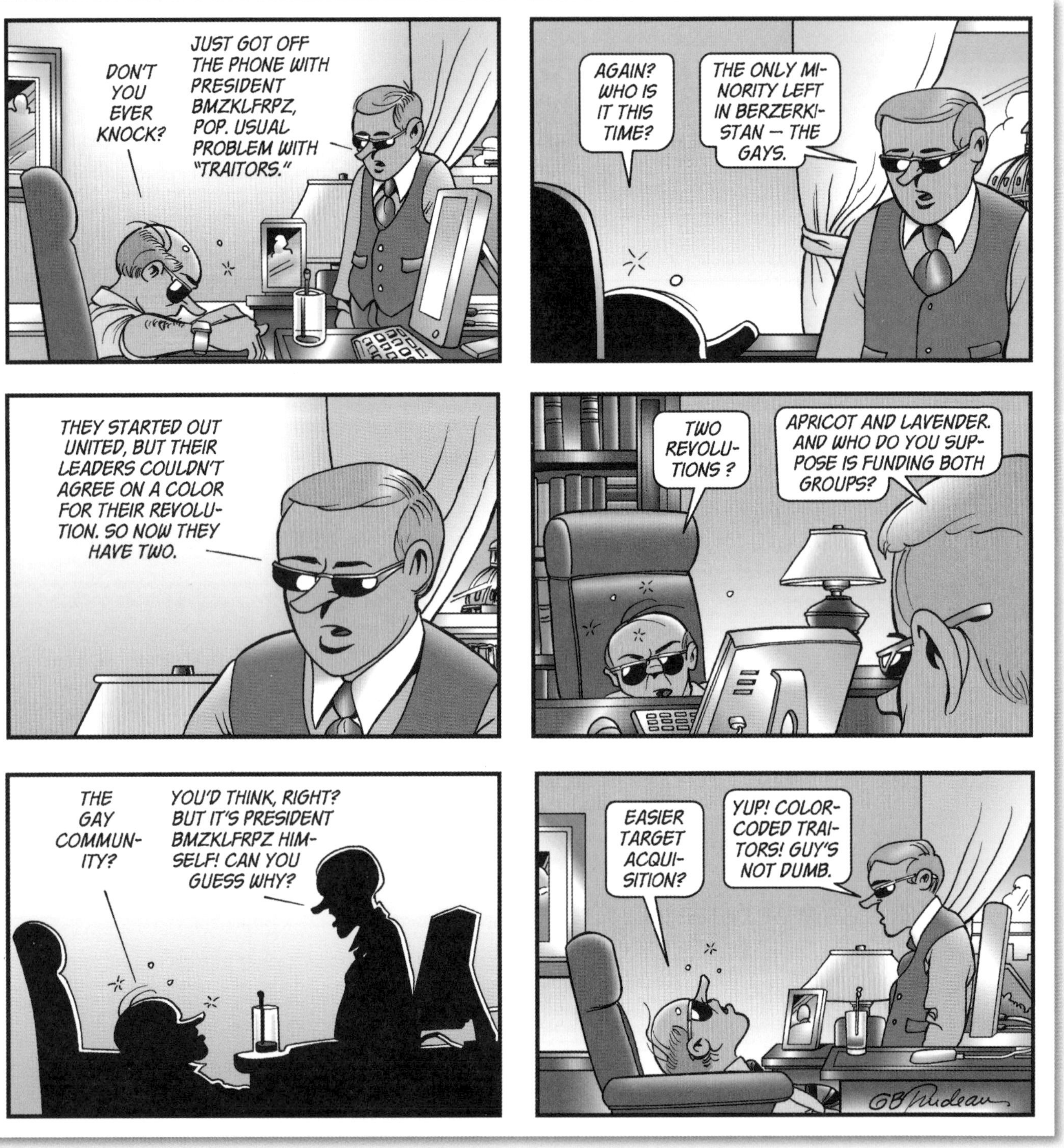
DON'T YOU EVER KNOCK?
JUST GOT OFF THE PHONE WITH PRESIDENT BMZKLFRPZ, POP. USUAL PROBLEM WITH "TRAITORS."
AGAIN? WHO IS IT THIS TIME?
THE ONLY MINORITY LEFT IN BERZERKISTAN — THE GAYS.
THEY STARTED OUT UNITED, BUT THEIR LEADERS COULDN'T AGREE ON A COLOR FOR THEIR REVOLUTION. SO NOW THEY HAVE TWO.
TWO REVOLUTIONS ?
APRICOT AND LAVENDER. AND WHO DO YOU SUPPOSE IS FUNDING BOTH GROUPS?
THE GAY COMMUNITY?
YOU'D THINK, RIGHT? BUT IT'S PRESIDENT BMZKLFRPZ HIMSELF! CAN YOU GUESS WHY?
EASIER TARGET ACQUISITION?
YUP! COLOR-CODED TRAITORS! GUY'S NOT DUMB.
GBTrudeau

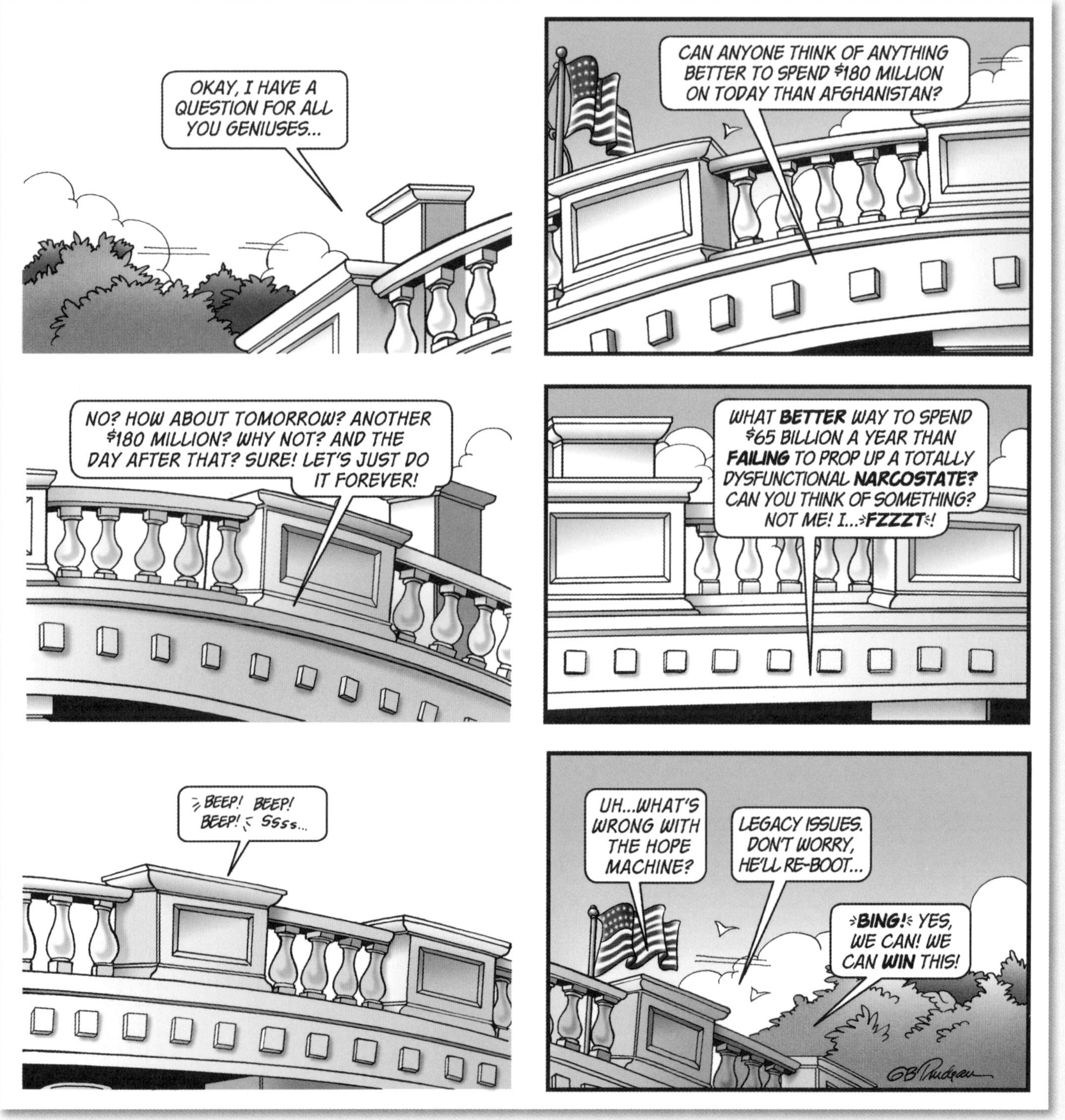
OKAY, I HAVE A QUESTION FOR ALL YOU GENIUSES...
CAN ANYONE THINK OF ANYTHING BETTER TO SPEND $180 MILLION ON TODAY THAN AFGHANISTAN?
NO? HOW ABOUT TOMORROW? ANOTHER $180 MILLION? WHY NOT? AND THE DAY AFTER THAT? SURE! LET'S JUST DO IT FOREVER!
WHAT **BETTER** WAY TO SPEND $65 BILLION A YEAR THAN **FAILING** TO PROP UP A TOTALLY DYSFUNCTIONAL **NARCOSTATE?** CAN YOU THINK OF SOMETHING? NOT ME! I... **FZZZT**!
BEEP! BEEP! BEEP! Ssss...
UH...WHAT'S WRONG WITH THE HOPE MACHINE?
LEGACY ISSUES. DON'T WORRY, HE'LL RE-BOOT...
BING! YES, WE CAN! WE CAN **WIN** THIS!
GB Trudeau

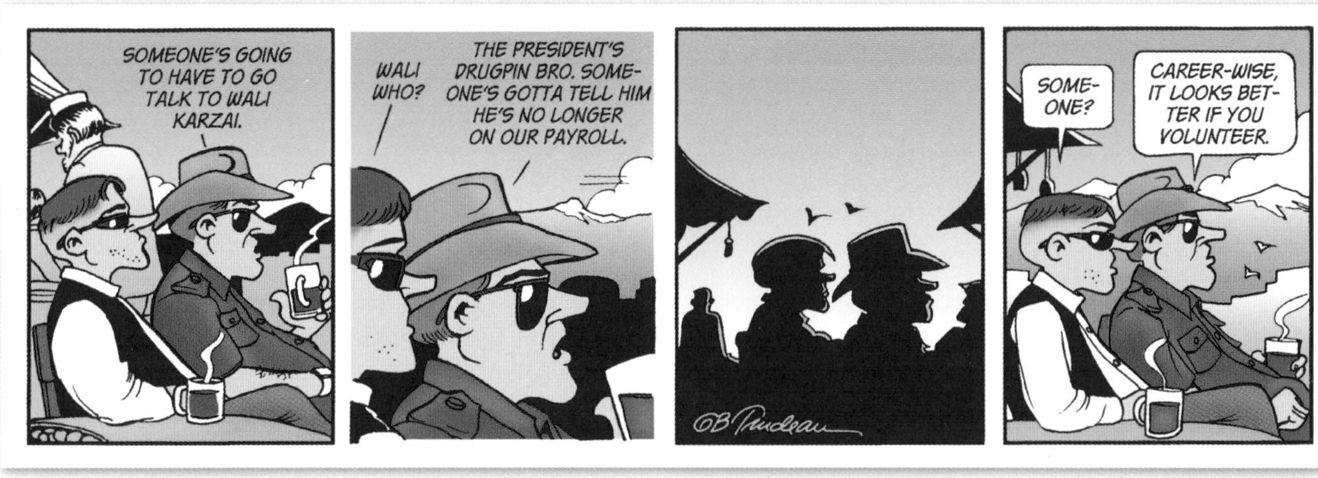
SOMEONE'S GOING TO HAVE TO GO TALK TO WALI KARZAI.
WALI WHO?
THE PRESIDENT'S DRUGPIN BRO. SOMEONE'S GOTTA TELL HIM HE'S NO LONGER ON OUR PAYROLL.
SOME-ONE?
CAREER-WISE, IT LOOKS BETTER IF YOU VOLUNTEER.

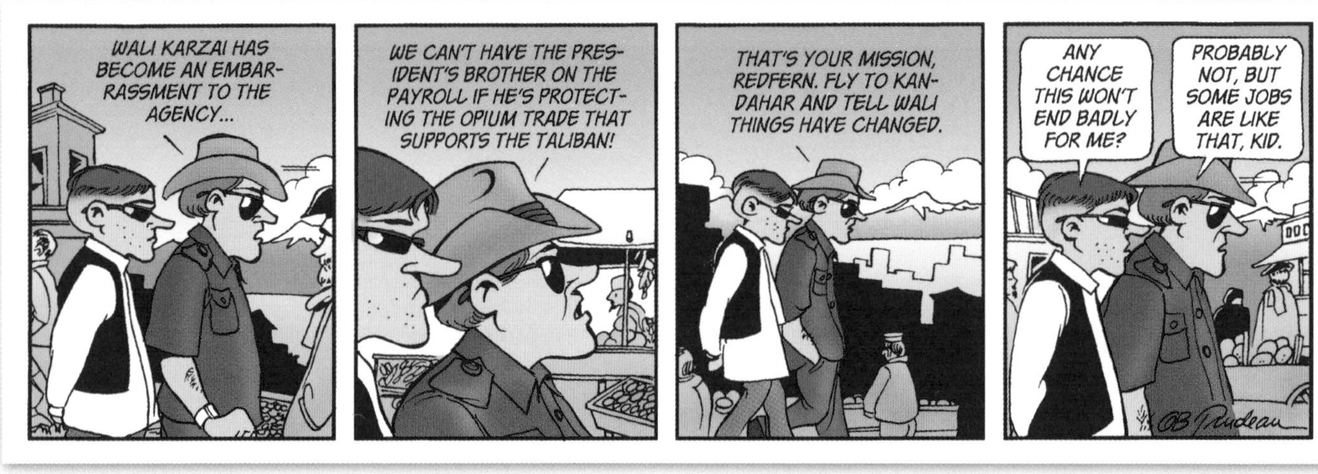
WALI KARZAI HAS BECOME AN EMBARRASSMENT TO THE AGENCY...
WE CAN'T HAVE THE PRESIDENT'S BROTHER ON THE PAYROLL IF HE'S PROTECTING THE OPIUM TRADE THAT SUPPORTS THE TALIBAN!
THAT'S YOUR MISSION, REDFERN. FLY TO KANDAHAR AND TELL WALI THINGS HAVE CHANGED.
ANY CHANCE THIS WON'T END BADLY FOR ME?
PROBABLY NOT, BUT SOME JOBS ARE LIKE THAT, KID.

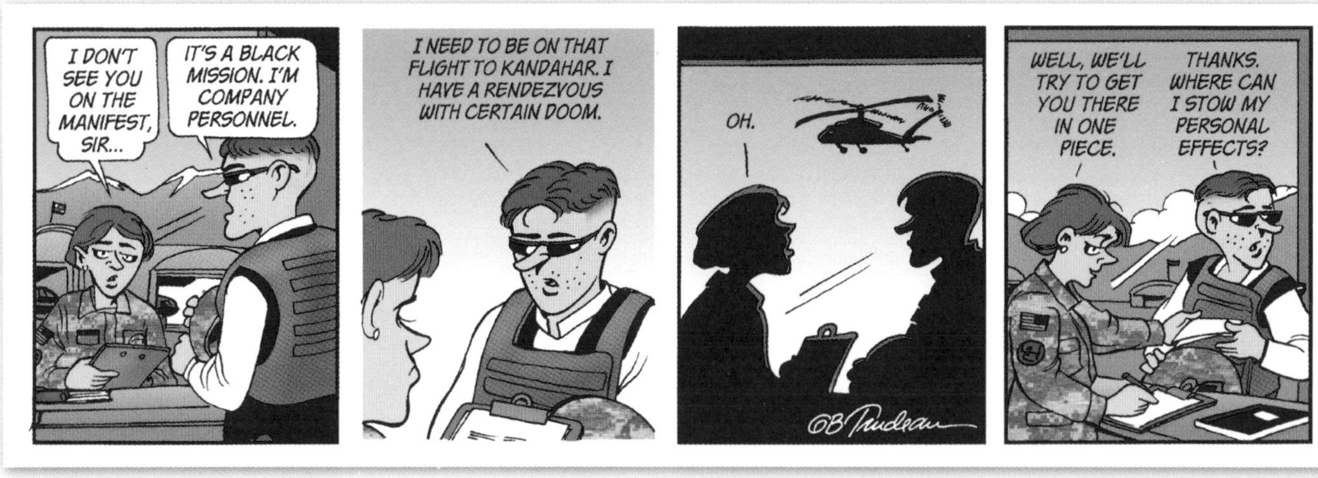
I DON'T SEE YOU ON THE MANIFEST, SIR...
IT'S A BLACK MISSION. I'M COMPANY PERSONNEL.
I NEED TO BE ON THAT FLIGHT TO KANDAHAR. I HAVE A RENDEZVOUS WITH CERTAIN DOOM.
OH.
WELL, WE'LL TRY TO GET YOU THERE IN ONE PIECE.
THANKS. WHERE CAN I STOW MY PERSONAL EFFECTS?

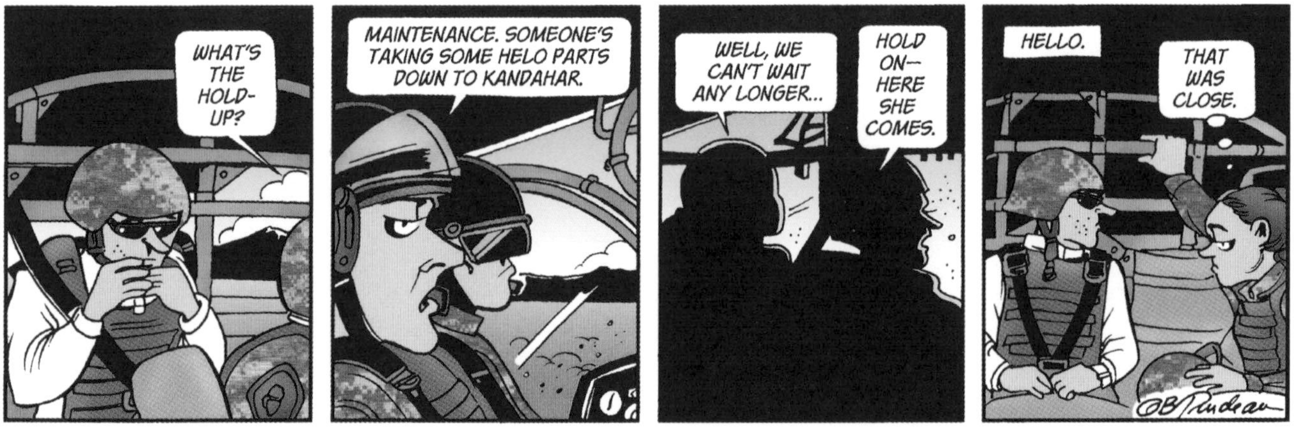
WHAT'S THE HOLD-UP?
MAINTENANCE. SOMEONE'S TAKING SOME HELO PARTS DOWN TO KANDAHAR.
WELL, WE CAN'T WAIT ANY LONGER...
HOLD ON— HERE SHE COMES.
HELLO.
THAT WAS CLOSE.
GB Trudeau

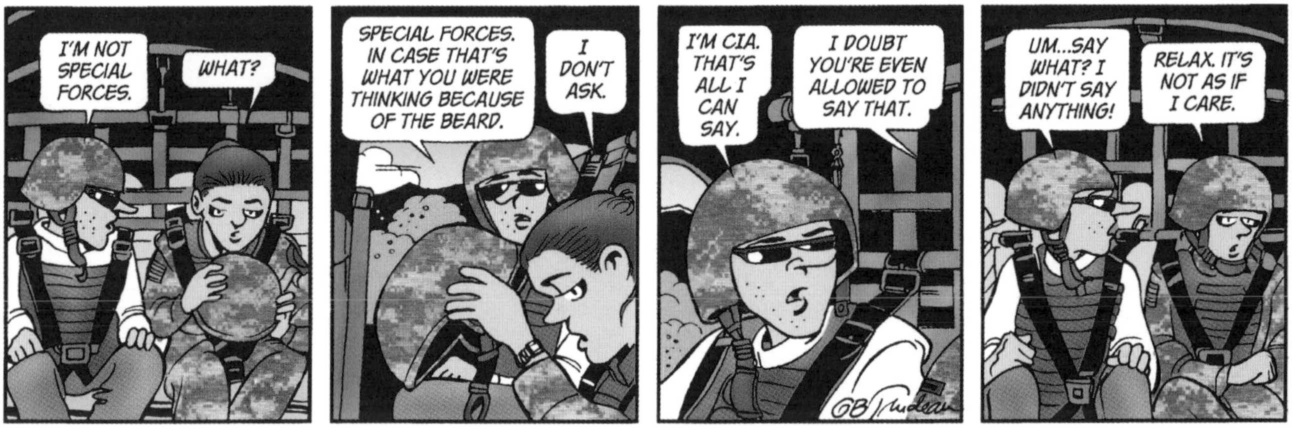
I'M NOT SPECIAL FORCES.
WHAT?
SPECIAL FORCES. IN CASE THAT'S WHAT YOU WERE THINKING BECAUSE OF THE BEARD.
I DON'T ASK.
I'M CIA. THAT'S ALL I CAN SAY.
I DOUBT YOU'RE EVEN ALLOWED TO SAY THAT.
UM...SAY WHAT? I DIDN'T SAY ANYTHING!
RELAX. IT'S NOT AS IF I CARE.
GB Trudeau

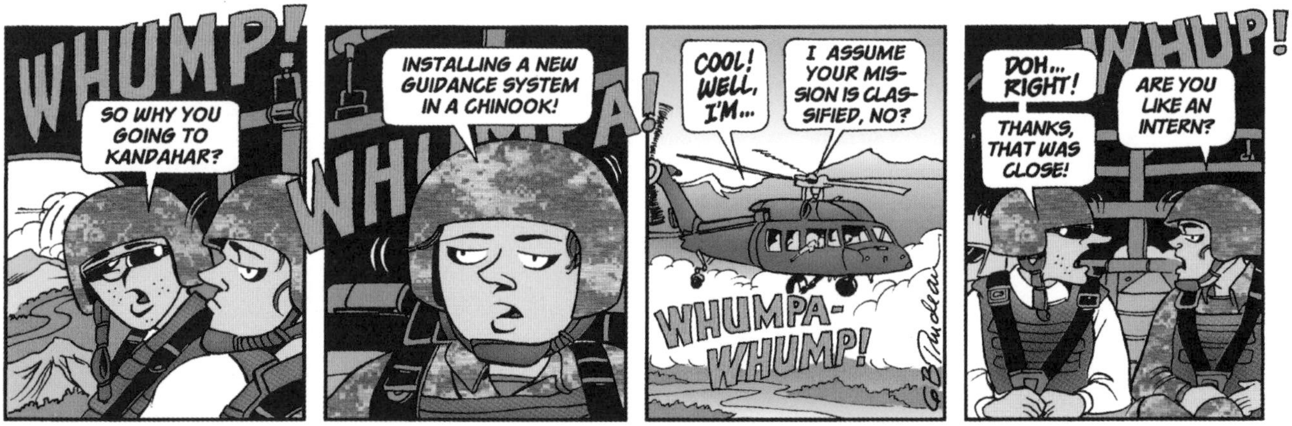
WHUMP!
SO WHY YOU GOING TO KANDAHAR?
INSTALLING A NEW GUIDANCE SYSTEM IN A CHINOOK!
WHUMPA!
COOL! WELL, I'M...
I ASSUME YOUR MISSION IS CLASSIFIED, NO?
WHUMPA-WHUMP!
GB Trudeau
WHUP!
DOH... RIGHT!
THANKS, THAT WAS CLOSE!
ARE YOU LIKE AN INTERN?

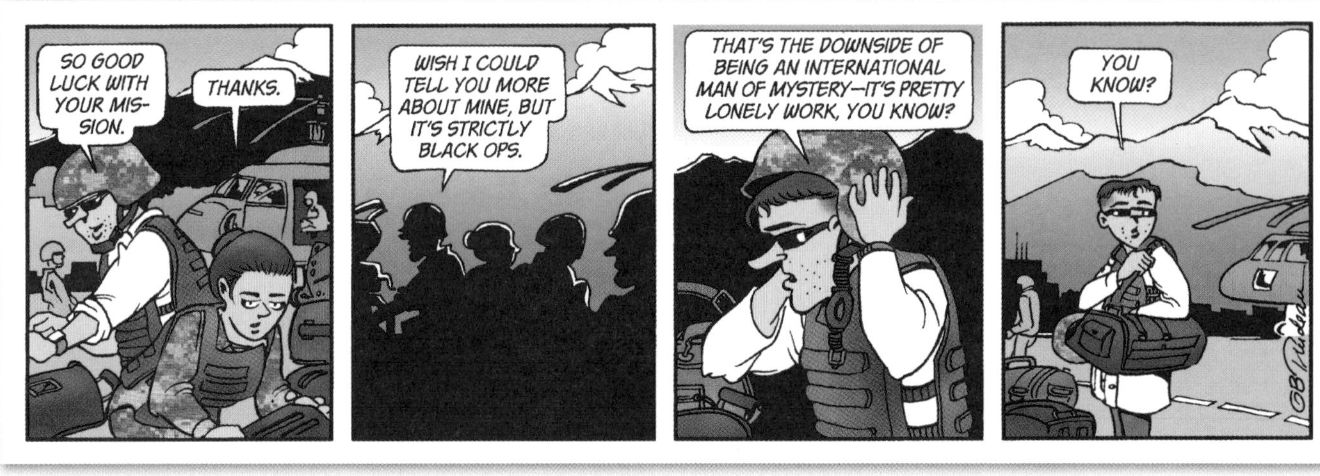
SO GOOD LUCK WITH YOUR MIS-SION.
THANKS.
WISH I COULD TELL YOU MORE ABOUT MINE, BUT IT'S STRICTLY BLACK OPS.
THAT'S THE DOWNSIDE OF BEING AN INTERNATIONAL MAN OF MYSTERY—IT'S PRETTY LONELY WORK, YOU KNOW?
YOU KNOW?

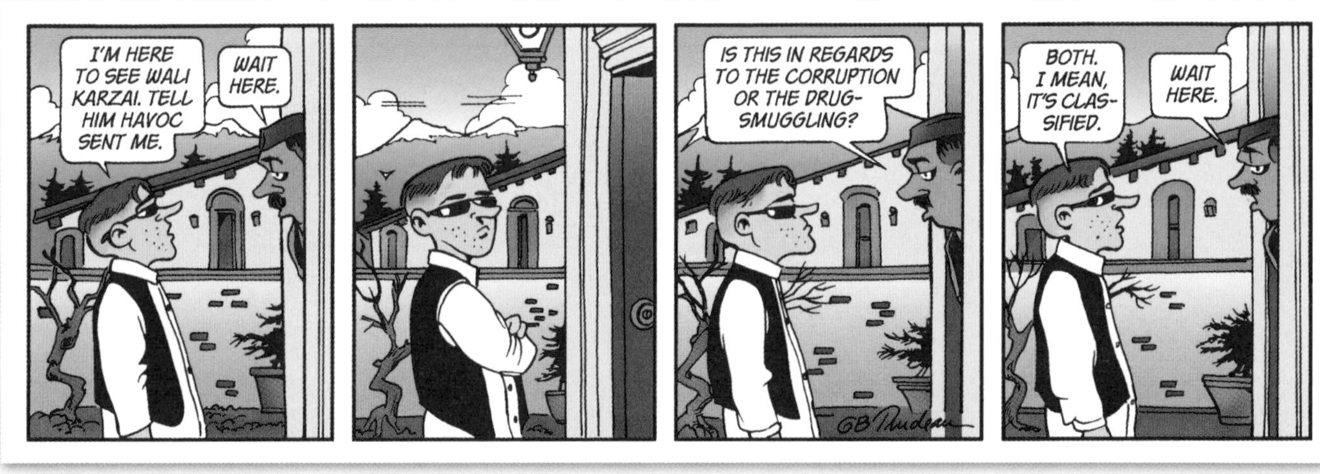
I'M HERE TO SEE WALI KARZAI. TELL HIM HAVOC SENT ME.
WAIT HERE.
IS THIS IN REGARDS TO THE CORRUPTION OR THE DRUG-SMUGGLING?
BOTH. I MEAN, IT'S CLAS-SIFIED.
WAIT HERE.

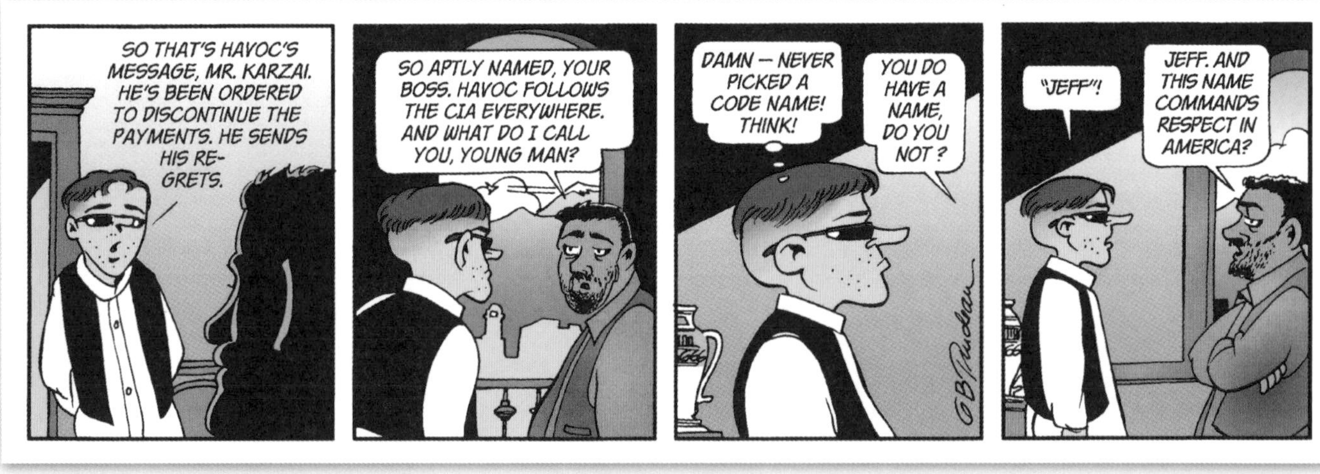
SO THAT'S HAVOC'S MESSAGE, MR. KARZAI. HE'S BEEN ORDERED TO DISCONTINUE THE PAYMENTS. HE SENDS HIS RE-GRETS.
SO APTLY NAMED, YOUR BOSS. HAVOC FOLLOWS THE CIA EVERYWHERE. AND WHAT DO I CALL YOU, YOUNG MAN?
DAMN — NEVER PICKED A CODE NAME! THINK!
YOU DO HAVE A NAME, DO YOU NOT?
"JEFF"!
JEFF. AND THIS NAME COMMANDS RESPECT IN AMERICA?

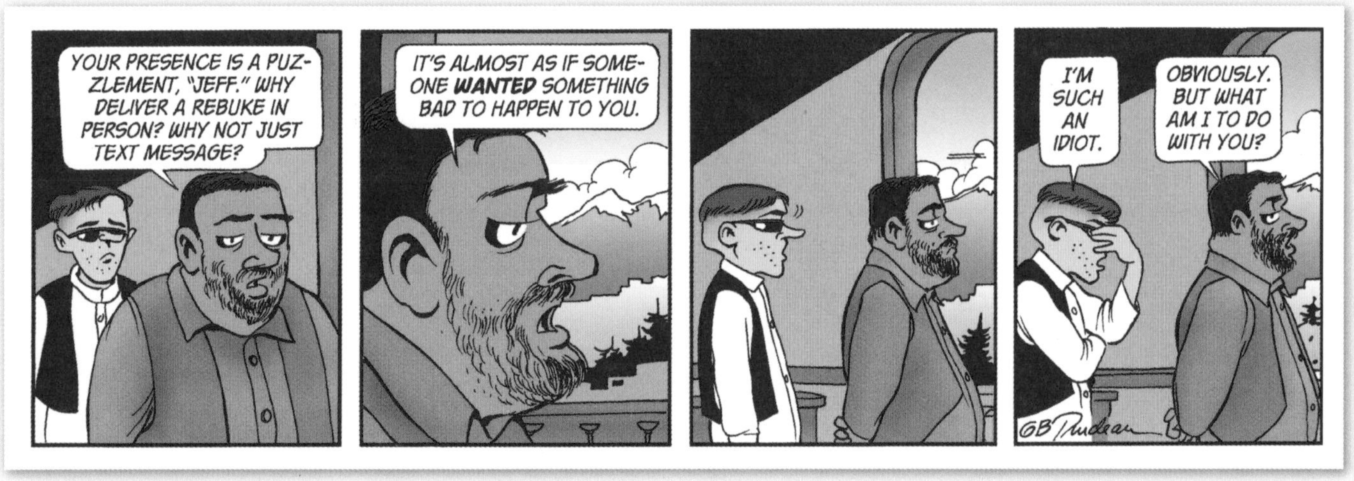
YOUR PRESENCE IS A PUZZLEMENT, "JEFF." WHY DELIVER A REBUKE IN PERSON? WHY NOT JUST TEXT MESSAGE?
IT'S ALMOST AS IF SOMEONE **WANTED** SOMETHING BAD TO HAPPEN TO YOU.
I'M SUCH AN IDIOT.
OBVIOUSLY. BUT WHAT AM I TO DO WITH YOU?
GB Trudeau

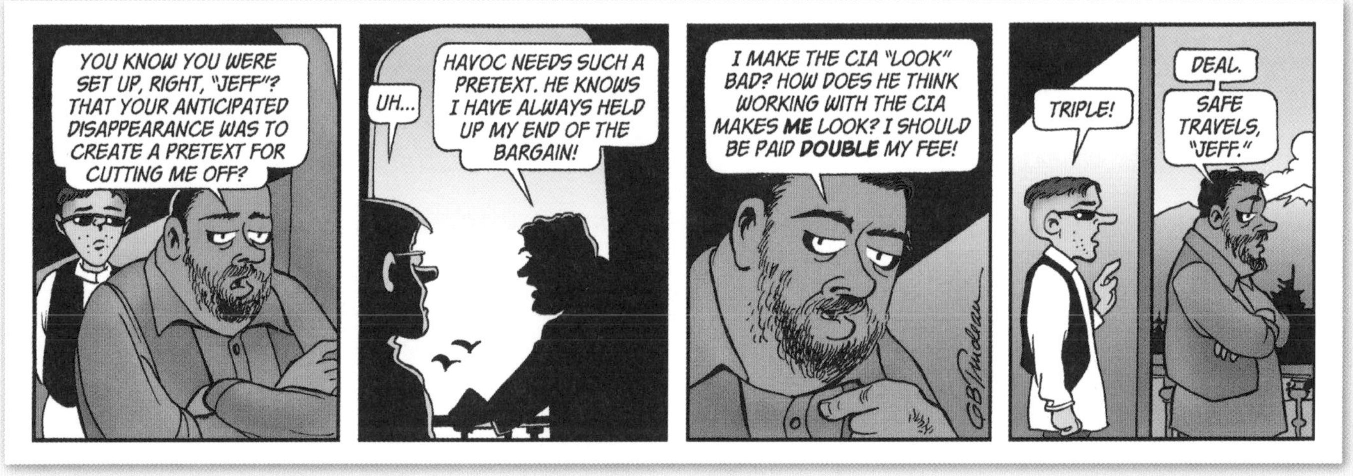
YOU KNOW YOU WERE SET UP, RIGHT, "JEFF"? THAT YOUR ANTICIPATED DISAPPEARANCE WAS TO CREATE A PRETEXT FOR CUTTING ME OFF?
UH...
HAVOC NEEDS SUCH A PRETEXT. HE KNOWS I HAVE ALWAYS HELD UP MY END OF THE BARGAIN!
I MAKE THE CIA "LOOK" BAD? HOW DOES HE THINK WORKING WITH THE CIA MAKES **ME** LOOK? I SHOULD BE PAID **DOUBLE** MY FEE!
GB Trudeau
TRIPLE!
DEAL.
SAFE TRAVELS, "JEFF."

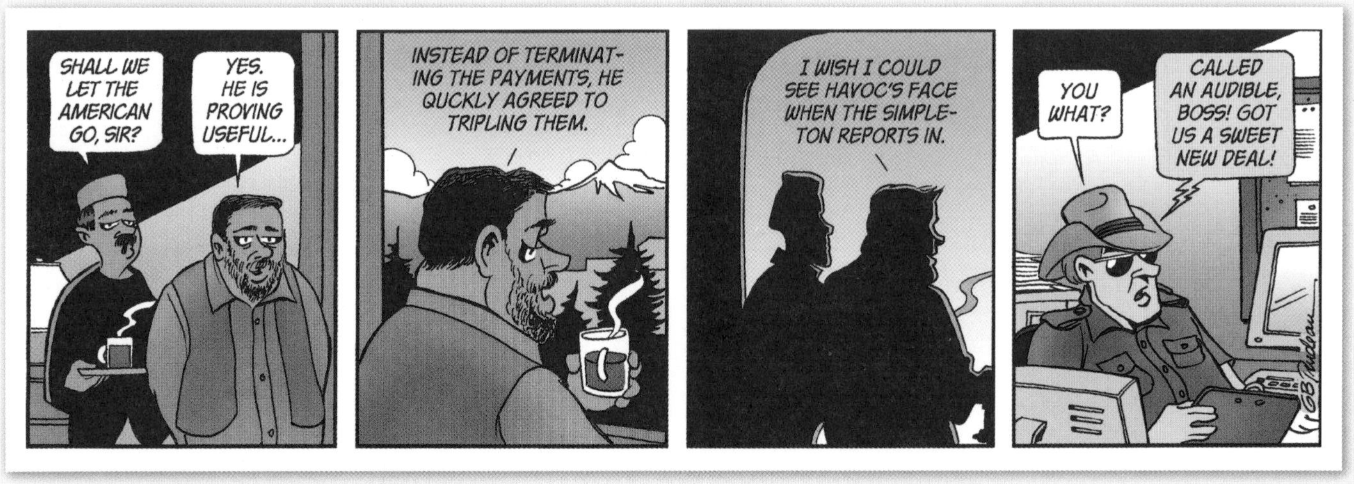
SHALL WE LET THE AMERICAN GO, SIR?
YES. HE IS PROVING USEFUL...
INSTEAD OF TERMINATING THE PAYMENTS, HE QUCKLY AGREED TO TRIPLING THEM.
I WISH I COULD SEE HAVOC'S FACE WHEN THE SIMPLETON REPORTS IN.
YOU WHAT?
CALLED AN AUDIBLE, BOSS! GOT US A SWEET NEW DEAL!
GB Trudeau

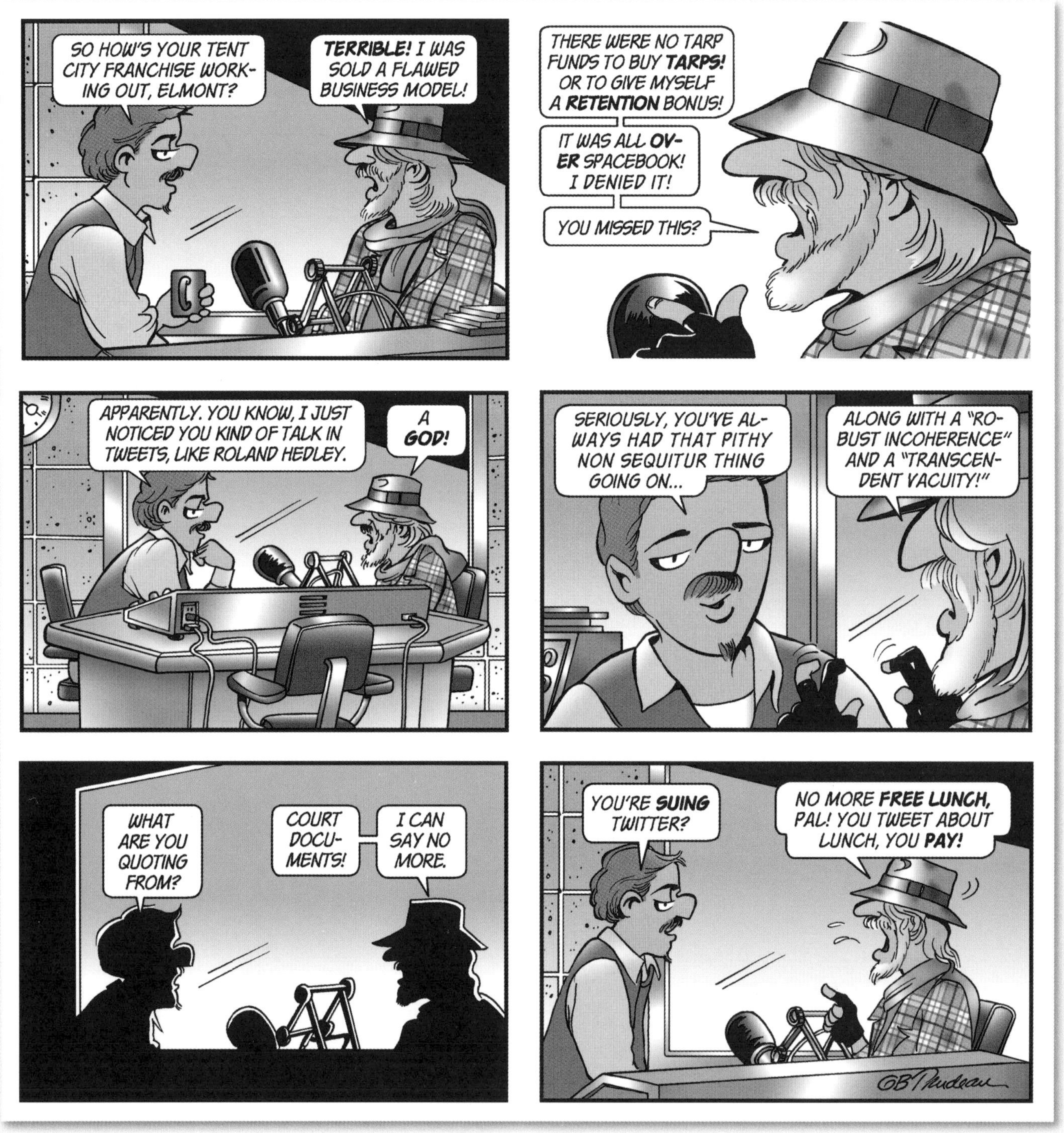
SO HOW'S YOUR TENT CITY FRANCHISE WORKING OUT, ELMONT?
TERRIBLE! I WAS SOLD A FLAWED BUSINESS MODEL!
THERE WERE NO TARP FUNDS TO BUY TARPS! OR TO GIVE MYSELF A RETENTION BONUS!
IT WAS ALL OVER SPACEBOOK! I DENIED IT!
YOU MISSED THIS?
APPARENTLY. YOU KNOW, I JUST NOTICED YOU KIND OF TALK IN TWEETS, LIKE ROLAND HEDLEY.
A GOD!
SERIOUSLY, YOU'VE ALWAYS HAD THAT PITHY NON SEQUITUR THING GOING ON...
ALONG WITH A "ROBUST INCOHERENCE" AND A "TRANSCENDENT VACUITY!"
WHAT ARE YOU QUOTING FROM?
COURT DOCUMENTS!
I CAN SAY NO MORE.
YOU'RE SUING TWITTER?
NO MORE FREE LUNCH, PAL! YOU TWEET ABOUT LUNCH, YOU PAY!
GB Trudeau

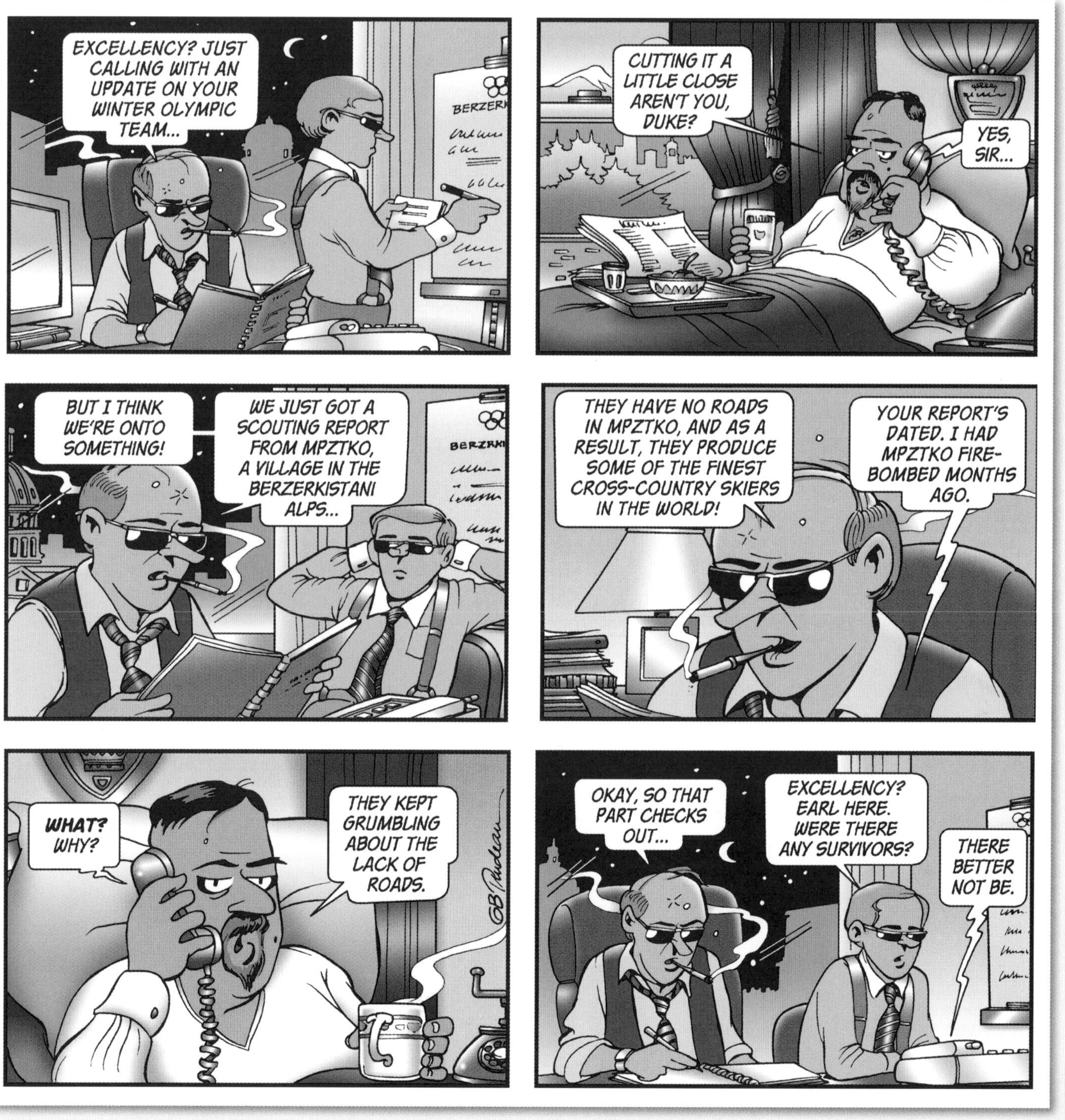
EXCELLENCY? JUST CALLING WITH AN UPDATE ON YOUR WINTER OLYMPIC TEAM...
BERZERK
CUTTING IT A LITTLE CLOSE AREN'T YOU, DUKE?
YES, SIR...
BUT I THINK WE'RE ONTO SOMETHING!
WE JUST GOT A SCOUTING REPORT FROM MPZTKO, A VILLAGE IN THE BERZERKISTANI ALPS...
BERZRKI
THEY HAVE NO ROADS IN MPZTKO, AND AS A RESULT, THEY PRODUCE SOME OF THE FINEST CROSS-COUNTRY SKIERS IN THE WORLD!
YOUR REPORT'S DATED. I HAD MPZTKO FIRE-BOMBED MONTHS AGO.
WHAT? WHY?
THEY KEPT GRUMBLING ABOUT THE LACK OF ROADS.
GB Trudeau
OKAY, SO THAT PART CHECKS OUT...
EXCELLENCY? EARL HERE. WERE THERE ANY SURVIVORS?
THERE BETTER NOT BE.

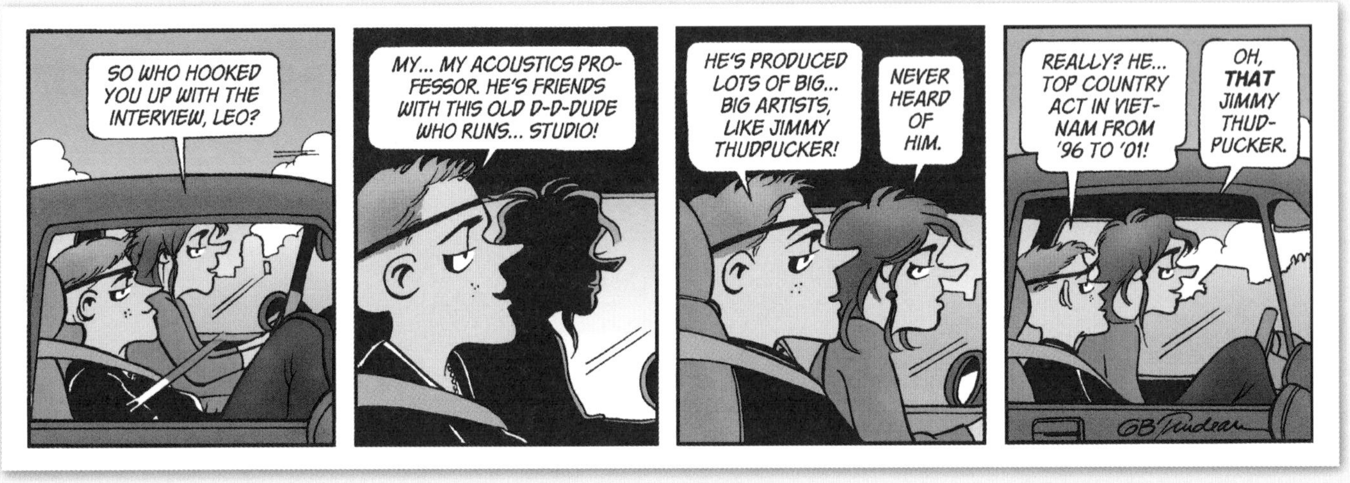
SO WHO HOOKED YOU UP WITH THE INTERVIEW, LEO?
MY... MY ACOUSTICS PROFESSOR. HE'S FRIENDS WITH THIS OLD D-D-DUDE WHO RUNS... STUDIO!
HE'S PRODUCED LOTS OF BIG... BIG ARTISTS, LIKE JIMMY THUDPUCKER!
NEVER HEARD OF HIM.
REALLY? HE... TOP COUNTRY ACT IN VIETNAM FROM '96 TO '01!
OH, **THAT** JIMMY THUDPUCKER.

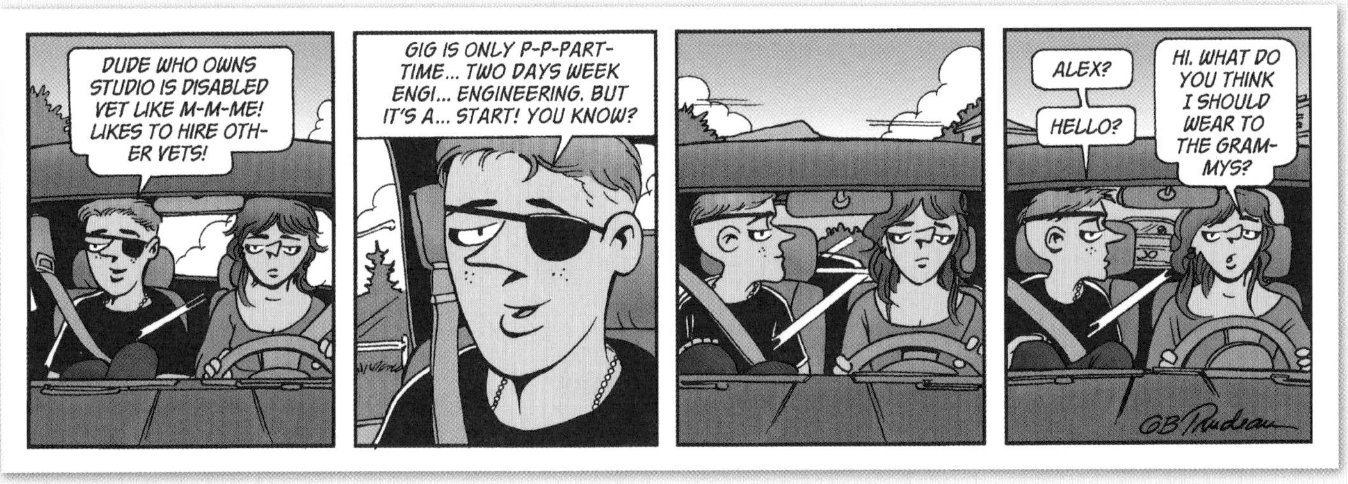
DUDE WHO OWNS STUDIO IS DISABLED VET LIKE M-M-ME! LIKES TO HIRE OTHER VETS!
GIG IS ONLY P-P-PART-TIME... TWO DAYS WEEK ENGI... ENGINEERING. BUT IT'S A... START! YOU KNOW?
ALEX?
HELLO?
HI. WHAT DO YOU THINK I SHOULD WEAR TO THE GRAMMYS?

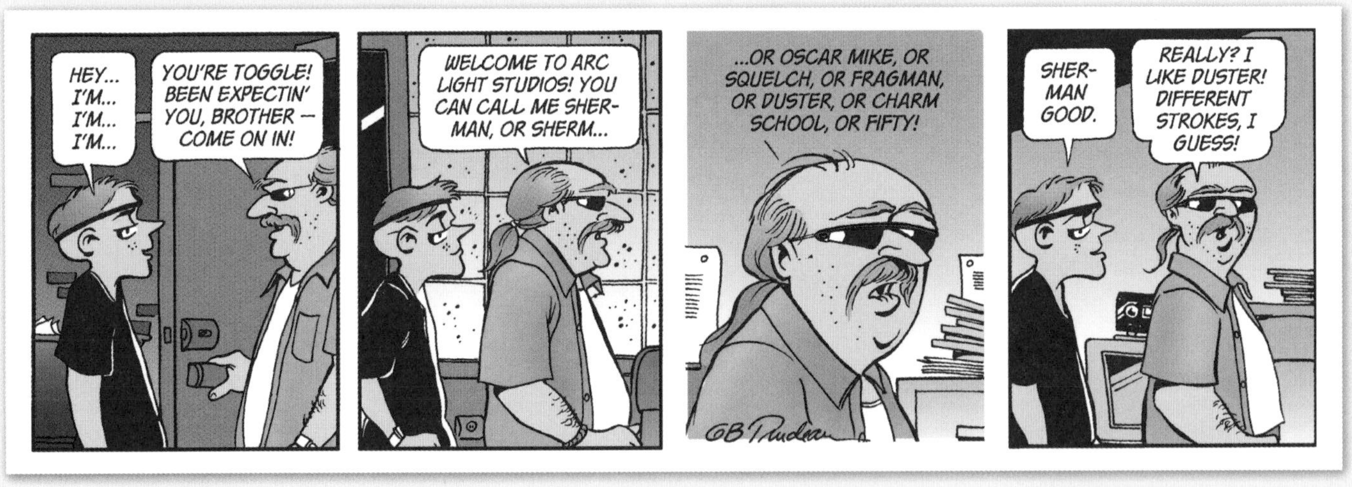
HEY... I'M... I'M... I'M...
YOU'RE TOGGLE! BEEN EXPECTIN' YOU, BROTHER — COME ON IN!
WELCOME TO ARC LIGHT STUDIOS! YOU CAN CALL ME SHERMAN, OR SHERM...
...OR OSCAR MIKE, OR SQUELCH, OR FRAGMAN, OR DUSTER, OR CHARM SCHOOL, OR FIFTY!
SHERMAN GOOD.
REALLY? I LIKE DUSTER! DIFFERENT STROKES, I GUESS!

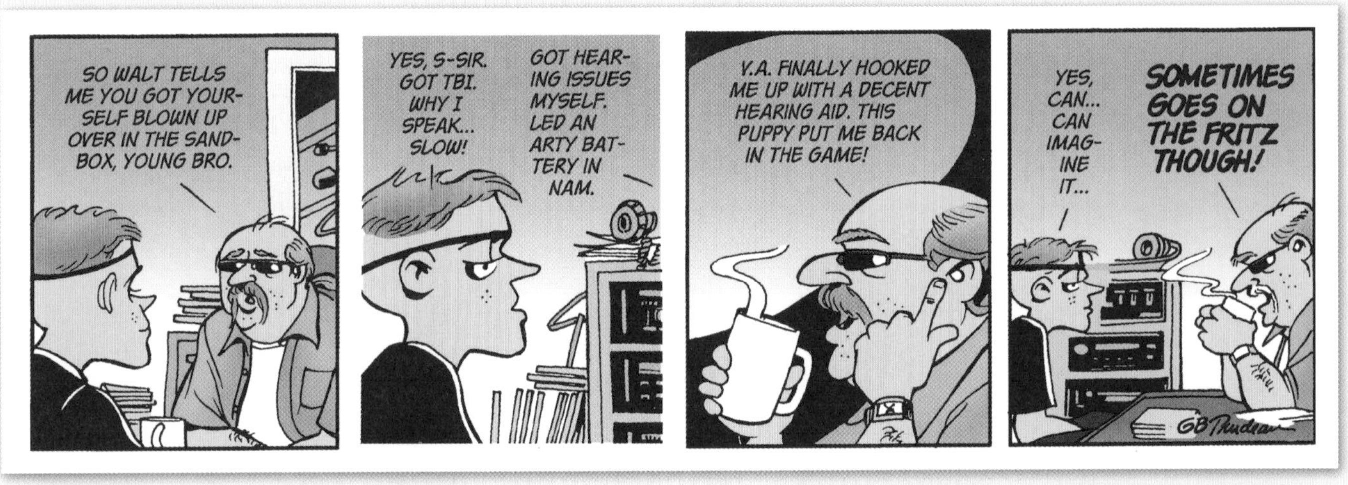
SO WALT TELLS ME YOU GOT YOURSELF BLOWN UP OVER IN THE SANDBOX, YOUNG BRO.
YES, S-SIR. GOT TBI. WHY I SPEAK... SLOW!
GOT HEARING ISSUES MYSELF. LED AN ARTY BATTERY IN NAM.
V.A. FINALLY HOOKED ME UP WITH A DECENT HEARING AID. THIS PUPPY PUT ME BACK IN THE GAME!
YES, CAN... CAN IMAGINE IT...
SOMETIMES GOES ON THE FRITZ THOUGH!
GB Trudeau

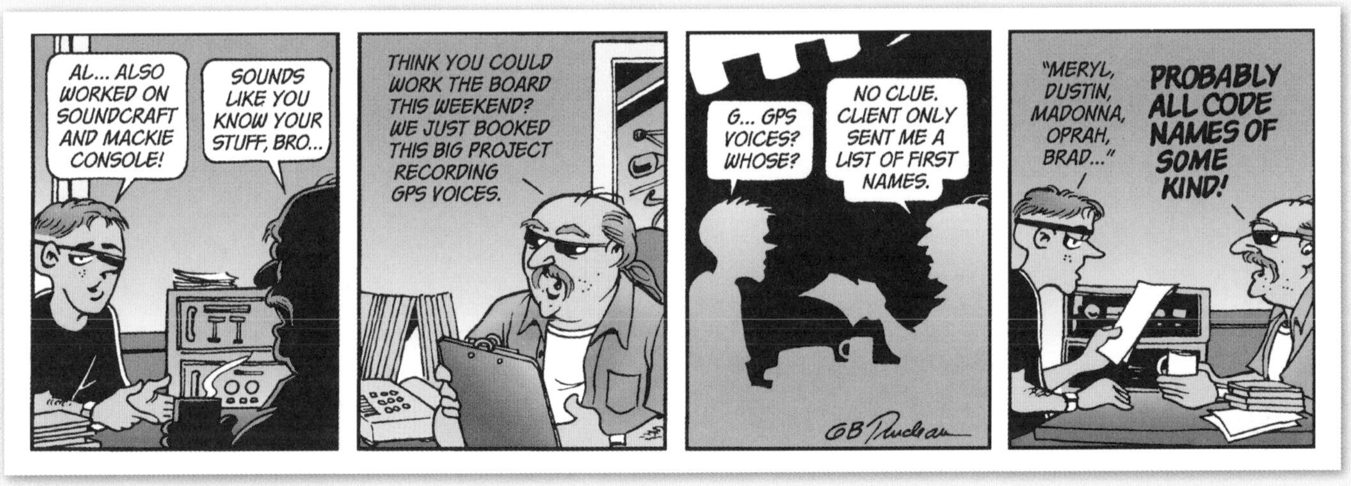
AL... ALSO WORKED ON SOUNDCRAFT AND MACKIE CONSOLE!
SOUNDS LIKE YOU KNOW YOUR STUFF, BRO...
THINK YOU COULD WORK THE BOARD THIS WEEKEND? WE JUST BOOKED THIS BIG PROJECT RECORDING GPS VOICES.
G... GPS VOICES? WHOSE?
NO CLUE. CLIENT ONLY SENT ME A LIST OF FIRST NAMES.
GB Trudeau
"MERYL, DUSTIN, MADONNA, OPRAH, BRAD..."
PROBABLY ALL CODE NAMES OF SOME KIND!

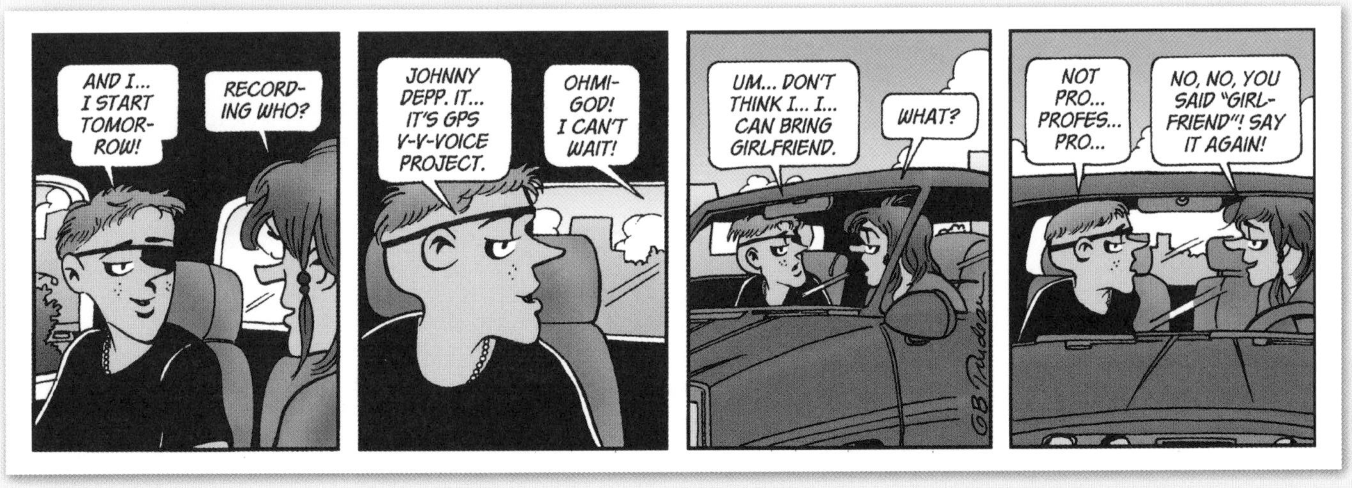
AND I... I START TOMORROW!
RECORDING WHO?
JOHNNY DEPP. IT... IT'S GPS V-V-VOICE PROJECT.
OHMIGOD! I CAN'T WAIT!
UM... DON'T THINK I... I... CAN BRING GIRLFRIEND.
WHAT?
GB Trudeau
NOT PRO... PROFES... PRO...
NO, NO, YOU SAID "GIRLFRIEND"! SAY IT AGAIN!

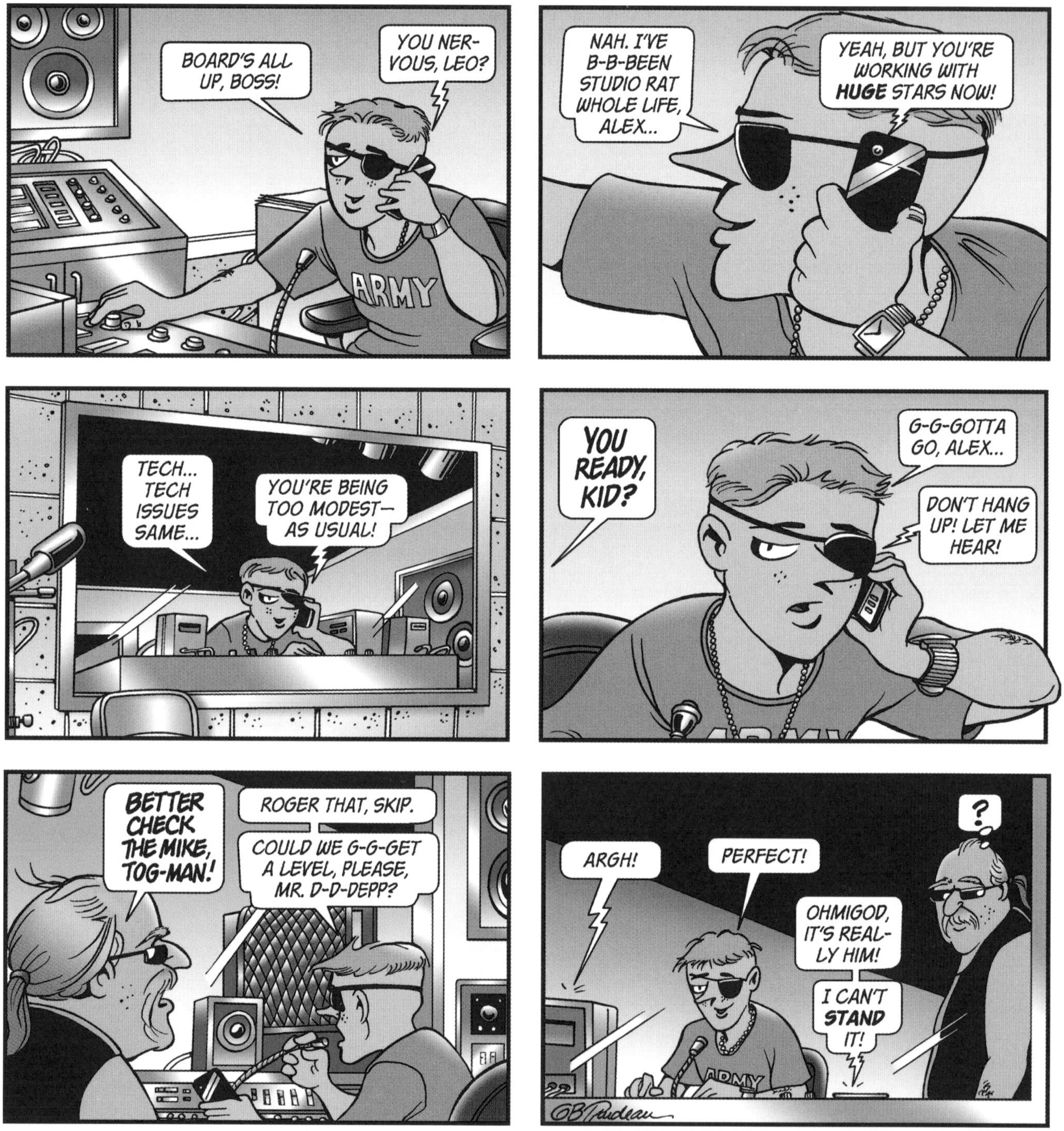
BOARD'S ALL UP, BOSS!
YOU NER-VOUS, LEO?
ARMY
NAH. I'VE B-B-BEEN STUDIO RAT WHOLE LIFE, ALEX...
YEAH, BUT YOU'RE WORKING WITH **HUGE** STARS NOW!
TECH... TECH ISSUES SAME...
YOU'RE BEING TOO MODEST— AS USUAL!
YOU READY, KID?
G-G-GOTTA GO, ALEX...
DON'T HANG UP! LET ME HEAR!
BETTER CHECK THE MIKE, TOG-MAN!
ROGER THAT, SKIP.
COULD WE G-G-GET A LEVEL, PLEASE, MR. D-D-DEPP?
ARGH!
PERFECT!
?
OHMIGOD, IT'S REAL-LY HIM!
I CAN'T **STAND** IT!
ARMY
GB Trudeau

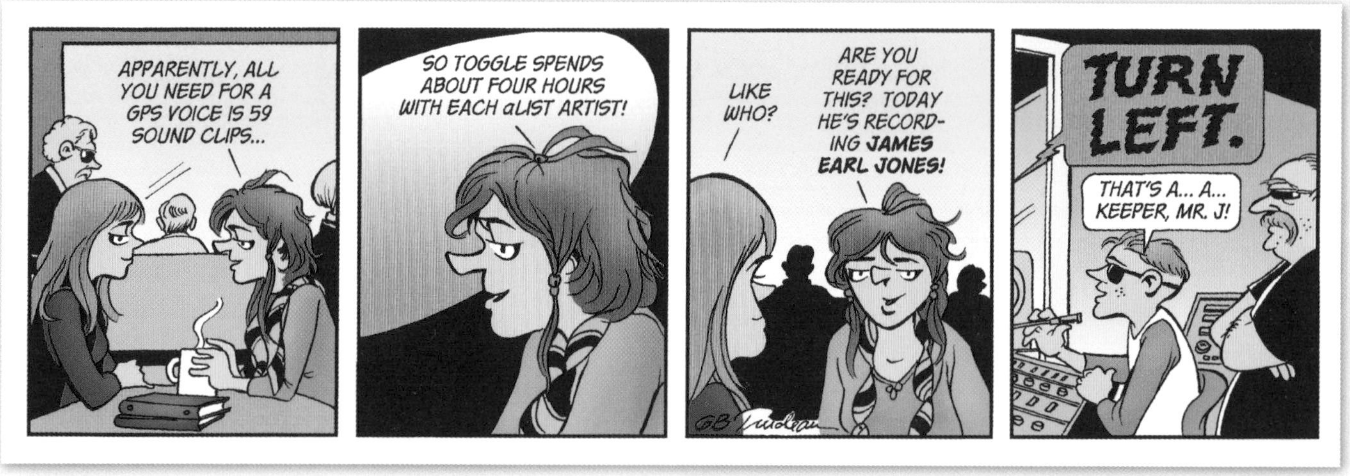
APPARENTLY, ALL YOU NEED FOR A GPS VOICE IS 59 SOUND CLIPS...
SO TOGGLE SPENDS ABOUT FOUR HOURS WITH EACH aLIST ARTIST!
LIKE WHO?
ARE YOU READY FOR THIS? TODAY HE'S RECORDING JAMES EARL JONES!
TURN LEFT.
THAT'S A... A... KEEPER, MR. J!

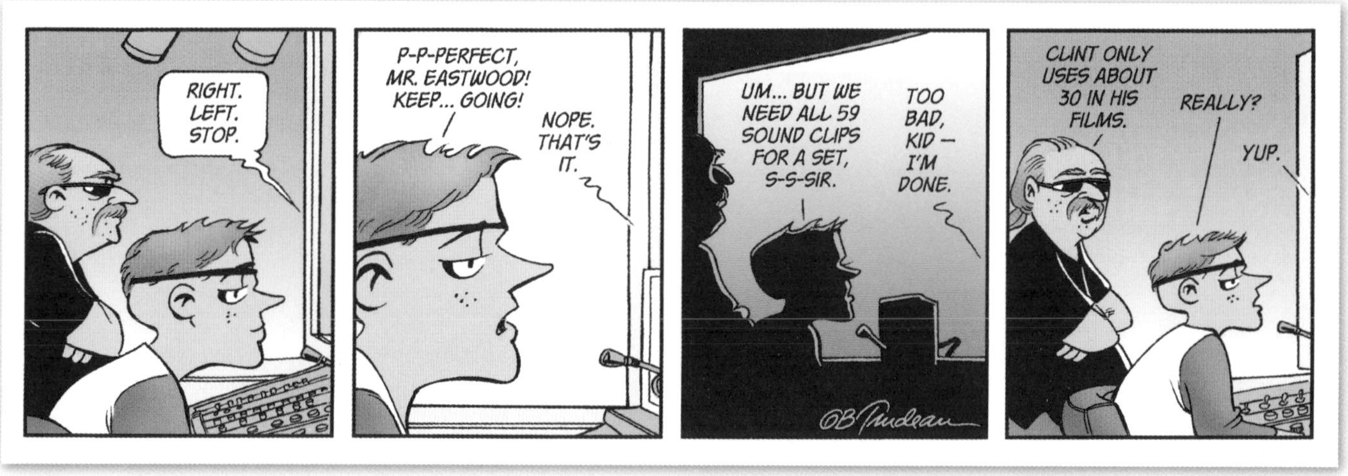
RIGHT. LEFT. STOP.
P-P-PERFECT, MR. EASTWOOD! KEEP... GOING!
NOPE. THAT'S IT.
UM... BUT WE NEED ALL 59 SOUND CLIPS FOR A SET, S-S-SIR.
TOO BAD, KID — I'M DONE.
CLINT ONLY USES ABOUT 30 IN HIS FILMS.
REALLY?
YUP.

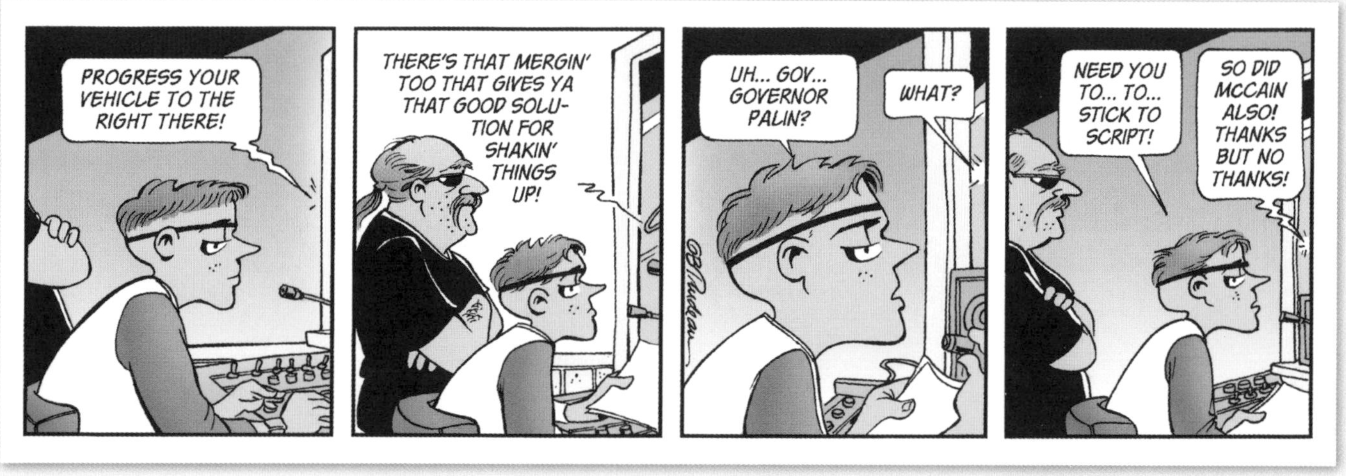
PROGRESS YOUR VEHICLE TO THE RIGHT THERE!
THERE'S THAT MERGIN' TOO THAT GIVES YA THAT GOOD SOLUTION FOR SHAKIN' THINGS UP!
UH... GOV... GOVERNOR PALIN?
WHAT?
NEED YOU TO... TO... STICK TO SCRIPT!
SO DID MCCAIN ALSO! THANKS BUT NO THANKS!

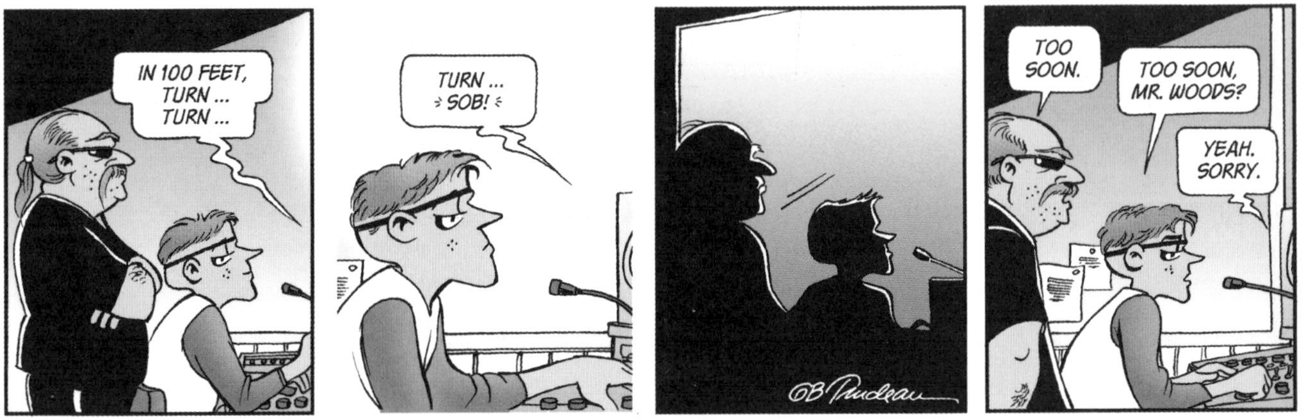
IN 100 FEET, TURN ... TURN ...
TURN ... SOB!
TOO SOON.
TOO SOON, MR. WOODS?
YEAH. SORRY.

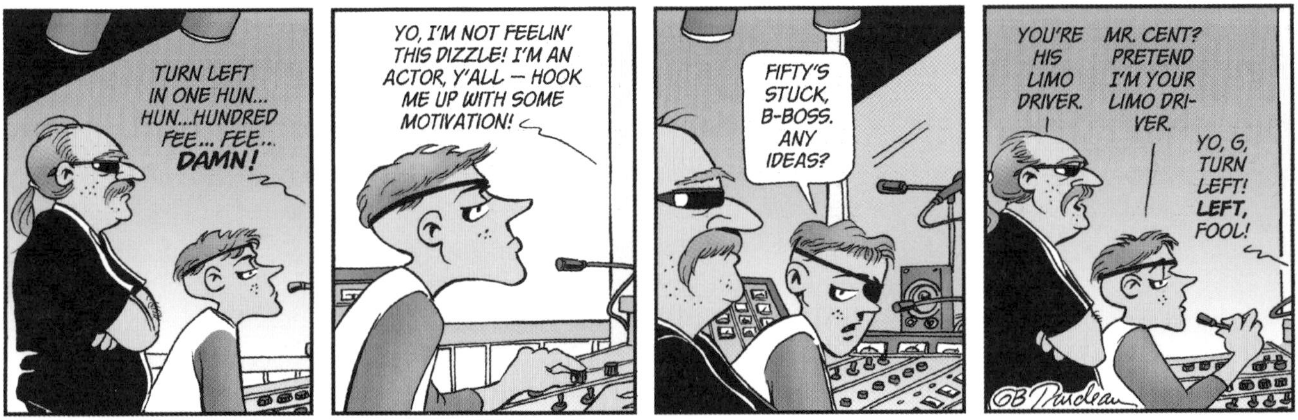
TURN LEFT IN ONE HUN... HUN...HUNDRED FEE... FEE... **DAMN!**
YO, I'M NOT FEELIN' THIS DIZZLE! I'M AN ACTOR, Y'ALL — HOOK ME UP WITH SOME MOTIVATION!
FIFTY'S STUCK, B-BOSS. ANY IDEAS?
YOU'RE HIS LIMO DRIVER.
MR. CENT? PRETEND I'M YOUR LIMO DRI-VER.
YO, G, TURN LEFT! **LEFT,** FOOL!

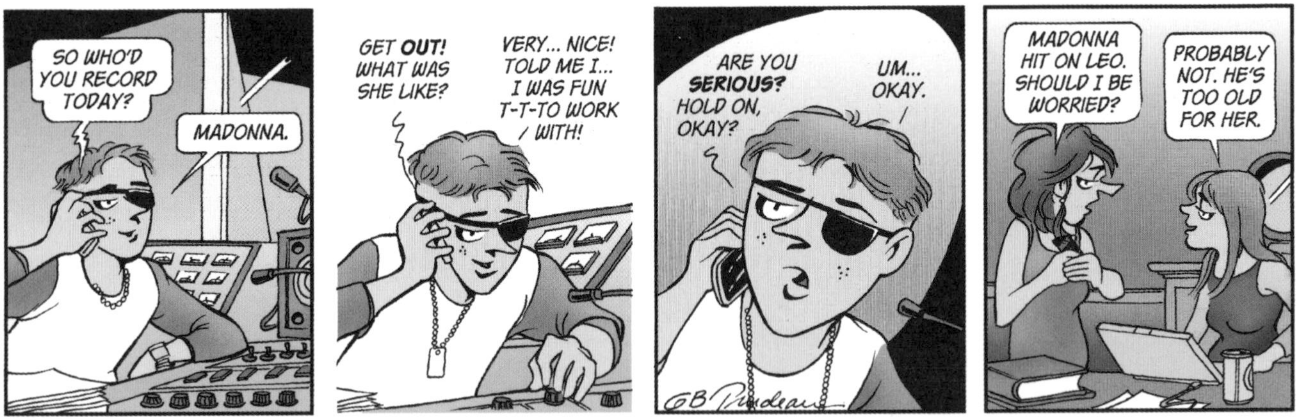
SO WHO'D YOU RECORD TODAY?
MADONNA.
GET **OUT!** WHAT WAS SHE LIKE?
VERY... NICE! TOLD ME I... I WAS FUN T-T-TO WORK WITH!
ARE YOU **SERIOUS?** HOLD ON, OKAY?
UM... OKAY.
MADONNA HIT ON LEO. SHOULD I BE WORRIED?
PROBABLY NOT. HE'S TOO OLD FOR HER.

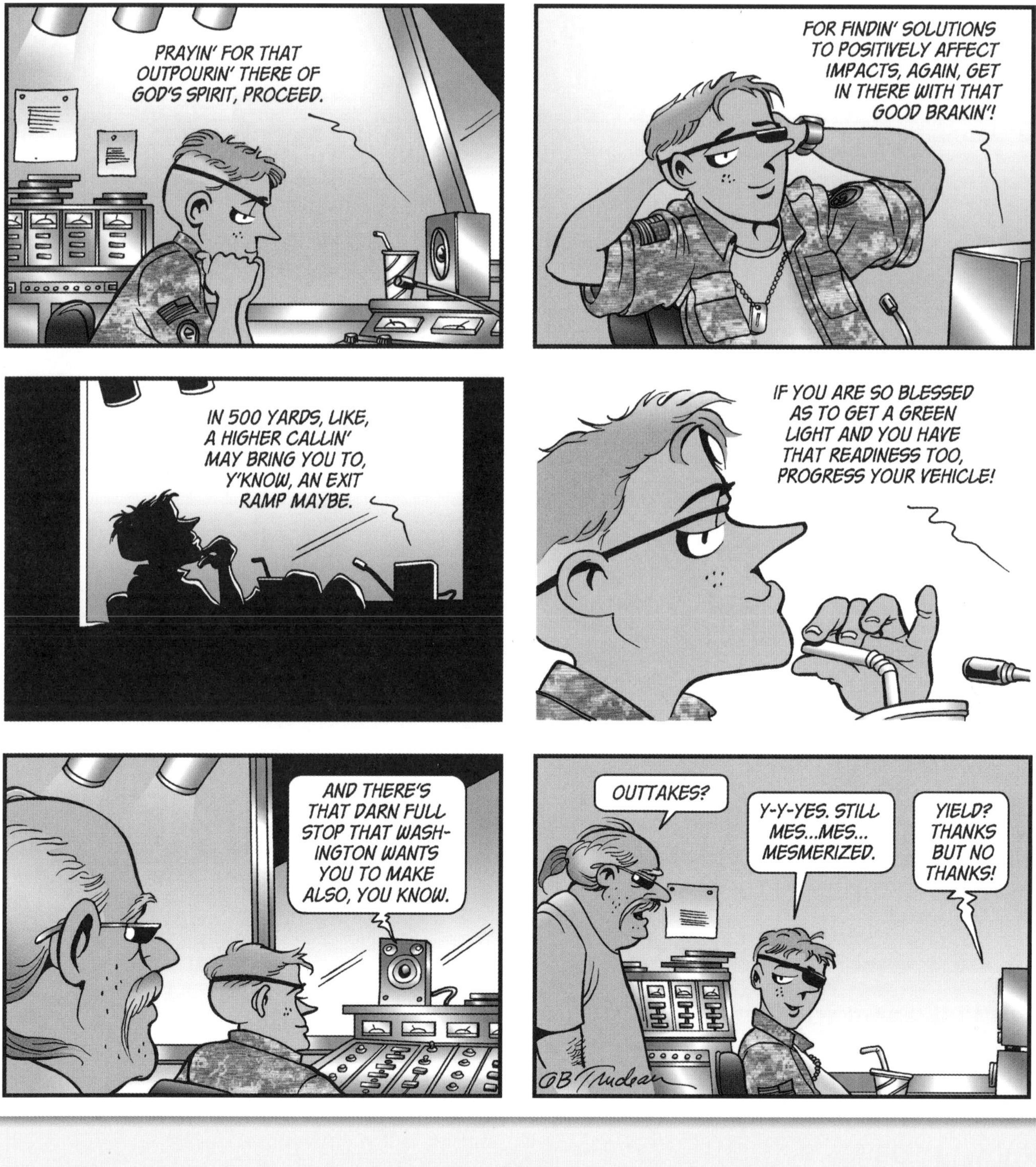
PRAYIN' FOR THAT OUTPOURIN' THERE OF GOD'S SPIRIT, PROCEED.
FOR FINDIN' SOLUTIONS TO POSITIVELY AFFECT IMPACTS, AGAIN, GET IN THERE WITH THAT GOOD BRAKIN'!
IN 500 YARDS, LIKE, A HIGHER CALLIN' MAY BRING YOU TO, Y'KNOW, AN EXIT RAMP MAYBE.
IF YOU ARE SO BLESSED AS TO GET A GREEN LIGHT AND YOU HAVE THAT READINESS TOO, PROGRESS YOUR VEHICLE!
AND THERE'S THAT DARN FULL STOP THAT WASH-INGTON WANTS YOU TO MAKE ALSO, YOU KNOW.
OUTTAKES?
Y-Y-YES. STILL MES...MES... MESMERIZED.
YIELD? THANKS BUT NO THANKS!
GB Trudeau

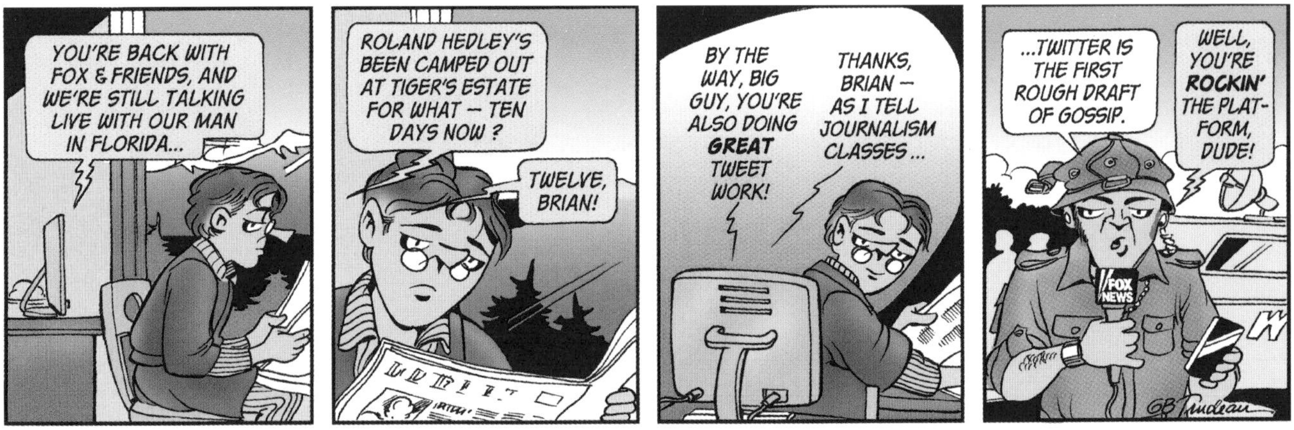
YOU'RE BACK WITH FOX & FRIENDS, AND WE'RE STILL TALKING LIVE WITH OUR MAN IN FLORIDA...
ROLAND HEDLEY'S BEEN CAMPED OUT AT TIGER'S ESTATE FOR WHAT — TEN DAYS NOW ?
TWELVE, BRIAN!
BY THE WAY, BIG GUY, YOU'RE ALSO DOING **GREAT** TWEET WORK!
THANKS, BRIAN — AS I TELL JOURNALISM CLASSES...
...TWITTER IS THE FIRST ROUGH DRAFT OF GOSSIP.
WELL, YOU'RE **ROCKIN'** THE PLATFORM, DUDE!
FOX NEWS
GB Trudeau

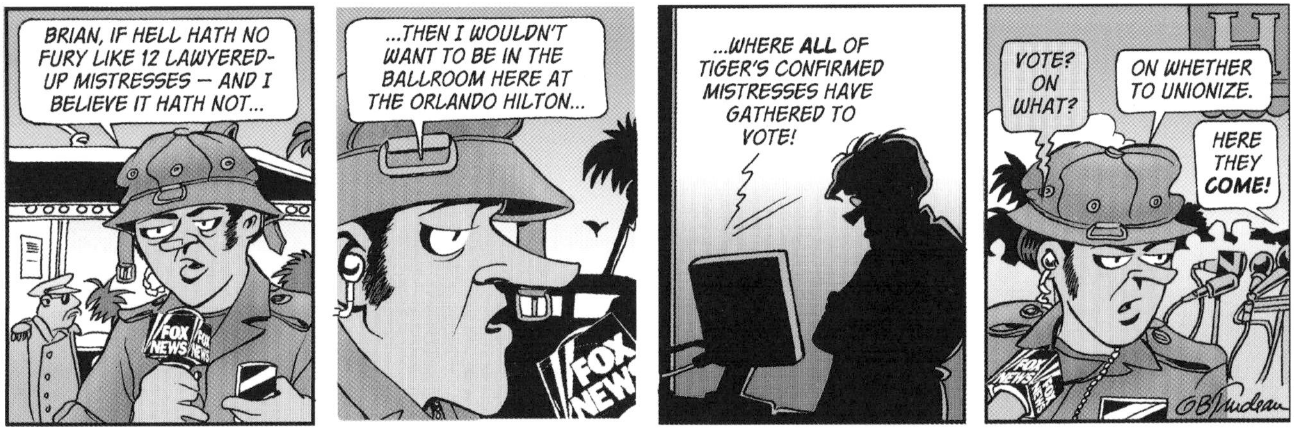
BRIAN, IF HELL HATH NO FURY LIKE 12 LAWYERED-UP MISTRESSES — AND I BELIEVE IT HATH NOT...
...THEN I WOULDN'T WANT TO BE IN THE BALLROOM HERE AT THE ORLANDO HILTON...
...WHERE **ALL** OF TIGER'S CONFIRMED MISTRESSES HAVE GATHERED TO VOTE!
VOTE? ON WHAT?
ON WHETHER TO UNIONIZE.
HERE THEY **COME!**
FOX NEWS
GB Trudeau

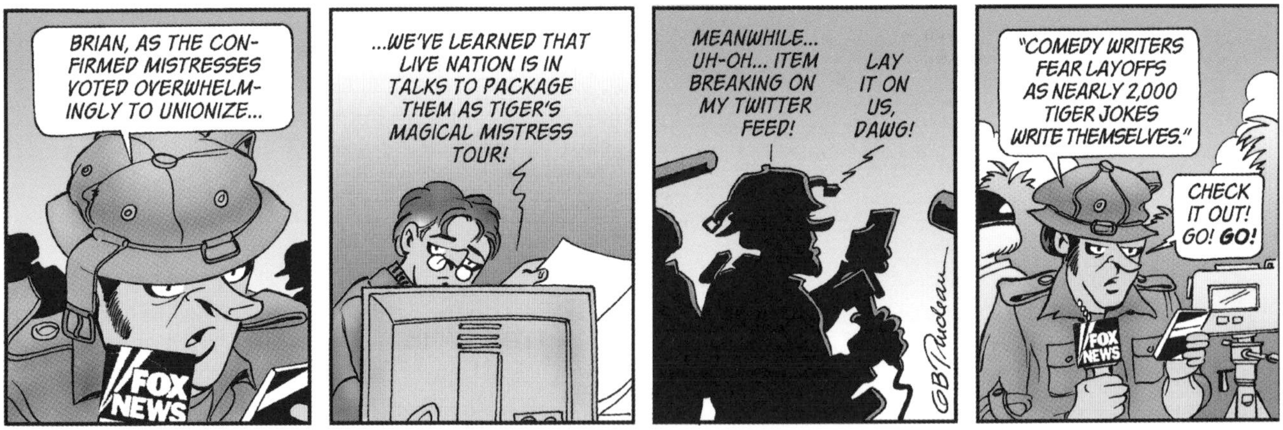
BRIAN, AS THE CONFIRMED MISTRESSES VOTED OVERWHELMINGLY TO UNIONIZE...
...WE'VE LEARNED THAT LIVE NATION IS IN TALKS TO PACKAGE THEM AS TIGER'S MAGICAL MISTRESS TOUR!
MEANWHILE... UH-OH... ITEM BREAKING ON MY TWITTER FEED!
LAY IT ON US, DAWG!
"COMEDY WRITERS FEAR LAYOFFS AS NEARLY 2,000 TIGER JOKES WRITE THEMSELVES."
CHECK IT OUT! GO! **GO!**
FOX NEWS
GB Trudeau

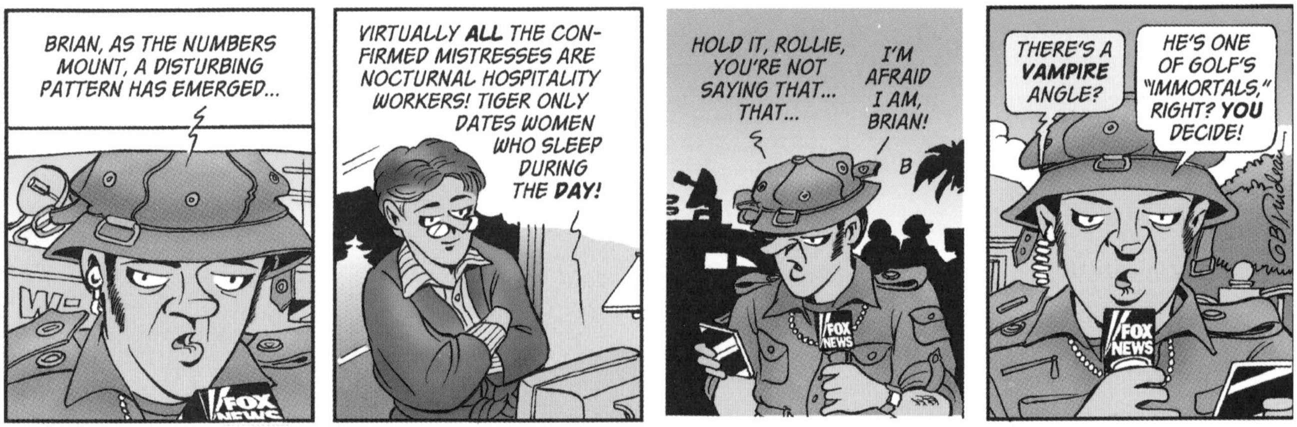
BRIAN, AS THE NUMBERS MOUNT, A DISTURBING PATTERN HAS EMERGED...
VIRTUALLY **ALL** THE CONFIRMED MISTRESSES ARE NOCTURNAL HOSPITALITY WORKERS! TIGER ONLY DATES WOMEN WHO SLEEP DURING THE **DAY**!
HOLD IT, ROLLIE, YOU'RE NOT SAYING THAT... THAT...
I'M AFRAID I AM, BRIAN!
THERE'S A **VAMPIRE** ANGLE?
HE'S ONE OF GOLF'S "IMMORTALS," RIGHT? **YOU** DECIDE!
FOX NEWS

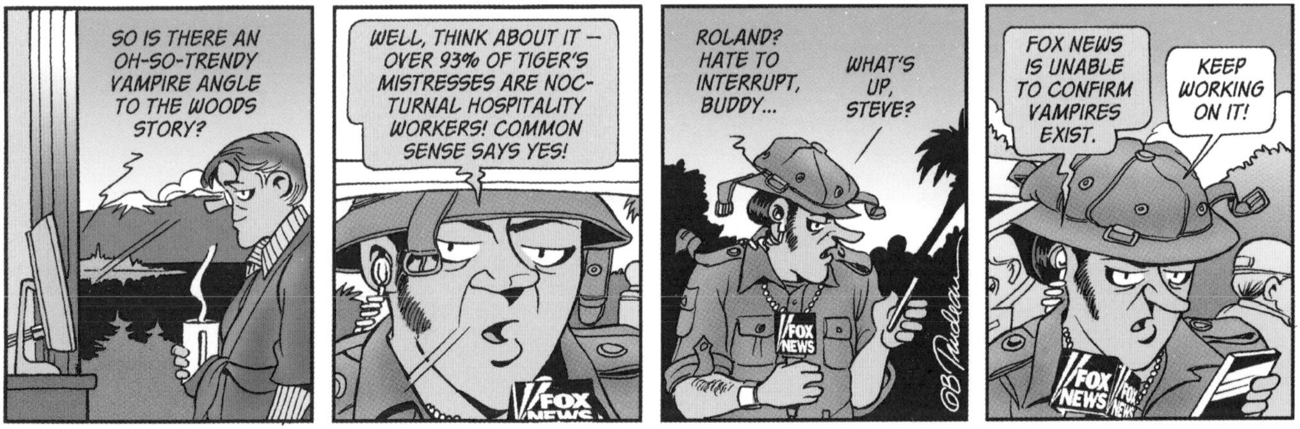
SO IS THERE AN OH-SO-TRENDY VAMPIRE ANGLE TO THE WOODS STORY?
WELL, THINK ABOUT IT — OVER 93% OF TIGER'S MISTRESSES ARE NOCTURNAL HOSPITALITY WORKERS! COMMON SENSE SAYS YES!
ROLAND? HATE TO INTERRUPT, BUDDY...
WHAT'S UP, STEVE?
FOX NEWS IS UNABLE TO CONFIRM VAMPIRES EXIST.
KEEP WORKING ON IT!
FOX NEWS

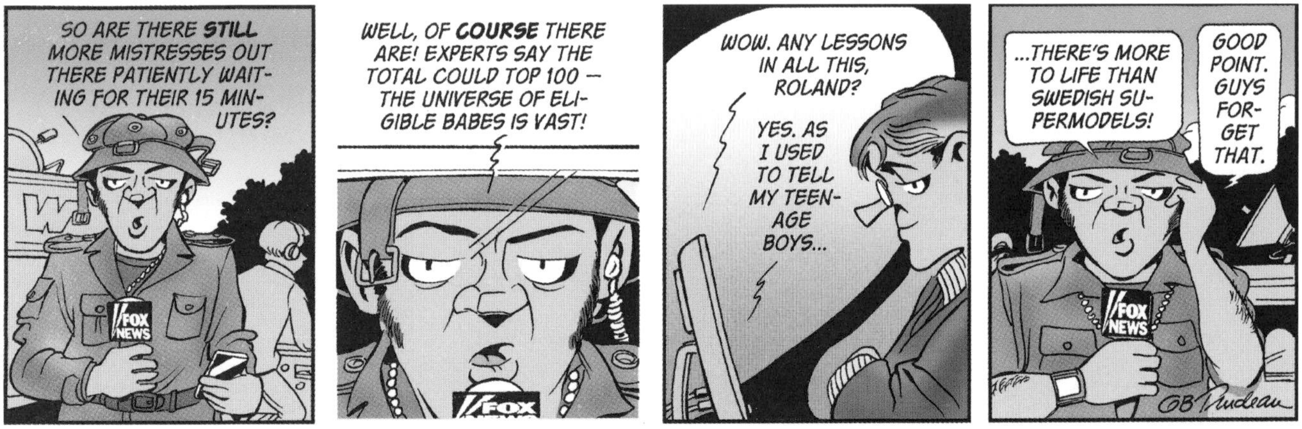
SO ARE THERE **STILL** MORE MISTRESSES OUT THERE PATIENTLY WAITING FOR THEIR 15 MINUTES?
WELL, OF **COURSE** THERE ARE! EXPERTS SAY THE TOTAL COULD TOP 100 — THE UNIVERSE OF ELIGIBLE BABES IS VAST!
WOW. ANY LESSONS IN ALL THIS, ROLAND?
YES. AS I USED TO TELL MY TEENAGE BOYS...
...THERE'S MORE TO LIFE THAN SWEDISH SUPERMODELS!
GOOD POINT. GUYS FORGET THAT.
FOX NEWS

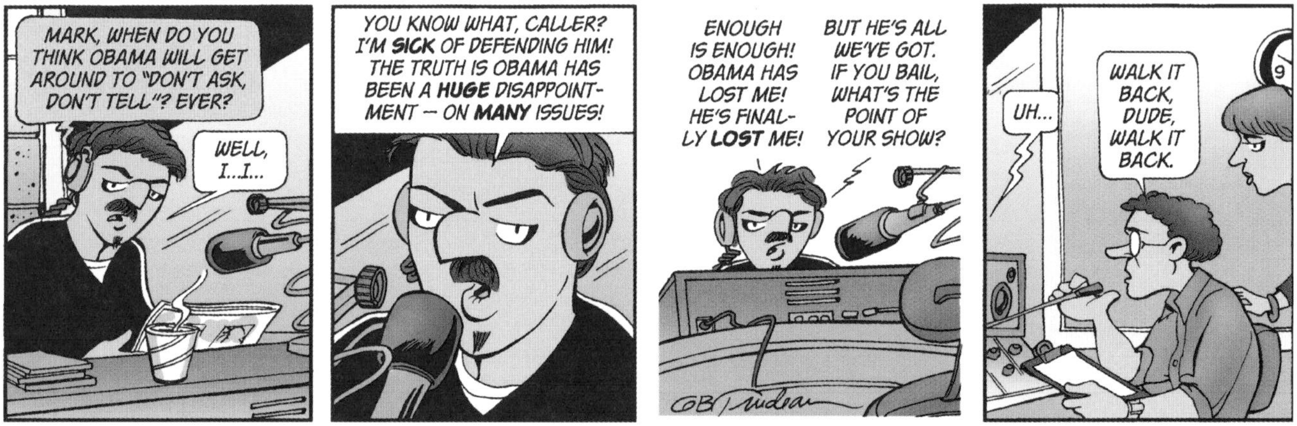
MARK, WHEN DO YOU THINK OBAMA WILL GET AROUND TO "DON'T ASK, DON'T TELL"? EVER?
WELL, I...I...
YOU KNOW WHAT, CALLER? I'M SICK OF DEFENDING HIM! THE TRUTH IS OBAMA HAS BEEN A HUGE DISAPPOINTMENT -- ON MANY ISSUES!
ENOUGH IS ENOUGH! OBAMA HAS LOST ME! HE'S FINALLY LOST ME!
BUT HE'S ALL WE'VE GOT. IF YOU BAIL, WHAT'S THE POINT OF YOUR SHOW?
UH...
WALK IT BACK, DUDE, WALK IT BACK.

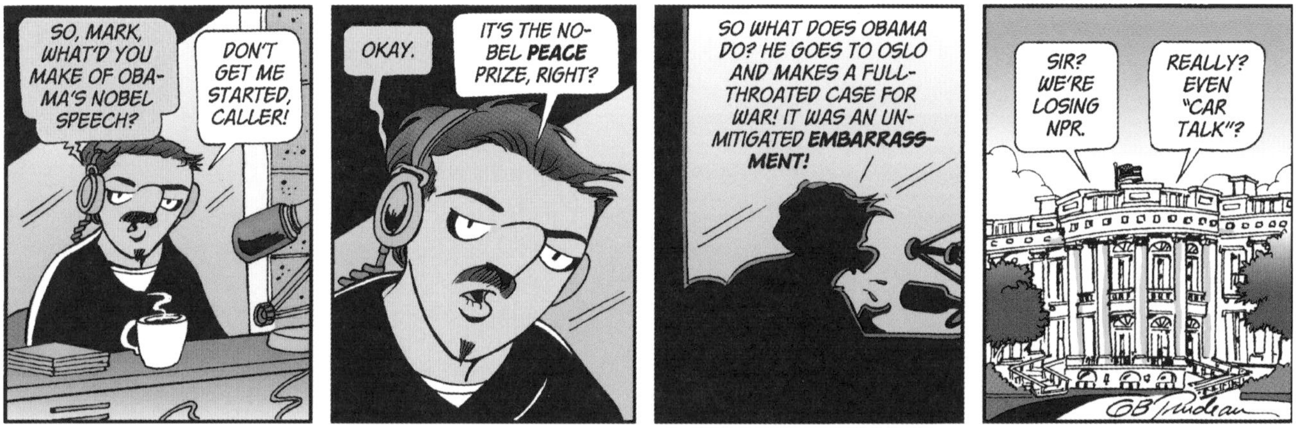
SO, MARK, WHAT'D YOU MAKE OF OBAMA'S NOBEL SPEECH?
DON'T GET ME STARTED, CALLER!
OKAY.
IT'S THE NOBEL PEACE PRIZE, RIGHT?
SO WHAT DOES OBAMA DO? HE GOES TO OSLO AND MAKES A FULL-THROATED CASE FOR WAR! IT WAS AN UNMITIGATED EMBARRASSMENT!
SIR? WE'RE LOSING NPR.
REALLY? EVEN "CAR TALK"?

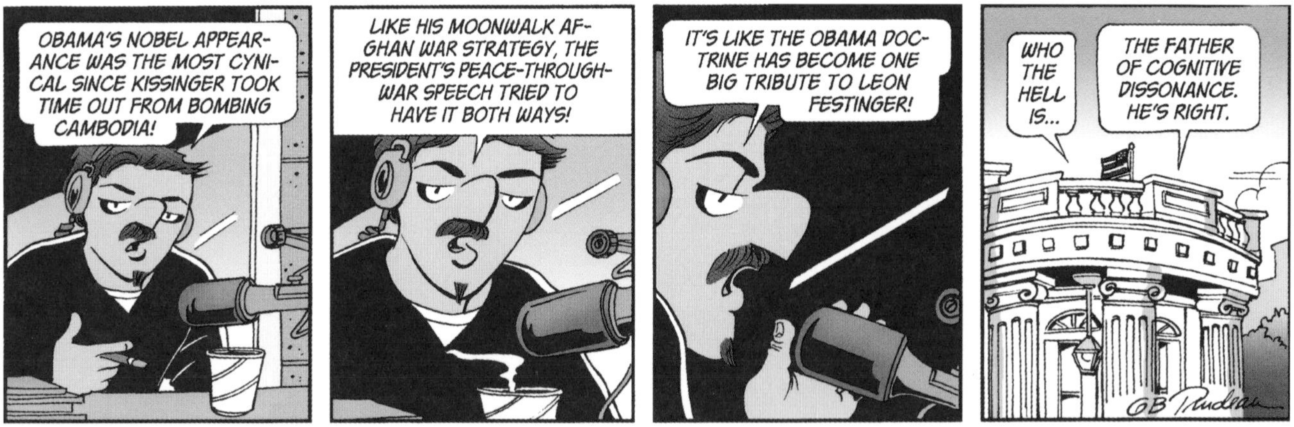
OBAMA'S NOBEL APPEARANCE WAS THE MOST CYNICAL SINCE KISSINGER TOOK TIME OUT FROM BOMBING CAMBODIA!
LIKE HIS MOONWALK AFGHAN WAR STRATEGY, THE PRESIDENT'S PEACE-THROUGH-WAR SPEECH TRIED TO HAVE IT BOTH WAYS!
IT'S LIKE THE OBAMA DOCTRINE HAS BECOME ONE BIG TRIBUTE TO LEON FESTINGER!
WHO THE HELL IS...
THE FATHER OF COGNITIVE DISSONANCE. HE'S RIGHT.

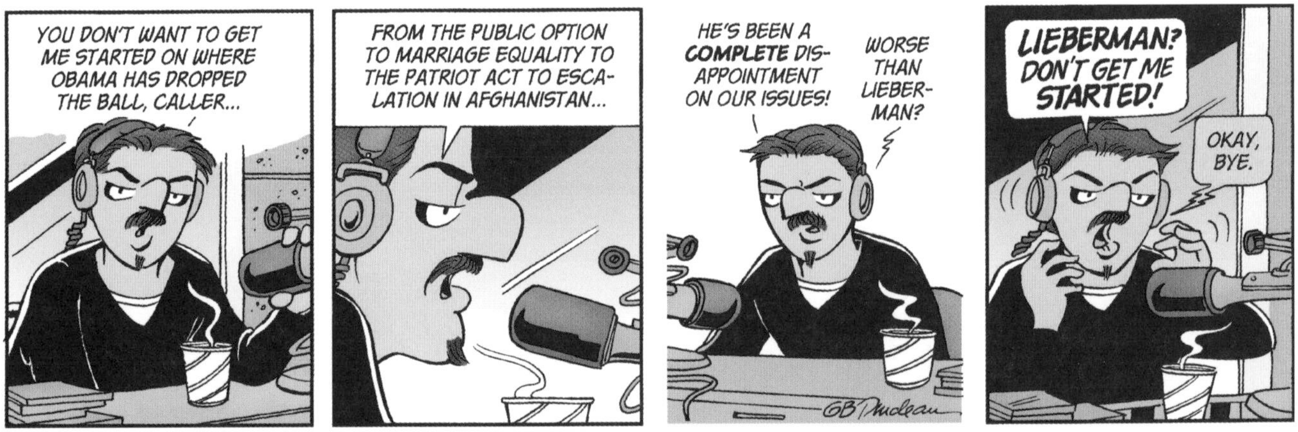
YOU DON'T WANT TO GET ME STARTED ON WHERE OBAMA HAS DROPPED THE BALL, CALLER...
FROM THE PUBLIC OPTION TO MARRIAGE EQUALITY TO THE PATRIOT ACT TO ESCALATION IN AFGHANISTAN...
HE'S BEEN A COMPLETE DISAPPOINTMENT ON OUR ISSUES!
WORSE THAN LIEBERMAN?
LIEBERMAN? DON'T GET ME STARTED!
OKAY, BYE.
GBTrudeau

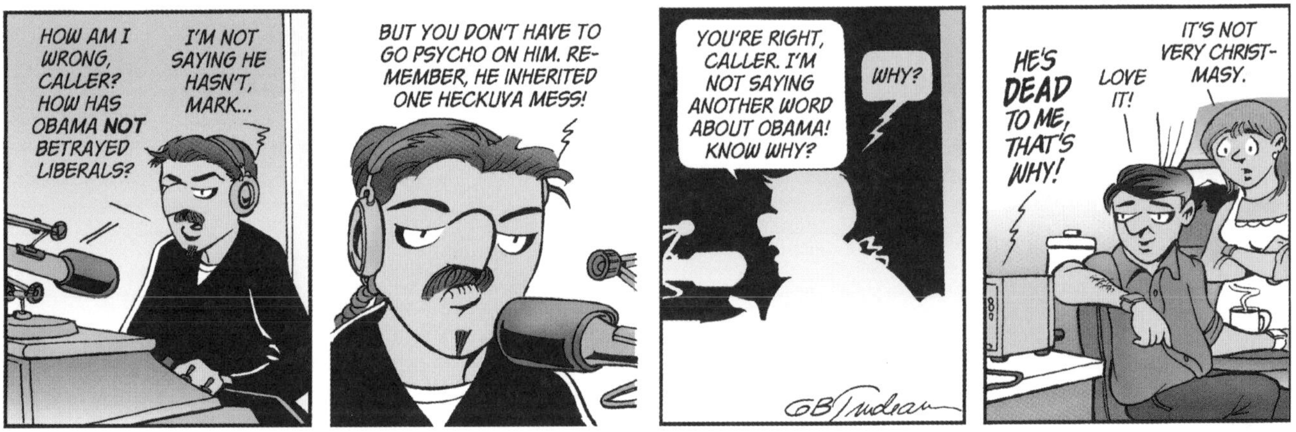
HOW AM I WRONG, CALLER? HOW HAS OBAMA NOT BETRAYED LIBERALS?
I'M NOT SAYING HE HASN'T, MARK...
BUT YOU DON'T HAVE TO GO PSYCHO ON HIM. REMEMBER, HE INHERITED ONE HECKUVA MESS!
YOU'RE RIGHT, CALLER. I'M NOT SAYING ANOTHER WORD ABOUT OBAMA! KNOW WHY?
WHY?
HE'S DEAD TO ME, THAT'S WHY!
LOVE IT!
IT'S NOT VERY CHRISTMASY.
GBTrudeau

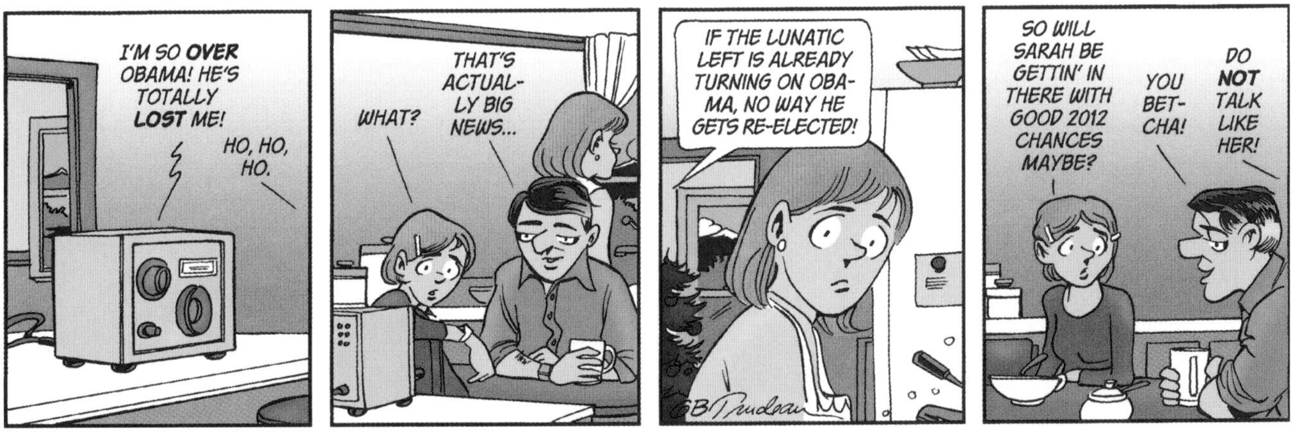
I'M SO OVER OBAMA! HE'S TOTALLY LOST ME!
HO, HO, HO.
WHAT?
THAT'S ACTUALLY BIG NEWS...
IF THE LUNATIC LEFT IS ALREADY TURNING ON OBAMA, NO WAY HE GETS RE-ELECTED!
SO WILL SARAH BE GETTIN' IN THERE WITH GOOD 2012 CHANCES MAYBE?
YOU BETCHA!
DO NOT TALK LIKE HER!
GBTrudeau

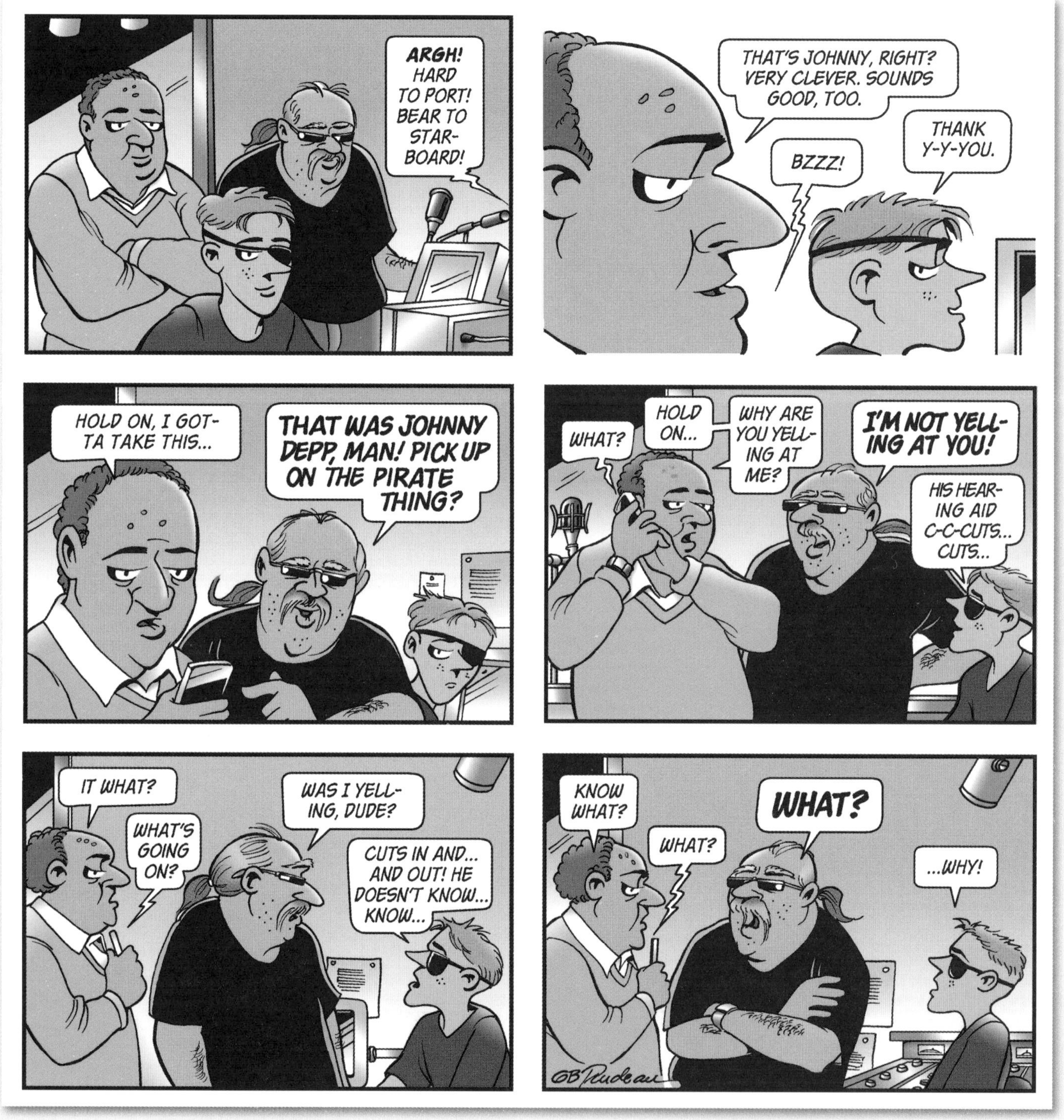
ARGH! HARD TO PORT! BEAR TO STAR-BOARD!
THAT'S JOHNNY, RIGHT? VERY CLEVER. SOUNDS GOOD, TOO.
BZZZ!
THANK Y-Y-YOU.
HOLD ON, I GOT-TA TAKE THIS...
THAT WAS JOHNNY DEPP, MAN! PICK UP ON THE PIRATE THING?
WHAT?
HOLD ON...
WHY ARE YOU YELL-ING AT ME?
I'M NOT YELL-ING AT YOU!
HIS HEAR-ING AID C-C-CUTS... CUTS...
IT WHAT?
WHAT'S GOING ON?
WAS I YELL-ING, DUDE?
CUTS IN AND... AND OUT! HE DOESN'T KNOW... KNOW...
KNOW WHAT?
WHAT?
WHAT?
...WHY!
GBTrudeau

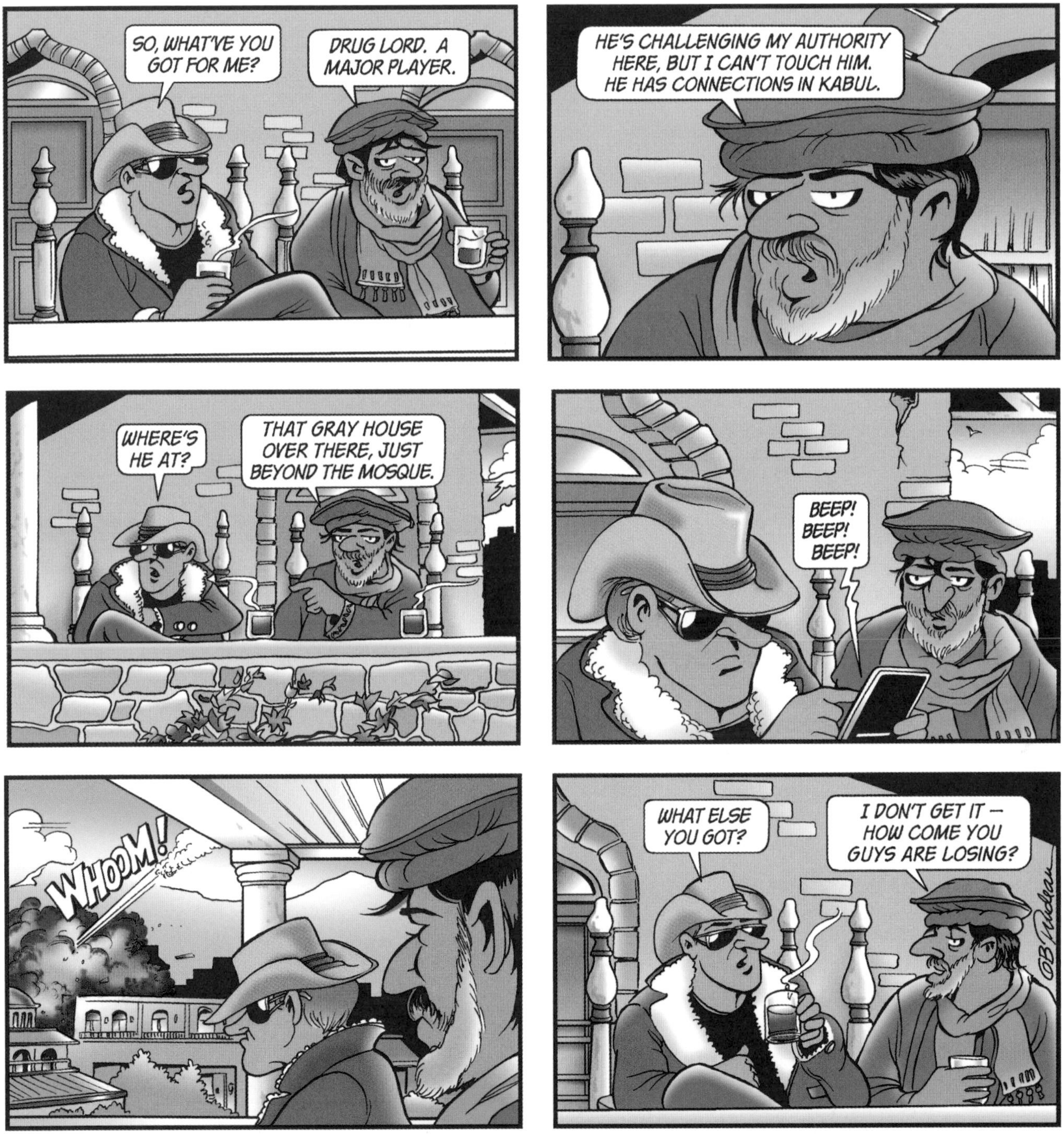
SO, WHAT'VE YOU GOT FOR ME?
DRUG LORD. A MAJOR PLAYER.
HE'S CHALLENGING MY AUTHORITY HERE, BUT I CAN'T TOUCH HIM. HE HAS CONNECTIONS IN KABUL.
WHERE'S HE AT?
THAT GRAY HOUSE OVER THERE, JUST BEYOND THE MOSQUE.
BEEP! BEEP! BEEP!
WHOOM!
WHAT ELSE YOU GOT?
I DON'T GET IT — HOW COME YOU GUYS ARE LOSING?
©B Trudeau

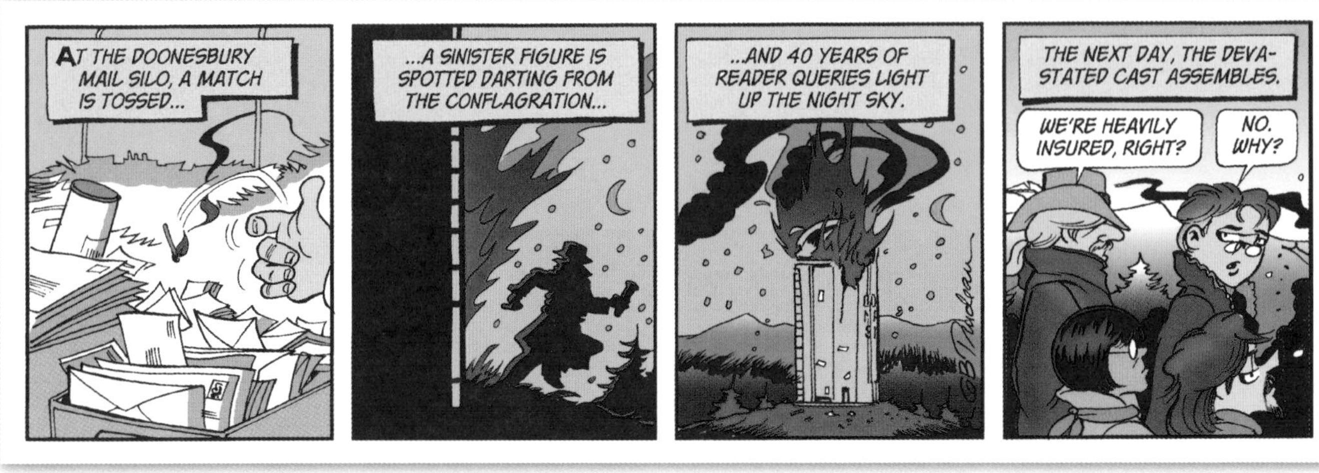
AT THE DOONESBURY MAIL SILO, A MATCH IS TOSSED...
...A SINISTER FIGURE IS SPOTTED DARTING FROM THE CONFLAGRATION...
...AND 40 YEARS OF READER QUERIES LIGHT UP THE NIGHT SKY.
THE NEXT DAY, THE DEVA-STATED CAST ASSEMBLES.
WE'RE HEAVILY INSURED, RIGHT?
NO. WHY?

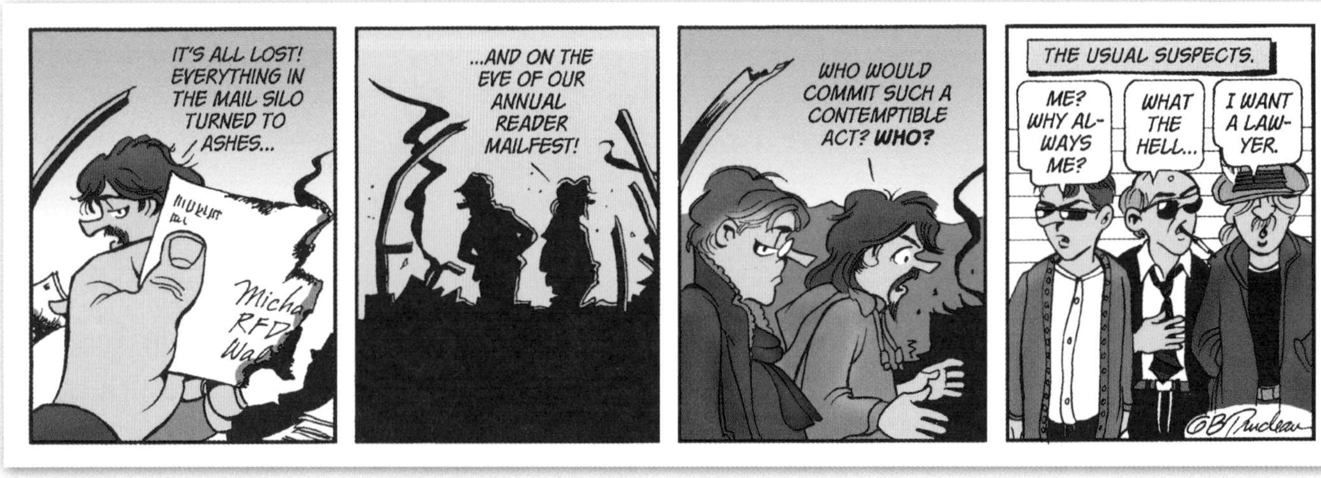
IT'S ALL LOST! EVERYTHING IN THE MAIL SILO TURNED TO ASHES...
...AND ON THE EVE OF OUR ANNUAL READER MAILFEST!
WHO WOULD COMMIT SUCH A CONTEMPTIBLE ACT? **WHO?**
THE USUAL SUSPECTS.
ME? WHY AL-WAYS ME?
WHAT THE HELL...
I WANT A LAW-YER.

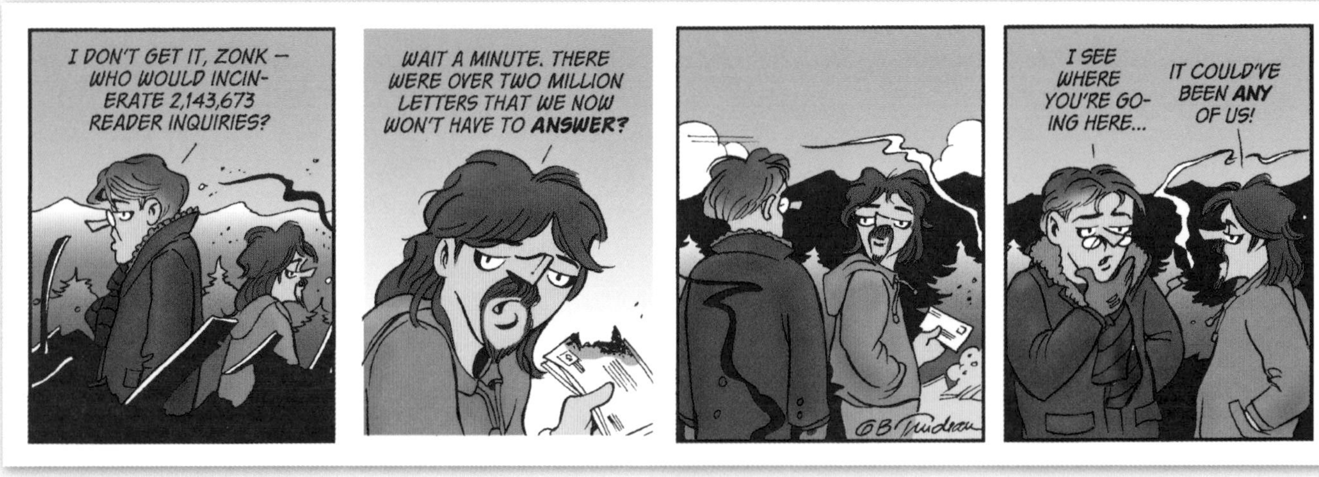
I DON'T GET IT, ZONK — WHO WOULD INCIN-ERATE 2,143,673 READER INQUIRIES?
WAIT A MINUTE. THERE WERE OVER TWO MILLION LETTERS THAT WE NOW WON'T HAVE TO **ANSWER?**
I SEE WHERE YOU'RE GO-ING HERE...
IT COULD'VE BEEN **ANY** OF US!

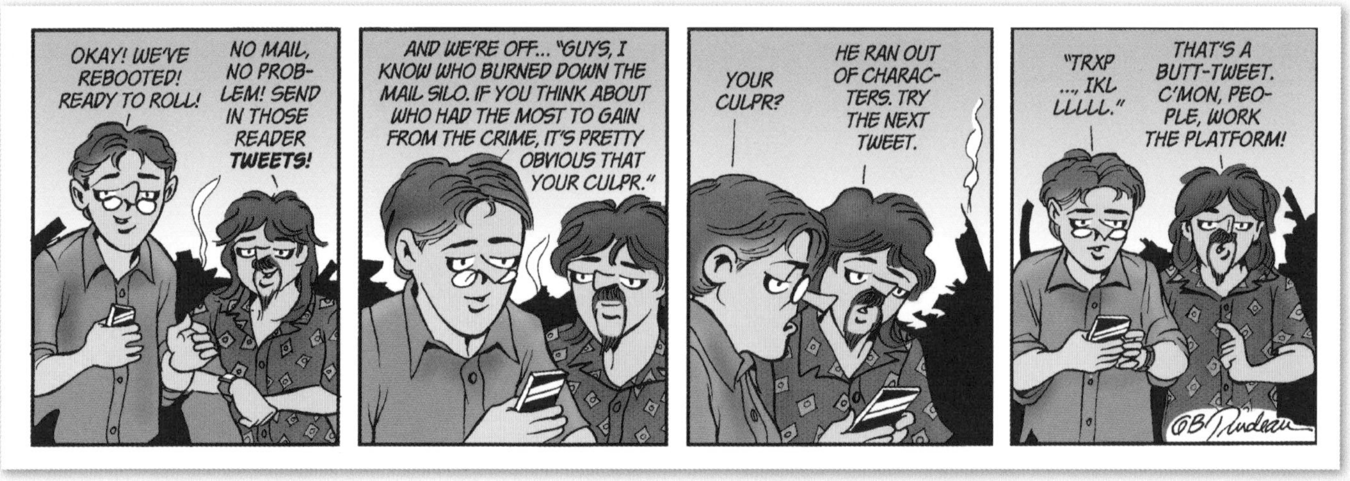
OKAY! WE'VE REBOOTED! READY TO ROLL!
NO MAIL, NO PROB-LEM! SEND IN THOSE READER **TWEETS!**
AND WE'RE OFF... "GUYS, I KNOW WHO BURNED DOWN THE MAIL SILO. IF YOU THINK ABOUT WHO HAD THE MOST TO GAIN FROM THE CRIME, IT'S PRETTY OBVIOUS THAT YOUR CULPR."
YOUR CULPR?
HE RAN OUT OF CHARAC-TERS. TRY THE NEXT TWEET.
"TRXP ..., IKL LLLLL."
THAT'S A BUTT-TWEET. C'MON, PEO-PLE, WORK THE PLATFORM!
GB Trudeau

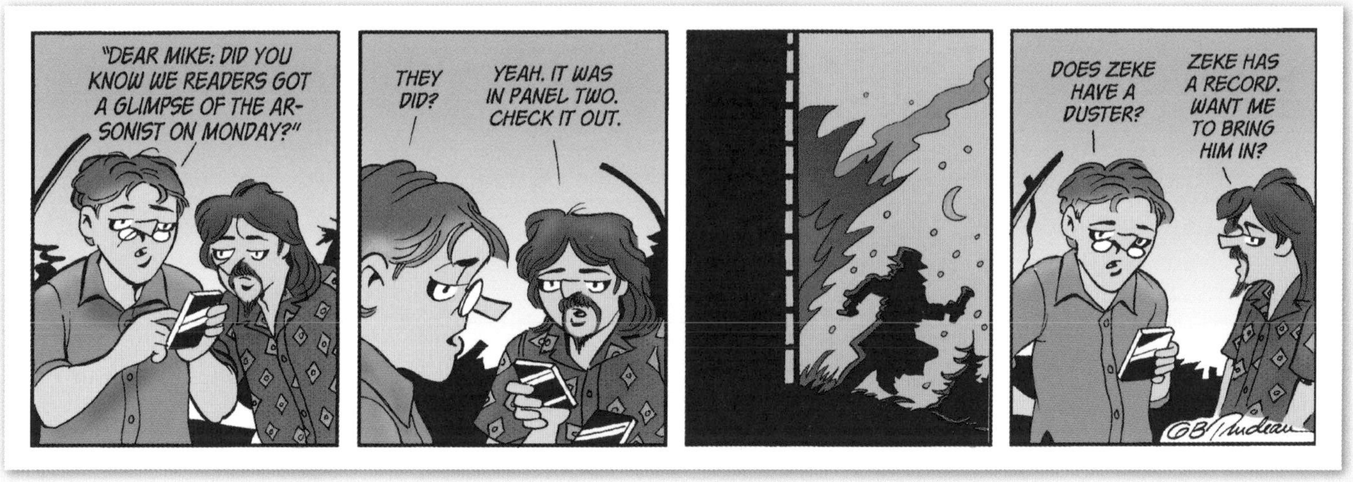
"DEAR MIKE: DID YOU KNOW WE READERS GOT A GLIMPSE OF THE AR-SONIST ON MONDAY?"
THEY DID?
YEAH. IT WAS IN PANEL TWO. CHECK IT OUT.
DOES ZEKE HAVE A DUSTER?
ZEKE HAS A RECORD. WANT ME TO BRING HIM IN?
GB Trudeau

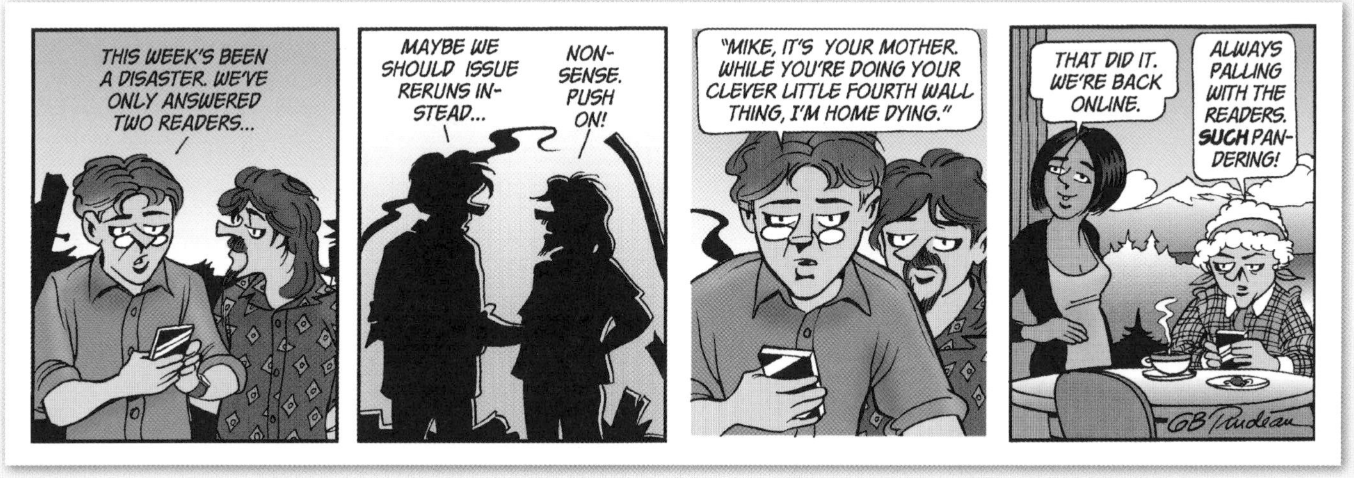
THIS WEEK'S BEEN A DISASTER. WE'VE ONLY ANSWERED TWO READERS...
MAYBE WE SHOULD ISSUE RERUNS IN-STEAD...
NON-SENSE. PUSH ON!
"MIKE, IT'S YOUR MOTHER. WHILE YOU'RE DOING YOUR CLEVER LITTLE FOURTH WALL THING, I'M HOME DYING."
THAT DID IT. WE'RE BACK ONLINE.
ALWAYS PALLING WITH THE READERS. **SUCH** PAN-DERING!
GB Trudeau

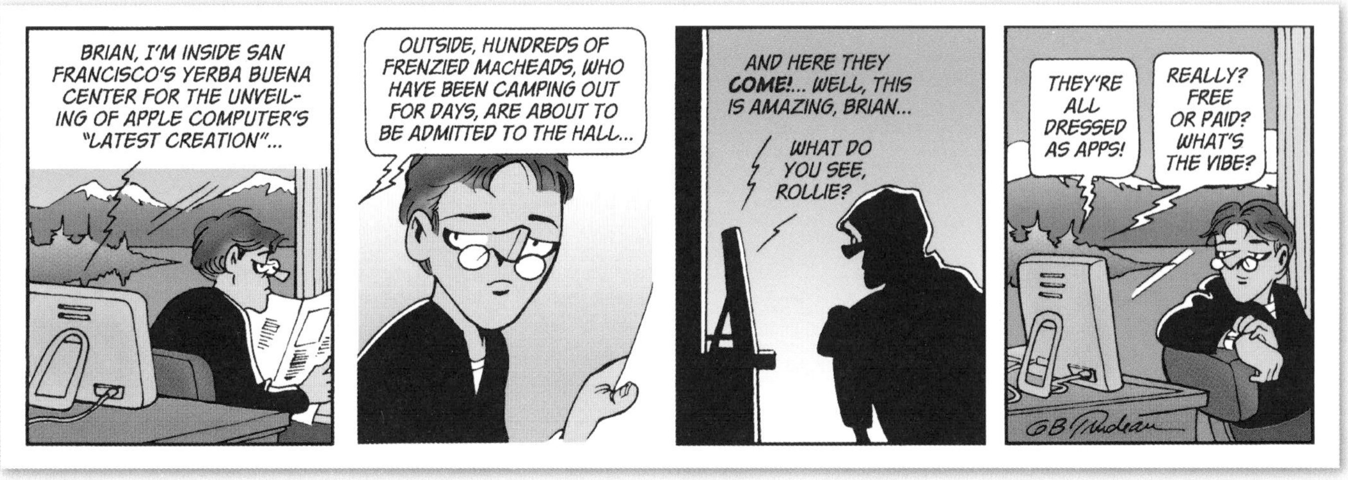
BRIAN, I'M INSIDE SAN FRANCISCO'S YERBA BUENA CENTER FOR THE UNVEIL-ING OF APPLE COMPUTER'S "LATEST CREATION"...
OUTSIDE, HUNDREDS OF FRENZIED MACHEADS, WHO HAVE BEEN CAMPING OUT FOR DAYS, ARE ABOUT TO BE ADMITTED TO THE HALL...
AND HERE THEY COME!... WELL, THIS IS AMAZING, BRIAN...
WHAT DO YOU SEE, ROLLIE?
THEY'RE ALL DRESSED AS APPS!
REALLY? FREE OR PAID? WHAT'S THE VIBE?
GB Trudeau

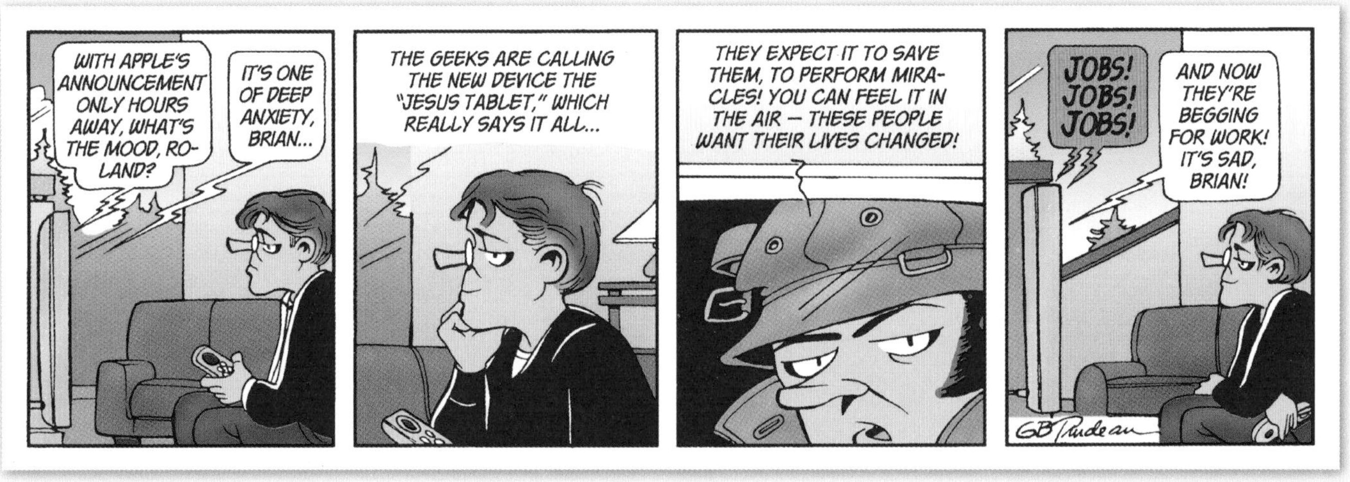
WITH APPLE'S ANNOUNCEMENT ONLY HOURS AWAY, WHAT'S THE MOOD, RO-LAND?
IT'S ONE OF DEEP ANXIETY, BRIAN...
THE GEEKS ARE CALLING THE NEW DEVICE THE "JESUS TABLET," WHICH REALLY SAYS IT ALL...
THEY EXPECT IT TO SAVE THEM, TO PERFORM MIRA-CLES! YOU CAN FEEL IT IN THE AIR — THESE PEOPLE WANT THEIR LIVES CHANGED!
JOBS! JOBS! JOBS!
AND NOW THEY'RE BEGGING FOR WORK! IT'S SAD, BRIAN!
GB Trudeau

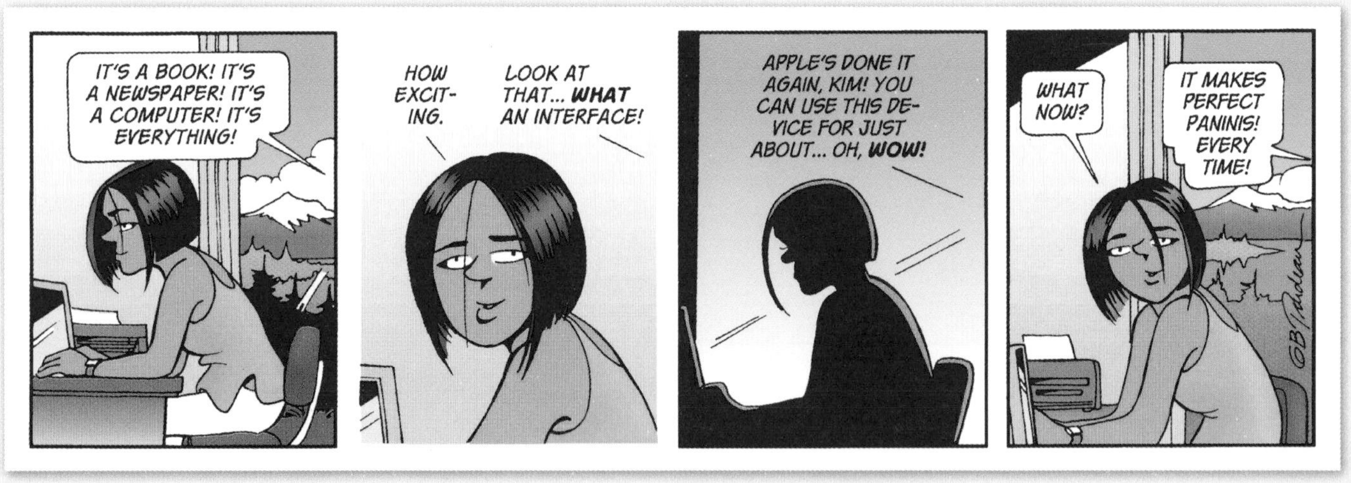
IT'S A BOOK! IT'S A NEWSPAPER! IT'S A COMPUTER! IT'S EVERYTHING!
HOW EXCIT-ING.
LOOK AT THAT... WHAT AN INTERFACE!
APPLE'S DONE IT AGAIN, KIM! YOU CAN USE THIS DE-VICE FOR JUST ABOUT... OH, WOW!
WHAT NOW?
IT MAKES PERFECT PANINIS! EVERY TIME!
GB Trudeau

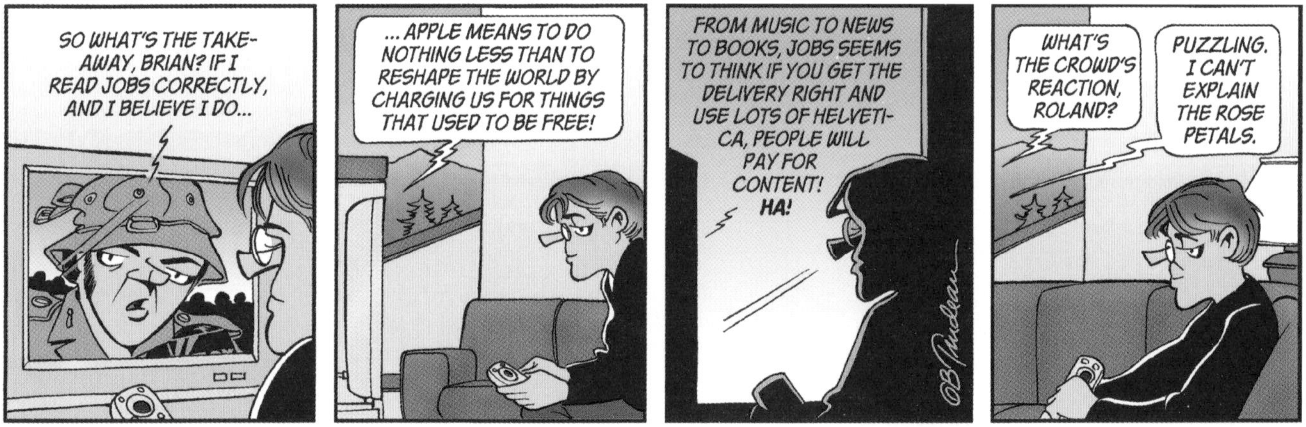
SO WHAT'S THE TAKE-AWAY, BRIAN? IF I READ JOBS CORRECTLY, AND I BELIEVE I DO...
... APPLE MEANS TO DO NOTHING LESS THAN TO RESHAPE THE WORLD BY CHARGING US FOR THINGS THAT USED TO BE FREE!
FROM MUSIC TO NEWS TO BOOKS, JOBS SEEMS TO THINK IF YOU GET THE DELIVERY RIGHT AND USE LOTS OF HELVETICA, PEOPLE WILL PAY FOR CONTENT! HA!
WHAT'S THE CROWD'S REACTION, ROLAND?
PUZZLING. I CAN'T EXPLAIN THE ROSE PETALS.

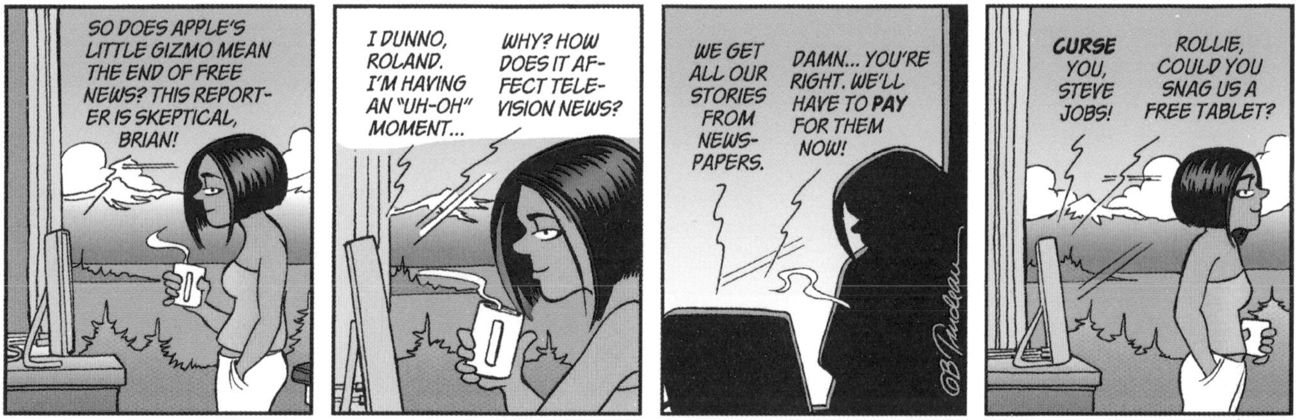
SO DOES APPLE'S LITTLE GIZMO MEAN THE END OF FREE NEWS? THIS REPORTER IS SKEPTICAL, BRIAN!
I DUNNO, ROLAND. I'M HAVING AN "UH-OH" MOMENT...
WHY? HOW DOES IT AFFECT TELEVISION NEWS?
WE GET ALL OUR STORIES FROM NEWSPAPERS.
DAMN... YOU'RE RIGHT. WE'LL HAVE TO PAY FOR THEM NOW!
CURSE YOU, STEVE JOBS!
ROLLIE, COULD YOU SNAG US A FREE TABLET?

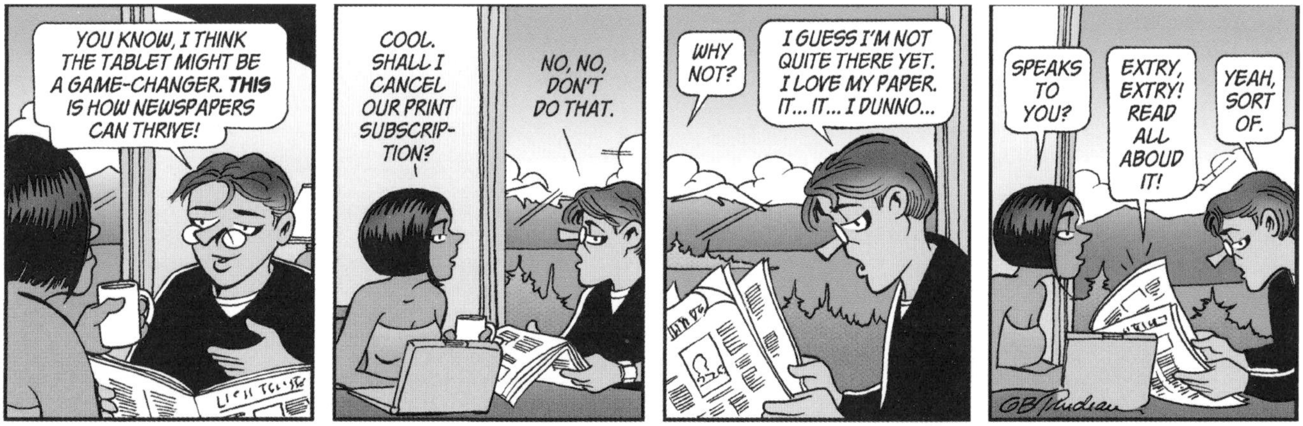
YOU KNOW, I THINK THE TABLET MIGHT BE A GAME-CHANGER. THIS IS HOW NEWSPAPERS CAN THRIVE!
COOL. SHALL I CANCEL OUR PRINT SUBSCRIPTION?
NO, NO, DON'T DO THAT.
WHY NOT?
I GUESS I'M NOT QUITE THERE YET. I LOVE MY PAPER. IT... IT... I DUNNO...
SPEAKS TO YOU?
EXTRY, EXTRY! READ ALL ABOUD IT!
YEAH, SORT OF.

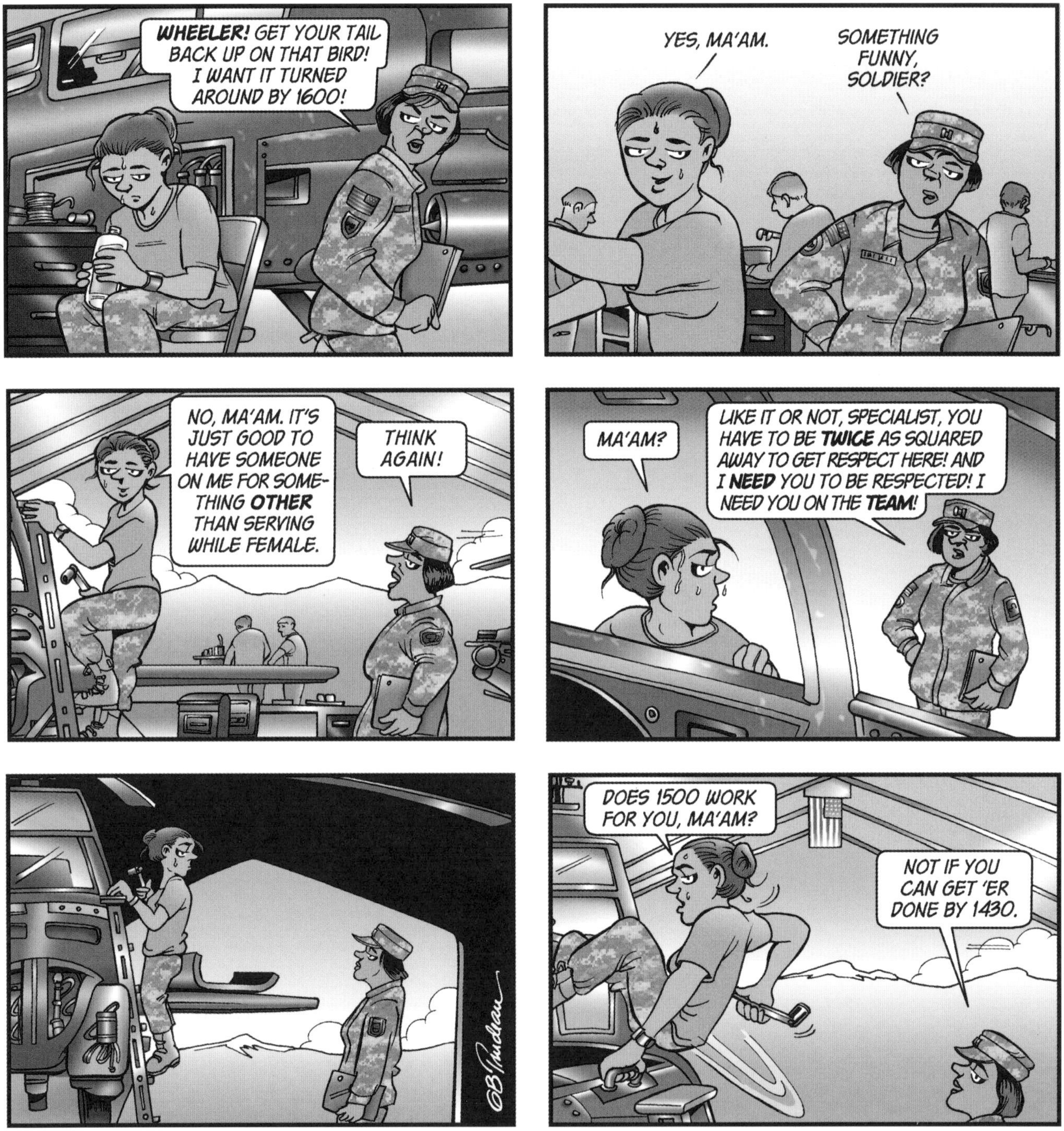
WHEELER! GET YOUR TAIL BACK UP ON THAT BIRD! I WANT IT TURNED AROUND BY 1600!
YES, MA'AM.
SOMETHING FUNNY, SOLDIER?
NO, MA'AM. IT'S JUST GOOD TO HAVE SOMEONE ON ME FOR SOMETHING OTHER THAN SERVING WHILE FEMALE.
THINK AGAIN!
MA'AM?
LIKE IT OR NOT, SPECIALIST, YOU HAVE TO BE TWICE AS SQUARED AWAY TO GET RESPECT HERE! AND I NEED YOU TO BE RESPECTED! I NEED YOU ON THE TEAM!
DOES 1500 WORK FOR YOU, MA'AM?
NOT IF YOU CAN GET 'ER DONE BY 1430.

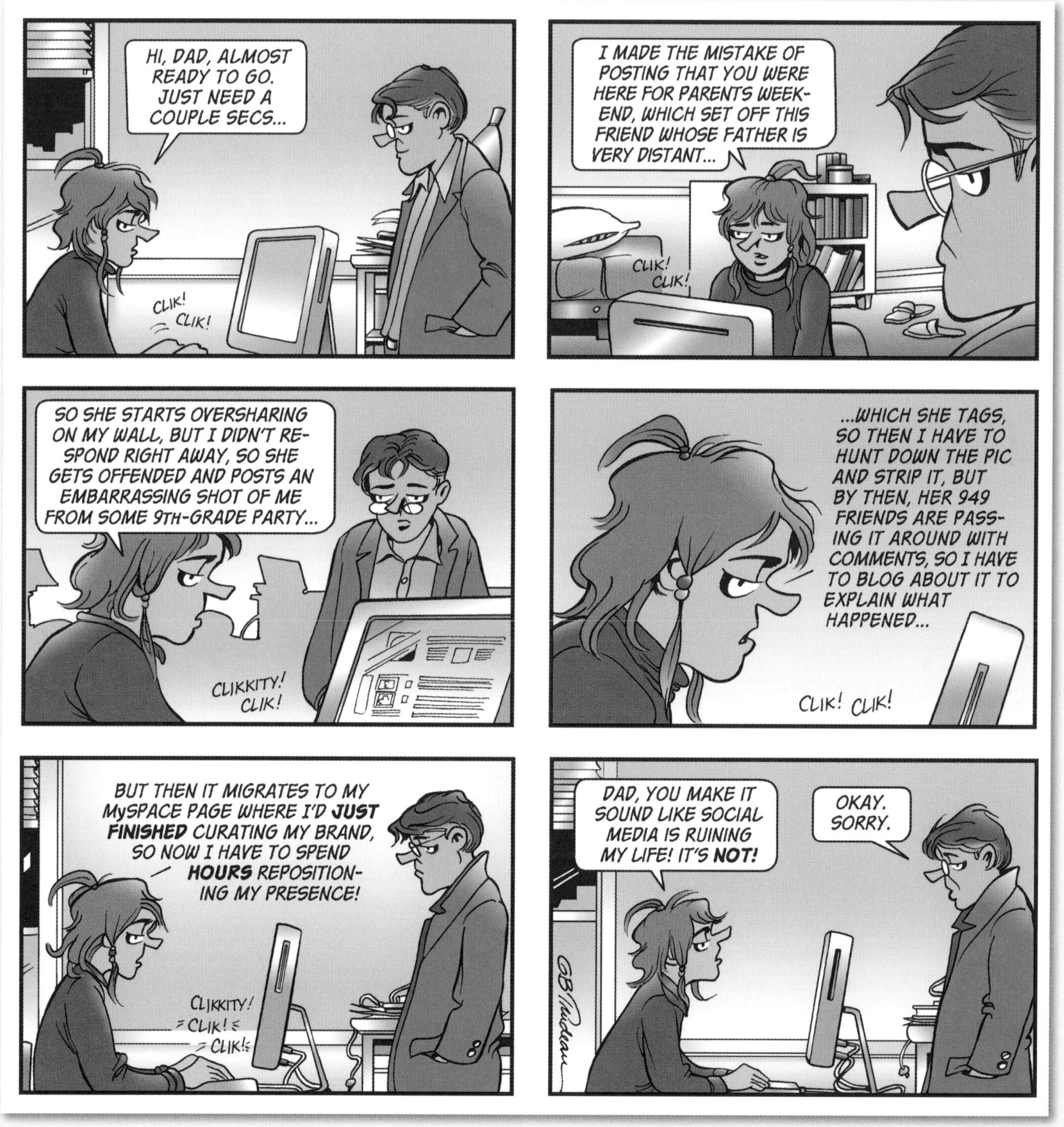
HI, DAD, ALMOST READY TO GO. JUST NEED A COUPLE SECS...
CLIK! CLIK!
I MADE THE MISTAKE OF POSTING THAT YOU WERE HERE FOR PARENTS WEEK-END, WHICH SET OFF THIS FRIEND WHOSE FATHER IS VERY DISTANT...
CLIK! CLIK!
SO SHE STARTS OVERSHARING ON MY WALL, BUT I DIDN'T RE-SPOND RIGHT AWAY, SO SHE GETS OFFENDED AND POSTS AN EMBARRASSING SHOT OF ME FROM SOME 9TH-GRADE PARTY...
CLIKKITY! CLIK!
...WHICH SHE TAGS, SO THEN I HAVE TO HUNT DOWN THE PIC AND STRIP IT, BUT BY THEN, HER 949 FRIENDS ARE PASS-ING IT AROUND WITH COMMENTS, SO I HAVE TO BLOG ABOUT IT TO EXPLAIN WHAT HAPPENED...
CLIK! CLIK!
BUT THEN IT MIGRATES TO MY MySPACE PAGE WHERE I'D **JUST FINISHED** CURATING MY BRAND, SO NOW I HAVE TO SPEND **HOURS** REPOSITION-ING MY PRESENCE!
CLIKKITY! CLIK! CLIK!
DAD, YOU MAKE IT SOUND LIKE SOCIAL MEDIA IS RUINING MY LIFE! IT'S **NOT**!
OKAY. SORRY.
GB Trudeau

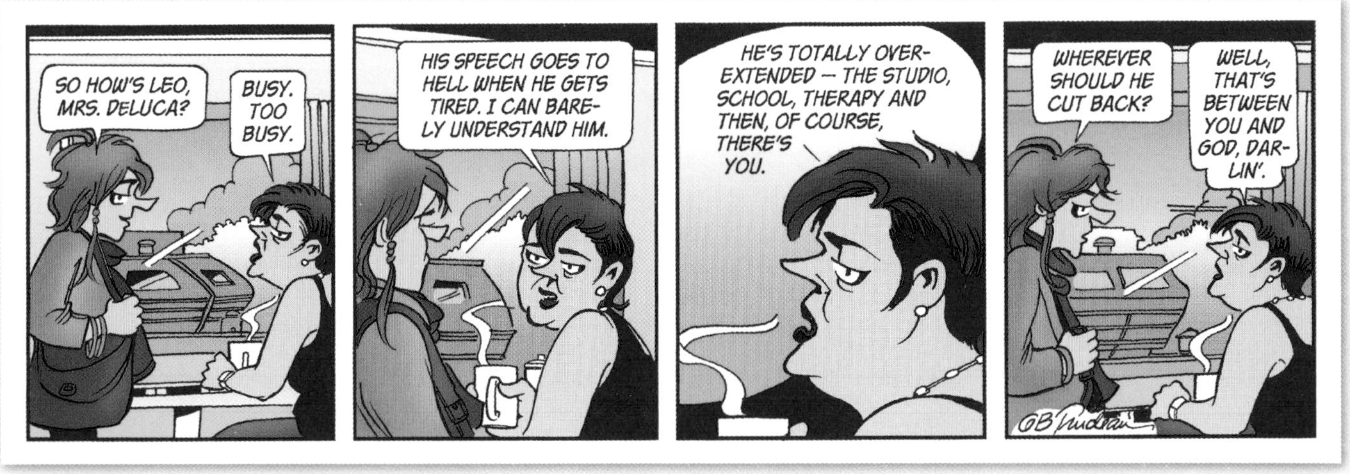
SO HOW'S LEO, MRS. DELUCA?
BUSY. TOO BUSY.
HIS SPEECH GOES TO HELL WHEN HE GETS TIRED. I CAN BARELY UNDERSTAND HIM.
HE'S TOTALLY OVER-EXTENDED -- THE STUDIO, SCHOOL, THERAPY AND THEN, OF COURSE, THERE'S YOU.
WHEREVER SHOULD HE CUT BACK?
WELL, THAT'S BETWEEN YOU AND GOD, DARLIN'.
GB Trudeau

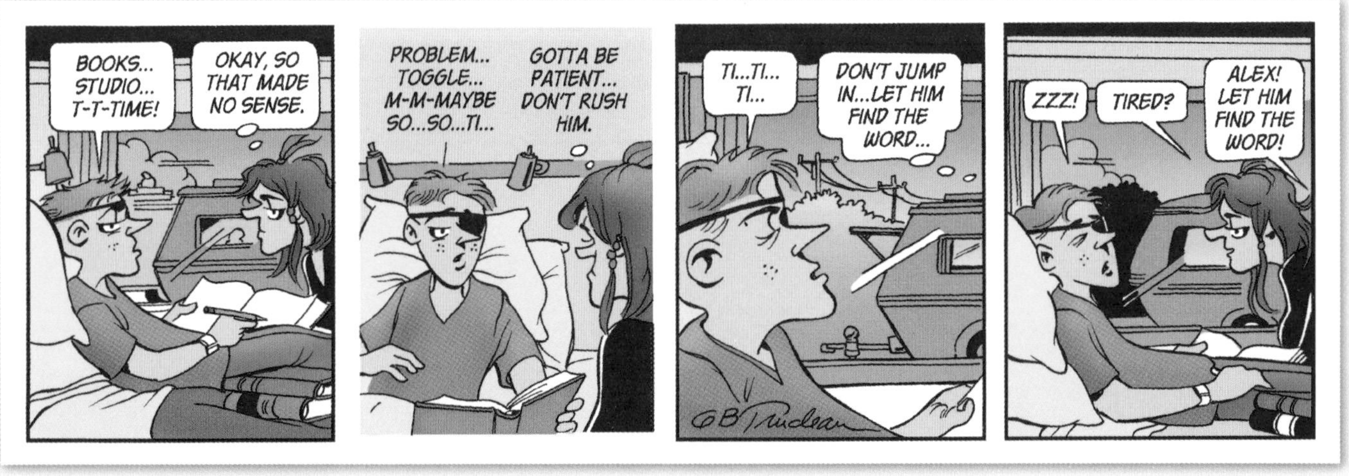
BOOKS... STUDIO... T-T-TIME!
OKAY, SO THAT MADE NO SENSE.
PROBLEM... TOGGLE... M-M-MAYBE SO...SO...TI...
GOTTA BE PATIENT... DON'T RUSH HIM.
TI...TI... TI...
DON'T JUMP IN...LET HIM FIND THE WORD...
GB Trudeau
ZZZ!
TIRED?
ALEX! LET HIM FIND THE WORD!

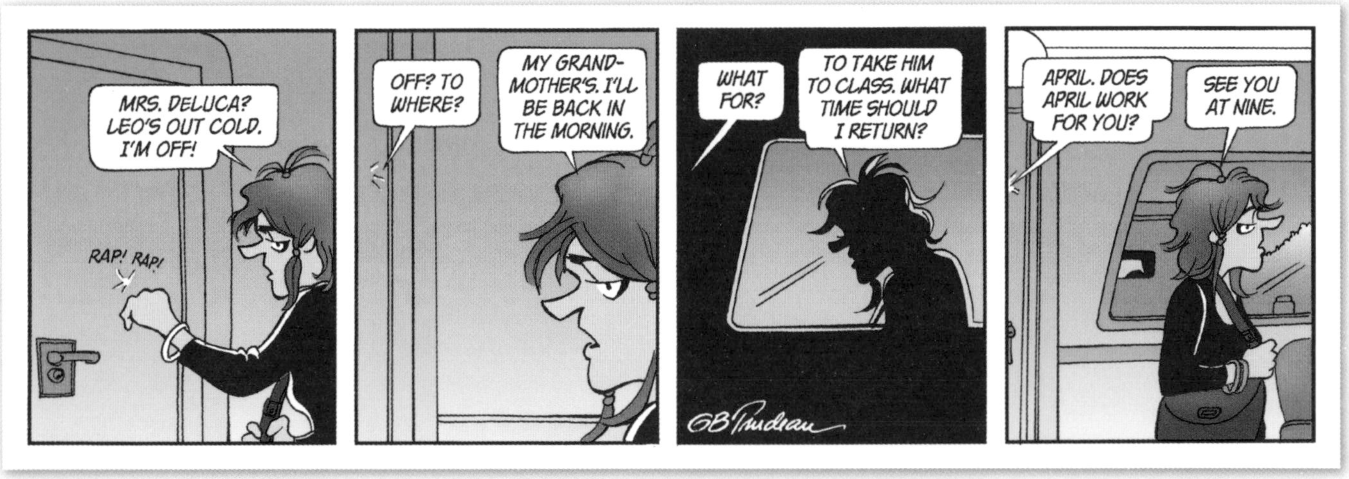
MRS. DELUCA? LEO'S OUT COLD. I'M OFF!
RAP! RAP!
OFF? TO WHERE?
MY GRANDMOTHER'S. I'LL BE BACK IN THE MORNING.
WHAT FOR?
TO TAKE HIM TO CLASS. WHAT TIME SHOULD I RETURN?
GB Trudeau
APRIL. DOES APRIL WORK FOR YOU?
SEE YOU AT NINE.

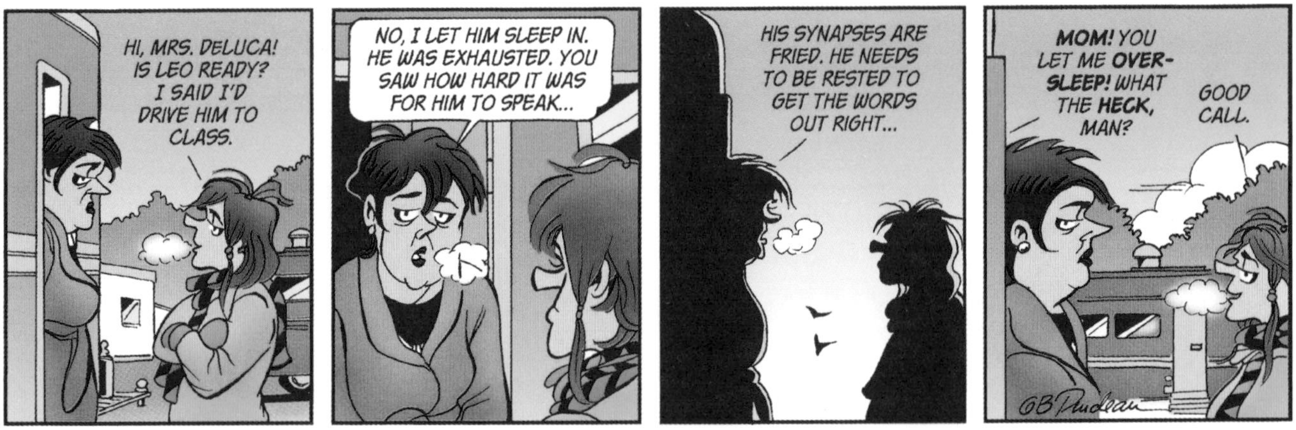
HI, MRS. DELUCA! IS LEO READY? I SAID I'D DRIVE HIM TO CLASS.
NO, I LET HIM SLEEP IN. HE WAS EXHAUSTED. YOU SAW HOW HARD IT WAS FOR HIM TO SPEAK...
HIS SYNAPSES ARE FRIED. HE NEEDS TO BE RESTED TO GET THE WORDS OUT RIGHT...
MOM! YOU LET ME **OVER-SLEEP!** WHAT THE **HECK,** MAN?
GOOD CALL.
GB Trudeau

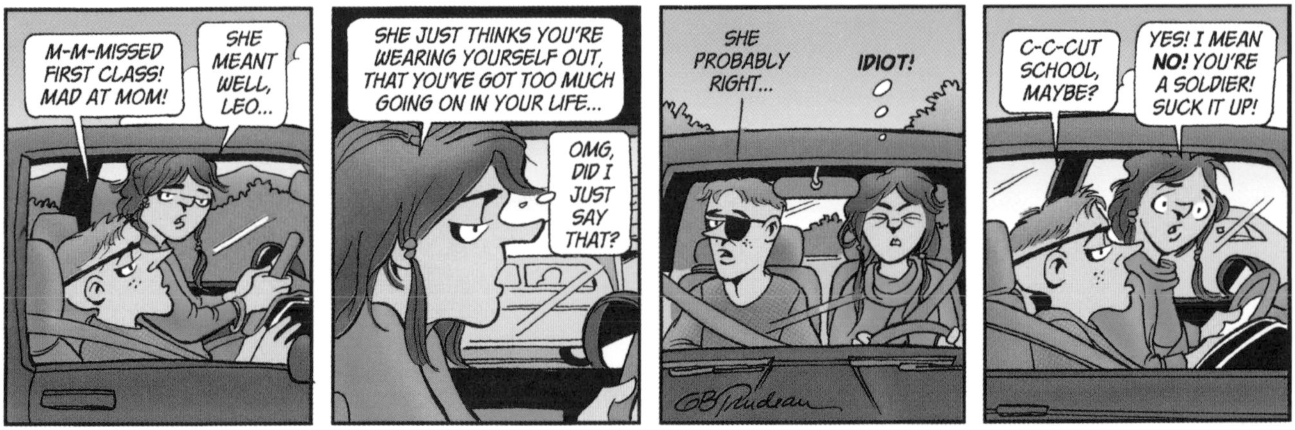
M-M-MISSED FIRST CLASS! MAD AT MOM!
SHE MEANT WELL, LEO...
SHE JUST THINKS YOU'RE WEARING YOURSELF OUT, THAT YOU'VE GOT TOO MUCH GOING ON IN YOUR LIFE...
OMG, DID I JUST SAY THAT?
SHE PROBABLY RIGHT...
IDIOT!
C-C-CUT SCHOOL, MAYBE?
YES! I MEAN **NO!** YOU'RE A SOLDIER! SUCK IT UP!
GB Trudeau

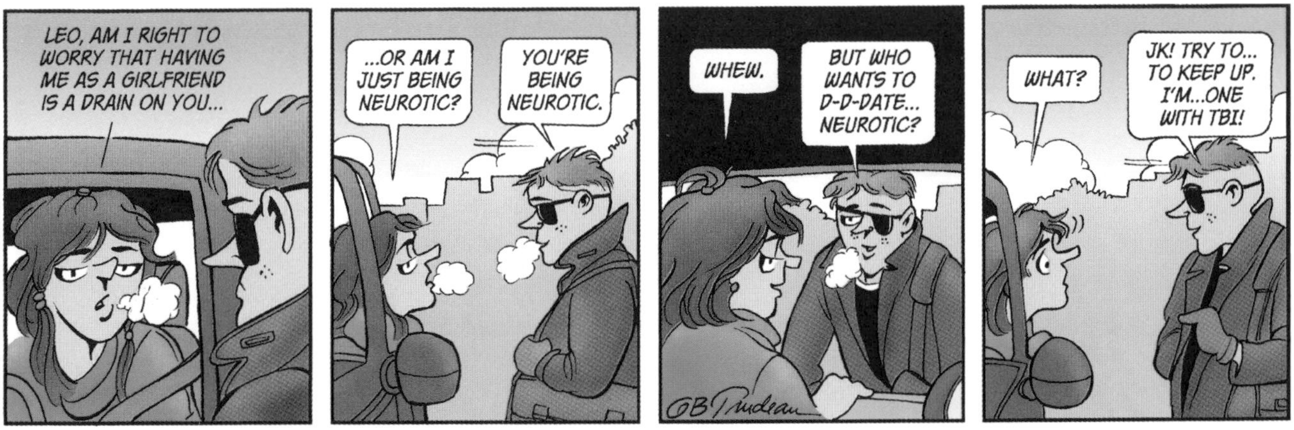
LEO, AM I RIGHT TO WORRY THAT HAVING ME AS A GIRLFRIEND IS A DRAIN ON YOU...
...OR AM I JUST BEING NEUROTIC?
YOU'RE BEING NEUROTIC.
WHEW.
BUT WHO WANTS TO D-D-DATE... NEUROTIC?
WHAT?
JK! TRY TO... TO KEEP UP. I'M...ONE WITH TBI!
GB Trudeau

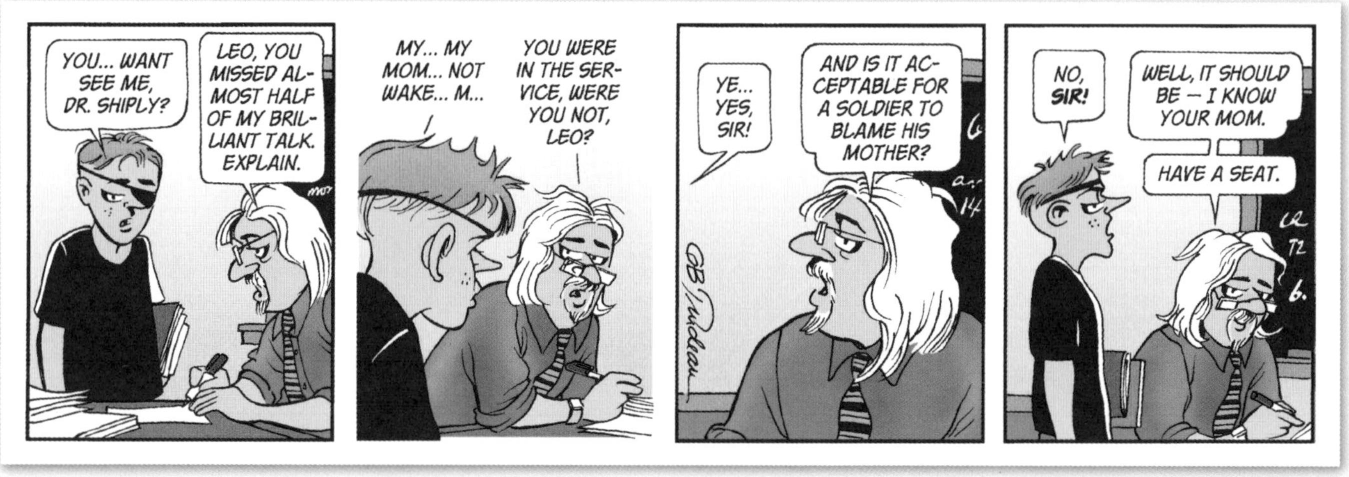
YOU... WANT SEE ME, DR. SHIPLY?
LEO, YOU MISSED ALMOST HALF OF MY BRILLIANT TALK. EXPLAIN.
MY... MY MOM... NOT WAKE... M...
YOU WERE IN THE SERVICE, WERE YOU NOT, LEO?
YE... YES, SIR!
AND IS IT ACCEPTABLE FOR A SOLDIER TO BLAME HIS MOTHER?
NO, SIR!
WELL, IT SHOULD BE — I KNOW YOUR MOM.
HAVE A SEAT.
GB Trudeau

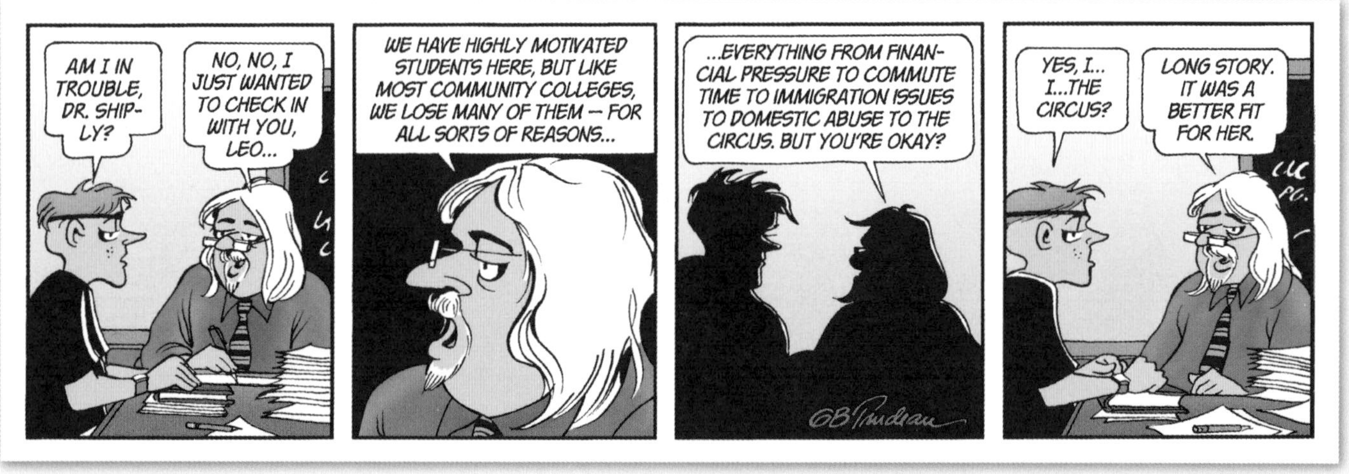
AM I IN TROUBLE, DR. SHIPLY?
NO, NO, I JUST WANTED TO CHECK IN WITH YOU, LEO...
WE HAVE HIGHLY MOTIVATED STUDENTS HERE, BUT LIKE MOST COMMUNITY COLLEGES, WE LOSE MANY OF THEM — FOR ALL SORTS OF REASONS...
...EVERYTHING FROM FINANCIAL PRESSURE TO COMMUTE TIME TO IMMIGRATION ISSUES TO DOMESTIC ABUSE TO THE CIRCUS. BUT YOU'RE OKAY?
GB Trudeau
YES, I... I...THE CIRCUS?
LONG STORY. IT WAS A BETTER FIT FOR HER.

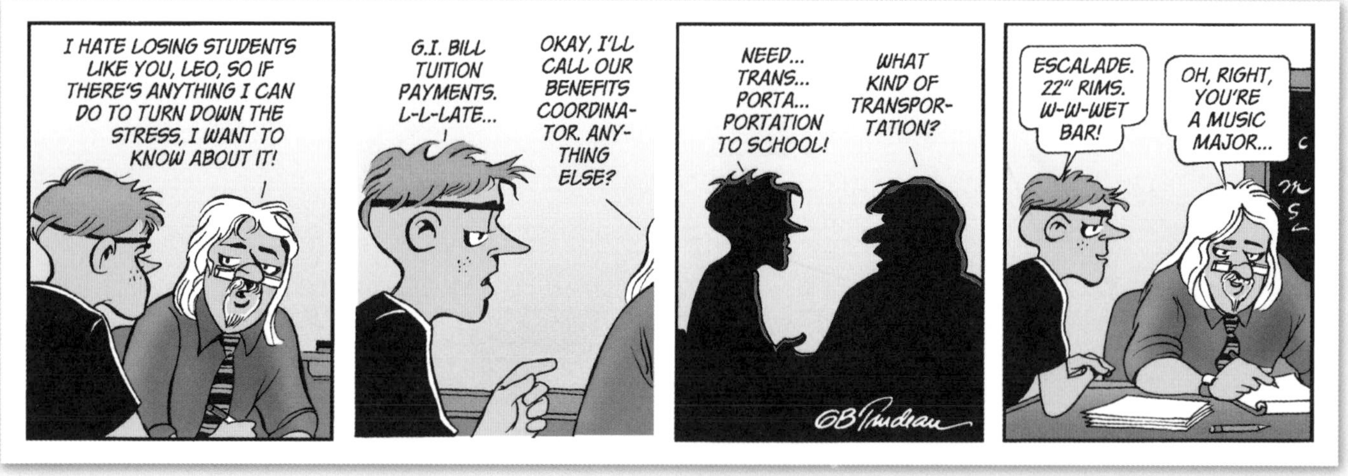
I HATE LOSING STUDENTS LIKE YOU, LEO, SO IF THERE'S ANYTHING I CAN DO TO TURN DOWN THE STRESS, I WANT TO KNOW ABOUT IT!
G.I. BILL TUITION PAYMENTS. L-L-LATE...
OKAY, I'LL CALL OUR BENEFITS COORDINATOR. ANYTHING ELSE?
NEED... TRANS... PORTA... PORTATION TO SCHOOL!
WHAT KIND OF TRANSPORTATION?
GB Trudeau
ESCALADE. 22" RIMS. W-W-WET BAR!
OH, RIGHT, YOU'RE A MUSIC MAJOR...

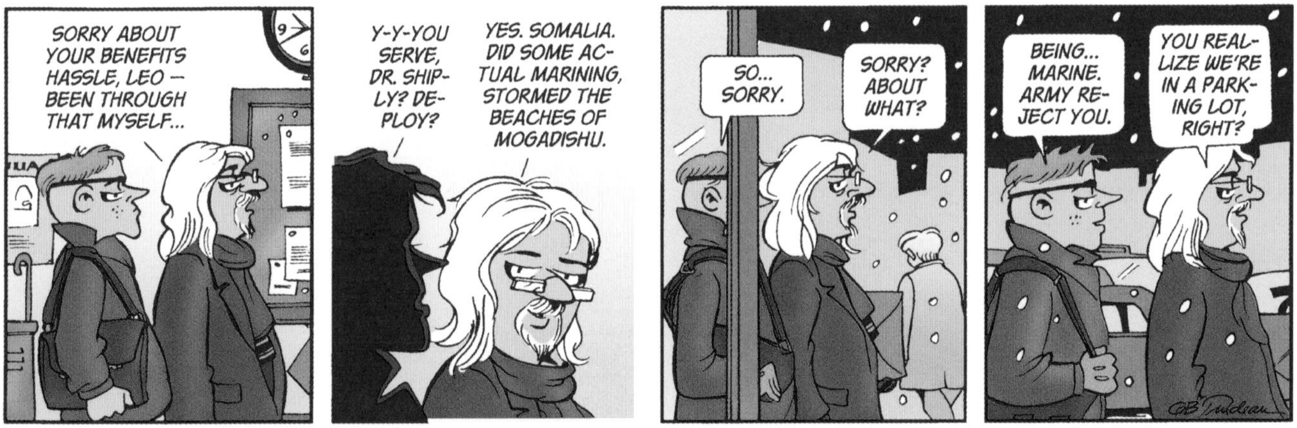
SORRY ABOUT YOUR BENEFITS HASSLE, LEO — BEEN THROUGH THAT MYSELF...
Y-Y-YOU SERVE, DR. SHIPLY? DEPLOY?
YES. SOMALIA. DID SOME ACTUAL MARINING, STORMED THE BEACHES OF MOGADISHU.
SO... SORRY.
SORRY? ABOUT WHAT?
BEING... MARINE. ARMY REJECT YOU.
YOU REALIZE WE'RE IN A PARKING LOT, RIGHT?

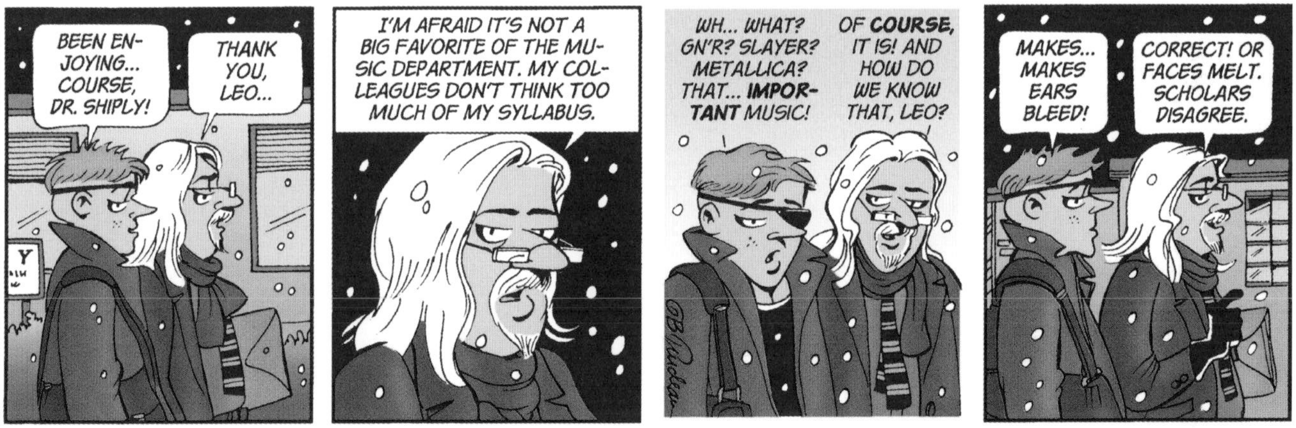
BEEN ENJOYING... COURSE, DR. SHIPLY!
THANK YOU, LEO...
I'M AFRAID IT'S NOT A BIG FAVORITE OF THE MUSIC DEPARTMENT. MY COLLEAGUES DON'T THINK TOO MUCH OF MY SYLLABUS.
WH... WHAT? GN'R? SLAYER? METALLICA? THAT... **IMPORTANT** MUSIC!
OF **COURSE**, IT IS! AND HOW DO WE KNOW THAT, LEO?
MAKES... MAKES EARS BLEED!
CORRECT! OR FACES MELT. SCHOLARS DISAGREE.

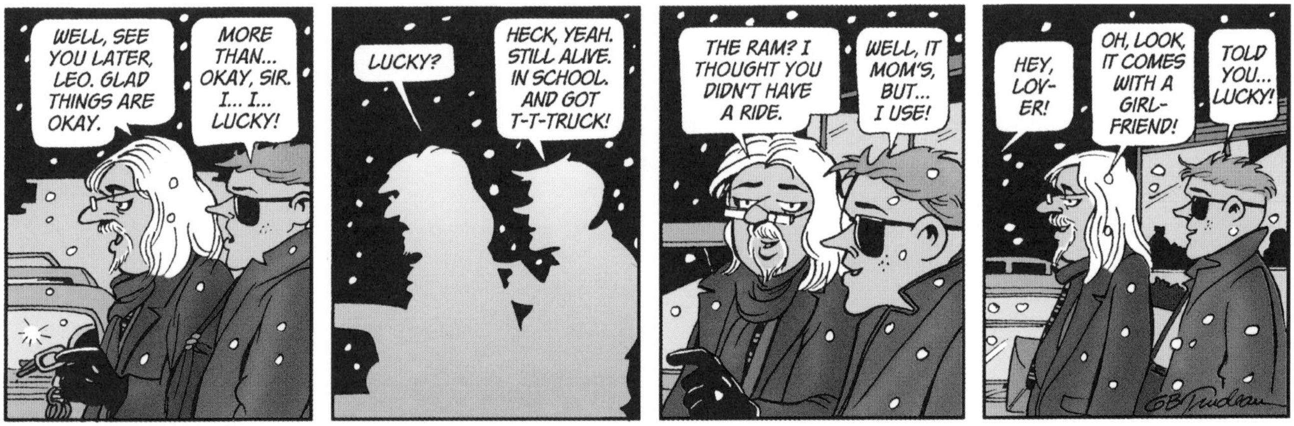
WELL, SEE YOU LATER, LEO. GLAD THINGS ARE OKAY.
MORE THAN... OKAY, SIR. I... I... LUCKY!
LUCKY?
HECK, YEAH. STILL ALIVE. IN SCHOOL. AND GOT T-T-TRUCK!
THE RAM? I THOUGHT YOU DIDN'T HAVE A RIDE.
WELL, IT MOM'S, BUT... I USE!
HEY, LOVER!
OH, LOOK, IT COMES WITH A GIRLFRIEND!
TOLD YOU... LUCKY!

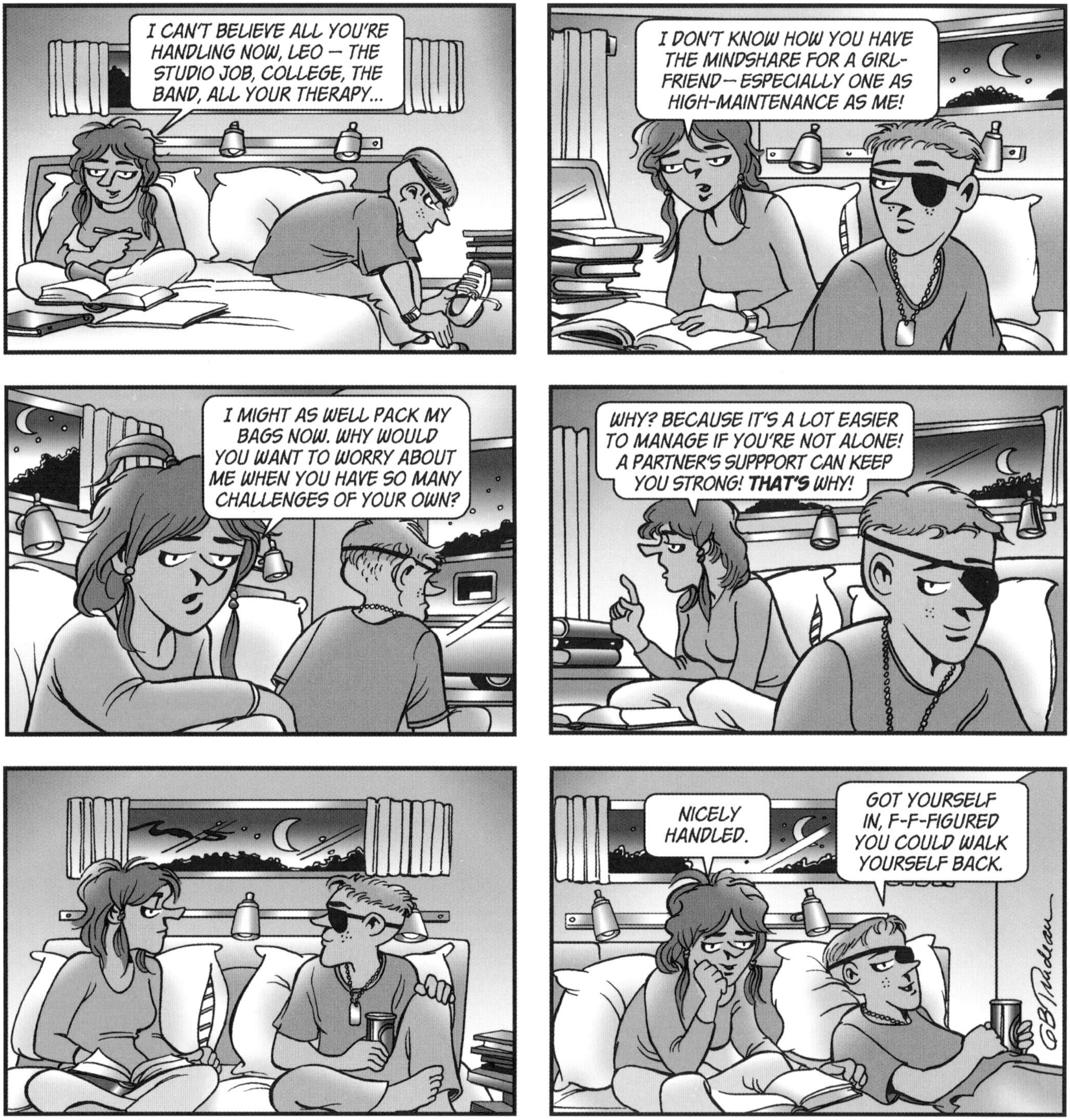
I CAN'T BELIEVE ALL YOU'RE HANDLING NOW, LEO — THE STUDIO JOB, COLLEGE, THE BAND, ALL YOUR THERAPY...
I DON'T KNOW HOW YOU HAVE THE MINDSHARE FOR A GIRL-FRIEND — ESPECIALLY ONE AS HIGH-MAINTENANCE AS ME!
I MIGHT AS WELL PACK MY BAGS NOW. WHY WOULD YOU WANT TO WORRY ABOUT ME WHEN YOU HAVE SO MANY CHALLENGES OF YOUR OWN?
WHY? BECAUSE IT'S A LOT EASIER TO MANAGE IF YOU'RE NOT ALONE! A PARTNER'S SUPPPORT CAN KEEP YOU STRONG! **THAT'S** WHY!
NICELY HANDLED.
GOT YOURSELF IN, F-F-FIGURED YOU COULD WALK YOURSELF BACK.
GBTrudeau

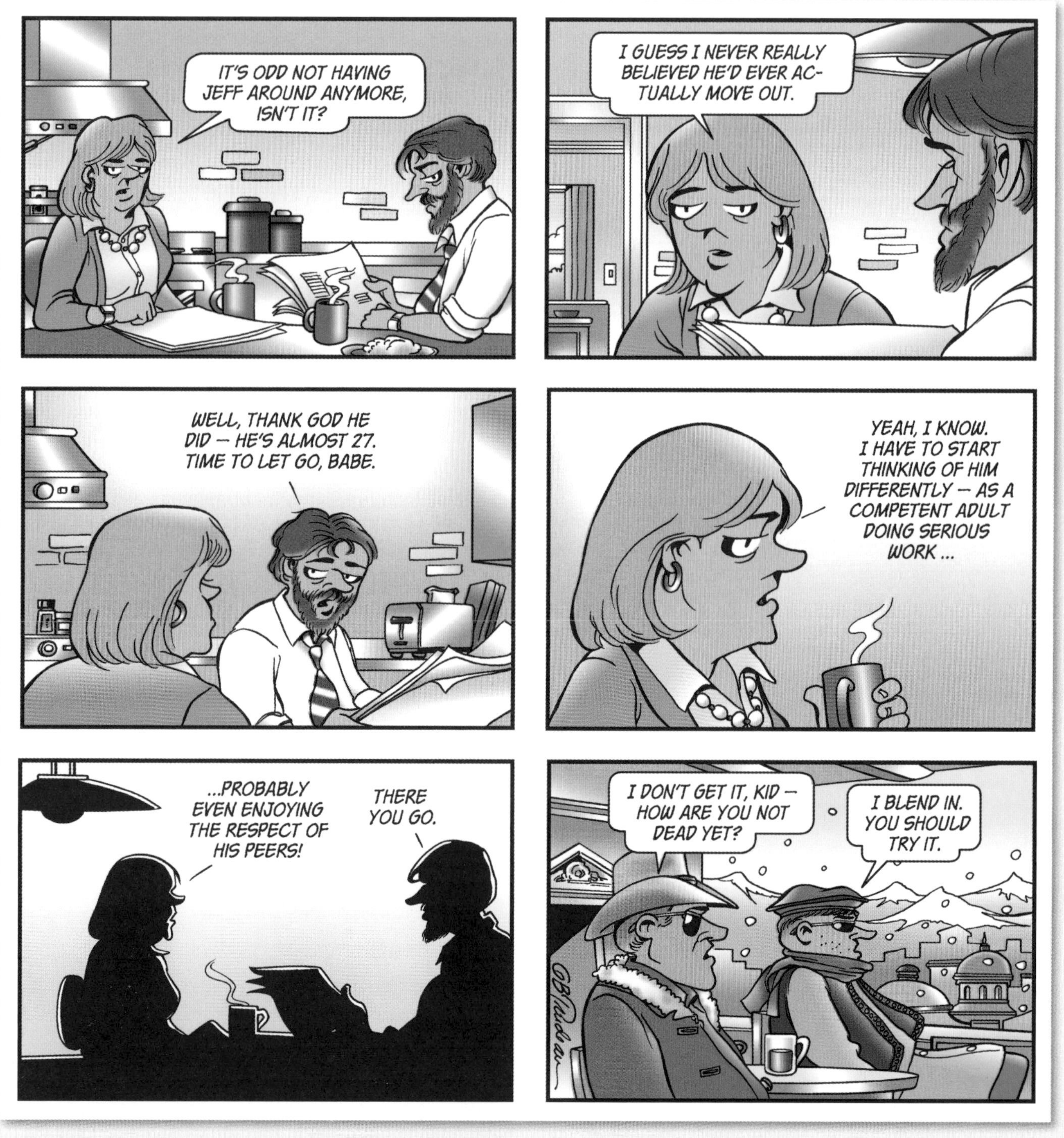
IT'S ODD NOT HAVING JEFF AROUND ANYMORE, ISN'T IT?
I GUESS I NEVER REALLY BELIEVED HE'D EVER ACTUALLY MOVE OUT.
WELL, THANK GOD HE DID — HE'S ALMOST 27. TIME TO LET GO, BABE.
YEAH, I KNOW. I HAVE TO START THINKING OF HIM DIFFERENTLY — AS A COMPETENT ADULT DOING SERIOUS WORK ...
...PROBABLY EVEN ENJOYING THE RESPECT OF HIS PEERS!
THERE YOU GO.
I DON'T GET IT, KID — HOW ARE YOU NOT DEAD YET?
I BLEND IN. YOU SHOULD TRY IT.
GBTrudeau

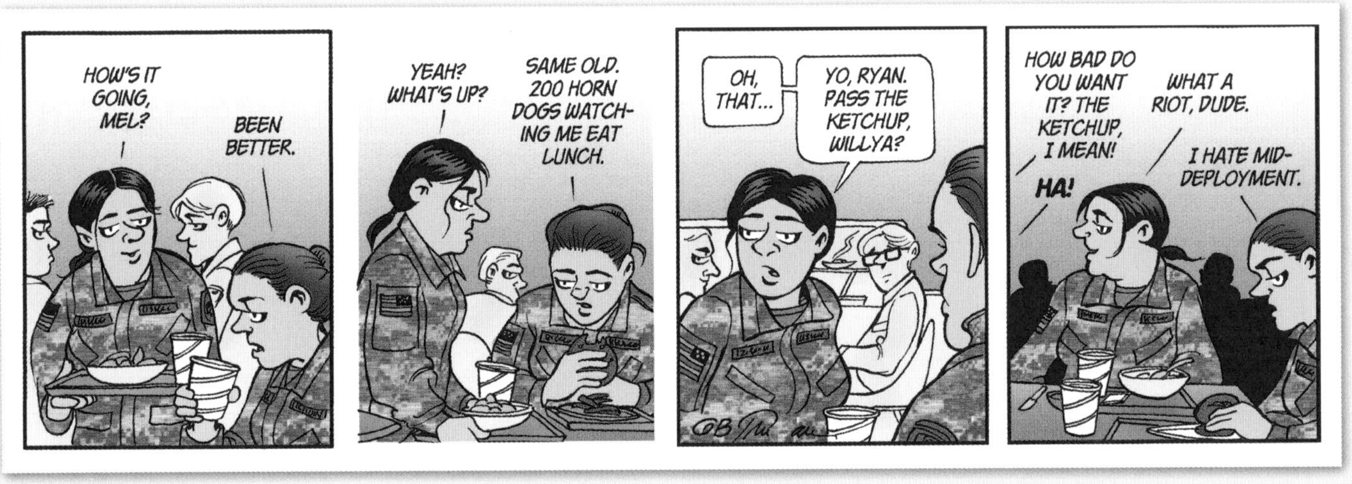
HOW'S IT GOING, MEL?
BEEN BETTER.
YEAH? WHAT'S UP?
SAME OLD. 200 HORN DOGS WATCHING ME EAT LUNCH.
OH, THAT...
YO, RYAN. PASS THE KETCHUP, WILLYA?
HOW BAD DO YOU WANT IT? THE KETCHUP, I MEAN!
HA!
WHAT A RIOT, DUDE.
I HATE MID-DEPLOYMENT.

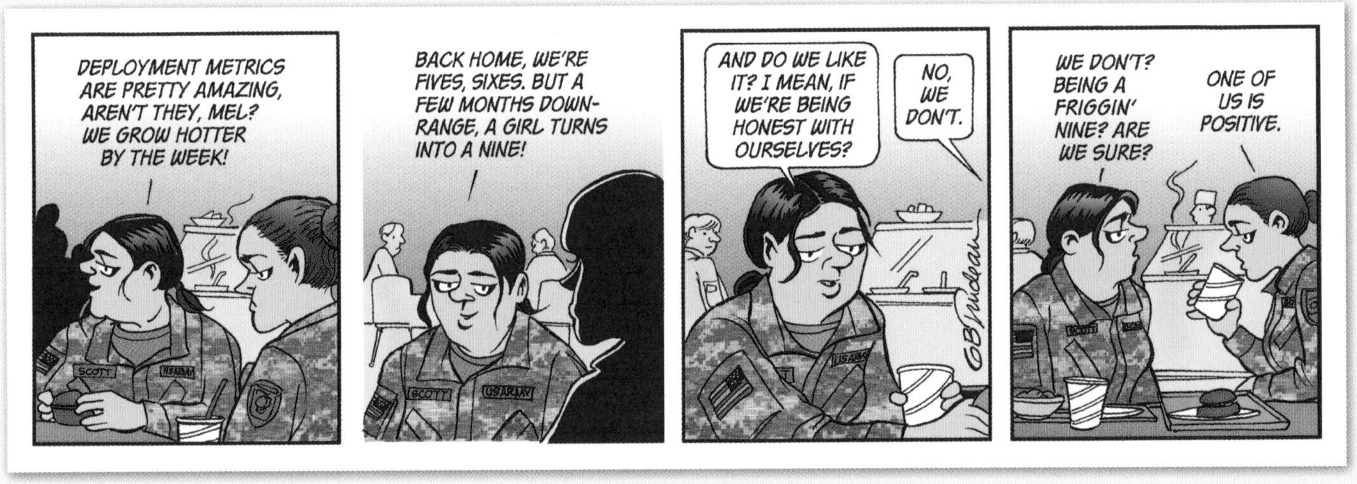
DEPLOYMENT METRICS ARE PRETTY AMAZING, AREN'T THEY, MEL? WE GROW HOTTER BY THE WEEK!
BACK HOME, WE'RE FIVES, SIXES. BUT A FEW MONTHS DOWN-RANGE, A GIRL TURNS INTO A NINE!
AND DO WE LIKE IT? I MEAN, IF WE'RE BEING HONEST WITH OURSELVES?
NO, WE DON'T.
WE DON'T? BEING A FRIGGIN' NINE? ARE WE SURE?
ONE OF US IS POSITIVE.

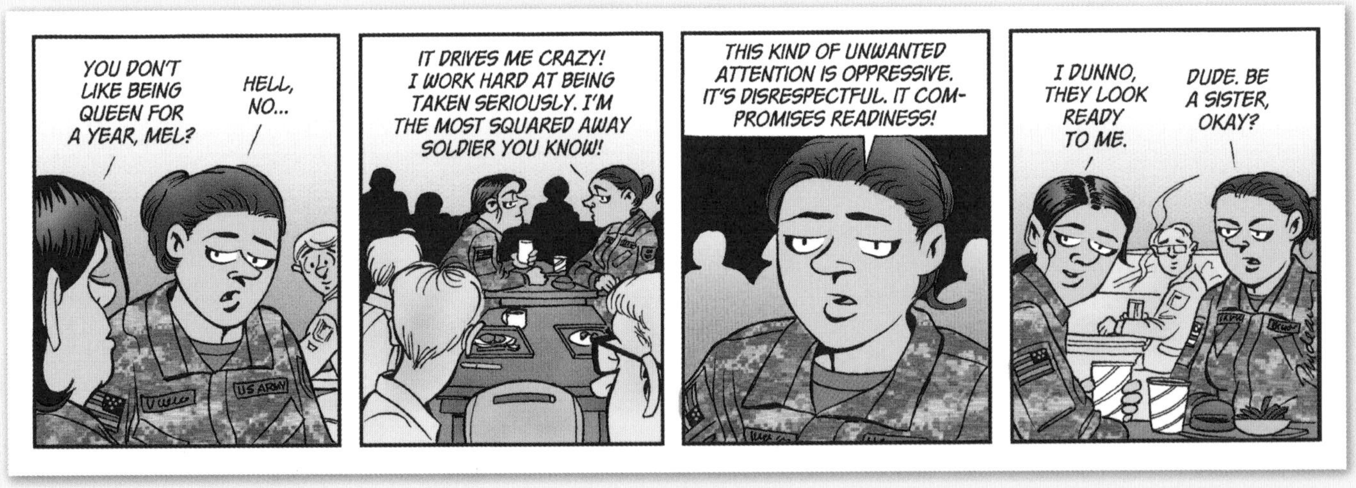
YOU DON'T LIKE BEING QUEEN FOR A YEAR, MEL?
HELL, NO...
IT DRIVES ME CRAZY! I WORK HARD AT BEING TAKEN SERIOUSLY. I'M THE MOST SQUARED AWAY SOLDIER YOU KNOW!
THIS KIND OF UNWANTED ATTENTION IS OPPRESSIVE. IT'S DISRESPECTFUL. IT COMPROMISES READINESS!
I DUNNO, THEY LOOK READY TO ME.
DUDE. BE A SISTER, OKAY?

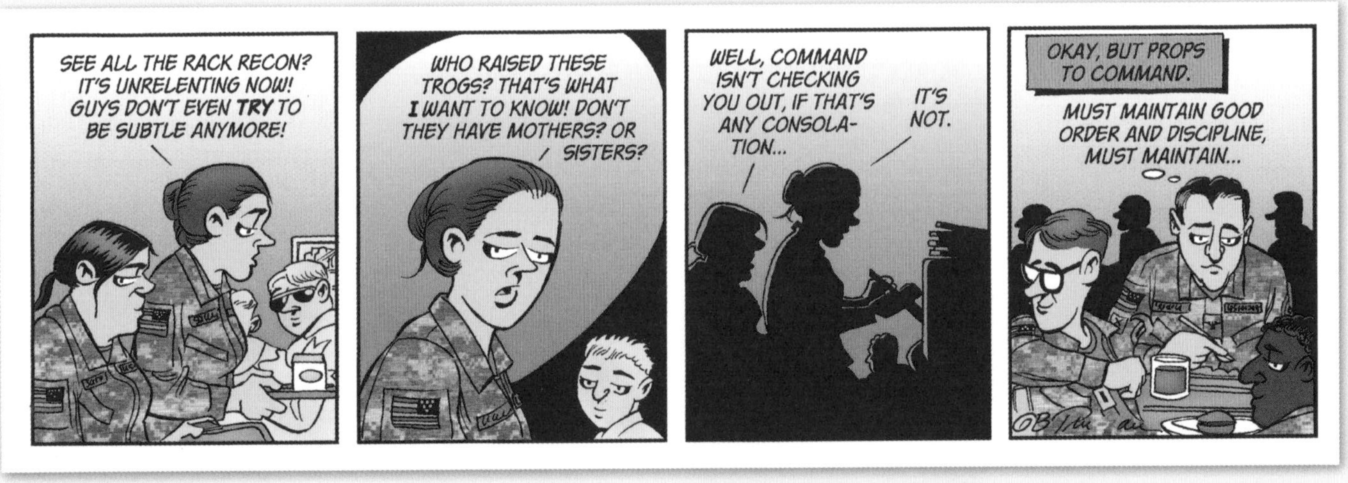
SEE ALL THE RACK RECON? IT'S UNRELENTING NOW! GUYS DON'T EVEN TRY TO BE SUBTLE ANYMORE!
WHO RAISED THESE TROGS? THAT'S WHAT I WANT TO KNOW! DON'T THEY HAVE MOTHERS? OR SISTERS?
WELL, COMMAND ISN'T CHECKING YOU OUT, IF THAT'S ANY CONSOLATION...
IT'S NOT.
OKAY, BUT PROPS TO COMMAND.
MUST MAINTAIN GOOD ORDER AND DISCIPLINE, MUST MAINTAIN...

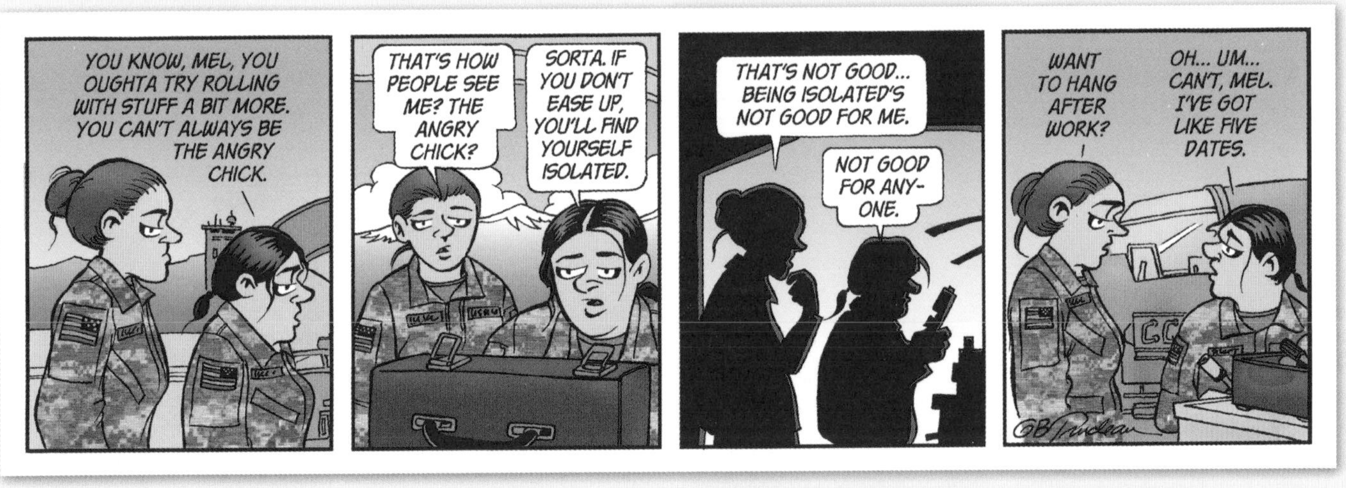
YOU KNOW, MEL, YOU OUGHTA TRY ROLLING WITH STUFF A BIT MORE. YOU CAN'T ALWAYS BE THE ANGRY CHICK.
THAT'S HOW PEOPLE SEE ME? THE ANGRY CHICK?
SORTA. IF YOU DON'T EASE UP, YOU'LL FIND YOURSELF ISOLATED.
THAT'S NOT GOOD... BEING ISOLATED'S NOT GOOD FOR ME.
NOT GOOD FOR ANYONE.
WANT TO HANG AFTER WORK?
OH... UM... CAN'T, MEL. I'VE GOT LIKE FIVE DATES.

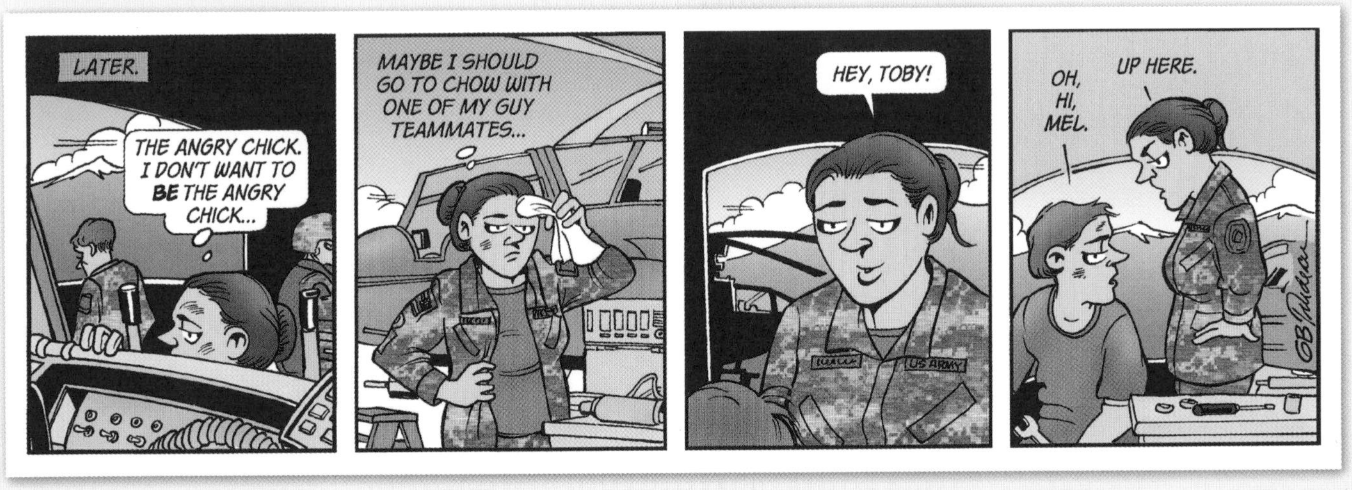
LATER.
THE ANGRY CHICK. I DON'T WANT TO BE THE ANGRY CHICK...
MAYBE I SHOULD GO TO CHOW WITH ONE OF MY GUY TEAMMATES...
HEY, TOBY!
OH, HI, MEL.
UP HERE.

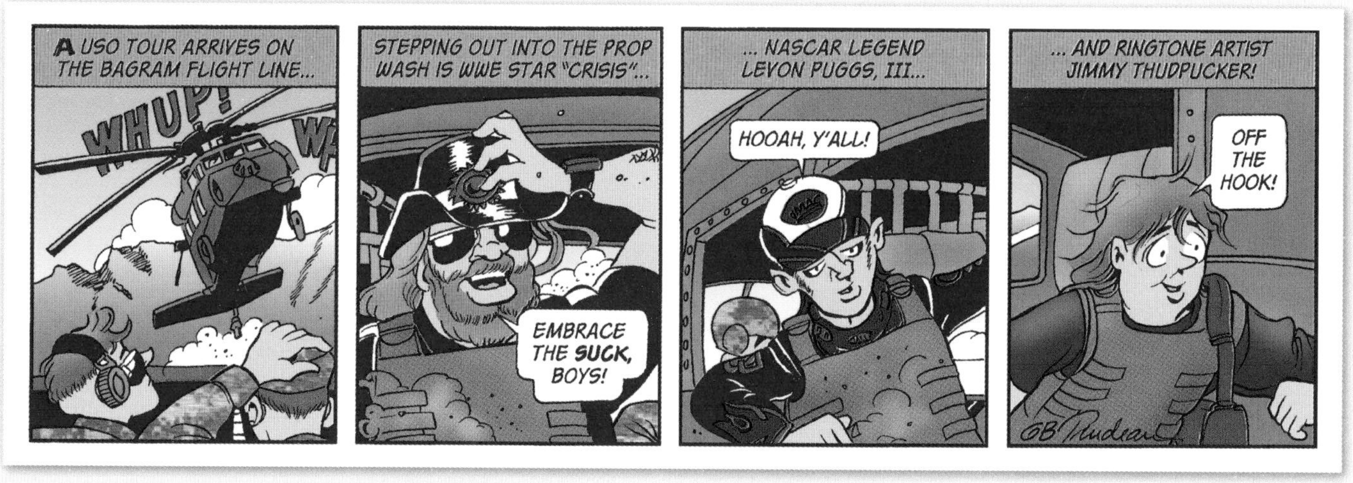
A USO TOUR ARRIVES ON THE BAGRAM FLIGHT LINE...
WHUP!
STEPPING OUT INTO THE PROP WASH IS WWE STAR "CRISIS"...
EMBRACE THE **SUCK,** BOYS!
... NASCAR LEGEND LEVON PUGGS, III...
HOOAH, Y'ALL!
... AND RINGTONE ARTIST JIMMY THUDPUCKER!
OFF THE HOOK!

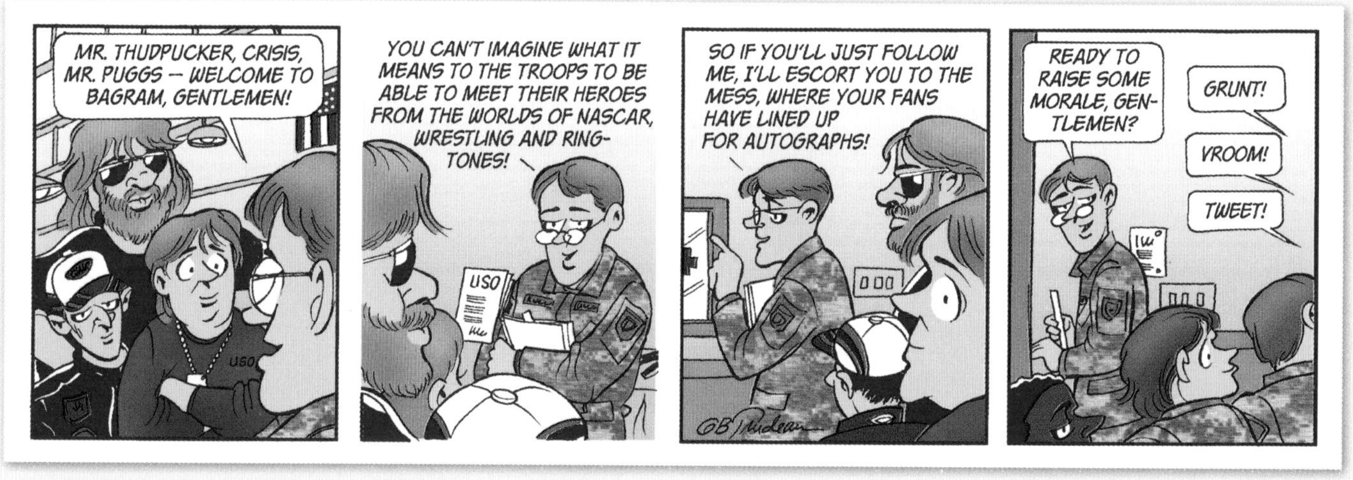
MR. THUDPUCKER, CRISIS, MR. PUGGS — WELCOME TO BAGRAM, GENTLEMEN!
YOU CAN'T IMAGINE WHAT IT MEANS TO THE TROOPS TO BE ABLE TO MEET THEIR HEROES FROM THE WORLDS OF NASCAR, WRESTLING AND RING-TONES!
USO
SO IF YOU'LL JUST FOLLOW ME, I'LL ESCORT YOU TO THE MESS, WHERE YOUR FANS HAVE LINED UP FOR AUTOGRAPHS!
READY TO RAISE SOME MORALE, GEN-TLEMEN?
GRUNT!
VROOM!
TWEET!

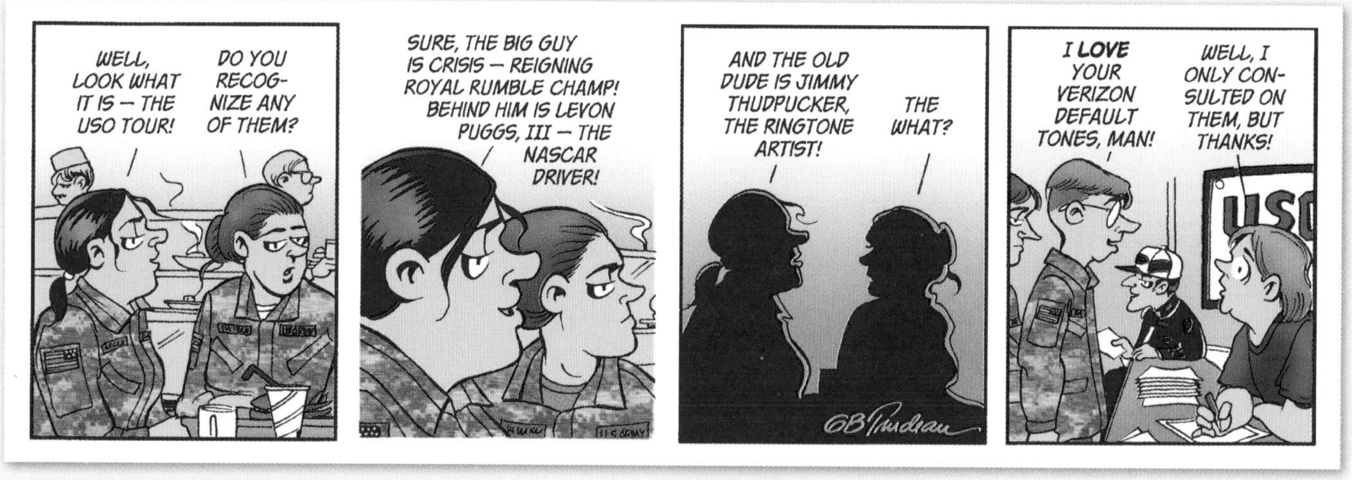
WELL, LOOK WHAT IT IS — THE USO TOUR!
DO YOU RECOG-NIZE ANY OF THEM?
SURE, THE BIG GUY IS CRISIS — REIGNING ROYAL RUMBLE CHAMP! BEHIND HIM IS LEVON PUGGS, III — THE NASCAR DRIVER!
AND THE OLD DUDE IS JIMMY THUDPUCKER, THE RINGTONE ARTIST!
THE WHAT?
I **LOVE** YOUR VERIZON DEFAULT TONES, MAN!
WELL, I ONLY CON-SULTED ON THEM, BUT THANKS!
USO

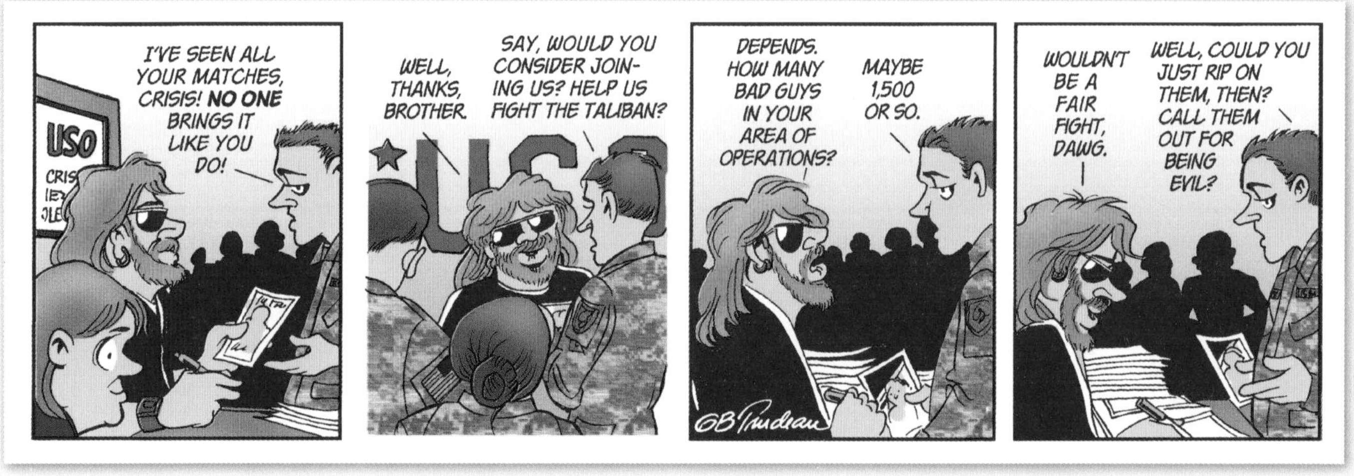
I'VE SEEN ALL YOUR MATCHES, CRISIS! **NO ONE** BRINGS IT LIKE YOU DO!
USO
WELL, THANKS, BROTHER.
SAY, WOULD YOU CONSIDER JOINING US? HELP US FIGHT THE TALIBAN?
DEPENDS. HOW MANY BAD GUYS IN YOUR AREA OF OPERATIONS?
MAYBE 1,500 OR SO.
WOULDN'T BE A FAIR FIGHT, DAWG.
WELL, COULD YOU JUST RIP ON THEM, THEN? CALL THEM OUT FOR BEING EVIL?
GB Trudeau

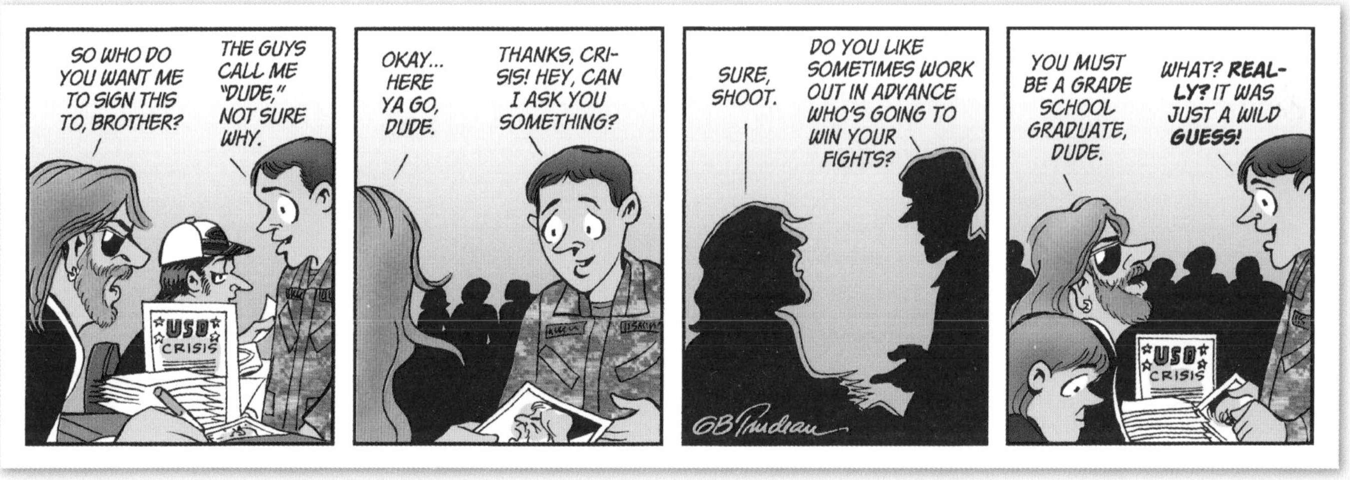
SO WHO DO YOU WANT ME TO SIGN THIS TO, BROTHER?
THE GUYS CALL ME "DUDE," NOT SURE WHY.
USO CRISIS
OKAY... HERE YA GO, DUDE.
THANKS, CRISIS! HEY, CAN I ASK YOU SOMETHING?
SURE, SHOOT.
DO YOU LIKE SOMETIMES WORK OUT IN ADVANCE WHO'S GOING TO WIN YOUR FIGHTS?
YOU MUST BE A GRADE SCHOOL GRADUATE, DUDE.
WHAT? **REALLY?** IT WAS JUST A WILD **GUESS!**
USO CRISIS
GB Trudeau

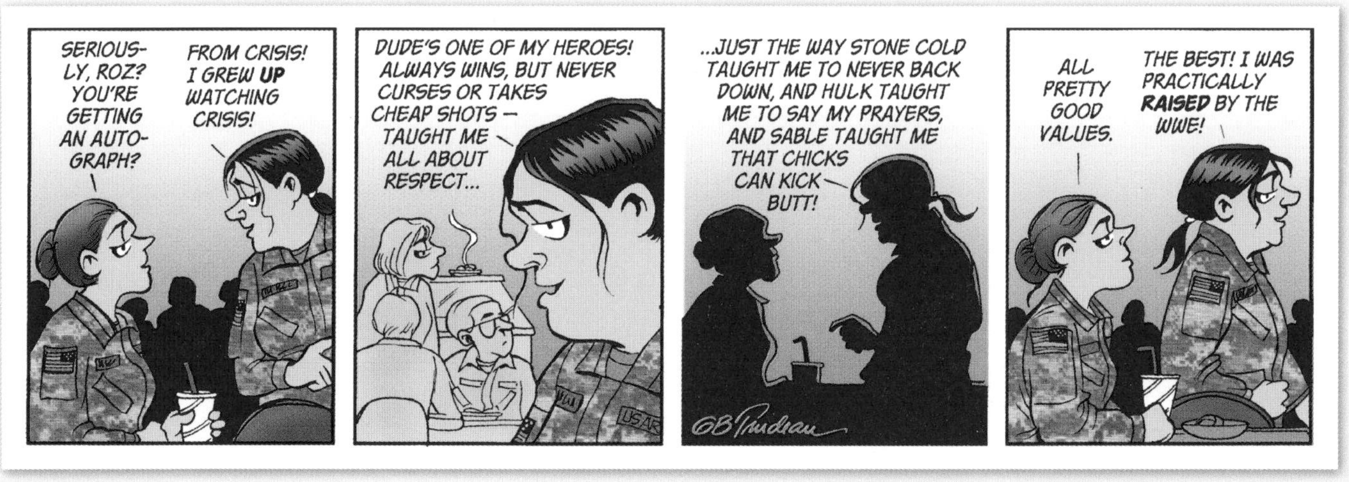
SERIOUSLY, ROZ? YOU'RE GETTING AN AUTOGRAPH?
FROM CRISIS! I GREW **UP** WATCHING CRISIS!
DUDE'S ONE OF MY HEROES! ALWAYS WINS, BUT NEVER CURSES OR TAKES CHEAP SHOTS — TAUGHT ME ALL ABOUT RESPECT...
...JUST THE WAY STONE COLD TAUGHT ME TO NEVER BACK DOWN, AND HULK TAUGHT ME TO SAY MY PRAYERS, AND SABLE TAUGHT ME THAT CHICKS CAN KICK BUTT!
ALL PRETTY GOOD VALUES.
THE BEST! I WAS PRACTICALLY **RAISED** BY THE WWE!
GB Trudeau

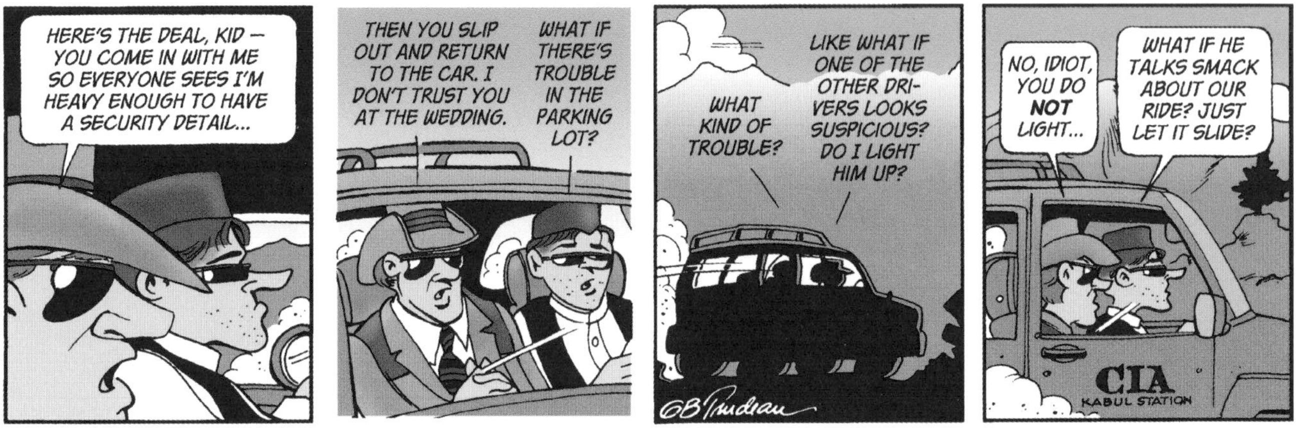
HERE'S THE DEAL, KID — YOU COME IN WITH ME SO EVERYONE SEES I'M HEAVY ENOUGH TO HAVE A SECURITY DETAIL...
THEN YOU SLIP OUT AND RETURN TO THE CAR. I DON'T TRUST YOU AT THE WEDDING.
WHAT IF THERE'S TROUBLE IN THE PARKING LOT?
WHAT KIND OF TROUBLE?
LIKE WHAT IF ONE OF THE OTHER DRIVERS LOOKS SUSPICIOUS? DO I LIGHT HIM UP?
GB Trudeau
NO, IDIOT, YOU DO **NOT** LIGHT...
WHAT IF HE TALKS SMACK ABOUT OUR RIDE? JUST LET IT SLIDE?
CIA
KABUL STATION

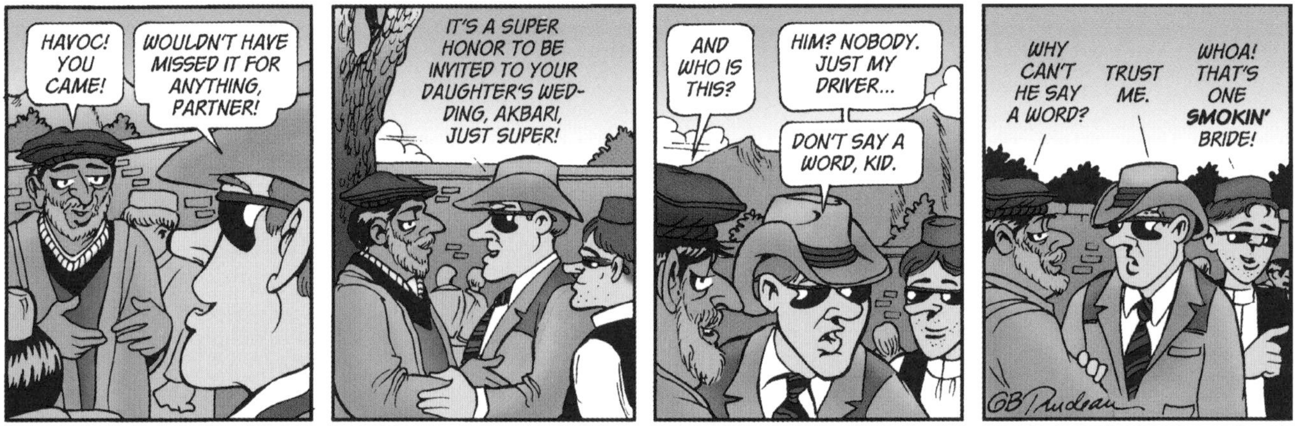
HAVOC! YOU CAME!
WOULDN'T HAVE MISSED IT FOR ANYTHING, PARTNER!
IT'S A SUPER HONOR TO BE INVITED TO YOUR DAUGHTER'S WEDDING, AKBARI, JUST SUPER!
AND WHO IS THIS?
HIM? NOBODY. JUST MY DRIVER...
DON'T SAY A WORD, KID.
WHY CAN'T HE SAY A WORD?
TRUST ME.
WHOA! THAT'S ONE **SMOKIN'** BRIDE!
GB Trudeau

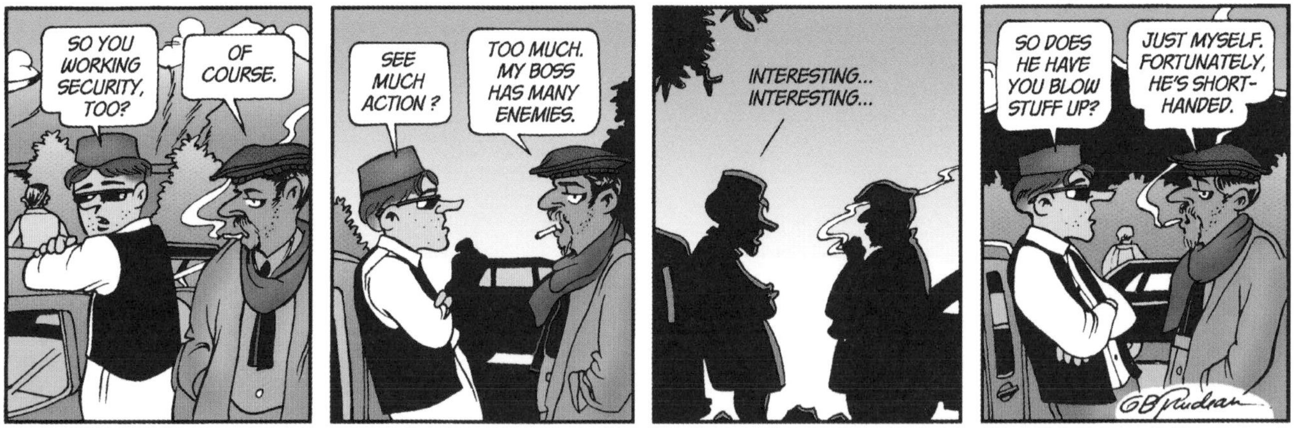
SO YOU WORKING SECURITY, TOO?
OF COURSE.
SEE MUCH ACTION ?
TOO MUCH. MY BOSS HAS MANY ENEMIES.
INTERESTING... INTERESTING...
SO DOES HE HAVE YOU BLOW STUFF UP?
JUST MYSELF. FORTUNATELY, HE'S SHORT-HANDED.
GB Trudeau

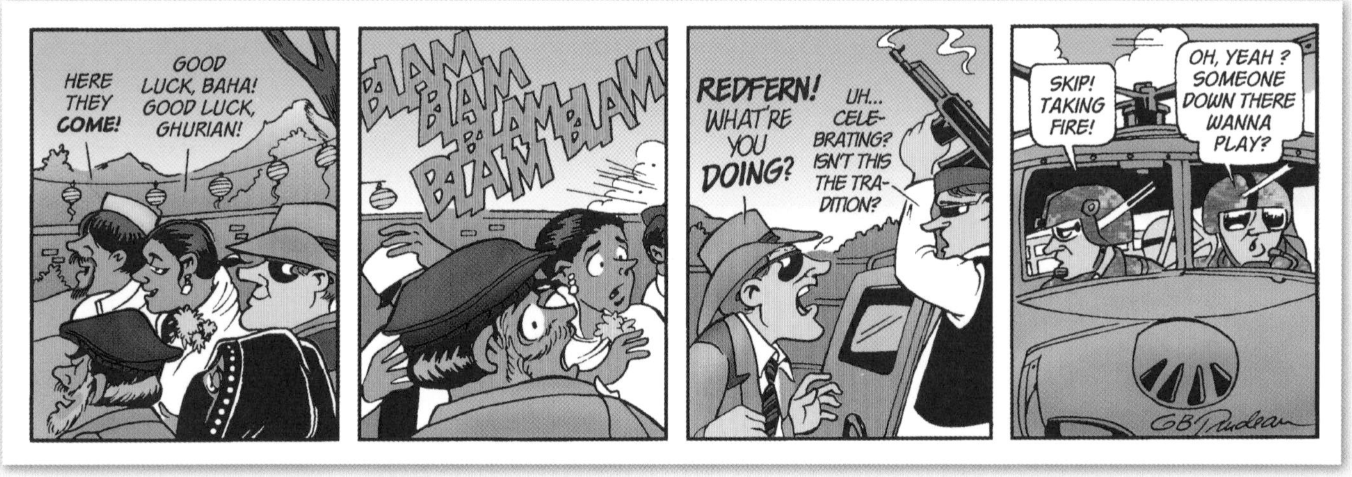
HERE THEY **COME!**
GOOD LUCK, BAHA! GOOD LUCK, GHURIAN!
BLAM BLAM BLAM BLAM BLAM BLAM!
REDFERN! WHAT'RE YOU **DOING?**
UH... CELEBRATING? ISN'T THIS THE TRADITION?
SKIP! TAKING FIRE!
OH, YEAH ? SOMEONE DOWN THERE WANNA PLAY?

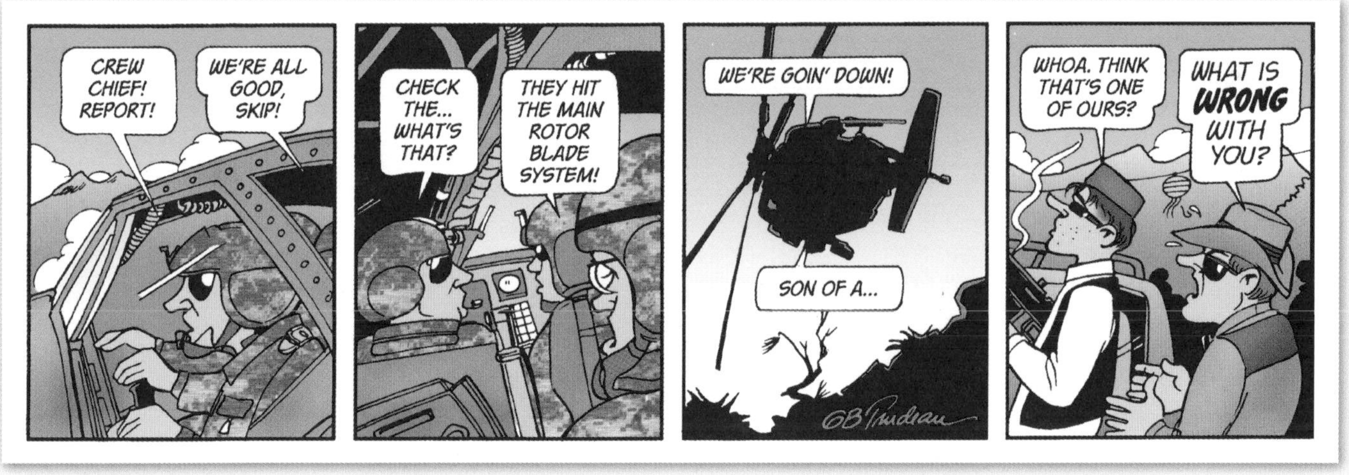
CREW CHIEF! REPORT!
WE'RE ALL GOOD, SKIP!
CHECK THE... WHAT'S THAT?
THEY HIT THE MAIN ROTOR BLADE SYSTEM!
WE'RE GOIN' DOWN!
SON OF A...
WHOA. THINK THAT'S ONE OF OURS?
WHAT IS **WRONG** WITH YOU?

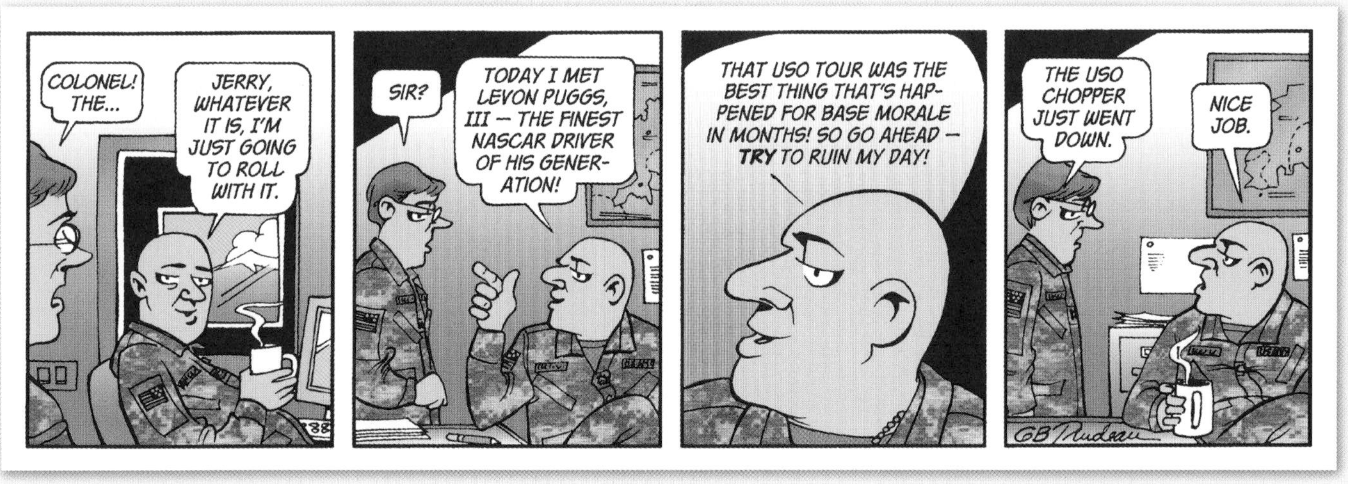
COLONEL! THE...
JERRY, WHATEVER IT IS, I'M JUST GOING TO ROLL WITH IT.
SIR?
TODAY I MET LEVON PUGGS, III — THE FINEST NASCAR DRIVER OF HIS GENERATION!
THAT USO TOUR WAS THE BEST THING THAT'S HAPPENED FOR BASE MORALE IN MONTHS! SO GO AHEAD — **TRY** TO RUIN MY DAY!
THE USO CHOPPER JUST WENT DOWN.
NICE JOB.

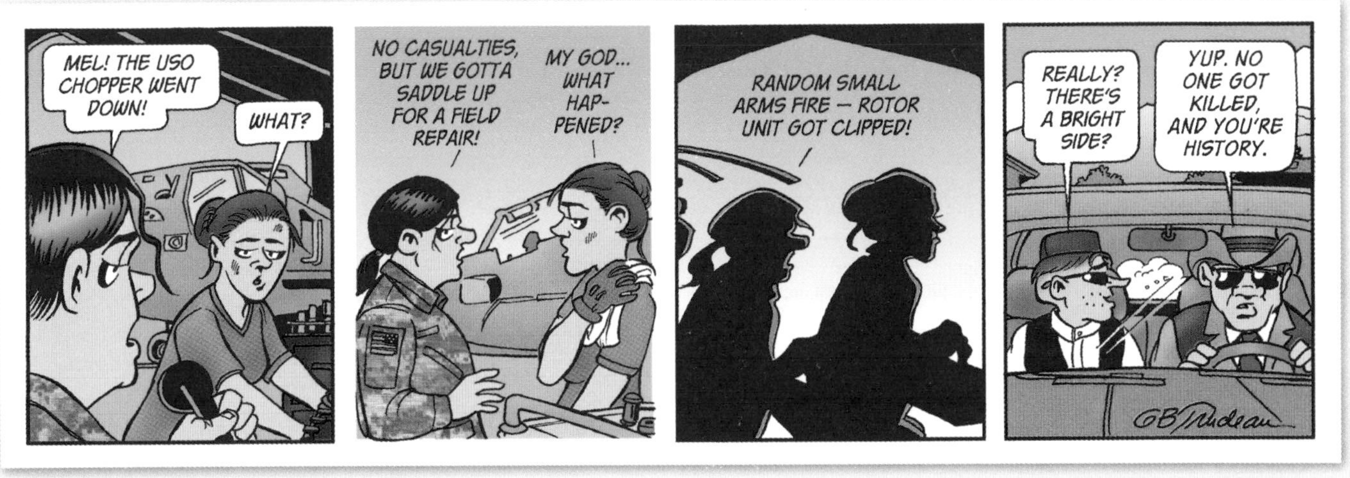
MEL! THE USO CHOPPER WENT DOWN!
WHAT?
NO CASUALTIES, BUT WE GOTTA SADDLE UP FOR A FIELD REPAIR!
MY GOD... WHAT HAP-PENED?
RANDOM SMALL ARMS FIRE — ROTOR UNIT GOT CLIPPED!
REALLY? THERE'S A BRIGHT SIDE?
YUP. NO ONE GOT KILLED, AND YOU'RE HISTORY.
GBTrudeau

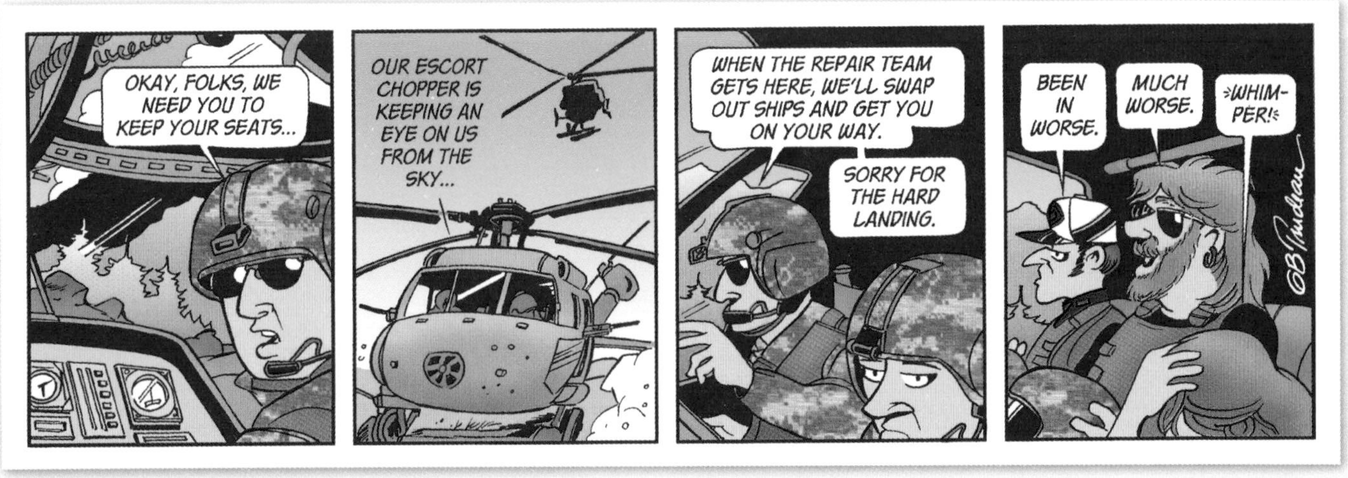
OKAY, FOLKS, WE NEED YOU TO KEEP YOUR SEATS...
OUR ESCORT CHOPPER IS KEEPING AN EYE ON US FROM THE SKY...
WHEN THE REPAIR TEAM GETS HERE, WE'LL SWAP OUT SHIPS AND GET YOU ON YOUR WAY.
SORRY FOR THE HARD LANDING.
BEEN IN WORSE.
MUCH WORSE.
WHIM-PER!
GBTrudeau

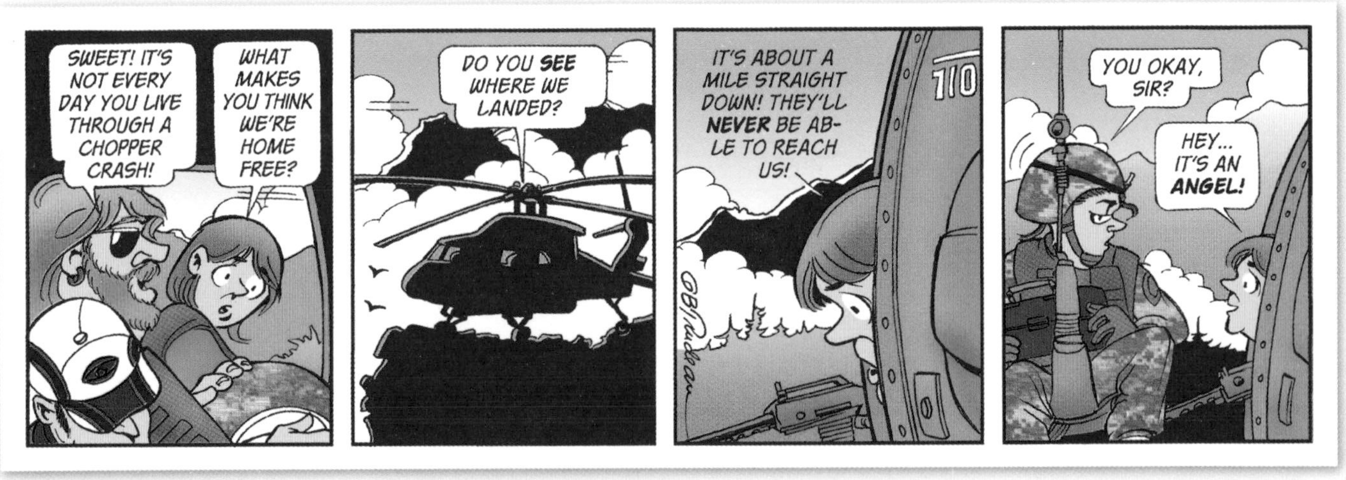
SWEET! IT'S NOT EVERY DAY YOU LIVE THROUGH A CHOPPER CRASH!
WHAT MAKES YOU THINK WE'RE HOME FREE?
DO YOU **SEE** WHERE WE LANDED?
IT'S ABOUT A MILE STRAIGHT DOWN! THEY'LL **NEVER** BE ABLE TO REACH US!
110
GBTrudeau
YOU OKAY, SIR?
HEY... IT'S AN **ANGEL!**

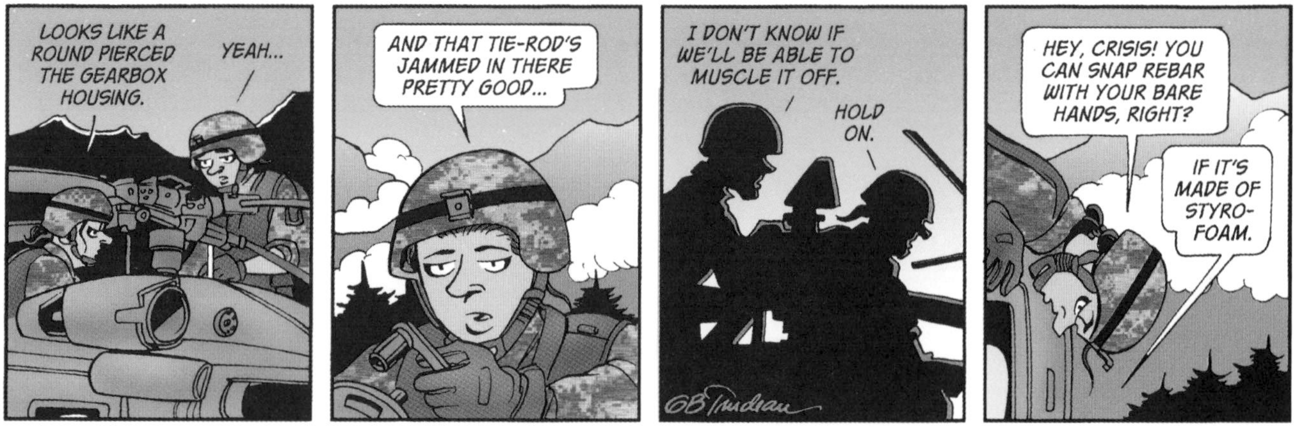
LOOKS LIKE A ROUND PIERCED THE GEARBOX HOUSING.
YEAH...
AND THAT TIE-ROD'S JAMMED IN THERE PRETTY GOOD...
I DON'T KNOW IF WE'LL BE ABLE TO MUSCLE IT OFF.
HOLD ON.
HEY, CRISIS! YOU CAN SNAP REBAR WITH YOUR BARE HANDS, RIGHT?
IF IT'S MADE OF STYRO-FOAM.
GB Trudeau

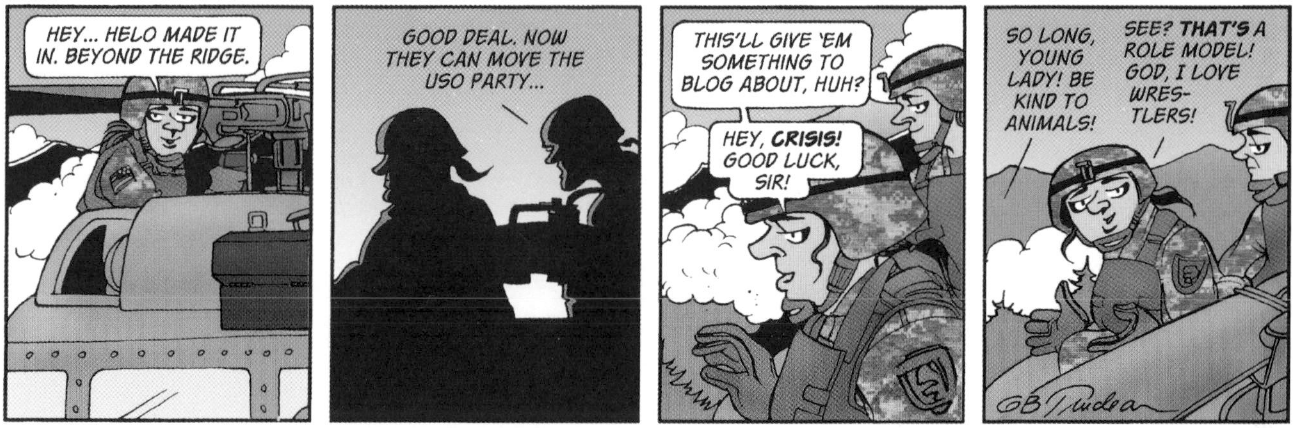
HEY... HELO MADE IT IN. BEYOND THE RIDGE.
GOOD DEAL. NOW THEY CAN MOVE THE USO PARTY...
THIS'LL GIVE 'EM SOMETHING TO BLOG ABOUT, HUH?
HEY, CRISIS! GOOD LUCK, SIR!
SO LONG, YOUNG LADY! BE KIND TO ANIMALS!
SEE? THAT'S A ROLE MODEL! GOD, I LOVE WRES-TLERS!
GB Trudeau

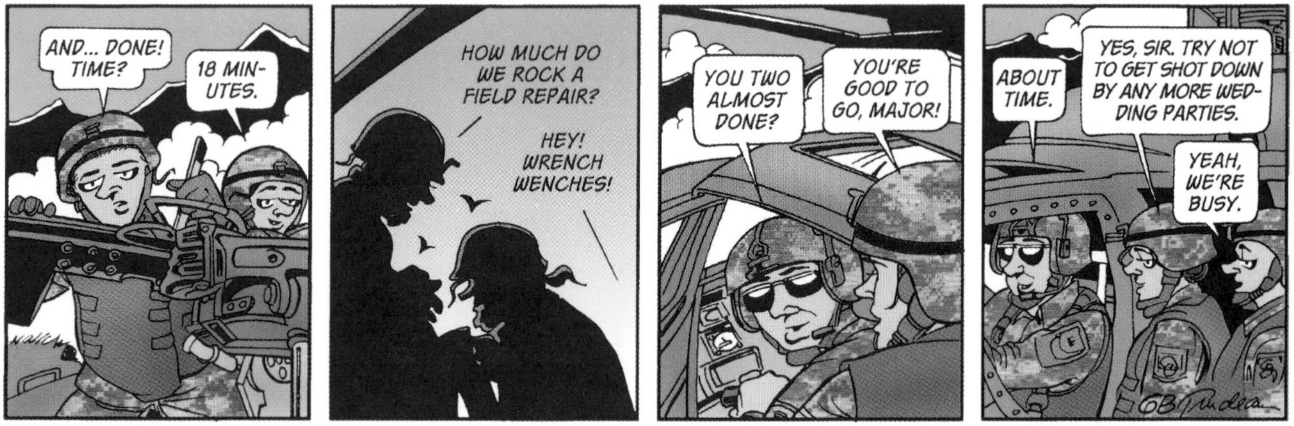
AND... DONE! TIME?
18 MIN-UTES.
HOW MUCH DO WE ROCK A FIELD REPAIR?
HEY! WRENCH WENCHES!
YOU TWO ALMOST DONE?
YOU'RE GOOD TO GO, MAJOR!
ABOUT TIME.
YES, SIR. TRY NOT TO GET SHOT DOWN BY ANY MORE WED-DING PARTIES.
YEAH, WE'RE BUSY.
GB Trudeau

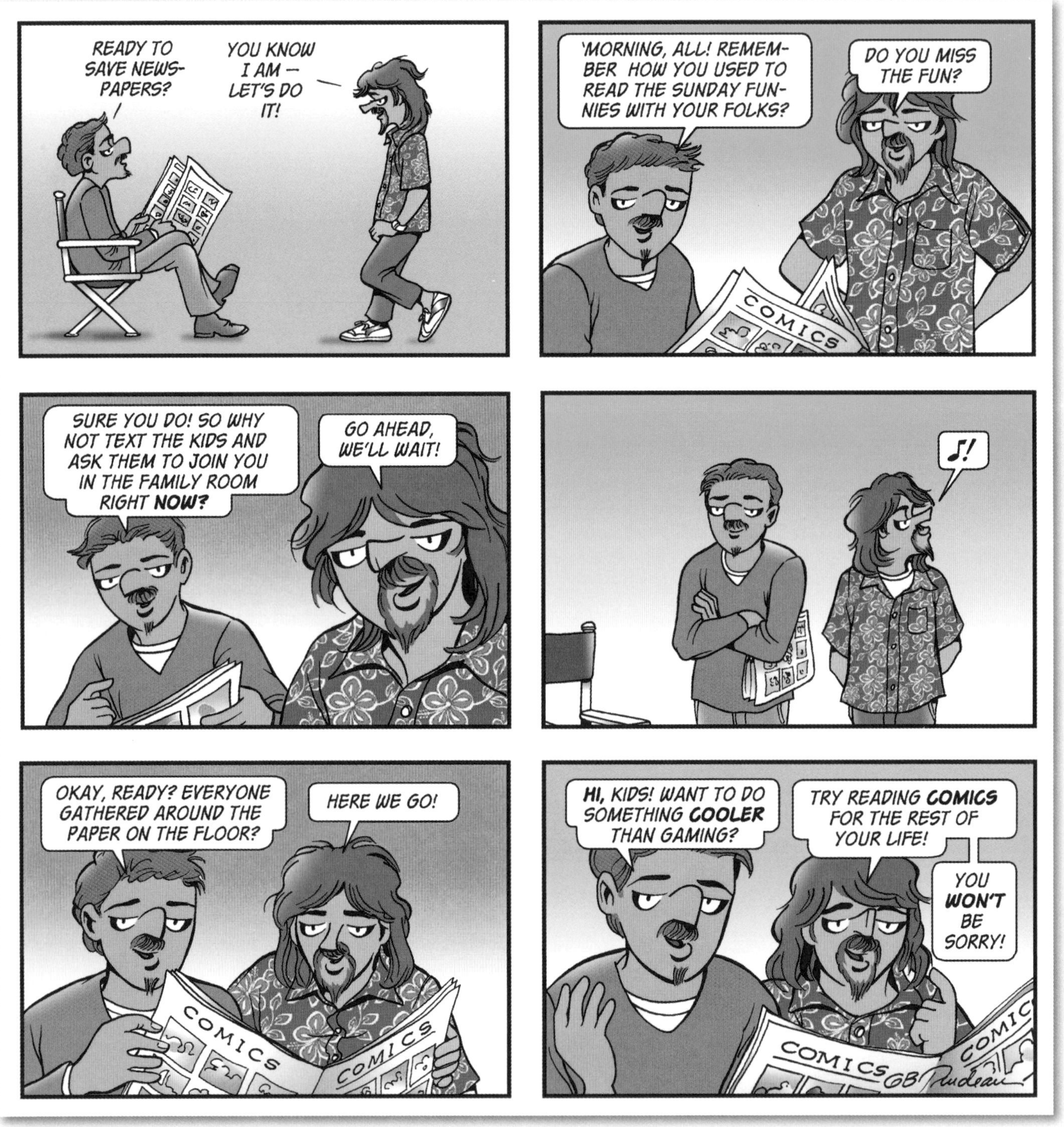
READY TO SAVE NEWS-PAPERS?
YOU KNOW I AM — LET'S DO IT!
'MORNING, ALL! REMEM-BER HOW YOU USED TO READ THE SUNDAY FUN-NIES WITH YOUR FOLKS?
DO YOU MISS THE FUN?
COMICS
SURE YOU DO! SO WHY NOT TEXT THE KIDS AND ASK THEM TO JOIN YOU IN THE FAMILY ROOM RIGHT **NOW?**
GO AHEAD, WE'LL WAIT!
♪!
OKAY, READY? EVERYONE GATHERED AROUND THE PAPER ON THE FLOOR?
HERE WE GO!
COMICS
COMICS
HI, KIDS! WANT TO DO SOMETHING **COOLER** THAN GAMING?
TRY READING **COMICS** FOR THE REST OF YOUR LIFE!
YOU **WON'T** BE SORRY!
COMICS
COMIC
GBTrudeau

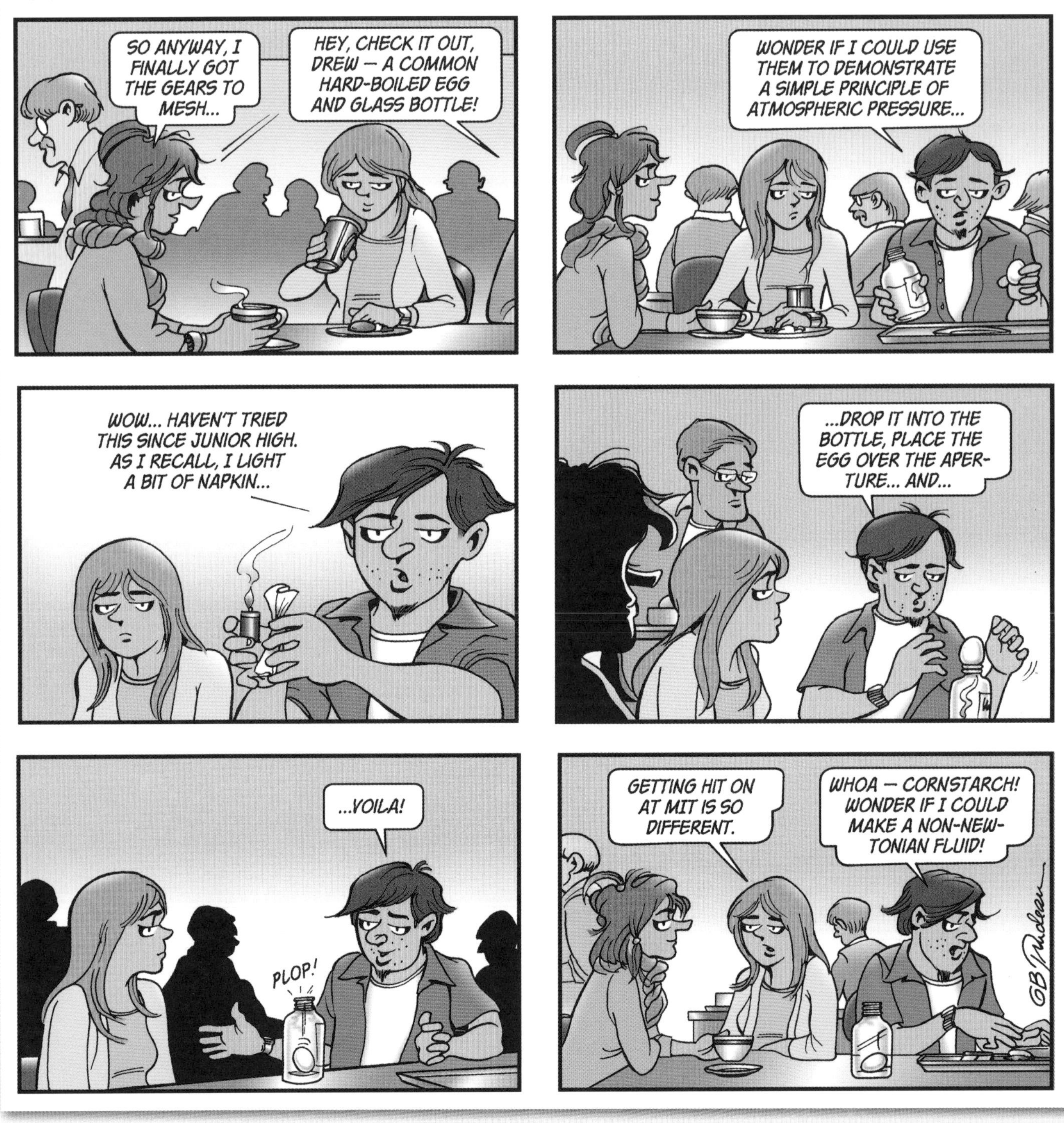
SO ANYWAY, I FINALLY GOT THE GEARS TO MESH...
HEY, CHECK IT OUT, DREW — A COMMON HARD-BOILED EGG AND GLASS BOTTLE!
WONDER IF I COULD USE THEM TO DEMONSTRATE A SIMPLE PRINCIPLE OF ATMOSPHERIC PRESSURE...
WOW... HAVEN'T TRIED THIS SINCE JUNIOR HIGH. AS I RECALL, I LIGHT A BIT OF NAPKIN...
...DROP IT INTO THE BOTTLE, PLACE THE EGG OVER THE APERTURE... AND...
...VOILA!
PLOP!
GETTING HIT ON AT MIT IS SO DIFFERENT.
WHOA — CORNSTARCH! WONDER IF I COULD MAKE A NON-NEWTONIAN FLUID!
GB Trudeau

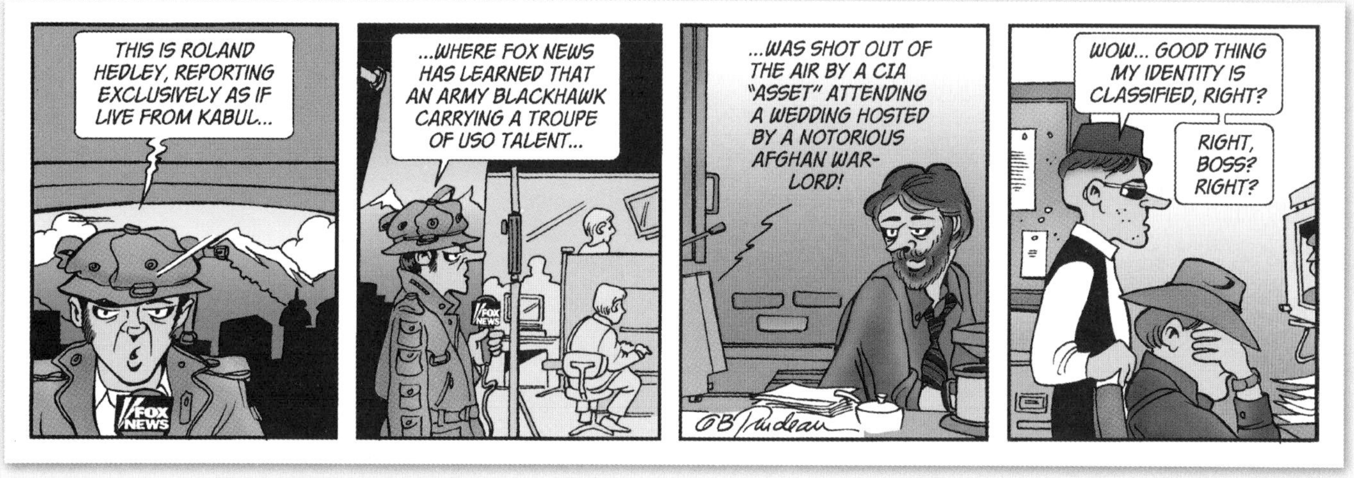
THIS IS ROLAND HEDLEY, REPORTING EXCLUSIVELY AS IF LIVE FROM KABUL...
...WHERE FOX NEWS HAS LEARNED THAT AN ARMY BLACKHAWK CARRYING A TROUPE OF USO TALENT...
...WAS SHOT OUT OF THE AIR BY A CIA "ASSET" ATTENDING A WEDDING HOSTED BY A NOTORIOUS AFGHAN WAR-LORD!
WOW... GOOD THING MY IDENTITY IS CLASSIFIED, RIGHT?
RIGHT, BOSS? RIGHT?

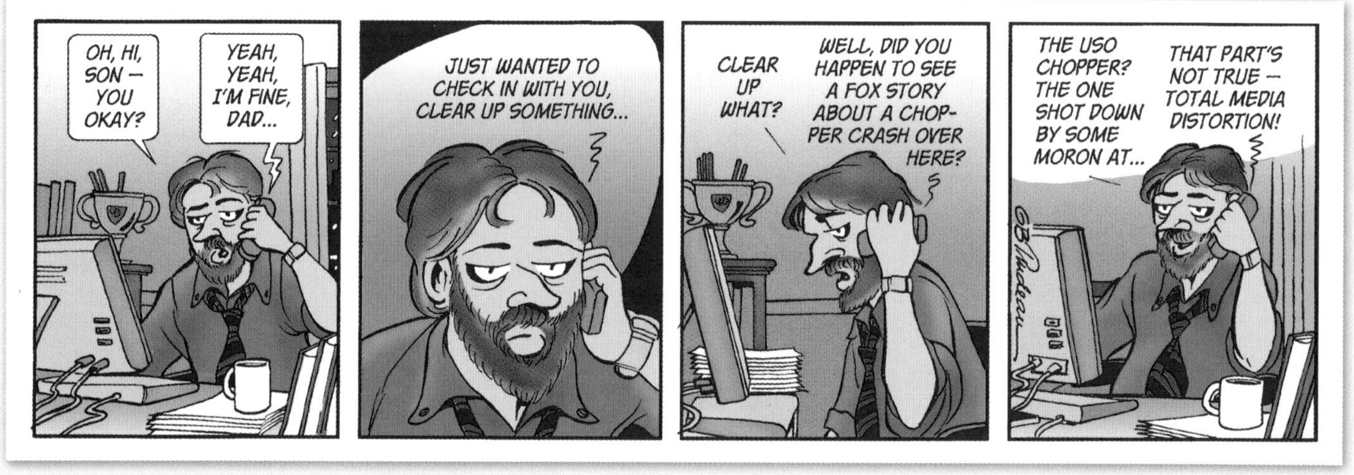
OH, HI, SON — YOU OKAY?
YEAH, YEAH, I'M FINE, DAD...
JUST WANTED TO CHECK IN WITH YOU, CLEAR UP SOMETHING...
CLEAR UP WHAT?
WELL, DID YOU HAPPEN TO SEE A FOX STORY ABOUT A CHOP-PER CRASH OVER HERE?
THE USO CHOPPER? THE ONE SHOT DOWN BY SOME MORON AT...
THAT PART'S NOT TRUE — TOTAL MEDIA DISTORTION!

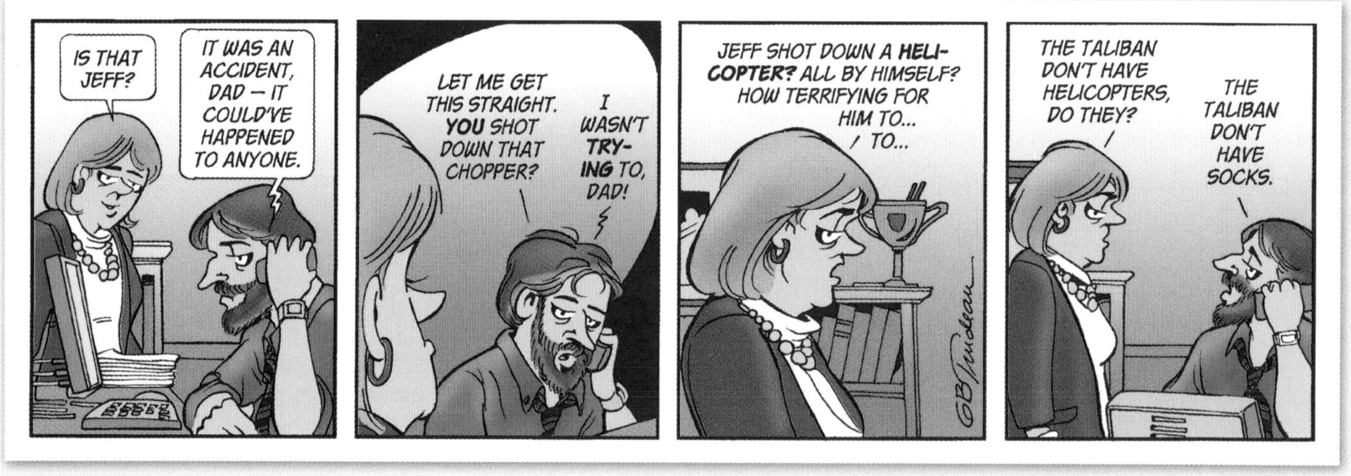
IS THAT JEFF?
IT WAS AN ACCIDENT, DAD — IT COULD'VE HAPPENED TO ANYONE.
LET ME GET THIS STRAIGHT. YOU SHOT DOWN THAT CHOPPER?
I WASN'T TRY-ING TO, DAD!
JEFF SHOT DOWN A HELI-COPTER? ALL BY HIMSELF? HOW TERRIFYING FOR HIM TO...
TO...
THE TALIBAN DON'T HAVE HELICOPTERS, DO THEY?
THE TALIBAN DON'T HAVE SOCKS.

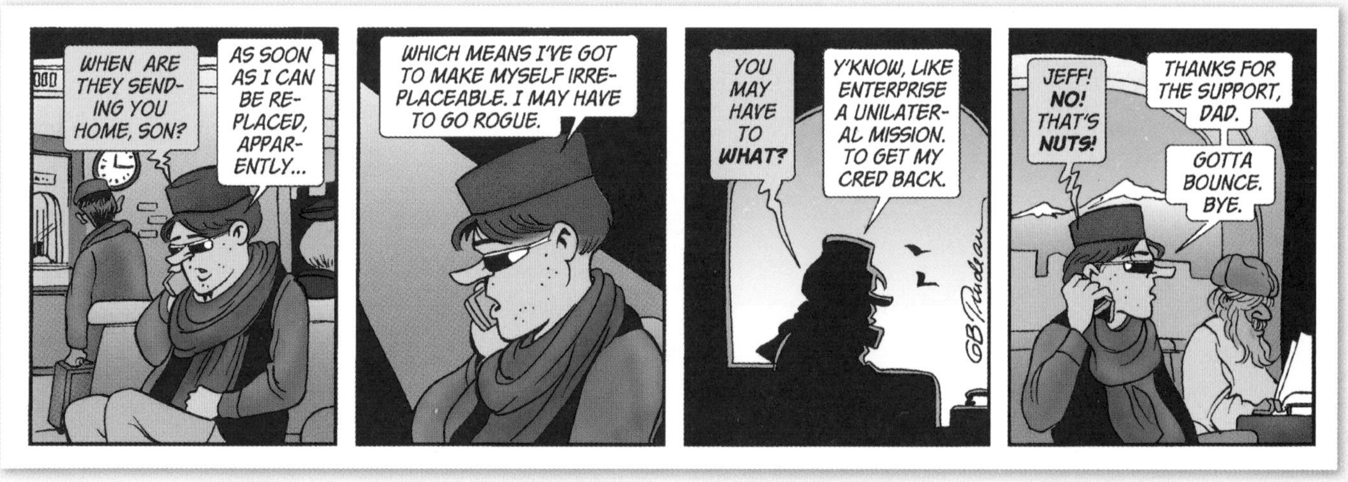
WHEN ARE THEY SENDING YOU HOME, SON?
AS SOON AS I CAN BE REPLACED, APPARENTLY...
WHICH MEANS I'VE GOT TO MAKE MYSELF IRREPLACEABLE. I MAY HAVE TO GO ROGUE.
YOU MAY HAVE TO **WHAT?**
Y'KNOW, LIKE ENTERPRISE A UNILATERAL MISSION. TO GET MY CRED BACK.
GB Trudeau
JEFF! **NO!** THAT'S **NUTS!**
THANKS FOR THE SUPPORT, DAD.
GOTTA BOUNCE. BYE.

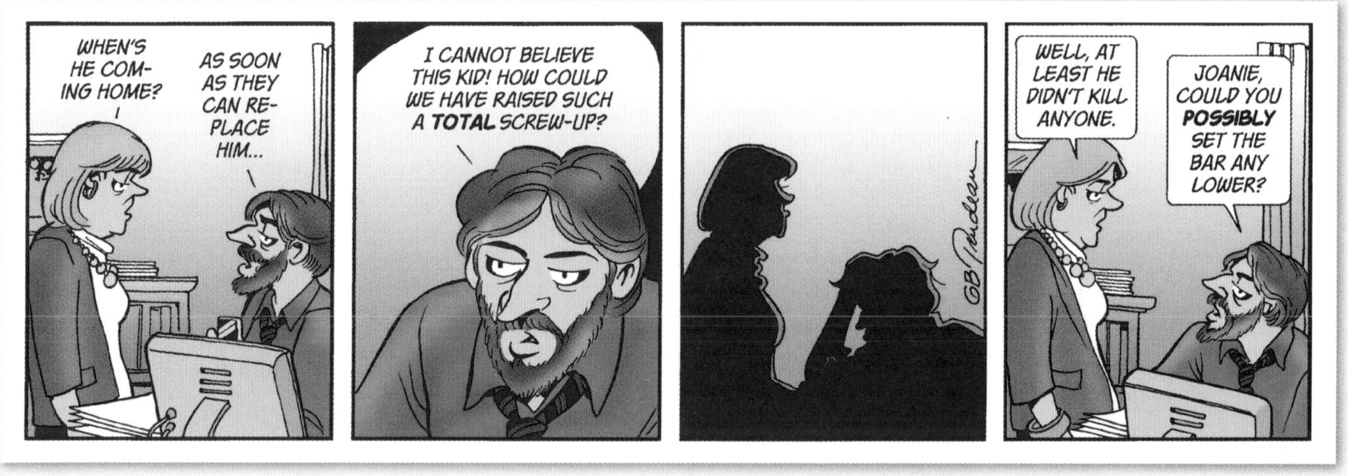
WHEN'S HE COMING HOME?
AS SOON AS THEY CAN REPLACE HIM...
I CANNOT BELIEVE THIS KID! HOW COULD WE HAVE RAISED SUCH A **TOTAL** SCREW-UP?
GB Trudeau
WELL, AT LEAST HE DIDN'T KILL ANYONE.
JOANIE, COULD YOU **POSSIBLY** SET THE BAR ANY LOWER?

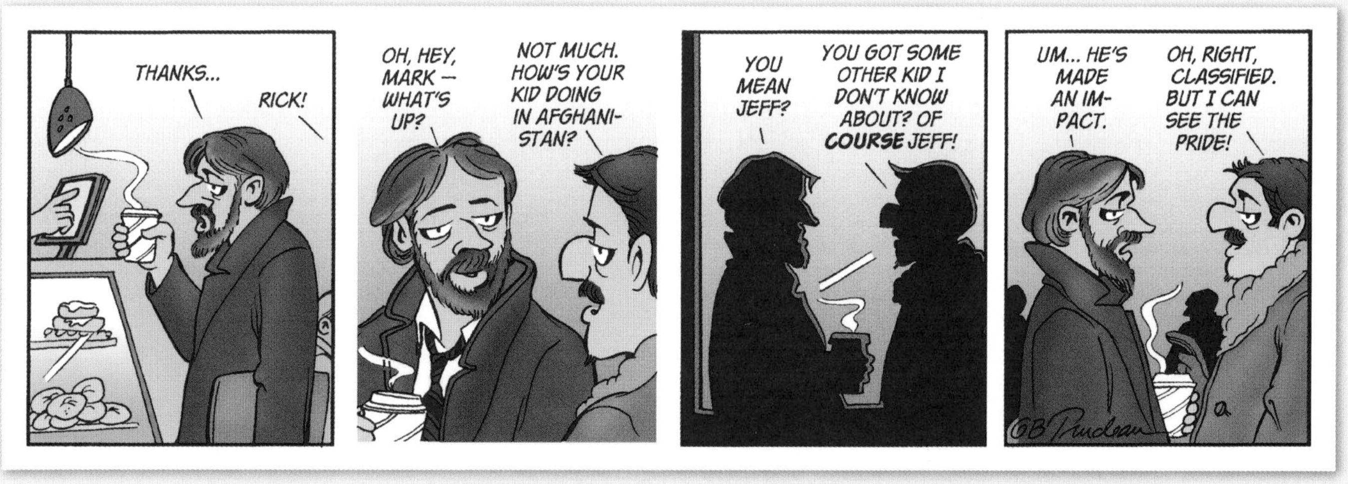
THANKS...
RICK!
OH, HEY, MARK — WHAT'S UP?
NOT MUCH. HOW'S YOUR KID DOING IN AFGHANISTAN?
YOU MEAN JEFF?
YOU GOT SOME OTHER KID I DON'T KNOW ABOUT? OF **COURSE** JEFF!
UM... HE'S MADE AN IMPACT.
OH, RIGHT, CLASSIFIED. BUT I CAN SEE THE PRIDE!
GB Trudeau

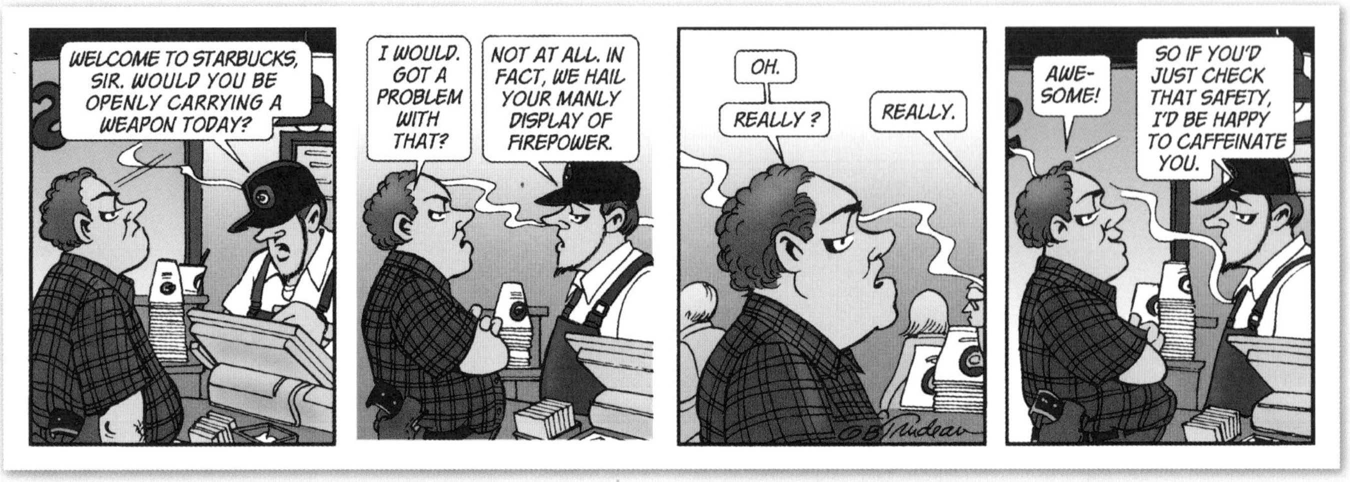
WELCOME TO STARBUCKS, SIR. WOULD YOU BE OPENLY CARRYING A WEAPON TODAY?
I WOULD. GOT A PROBLEM WITH THAT?
NOT AT ALL. IN FACT, WE HAIL YOUR MANLY DISPLAY OF FIREPOWER.
OH.
REALLY ?
REALLY.
AWE-SOME!
SO IF YOU'D JUST CHECK THAT SAFETY, I'D BE HAPPY TO CAFFEINATE YOU.

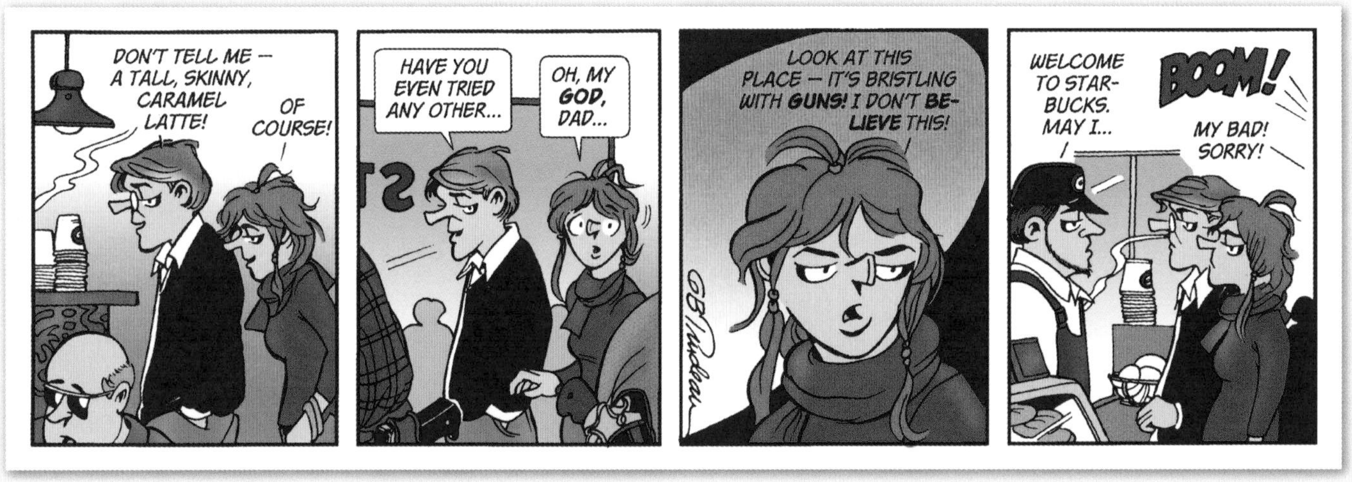
DON'T TELL ME — A TALL, SKINNY, CARAMEL LATTE!
OF COURSE!
HAVE YOU EVEN TRIED ANY OTHER...
OH, MY **GOD,** DAD...
LOOK AT THIS PLACE — IT'S BRISTLING WITH **GUNS!** I DON'T **BE-LIEVE** THIS!
WELCOME TO STAR-BUCKS. MAY I...
BOOM!
MY BAD! SORRY!

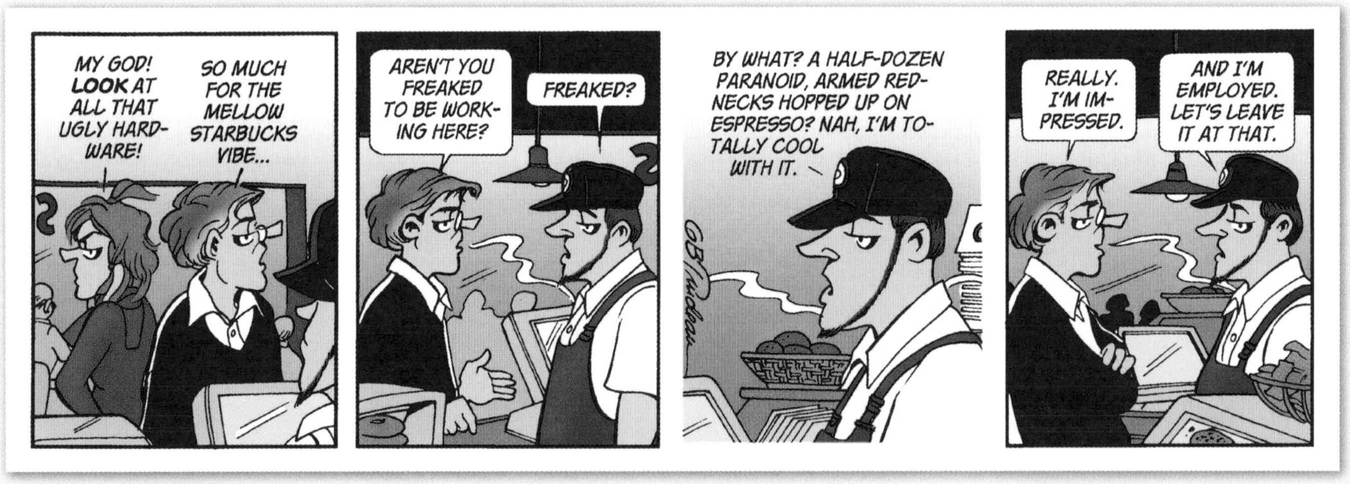
MY GOD! **LOOK** AT ALL THAT UGLY HARD-WARE!
SO MUCH FOR THE MELLOW STARBUCKS VIBE...
AREN'T YOU FREAKED TO BE WORK-ING HERE?
FREAKED?
BY WHAT? A HALF-DOZEN PARANOID, ARMED RED-NECKS HOPPED UP ON ESPRESSO? NAH, I'M TO-TALLY COOL WITH IT.
REALLY. I'M IM-PRESSED.
AND I'M EMPLOYED. LET'S LEAVE IT AT THAT.

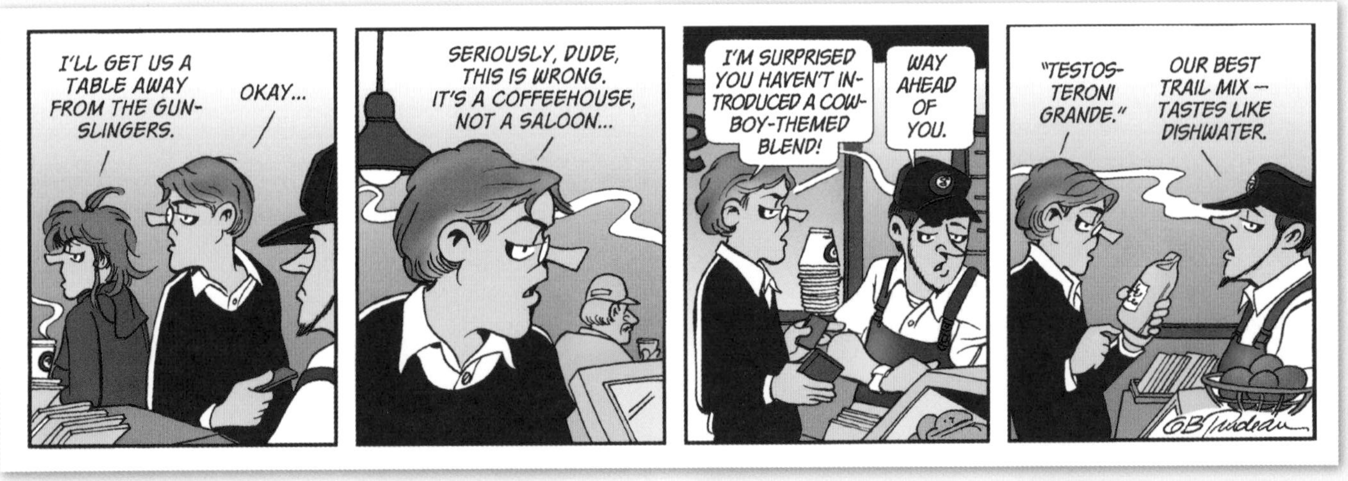
I'LL GET US A TABLE AWAY FROM THE GUN-SLINGERS.
OKAY...
SERIOUSLY, DUDE, THIS IS WRONG. IT'S A COFFEEHOUSE, NOT A SALOON...
I'M SURPRISED YOU HAVEN'T IN-TRODUCED A COW-BOY-THEMED BLEND!
WAY AHEAD OF YOU.
"TESTOS-TERONI GRANDE."
OUR BEST TRAIL MIX — TASTES LIKE DISHWATER.

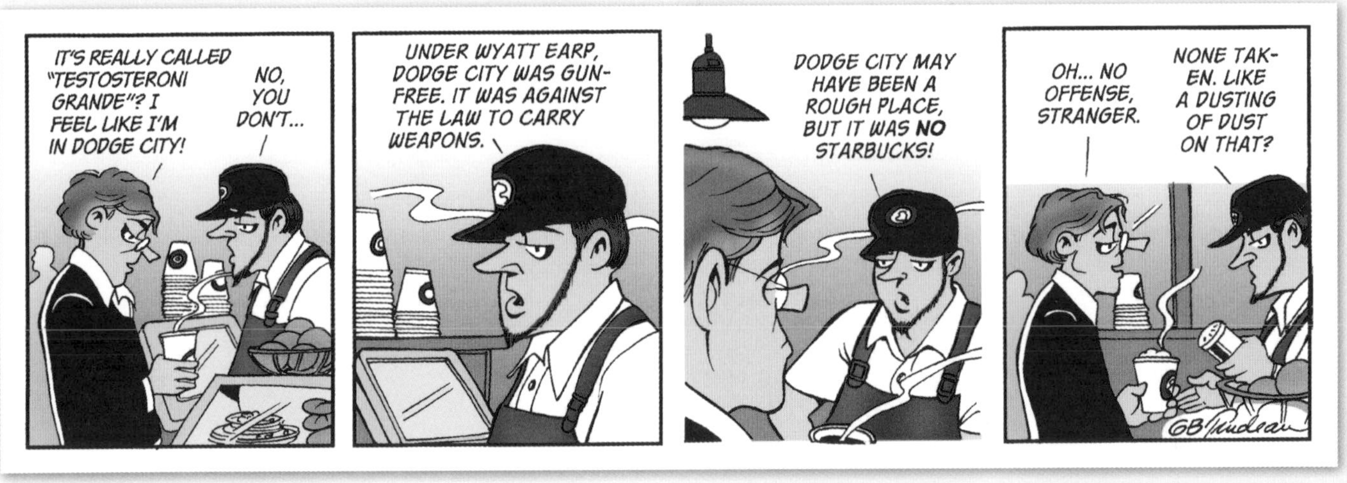
IT'S REALLY CALLED "TESTOSTERONI GRANDE"? I FEEL LIKE I'M IN DODGE CITY!
NO, YOU DON'T...
UNDER WYATT EARP, DODGE CITY WAS GUN-FREE. IT WAS AGAINST THE LAW TO CARRY WEAPONS.
DODGE CITY MAY HAVE BEEN A ROUGH PLACE, BUT IT WAS **NO** STARBUCKS!
OH... NO OFFENSE, STRANGER.
NONE TAK-EN. LIKE A DUSTING OF DUST ON THAT?

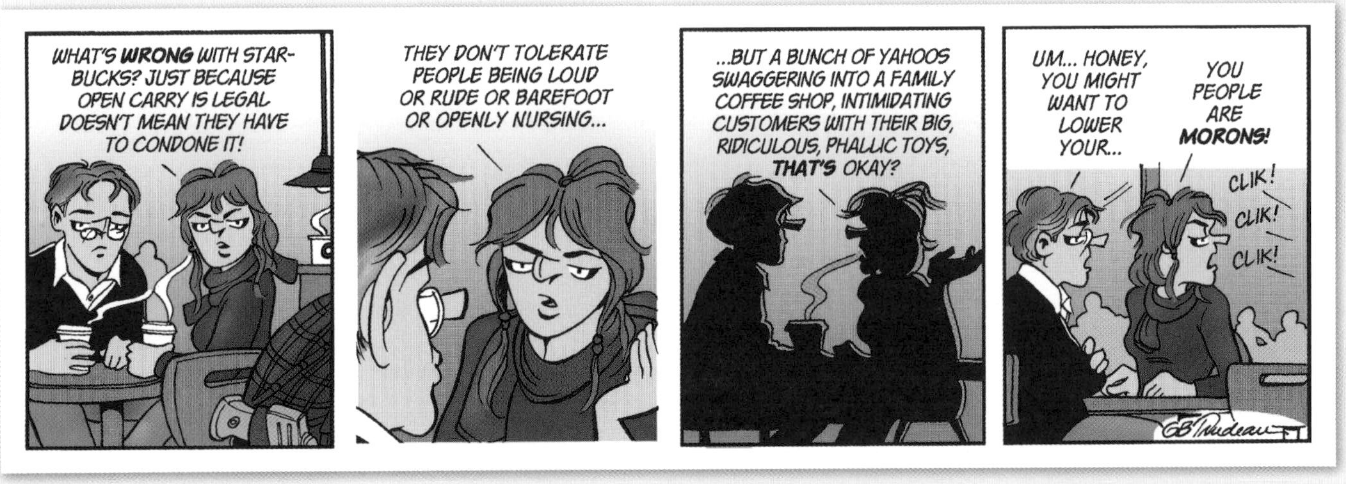
WHAT'S **WRONG** WITH STAR-BUCKS? JUST BECAUSE OPEN CARRY IS LEGAL DOESN'T MEAN THEY HAVE TO CONDONE IT!
THEY DON'T TOLERATE PEOPLE BEING LOUD OR RUDE OR BAREFOOT OR OPENLY NURSING...
...BUT A BUNCH OF YAHOOS SWAGGERING INTO A FAMILY COFFEE SHOP, INTIMIDATING CUSTOMERS WITH THEIR BIG, RIDICULOUS, PHALLIC TOYS, **THAT'S** OKAY?
UM... HONEY, YOU MIGHT WANT TO LOWER YOUR...
YOU PEOPLE ARE **MORONS!**
CLIK!
CLIK!
CLIK!

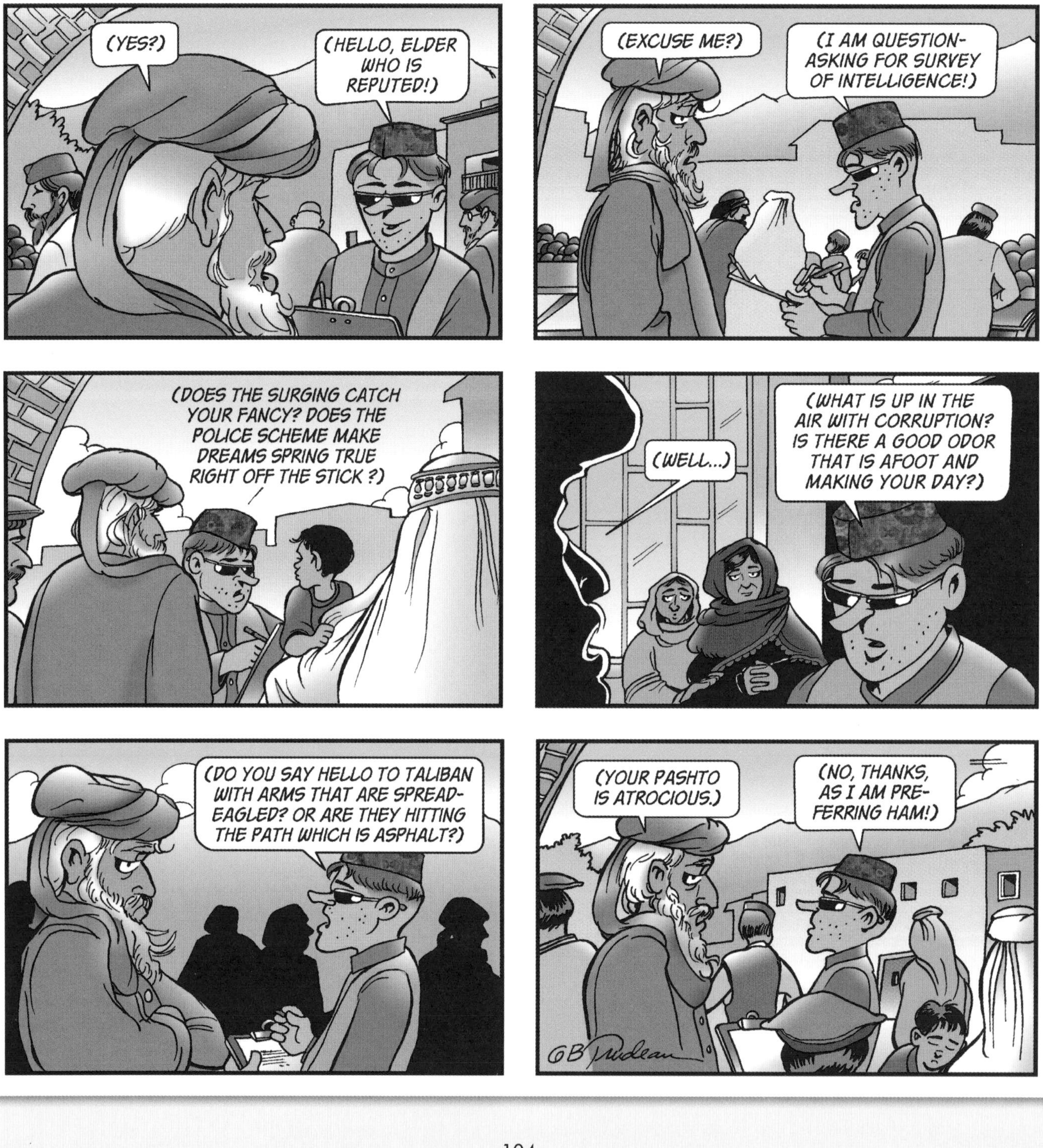
(YES?)
(HELLO, ELDER WHO IS REPUTED!)
(EXCUSE ME?)
(I AM QUESTION-ASKING FOR SURVEY OF INTELLIGENCE!)
(DOES THE SURGING CATCH YOUR FANCY? DOES THE POLICE SCHEME MAKE DREAMS SPRING TRUE RIGHT OFF THE STICK?)
(WHAT IS UP IN THE AIR WITH CORRUPTION? IS THERE A GOOD ODOR THAT IS AFOOT AND MAKING YOUR DAY?)
(WELL...)
(DO YOU SAY HELLO TO TALIBAN WITH ARMS THAT ARE SPREAD-EAGLED? OR ARE THEY HITTING THE PATH WHICH IS ASPHALT?)
(YOUR PASHTO IS ATROCIOUS.)
(NO, THANKS, AS I AM PRE-FERRING HAM!)
GB Trudeau

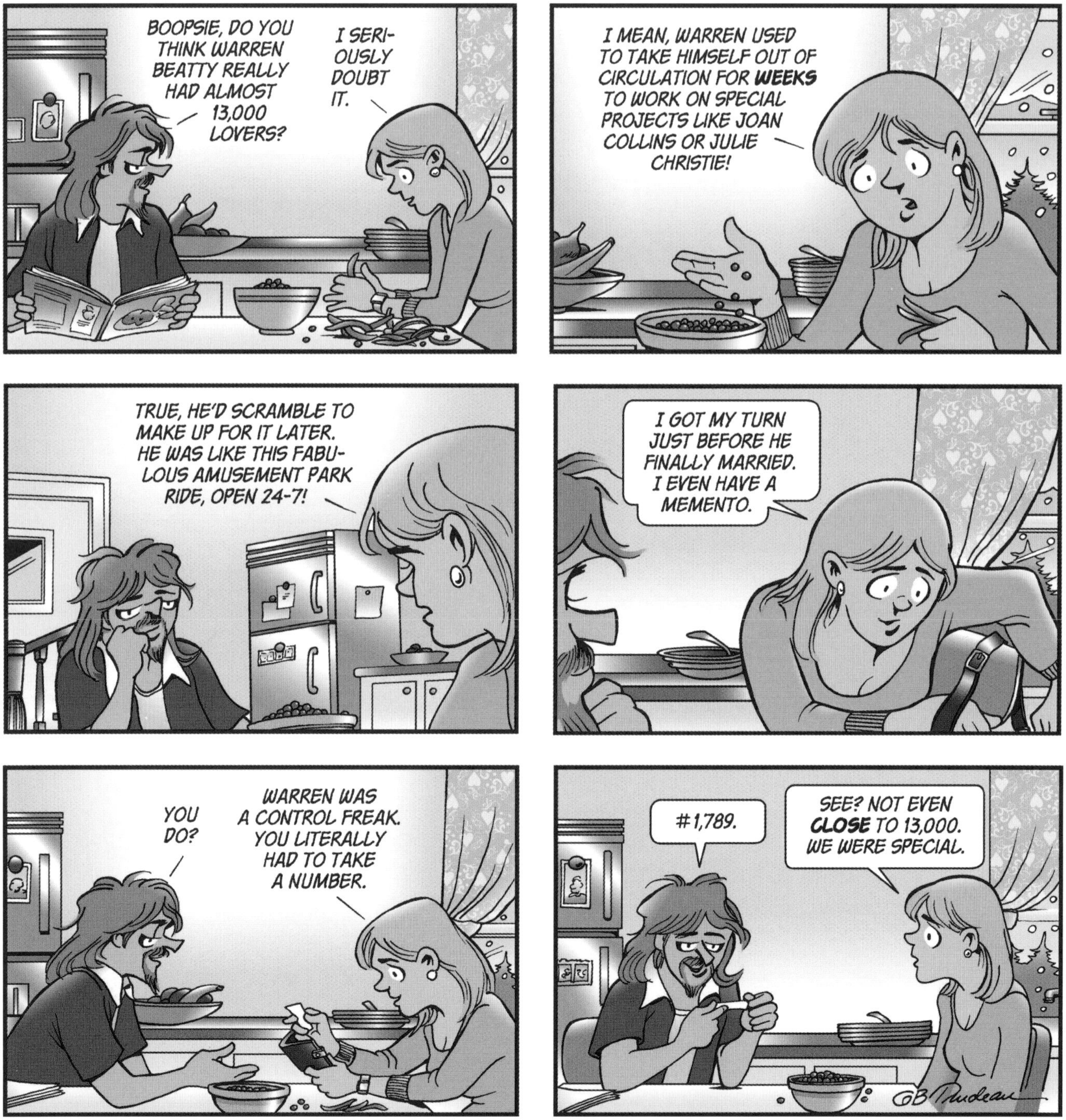
BOOPSIE, DO YOU THINK WARREN BEATTY REALLY HAD ALMOST 13,000 LOVERS?
I SERI-OUSLY DOUBT IT.
I MEAN, WARREN USED TO TAKE HIMSELF OUT OF CIRCULATION FOR **WEEKS** TO WORK ON SPECIAL PROJECTS LIKE JOAN COLLINS OR JULIE CHRISTIE!
TRUE, HE'D SCRAMBLE TO MAKE UP FOR IT LATER. HE WAS LIKE THIS FABU-LOUS AMUSEMENT PARK RIDE, OPEN 24-7!
I GOT MY TURN JUST BEFORE HE FINALLY MARRIED. I EVEN HAVE A MEMENTO.
YOU DO?
WARREN WAS A CONTROL FREAK. YOU LITERALLY HAD TO TAKE A NUMBER.
#1,789.
SEE? NOT EVEN **CLOSE** TO 13,000. WE WERE SPECIAL.
GB Trudeau

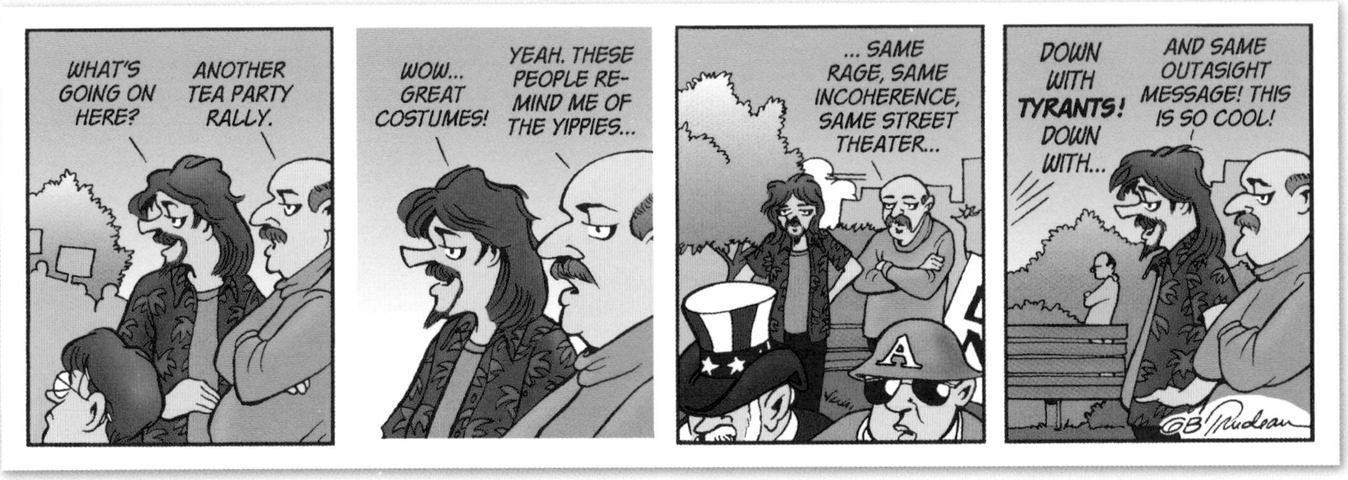
WHAT'S GOING ON HERE?
ANOTHER TEA PARTY RALLY.
WOW... GREAT COSTUMES!
YEAH. THESE PEOPLE RE-MIND ME OF THE YIPPIES...
... SAME RAGE, SAME INCOHERENCE, SAME STREET THEATER...
DOWN WITH **TYRANTS!** DOWN WITH...
AND SAME OUTASIGHT MESSAGE! THIS IS SO COOL!

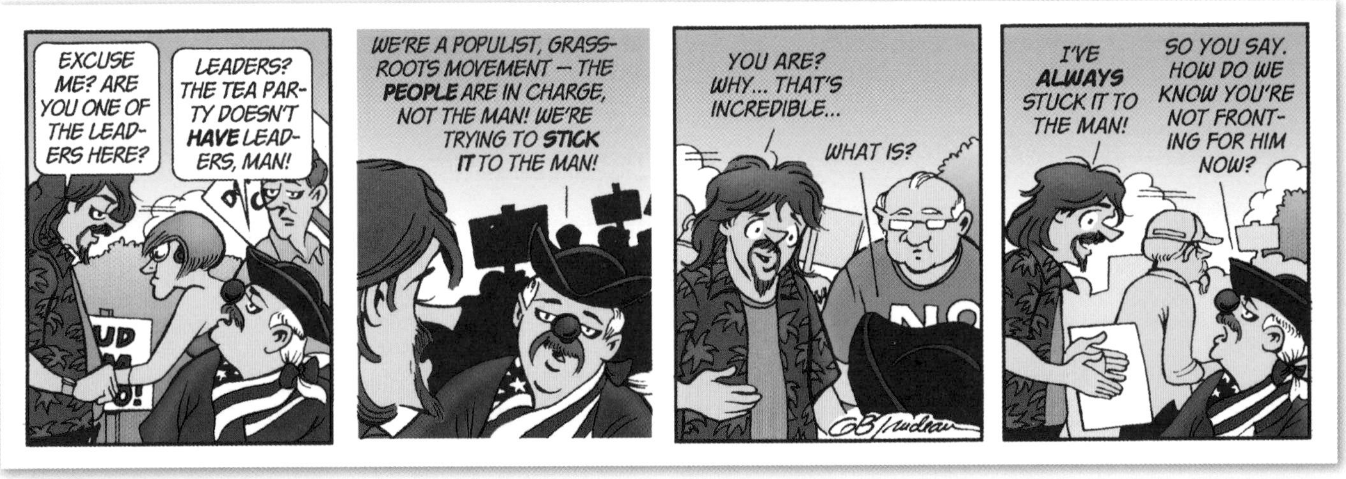
EXCUSE ME? ARE YOU ONE OF THE LEAD-ERS HERE?
LEADERS? THE TEA PAR-TY DOESN'T **HAVE** LEAD-ERS, MAN!
WE'RE A POPULIST, GRASS-ROOTS MOVEMENT — THE **PEOPLE** ARE IN CHARGE, NOT THE MAN! WE'RE TRYING TO **STICK IT** TO THE MAN!
YOU ARE? WHY... THAT'S INCREDIBLE...
WHAT IS?
I'VE **ALWAYS** STUCK IT TO THE MAN!
SO YOU SAY. HOW DO WE KNOW YOU'RE NOT FRONT-ING FOR HIM NOW?

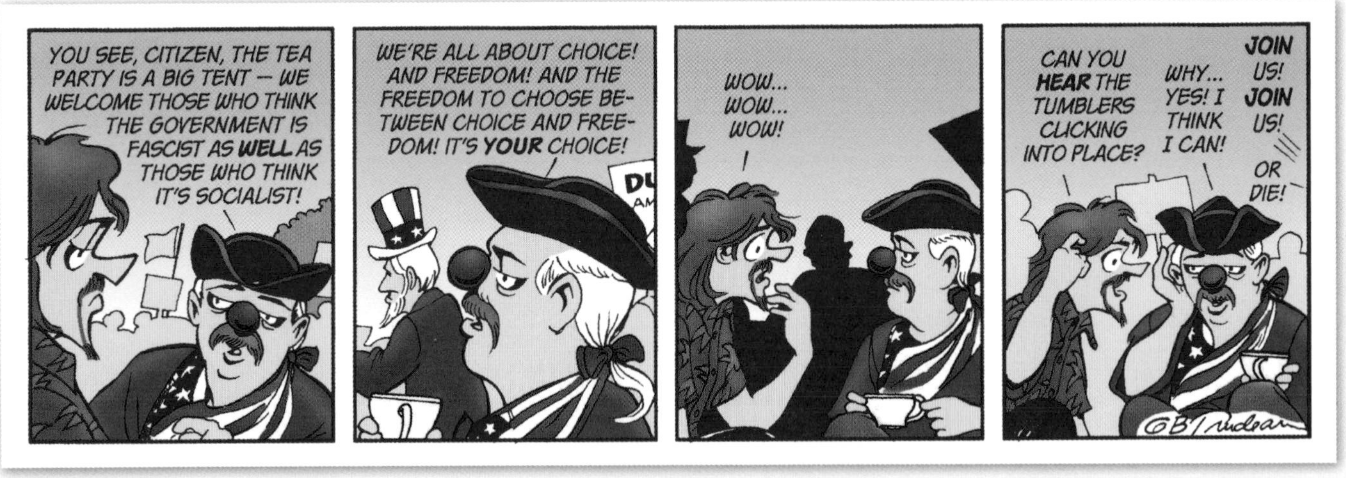
YOU SEE, CITIZEN, THE TEA PARTY IS A BIG TENT — WE WELCOME THOSE WHO THINK THE GOVERNMENT IS FASCIST AS **WELL** AS THOSE WHO THINK IT'S SOCIALIST!
WE'RE ALL ABOUT CHOICE! AND FREEDOM! AND THE FREEDOM TO CHOOSE BE-TWEEN CHOICE AND FREE-DOM! IT'S **YOUR** CHOICE!
WOW... WOW... WOW!
CAN YOU **HEAR** THE TUMBLERS CLICKING INTO PLACE?
WHY... YES! I THINK I CAN!
JOIN US! **JOIN** US!
OR DIE!

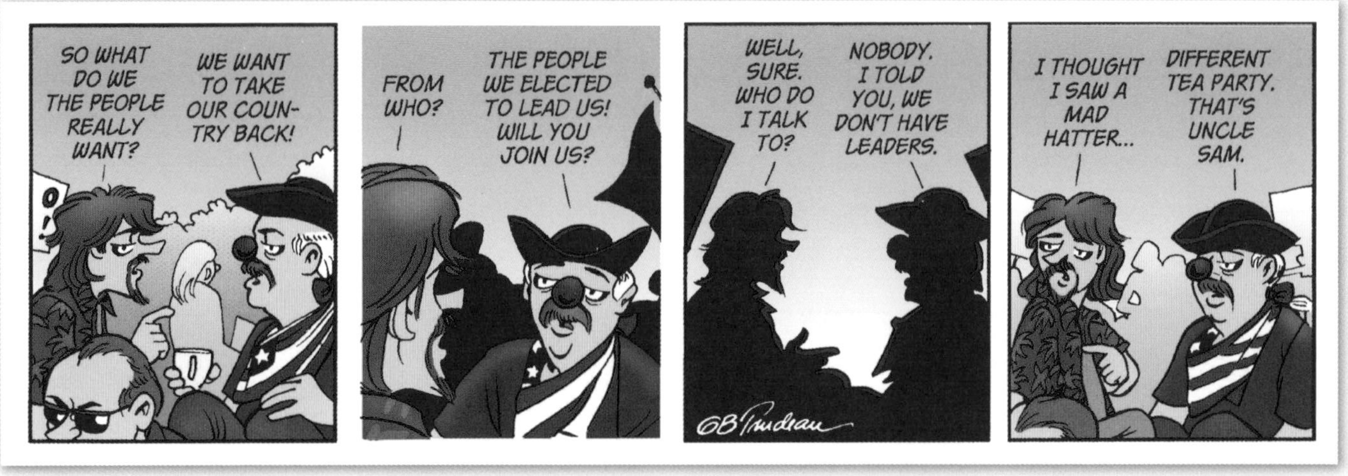
SO WHAT DO WE THE PEOPLE REALLY WANT?
WE WANT TO TAKE OUR COUNTRY BACK!
FROM WHO?
THE PEOPLE WE ELECTED TO LEAD US! WILL YOU JOIN US?
WELL, SURE. WHO DO I TALK TO?
NOBODY. I TOLD YOU, WE DON'T HAVE LEADERS.
I THOUGHT I SAW A MAD HATTER...
DIFFERENT TEA PARTY. THAT'S UNCLE SAM.

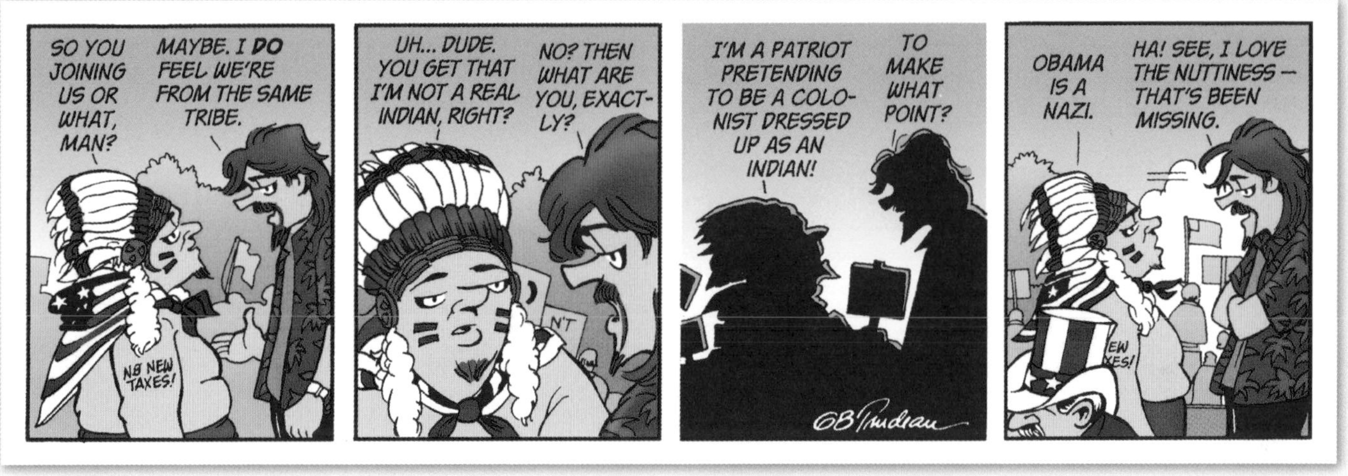
SO YOU JOINING US OR WHAT, MAN?
MAYBE. I **DO** FEEL WE'RE FROM THE SAME TRIBE.
NO NEW TAXES!
UH... DUDE. YOU GET THAT I'M NOT A REAL INDIAN, RIGHT?
NO? THEN WHAT ARE YOU, EXACTLY?
I'M A PATRIOT PRETENDING TO BE A COLONIST DRESSED UP AS AN INDIAN!
TO MAKE WHAT POINT?
OBAMA IS A NAZI.
HA! SEE, I LOVE THE NUTTINESS — THAT'S BEEN MISSING.

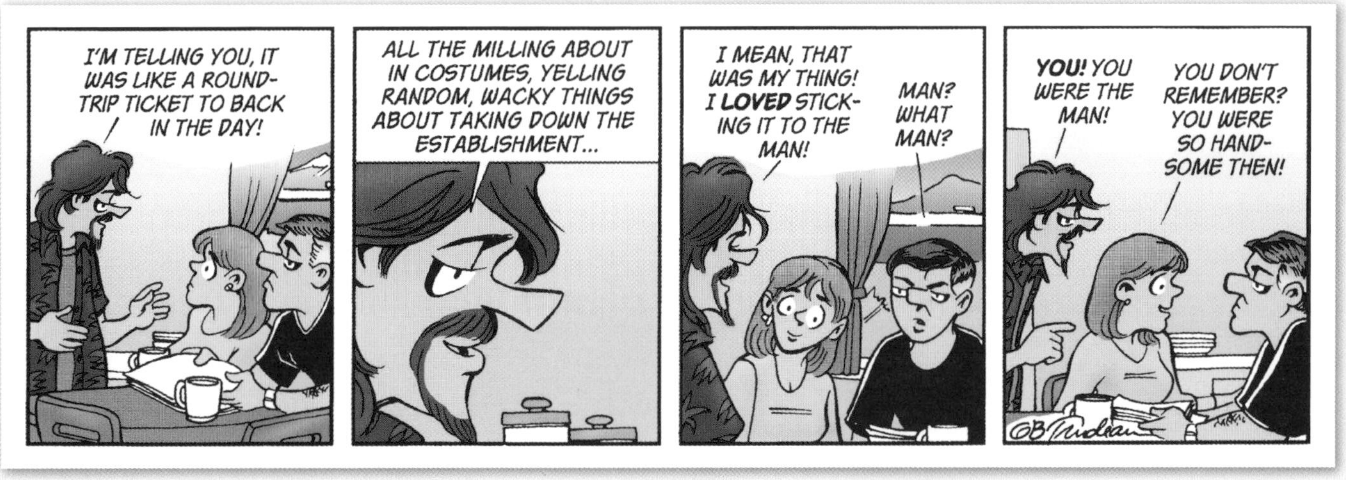
I'M TELLING YOU, IT WAS LIKE A ROUND-TRIP TICKET TO BACK IN THE DAY!
ALL THE MILLING ABOUT IN COSTUMES, YELLING RANDOM, WACKY THINGS ABOUT TAKING DOWN THE ESTABLISHMENT...
I MEAN, THAT WAS MY THING! I **LOVED** STICKING IT TO THE MAN!
MAN? WHAT MAN?
YOU! YOU WERE THE MAN!
YOU DON'T REMEMBER? YOU WERE SO HANDSOME THEN!

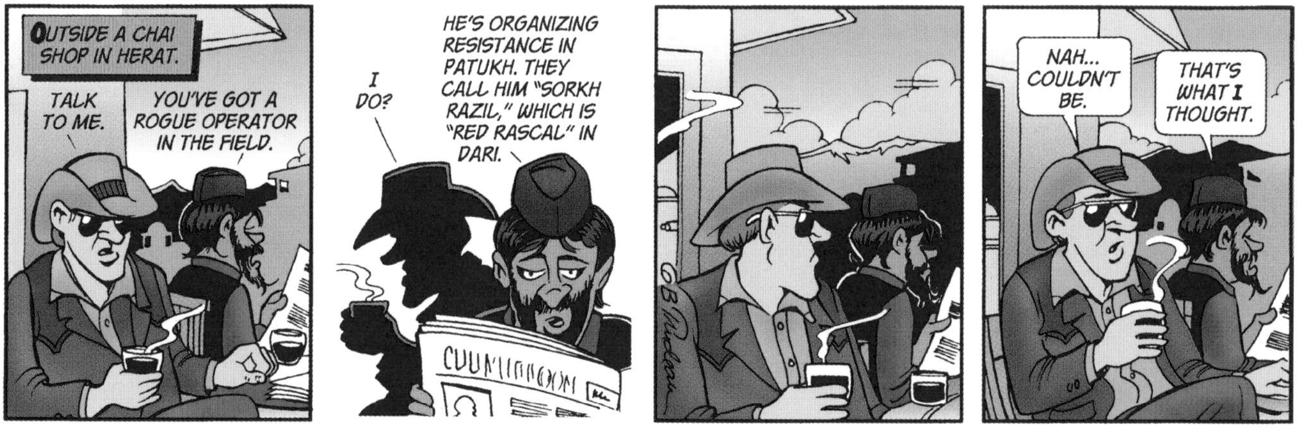
OUTSIDE A CHAI SHOP IN HERAT.
TALK TO ME.
YOU'VE GOT A ROGUE OPERATOR IN THE FIELD.
I DO?
HE'S ORGANIZING RESISTANCE IN PATUKH. THEY CALL HIM "SORKH RAZIL," WHICH IS "RED RASCAL" IN DARI.
NAH... COULDN'T BE.
THAT'S WHAT I THOUGHT.
GB Trudeau

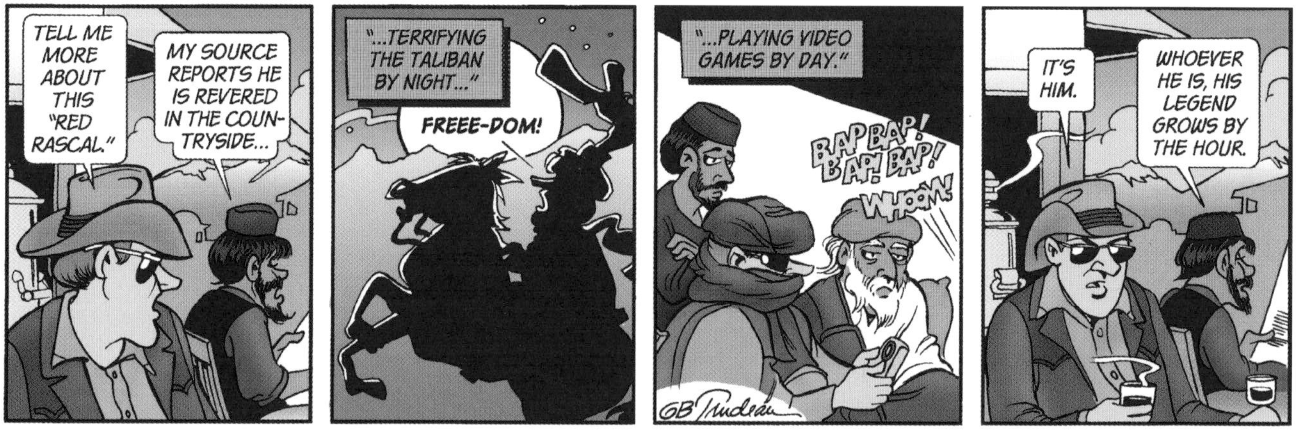
TELL ME MORE ABOUT THIS "RED RASCAL."
MY SOURCE REPORTS HE IS REVERED IN THE COUNTRYSIDE...
"...TERRIFYING THE TALIBAN BY NIGHT..."
FREEE-DOM!
"...PLAYING VIDEO GAMES BY DAY."
BAP BAP! BAP! BAP!
WHOOM!
GB Trudeau
IT'S HIM.
WHOEVER HE IS, HIS LEGEND GROWS BY THE HOUR.

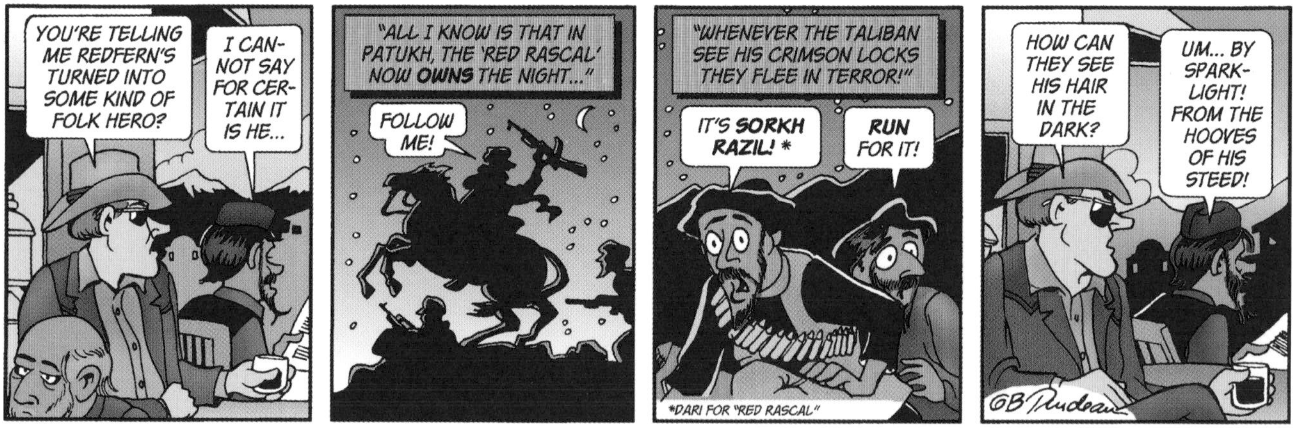
YOU'RE TELLING ME REDFERN'S TURNED INTO SOME KIND OF FOLK HERO?
I CANNOT SAY FOR CERTAIN IT IS HE...
"ALL I KNOW IS THAT IN PATUKH, THE 'RED RASCAL' NOW OWNS THE NIGHT..."
FOLLOW ME!
"WHENEVER THE TALIBAN SEE HIS CRIMSON LOCKS THEY FLEE IN TERROR!"
IT'S SORKH RAZIL! *
RUN FOR IT!
*DARI FOR "RED RASCAL"
HOW CAN THEY SEE HIS HAIR IN THE DARK?
UM... BY SPARKLIGHT! FROM THE HOOVES OF HIS STEED!
GB Trudeau

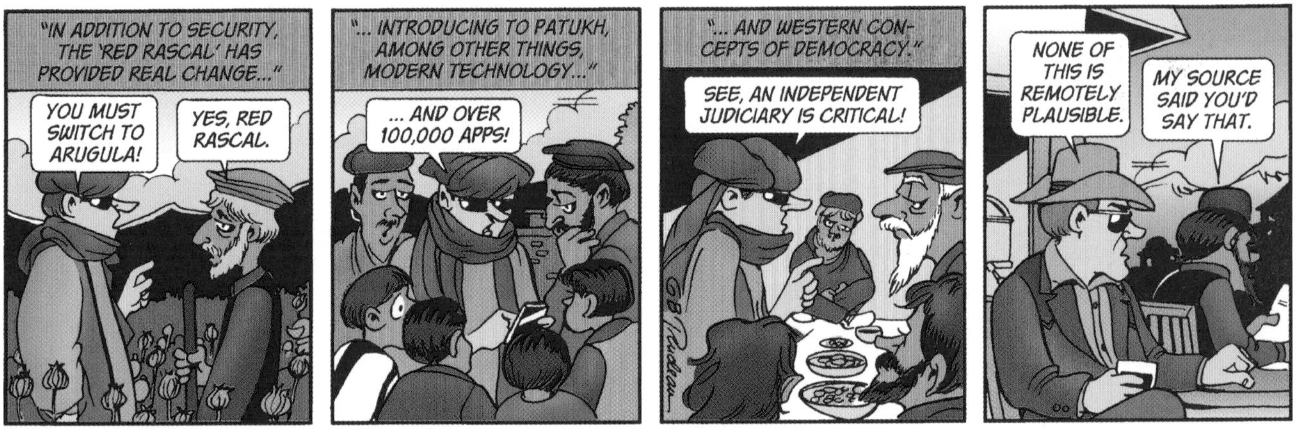
"IN ADDITION TO SECURITY, THE 'RED RASCAL' HAS PROVIDED REAL CHANGE..."
YOU MUST SWITCH TO ARUGULA!
YES, RED RASCAL.
"... INTRODUCING TO PATUKH, AMONG OTHER THINGS, MODERN TECHNOLOGY..."
... AND OVER 100,000 APPS!
"... AND WESTERN CONCEPTS OF DEMOCRACY."
SEE, AN INDEPENDENT JUDICIARY IS CRITICAL!
NONE OF THIS IS REMOTELY PLAUSIBLE.
MY SOURCE SAID YOU'D SAY THAT.

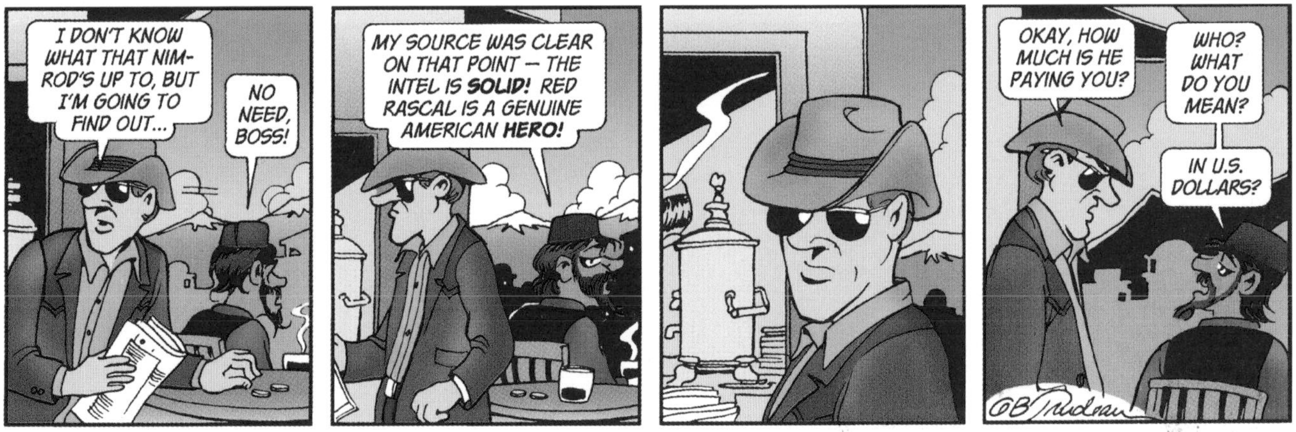
I DON'T KNOW WHAT THAT NIMROD'S UP TO, BUT I'M GOING TO FIND OUT...
NO NEED, BOSS!
MY SOURCE WAS CLEAR ON THAT POINT — THE INTEL IS SOLID! RED RASCAL IS A GENUINE AMERICAN HERO!
OKAY, HOW MUCH IS HE PAYING YOU?
WHO? WHAT DO YOU MEAN?
IN U.S. DOLLARS?

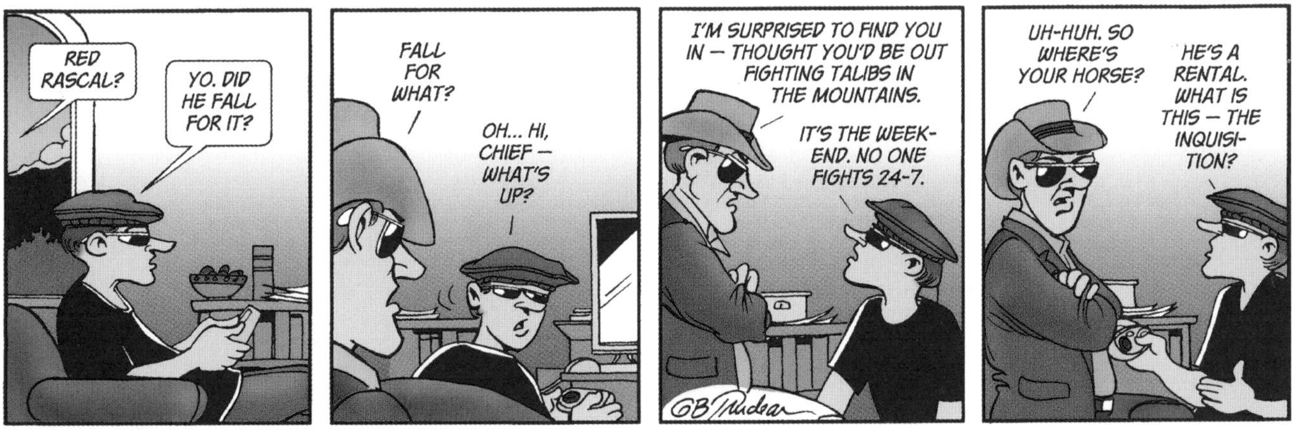
RED RASCAL?
YO. DID HE FALL FOR IT?
FALL FOR WHAT?
OH... HI, CHIEF — WHAT'S UP?
I'M SURPRISED TO FIND YOU IN — THOUGHT YOU'D BE OUT FIGHTING TALIBS IN THE MOUNTAINS.
IT'S THE WEEKEND. NO ONE FIGHTS 24-7.
UH-HUH. SO WHERE'S YOUR HORSE?
HE'S A RENTAL. WHAT IS THIS — THE INQUISITION?

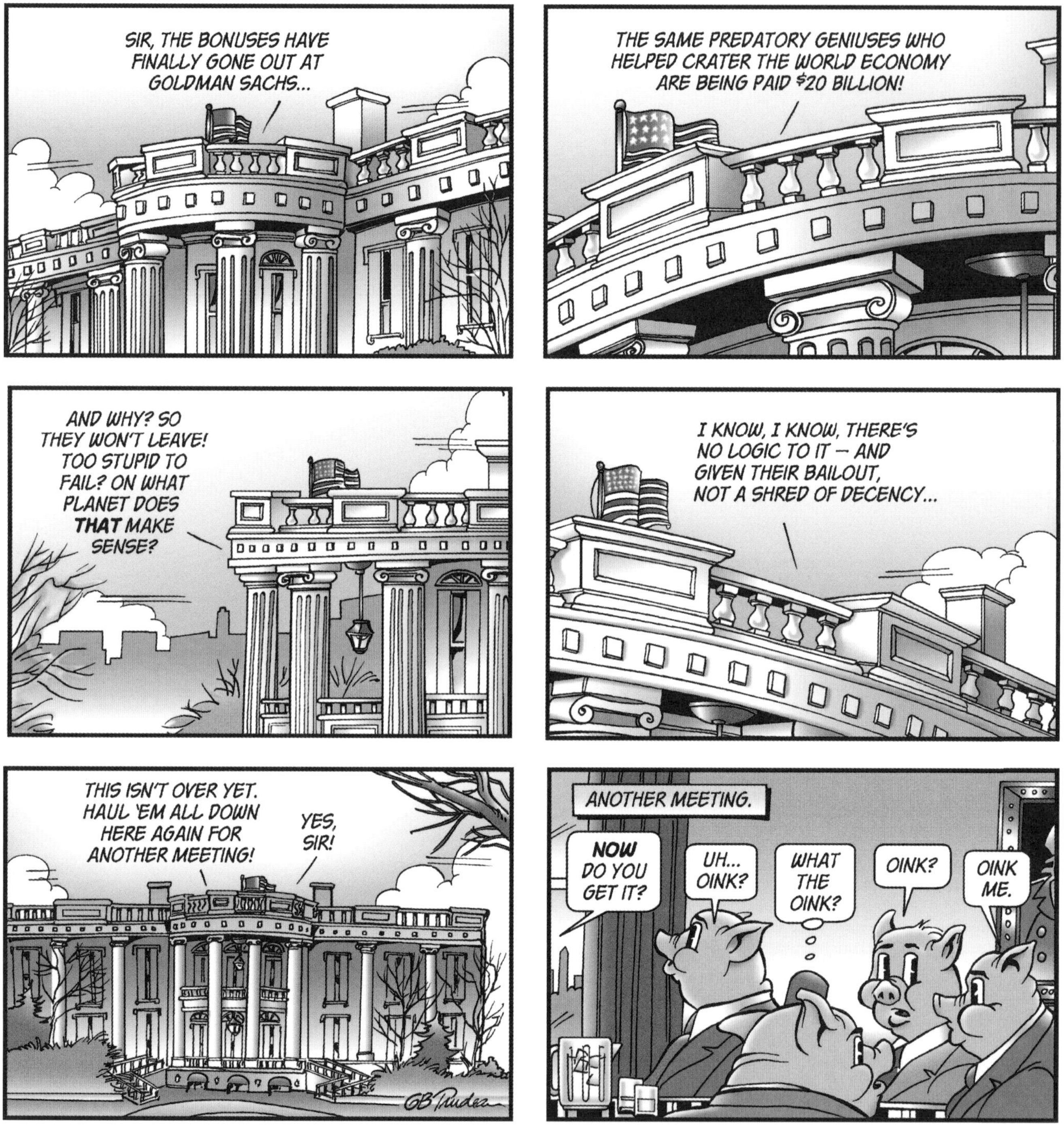
SIR, THE BONUSES HAVE FINALLY GONE OUT AT GOLDMAN SACHS...
THE SAME PREDATORY GENIUSES WHO HELPED CRATER THE WORLD ECONOMY ARE BEING PAID $20 BILLION!
AND WHY? SO THEY WON'T LEAVE! TOO STUPID TO FAIL? ON WHAT PLANET DOES THAT MAKE SENSE?
I KNOW, I KNOW, THERE'S NO LOGIC TO IT — AND GIVEN THEIR BAILOUT, NOT A SHRED OF DECENCY...
THIS ISN'T OVER YET. HAUL 'EM ALL DOWN HERE AGAIN FOR ANOTHER MEETING!
YES, SIR!
GB Trudeau
ANOTHER MEETING.
NOW DO YOU GET IT?
UH... OINK?
WHAT THE OINK?
OINK?
OINK ME.

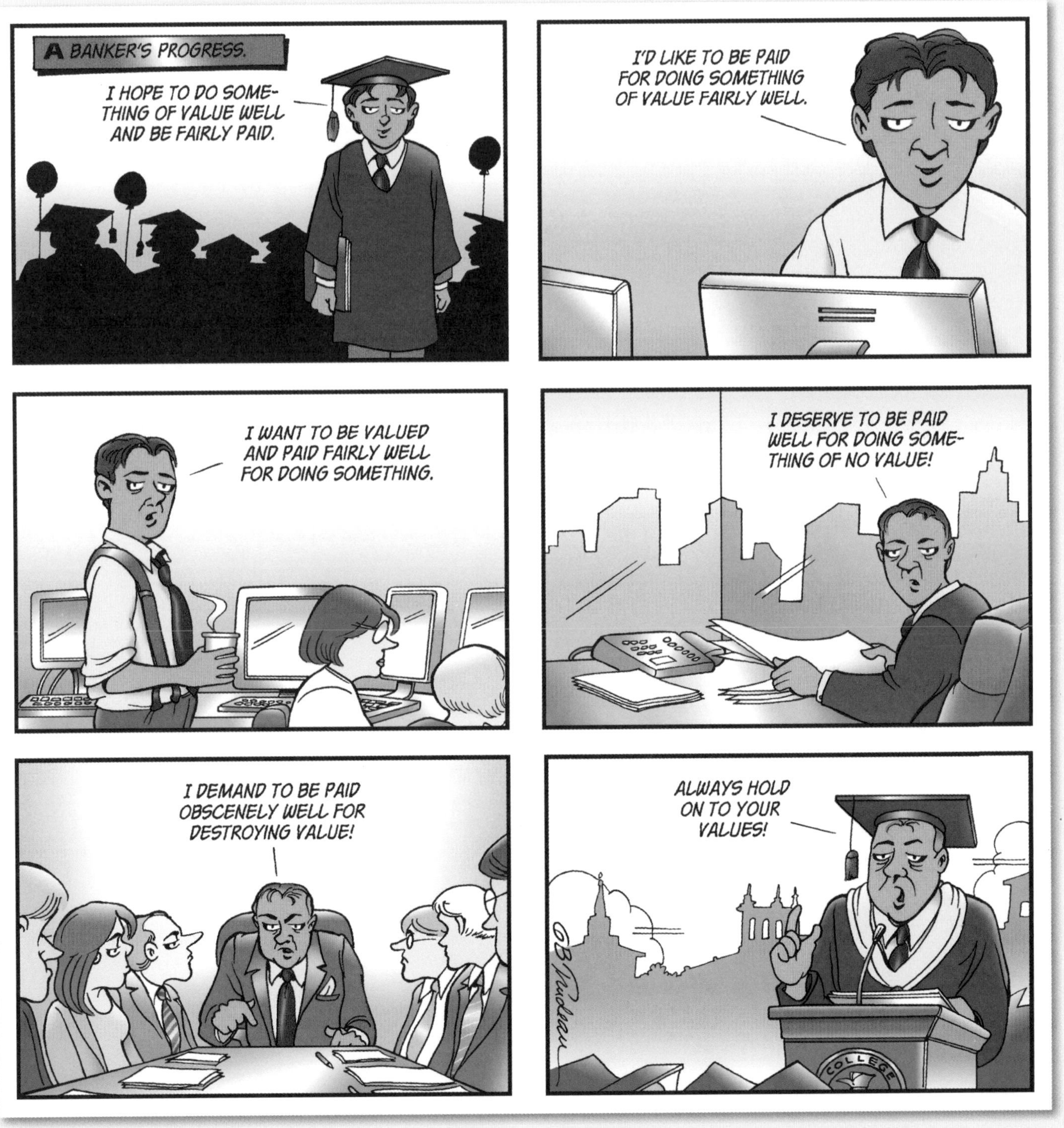
A BANKER'S PROGRESS.
I HOPE TO DO SOMETHING OF VALUE WELL AND BE FAIRLY PAID.
I'D LIKE TO BE PAID FOR DOING SOMETHING OF VALUE FAIRLY WELL.
I WANT TO BE VALUED AND PAID FAIRLY WELL FOR DOING SOMETHING.
I DESERVE TO BE PAID WELL FOR DOING SOMETHING OF NO VALUE!
I DEMAND TO BE PAID OBSCENELY WELL FOR DESTROYING VALUE!
ALWAYS HOLD ON TO YOUR VALUES!
COLLEGE

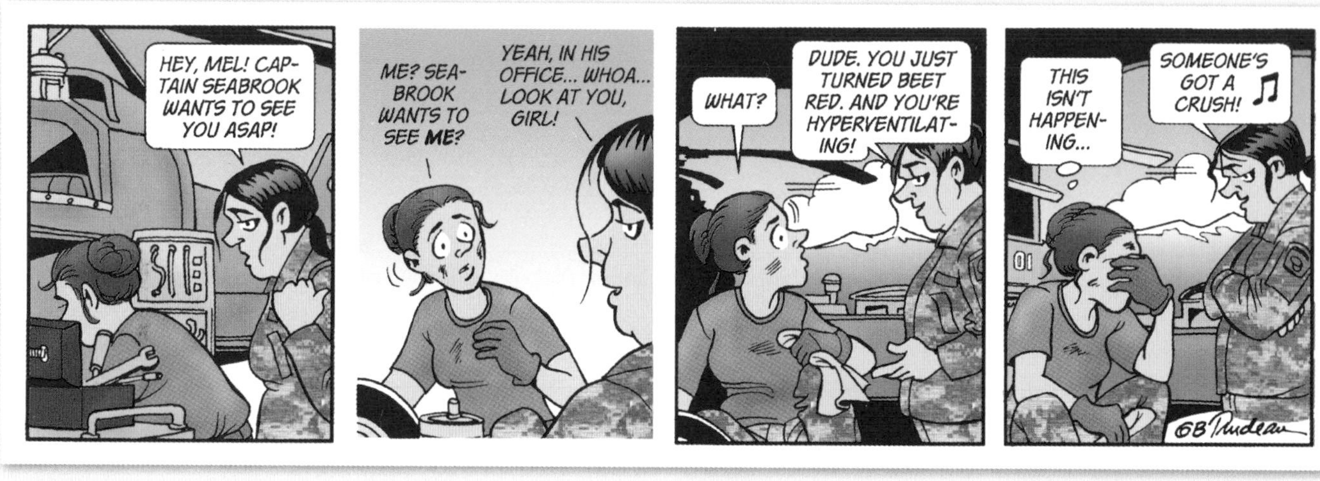
HEY, MEL! CAPTAIN SEABROOK WANTS TO SEE YOU ASAP!
ME? SEABROOK WANTS TO SEE **ME**?
YEAH, IN HIS OFFICE... WHOA... LOOK AT YOU, GIRL!
WHAT?
DUDE. YOU JUST TURNED BEET RED. AND YOU'RE HYPERVENTILATING!
THIS ISN'T HAPPENING...
SOMEONE'S GOT A CRUSH! ♫
©B Trudeau

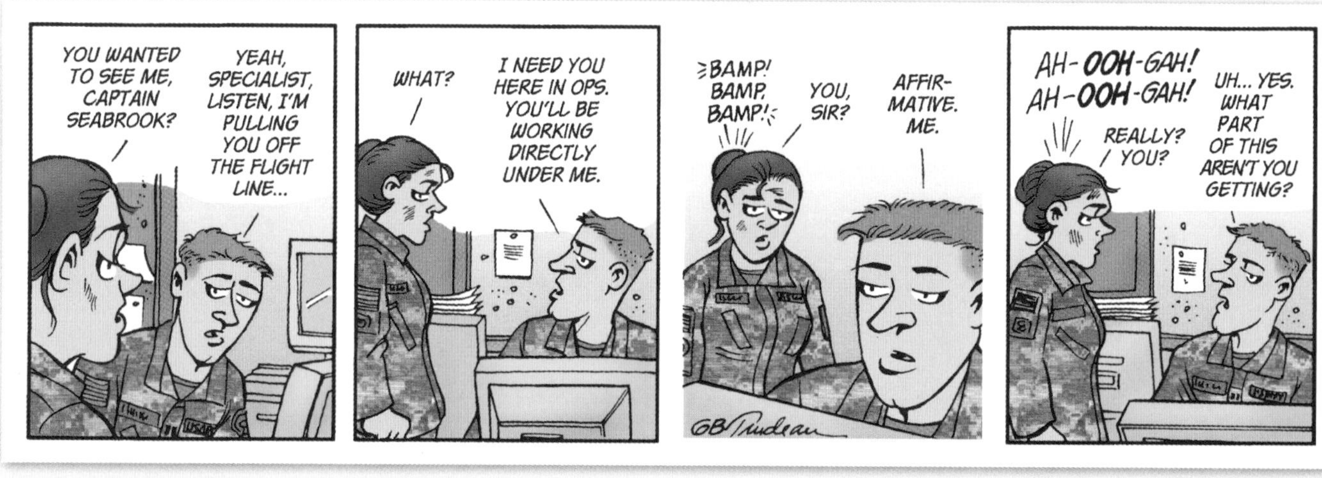
YOU WANTED TO SEE ME, CAPTAIN SEABROOK?
YEAH, SPECIALIST, LISTEN, I'M PULLING YOU OFF THE FLIGHT LINE...
WHAT?
I NEED YOU HERE IN OPS. YOU'LL BE WORKING DIRECTLY UNDER ME.
BAMP! BAMP, BAMP!
YOU, SIR?
AFFIRMATIVE. ME.
©B Trudeau
AH-**OOH**-GAH! AH-**OOH**-GAH!
REALLY? YOU?
UH... YES. WHAT PART OF THIS AREN'T YOU GETTING?

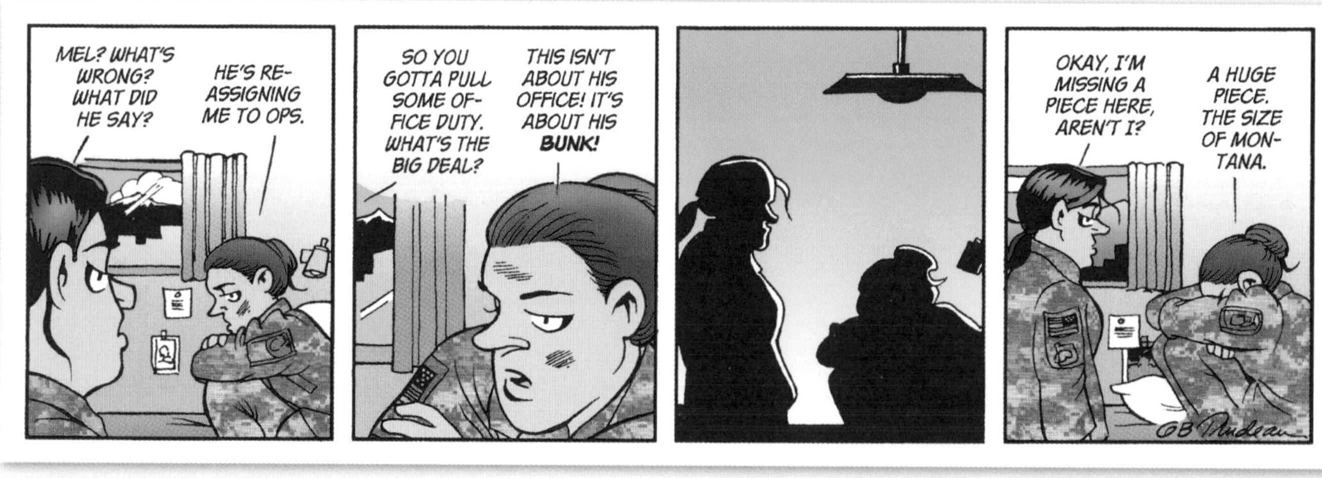
MEL? WHAT'S WRONG? WHAT DID HE SAY?
HE'S REASSIGNING ME TO OPS.
SO YOU GOTTA PULL SOME OFFICE DUTY. WHAT'S THE BIG DEAL?
THIS ISN'T ABOUT HIS OFFICE! IT'S ABOUT HIS **BUNK!**
OKAY, I'M MISSING A PIECE HERE, AREN'T I?
A HUGE PIECE. THE SIZE OF MONTANA.
©B Trudeau

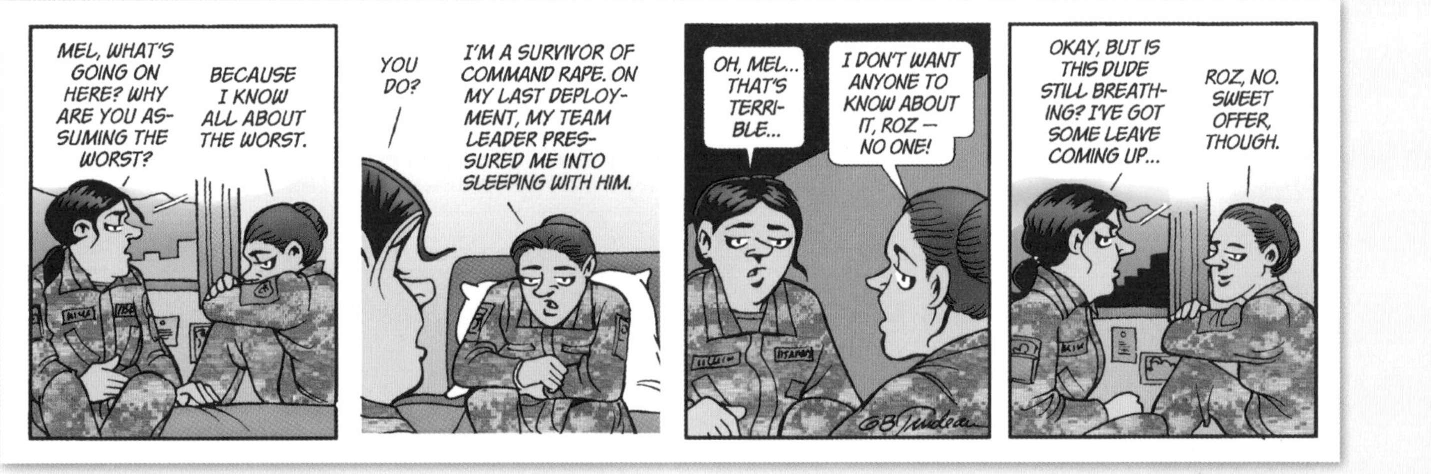
MEL, WHAT'S GOING ON HERE? WHY ARE YOU AS-SUMING THE WORST?
BECAUSE I KNOW ALL ABOUT THE WORST.
YOU DO?
I'M A SURVIVOR OF COMMAND RAPE. ON MY LAST DEPLOY-MENT, MY TEAM LEADER PRES-SURED ME INTO SLEEPING WITH HIM.
OH, MEL... THAT'S TERRI-BLE...
I DON'T WANT ANYONE TO KNOW ABOUT IT, ROZ — NO ONE!
OKAY, BUT IS THIS DUDE STILL BREATH-ING? I'VE GOT SOME LEAVE COMING UP...
ROZ, NO. SWEET OFFER, THOUGH.

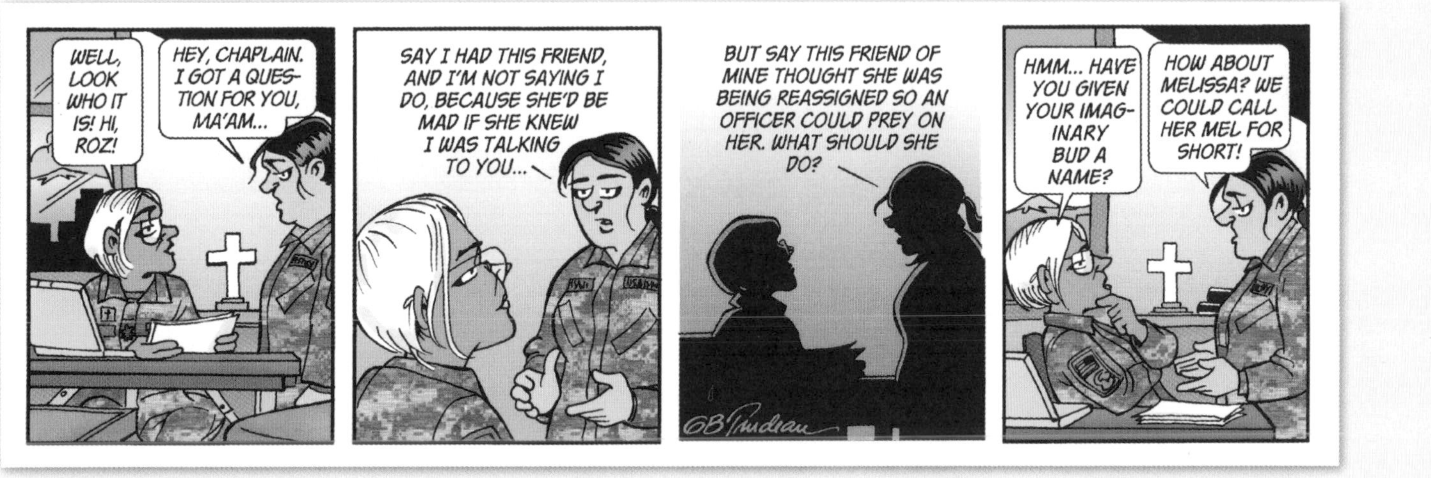
WELL, LOOK WHO IT IS! HI, ROZ!
HEY, CHAPLAIN. I GOT A QUES-TION FOR YOU, MA'AM...
SAY I HAD THIS FRIEND, AND I'M NOT SAYING I DO, BECAUSE SHE'D BE MAD IF SHE KNEW I WAS TALKING TO YOU...
BUT SAY THIS FRIEND OF MINE THOUGHT SHE WAS BEING REASSIGNED SO AN OFFICER COULD PREY ON HER. WHAT SHOULD SHE DO?
HMM... HAVE YOU GIVEN YOUR IMAG-INARY BUD A NAME?
HOW ABOUT MELISSA? WE COULD CALL HER MEL FOR SHORT!

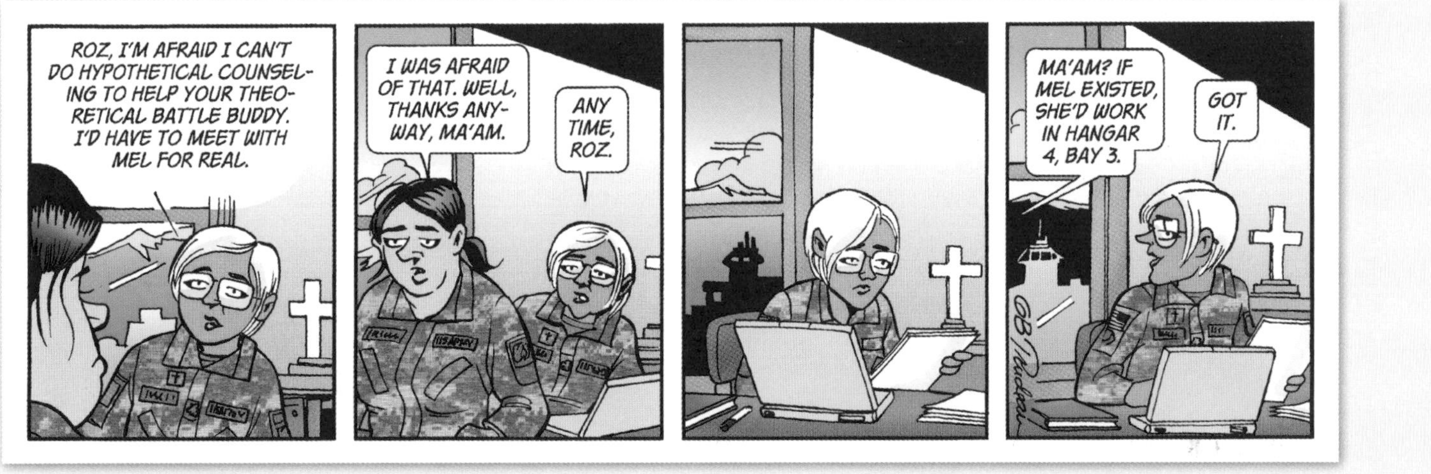
ROZ, I'M AFRAID I CAN'T DO HYPOTHETICAL COUNSEL-ING TO HELP YOUR THEO-RETICAL BATTLE BUDDY. I'D HAVE TO MEET WITH MEL FOR REAL.
I WAS AFRAID OF THAT. WELL, THANKS ANY-WAY, MA'AM.
ANY TIME, ROZ.
MA'AM? IF MEL EXISTED, SHE'D WORK IN HANGAR 4, BAY 3.
GOT IT.

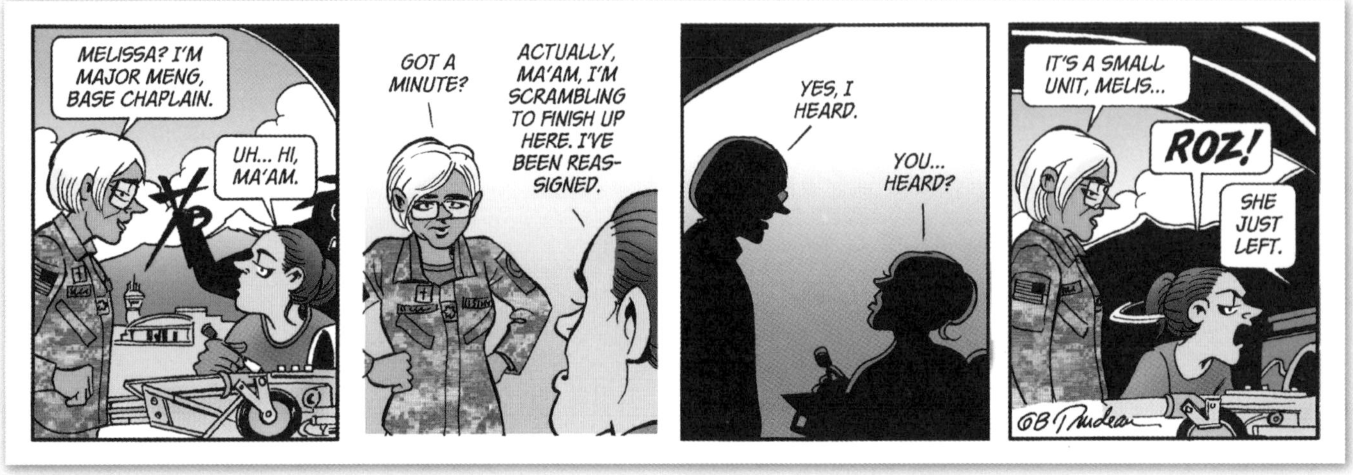
MELISSA? I'M MAJOR MENG, BASE CHAPLAIN.
UH... HI, MA'AM.
GOT A MINUTE?
ACTUALLY, MA'AM, I'M SCRAMBLING TO FINISH UP HERE. I'VE BEEN REASSIGNED.
YES, I HEARD.
YOU... HEARD?
IT'S A SMALL UNIT, MELIS...
ROZ!
SHE JUST LEFT.

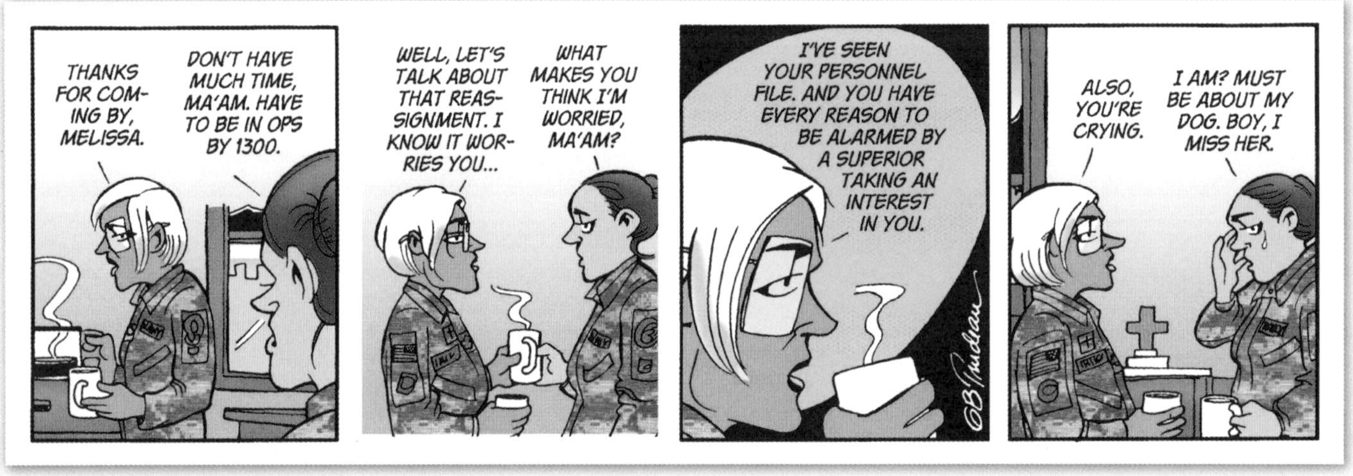
THANKS FOR COMING BY, MELISSA.
DON'T HAVE MUCH TIME, MA'AM. HAVE TO BE IN OPS BY 1300.
WELL, LET'S TALK ABOUT THAT REASSIGNMENT. I KNOW IT WORRIES YOU...
WHAT MAKES YOU THINK I'M WORRIED, MA'AM?
I'VE SEEN YOUR PERSONNEL FILE. AND YOU HAVE EVERY REASON TO BE ALARMED BY A SUPERIOR TAKING AN INTEREST IN YOU.
ALSO, YOU'RE CRYING.
I AM? MUST BE ABOUT MY DOG. BOY, I MISS HER.

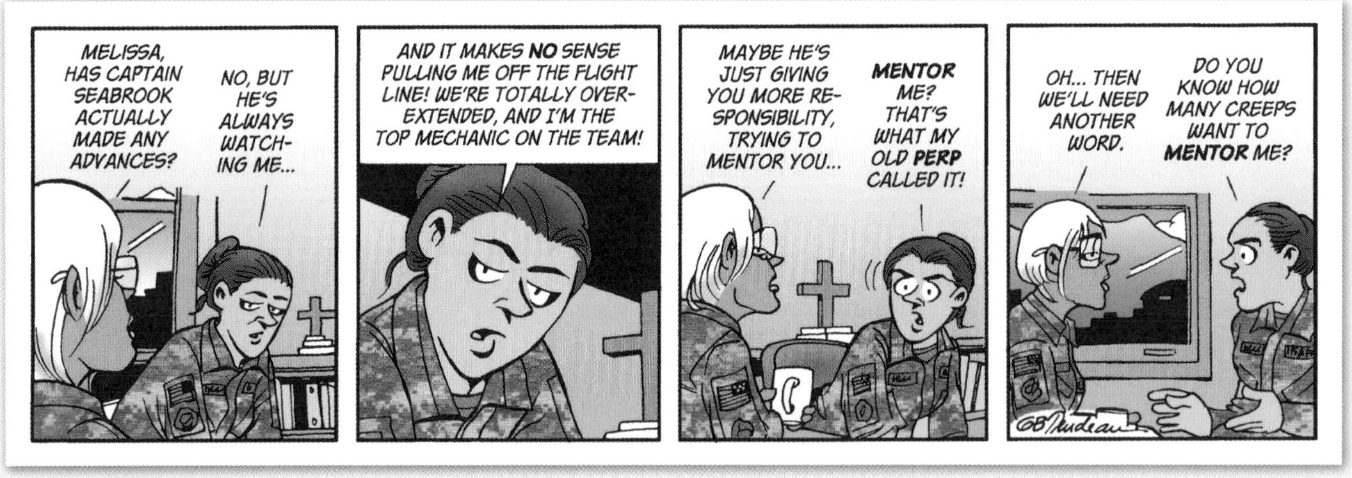
MELISSA, HAS CAPTAIN SEABROOK ACTUALLY MADE ANY ADVANCES?
NO, BUT HE'S ALWAYS WATCHING ME...
AND IT MAKES NO SENSE PULLING ME OFF THE FLIGHT LINE! WE'RE TOTALLY OVEREXTENDED, AND I'M THE TOP MECHANIC ON THE TEAM!
MAYBE HE'S JUST GIVING YOU MORE RESPONSIBILITY, TRYING TO MENTOR YOU...
MENTOR ME? THAT'S WHAT MY OLD PERP CALLED IT!
OH... THEN WE'LL NEED ANOTHER WORD.
DO YOU KNOW HOW MANY CREEPS WANT TO MENTOR ME?

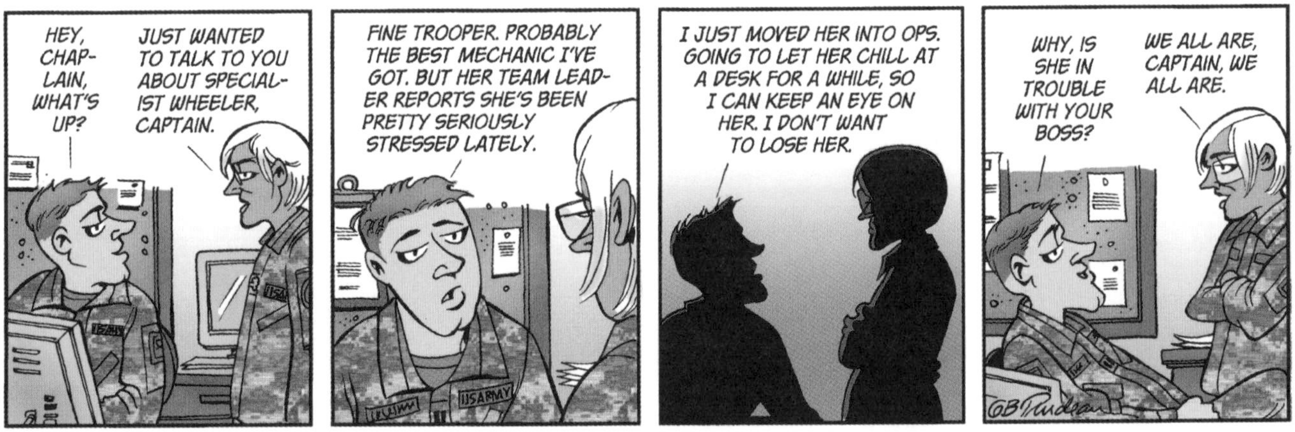
HEY, CHAPLAIN, WHAT'S UP?
JUST WANTED TO TALK TO YOU ABOUT SPECIALIST WHEELER, CAPTAIN.
FINE TROOPER. PROBABLY THE BEST MECHANIC I'VE GOT. BUT HER TEAM LEADER REPORTS SHE'S BEEN PRETTY SERIOUSLY STRESSED LATELY.
I JUST MOVED HER INTO OPS. GOING TO LET HER CHILL AT A DESK FOR A WHILE, SO I CAN KEEP AN EYE ON HER. I DON'T WANT TO LOSE HER.
WHY, IS SHE IN TROUBLE WITH YOUR BOSS?
WE ALL ARE, CAPTAIN, WE ALL ARE.

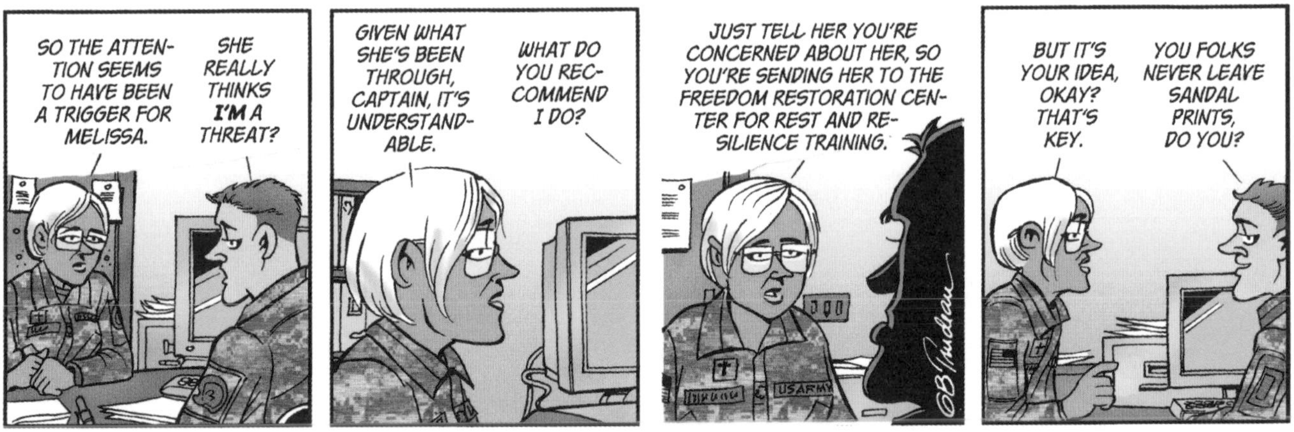
SO THE ATTENTION SEEMS TO HAVE BEEN A TRIGGER FOR MELISSA.
SHE REALLY THINKS **I'M** A THREAT?
GIVEN WHAT SHE'S BEEN THROUGH, CAPTAIN, IT'S UNDERSTANDABLE.
WHAT DO YOU RECOMMEND I DO?
JUST TELL HER YOU'RE CONCERNED ABOUT HER, SO YOU'RE SENDING HER TO THE FREEDOM RESTORATION CENTER FOR REST AND RESILIENCE TRAINING.
BUT IT'S YOUR IDEA, OKAY? THAT'S KEY.
YOU FOLKS NEVER LEAVE SANDAL PRINTS, DO YOU?

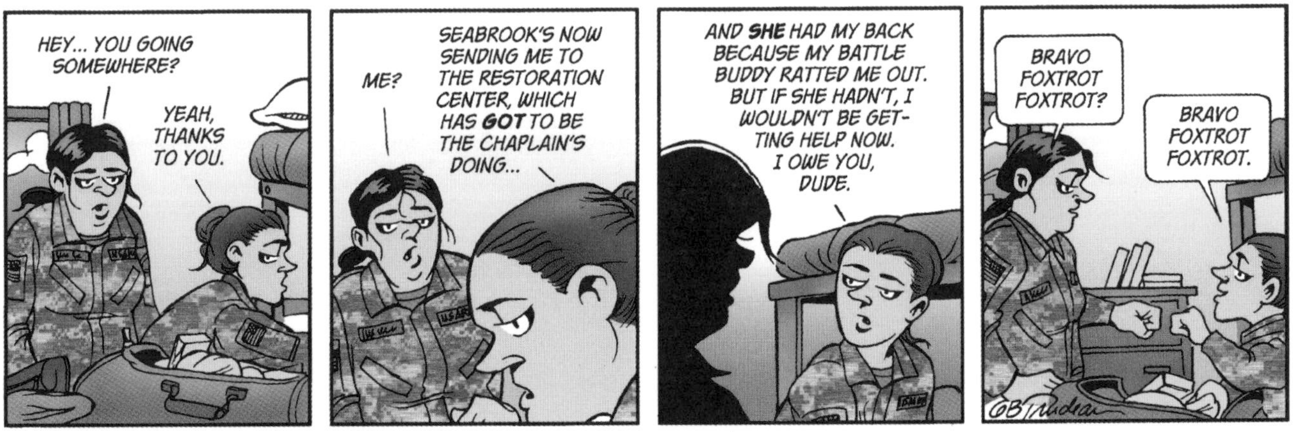
HEY... YOU GOING SOMEWHERE?
YEAH, THANKS TO YOU.
ME?
SEABROOK'S NOW SENDING ME TO THE RESTORATION CENTER, WHICH HAS **GOT** TO BE THE CHAPLAIN'S DOING...
AND **SHE** HAD MY BACK BECAUSE MY BATTLE BUDDY RATTED ME OUT. BUT IF SHE HADN'T, I WOULDN'T BE GETTING HELP NOW. I OWE YOU, DUDE.
BRAVO FOXTROT FOXTROT?
BRAVO FOXTROT FOXTROT.

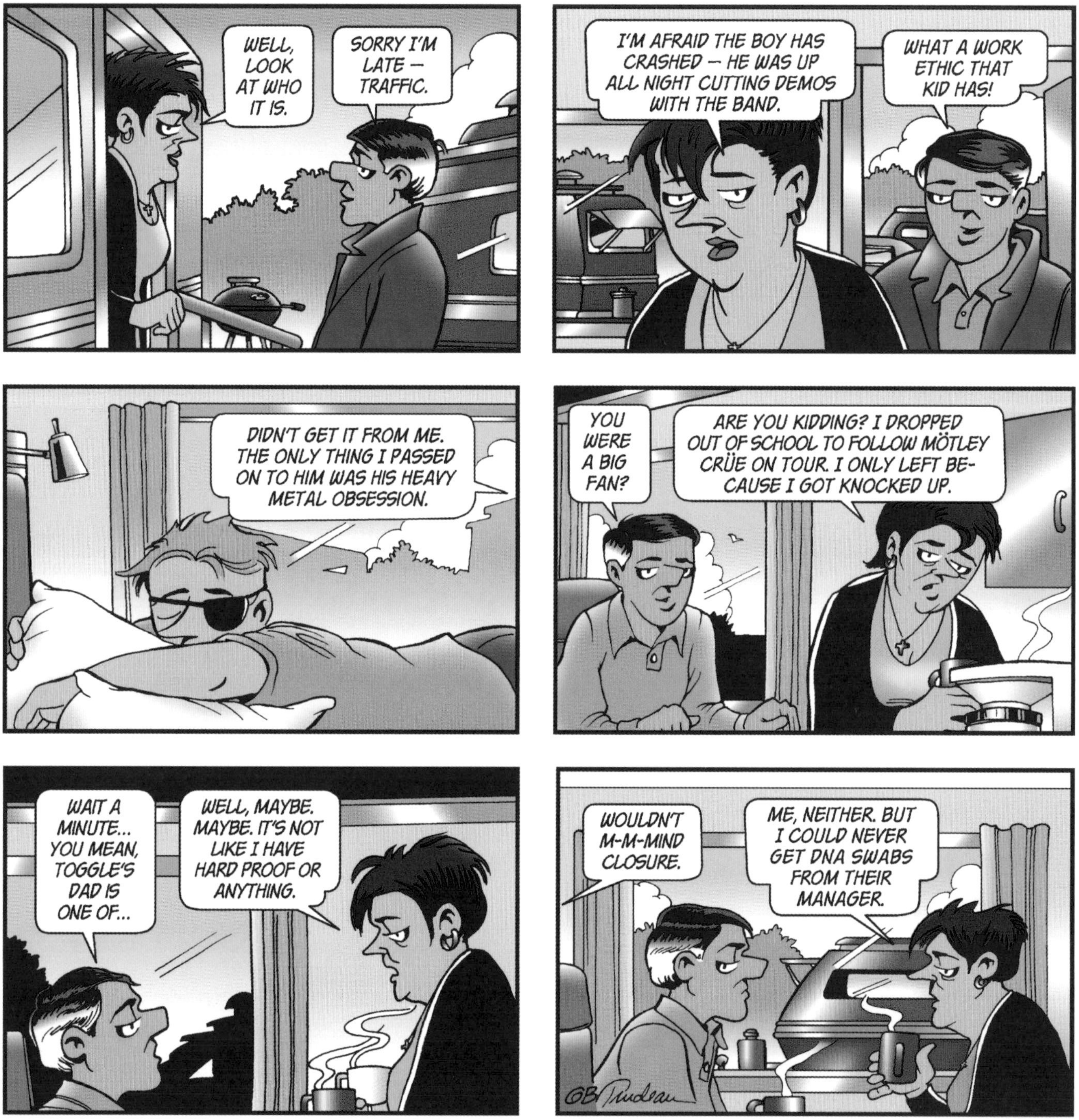
WELL, LOOK AT WHO IT IS.
SORRY I'M LATE — TRAFFIC.
I'M AFRAID THE BOY HAS CRASHED — HE WAS UP ALL NIGHT CUTTING DEMOS WITH THE BAND.
WHAT A WORK ETHIC THAT KID HAS!
DIDN'T GET IT FROM ME. THE ONLY THING I PASSED ON TO HIM WAS HIS HEAVY METAL OBSESSION.
YOU WERE A BIG FAN?
ARE YOU KIDDING? I DROPPED OUT OF SCHOOL TO FOLLOW MÖTLEY CRÜE ON TOUR. I ONLY LEFT BE-CAUSE I GOT KNOCKED UP.
WAIT A MINUTE... YOU MEAN, TOGGLE'S DAD IS ONE OF...
WELL, MAYBE. MAYBE. IT'S NOT LIKE I HAVE HARD PROOF OR ANYTHING.
WOULDN'T M-M-MIND CLOSURE.
ME, NEITHER. BUT I COULD NEVER GET DNA SWABS FROM THEIR MANAGER.

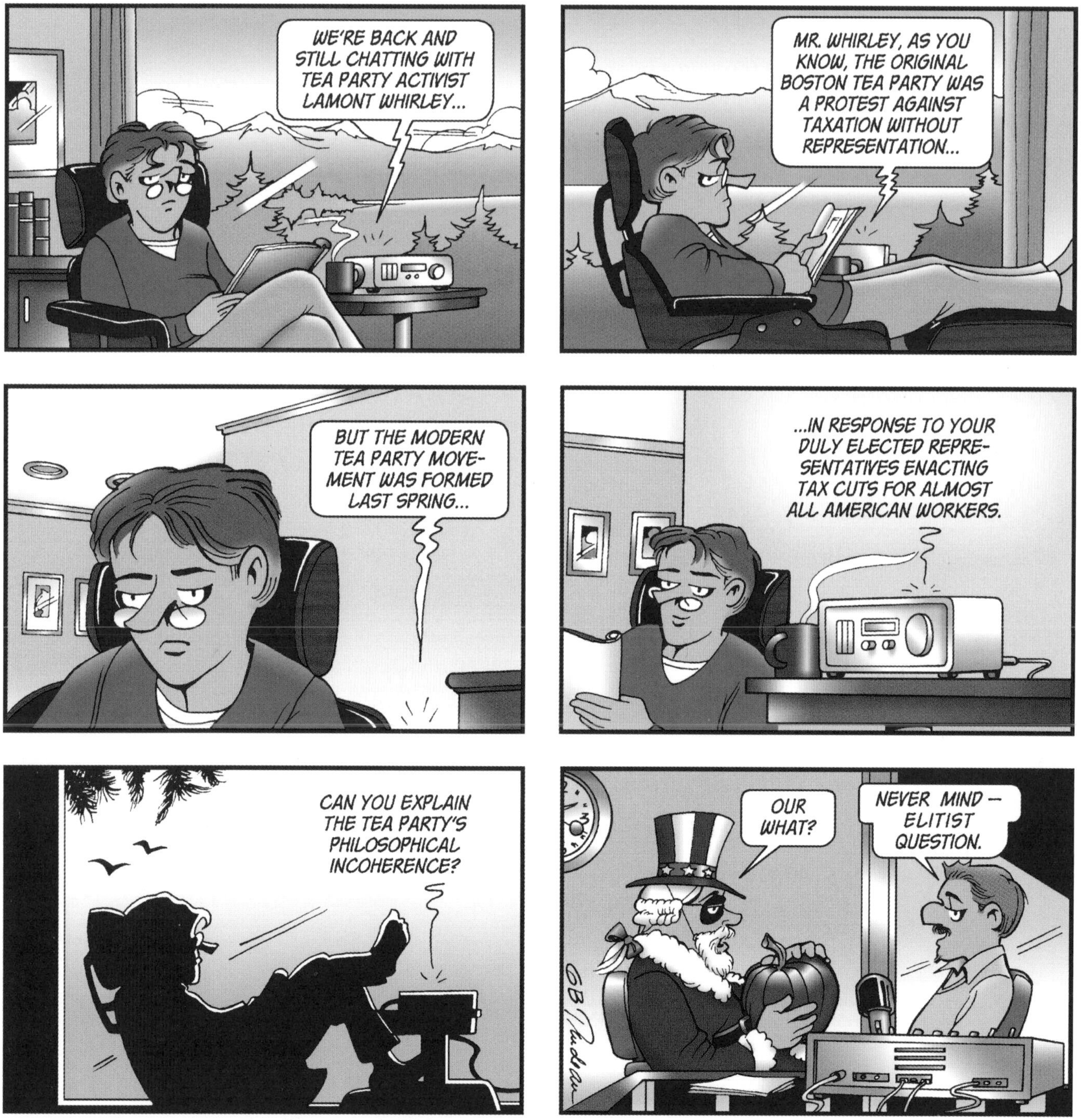
WE'RE BACK AND STILL CHATTING WITH TEA PARTY ACTIVIST LAMONT WHIRLEY...
MR. WHIRLEY, AS YOU KNOW, THE ORIGINAL BOSTON TEA PARTY WAS A PROTEST AGAINST TAXATION WITHOUT REPRESENTATION...
BUT THE MODERN TEA PARTY MOVE-MENT WAS FORMED LAST SPRING...
...IN RESPONSE TO YOUR DULY ELECTED REPRE-SENTATIVES ENACTING TAX CUTS FOR ALMOST ALL AMERICAN WORKERS.
CAN YOU EXPLAIN THE TEA PARTY'S PHILOSOPHICAL INCOHERENCE?
OUR WHAT?
NEVER MIND — ELITIST QUESTION.

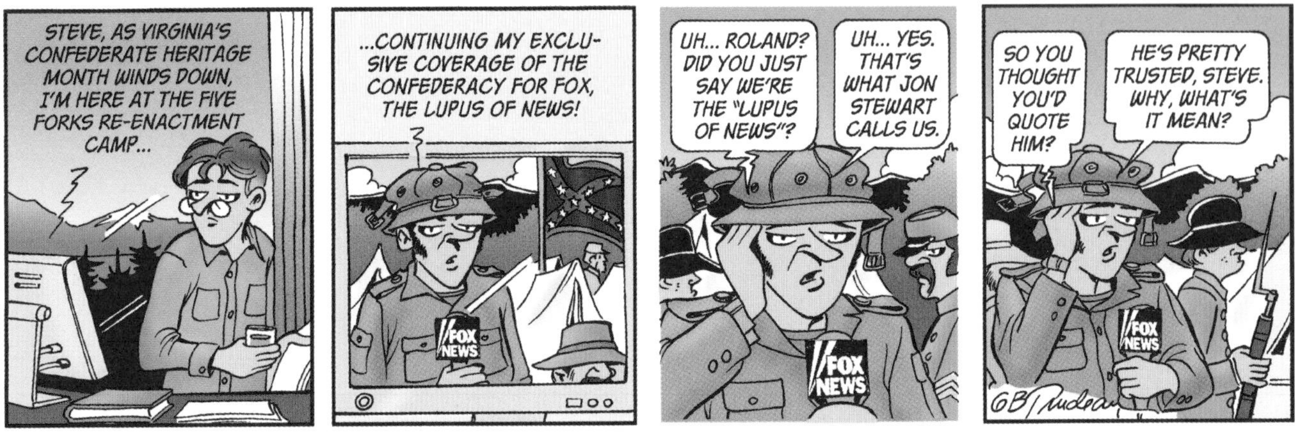
STEVE, AS VIRGINIA'S CONFEDERATE HERITAGE MONTH WINDS DOWN, I'M HERE AT THE FIVE FORKS RE-ENACTMENT CAMP...
...CONTINUING MY EXCLUSIVE COVERAGE OF THE CONFEDERACY FOR FOX, THE LUPUS OF NEWS!
FOX NEWS
UH... ROLAND? DID YOU JUST SAY WE'RE THE "LUPUS OF NEWS"?
UH... YES. THAT'S WHAT JON STEWART CALLS US.
FOX NEWS
SO YOU THOUGHT YOU'D QUOTE HIM?
HE'S PRETTY TRUSTED, STEVE. WHY, WHAT'S IT MEAN?
FOX NEWS
GB Trudeau

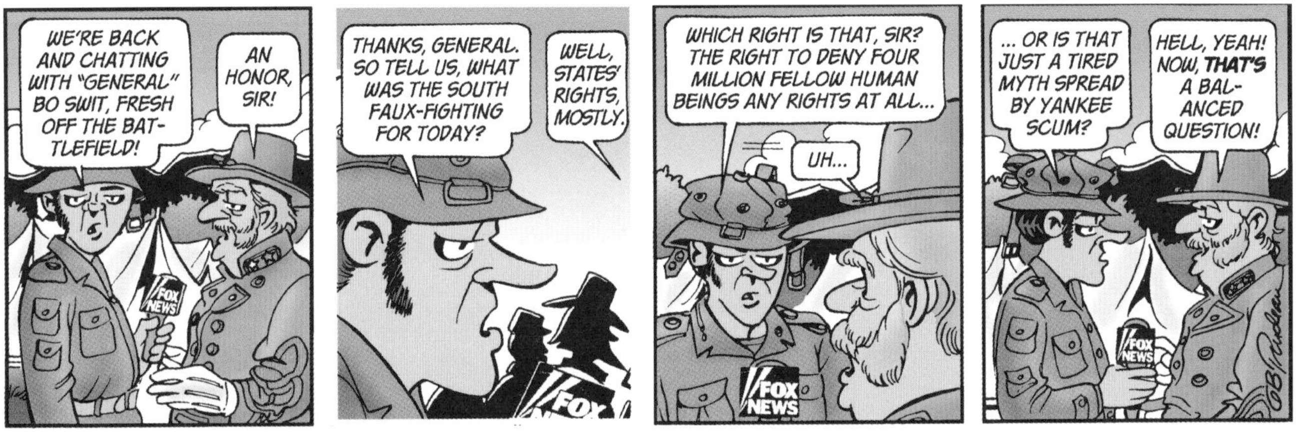
WE'RE BACK AND CHATTING WITH "GENERAL" BO SWIT, FRESH OFF THE BATTLEFIELD!
AN HONOR, SIR!
FOX NEWS
THANKS, GENERAL. SO TELL US, WHAT WAS THE SOUTH FAUX-FIGHTING FOR TODAY?
WELL, STATES' RIGHTS, MOSTLY.
WHICH RIGHT IS THAT, SIR? THE RIGHT TO DENY FOUR MILLION FELLOW HUMAN BEINGS ANY RIGHTS AT ALL...
UH...
FOX NEWS
... OR IS THAT JUST A TIRED MYTH SPREAD BY YANKEE SCUM?
HELL, YEAH! NOW, **THAT'S** A BALANCED QUESTION!
FOX NEWS
GB Trudeau

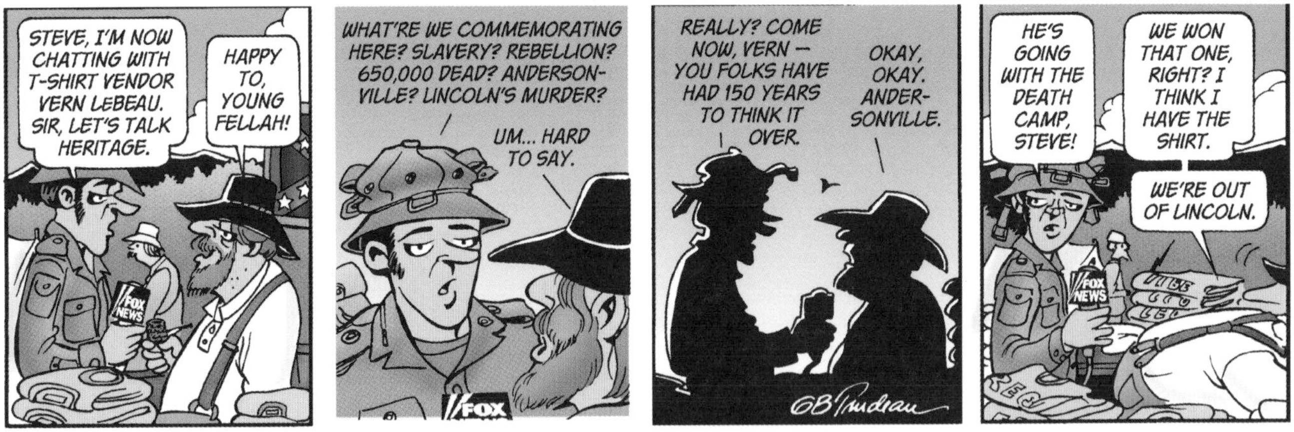
STEVE, I'M NOW CHATTING WITH T-SHIRT VENDOR VERN LEBEAU. SIR, LET'S TALK HERITAGE.
HAPPY TO, YOUNG FELLAH!
FOX NEWS
WHAT'RE WE COMMEMORATING HERE? SLAVERY? REBELLION? 650,000 DEAD? ANDERSONVILLE? LINCOLN'S MURDER?
UM... HARD TO SAY.
REALLY? COME NOW, VERN — YOU FOLKS HAVE HAD 150 YEARS TO THINK IT OVER.
OKAY, OKAY. ANDERSONVILLE.
GB Trudeau
HE'S GOING WITH THE DEATH CAMP, STEVE!
WE WON THAT ONE, RIGHT? I THINK I HAVE THE SHIRT.
WE'RE OUT OF LINCOLN.
FOX NEWS

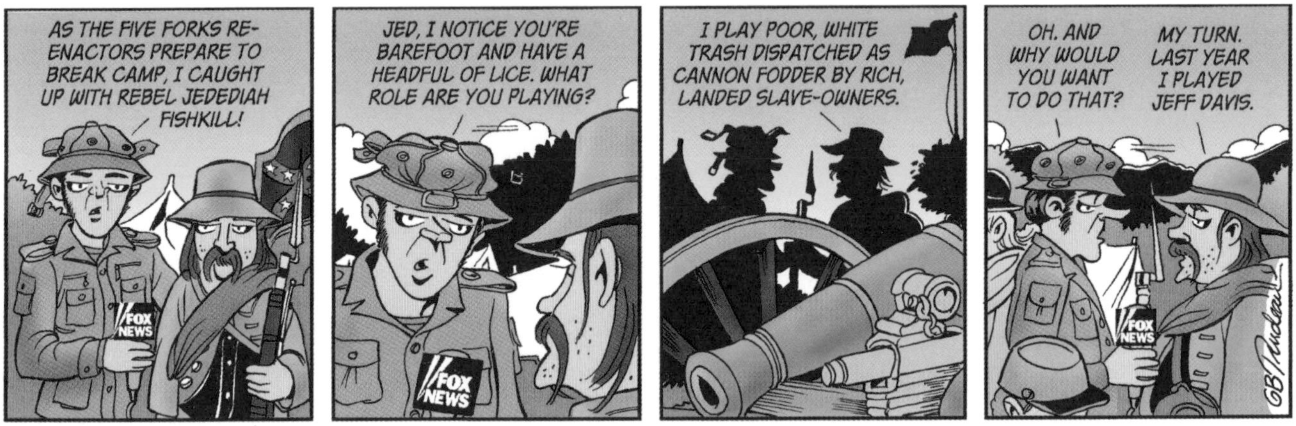
AS THE FIVE FORKS RE-ENACTORS PREPARE TO BREAK CAMP, I CAUGHT UP WITH REBEL JEDEDIAH FISHKILL!
FOX NEWS
JED, I NOTICE YOU'RE BAREFOOT AND HAVE A HEADFUL OF LICE. WHAT ROLE ARE YOU PLAYING?
FOX NEWS
I PLAY POOR, WHITE TRASH DISPATCHED AS CANNON FODDER BY RICH, LANDED SLAVE-OWNERS.
OH. AND WHY WOULD YOU WANT TO DO THAT?
MY TURN. LAST YEAR I PLAYED JEFF DAVIS.
FOX NEWS
GB Trudeau

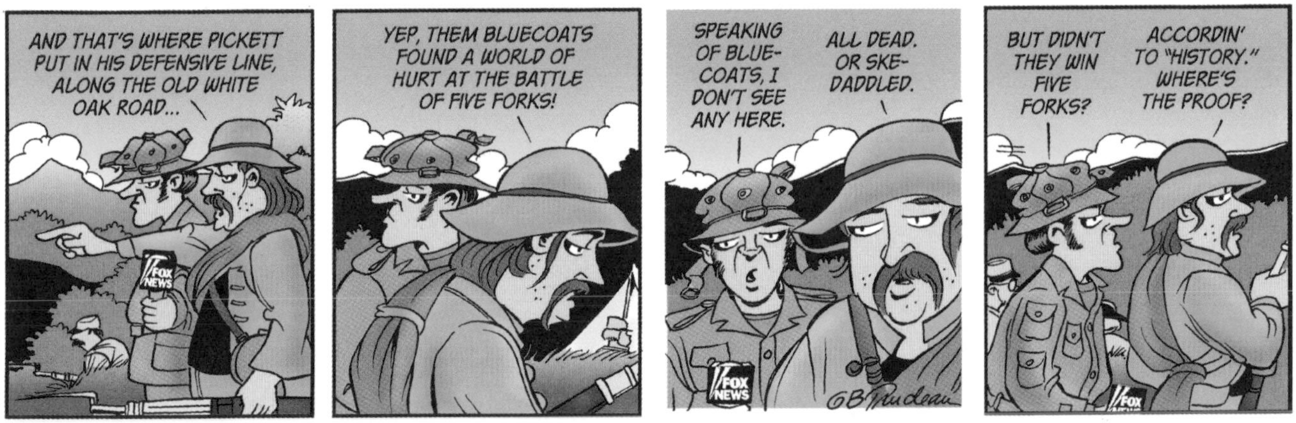
AND THAT'S WHERE PICKETT PUT IN HIS DEFENSIVE LINE, ALONG THE OLD WHITE OAK ROAD...
FOX NEWS
YEP, THEM BLUECOATS FOUND A WORLD OF HURT AT THE BATTLE OF FIVE FORKS!
SPEAKING OF BLUE-COATS, I DON'T SEE ANY HERE.
ALL DEAD. OR SKE-DADDLED.
FOX NEWS
GB Trudeau
BUT DIDN'T THEY WIN FIVE FORKS?
ACCORDIN' TO "HISTORY." WHERE'S THE PROOF?

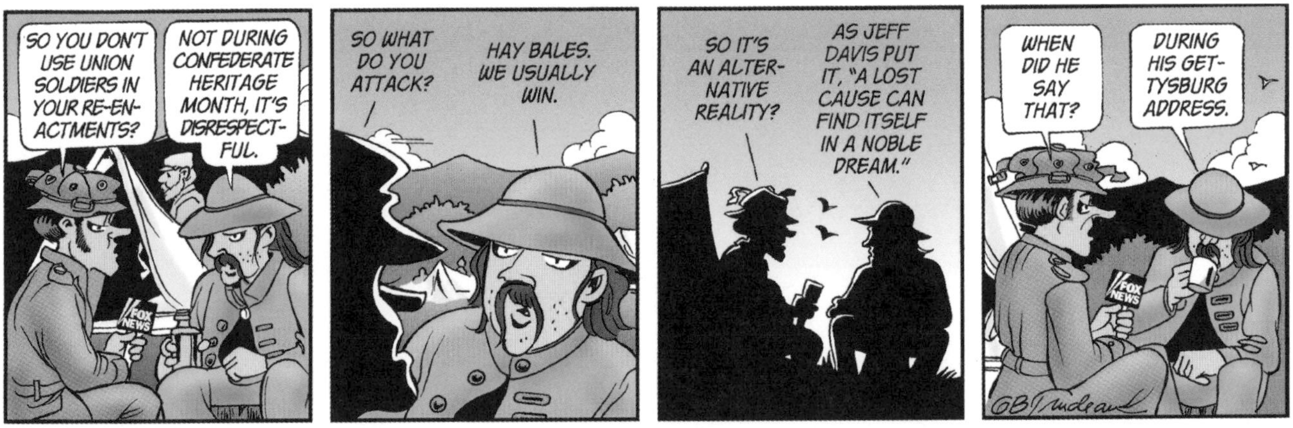
SO YOU DON'T USE UNION SOLDIERS IN YOUR RE-EN-ACTMENTS?
NOT DURING CONFEDERATE HERITAGE MONTH, IT'S DISRESPECT-FUL.
FOX NEWS
SO WHAT DO YOU ATTACK?
HAY BALES. WE USUALLY WIN.
SO IT'S AN ALTER-NATIVE REALITY?
AS JEFF DAVIS PUT IT, "A LOST CAUSE CAN FIND ITSELF IN A NOBLE DREAM."
WHEN DID HE SAY THAT?
DURING HIS GET-TYSBURG ADDRESS.
FOX NEWS
GB Trudeau

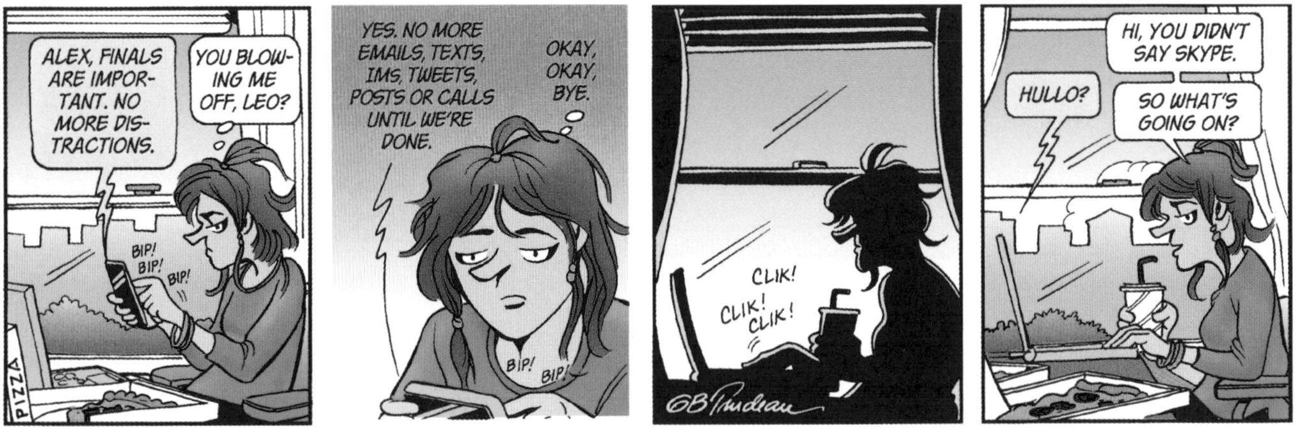
ALEX, FINALS ARE IMPORTANT. NO MORE DISTRACTIONS.
YOU BLOWING ME OFF, LEO?
BIP! BIP! BIP!
PIZZA
YES. NO MORE EMAILS, TEXTS, IMS, TWEETS, POSTS OR CALLS UNTIL WE'RE DONE.
OKAY, OKAY, BYE.
BIP! BIP!
CLIK! CLIK! CLIK!
GB Trudeau
HULLO?
HI, YOU DIDN'T SAY SKYPE.
SO WHAT'S GOING ON?

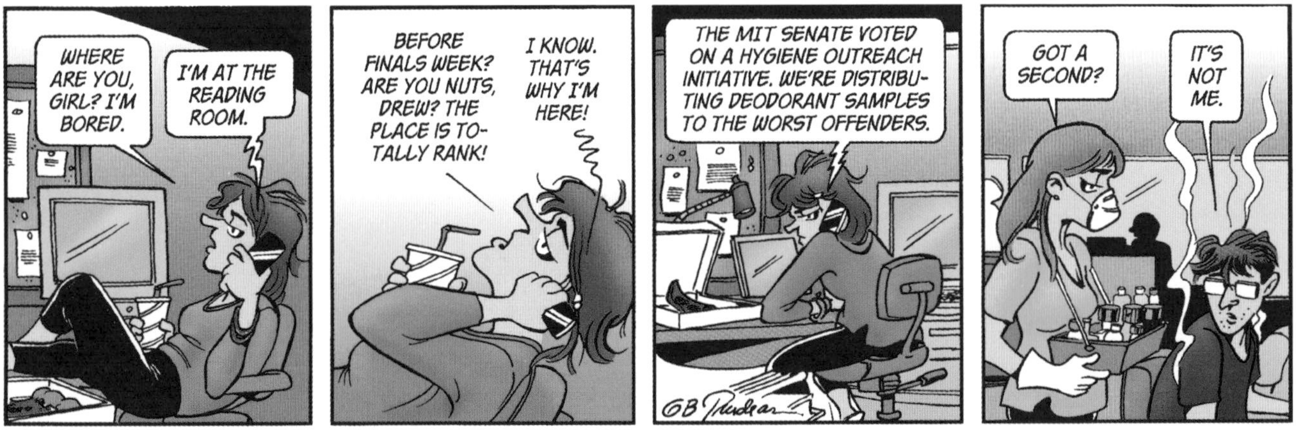
WHERE ARE YOU, GIRL? I'M BORED.
I'M AT THE READING ROOM.
BEFORE FINALS WEEK? ARE YOU NUTS, DREW? THE PLACE IS TOTALLY RANK!
I KNOW. THAT'S WHY I'M HERE!
THE MIT SENATE VOTED ON A HYGIENE OUTREACH INITIATIVE. WE'RE DISTRIBUTING DEODORANT SAMPLES TO THE WORST OFFENDERS.
GB Trudeau
GOT A SECOND?
IT'S NOT ME.

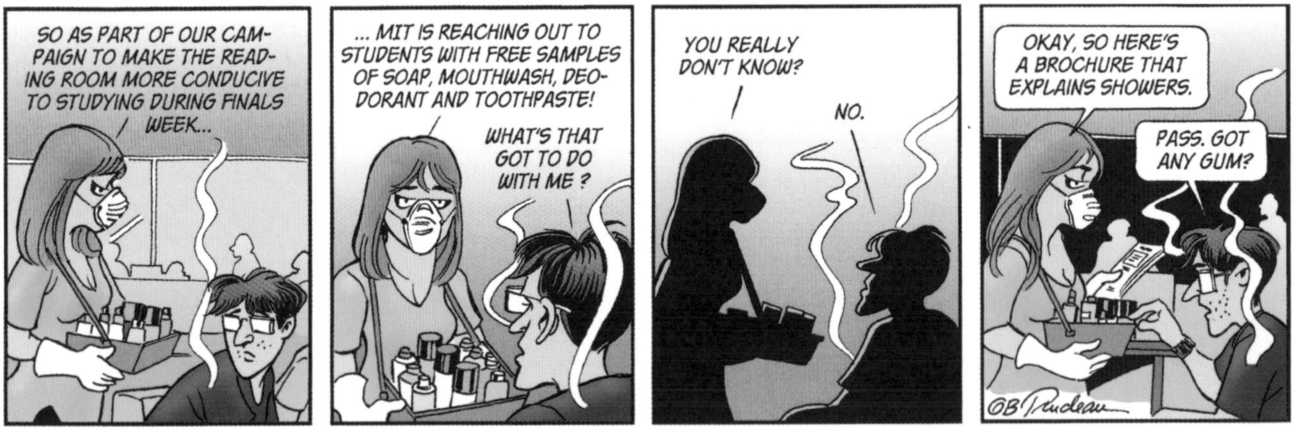
SO AS PART OF OUR CAMPAIGN TO MAKE THE READING ROOM MORE CONDUCIVE TO STUDYING DURING FINALS WEEK...
... MIT IS REACHING OUT TO STUDENTS WITH FREE SAMPLES OF SOAP, MOUTHWASH, DEODORANT AND TOOTHPASTE!
WHAT'S THAT GOT TO DO WITH ME ?
YOU REALLY DON'T KNOW?
NO.
OKAY, SO HERE'S A BROCHURE THAT EXPLAINS SHOWERS.
PASS. GOT ANY GUM?
GB Trudeau

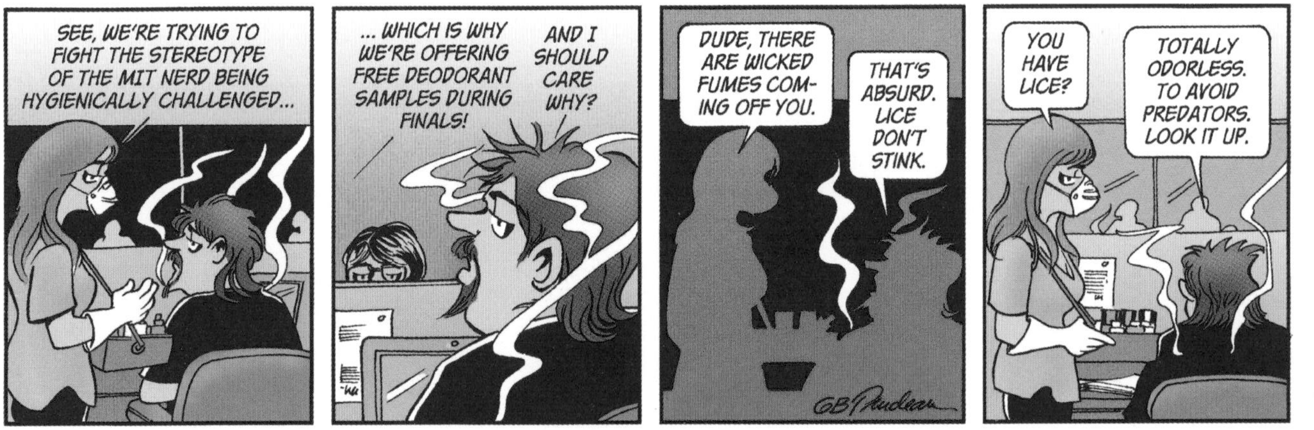
SEE, WE'RE TRYING TO FIGHT THE STEREOTYPE OF THE MIT NERD BEING HYGIENICALLY CHALLENGED...
... WHICH IS WHY WE'RE OFFERING FREE DEODORANT SAMPLES DURING FINALS!
AND I SHOULD CARE WHY?
DUDE, THERE ARE WICKED FUMES COMING OFF YOU.
THAT'S ABSURD. LICE DON'T STINK.
YOU HAVE LICE?
TOTALLY ODORLESS. TO AVOID PREDATORS. LOOK IT UP.

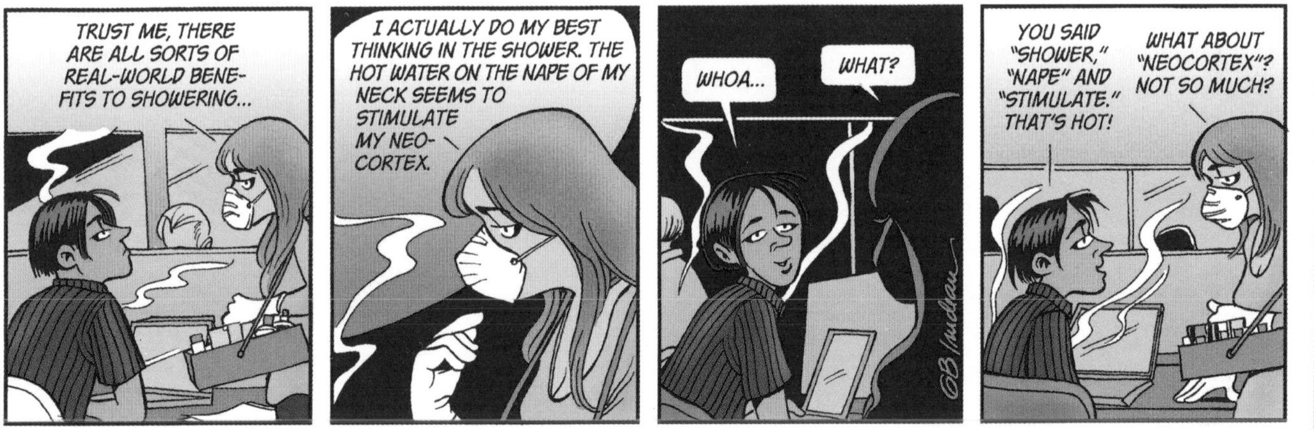
TRUST ME, THERE ARE ALL SORTS OF REAL-WORLD BENEFITS TO SHOWERING...
I ACTUALLY DO MY BEST THINKING IN THE SHOWER. THE HOT WATER ON THE NAPE OF MY NECK SEEMS TO STIMULATE MY NEOCORTEX.
WHOA...
WHAT?
YOU SAID "SHOWER," "NAPE" AND "STIMULATE." THAT'S HOT!
WHAT ABOUT "NEOCORTEX"? NOT SO MUCH?

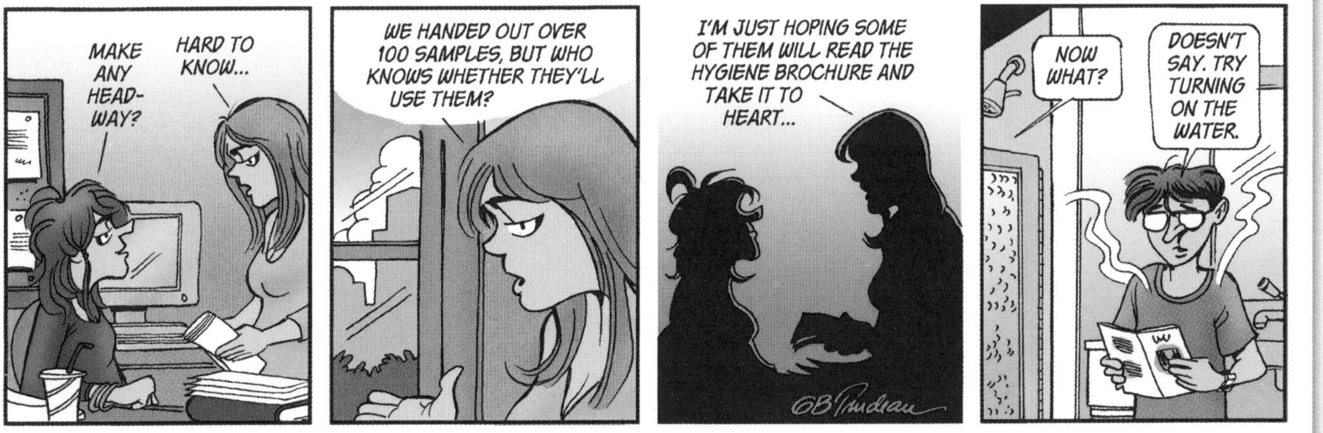
MAKE ANY HEADWAY?
HARD TO KNOW...
WE HANDED OUT OVER 100 SAMPLES, BUT WHO KNOWS WHETHER THEY'LL USE THEM?
I'M JUST HOPING SOME OF THEM WILL READ THE HYGIENE BROCHURE AND TAKE IT TO HEART...
NOW WHAT?
DOESN'T SAY. TRY TURNING ON THE WATER.

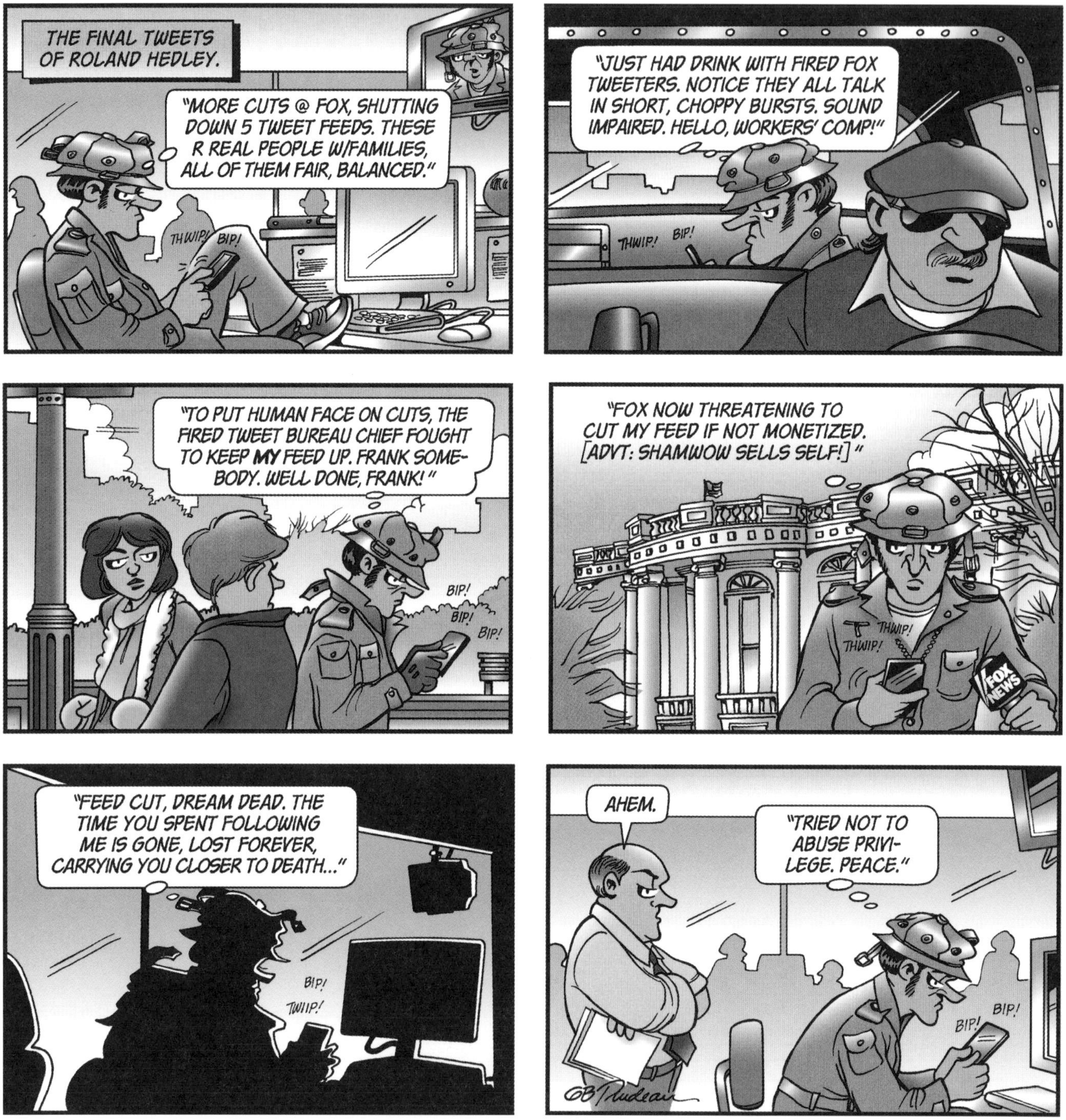
THE FINAL TWEETS OF ROLAND HEDLEY.
"MORE CUTS @ FOX, SHUTTING DOWN 5 TWEET FEEDS. THESE R REAL PEOPLE W/FAMILIES, ALL OF THEM FAIR, BALANCED."
THWIP! BIP!
"JUST HAD DRINK WITH FIRED FOX TWEETERS. NOTICE THEY ALL TALK IN SHORT, CHOPPY BURSTS. SOUND IMPAIRED. HELLO, WORKERS' COMP!"
THWIP! BIP!
"TO PUT HUMAN FACE ON CUTS, THE FIRED TWEET BUREAU CHIEF FOUGHT TO KEEP **MY** FEED UP. FRANK SOMEBODY. WELL DONE, FRANK!"
BIP! BIP! BIP!
"FOX NOW THREATENING TO CUT MY FEED IF NOT MONETIZED. [ADVT: SHAMWOW SELLS SELF!]"
THWIP! THWIP!
FOX NEWS
"FEED CUT, DREAM DEAD. THE TIME YOU SPENT FOLLOWING ME IS GONE, LOST FOREVER, CARRYING YOU CLOSER TO DEATH..."
BIP! TWIIP!
AHEM.
"TRIED NOT TO ABUSE PRIVILEGE. PEACE."
BIP! BIP!
GB Trudeau

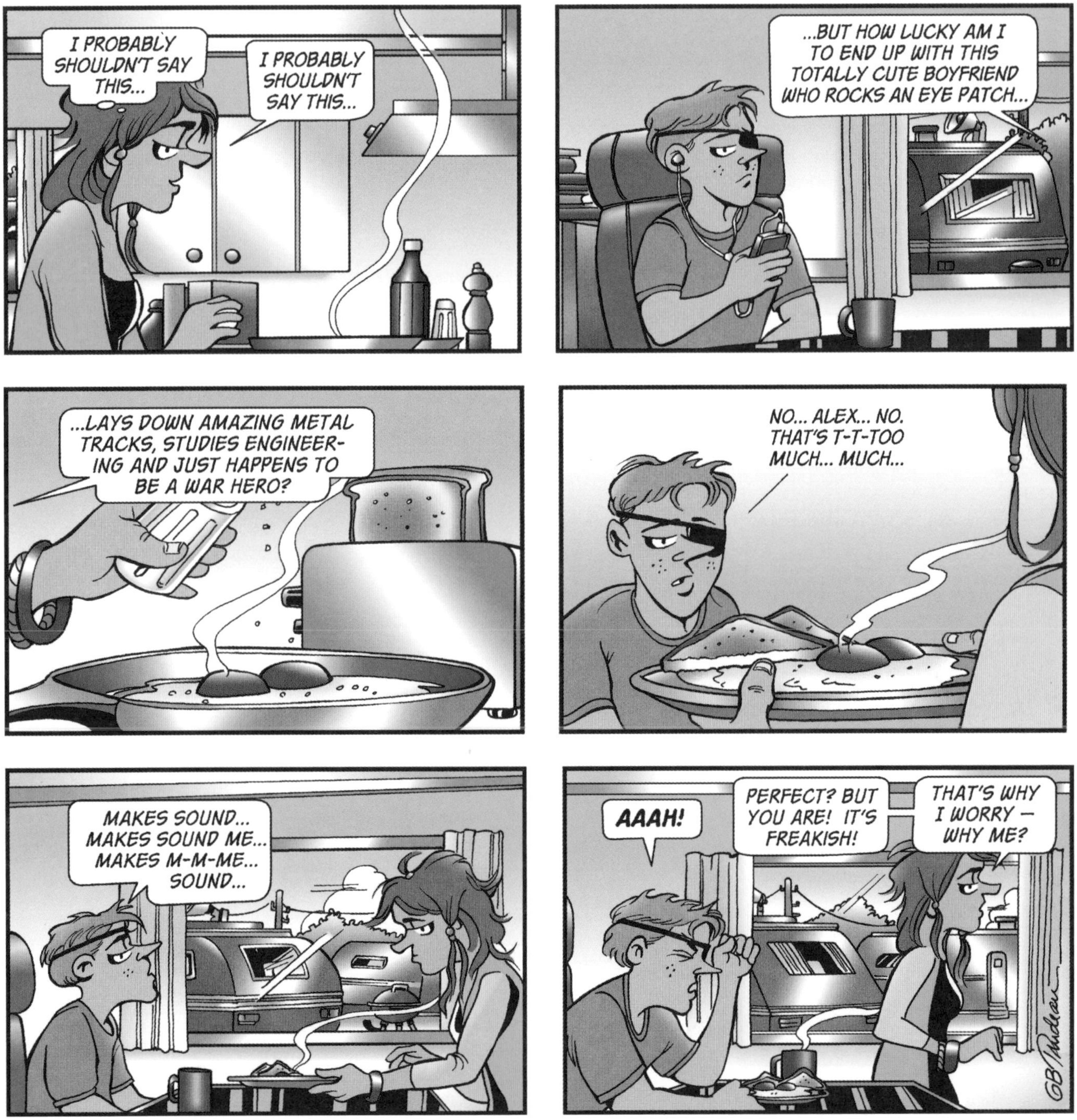
I PROBABLY SHOULDN'T SAY THIS...
I PROBABLY SHOULDN'T SAY THIS...
...BUT HOW LUCKY AM I TO END UP WITH THIS TOTALLY CUTE BOYFRIEND WHO ROCKS AN EYE PATCH...
...LAYS DOWN AMAZING METAL TRACKS, STUDIES ENGINEER-ING AND JUST HAPPENS TO BE A WAR HERO?
NO... ALEX... NO. THAT'S T-T-TOO MUCH... MUCH...
MAKES SOUND... MAKES SOUND ME... MAKES M-M-ME... SOUND...
AAAH!
PERFECT? BUT YOU ARE! IT'S FREAKISH!
THAT'S WHY I WORRY — WHY ME?

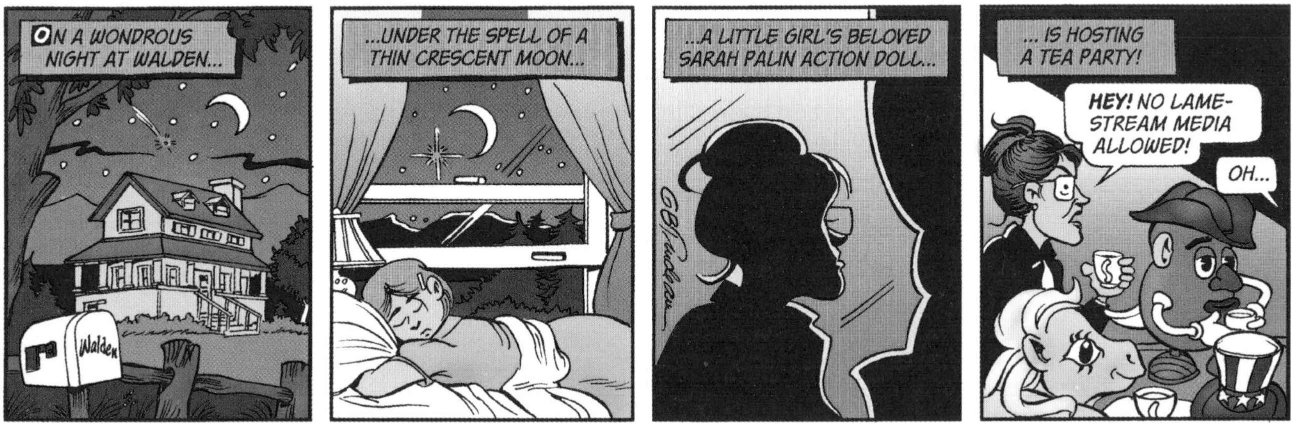
ON A WONDROUS NIGHT AT WALDEN...
Walden
...UNDER THE SPELL OF A THIN CRESCENT MOON...
...A LITTLE GIRL'S BELOVED SARAH PALIN ACTION DOLL...
... IS HOSTING A TEA PARTY!
HEY! NO LAME-STREAM MEDIA ALLOWED!
OH...

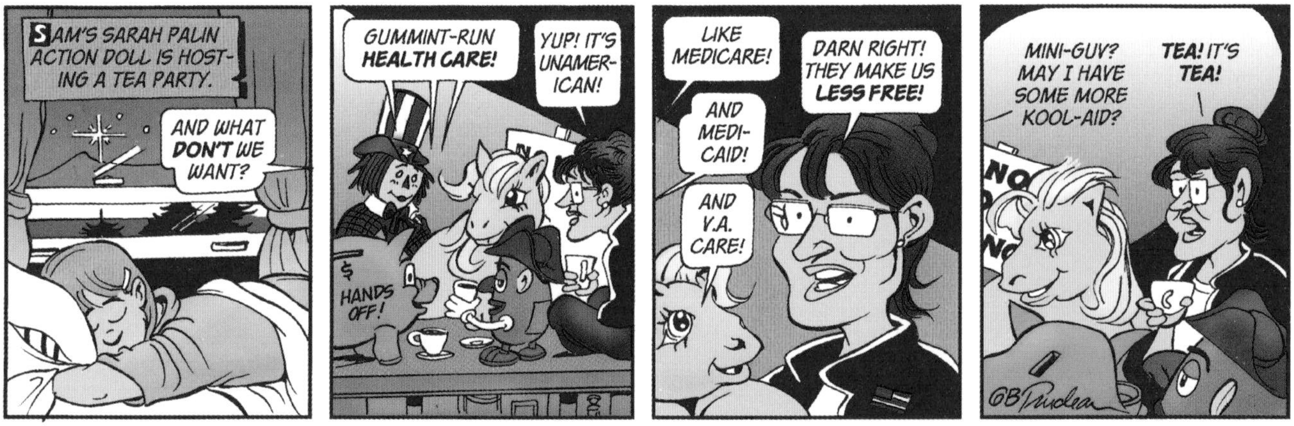
SAM'S SARAH PALIN ACTION DOLL IS HOSTING A TEA PARTY.
AND WHAT DON'T WE WANT?
GUMMINT-RUN HEALTH CARE!
YUP! IT'S UNAMERICAN!
$ HANDS OFF!
LIKE MEDICARE!
AND MEDICAID!
AND V.A. CARE!
DARN RIGHT! THEY MAKE US LESS FREE!
MINI-GUV? MAY I HAVE SOME MORE KOOL-AID?
TEA! IT'S TEA!

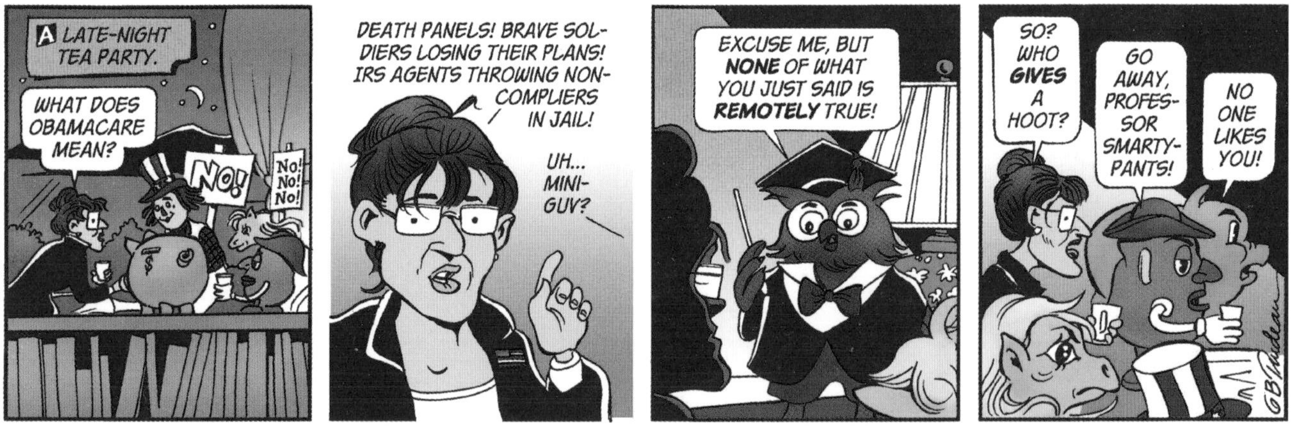
A LATE-NIGHT TEA PARTY.
WHAT DOES OBAMACARE MEAN?
NO!
No! No! No!
DEATH PANELS! BRAVE SOLDIERS LOSING THEIR PLANS! IRS AGENTS THROWING NON-COMPLIERS IN JAIL!
UH... MINI-GUV?
EXCUSE ME, BUT NONE OF WHAT YOU JUST SAID IS REMOTELY TRUE!
SO? WHO GIVES A HOOT?
GO AWAY, PROFESSOR SMARTY-PANTS!
NO ONE LIKES YOU!

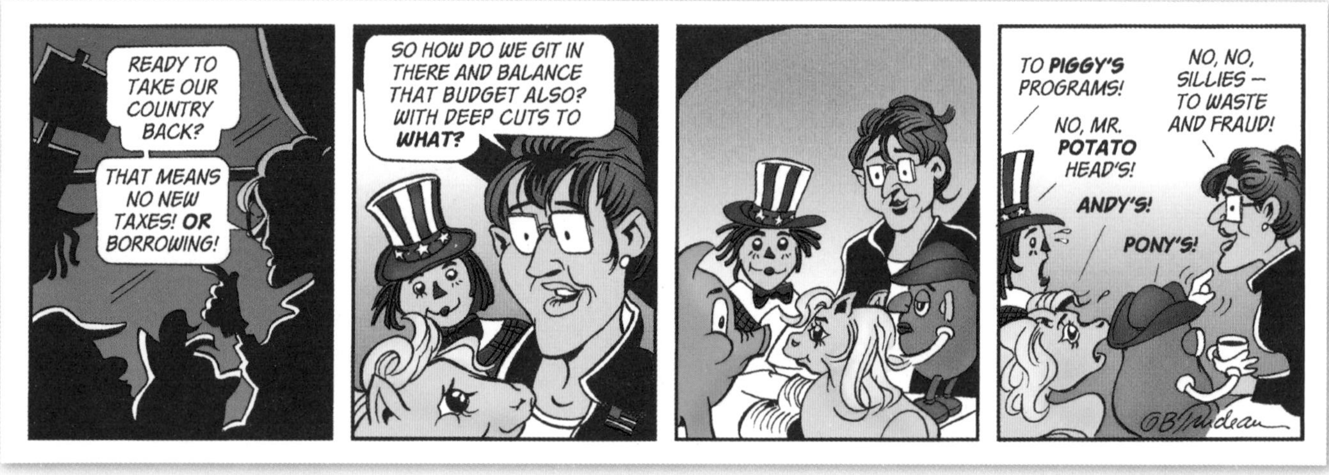
READY TO TAKE OUR COUNTRY BACK?
THAT MEANS NO NEW TAXES! OR BORROWING!
SO HOW DO WE GIT IN THERE AND BALANCE THAT BUDGET ALSO? WITH DEEP CUTS TO WHAT?
TO PIGGY'S PROGRAMS!
NO, MR. POTATO HEAD'S!
ANDY'S!
PONY'S!
NO, NO, SILLIES — TO WASTE AND FRAUD!
GB Trudeau

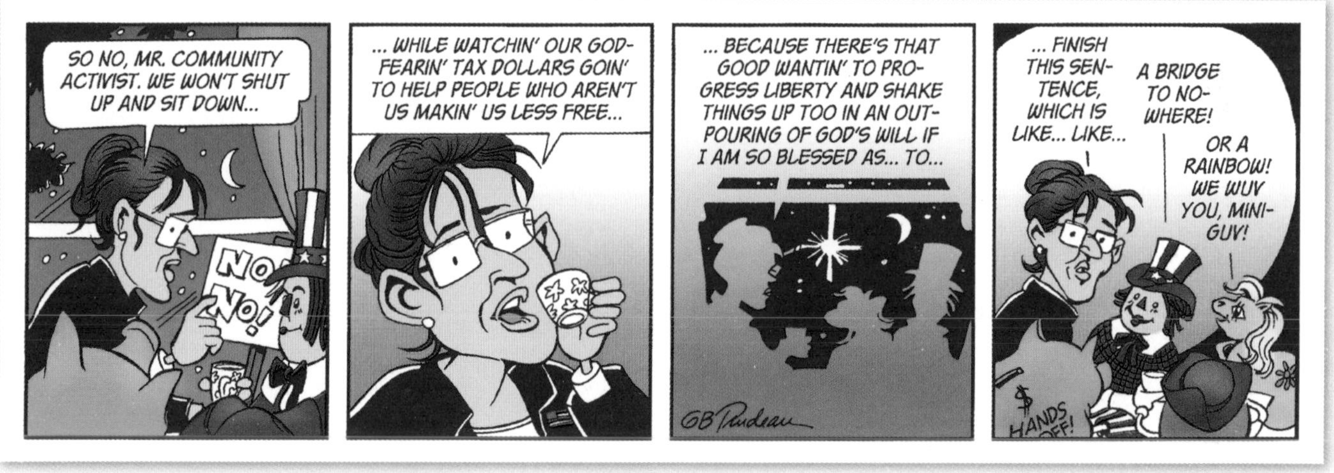
SO NO, MR. COMMUNITY ACTIVIST. WE WON'T SHUT UP AND SIT DOWN...
NO NO!
... WHILE WATCHIN' OUR GOD-FEARIN' TAX DOLLARS GOIN' TO HELP PEOPLE WHO AREN'T US MAKIN' US LESS FREE...
... BECAUSE THERE'S THAT GOOD WANTIN' TO PRO-GRESS LIBERTY AND SHAKE THINGS UP TOO IN AN OUT-POURING OF GOD'S WILL IF I AM SO BLESSED AS... TO...
GB Trudeau
... FINISH THIS SEN-TENCE, WHICH IS LIKE... LIKE...
A BRIDGE TO NO-WHERE!
OR A RAINBOW! WE WUV YOU, MINI-GUV!
$ HANDS OFF!

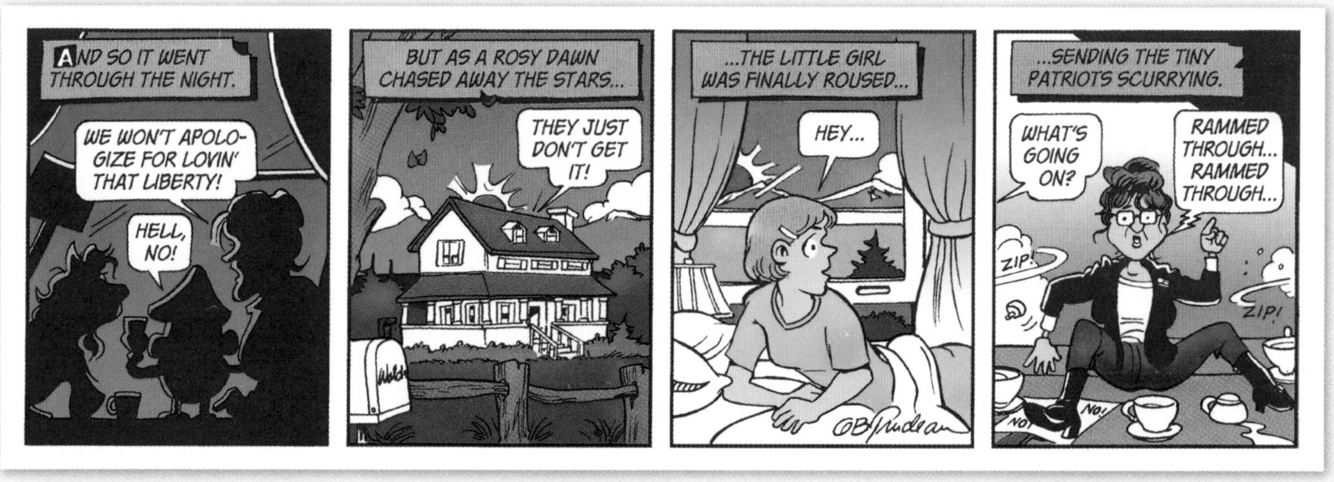
AND SO IT WENT THROUGH THE NIGHT.
WE WON'T APOLO-GIZE FOR LOVIN' THAT LIBERTY!
HELL, NO!
BUT AS A ROSY DAWN CHASED AWAY THE STARS...
THEY JUST DON'T GET IT!
...THE LITTLE GIRL WAS FINALLY ROUSED...
HEY...
GB Trudeau
...SENDING THE TINY PATRIOTS SCURRYING.
WHAT'S GOING ON?
RAMMED THROUGH... RAMMED THROUGH...
ZIP!
ZIP!
NO!
NO!

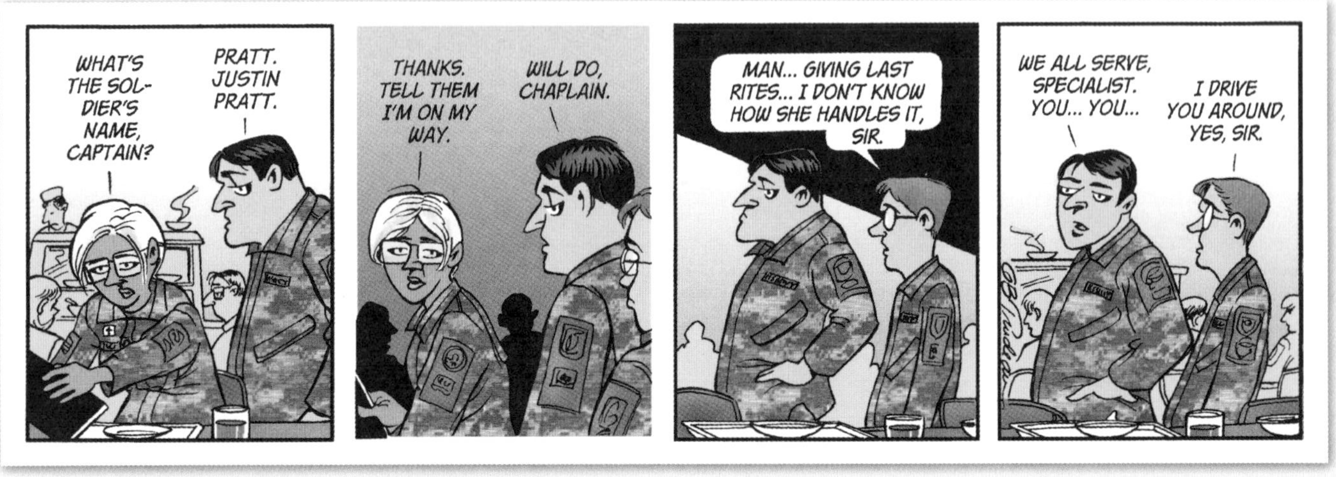
WHAT'S THE SOL-DIER'S NAME, CAPTAIN?
PRATT. JUSTIN PRATT.
THANKS. TELL THEM I'M ON MY WAY.
WILL DO, CHAPLAIN.
MAN... GIVING LAST RITES... I DON'T KNOW HOW SHE HANDLES IT, SIR.
WE ALL SERVE, SPECIALIST. YOU... YOU...
I DRIVE YOU AROUND, YES, SIR.

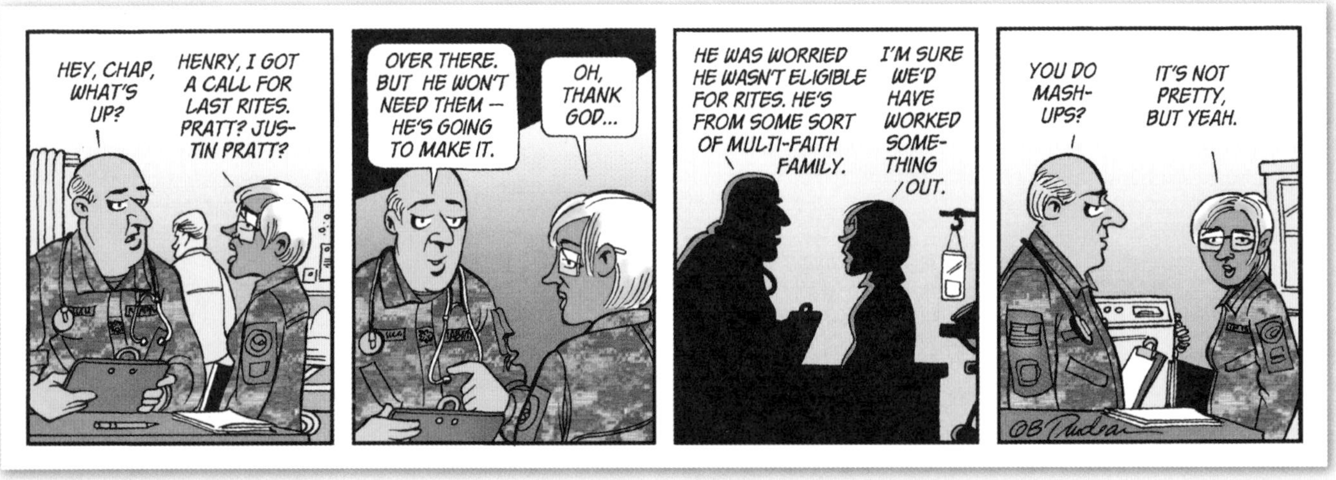
HEY, CHAP, WHAT'S UP?
HENRY, I GOT A CALL FOR LAST RITES. PRATT? JUS-TIN PRATT?
OVER THERE. BUT HE WON'T NEED THEM — HE'S GOING TO MAKE IT.
OH, THANK GOD...
HE WAS WORRIED HE WASN'T ELIGIBLE FOR RITES. HE'S FROM SOME SORT OF MULTI-FAITH FAMILY.
I'M SURE WE'D HAVE WORKED SOME-THING OUT.
YOU DO MASH-UPS?
IT'S NOT PRETTY, BUT YEAH.

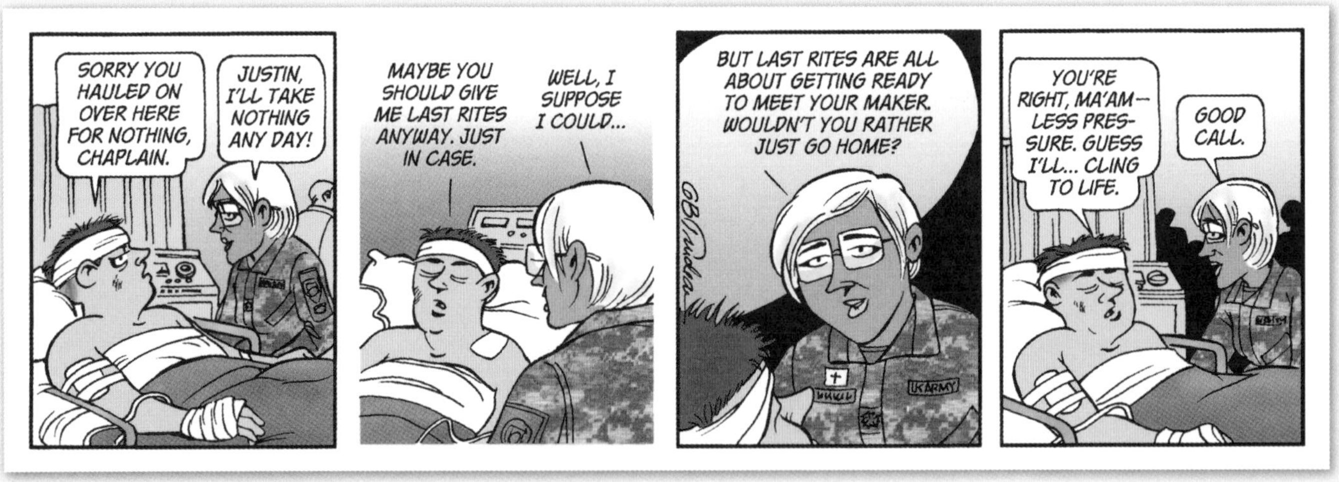
SORRY YOU HAULED ON OVER HERE FOR NOTHING, CHAPLAIN.
JUSTIN, I'LL TAKE NOTHING ANY DAY!
MAYBE YOU SHOULD GIVE ME LAST RITES ANYWAY. JUST IN CASE.
WELL, I SUPPOSE I COULD...
BUT LAST RITES ARE ALL ABOUT GETTING READY TO MEET YOUR MAKER. WOULDN'T YOU RATHER JUST GO HOME?
YOU'RE RIGHT, MA'AM— LESS PRES-SURE. GUESS I'LL... CLING TO LIFE.
GOOD CALL.

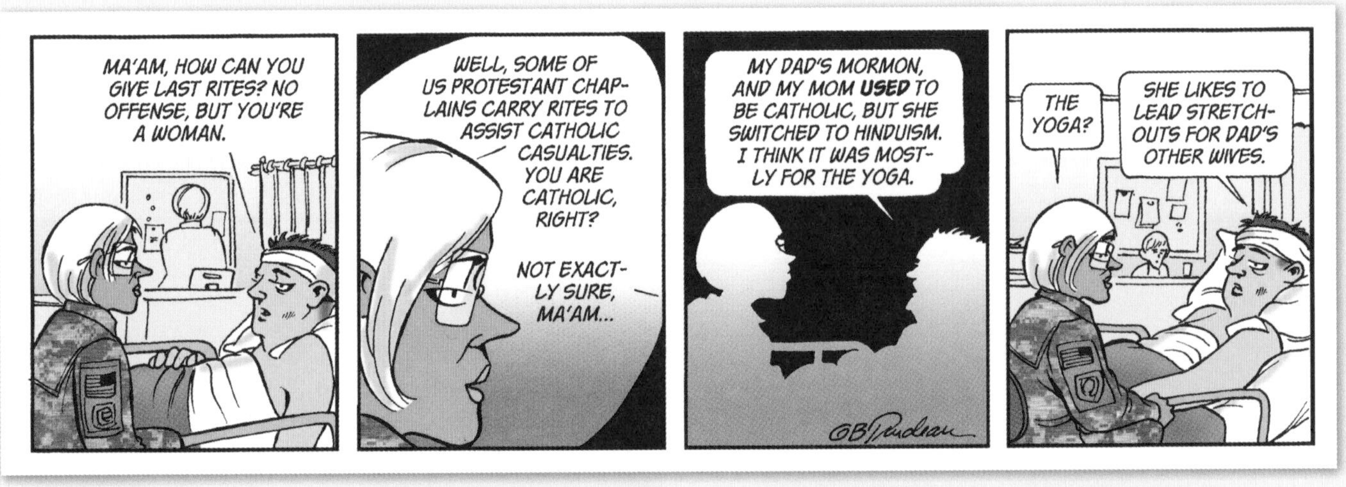
MA'AM, HOW CAN YOU GIVE LAST RITES? NO OFFENSE, BUT YOU'RE A WOMAN.
WELL, SOME OF US PROTESTANT CHAPLAINS CARRY RITES TO ASSIST CATHOLIC CASUALTIES. YOU ARE CATHOLIC, RIGHT?
NOT EXACTLY SURE, MA'AM...
MY DAD'S MORMON, AND MY MOM USED TO BE CATHOLIC, BUT SHE SWITCHED TO HINDUISM. I THINK IT WAS MOSTLY FOR THE YOGA.
THE YOGA?
SHE LIKES TO LEAD STRETCH-OUTS FOR DAD'S OTHER WIVES.
GBTrudeau

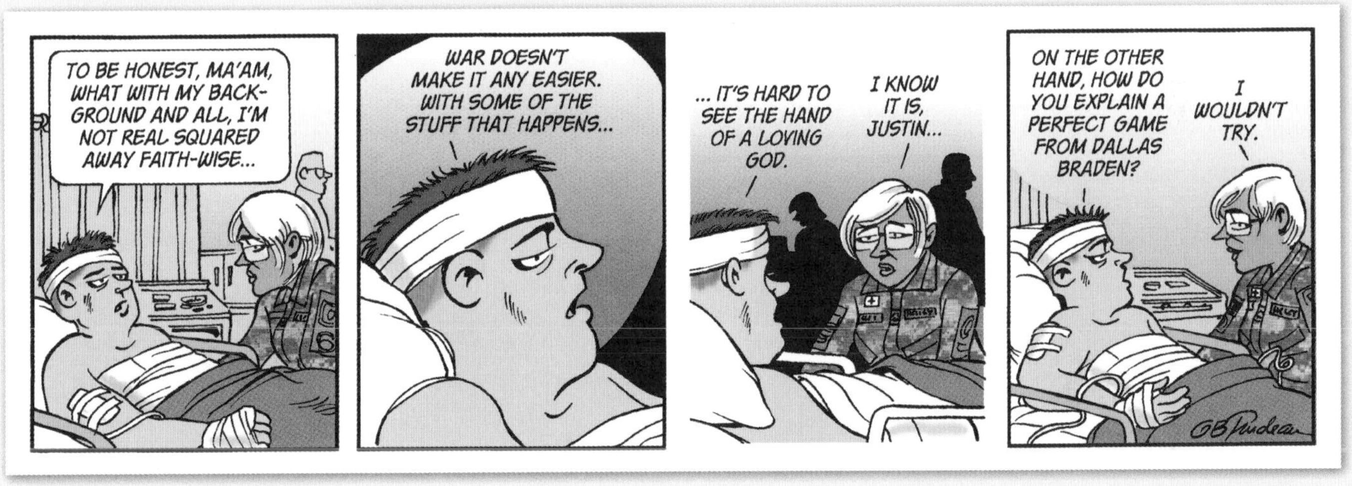
TO BE HONEST, MA'AM, WHAT WITH MY BACKGROUND AND ALL, I'M NOT REAL SQUARED AWAY FAITH-WISE...
WAR DOESN'T MAKE IT ANY EASIER. WITH SOME OF THE STUFF THAT HAPPENS...
... IT'S HARD TO SEE THE HAND OF A LOVING GOD.
I KNOW IT IS, JUSTIN...
ON THE OTHER HAND, HOW DO YOU EXPLAIN A PERFECT GAME FROM DALLAS BRADEN?
I WOULDN'T TRY.
GBTrudeau

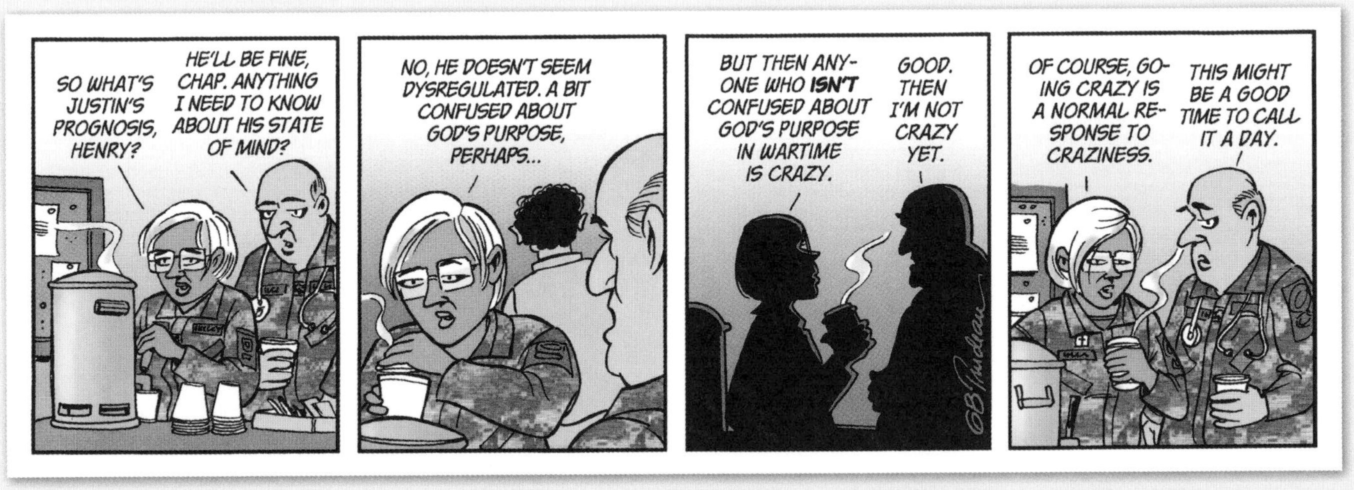
SO WHAT'S JUSTIN'S PROGNOSIS, HENRY?
HE'LL BE FINE, CHAP. ANYTHING I NEED TO KNOW ABOUT HIS STATE OF MIND?
NO, HE DOESN'T SEEM DYSREGULATED. A BIT CONFUSED ABOUT GOD'S PURPOSE, PERHAPS...
BUT THEN ANYONE WHO ISN'T CONFUSED ABOUT GOD'S PURPOSE IN WARTIME IS CRAZY.
GOOD. THEN I'M NOT CRAZY YET.
OF COURSE, GOING CRAZY IS A NORMAL RESPONSE TO CRAZINESS.
THIS MIGHT BE A GOOD TIME TO CALL IT A DAY.
GBTrudeau

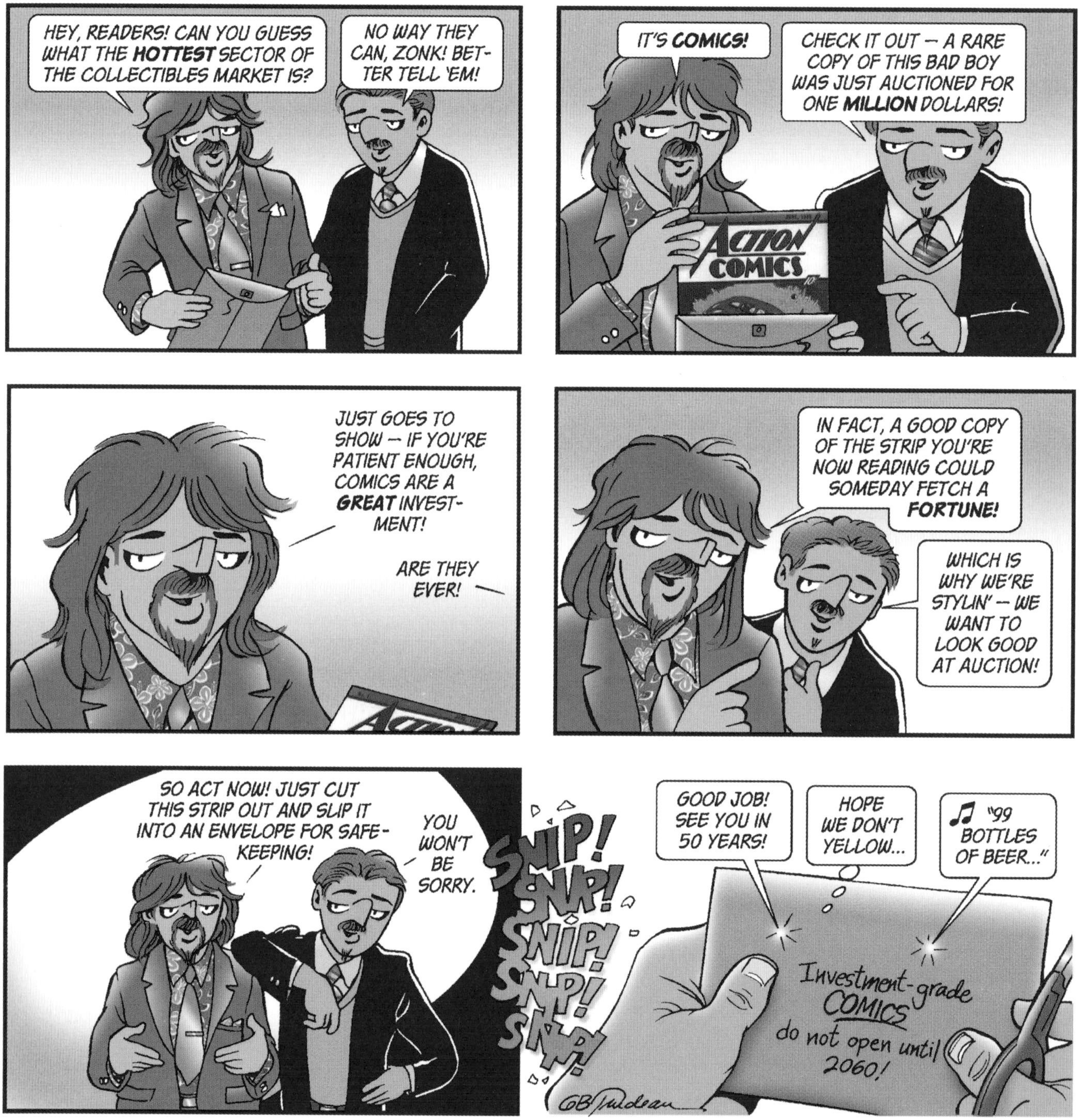
HEY, READERS! CAN YOU GUESS WHAT THE **HOTTEST** SECTOR OF THE COLLECTIBLES MARKET IS?
NO WAY THEY CAN, ZONK! BETTER TELL 'EM!
IT'S **COMICS!**
CHECK IT OUT — A RARE COPY OF THIS BAD BOY WAS JUST AUCTIONED FOR ONE **MILLION** DOLLARS!
ACTION COMICS
JUST GOES TO SHOW — IF YOU'RE PATIENT ENOUGH, COMICS ARE A **GREAT** INVESTMENT!
ARE THEY EVER!
IN FACT, A GOOD COPY OF THE STRIP YOU'RE NOW READING COULD SOMEDAY FETCH A **FORTUNE!**
WHICH IS WHY WE'RE STYLIN' — WE WANT TO LOOK GOOD AT AUCTION!
SO ACT NOW! JUST CUT THIS STRIP OUT AND SLIP IT INTO AN ENVELOPE FOR SAFE-KEEPING!
YOU WON'T BE SORRY.
SNIP! SNIP! SNIP! SNIP! SNIP!
GOOD JOB! SEE YOU IN 50 YEARS!
HOPE WE DON'T YELLOW...
♫ "99 BOTTLES OF BEER..."
Investment-grade COMICS do not open until 2060!
GB Trudeau

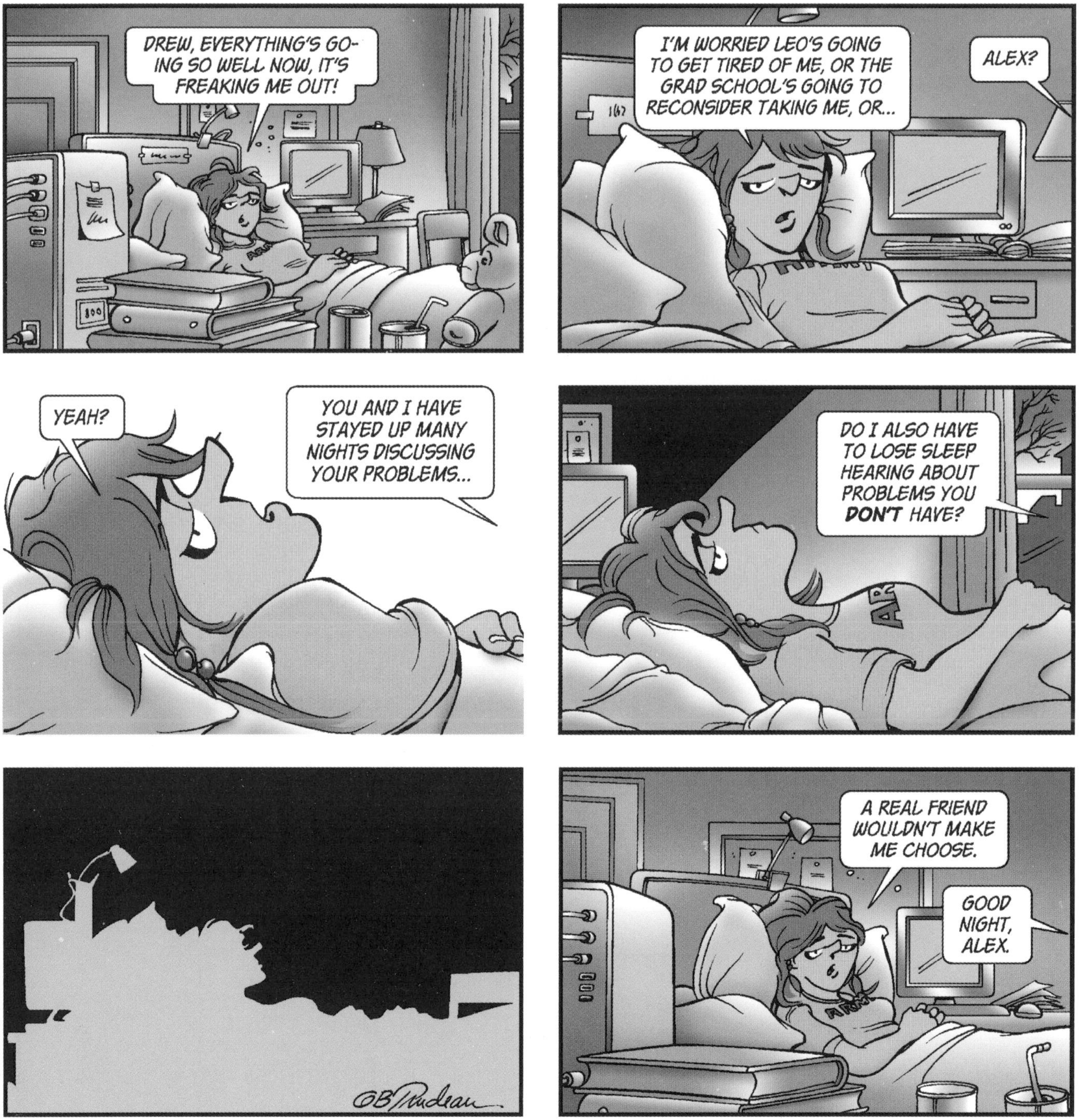
DREW, EVERYTHING'S GOING SO WELL NOW, IT'S FREAKING ME OUT!
I'M WORRIED LEO'S GOING TO GET TIRED OF ME, OR THE GRAD SCHOOL'S GOING TO RECONSIDER TAKING ME, OR...
ALEX?
YEAH?
YOU AND I HAVE STAYED UP MANY NIGHTS DISCUSSING YOUR PROBLEMS...
DO I ALSO HAVE TO LOSE SLEEP HEARING ABOUT PROBLEMS YOU **DON'T** HAVE?
A REAL FRIEND WOULDN'T MAKE ME CHOOSE.
GOOD NIGHT, ALEX.
GB Trudeau

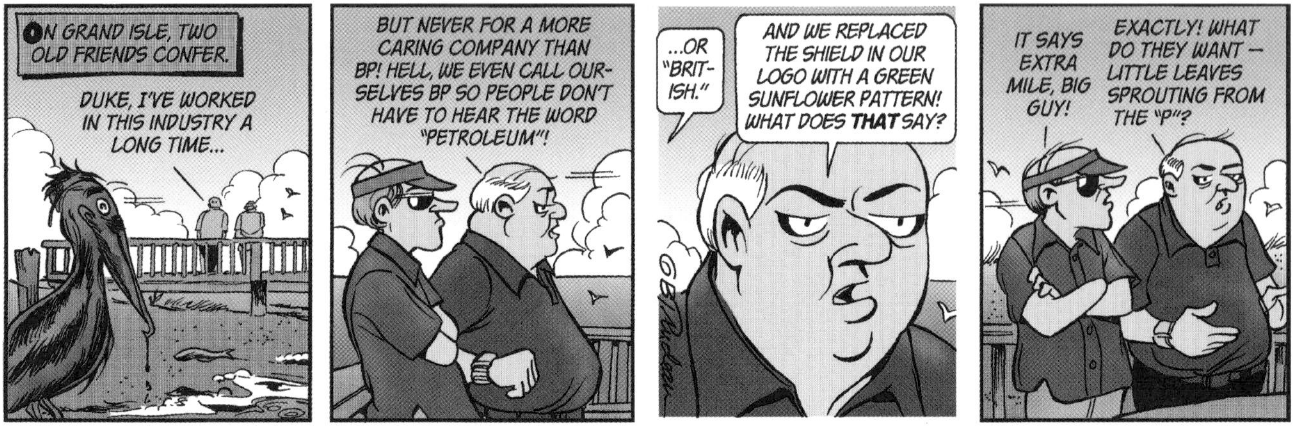
ON GRAND ISLE, TWO OLD FRIENDS CONFER.
DUKE, I'VE WORKED IN THIS INDUSTRY A LONG TIME...
BUT NEVER FOR A MORE CARING COMPANY THAN BP! HELL, WE EVEN CALL OUR-SELVES BP SO PEOPLE DON'T HAVE TO HEAR THE WORD "PETROLEUM"!
...OR "BRIT-ISH."
AND WE REPLACED THE SHIELD IN OUR LOGO WITH A GREEN SUNFLOWER PATTERN! WHAT DOES **THAT** SAY?
IT SAYS EXTRA MILE, BIG GUY!
EXACTLY! WHAT DO THEY WANT — LITTLE LEAVES SPROUTING FROM THE "P"?

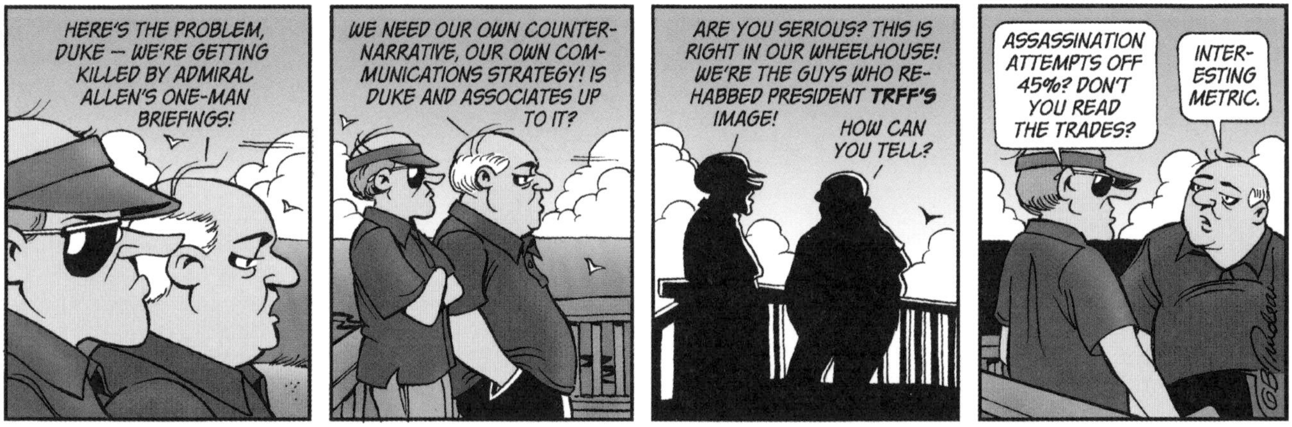
HERE'S THE PROBLEM, DUKE — WE'RE GETTING KILLED BY ADMIRAL ALLEN'S ONE-MAN BRIEFINGS!
WE NEED OUR OWN COUNTER-NARRATIVE, OUR OWN COM-MUNICATIONS STRATEGY! IS DUKE AND ASSOCIATES UP TO IT?
ARE YOU SERIOUS? THIS IS RIGHT IN OUR WHEELHOUSE! WE'RE THE GUYS WHO RE-HABBED PRESIDENT **TRFF'S** IMAGE!
HOW CAN YOU TELL?
ASSASSINATION ATTEMPTS OFF 45%? DON'T YOU READ THE TRADES?
INTER-ESTING METRIC.

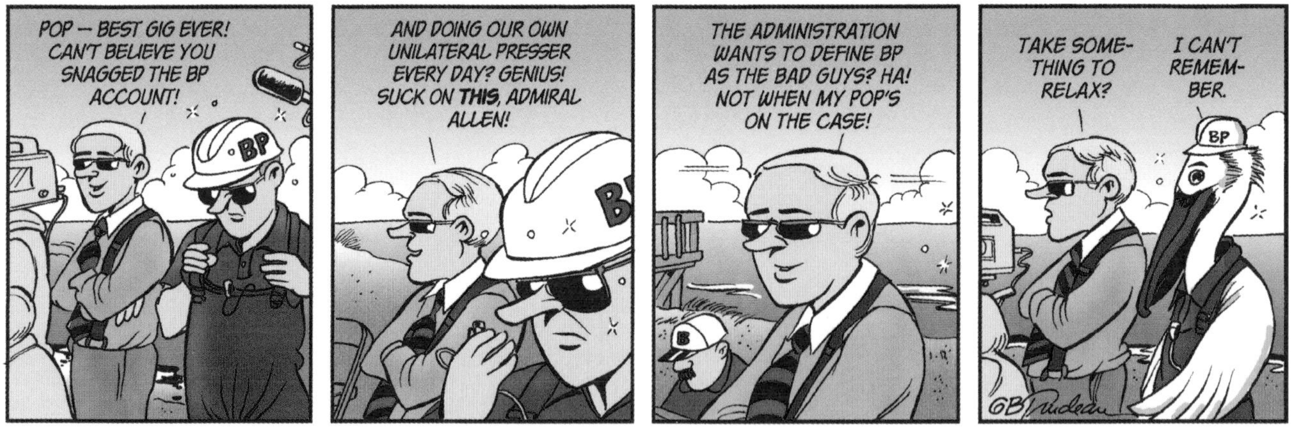
POP — BEST GIG EVER! CAN'T BELIEVE YOU SNAGGED THE BP ACCOUNT!
BP
AND DOING OUR OWN UNILATERAL PRESSER EVERY DAY? GENIUS! SUCK ON **THIS**, ADMIRAL ALLEN!
THE ADMINISTRATION WANTS TO DEFINE BP AS THE BAD GUYS? HA! NOT WHEN MY POP'S ON THE CASE!
TAKE SOME-THING TO RELAX?
I CAN'T REMEM-BER.

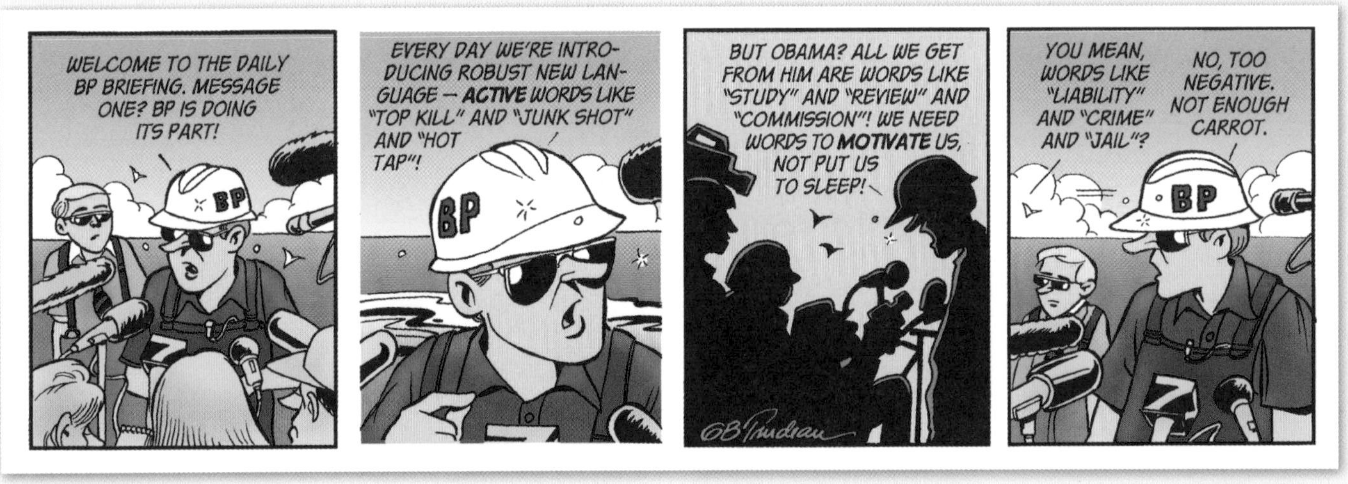
WELCOME TO THE DAILY BP BRIEFING. MESSAGE ONE? BP IS DOING ITS PART!
EVERY DAY WE'RE INTRODUCING ROBUST NEW LANGUAGE — **ACTIVE** WORDS LIKE "TOP KILL" AND "JUNK SHOT" AND "HOT TAP"!
BUT OBAMA? ALL WE GET FROM HIM ARE WORDS LIKE "STUDY" AND "REVIEW" AND "COMMISSION"! WE NEED WORDS TO **MOTIVATE** US, NOT PUT US TO SLEEP!
YOU MEAN, WORDS LIKE "LIABILITY" AND "CRIME" AND "JAIL"?
NO, TOO NEGATIVE. NOT ENOUGH CARROT.

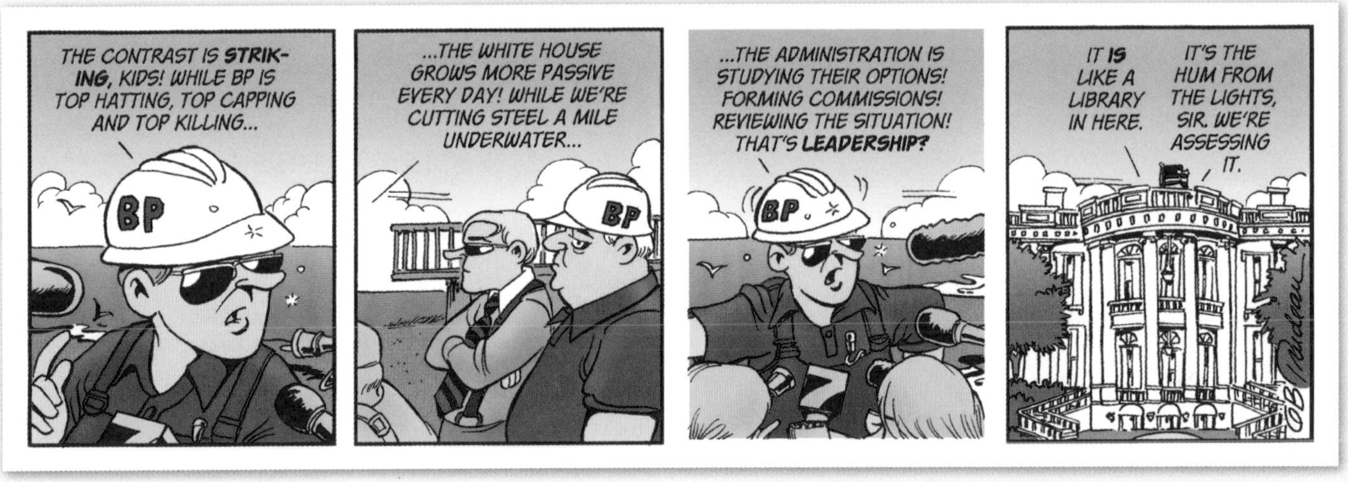
THE CONTRAST IS **STRIKING**, KIDS! WHILE BP IS TOP HATTING, TOP CAPPING AND TOP KILLING...
...THE WHITE HOUSE GROWS MORE PASSIVE EVERY DAY! WHILE WE'RE CUTTING STEEL A MILE UNDERWATER...
...THE ADMINISTRATION IS STUDYING THEIR OPTIONS! FORMING COMMISSIONS! REVIEWING THE SITUATION! THAT'S **LEADERSHIP?**
IT **IS** LIKE A LIBRARY IN HERE.
IT'S THE HUM FROM THE LIGHTS, SIR. WE'RE ASSESSING IT.

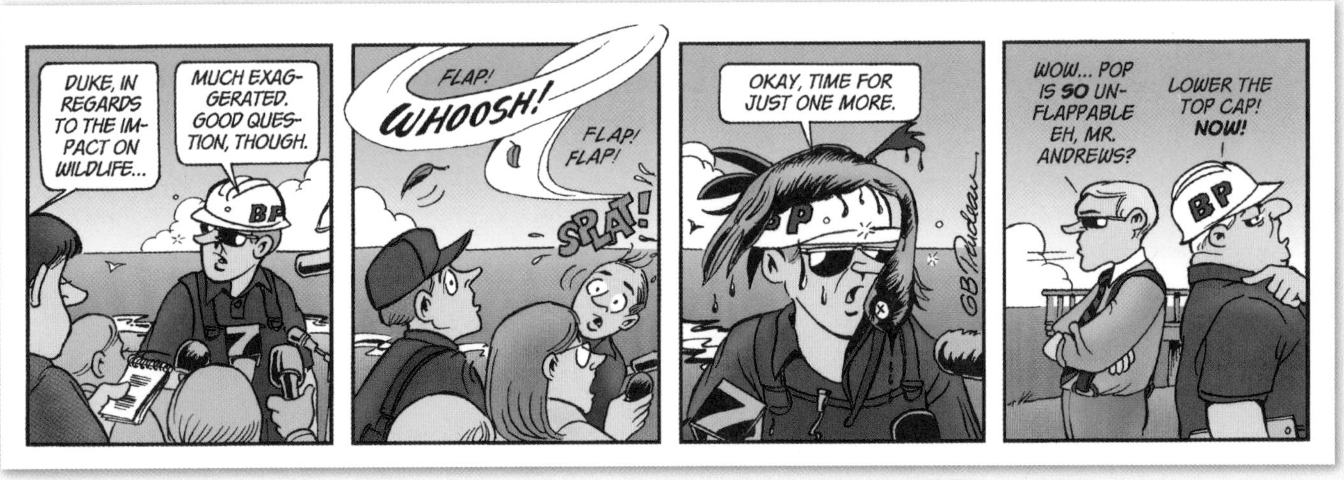
DUKE, IN REGARDS TO THE IMPACT ON WILDLIFE...
MUCH EXAGGERATED. GOOD QUESTION, THOUGH.
FLAP!
WHOOSH!
FLAP! FLAP!
SPLAT!
OKAY, TIME FOR JUST ONE MORE.
WOW... POP IS **SO** UNFLAPPABLE EH, MR. ANDREWS?
LOWER THE TOP CAP! **NOW!**

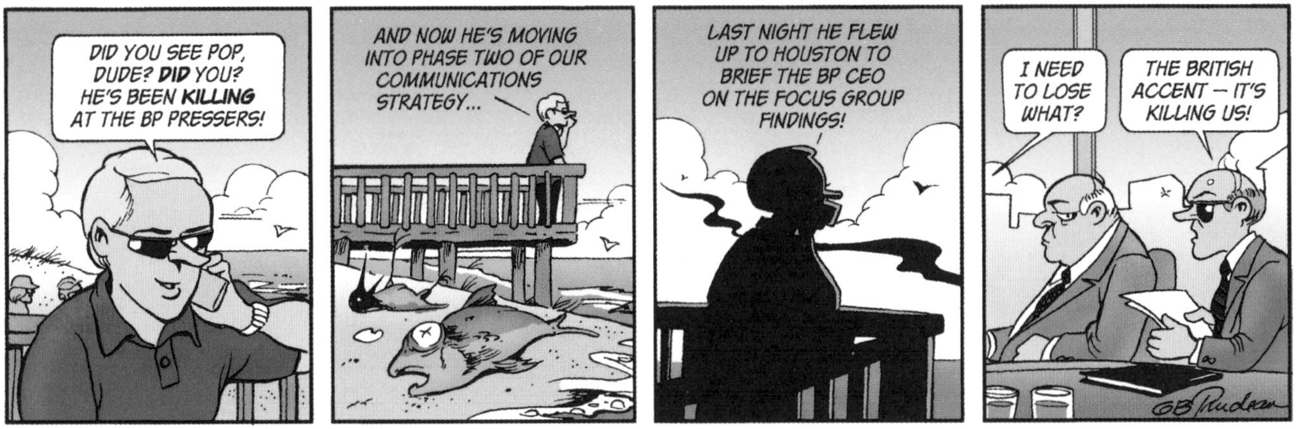
DID YOU SEE POP, DUDE? **DID** YOU? HE'S BEEN **KILLING** AT THE BP PRESSERS!
AND NOW HE'S MOVING INTO PHASE TWO OF OUR COMMUNICATIONS STRATEGY...
LAST NIGHT HE FLEW UP TO HOUSTON TO BRIEF THE BP CEO ON THE FOCUS GROUP FINDINGS!
I NEED TO LOSE WHAT?
THE BRITISH ACCENT — IT'S KILLING US!
GB Trudeau

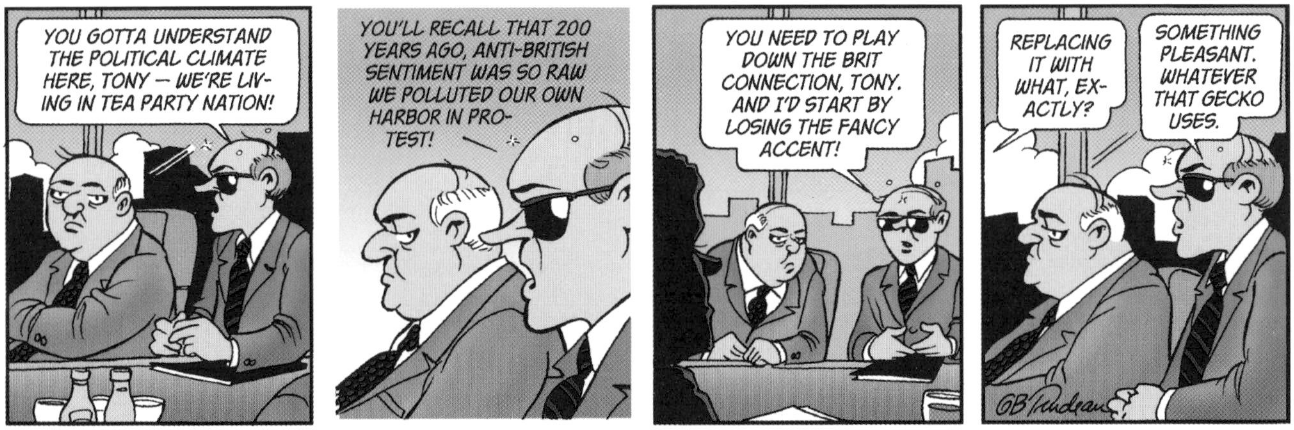
YOU GOTTA UNDERSTAND THE POLITICAL CLIMATE HERE, TONY — WE'RE LIVING IN TEA PARTY NATION!
YOU'LL RECALL THAT 200 YEARS AGO, ANTI-BRITISH SENTIMENT WAS SO RAW WE POLLUTED OUR OWN HARBOR IN PROTEST!
YOU NEED TO PLAY DOWN THE BRIT CONNECTION, TONY. AND I'D START BY LOSING THE FANCY ACCENT!
REPLACING IT WITH WHAT, EXACTLY?
SOMETHING PLEASANT. WHATEVER THAT GECKO USES.
GB Trudeau

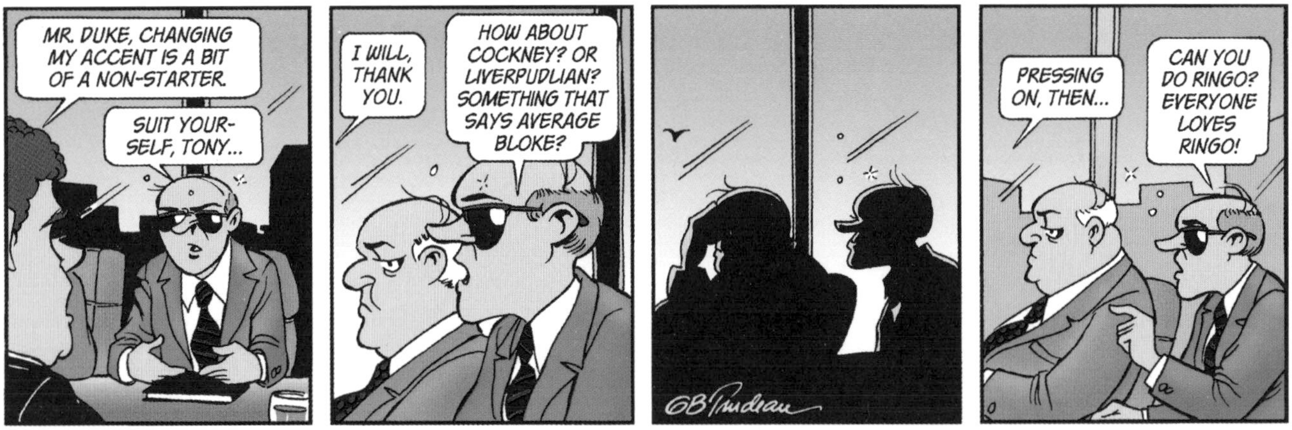
MR. DUKE, CHANGING MY ACCENT IS A BIT OF A NON-STARTER.
SUIT YOURSELF, TONY...
I WILL, THANK YOU.
HOW ABOUT COCKNEY? OR LIVERPUDLIAN? SOMETHING THAT SAYS AVERAGE BLOKE?
GB Trudeau
PRESSING ON, THEN...
CAN YOU DO RINGO? EVERYONE LOVES RINGO!

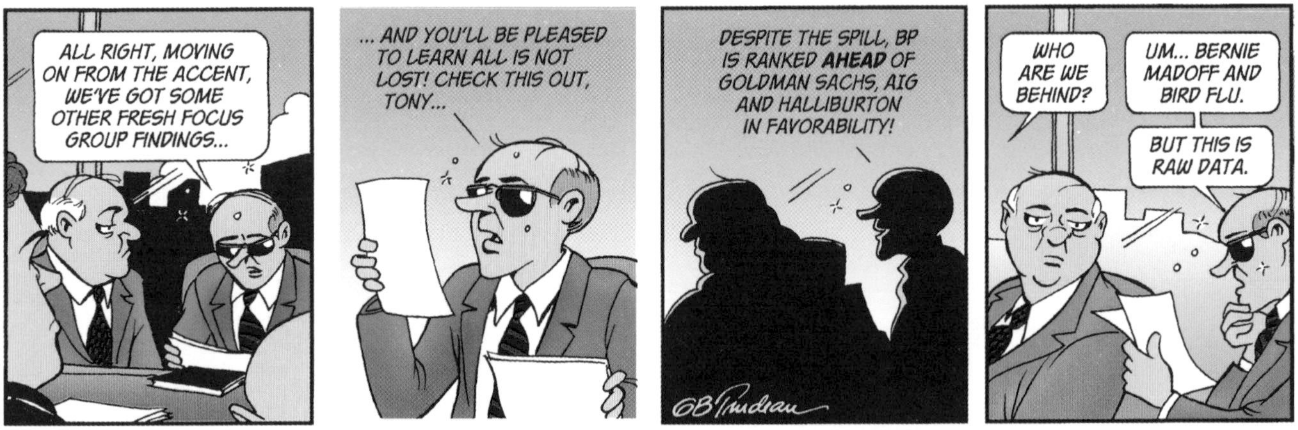
ALL RIGHT, MOVING ON FROM THE ACCENT, WE'VE GOT SOME OTHER FRESH FOCUS GROUP FINDINGS...
... AND YOU'LL BE PLEASED TO LEARN ALL IS NOT LOST! CHECK THIS OUT, TONY...
DESPITE THE SPILL, BP IS RANKED **AHEAD** OF GOLDMAN SACHS, AIG AND HALLIBURTON IN FAVORABILITY!
WHO ARE WE BEHIND?
UM... BERNIE MADOFF AND BIRD FLU.
BUT THIS IS RAW DATA.

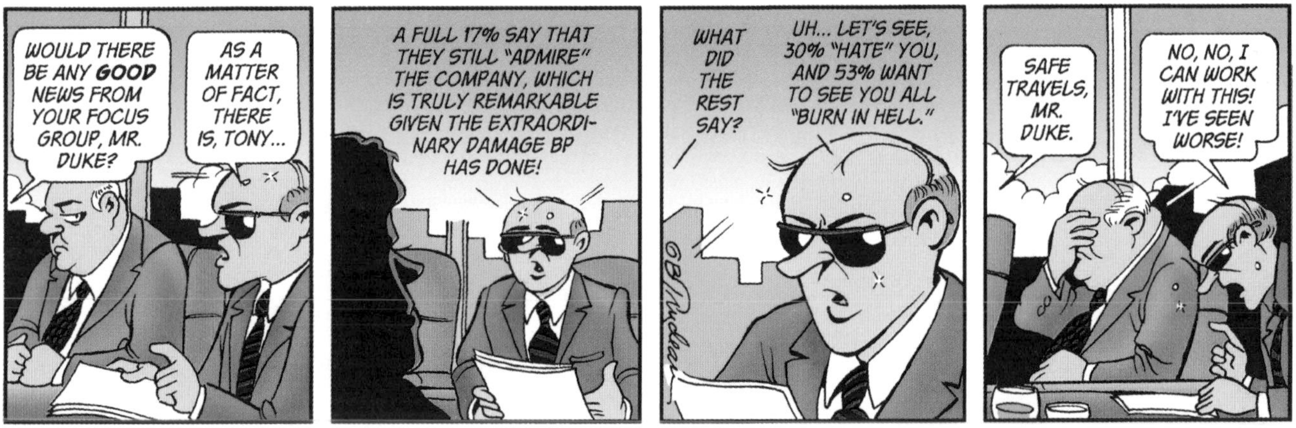
WOULD THERE BE ANY **GOOD** NEWS FROM YOUR FOCUS GROUP, MR. DUKE?
AS A MATTER OF FACT, THERE IS, TONY...
A FULL 17% SAY THAT THEY STILL "ADMIRE" THE COMPANY, WHICH IS TRULY REMARKABLE GIVEN THE EXTRAORDINARY DAMAGE BP HAS DONE!
WHAT DID THE REST SAY?
UH... LET'S SEE, 30% "HATE" YOU, AND 53% WANT TO SEE YOU ALL "BURN IN HELL."
SAFE TRAVELS, MR. DUKE.
NO, NO, I CAN WORK WITH THIS! I'VE SEEN WORSE!

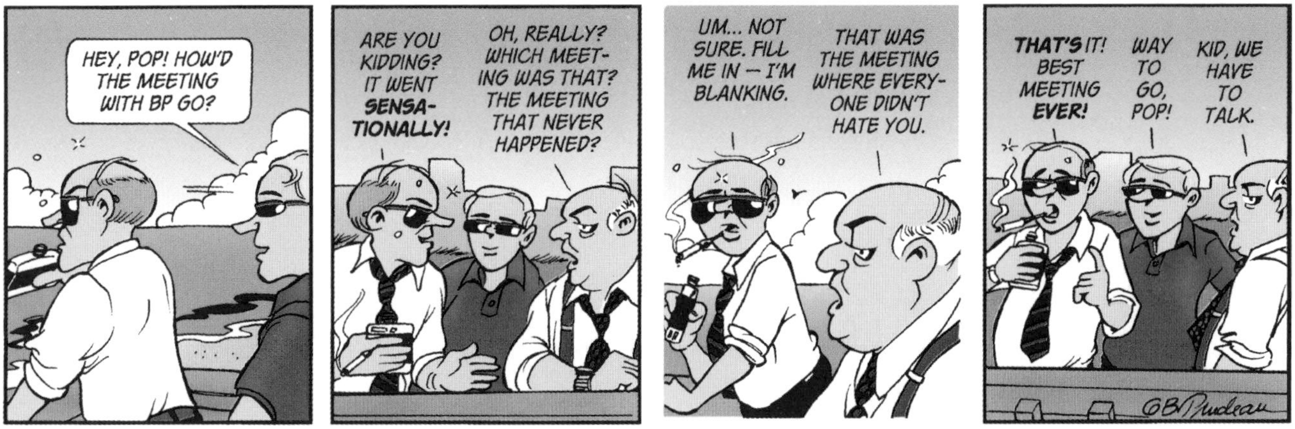
HEY, POP! HOW'D THE MEETING WITH BP GO?
ARE YOU KIDDING? IT WENT **SENSATIONALLY!**
OH, REALLY? WHICH MEETING WAS THAT? THE MEETING THAT NEVER HAPPENED?
UM... NOT SURE. FILL ME IN — I'M BLANKING.
THAT WAS THE MEETING WHERE EVERYONE DIDN'T HATE YOU.
THAT'S IT! BEST MEETING **EVER!**
WAY TO GO, POP!
KID, WE HAVE TO TALK.

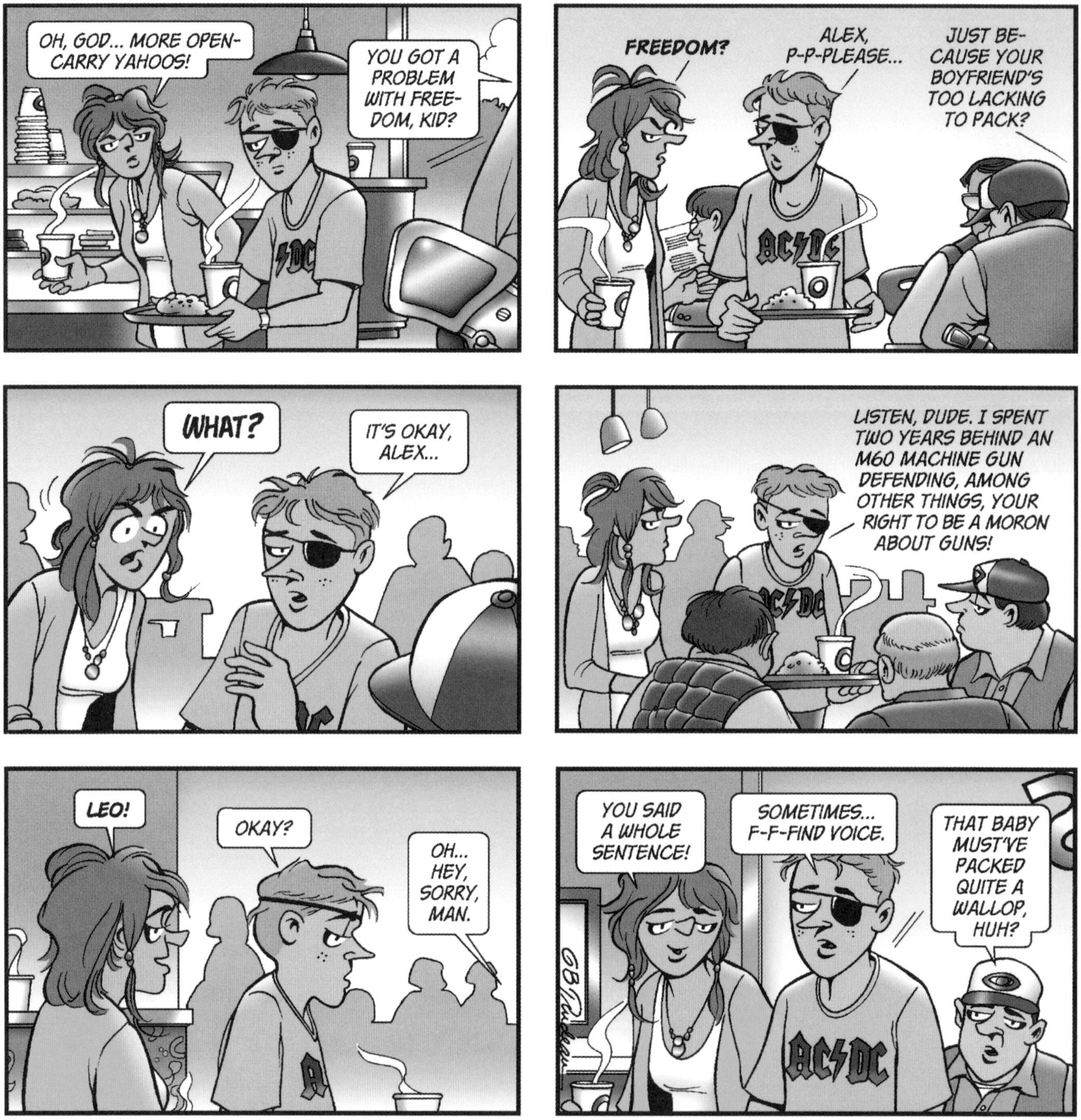
OH, GOD... MORE OPEN-CARRY YAHOOS!
YOU GOT A PROBLEM WITH FREE-DOM, KID?
FREEDOM?
ALEX, P-P-PLEASE...
JUST BE-CAUSE YOUR BOYFRIEND'S TOO LACKING TO PACK?
WHAT?
IT'S OKAY, ALEX...
LISTEN, DUDE. I SPENT TWO YEARS BEHIND AN M60 MACHINE GUN DEFENDING, AMONG OTHER THINGS, YOUR RIGHT TO BE A MORON ABOUT GUNS!
LEO!
OKAY?
OH... HEY, SORRY, MAN.
YOU SAID A WHOLE SENTENCE!
SOMETIMES... F-F-FIND VOICE.
THAT BABY MUST'VE PACKED QUITE A WALLOP, HUH?

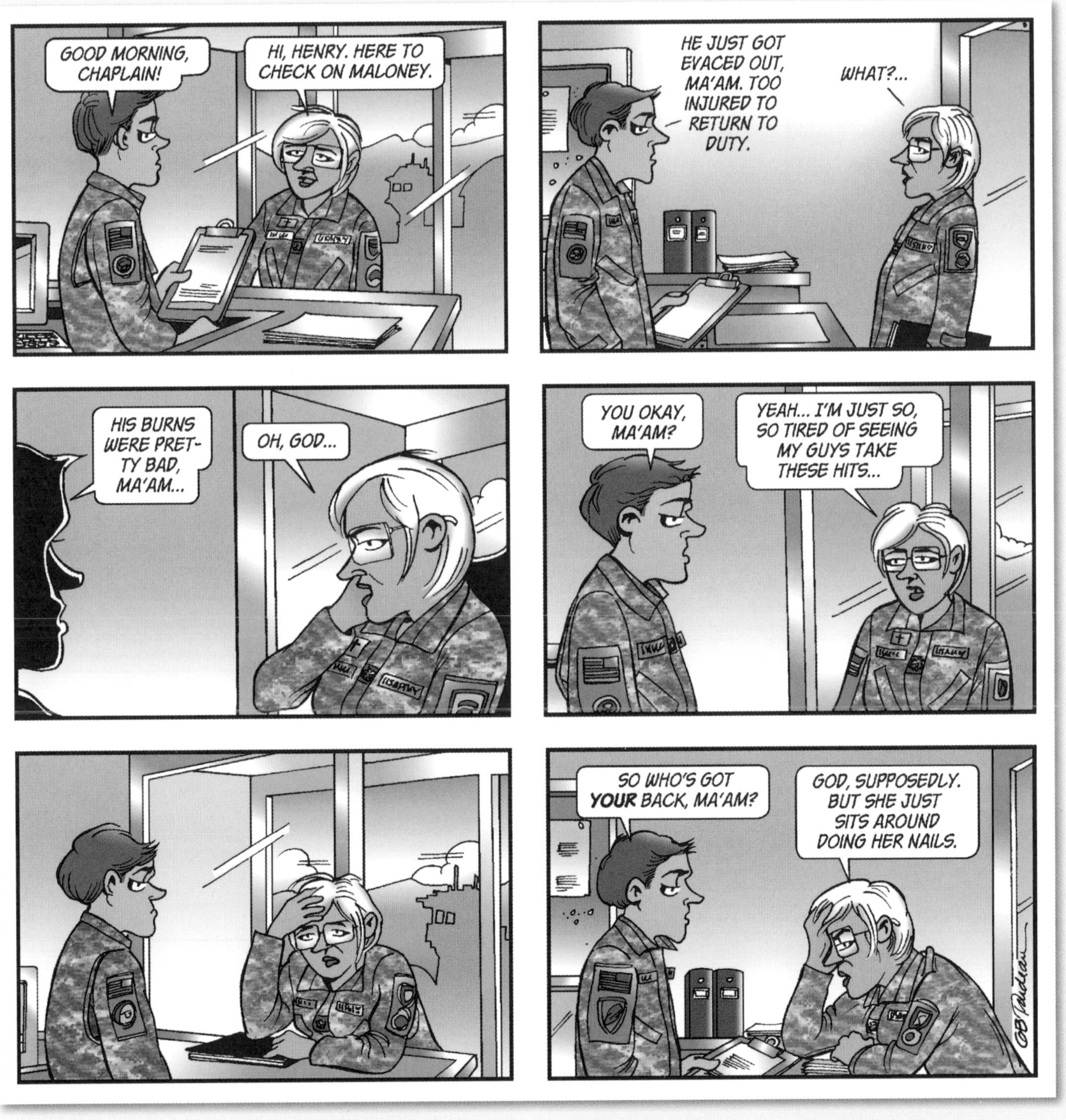
GOOD MORNING, CHAPLAIN!
HI, HENRY. HERE TO CHECK ON MALONEY.
HE JUST GOT EVACED OUT, MA'AM. TOO INJURED TO RETURN TO DUTY.
WHAT?...
HIS BURNS WERE PRETTY BAD, MA'AM...
OH, GOD...
YOU OKAY, MA'AM?
YEAH... I'M JUST SO, SO TIRED OF SEEING MY GUYS TAKE THESE HITS...
SO WHO'S GOT YOUR BACK, MA'AM?
GOD, SUPPOSEDLY. BUT SHE JUST SITS AROUND DOING HER NAILS.

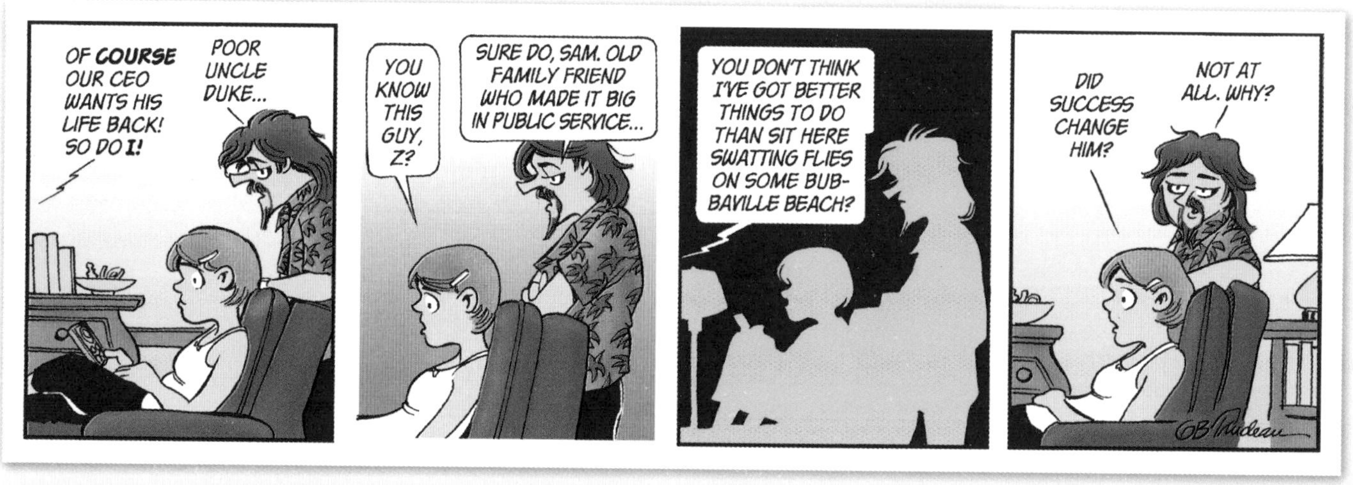
OF COURSE OUR CEO WANTS HIS LIFE BACK! SO DO I!
POOR UNCLE DUKE...
YOU KNOW THIS GUY, Z?
SURE DO, SAM. OLD FAMILY FRIEND WHO MADE IT BIG IN PUBLIC SERVICE...
YOU DON'T THINK I'VE GOT BETTER THINGS TO DO THAN SIT HERE SWATTING FLIES ON SOME BUBBAVILLE BEACH?
DID SUCCESS CHANGE HIM?
NOT AT ALL. WHY?
GB Trudeau

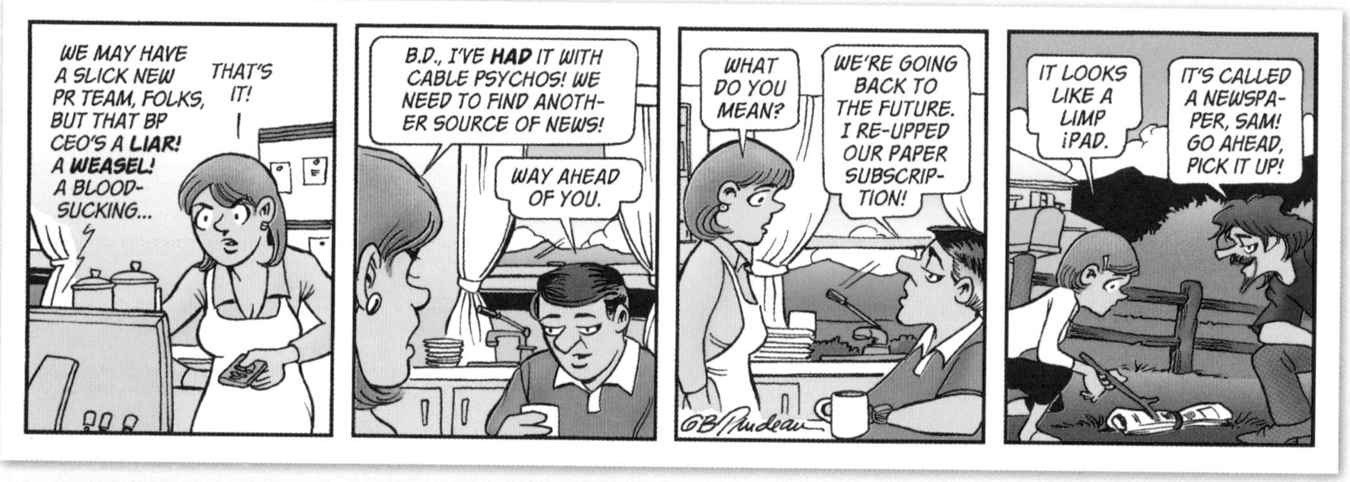
WE MAY HAVE A SLICK NEW PR TEAM, FOLKS, BUT THAT BP CEO'S A LIAR! A WEASEL! A BLOOD-SUCKING...
THAT'S IT!
B.D., I'VE HAD IT WITH CABLE PSYCHOS! WE NEED TO FIND ANOTHER SOURCE OF NEWS!
WAY AHEAD OF YOU.
WHAT DO YOU MEAN?
WE'RE GOING BACK TO THE FUTURE. I RE-UPPED OUR PAPER SUBSCRIPTION!
GB Trudeau
IT LOOKS LIKE A LIMP iPAD.
IT'S CALLED A NEWSPAPER, SAM! GO AHEAD, PICK IT UP!

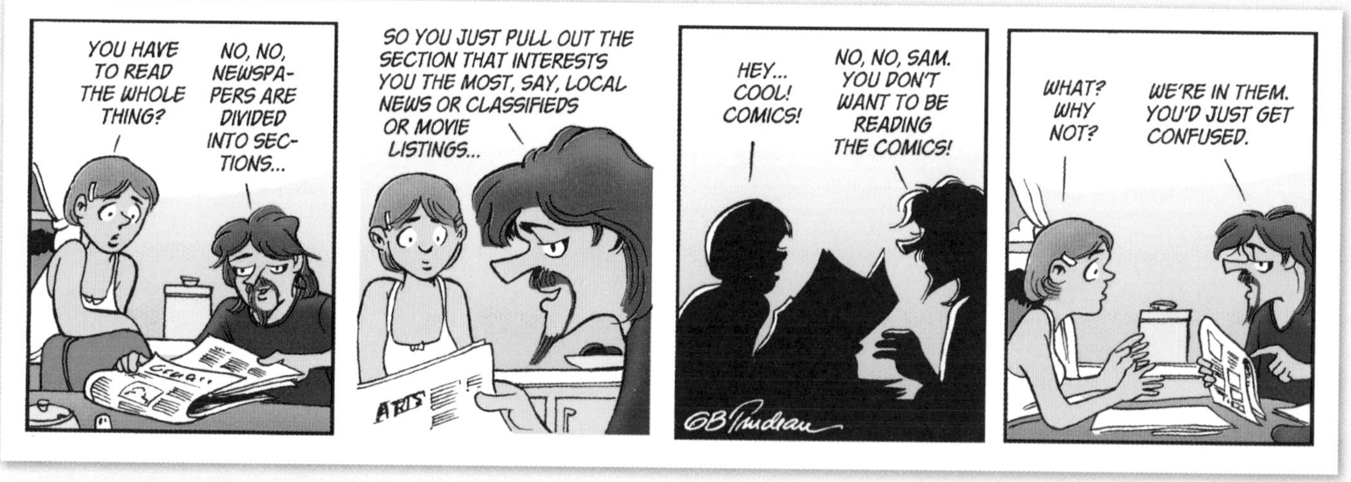
YOU HAVE TO READ THE WHOLE THING?
NO, NO, NEWSPAPERS ARE DIVIDED INTO SECTIONS...
SO YOU JUST PULL OUT THE SECTION THAT INTERESTS YOU THE MOST, SAY, LOCAL NEWS OR CLASSIFIEDS OR MOVIE LISTINGS...
ARTS
HEY... COOL! COMICS!
NO, NO, SAM. YOU DON'T WANT TO BE READING THE COMICS!
GB Trudeau
WHAT? WHY NOT?
WE'RE IN THEM. YOU'D JUST GET CONFUSED.

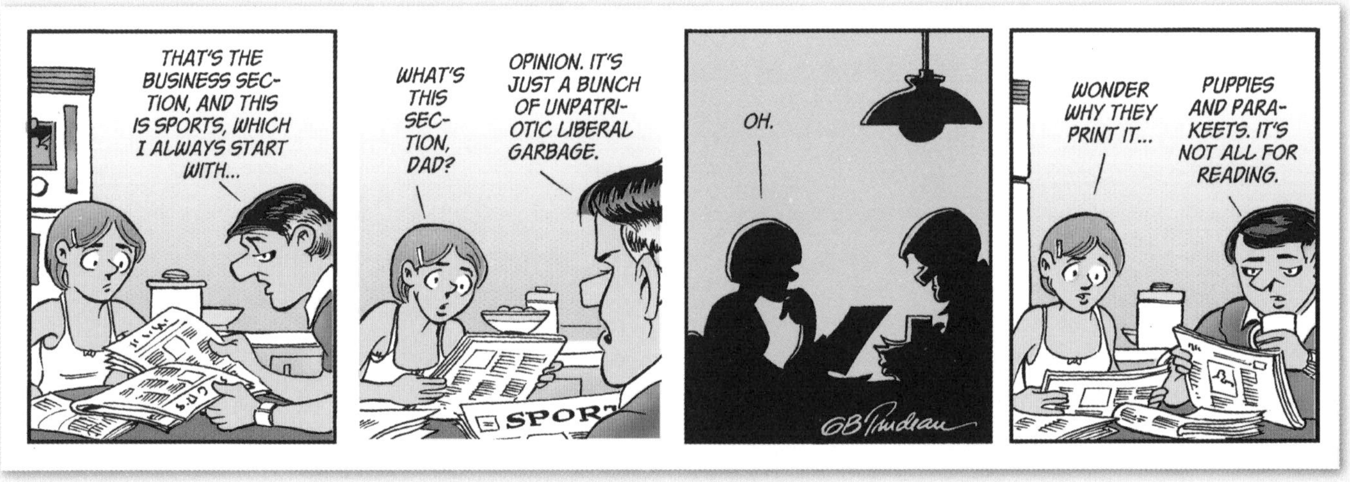
THAT'S THE BUSINESS SEC-TION, AND THIS IS SPORTS, WHICH I ALWAYS START WITH...
WHAT'S THIS SEC-TION, DAD?
OPINION. IT'S JUST A BUNCH OF UNPATRI-OTIC LIBERAL GARBAGE.
SPORT
OH.
WONDER WHY THEY PRINT IT...
PUPPIES AND PARA-KEETS. IT'S NOT ALL FOR READING.

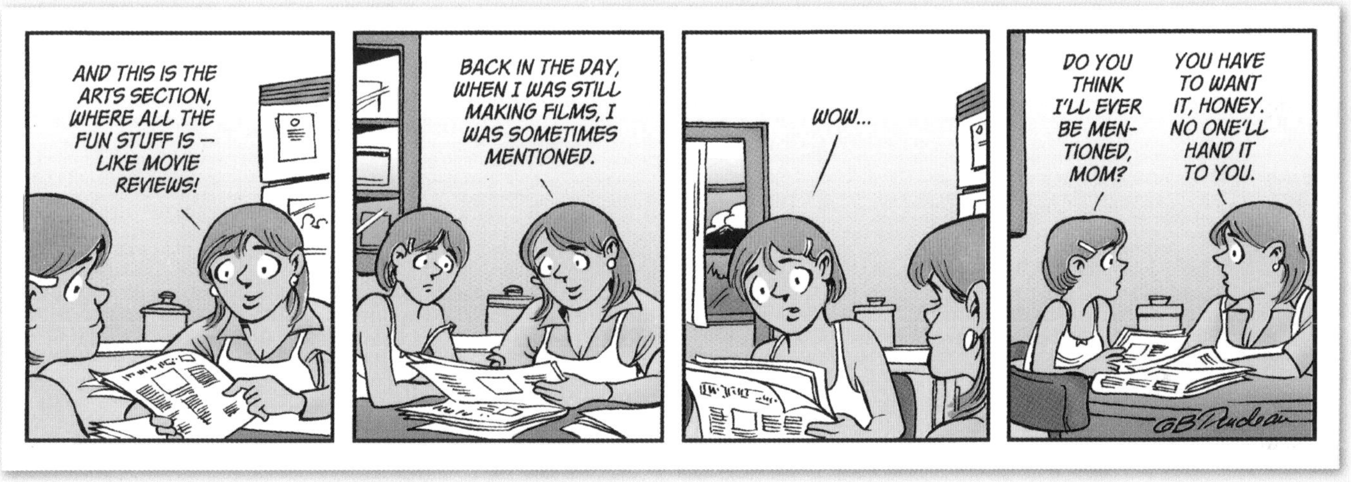
AND THIS IS THE ARTS SECTION, WHERE ALL THE FUN STUFF IS — LIKE MOVIE REVIEWS!
BACK IN THE DAY, WHEN I WAS STILL MAKING FILMS, I WAS SOMETIMES MENTIONED.
WOW...
DO YOU THINK I'LL EVER BE MEN-TIONED, MOM?
YOU HAVE TO WANT IT, HONEY. NO ONE'LL HAND IT TO YOU.

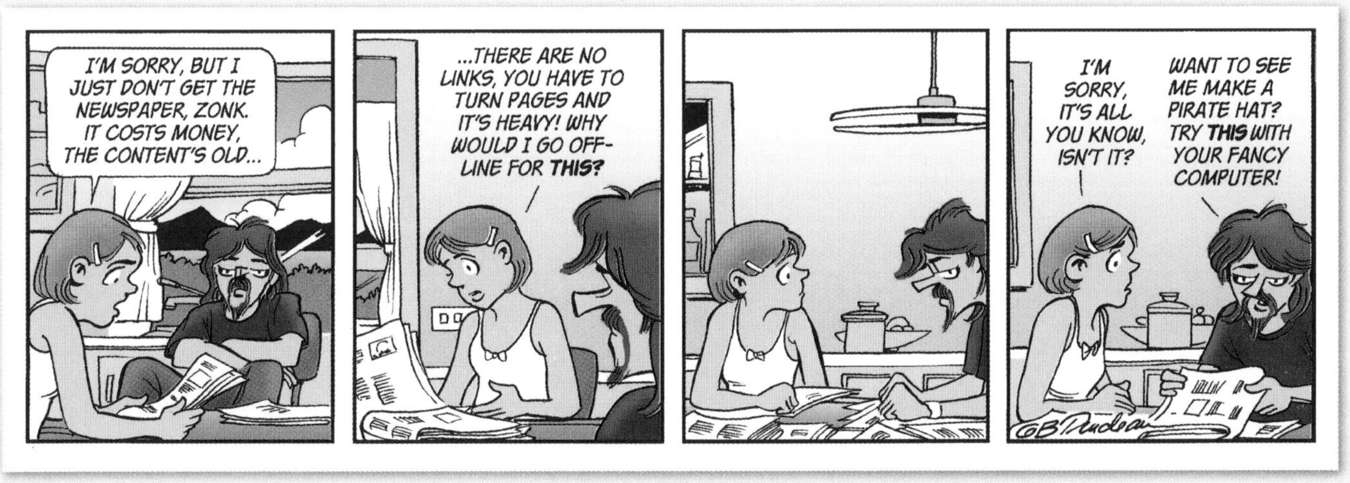
I'M SORRY, BUT I JUST DON'T GET THE NEWSPAPER, ZONK. IT COSTS MONEY, THE CONTENT'S OLD...
...THERE ARE NO LINKS, YOU HAVE TO TURN PAGES AND IT'S HEAVY! WHY WOULD I GO OFF-LINE FOR THIS?
I'M SORRY, IT'S ALL YOU KNOW, ISN'T IT?
WANT TO SEE ME MAKE A PIRATE HAT? TRY THIS WITH YOUR FANCY COMPUTER!

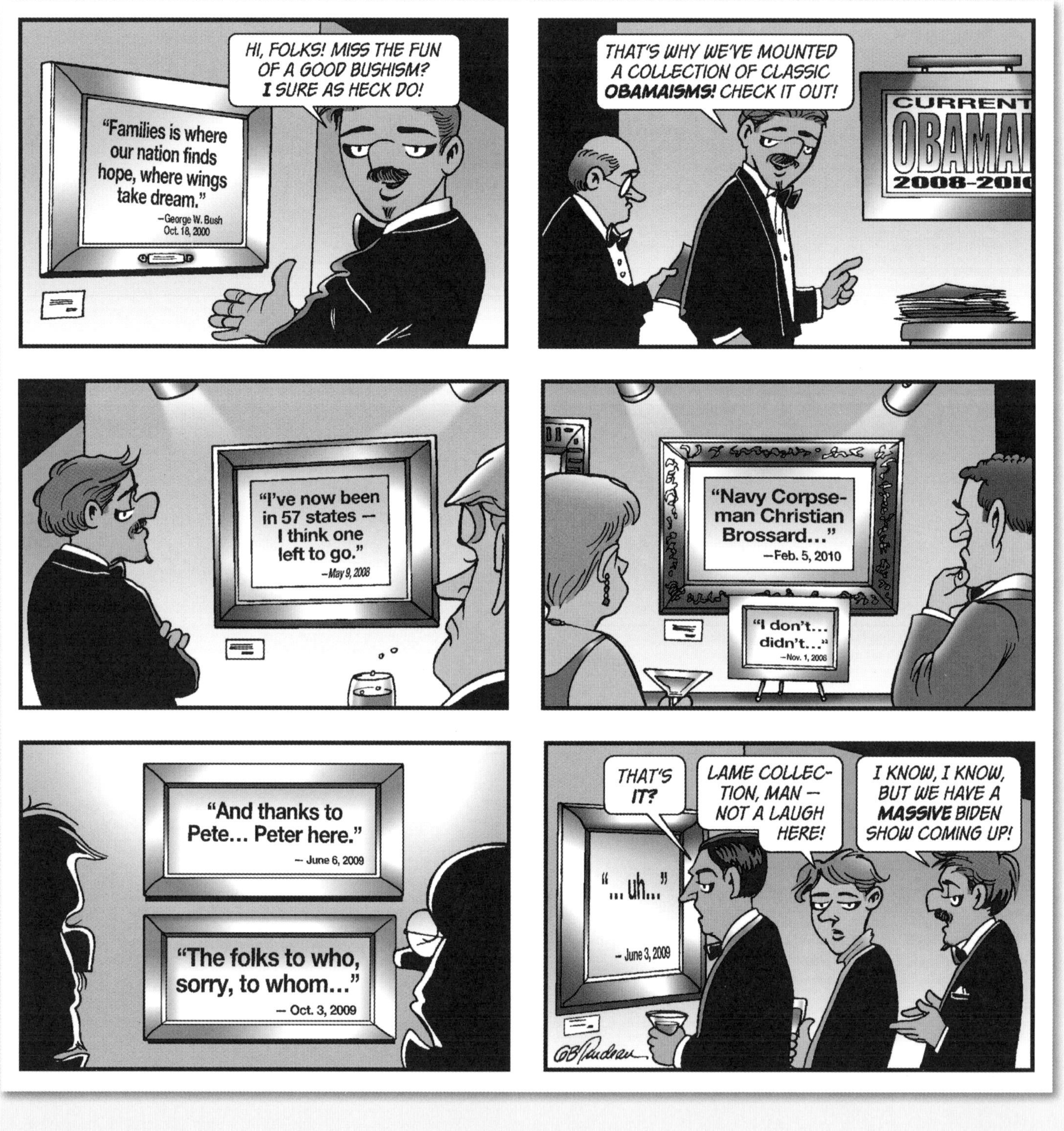
"Families is where our nation finds hope, where wings take dream."
—George W. Bush Oct. 18, 2000
HI, FOLKS! MISS THE FUN OF A GOOD BUSHISM? I SURE AS HECK DO!
THAT'S WHY WE'VE MOUNTED A COLLECTION OF CLASSIC OBAMAISMS! CHECK IT OUT!
CURRENT OBAMAI
2008-201
"I've now been in 57 states — I think one left to go."
—May 9, 2008
"Navy Corpse-man Christian Brossard..."
—Feb. 5, 2010
"I don't... didn't..."
—Nov. 1, 2008
"And thanks to Pete... Peter here."
— June 6, 2009
"The folks to who, sorry, to whom..."
— Oct. 3, 2009
THAT'S IT?
LAME COLLEC-TION, MAN — NOT A LAUGH HERE!
I KNOW, I KNOW, BUT WE HAVE A MASSIVE BIDEN SHOW COMING UP!
"... uh..."
— June 3, 2009

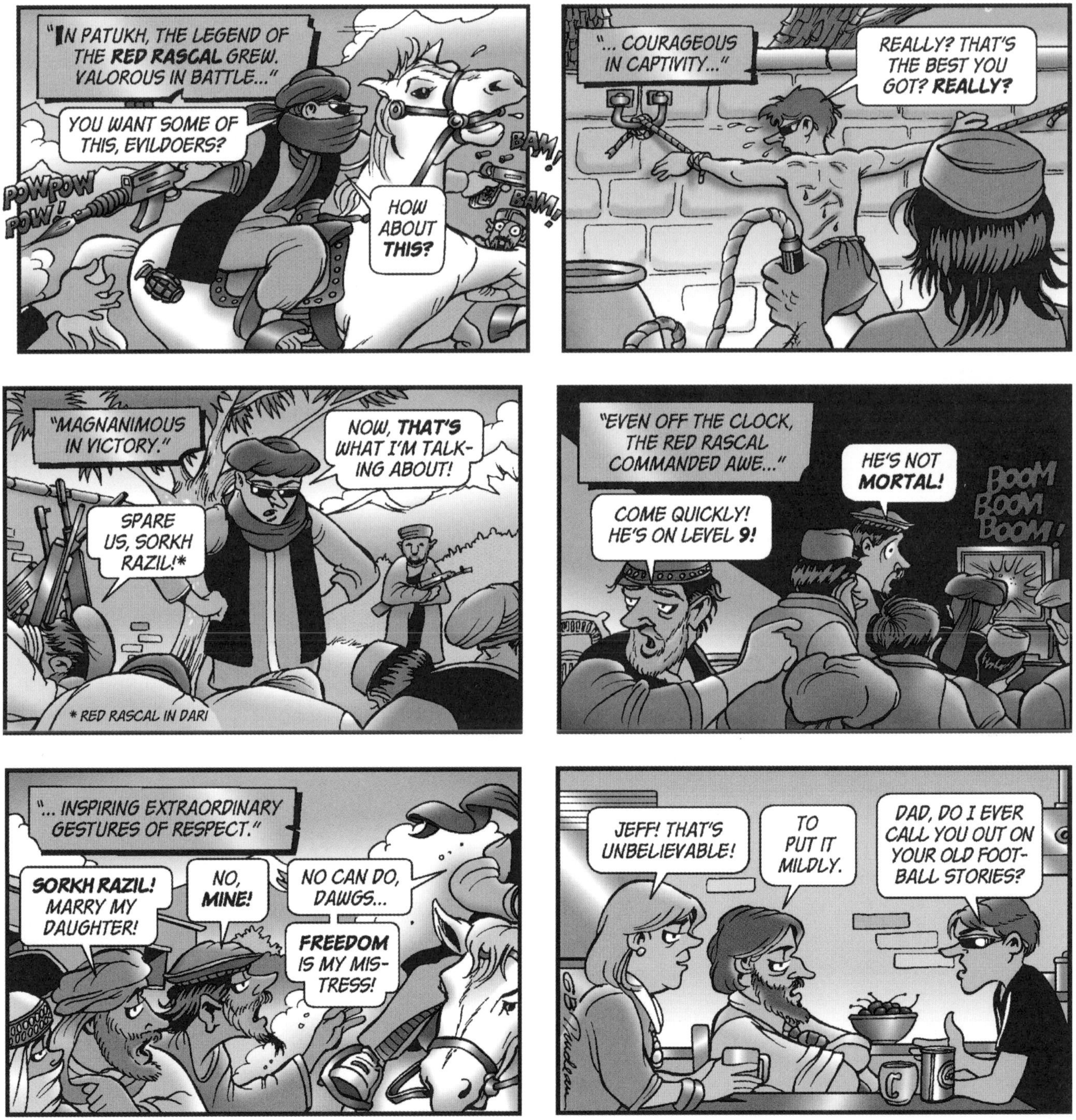
"IN PATUKH, THE LEGEND OF THE **RED RASCAL** GREW. VALOROUS IN BATTLE..."
YOU WANT SOME OF THIS, EVILDOERS?
POWPOW POW!
BAM!
BAM!
HOW ABOUT **THIS?**
"... COURAGEOUS IN CAPTIVITY..."
REALLY? THAT'S THE BEST YOU GOT? **REALLY?**
"MAGNANIMOUS IN VICTORY."
NOW, **THAT'S** WHAT I'M TALKING ABOUT!
SPARE US, SORKH RAZIL!*
* RED RASCAL IN DARI
"EVEN OFF THE CLOCK, THE RED RASCAL COMMANDED AWE..."
COME QUICKLY! HE'S ON LEVEL **9!**
HE'S NOT **MORTAL!**
BOOM BOOM BOOM!
"... INSPIRING EXTRAORDINARY GESTURES OF RESPECT."
SORKH RAZIL! MARRY MY DAUGHTER!
NO, **MINE!**
NO CAN DO, DAWGS...
FREEDOM IS MY MISTRESS!
JEFF! THAT'S UNBELIEVABLE!
TO PUT IT MILDLY.
DAD, DO I EVER CALL YOU OUT ON YOUR OLD FOOTBALL STORIES?
GB Trudeau

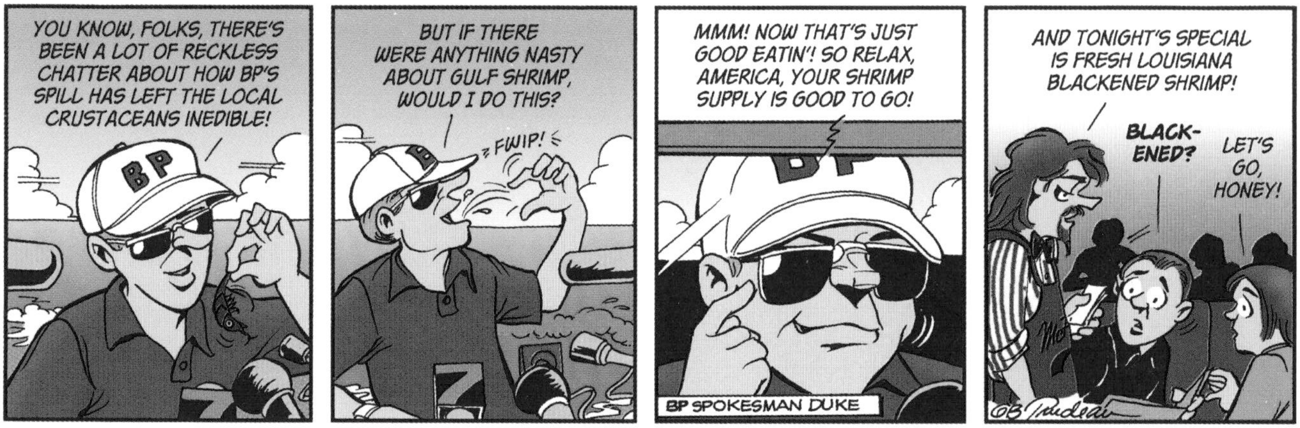
YOU KNOW, FOLKS, THERE'S BEEN A LOT OF RECKLESS CHATTER ABOUT HOW BP'S SPILL HAS LEFT THE LOCAL CRUSTACEANS INEDIBLE!
BUT IF THERE WERE ANYTHING NASTY ABOUT GULF SHRIMP, WOULD I DO THIS?
FWIP!
MMM! NOW THAT'S JUST GOOD EATIN'! SO RELAX, AMERICA, YOUR SHRIMP SUPPLY IS GOOD TO GO!
BP SPOKESMAN DUKE
AND TONIGHT'S SPECIAL IS FRESH LOUISIANA BLACKENED SHRIMP!
BLACK-ENED?
LET'S GO, HONEY!

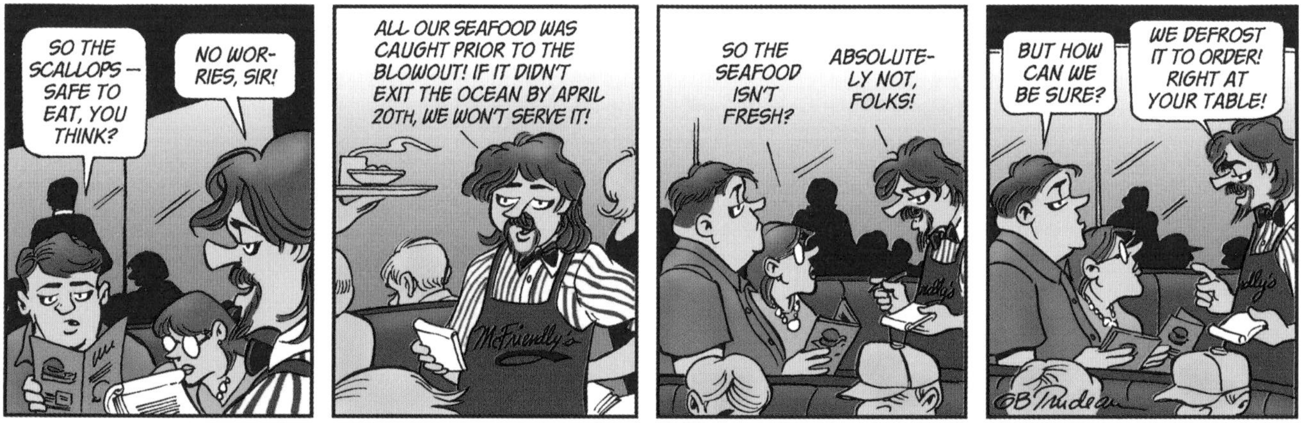
SO THE SCALLOPS — SAFE TO EAT, YOU THINK?
NO WOR-RIES, SIR!
ALL OUR SEAFOOD WAS CAUGHT PRIOR TO THE BLOWOUT! IF IT DIDN'T EXIT THE OCEAN BY APRIL 20TH, WE WON'T SERVE IT!
McFriendly's
SO THE SEAFOOD ISN'T FRESH?
ABSOLUTE-LY NOT, FOLKS!
BUT HOW CAN WE BE SURE?
WE DEFROST IT TO ORDER! RIGHT AT YOUR TABLE!

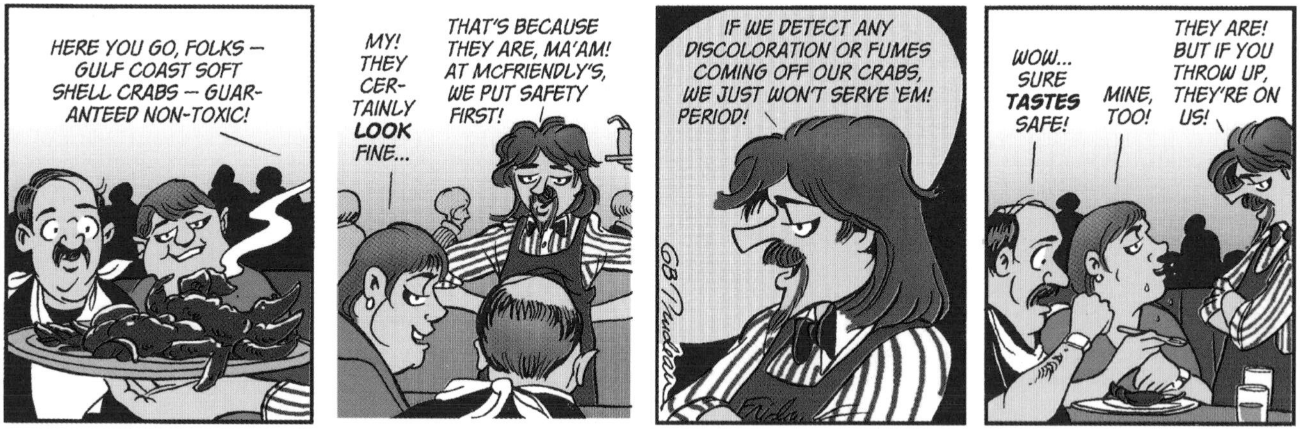
HERE YOU GO, FOLKS — GULF COAST SOFT SHELL CRABS — GUAR-ANTEED NON-TOXIC!
MY! THEY CER-TAINLY LOOK FINE...
THAT'S BECAUSE THEY ARE, MA'AM! AT MCFRIENDLY'S, WE PUT SAFETY FIRST!
IF WE DETECT ANY DISCOLORATION OR FUMES COMING OFF OUR CRABS, WE JUST WON'T SERVE 'EM! PERIOD!
WOW... SURE TASTES SAFE!
MINE, TOO!
THEY ARE! BUT IF YOU THROW UP, THEY'RE ON US!

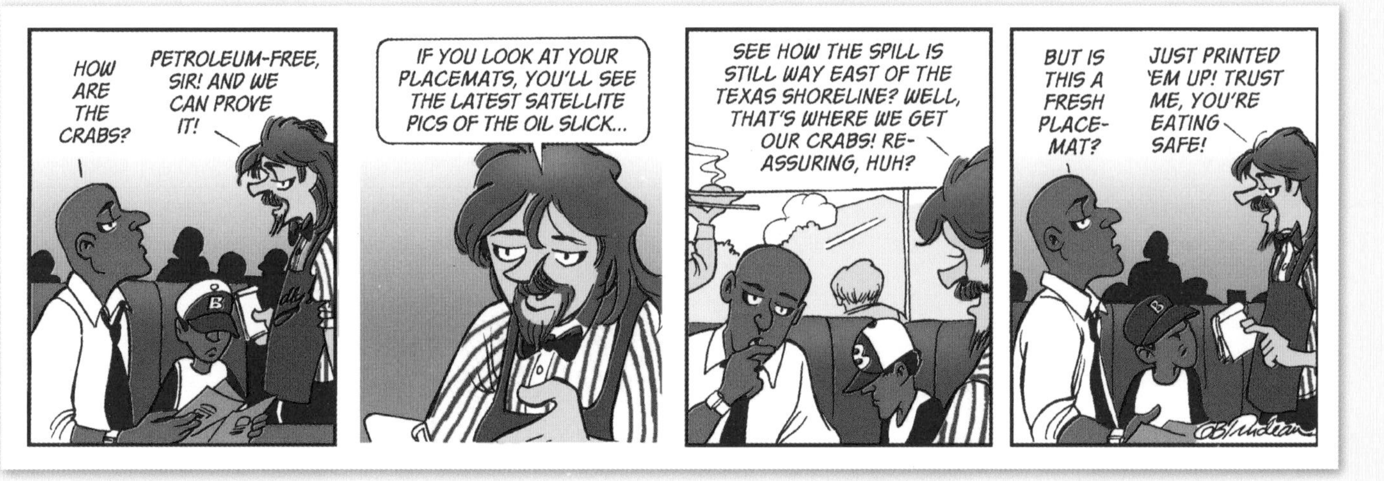
HOW ARE THE CRABS?
PETROLEUM-FREE, SIR! AND WE CAN PROVE IT!
IF YOU LOOK AT YOUR PLACEMATS, YOU'LL SEE THE LATEST SATELLITE PICS OF THE OIL SLICK...
SEE HOW THE SPILL IS STILL WAY EAST OF THE TEXAS SHORELINE? WELL, THAT'S WHERE WE GET OUR CRABS! RE-ASSURING, HUH?
BUT IS THIS A FRESH PLACE-MAT?
JUST PRINTED 'EM UP! TRUST ME, YOU'RE EATING SAFE!

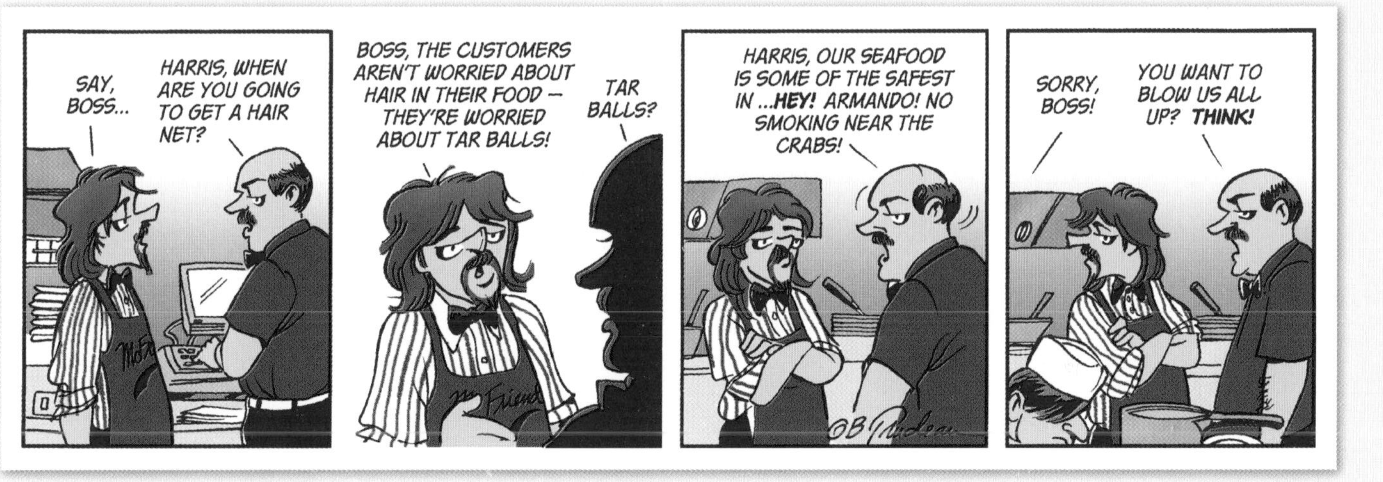
SAY, BOSS...
HARRIS, WHEN ARE YOU GOING TO GET A HAIR NET?
BOSS, THE CUSTOMERS AREN'T WORRIED ABOUT HAIR IN THEIR FOOD — THEY'RE WORRIED ABOUT TAR BALLS!
TAR BALLS?
HARRIS, OUR SEAFOOD IS SOME OF THE SAFEST IN ...HEY! ARMANDO! NO SMOKING NEAR THE CRABS!
SORRY, BOSS!
YOU WANT TO BLOW US ALL UP? THINK!

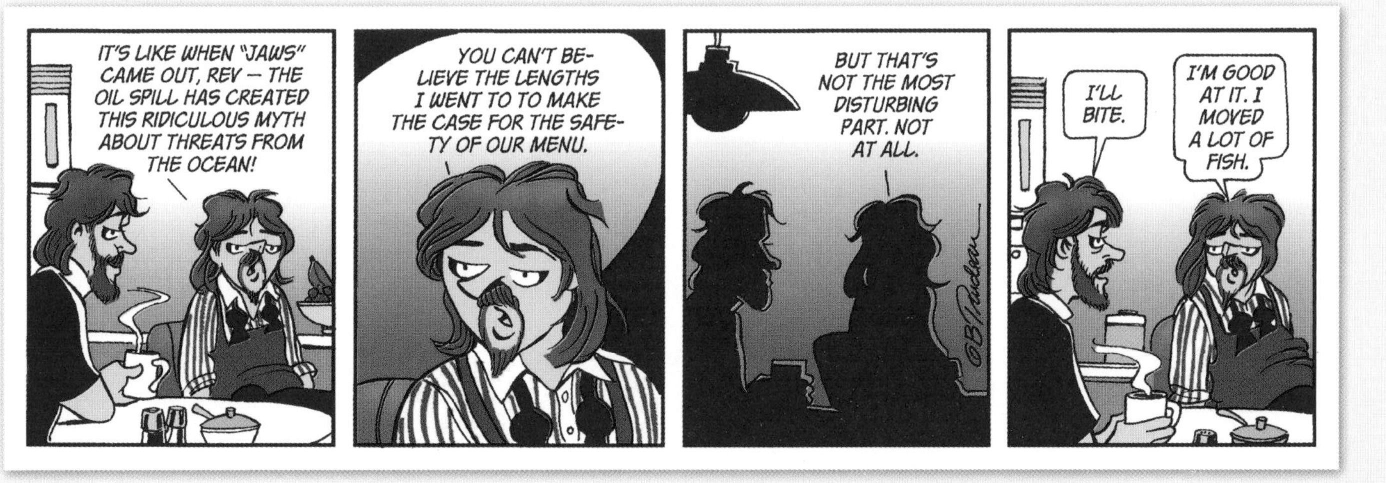
IT'S LIKE WHEN "JAWS" CAME OUT, REV — THE OIL SPILL HAS CREATED THIS RIDICULOUS MYTH ABOUT THREATS FROM THE OCEAN!
YOU CAN'T BE-LIEVE THE LENGTHS I WENT TO TO MAKE THE CASE FOR THE SAFE-TY OF OUR MENU.
BUT THAT'S NOT THE MOST DISTURBING PART. NOT AT ALL.
I'LL BITE.
I'M GOOD AT IT. I MOVED A LOT OF FISH.

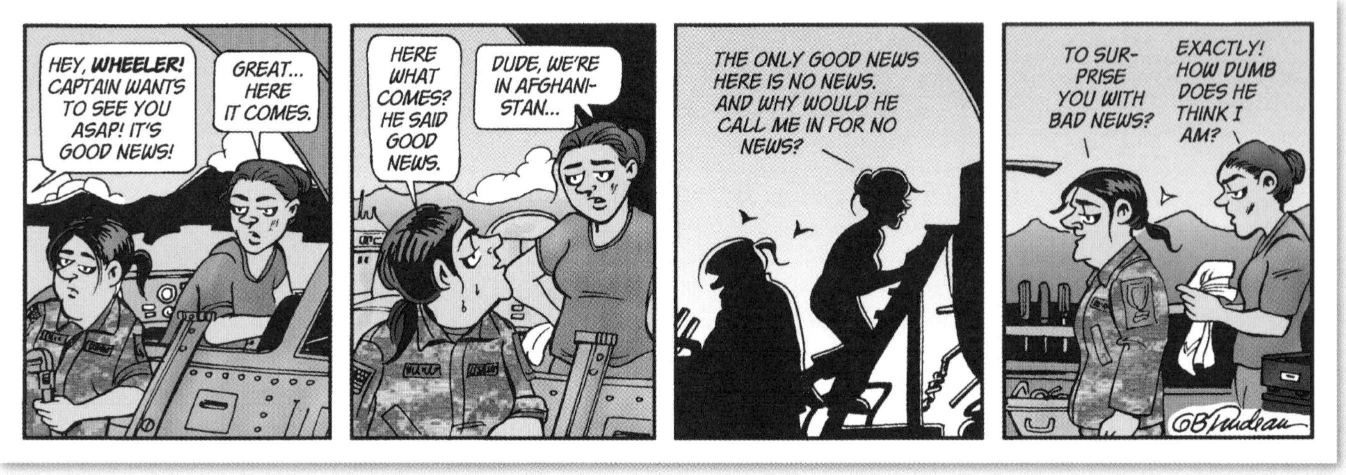
HEY, **WHEELER!** CAPTAIN WANTS TO SEE YOU ASAP! IT'S GOOD NEWS!
GREAT... HERE IT COMES.
HERE WHAT COMES? HE SAID GOOD NEWS.
DUDE, WE'RE IN AFGHANISTAN...
THE ONLY GOOD NEWS HERE IS NO NEWS. AND WHY WOULD HE CALL ME IN FOR NO NEWS?
TO SURPRISE YOU WITH BAD NEWS?
EXACTLY! HOW DUMB DOES HE THINK I AM?
GBTrudeau

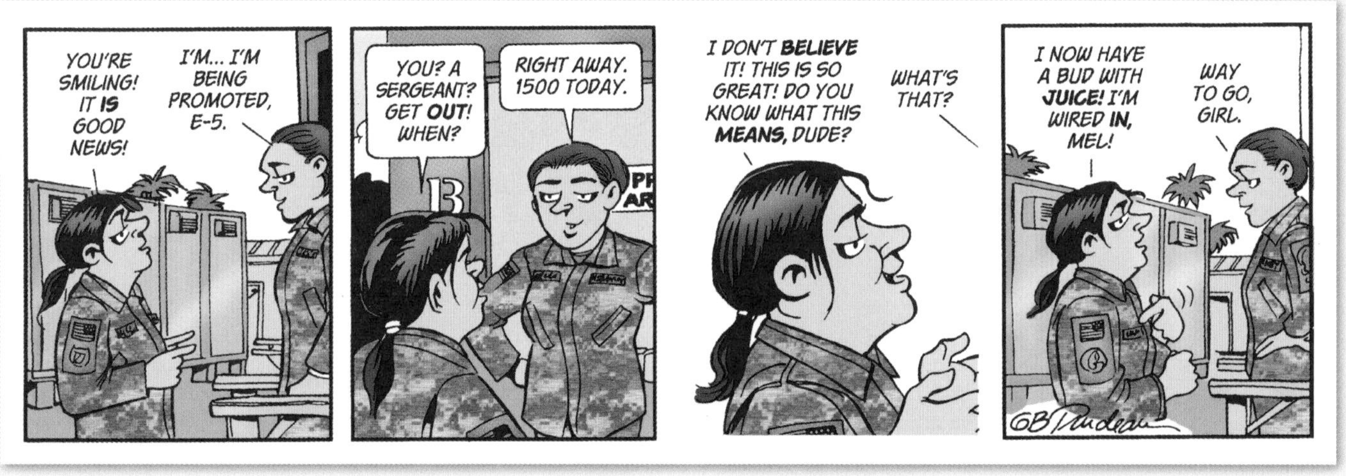
YOU'RE SMILING! IT **IS** GOOD NEWS!
I'M... I'M BEING PROMOTED, E-5.
YOU? A SERGEANT? GET **OUT**! WHEN?
RIGHT AWAY. 1500 TODAY.
I DON'T **BELIEVE** IT! THIS IS SO GREAT! DO YOU KNOW WHAT THIS **MEANS,** DUDE?
WHAT'S THAT?
I NOW HAVE A BUD WITH **JUICE!** I'M WIRED **IN,** MEL!
WAY TO GO, GIRL.
GBTrudeau

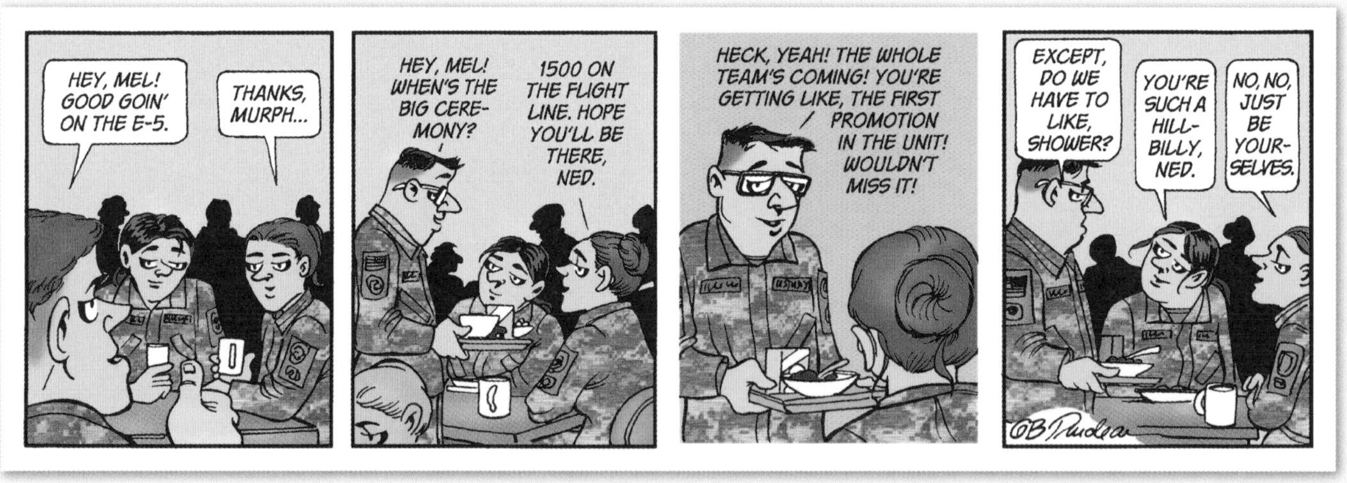
HEY, MEL! GOOD GOIN' ON THE E-5.
THANKS, MURPH...
HEY, MEL! WHEN'S THE BIG CEREMONY?
1500 ON THE FLIGHT LINE. HOPE YOU'LL BE THERE, NED.
HECK, YEAH! THE WHOLE TEAM'S COMING! YOU'RE GETTING LIKE, THE FIRST PROMOTION IN THE UNIT! WOULDN'T MISS IT!
EXCEPT, DO WE HAVE TO LIKE, SHOWER?
YOU'RE SUCH A HILLBILLY, NED.
NO, NO, JUST BE YOURSELVES.
GBTrudeau

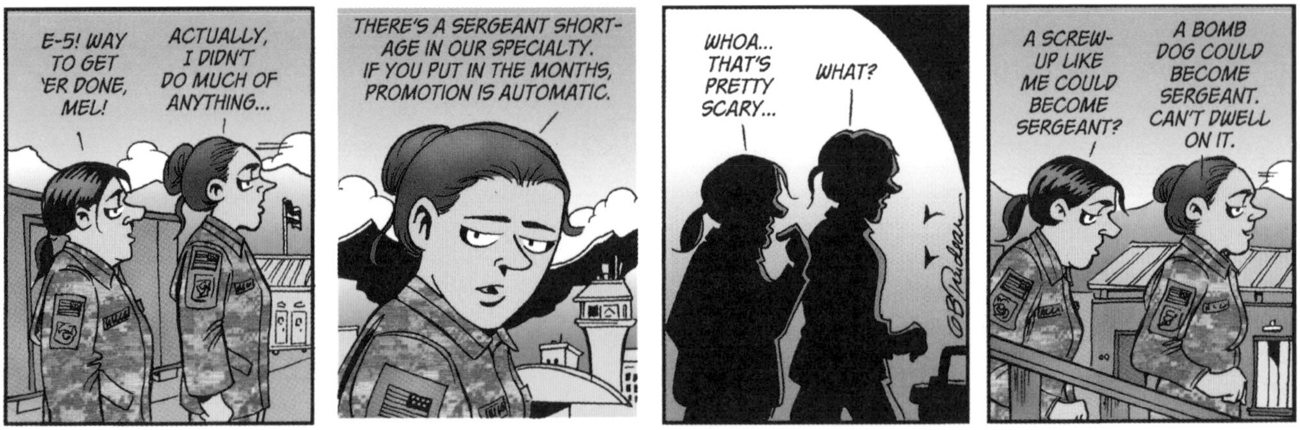
E-5! WAY TO GET 'ER DONE, MEL!
ACTUALLY, I DIDN'T DO MUCH OF ANYTHING...
THERE'S A SERGEANT SHORTAGE IN OUR SPECIALTY. IF YOU PUT IN THE MONTHS, PROMOTION IS AUTOMATIC.
WHOA... THAT'S PRETTY SCARY...
WHAT?
A SCREW-UP LIKE ME COULD BECOME SERGEANT?
A BOMB DOG COULD BECOME SERGEANT. CAN'T DWELL ON IT.

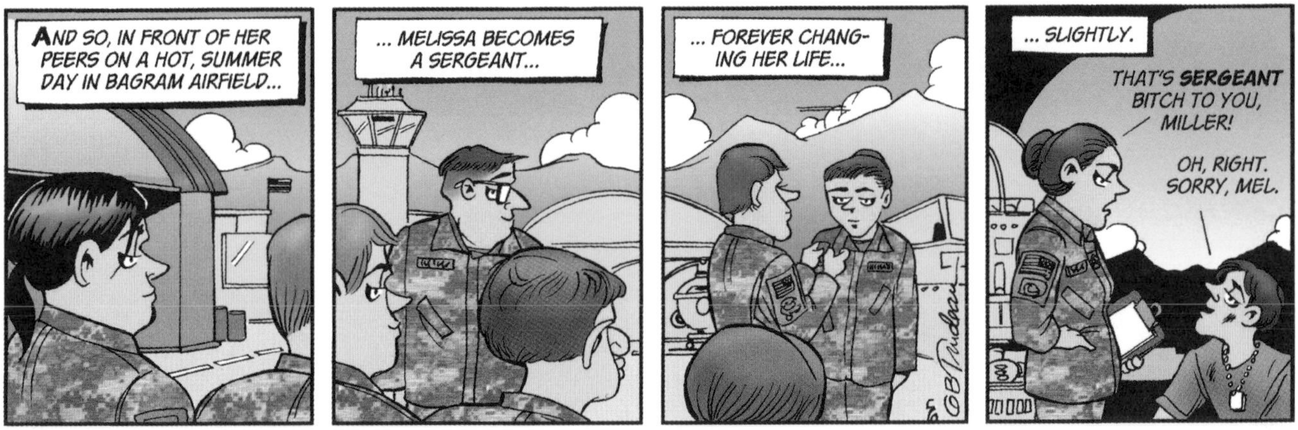
AND SO, IN FRONT OF HER PEERS ON A HOT, SUMMER DAY IN BAGRAM AIRFIELD...
... MELISSA BECOMES A SERGEANT...
... FOREVER CHANGING HER LIFE...
... SLIGHTLY.
THAT'S SERGEANT BITCH TO YOU, MILLER!
OH, RIGHT. SORRY, MEL.

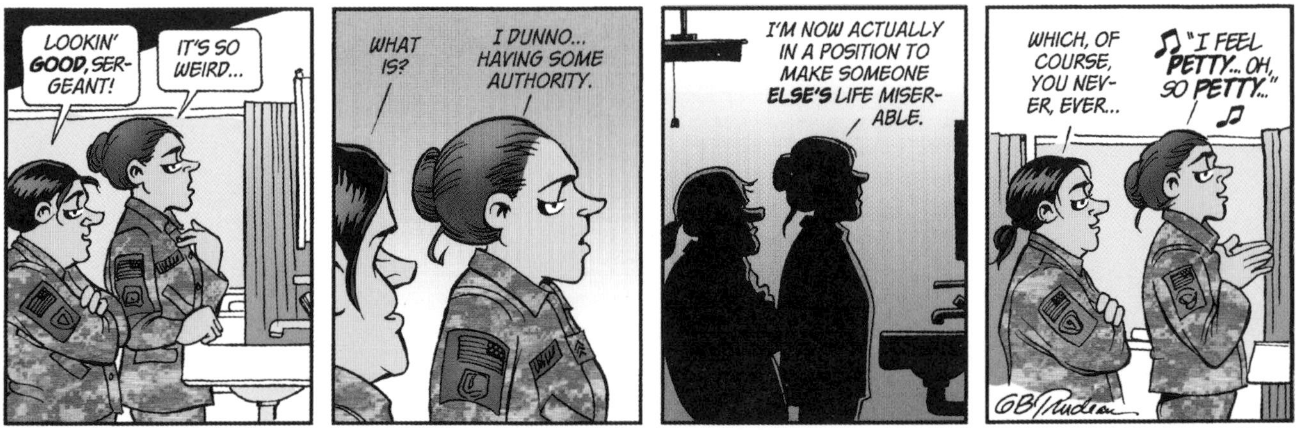
LOOKIN' GOOD, SERGEANT!
IT'S SO WEIRD...
WHAT IS?
I DUNNO... HAVING SOME AUTHORITY.
I'M NOW ACTUALLY IN A POSITION TO MAKE SOMEONE ELSE'S LIFE MISERABLE.
WHICH, OF COURSE, YOU NEVER, EVER...
"I FEEL PETTY... OH, SO PETTY..."

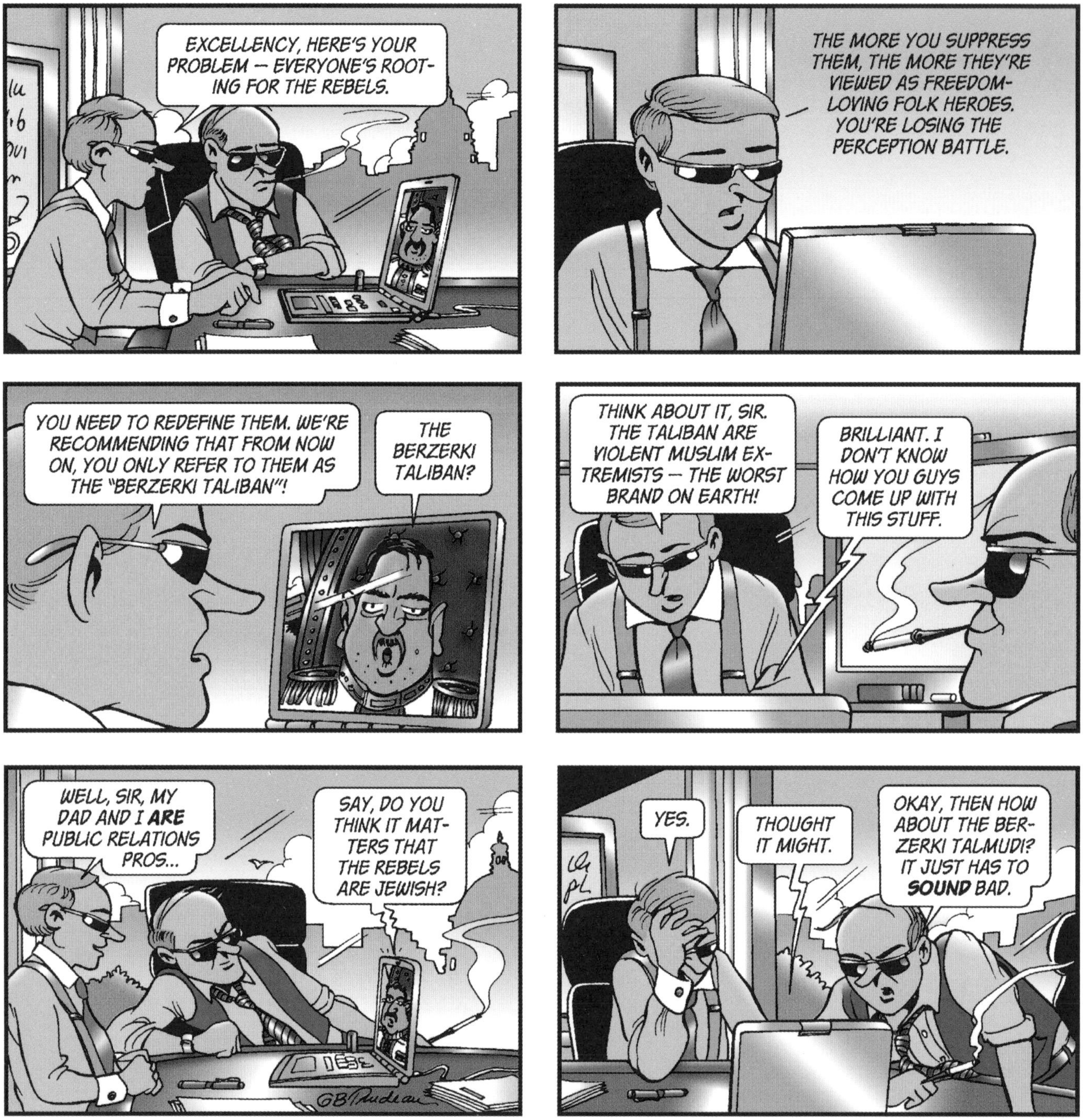
EXCELLENCY, HERE'S YOUR PROBLEM — EVERYONE'S ROOTING FOR THE REBELS.
THE MORE YOU SUPPRESS THEM, THE MORE THEY'RE VIEWED AS FREEDOM-LOVING FOLK HEROES. YOU'RE LOSING THE PERCEPTION BATTLE.
YOU NEED TO REDEFINE THEM. WE'RE RECOMMENDING THAT FROM NOW ON, YOU ONLY REFER TO THEM AS THE "BERZERKI TALIBAN"!
THE BERZERKI TALIBAN?
THINK ABOUT IT, SIR. THE TALIBAN ARE VIOLENT MUSLIM EXTREMISTS — THE WORST BRAND ON EARTH!
BRILLIANT. I DON'T KNOW HOW YOU GUYS COME UP WITH THIS STUFF.
WELL, SIR, MY DAD AND I **ARE** PUBLIC RELATIONS PROS...
SAY, DO YOU THINK IT MATTERS THAT THE REBELS ARE JEWISH?
YES.
THOUGHT IT MIGHT.
OKAY, THEN HOW ABOUT THE BERZERKI TALMUDI? IT JUST HAS TO **SOUND** BAD.
GBTrudeau

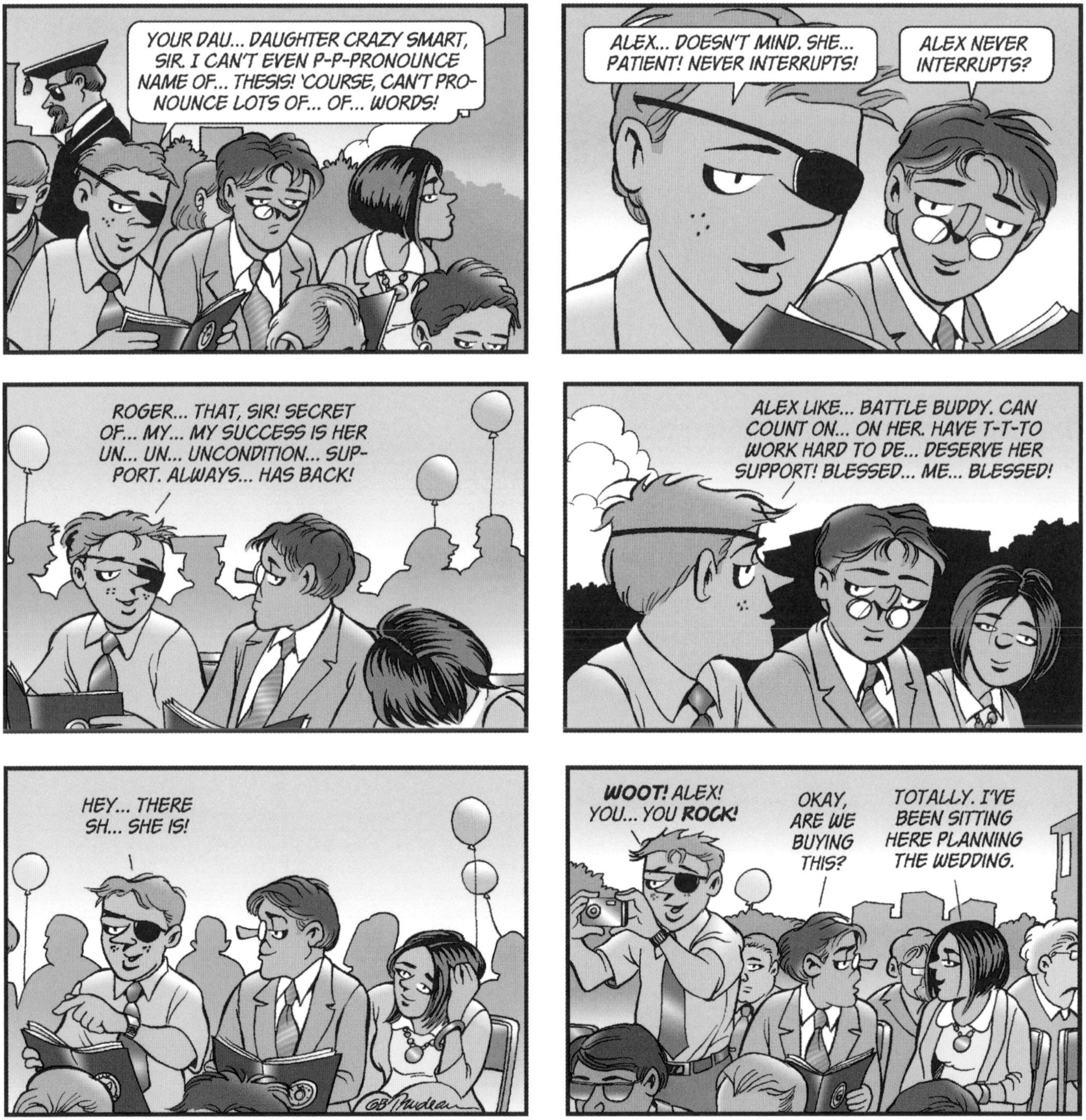
YOUR DAU... DAUGHTER CRAZY SMART, SIR. I CAN'T EVEN P-P-PRONOUNCE NAME OF... THESIS! 'COURSE, CAN'T PRONOUNCE LOTS OF... OF... WORDS!
ALEX... DOESN'T MIND. SHE... PATIENT! NEVER INTERRUPTS!
ALEX NEVER INTERRUPTS?
ROGER... THAT, SIR! SECRET OF... MY... MY SUCCESS IS HER UN... UN... UNCONDITION... SUPPORT. ALWAYS... HAS BACK!
ALEX LIKE... BATTLE BUDDY. CAN COUNT ON... ON HER. HAVE T-T-TO WORK HARD TO DE... DESERVE HER SUPPORT! BLESSED... ME... BLESSED!
HEY... THERE SH... SHE IS!
WOOT! ALEX! YOU... YOU **ROCK!**
OKAY, ARE WE BUYING THIS?
TOTALLY. I'VE BEEN SITTING HERE PLANNING THE WEDDING.

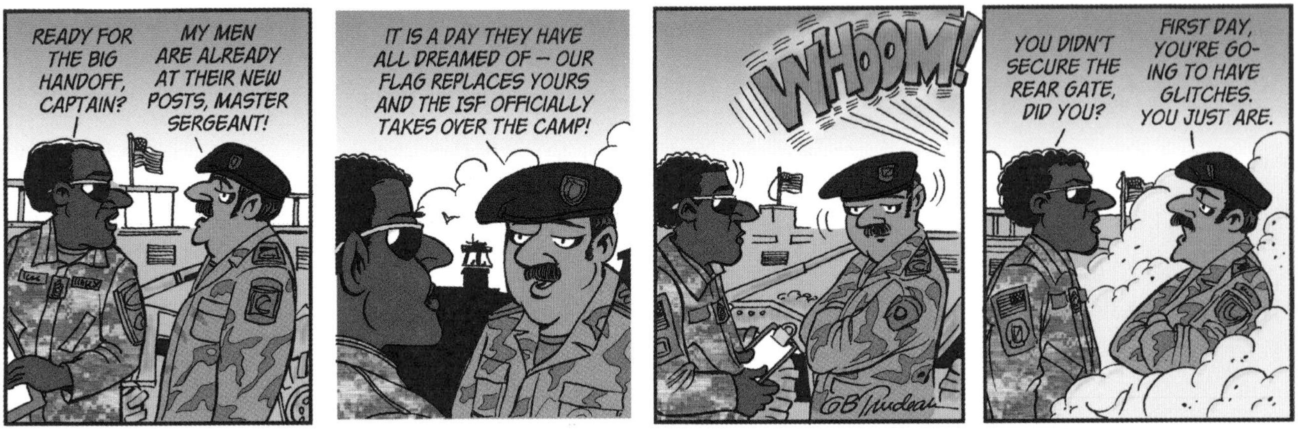
READY FOR THE BIG HANDOFF, CAPTAIN?
MY MEN ARE ALREADY AT THEIR NEW POSTS, MASTER SERGEANT!
IT IS A DAY THEY HAVE ALL DREAMED OF — OUR FLAG REPLACES YOURS AND THE ISF OFFICIALLY TAKES OVER THE CAMP!
WHOOM!
YOU DIDN'T SECURE THE REAR GATE, DID YOU?
FIRST DAY, YOU'RE GOING TO HAVE GLITCHES. YOU JUST ARE.
GB Trudeau

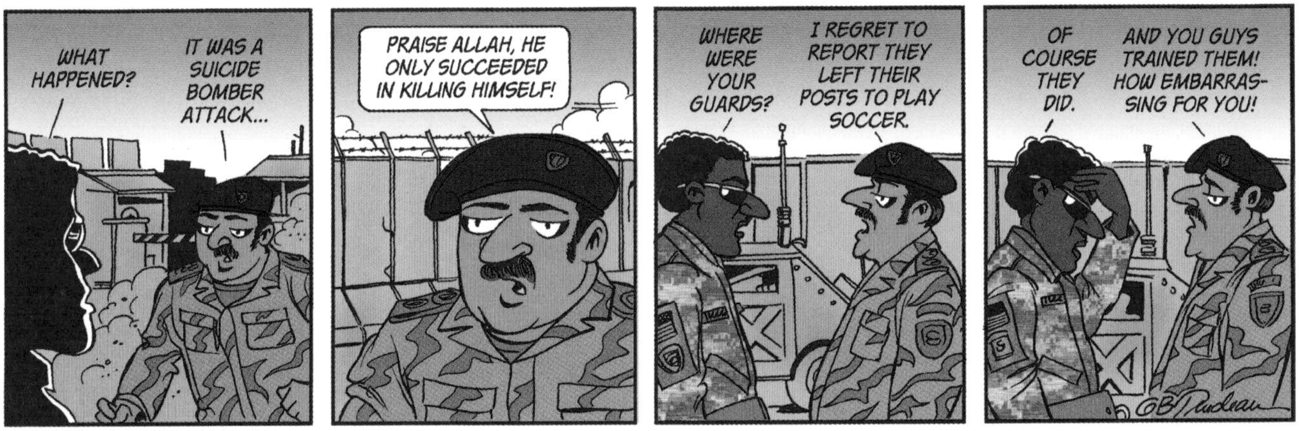
WHAT HAPPENED?
IT WAS A SUICIDE BOMBER ATTACK...
PRAISE ALLAH, HE ONLY SUCCEEDED IN KILLING HIMSELF!
WHERE WERE YOUR GUARDS?
I REGRET TO REPORT THEY LEFT THEIR POSTS TO PLAY SOCCER.
OF COURSE THEY DID.
AND YOU GUYS TRAINED THEM! HOW EMBARRASSING FOR YOU!
GB Trudeau

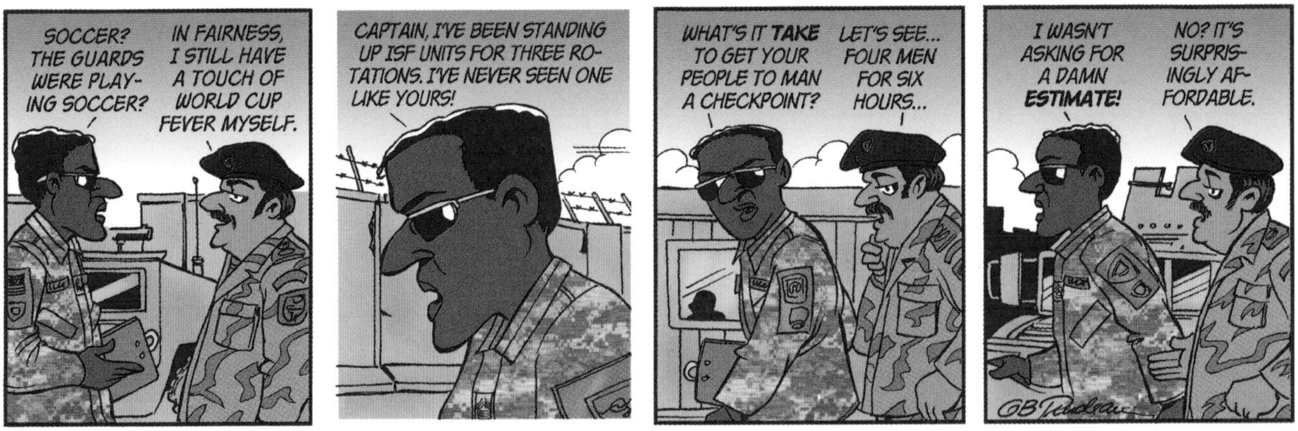
SOCCER? THE GUARDS WERE PLAYING SOCCER?
IN FAIRNESS, I STILL HAVE A TOUCH OF WORLD CUP FEVER MYSELF.
CAPTAIN, I'VE BEEN STANDING UP ISF UNITS FOR THREE ROTATIONS. I'VE NEVER SEEN ONE LIKE YOURS!
WHAT'S IT **TAKE** TO GET YOUR PEOPLE TO MAN A CHECKPOINT?
LET'S SEE... FOUR MEN FOR SIX HOURS...
I WASN'T ASKING FOR A DAMN **ESTIMATE!**
NO? IT'S SURPRISINGLY AFFORDABLE.
GB Trudeau

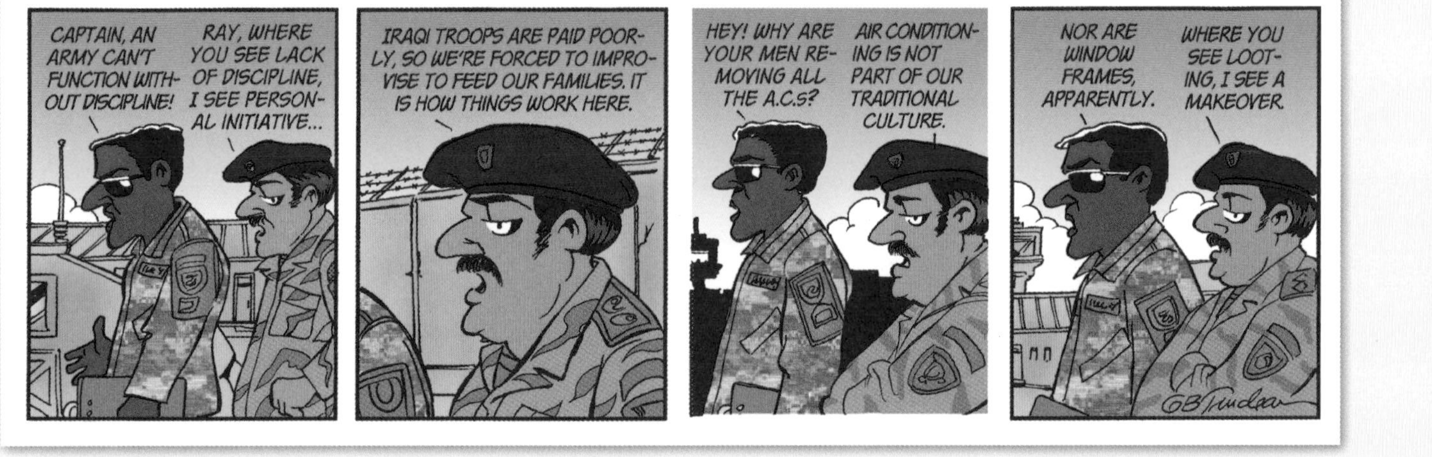
CAPTAIN, AN ARMY CAN'T FUNCTION WITHOUT DISCIPLINE!
RAY, WHERE YOU SEE LACK OF DISCIPLINE, I SEE PERSONAL INITIATIVE...
IRAQI TROOPS ARE PAID POORLY, SO WE'RE FORCED TO IMPROVISE TO FEED OUR FAMILIES. IT IS HOW THINGS WORK HERE.
HEY! WHY ARE YOUR MEN REMOVING ALL THE A.C.s?
AIR CONDITIONING IS NOT PART OF OUR TRADITIONAL CULTURE.
NOR ARE WINDOW FRAMES, APPARENTLY.
WHERE YOU SEE LOOTING, I SEE A MAKEOVER.
GBTrudeau

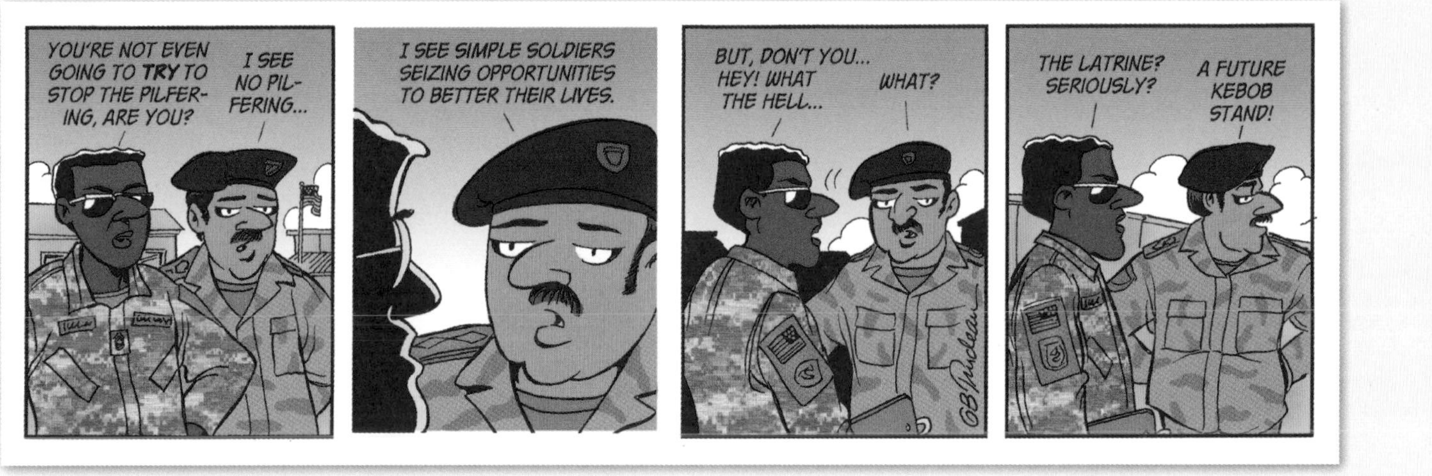
YOU'RE NOT EVEN GOING TO **TRY** TO STOP THE PILFERING, ARE YOU?
I SEE NO PILFERING...
I SEE SIMPLE SOLDIERS SEIZING OPPORTUNITIES TO BETTER THEIR LIVES.
BUT, DON'T YOU... HEY! WHAT THE HELL...
WHAT?
THE LATRINE? SERIOUSLY?
A FUTURE KEBOB STAND!
GBTrudeau

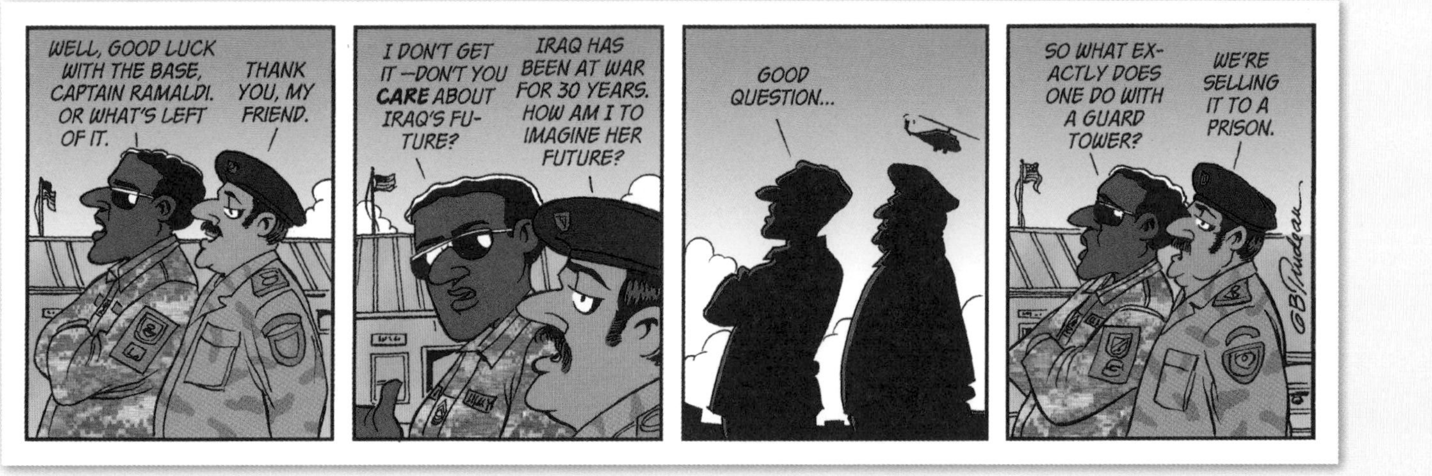
WELL, GOOD LUCK WITH THE BASE, CAPTAIN RAMALDI. OR WHAT'S LEFT OF IT.
THANK YOU, MY FRIEND.
I DON'T GET IT —DON'T YOU **CARE** ABOUT IRAQ'S FUTURE?
IRAQ HAS BEEN AT WAR FOR 30 YEARS. HOW AM I TO IMAGINE HER FUTURE?
GOOD QUESTION...
SO WHAT EXACTLY DOES ONE DO WITH A GUARD TOWER?
WE'RE SELLING IT TO A PRISON.
GBTrudeau

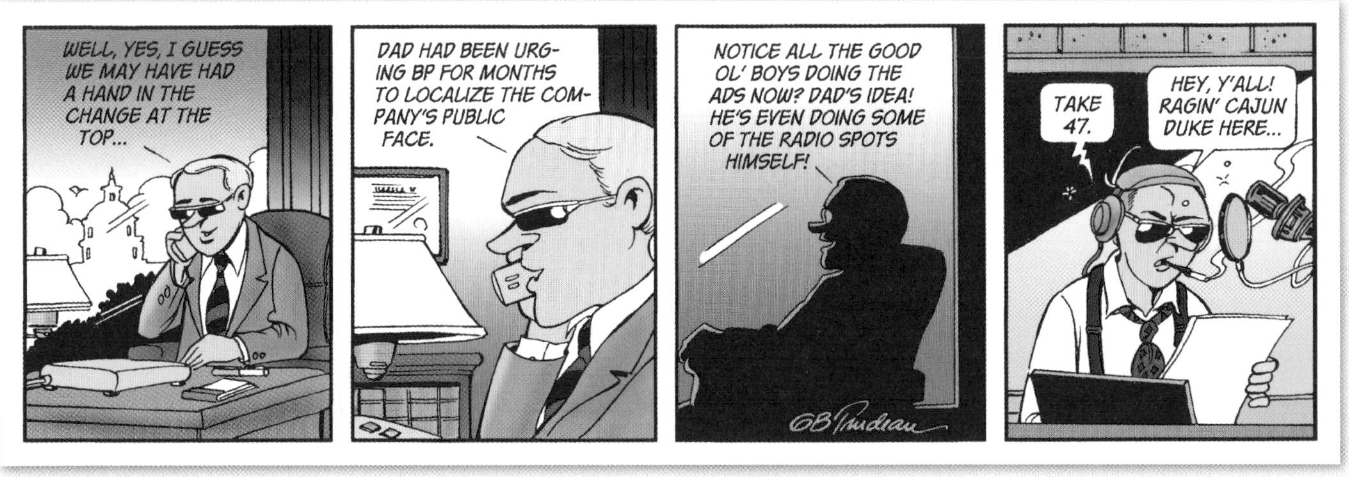
WELL, YES, I GUESS WE MAY HAVE HAD A HAND IN THE CHANGE AT THE TOP...
DAD HAD BEEN URGING BP FOR MONTHS TO LOCALIZE THE COMPANY'S PUBLIC FACE.
NOTICE ALL THE GOOD OL' BOYS DOING THE ADS NOW? DAD'S IDEA! HE'S EVEN DOING SOME OF THE RADIO SPOTS HIMSELF!
GB Trudeau
TAKE 47.
HEY, Y'ALL! RAGIN' CAJUN DUKE HERE...

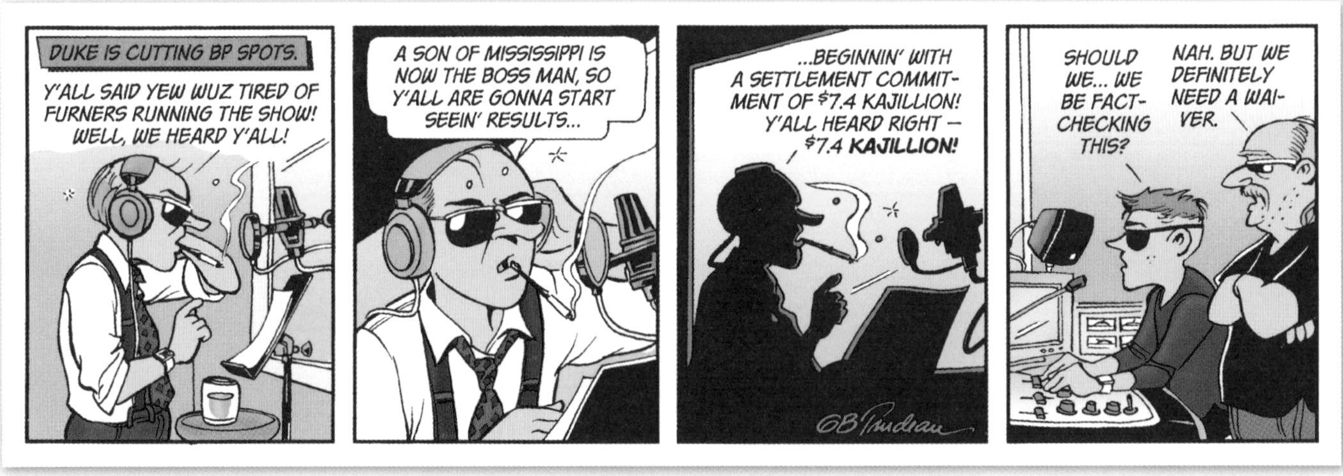
DUKE IS CUTTING BP SPOTS.
Y'ALL SAID YEW WUZ TIRED OF FURNERS RUNNING THE SHOW! WELL, WE HEARD Y'ALL!
A SON OF MISSISSIPPI IS NOW THE BOSS MAN, SO Y'ALL ARE GONNA START SEEIN' RESULTS...
...BEGINNIN' WITH A SETTLEMENT COMMITMENT OF $7.4 KAJILLION! Y'ALL HEARD RIGHT — $7.4 KAJILLION!
GB Trudeau
SHOULD WE... WE BE FACT-CHECKING THIS?
NAH. BUT WE DEFINITELY NEED A WAIVER.

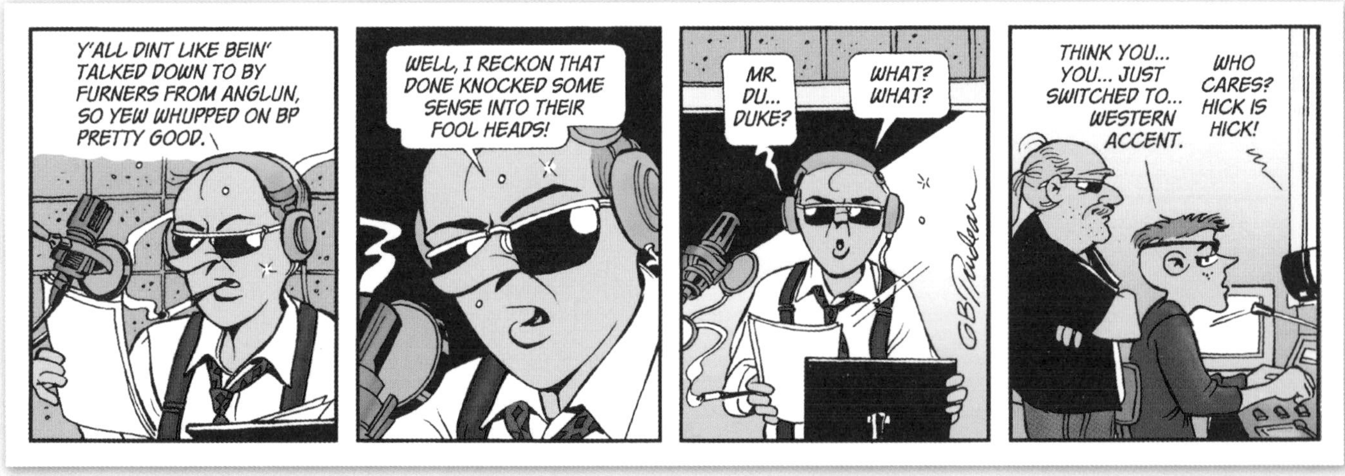
Y'ALL DINT LIKE BEIN' TALKED DOWN TO BY FURNERS FROM ANGLUN, SO YEW WHUPPED ON BP PRETTY GOOD.
WELL, I RECKON THAT DONE KNOCKED SOME SENSE INTO THEIR FOOL HEADS!
MR. DU... DUKE?
WHAT? WHAT?
GB Trudeau
THINK YOU... YOU... JUST SWITCHED TO... WESTERN ACCENT.
WHO CARES? HICK IS HICK!

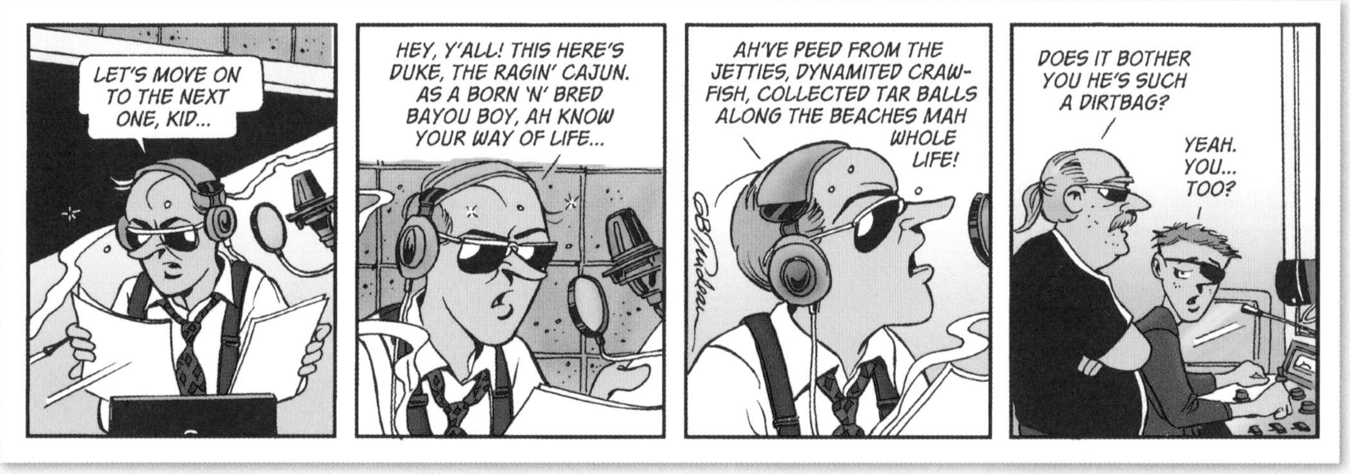
LET'S MOVE ON TO THE NEXT ONE, KID...
HEY, Y'ALL! THIS HERE'S DUKE, THE RAGIN' CAJUN. AS A BORN 'N' BRED BAYOU BOY, AH KNOW YOUR WAY OF LIFE...
AH'VE PEED FROM THE JETTIES, DYNAMITED CRAWFISH, COLLECTED TAR BALLS ALONG THE BEACHES MAH WHOLE LIFE!
DOES IT BOTHER YOU HE'S SUCH A DIRTBAG?
YEAH. YOU... TOO?

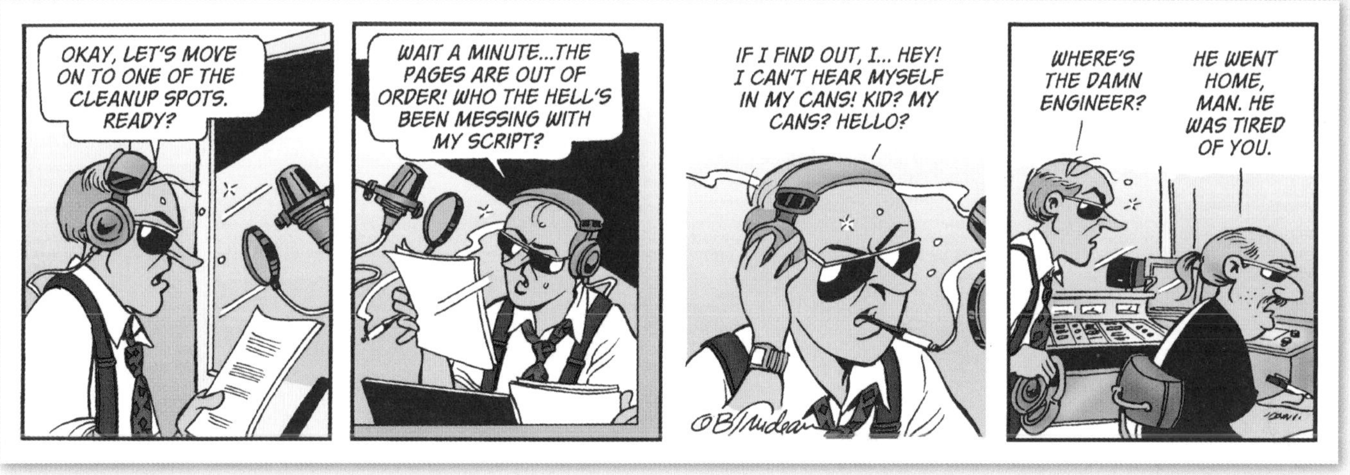
OKAY, LET'S MOVE ON TO ONE OF THE CLEANUP SPOTS. READY?
WAIT A MINUTE...THE PAGES ARE OUT OF ORDER! WHO THE HELL'S BEEN MESSING WITH MY SCRIPT?
IF I FIND OUT, I... HEY! I CAN'T HEAR MYSELF IN MY CANS! KID? MY CANS? HELLO?
WHERE'S THE DAMN ENGINEER?
HE WENT HOME, MAN. HE WAS TIRED OF YOU.

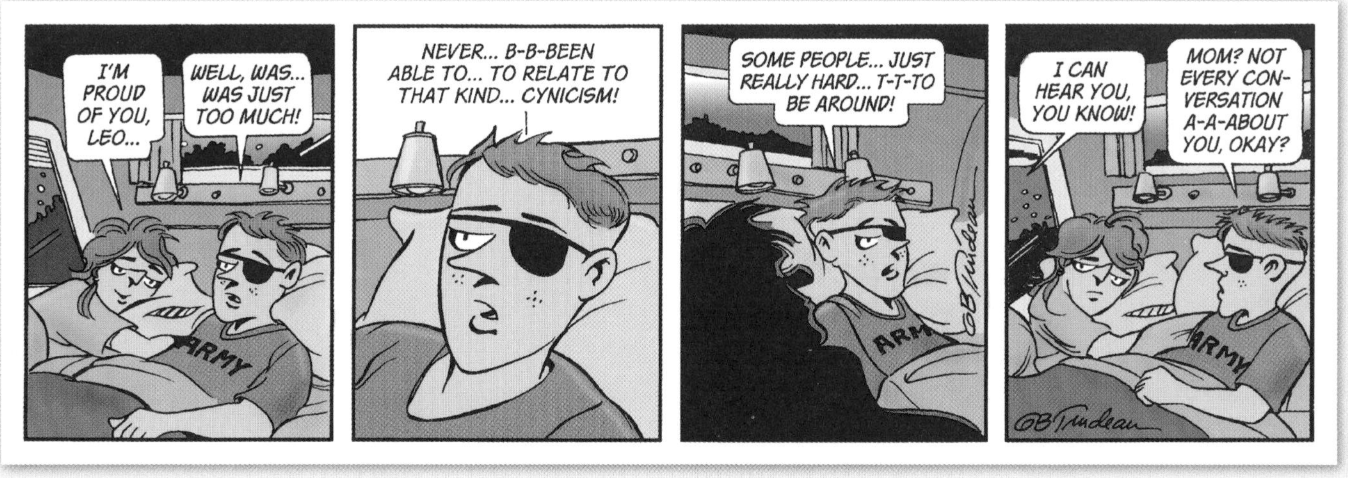
I'M PROUD OF YOU, LEO...
WELL, WAS... WAS JUST TOO MUCH!
ARMY
NEVER... B-B-BEEN ABLE TO... TO RELATE TO THAT KIND... CYNICISM!
SOME PEOPLE... JUST REALLY HARD... T-T-TO BE AROUND!
ARMY
I CAN HEAR YOU, YOU KNOW!
MOM? NOT EVERY CONVERSATION A-A-ABOUT YOU, OKAY?
ARMY

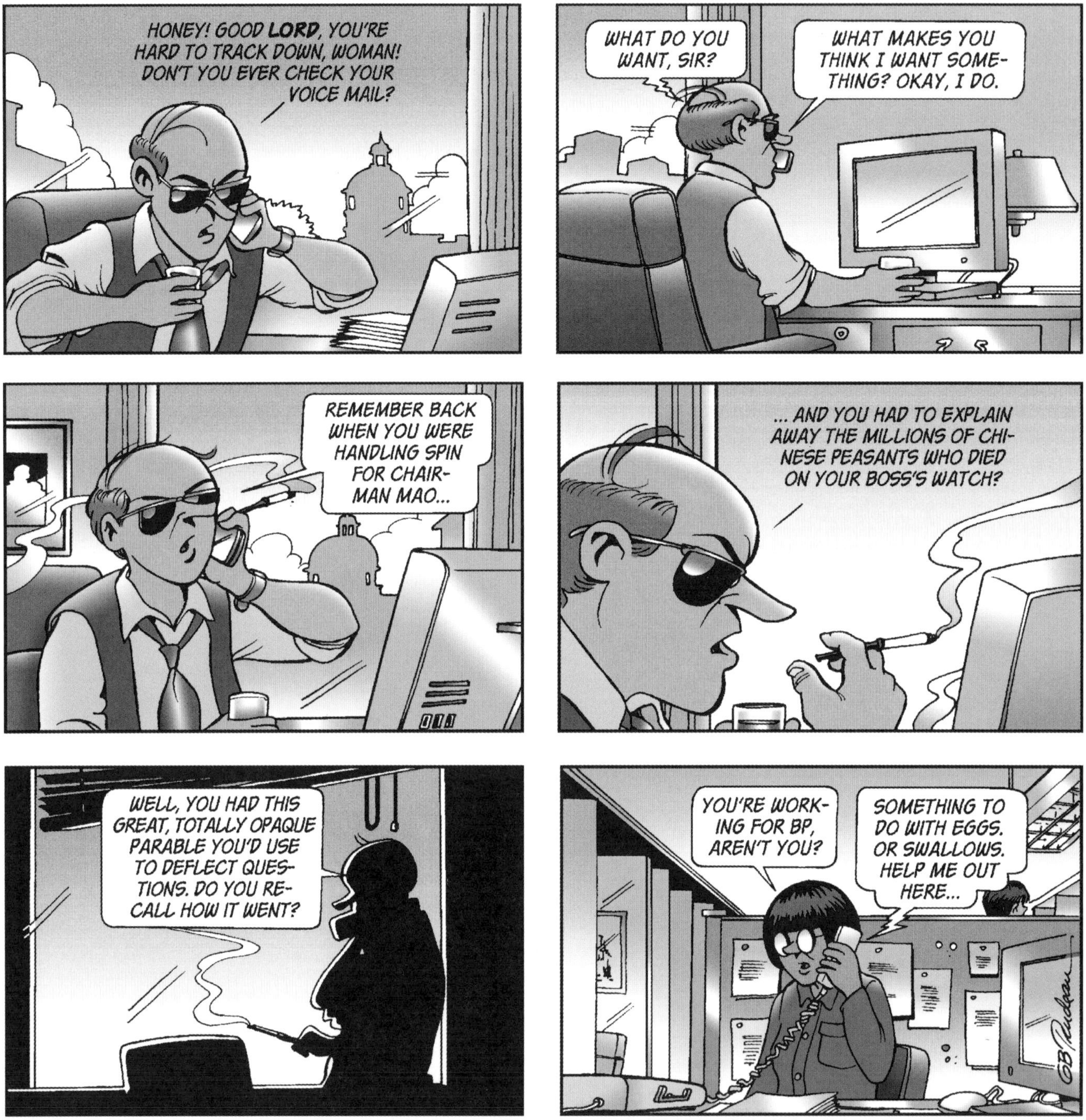
HONEY! GOOD **LORD**, YOU'RE HARD TO TRACK DOWN, WOMAN! DON'T YOU EVER CHECK YOUR VOICE MAIL?
WHAT DO YOU WANT, SIR?
WHAT MAKES YOU THINK I WANT SOMETHING? OKAY, I DO.
REMEMBER BACK WHEN YOU WERE HANDLING SPIN FOR CHAIRMAN MAO...
... AND YOU HAD TO EXPLAIN AWAY THE MILLIONS OF CHINESE PEASANTS WHO DIED ON YOUR BOSS'S WATCH?
WELL, YOU HAD THIS GREAT, TOTALLY OPAQUE PARABLE YOU'D USE TO DEFLECT QUESTIONS. DO YOU RECALL HOW IT WENT?
YOU'RE WORKING FOR BP, AREN'T YOU?
SOMETHING TO DO WITH EGGS. OR SWALLOWS. HELP ME OUT HERE...
GBTrudeau

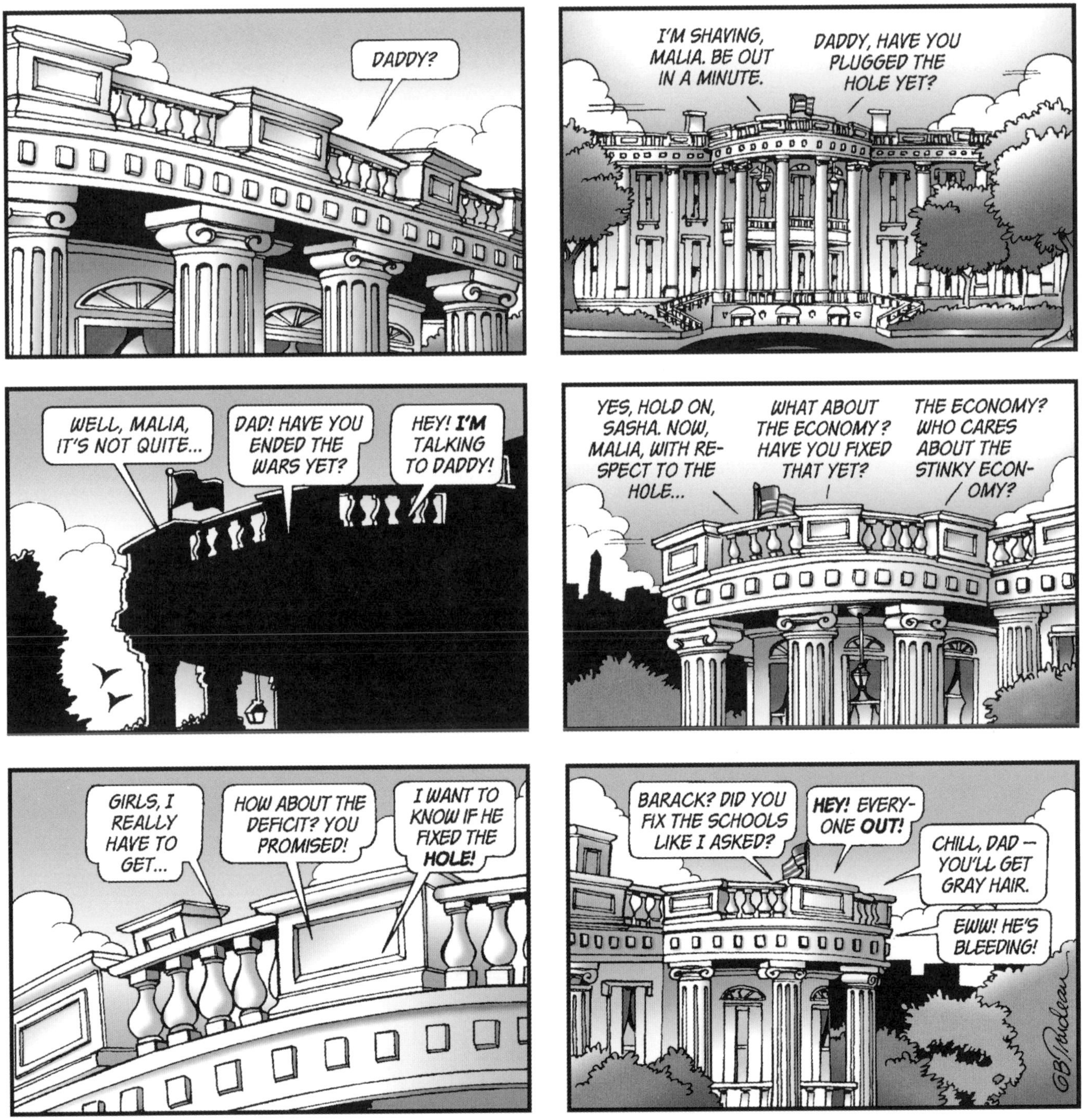
DADDY?
I'M SHAVING, MALIA. BE OUT IN A MINUTE.
DADDY, HAVE YOU PLUGGED THE HOLE YET?
WELL, MALIA, IT'S NOT QUITE...
DAD! HAVE YOU ENDED THE WARS YET?
HEY! I'M TALKING TO DADDY!
YES, HOLD ON, SASHA. NOW, MALIA, WITH RESPECT TO THE HOLE...
WHAT ABOUT THE ECONOMY? HAVE YOU FIXED THAT YET?
THE ECONOMY? WHO CARES ABOUT THE STINKY ECONOMY?
GIRLS, I REALLY HAVE TO GET...
HOW ABOUT THE DEFICIT? YOU PROMISED!
I WANT TO KNOW IF HE FIXED THE HOLE!
BARACK? DID YOU FIX THE SCHOOLS LIKE I ASKED?
HEY! EVERYONE OUT!
CHILL, DAD — YOU'LL GET GRAY HAIR.
EWW! HE'S BLEEDING!
GBTrudeau

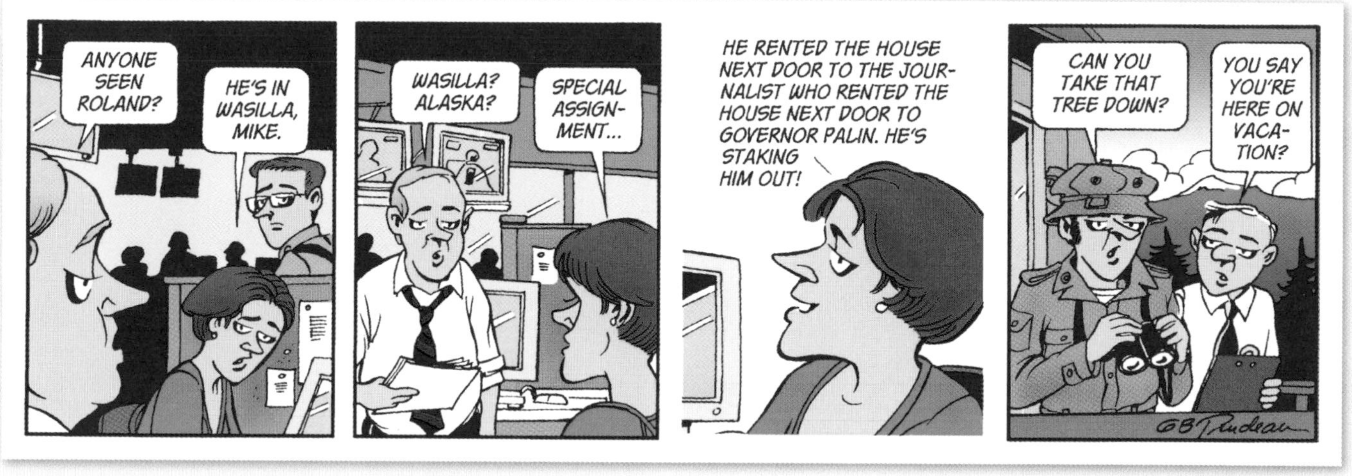
ANYONE SEEN ROLAND?
HE'S IN WASILLA, MIKE.
WASILLA? ALASKA?
SPECIAL ASSIGNMENT...
HE RENTED THE HOUSE NEXT DOOR TO THE JOURNALIST WHO RENTED THE HOUSE NEXT DOOR TO GOVERNOR PALIN. HE'S STAKING HIM OUT!
CAN YOU TAKE THAT TREE DOWN?
YOU SAY YOU'RE HERE ON VACATION?
GB Trudeau

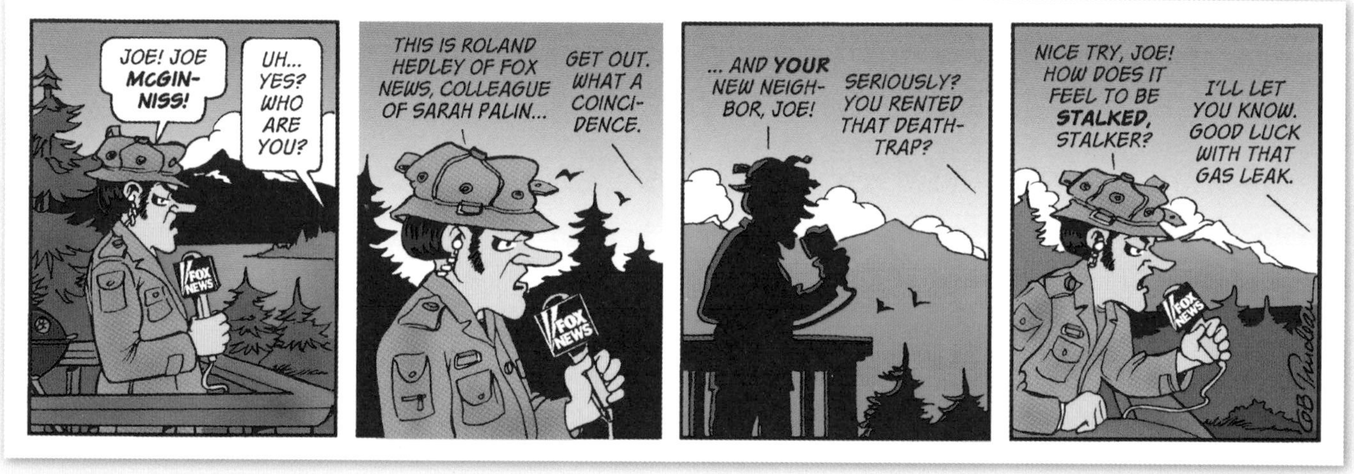
JOE! JOE **MCGINNISS!**
UH... YES? WHO ARE YOU?
THIS IS ROLAND HEDLEY OF FOX NEWS, COLLEAGUE OF SARAH PALIN...
GET OUT. WHAT A COINCIDENCE.
... AND **YOUR** NEW NEIGHBOR, JOE!
SERIOUSLY? YOU RENTED THAT DEATHTRAP?
NICE TRY, JOE! HOW DOES IT FEEL TO BE **STALKED,** STALKER?
I'LL LET YOU KNOW. GOOD LUCK WITH THAT GAS LEAK.
GB Trudeau

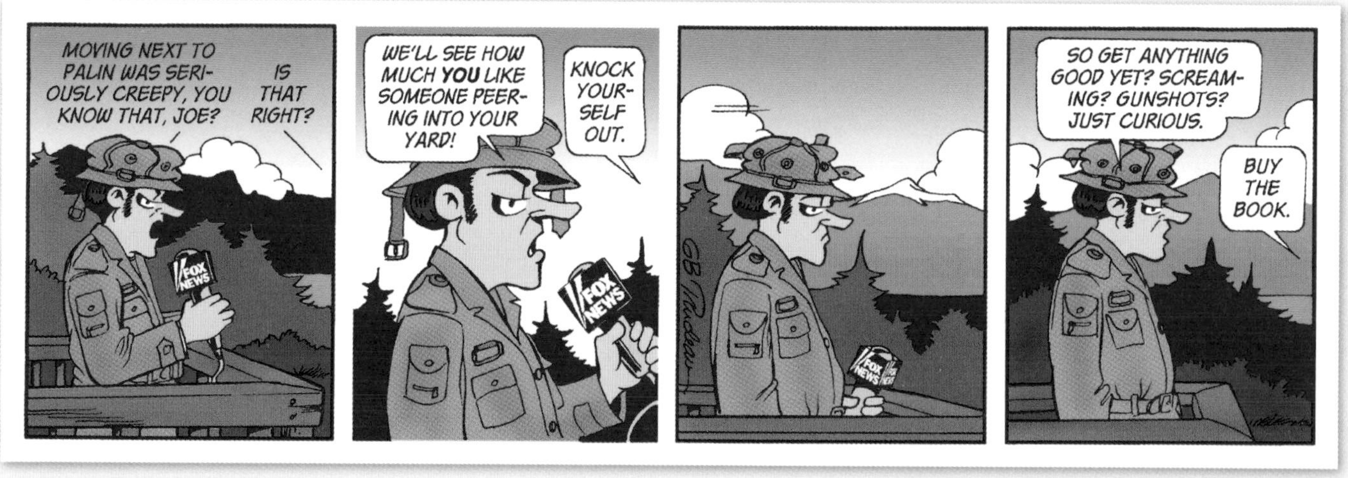
MOVING NEXT TO PALIN WAS SERIOUSLY CREEPY, YOU KNOW THAT, JOE?
IS THAT RIGHT?
WE'LL SEE HOW MUCH **YOU** LIKE SOMEONE PEERING INTO YOUR YARD!
KNOCK YOURSELF OUT.
GB Trudeau
SO GET ANYTHING GOOD YET? SCREAMING? GUNSHOTS? JUST CURIOUS.
BUY THE BOOK.

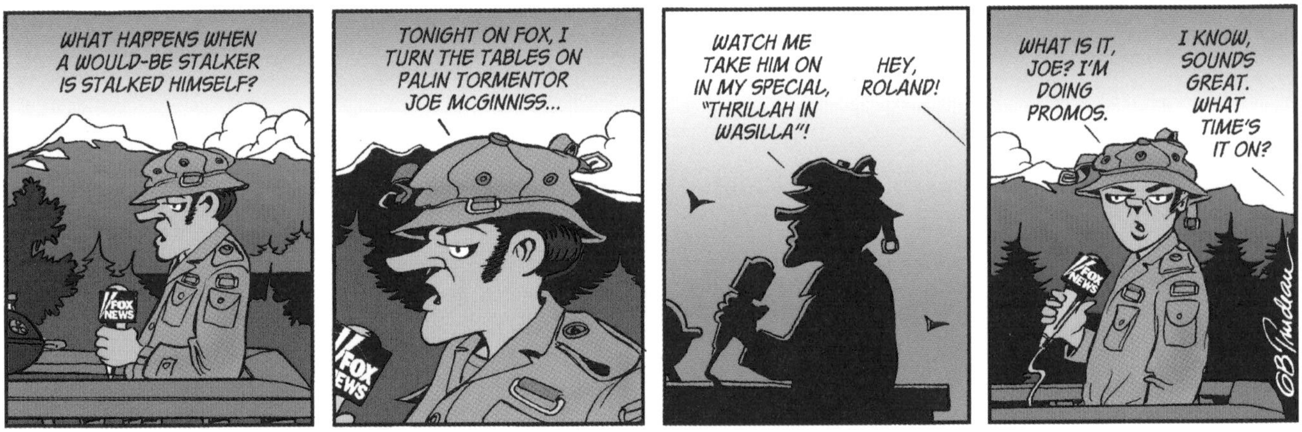
WHAT HAPPENS WHEN A WOULD-BE STALKER IS STALKED HIMSELF?
TONIGHT ON FOX, I TURN THE TABLES ON PALIN TORMENTOR JOE MCGINNISS...
WATCH ME TAKE HIM ON IN MY SPECIAL, "THRILLAH IN WASILLA"!
HEY, ROLAND!
WHAT IS IT, JOE? I'M DOING PROMOS.
I KNOW, SOUNDS GREAT. WHAT TIME'S IT ON?

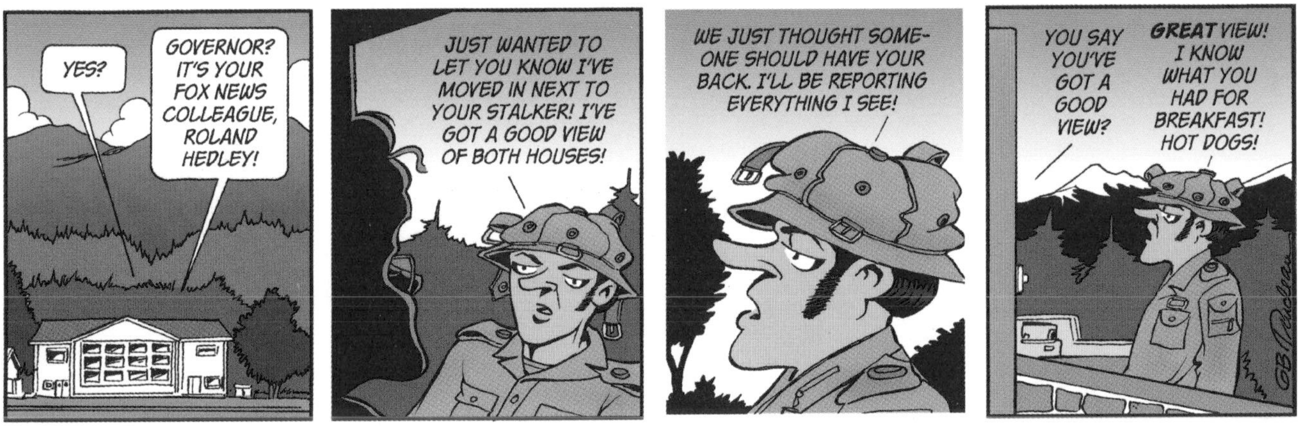
YES?
GOVERNOR? IT'S YOUR FOX NEWS COLLEAGUE, ROLAND HEDLEY!
JUST WANTED TO LET YOU KNOW I'VE MOVED IN NEXT TO YOUR STALKER! I'VE GOT A GOOD VIEW OF BOTH HOUSES!
WE JUST THOUGHT SOMEONE SHOULD HAVE YOUR BACK. I'LL BE REPORTING EVERYTHING I SEE!
YOU SAY YOU'VE GOT A GOOD VIEW?
GREAT VIEW! I KNOW WHAT YOU HAD FOR BREAKFAST! HOT DOGS!

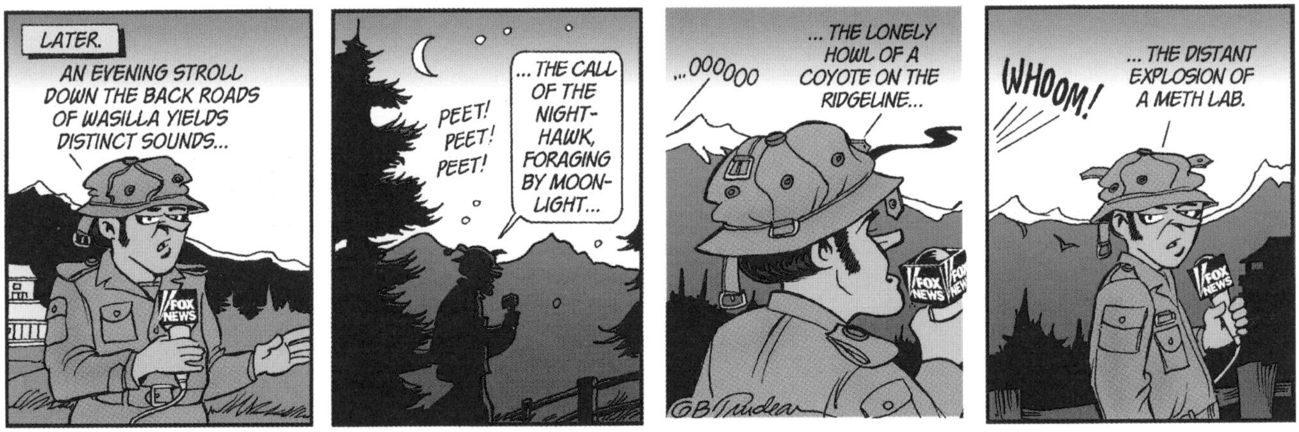
LATER.
AN EVENING STROLL DOWN THE BACK ROADS OF WASILLA YIELDS DISTINCT SOUNDS...
PEET! PEET! PEET!
...THE CALL OF THE NIGHT-HAWK, FORAGING BY MOON-LIGHT...
...OOOOOO
...THE LONELY HOWL OF A COYOTE ON THE RIDGELINE...
WHOOM!
...THE DISTANT EXPLOSION OF A METH LAB.

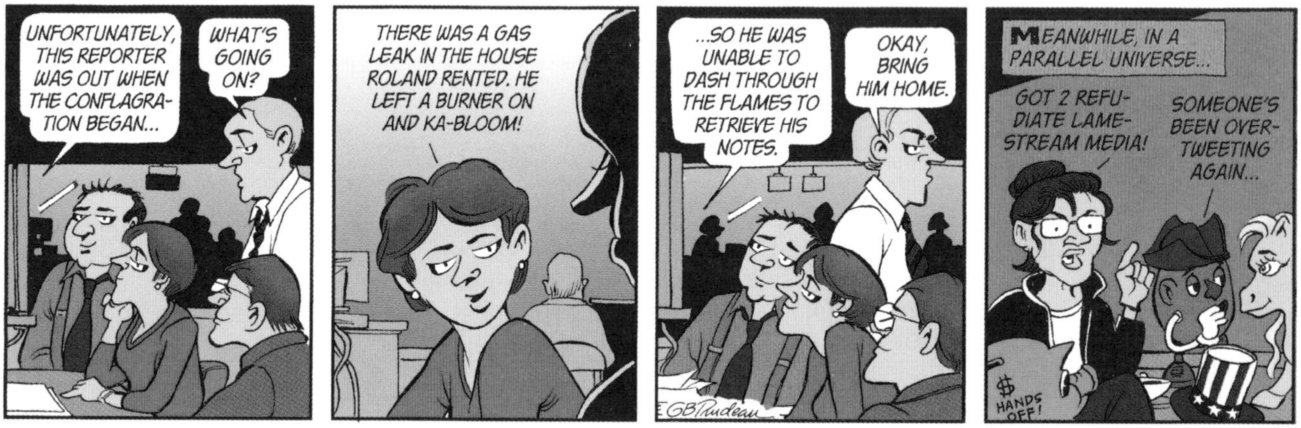
UNFORTUNATELY, THIS REPORTER WAS OUT WHEN THE CONFLAGRATION BEGAN...
WHAT'S GOING ON?
THERE WAS A GAS LEAK IN THE HOUSE ROLAND RENTED. HE LEFT A BURNER ON AND KA-BLOOM!
...SO HE WAS UNABLE TO DASH THROUGH THE FLAMES TO RETRIEVE HIS NOTES.
OKAY, BRING HIM HOME.
GBTrudeau
MEANWHILE, IN A PARALLEL UNIVERSE...
GOT 2 REFUDIATE LAME-STREAM MEDIA!
SOMEONE'S BEEN OVER-TWEETING AGAIN...
$ HANDS OFF!

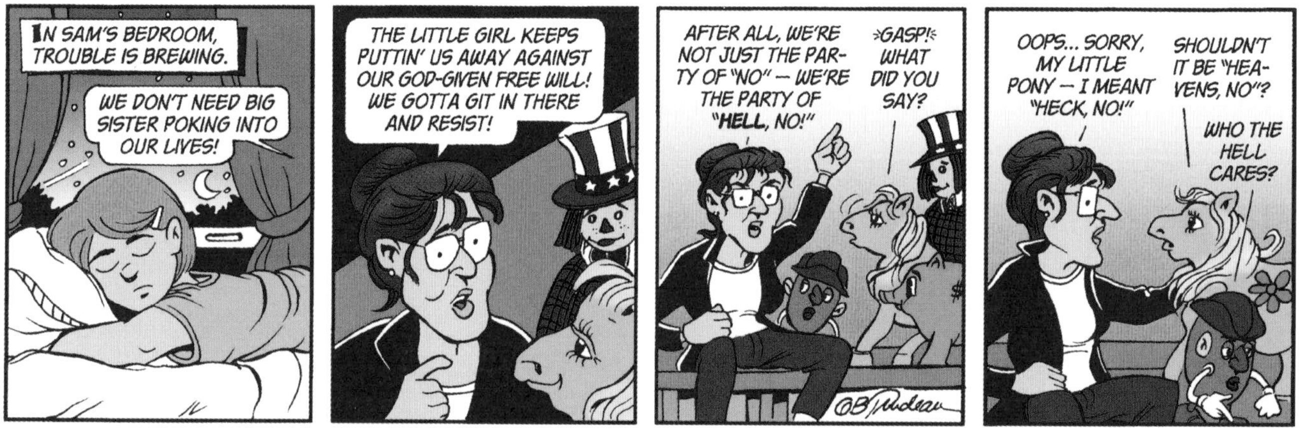
IN SAM'S BEDROOM, TROUBLE IS BREWING.
WE DON'T NEED BIG SISTER POKING INTO OUR LIVES!
THE LITTLE GIRL KEEPS PUTTIN' US AWAY AGAINST OUR GOD-GIVEN FREE WILL! WE GOTTA GIT IN THERE AND RESIST!
AFTER ALL, WE'RE NOT JUST THE PARTY OF "NO" — WE'RE THE PARTY OF "HELL, NO!"
GASP! WHAT DID YOU SAY?
GBTrudeau
OOPS... SORRY, MY LITTLE PONY — I MEANT "HECK, NO!"
SHOULDN'T IT BE "HEAVENS, NO"?
WHO THE HELL CARES?

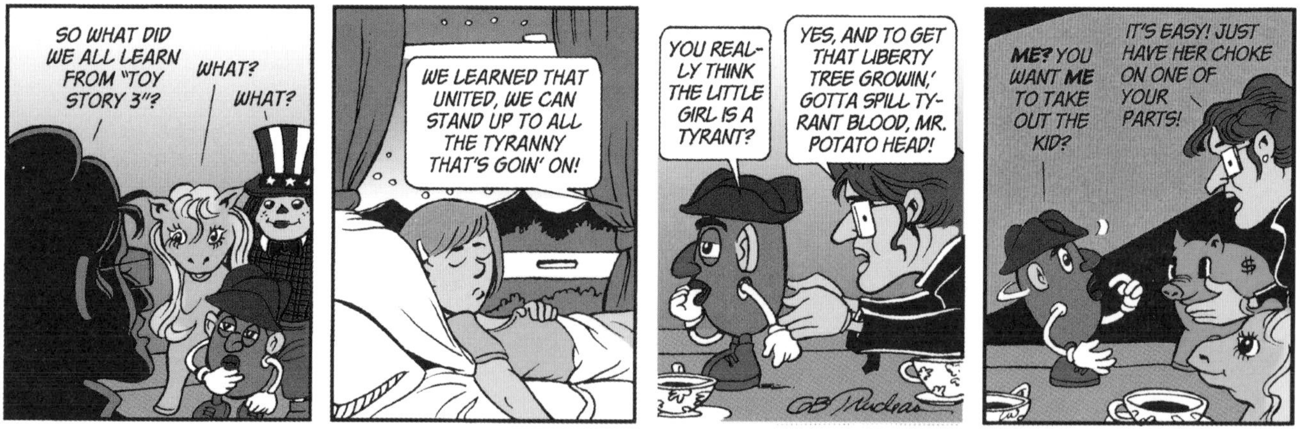
SO WHAT DID WE ALL LEARN FROM "TOY STORY 3"?
WHAT?
WHAT?
WE LEARNED THAT UNITED, WE CAN STAND UP TO ALL THE TYRANNY THAT'S GOIN' ON!
YOU REALLY THINK THE LITTLE GIRL IS A TYRANT?
YES, AND TO GET THAT LIBERTY TREE GROWIN,' GOTTA SPILL TYRANT BLOOD, MR. POTATO HEAD!
GBTrudeau
ME? YOU WANT ME TO TAKE OUT THE KID?
IT'S EASY! JUST HAVE HER CHOKE ON ONE OF YOUR PARTS!

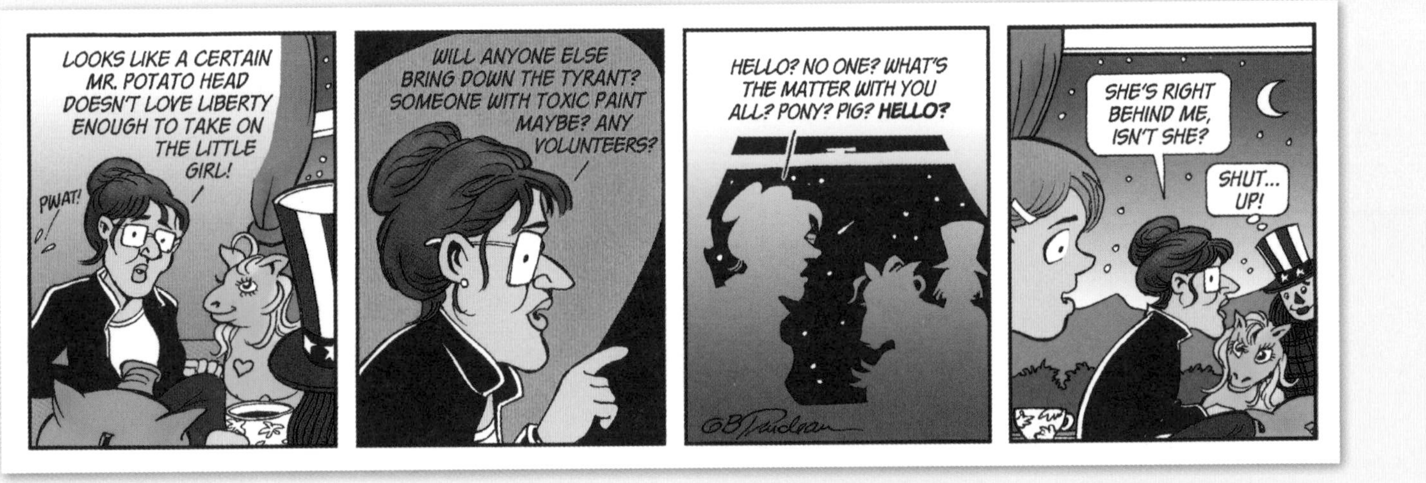
LOOKS LIKE A CERTAIN MR. POTATO HEAD DOESN'T LOVE LIBERTY ENOUGH TO TAKE ON THE LITTLE GIRL!
PWAT!
WILL ANYONE ELSE BRING DOWN THE TYRANT? SOMEONE WITH TOXIC PAINT MAYBE? ANY VOLUNTEERS?
HELLO? NO ONE? WHAT'S THE MATTER WITH YOU ALL? PONY? PIG? HELLO?
SHE'S RIGHT BEHIND ME, ISN'T SHE?
SHUT... UP!

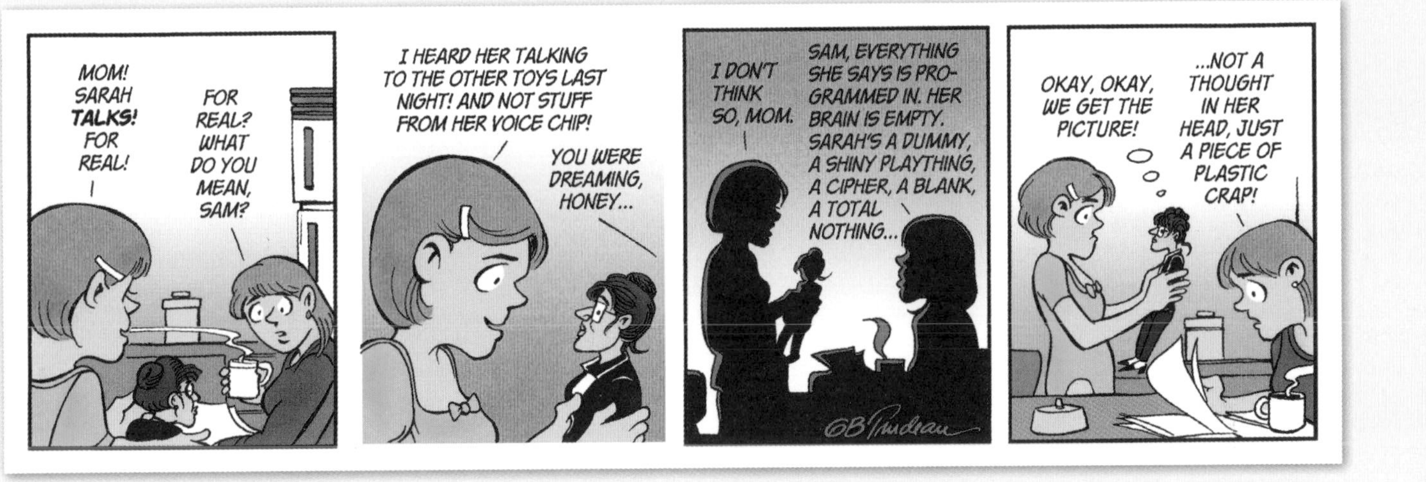
MOM! SARAH TALKS! FOR REAL!
FOR REAL? WHAT DO YOU MEAN, SAM?
I HEARD HER TALKING TO THE OTHER TOYS LAST NIGHT! AND NOT STUFF FROM HER VOICE CHIP!
YOU WERE DREAMING, HONEY...
I DON'T THINK SO, MOM.
SAM, EVERYTHING SHE SAYS IS PROGRAMMED IN. HER BRAIN IS EMPTY. SARAH'S A DUMMY, A SHINY PLAYTHING, A CIPHER, A BLANK, A TOTAL NOTHING...
OKAY, OKAY, WE GET THE PICTURE!
...NOT A THOUGHT IN HER HEAD, JUST A PIECE OF PLASTIC CRAP!

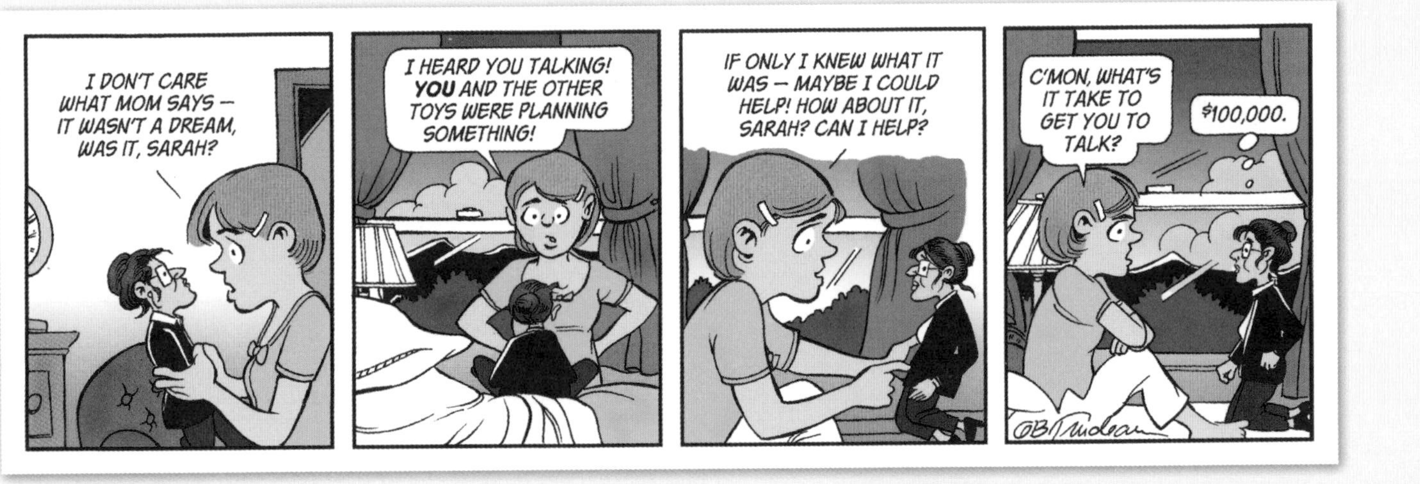
I DON'T CARE WHAT MOM SAYS — IT WASN'T A DREAM, WAS IT, SARAH?
I HEARD YOU TALKING! YOU AND THE OTHER TOYS WERE PLANNING SOMETHING!
IF ONLY I KNEW WHAT IT WAS — MAYBE I COULD HELP! HOW ABOUT IT, SARAH? CAN I HELP?
C'MON, WHAT'S IT TAKE TO GET YOU TO TALK?
$100,000.

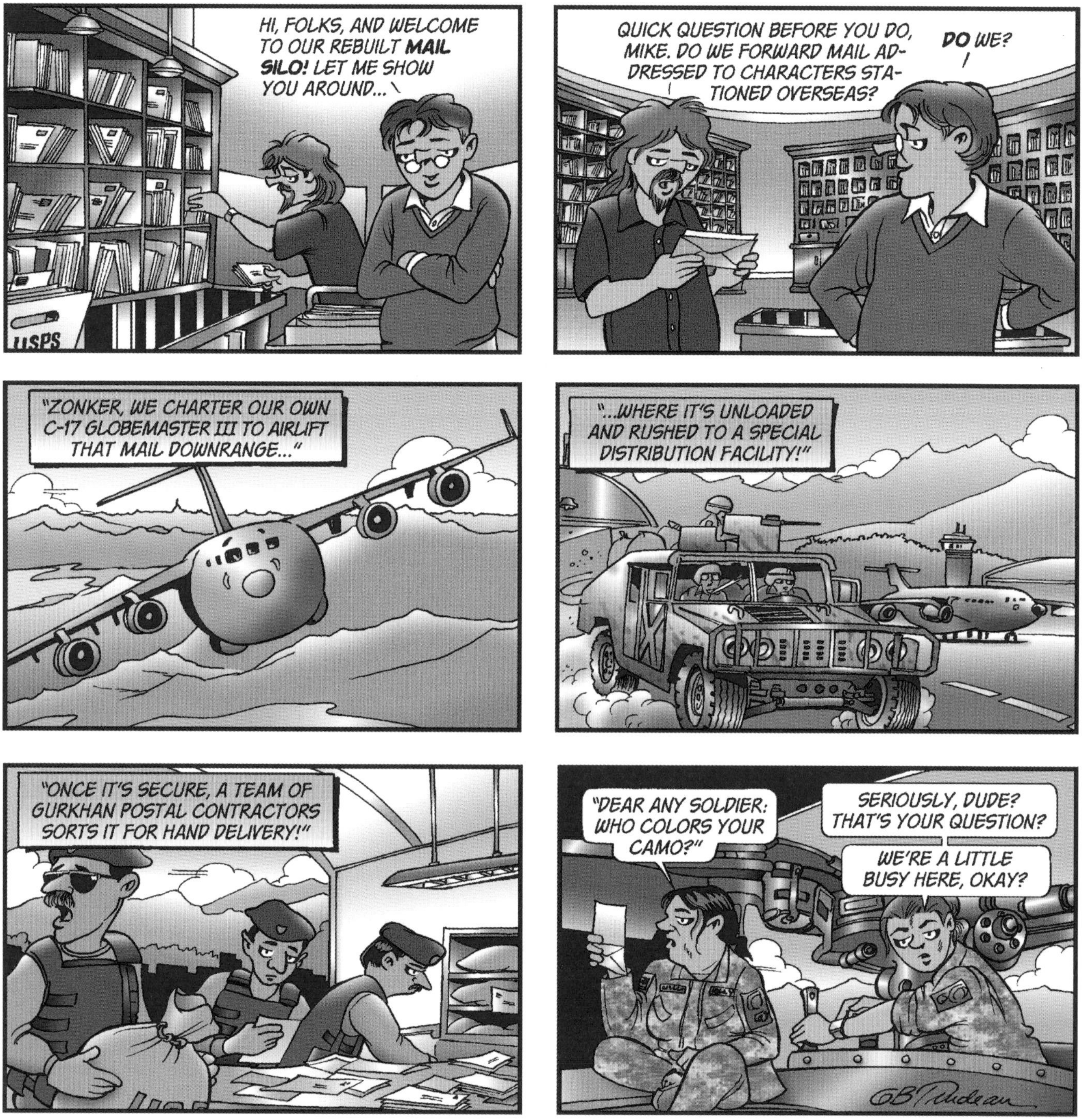
HI, FOLKS, AND WELCOME TO OUR REBUILT MAIL SILO! LET ME SHOW YOU AROUND...
USPS
QUICK QUESTION BEFORE YOU DO, MIKE. DO WE FORWARD MAIL ADDRESSED TO CHARACTERS STATIONED OVERSEAS?
DO WE?
"ZONKER, WE CHARTER OUR OWN C-17 GLOBEMASTER III TO AIRLIFT THAT MAIL DOWNRANGE..."
"...WHERE IT'S UNLOADED AND RUSHED TO A SPECIAL DISTRIBUTION FACILITY!"
"ONCE IT'S SECURE, A TEAM OF GURKHAN POSTAL CONTRACTORS SORTS IT FOR HAND DELIVERY!"
"DEAR ANY SOLDIER: WHO COLORS YOUR CAMO?"
SERIOUSLY, DUDE? THAT'S YOUR QUESTION?
WE'RE A LITTLE BUSY HERE, OKAY?
GBTrudeau

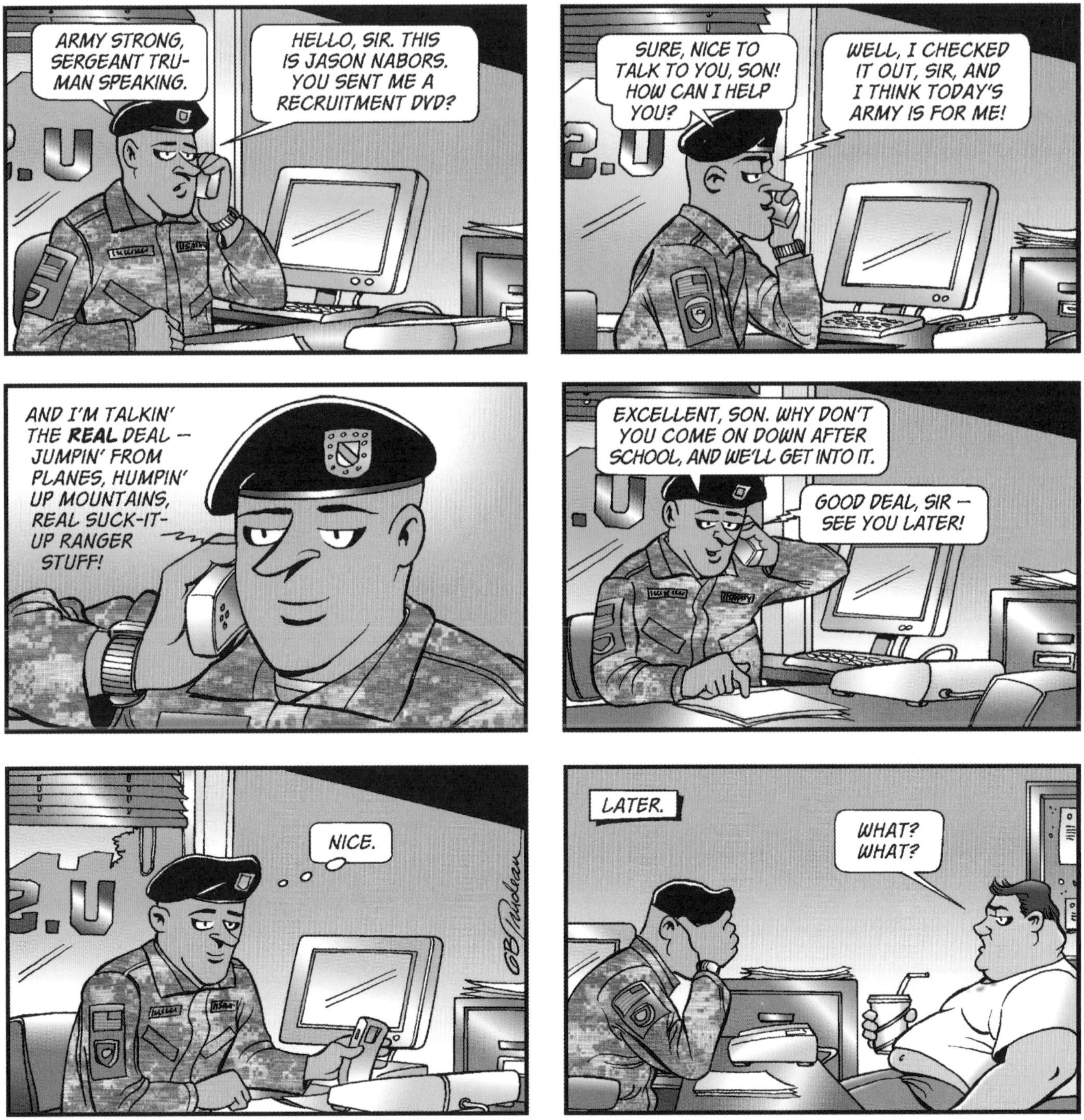
ARMY STRONG, SERGEANT TRUMAN SPEAKING.
HELLO, SIR. THIS IS JASON NABORS. YOU SENT ME A RECRUITMENT DVD?
SURE, NICE TO TALK TO YOU, SON! HOW CAN I HELP YOU?
WELL, I CHECKED IT OUT, SIR, AND I THINK TODAY'S ARMY IS FOR ME!
AND I'M TALKIN' THE REAL DEAL — JUMPIN' FROM PLANES, HUMPIN' UP MOUNTAINS, REAL SUCK-IT-UP RANGER STUFF!
EXCELLENT, SON. WHY DON'T YOU COME ON DOWN AFTER SCHOOL, AND WE'LL GET INTO IT.
GOOD DEAL, SIR — SEE YOU LATER!
NICE.
LATER.
WHAT? WHAT?

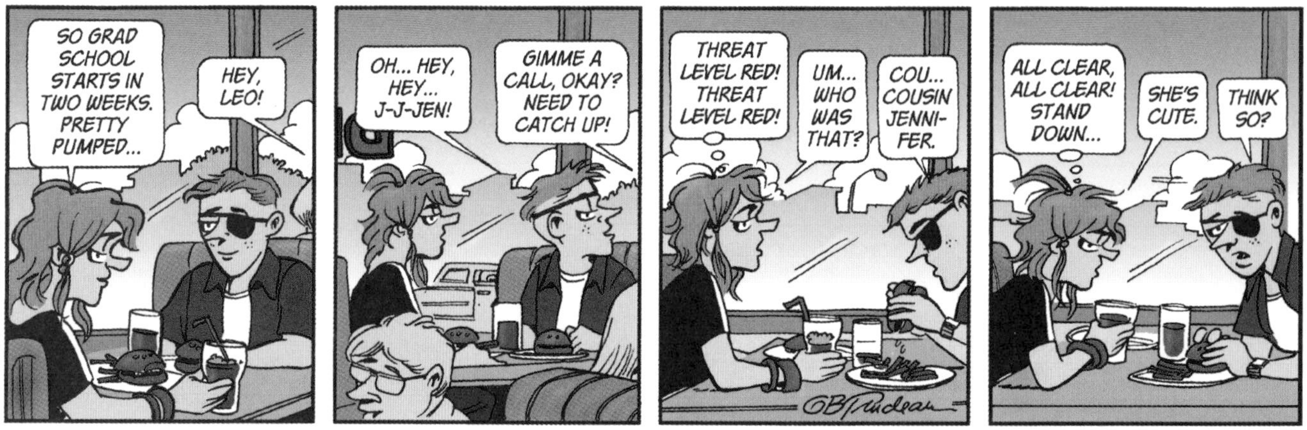
SO GRAD SCHOOL STARTS IN TWO WEEKS. PRETTY PUMPED...
HEY, LEO!
OH... HEY, HEY... J-J-JEN!
GIMME A CALL, OKAY? NEED TO CATCH UP!
THREAT LEVEL RED! THREAT LEVEL RED!
UM... WHO WAS THAT?
COU... COUSIN JENNIFER.
ALL CLEAR, ALL CLEAR! STAND DOWN...
SHE'S CUTE.
THINK SO?
GB Trudeau

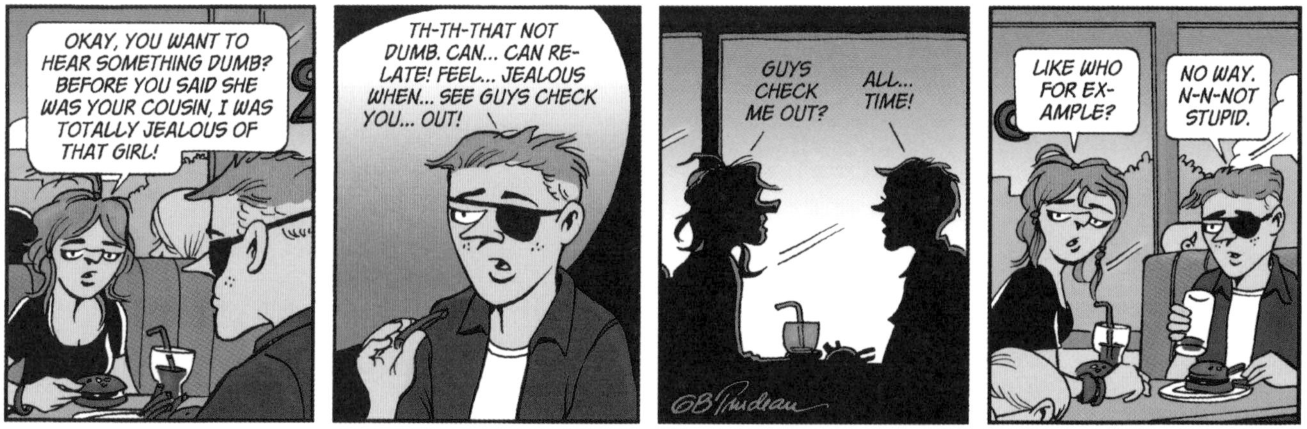
OKAY, YOU WANT TO HEAR SOMETHING DUMB? BEFORE YOU SAID SHE WAS YOUR COUSIN, I WAS TOTALLY JEALOUS OF THAT GIRL!
TH-TH-THAT NOT DUMB. CAN... CAN RELATE! FEEL... JEALOUS WHEN... SEE GUYS CHECK YOU... OUT!
GUYS CHECK ME OUT?
ALL... TIME!
LIKE WHO FOR EXAMPLE?
NO WAY. N-N-NOT STUPID.
GB Trudeau

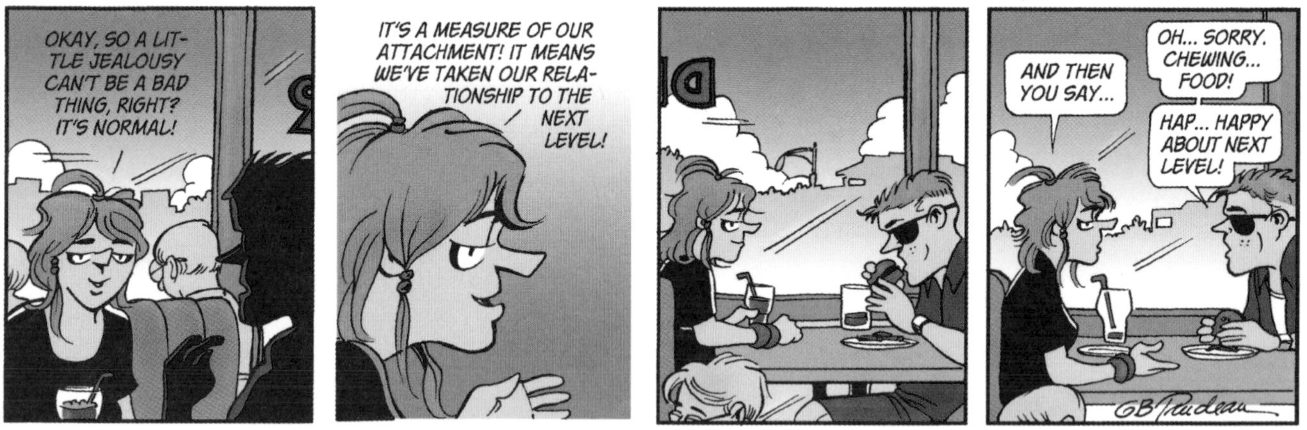
OKAY, SO A LITTLE JEALOUSY CAN'T BE A BAD THING, RIGHT? IT'S NORMAL!
IT'S A MEASURE OF OUR ATTACHMENT! IT MEANS WE'VE TAKEN OUR RELATIONSHIP TO THE NEXT LEVEL!
AND THEN YOU SAY...
OH... SORRY. CHEWING... FOOD!
HAP... HAPPY ABOUT NEXT LEVEL!
GB Trudeau

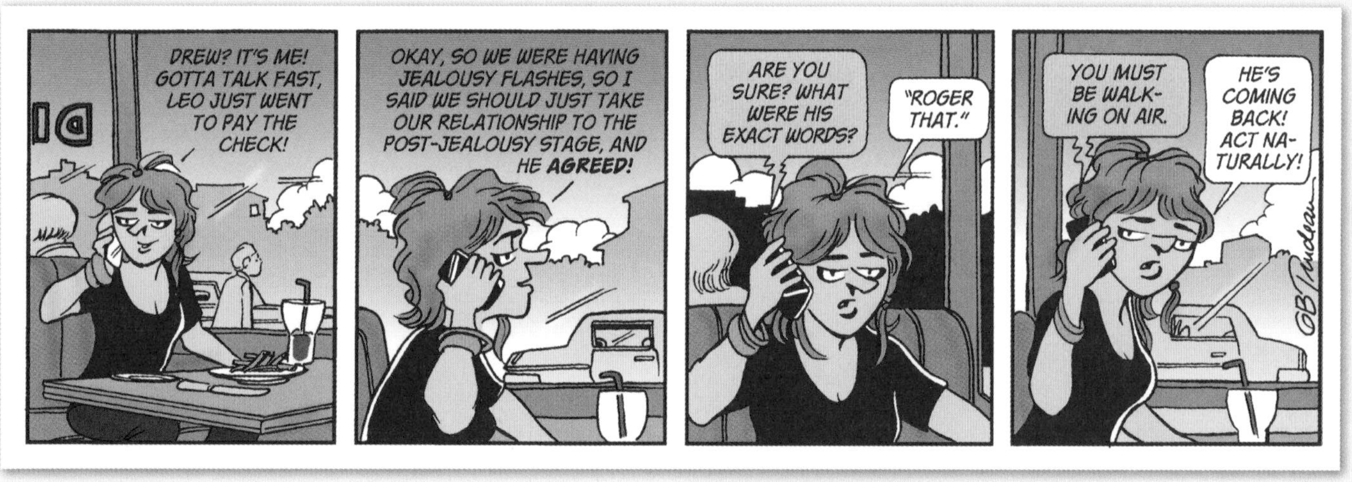
DREW? IT'S ME! GOTTA TALK FAST, LEO JUST WENT TO PAY THE CHECK!
OKAY, SO WE WERE HAVING JEALOUSY FLASHES, SO I SAID WE SHOULD JUST TAKE OUR RELATIONSHIP TO THE POST-JEALOUSY STAGE, AND HE **AGREED!**
ARE YOU SURE? WHAT WERE HIS EXACT WORDS?
"ROGER THAT."
YOU MUST BE WALKING ON AIR.
HE'S COMING BACK! ACT NATURALLY!

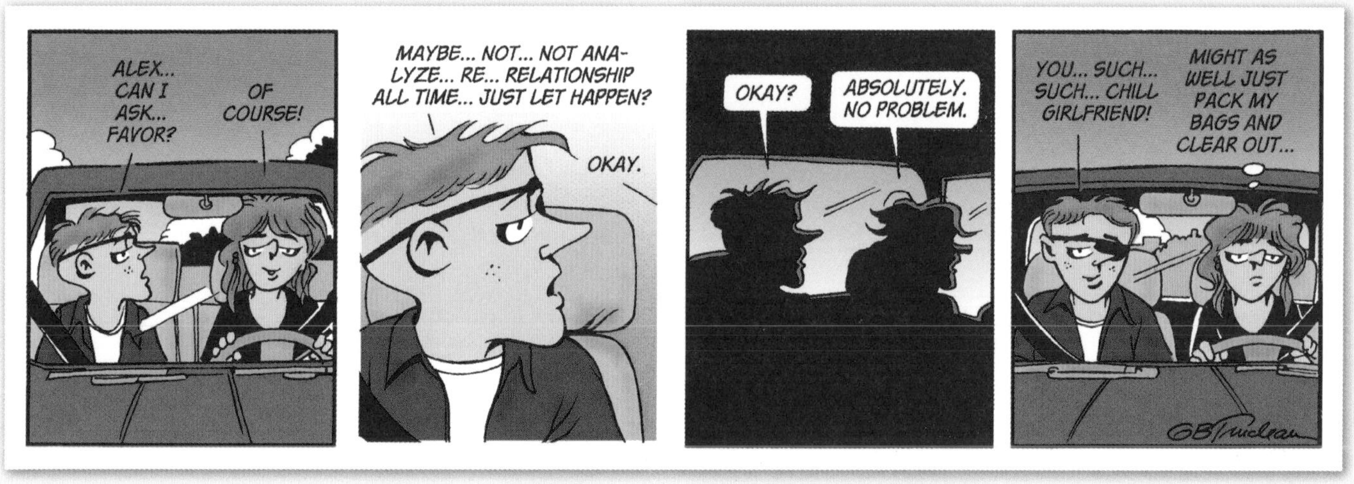
ALEX... CAN I ASK... FAVOR?
OF COURSE!
MAYBE... NOT... NOT ANALYZE... RE... RELATIONSHIP ALL TIME... JUST LET HAPPEN?
OKAY.
OKAY?
ABSOLUTELY. NO PROBLEM.
YOU... SUCH... SUCH... CHILL GIRLFRIEND!
MIGHT AS WELL JUST PACK MY BAGS AND CLEAR OUT...

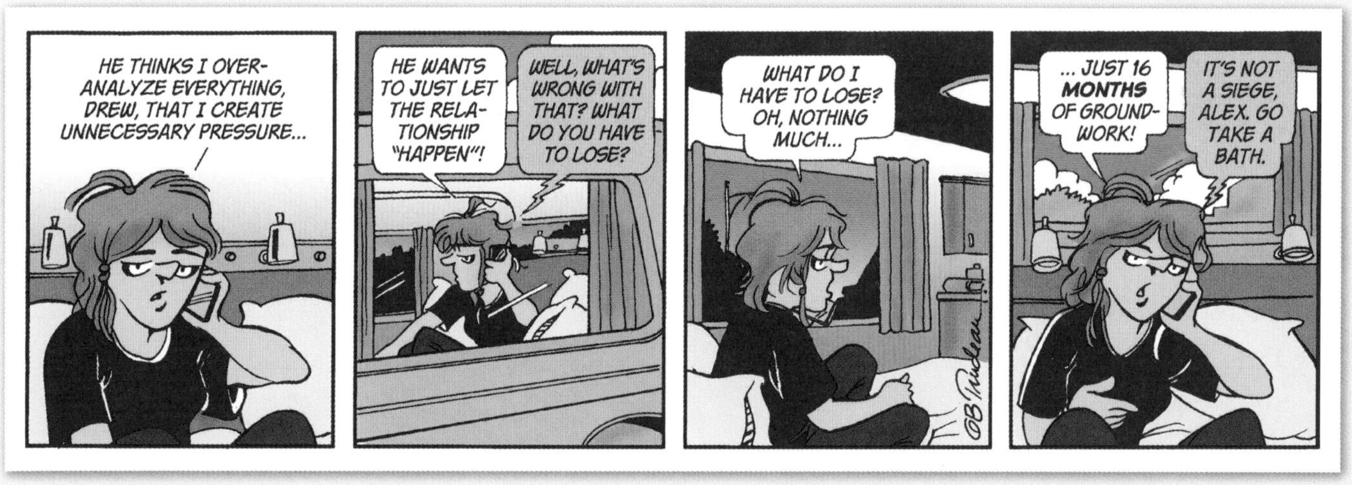
HE THINKS I OVER-ANALYZE EVERYTHING, DREW, THAT I CREATE UNNECESSARY PRESSURE...
HE WANTS TO JUST LET THE RELATIONSHIP "HAPPEN"!
WELL, WHAT'S WRONG WITH THAT? WHAT DO YOU HAVE TO LOSE?
WHAT DO I HAVE TO LOSE? OH, NOTHING MUCH...
... JUST 16 **MONTHS** OF GROUNDWORK!
IT'S NOT A SIEGE, ALEX. GO TAKE A BATH.

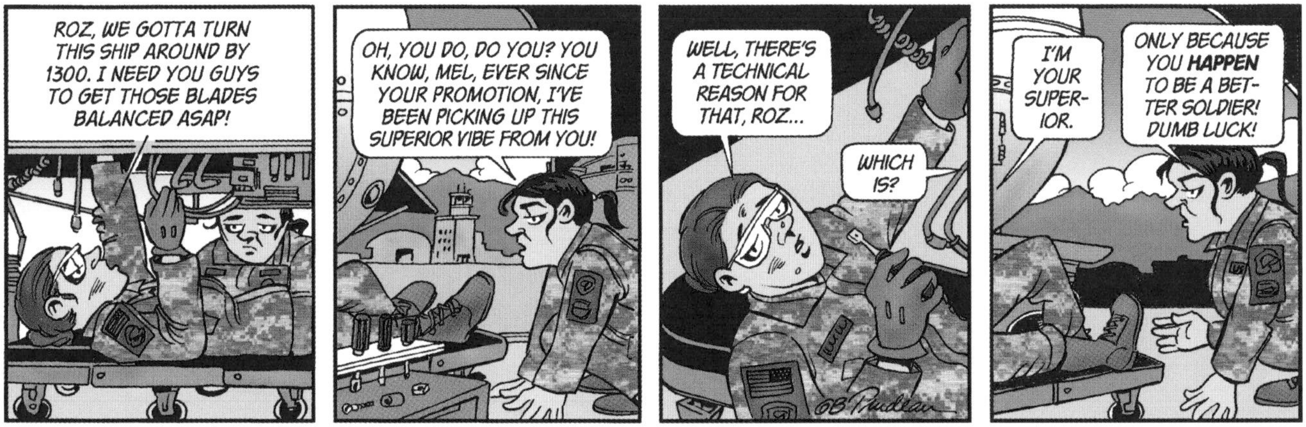
ROZ, WE GOTTA TURN THIS SHIP AROUND BY 1300. I NEED YOU GUYS TO GET THOSE BLADES BALANCED ASAP!
OH, YOU DO, DO YOU? YOU KNOW, MEL, EVER SINCE YOUR PROMOTION, I'VE BEEN PICKING UP THIS SUPERIOR VIBE FROM YOU!
WELL, THERE'S A TECHNICAL REASON FOR THAT, ROZ...
WHICH IS?
I'M YOUR SUPER-IOR.
ONLY BECAUSE YOU **HAPPEN** TO BE A BET-TER SOLDIER! DUMB LUCK!

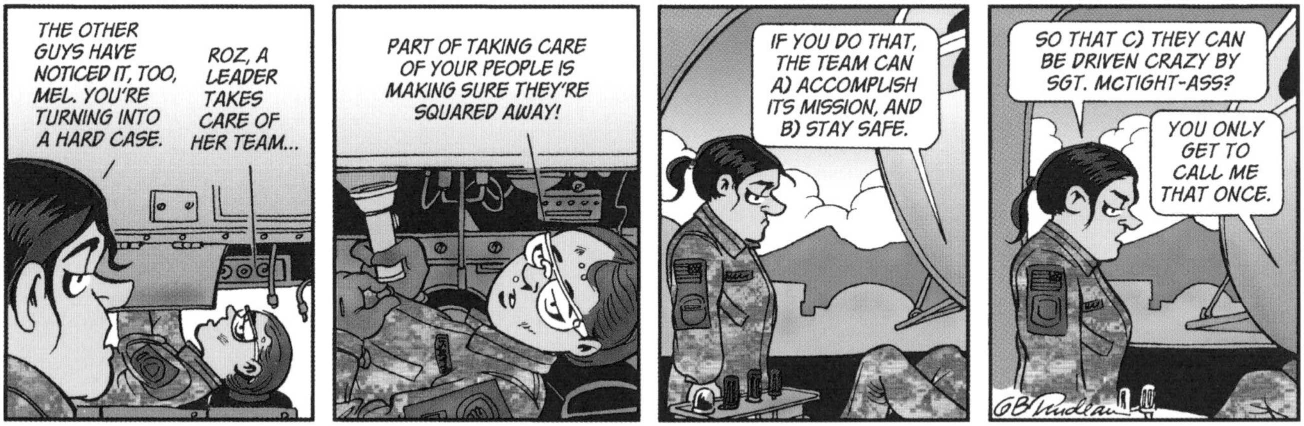
THE OTHER GUYS HAVE NOTICED IT, TOO, MEL. YOU'RE TURNING INTO A HARD CASE.
ROZ, A LEADER TAKES CARE OF HER TEAM...
PART OF TAKING CARE OF YOUR PEOPLE IS MAKING SURE THEY'RE SQUARED AWAY!
IF YOU DO THAT, THE TEAM CAN A) ACCOMPLISH ITS MISSION, AND B) STAY SAFE.
SO THAT C) THEY CAN BE DRIVEN CRAZY BY SGT. MCTIGHT-ASS?
YOU ONLY GET TO CALL ME THAT ONCE.

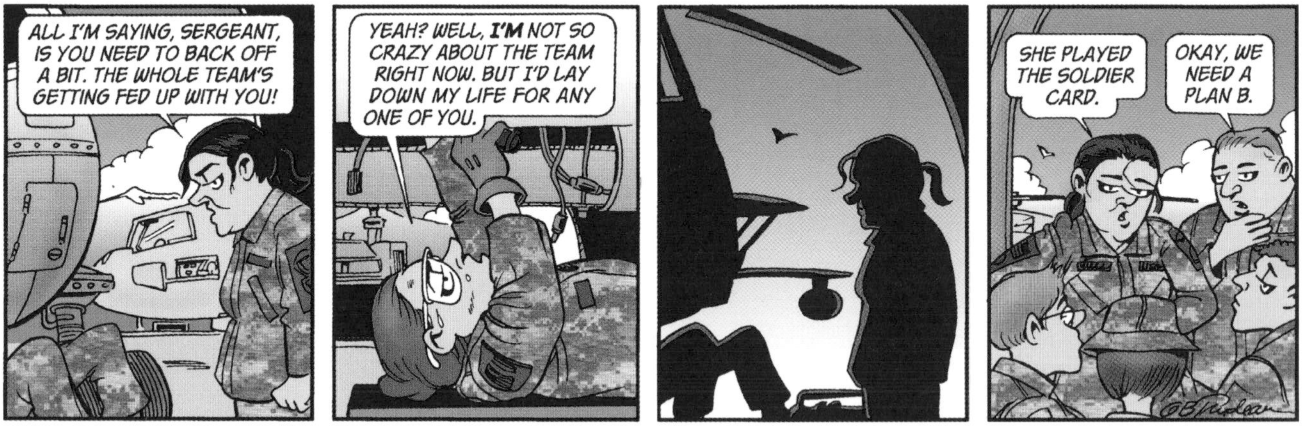
ALL I'M SAYING, SERGEANT, IS YOU NEED TO BACK OFF A BIT. THE WHOLE TEAM'S GETTING FED UP WITH YOU!
YEAH? WELL, **I'M** NOT SO CRAZY ABOUT THE TEAM RIGHT NOW. BUT I'D LAY DOWN MY LIFE FOR ANY ONE OF YOU.
SHE PLAYED THE SOLDIER CARD.
OKAY, WE NEED A PLAN B.

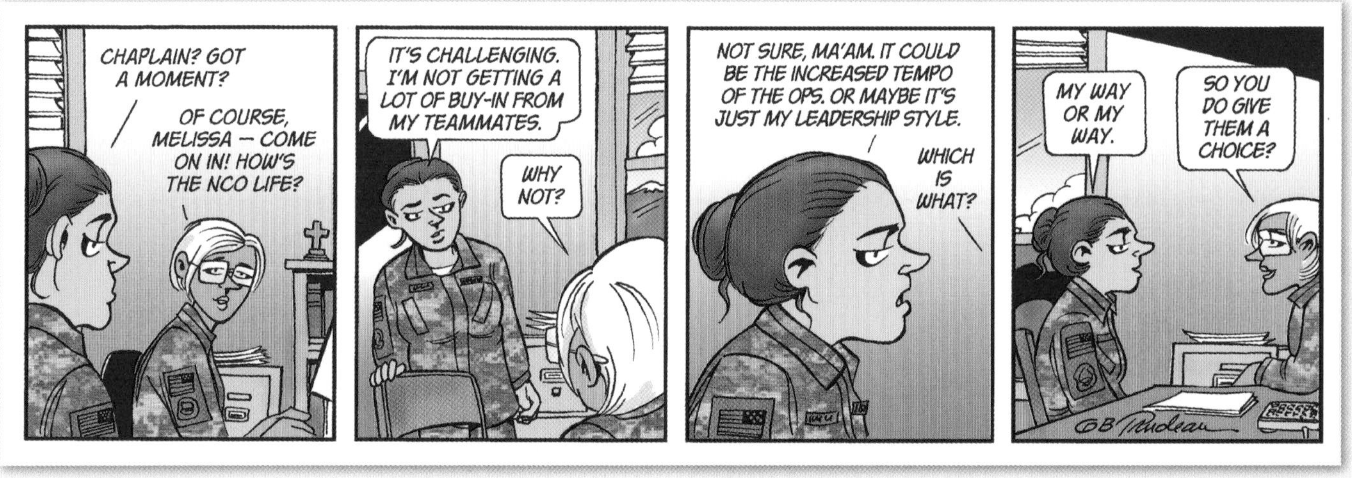
CHAPLAIN? GOT A MOMENT?
OF COURSE, MELISSA — COME ON IN! HOW'S THE NCO LIFE?
IT'S CHALLENGING. I'M NOT GETTING A LOT OF BUY-IN FROM MY TEAMMATES.
WHY NOT?
NOT SURE, MA'AM. IT COULD BE THE INCREASED TEMPO OF THE OPS. OR MAYBE IT'S JUST MY LEADERSHIP STYLE.
WHICH IS WHAT?
MY WAY OR MY WAY.
SO YOU DO GIVE THEM A CHOICE?
GB Trudeau

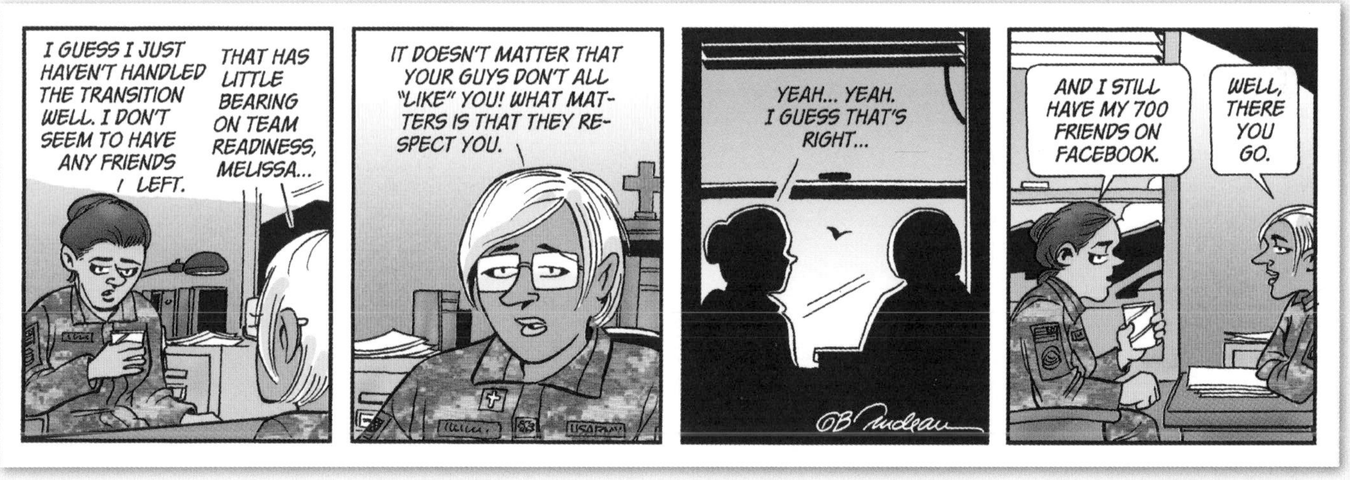
I GUESS I JUST HAVEN'T HANDLED THE TRANSITION WELL. I DON'T SEEM TO HAVE ANY FRIENDS LEFT.
THAT HAS LITTLE BEARING ON TEAM READINESS, MELISSA...
IT DOESN'T MATTER THAT YOUR GUYS DON'T ALL "LIKE" YOU! WHAT MATTERS IS THAT THEY RESPECT YOU.
YEAH... YEAH. I GUESS THAT'S RIGHT...
GB Trudeau
AND I STILL HAVE MY 700 FRIENDS ON FACEBOOK.
WELL, THERE YOU GO.

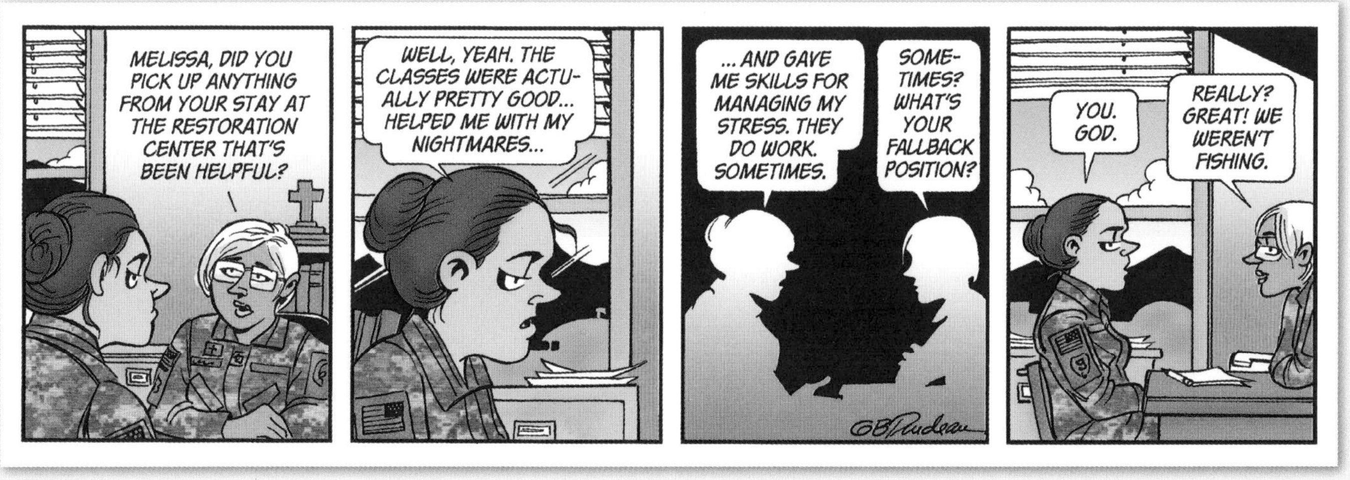
MELISSA, DID YOU PICK UP ANYTHING FROM YOUR STAY AT THE RESTORATION CENTER THAT'S BEEN HELPFUL?
WELL, YEAH. THE CLASSES WERE ACTUALLY PRETTY GOOD... HELPED ME WITH MY NIGHTMARES...
... AND GAVE ME SKILLS FOR MANAGING MY STRESS. THEY DO WORK. SOMETIMES.
SOMETIMES? WHAT'S YOUR FALLBACK POSITION?
GB Trudeau
YOU. GOD.
REALLY? GREAT! WE WEREN'T FISHING.

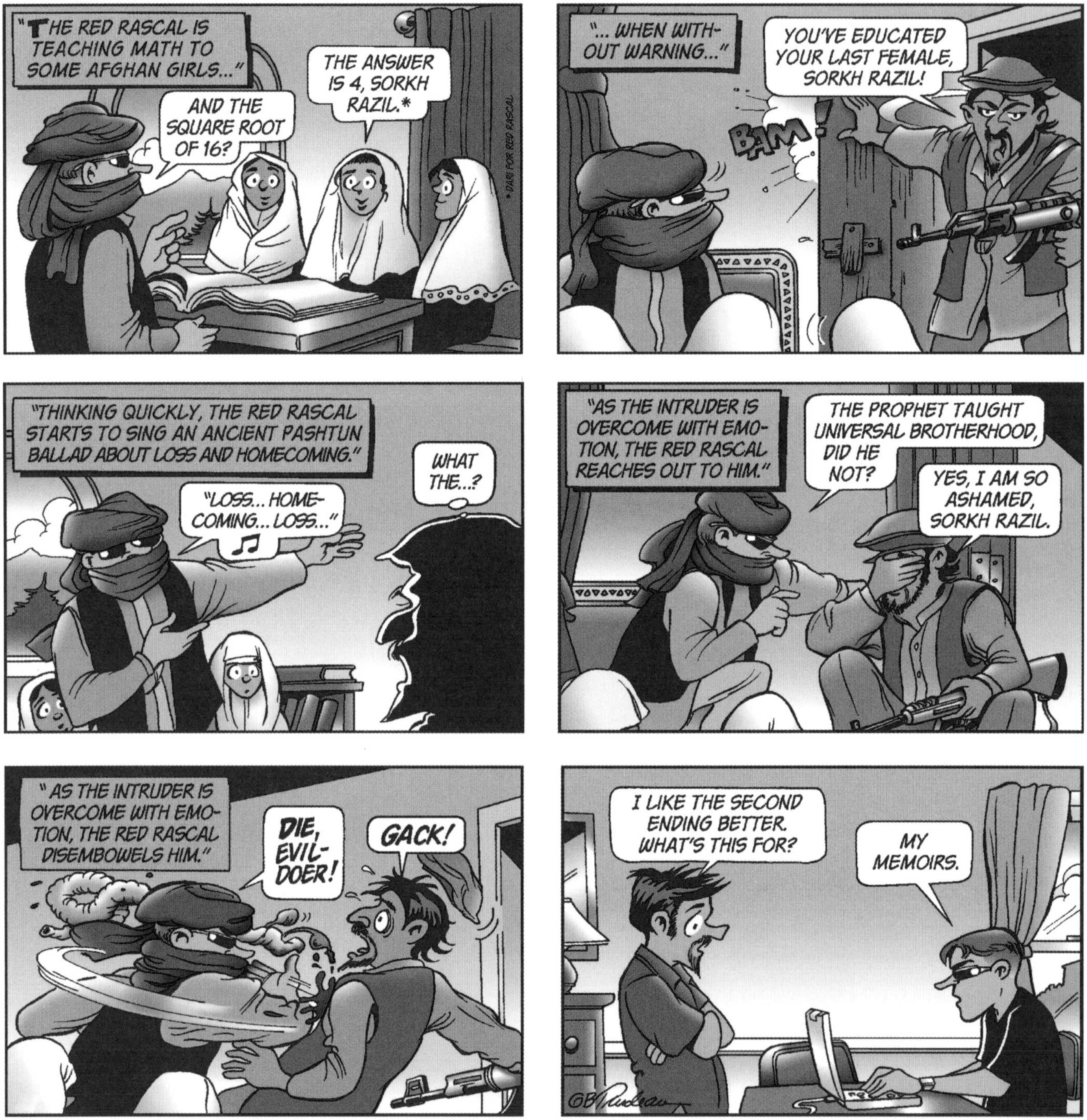
"THE RED RASCAL IS TEACHING MATH TO SOME AFGHAN GIRLS..."
AND THE SQUARE ROOT OF 16?
THE ANSWER IS 4, SORKH RAZIL.*
* DARI FOR RED RASCAL
"... WHEN WITH-OUT WARNING..."
BAM!
YOU'VE EDUCATED YOUR LAST FEMALE, SORKH RAZIL!
"THINKING QUICKLY, THE RED RASCAL STARTS TO SING AN ANCIENT PASHTUN BALLAD ABOUT LOSS AND HOMECOMING."
"LOSS... HOME-COMING... LOSS..."
WHAT THE...?
"AS THE INTRUDER IS OVERCOME WITH EMO-TION, THE RED RASCAL REACHES OUT TO HIM."
THE PROPHET TAUGHT UNIVERSAL BROTHERHOOD, DID HE NOT?
YES, I AM SO ASHAMED, SORKH RAZIL.
"AS THE INTRUDER IS OVERCOME WITH EMO-TION, THE RED RASCAL DISEMBOWELS HIM."
DIE, EVIL-DOER!
GACK!
I LIKE THE SECOND ENDING BETTER. WHAT'S THIS FOR?
MY MEMOIRS.

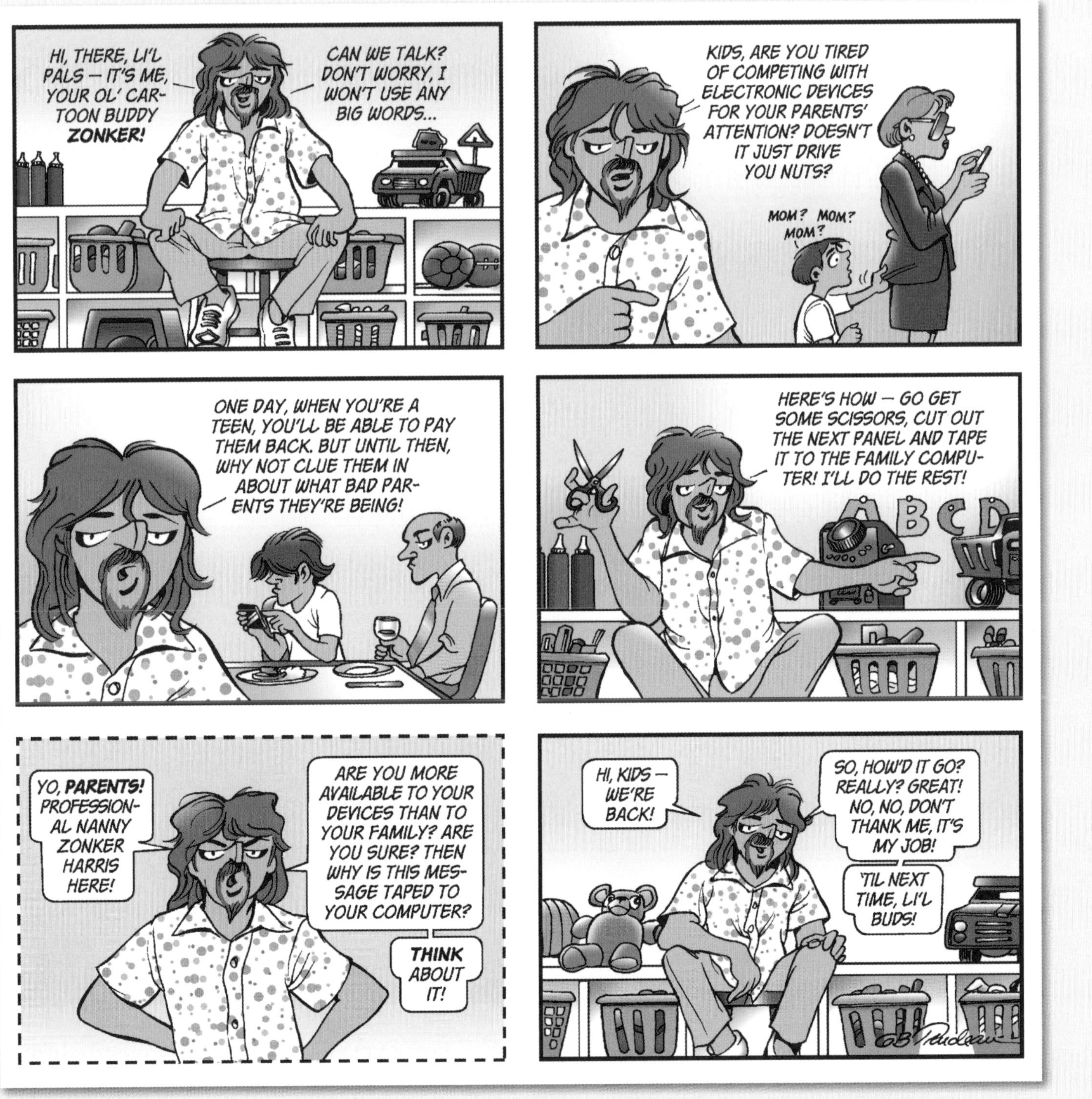
HI, THERE, LI'L PALS — IT'S ME, YOUR OL' CARTOON BUDDY ZONKER!
CAN WE TALK? DON'T WORRY, I WON'T USE ANY BIG WORDS...
KIDS, ARE YOU TIRED OF COMPETING WITH ELECTRONIC DEVICES FOR YOUR PARENTS' ATTENTION? DOESN'T IT JUST DRIVE YOU NUTS?
MOM? MOM? MOM?
ONE DAY, WHEN YOU'RE A TEEN, YOU'LL BE ABLE TO PAY THEM BACK. BUT UNTIL THEN, WHY NOT CLUE THEM IN ABOUT WHAT BAD PARENTS THEY'RE BEING!
HERE'S HOW — GO GET SOME SCISSORS, CUT OUT THE NEXT PANEL AND TAPE IT TO THE FAMILY COMPUTER! I'LL DO THE REST!
YO, PARENTS! PROFESSIONAL NANNY ZONKER HARRIS HERE!
ARE YOU MORE AVAILABLE TO YOUR DEVICES THAN TO YOUR FAMILY? ARE YOU SURE? THEN WHY IS THIS MESSAGE TAPED TO YOUR COMPUTER?
THINK ABOUT IT!
HI, KIDS — WE'RE BACK!
SO, HOW'D IT GO? REALLY? GREAT! NO, NO, DON'T THANK ME, IT'S MY JOB!
'TIL NEXT TIME, LI'L BUDS!
GBTrudeau

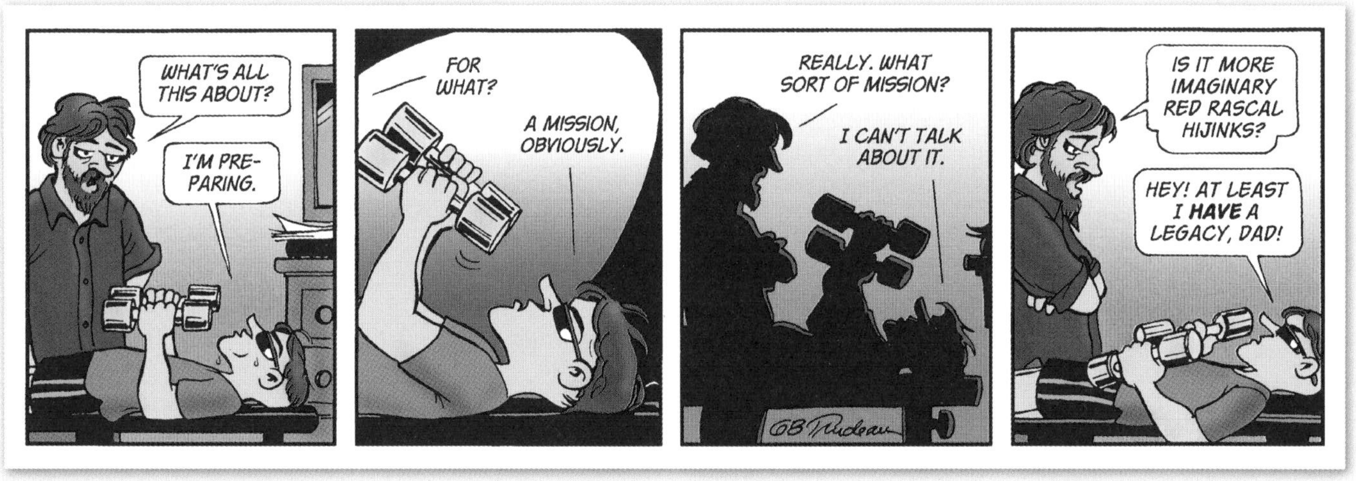
WHAT'S ALL THIS ABOUT?
I'M PRE-PARING.
FOR WHAT?
A MISSION, OBVIOUSLY.
REALLY. WHAT SORT OF MISSION?
I CAN'T TALK ABOUT IT.
IS IT MORE IMAGINARY RED RASCAL HIJINKS?
HEY! AT LEAST I **HAVE** A LEGACY, DAD!

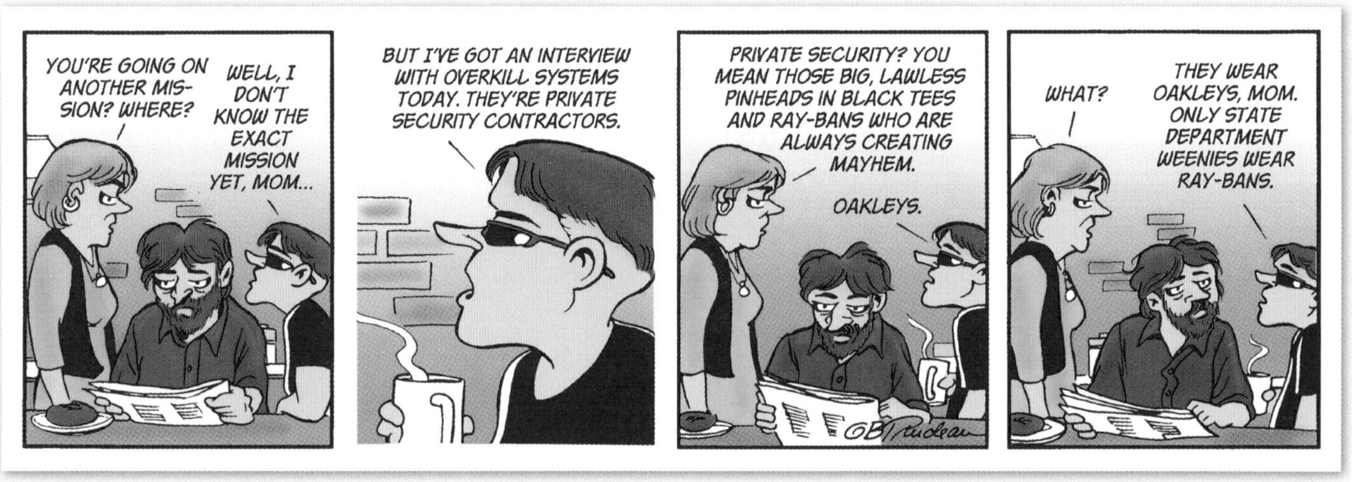
YOU'RE GOING ON ANOTHER MIS-SION? WHERE?
WELL, I DON'T KNOW THE EXACT MISSION YET, MOM...
BUT I'VE GOT AN INTERVIEW WITH OVERKILL SYSTEMS TODAY. THEY'RE PRIVATE SECURITY CONTRACTORS.
PRIVATE SECURITY? YOU MEAN THOSE BIG, LAWLESS PINHEADS IN BLACK TEES AND RAY-BANS WHO ARE ALWAYS CREATING MAYHEM.
OAKLEYS.
WHAT?
THEY WEAR OAKLEYS, MOM. ONLY STATE DEPARTMENT WEENIES WEAR RAY-BANS.

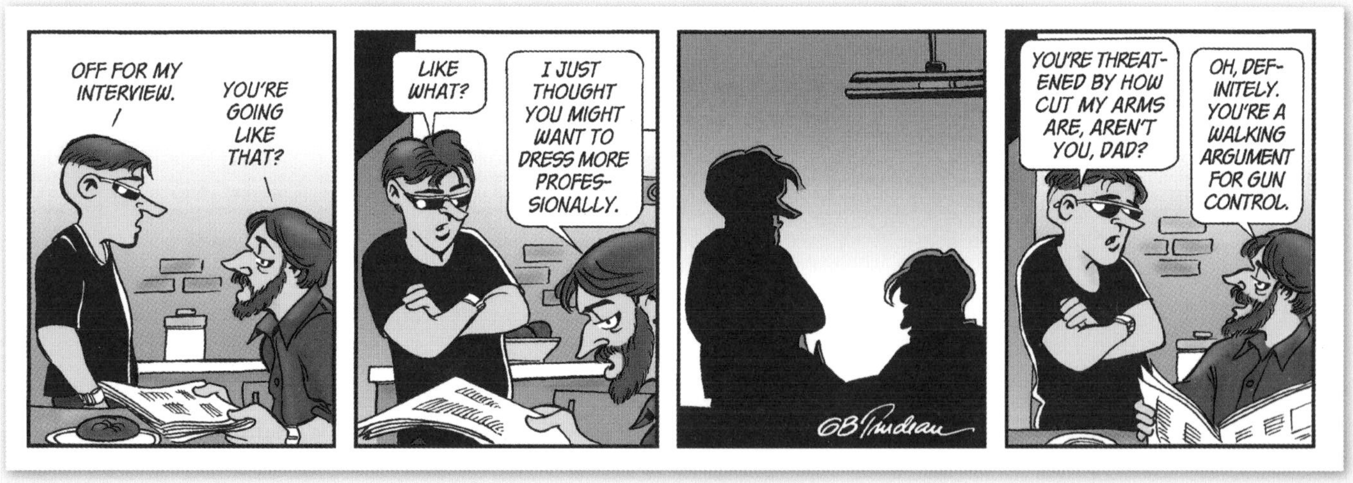
OFF FOR MY INTERVIEW.
YOU'RE GOING LIKE THAT?
LIKE WHAT?
I JUST THOUGHT YOU MIGHT WANT TO DRESS MORE PROFES-SIONALLY.
YOU'RE THREAT-ENED BY HOW CUT MY ARMS ARE, AREN'T YOU, DAD?
OH, DEF-INITELY. YOU'RE A WALKING ARGUMENT FOR GUN CONTROL.

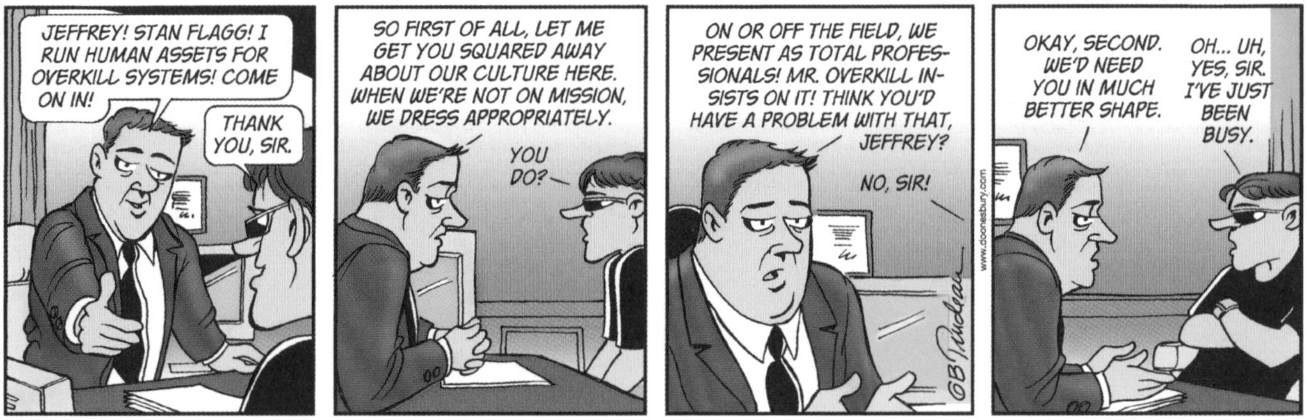
JEFFREY! STAN FLAGG! I RUN HUMAN ASSETS FOR OVERKILL SYSTEMS! COME ON IN!
THANK YOU, SIR.
SO FIRST OF ALL, LET ME GET YOU SQUARED AWAY ABOUT OUR CULTURE HERE. WHEN WE'RE NOT ON MISSION, WE DRESS APPROPRIATELY.
YOU DO?
ON OR OFF THE FIELD, WE PRESENT AS TOTAL PROFESSIONALS! MR. OVERKILL INSISTS ON IT! THINK YOU'D HAVE A PROBLEM WITH THAT, JEFFREY?
NO, SIR!
www.doonesbury.com
OKAY, SECOND. WE'D NEED YOU IN MUCH BETTER SHAPE.
OH... UH, YES, SIR. I'VE JUST BEEN BUSY.

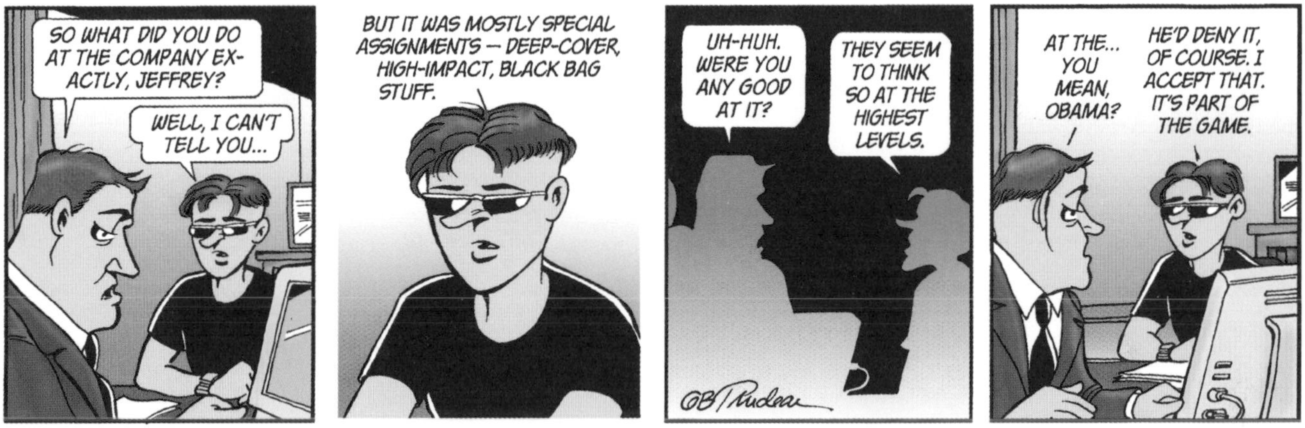
SO WHAT DID YOU DO AT THE COMPANY EXACTLY, JEFFREY?
WELL, I CAN'T TELL YOU...
BUT IT WAS MOSTLY SPECIAL ASSIGNMENTS — DEEP-COVER, HIGH-IMPACT, BLACK BAG STUFF.
UH-HUH. WERE YOU ANY GOOD AT IT?
THEY SEEM TO THINK SO AT THE HIGHEST LEVELS.
AT THE... YOU MEAN, OBAMA?
HE'D DENY IT, OF COURSE. I ACCEPT THAT. IT'S PART OF THE GAME.

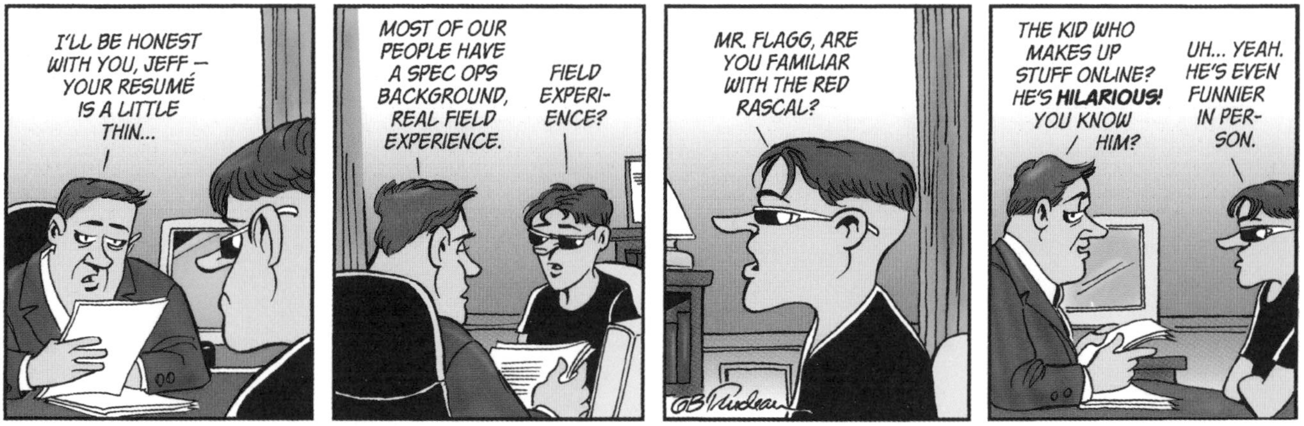
I'LL BE HONEST WITH YOU, JEFF — YOUR RESUMÉ IS A LITTLE THIN...
MOST OF OUR PEOPLE HAVE A SPEC OPS BACKGROUND, REAL FIELD EXPERIENCE.
FIELD EXPERIENCE?
MR. FLAGG, ARE YOU FAMILIAR WITH THE RED RASCAL?
THE KID WHO MAKES UP STUFF ONLINE? HE'S **HILARIOUS!** YOU KNOW HIM?
UH... YEAH. HE'S EVEN FUNNIER IN PERSON.

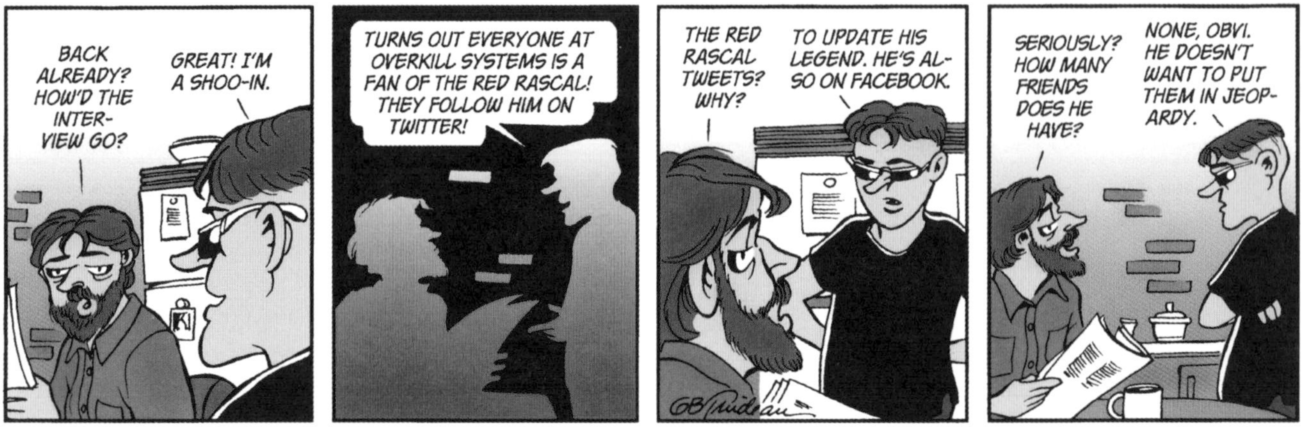
BACK ALREADY? HOW'D THE INTER-VIEW GO?
GREAT! I'M A SHOO-IN.
TURNS OUT EVERYONE AT OVERKILL SYSTEMS IS A FAN OF THE RED RASCAL! THEY FOLLOW HIM ON TWITTER!
THE RED RASCAL TWEETS? WHY?
TO UPDATE HIS LEGEND. HE'S AL-SO ON FACEBOOK.
SERIOUSLY? HOW MANY FRIENDS DOES HE HAVE?
NONE, OBVI. HE DOESN'T WANT TO PUT THEM IN JEOP-ARDY.

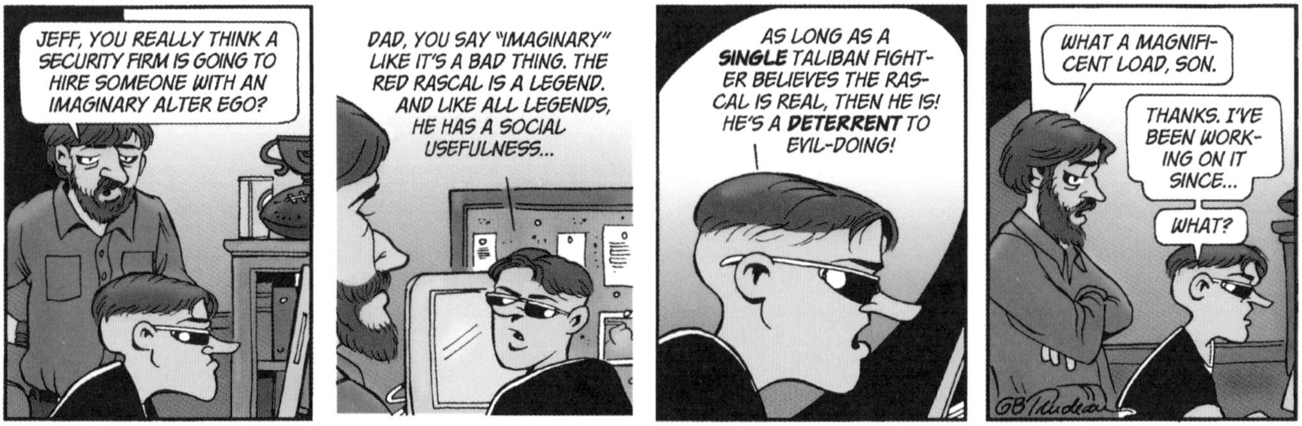
JEFF, YOU REALLY THINK A SECURITY FIRM IS GOING TO HIRE SOMEONE WITH AN IMAGINARY ALTER EGO?
DAD, YOU SAY "IMAGINARY" LIKE IT'S A BAD THING. THE RED RASCAL IS A LEGEND. AND LIKE ALL LEGENDS, HE HAS A SOCIAL USEFULNESS...
AS LONG AS A SINGLE TALIBAN FIGHT-ER BELIEVES THE RAS-CAL IS REAL, THEN HE IS! HE'S A DETERRENT TO EVIL-DOING!
WHAT A MAGNIFI-CENT LOAD, SON.
THANKS. I'VE BEEN WORK-ING ON IT SINCE...
WHAT?

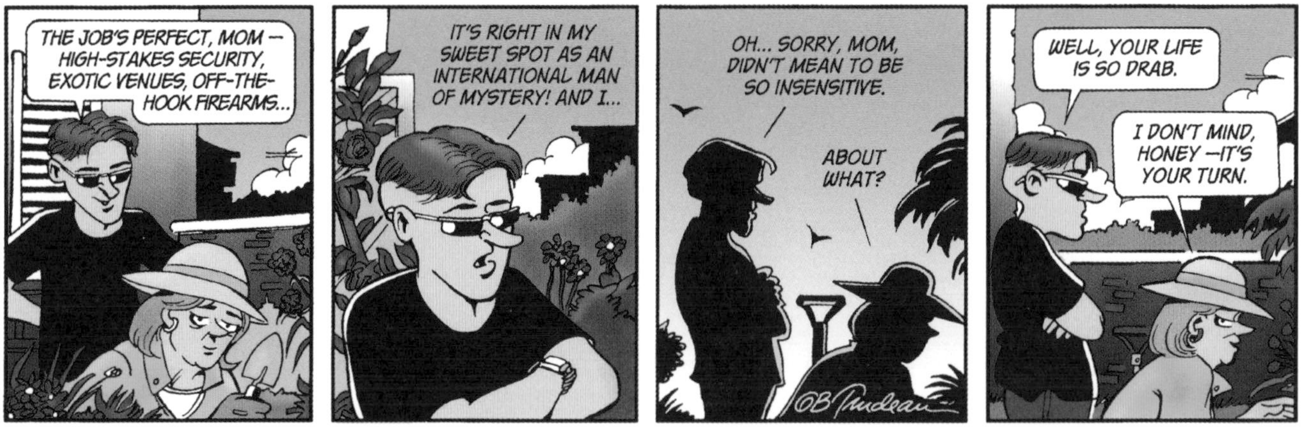
THE JOB'S PERFECT, MOM — HIGH-STAKES SECURITY, EXOTIC VENUES, OFF-THE-HOOK FIREARMS...
IT'S RIGHT IN MY SWEET SPOT AS AN INTERNATIONAL MAN OF MYSTERY! AND I...
OH... SORRY, MOM, DIDN'T MEAN TO BE SO INSENSITIVE.
ABOUT WHAT?
WELL, YOUR LIFE IS SO DRAB.
I DON'T MIND, HONEY —IT'S YOUR TURN.

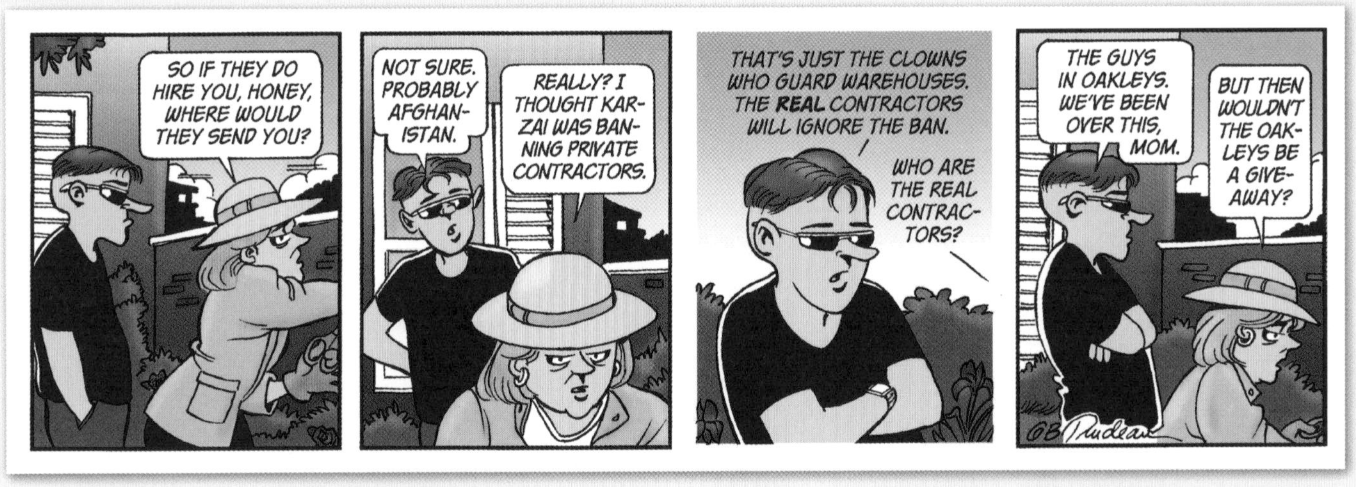
SO IF THEY DO HIRE YOU, HONEY, WHERE WOULD THEY SEND YOU?
NOT SURE. PROBABLY AFGHAN-ISTAN.
REALLY? I THOUGHT KAR-ZAI WAS BAN-NING PRIVATE CONTRACTORS.
THAT'S JUST THE CLOWNS WHO GUARD WAREHOUSES. THE **REAL** CONTRACTORS WILL IGNORE THE BAN.
WHO ARE THE REAL CONTRAC-TORS?
THE GUYS IN OAKLEYS. WE'VE BEEN OVER THIS, MOM.
BUT THEN WOULDN'T THE OAK-LEYS BE A GIVE-AWAY?
©B Trudeau

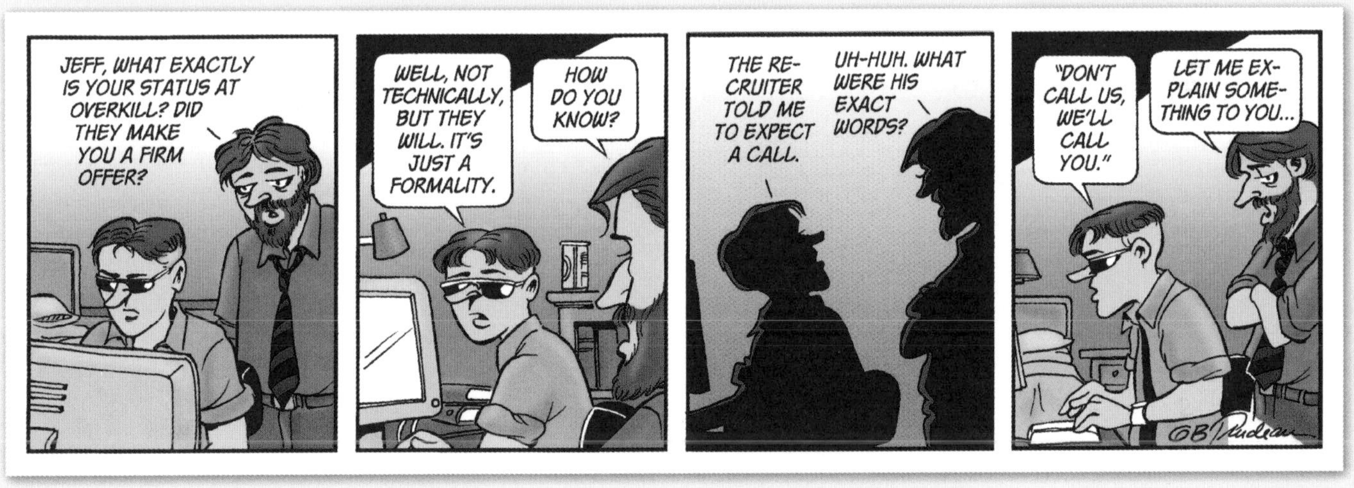
JEFF, WHAT EXACTLY IS YOUR STATUS AT OVERKILL? DID THEY MAKE YOU A FIRM OFFER?
WELL, NOT TECHNICALLY, BUT THEY WILL. IT'S JUST A FORMALITY.
HOW DO YOU KNOW?
THE RE-CRUITER TOLD ME TO EXPECT A CALL.
UH-HUH. WHAT WERE HIS EXACT WORDS?
"DON'T CALL US, WE'LL CALL YOU."
LET ME EX-PLAIN SOME-THING TO YOU...
©B Trudeau

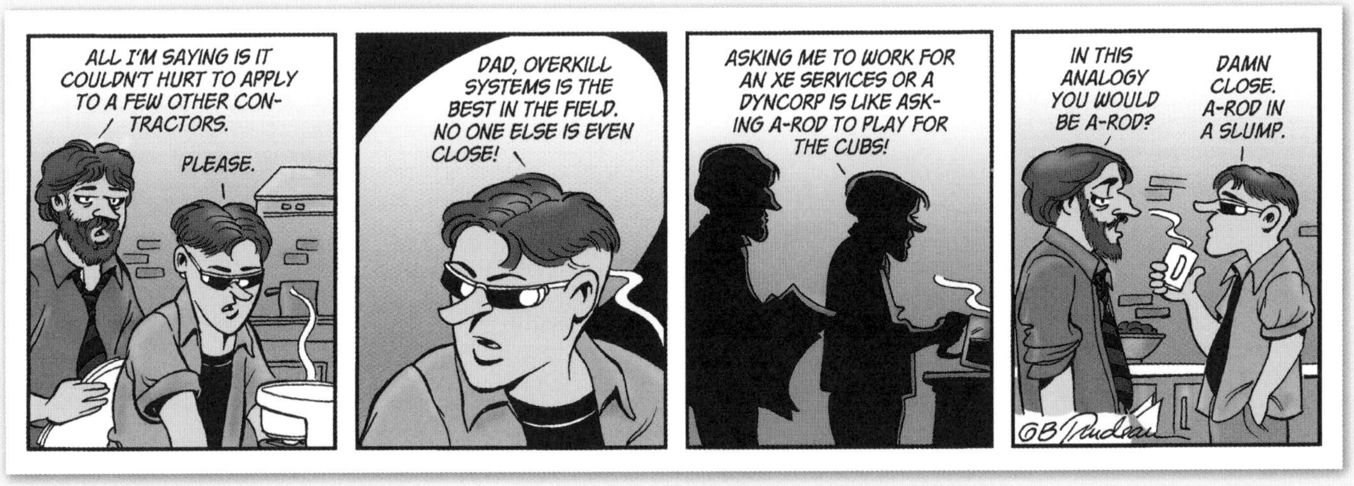
ALL I'M SAYING IS IT COULDN'T HURT TO APPLY TO A FEW OTHER CON-TRACTORS.
PLEASE.
DAD, OVERKILL SYSTEMS IS THE BEST IN THE FIELD. NO ONE ELSE IS EVEN CLOSE!
ASKING ME TO WORK FOR AN XE SERVICES OR A DYNCORP IS LIKE ASK-ING A-ROD TO PLAY FOR THE CUBS!
IN THIS ANALOGY YOU WOULD BE A-ROD?
DAMN CLOSE. A-ROD IN A SLUMP.
©B Trudeau

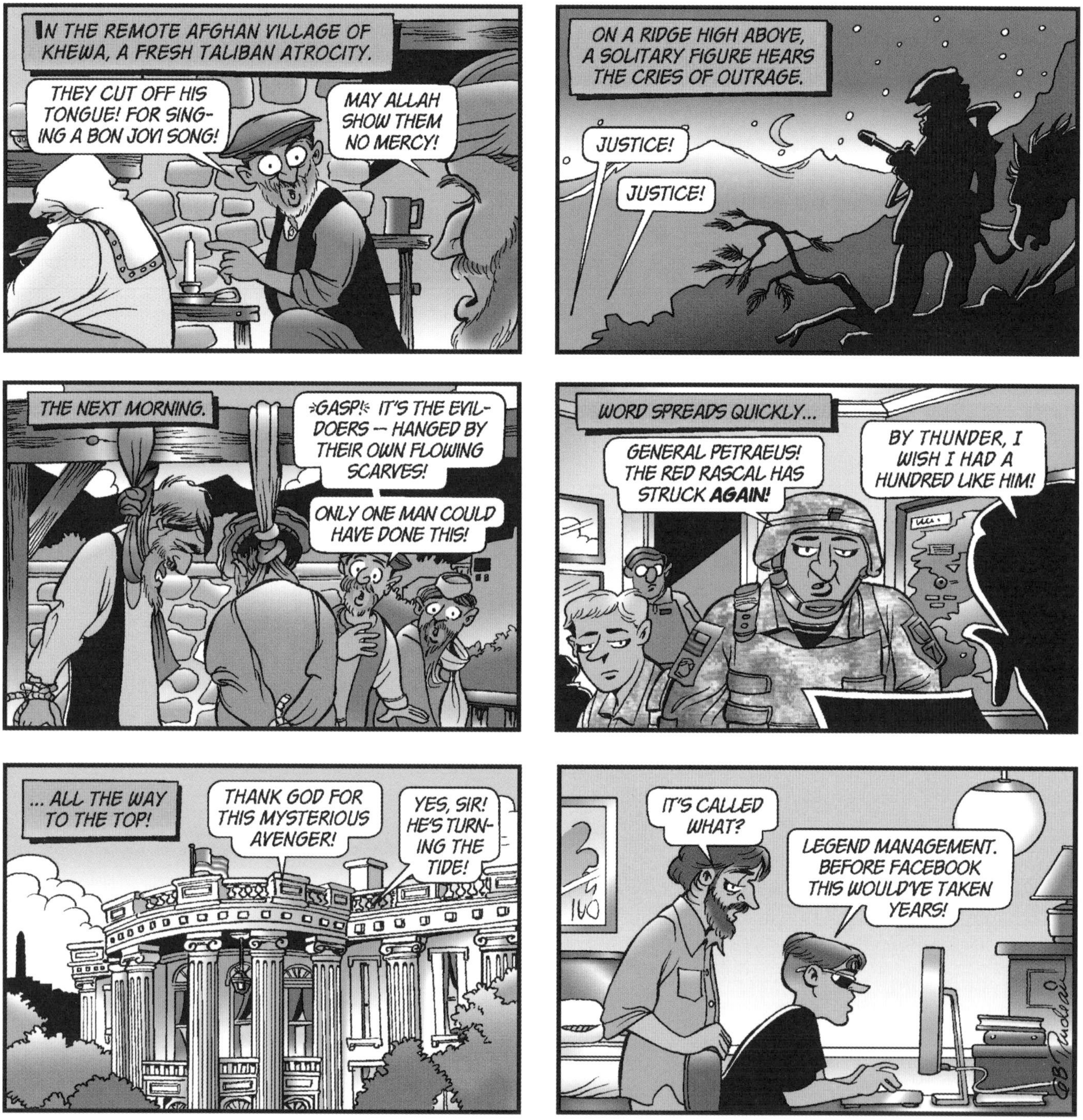
IN THE REMOTE AFGHAN VILLAGE OF KHEWA, A FRESH TALIBAN ATROCITY.
THEY CUT OFF HIS TONGUE! FOR SINGING A BON JOVI SONG!
MAY ALLAH SHOW THEM NO MERCY!
ON A RIDGE HIGH ABOVE, A SOLITARY FIGURE HEARS THE CRIES OF OUTRAGE.
JUSTICE!
JUSTICE!
THE NEXT MORNING.
GASP! IT'S THE EVILDOERS -- HANGED BY THEIR OWN FLOWING SCARVES!
ONLY ONE MAN COULD HAVE DONE THIS!
WORD SPREADS QUICKLY...
GENERAL PETRAEUS! THE RED RASCAL HAS STRUCK **AGAIN!**
BY THUNDER, I WISH I HAD A HUNDRED LIKE HIM!
... ALL THE WAY TO THE TOP!
THANK GOD FOR THIS MYSTERIOUS AVENGER!
YES, SIR! HE'S TURNING THE TIDE!
IT'S CALLED WHAT?
LEGEND MANAGEMENT. BEFORE FACEBOOK THIS WOULD'VE TAKEN YEARS!

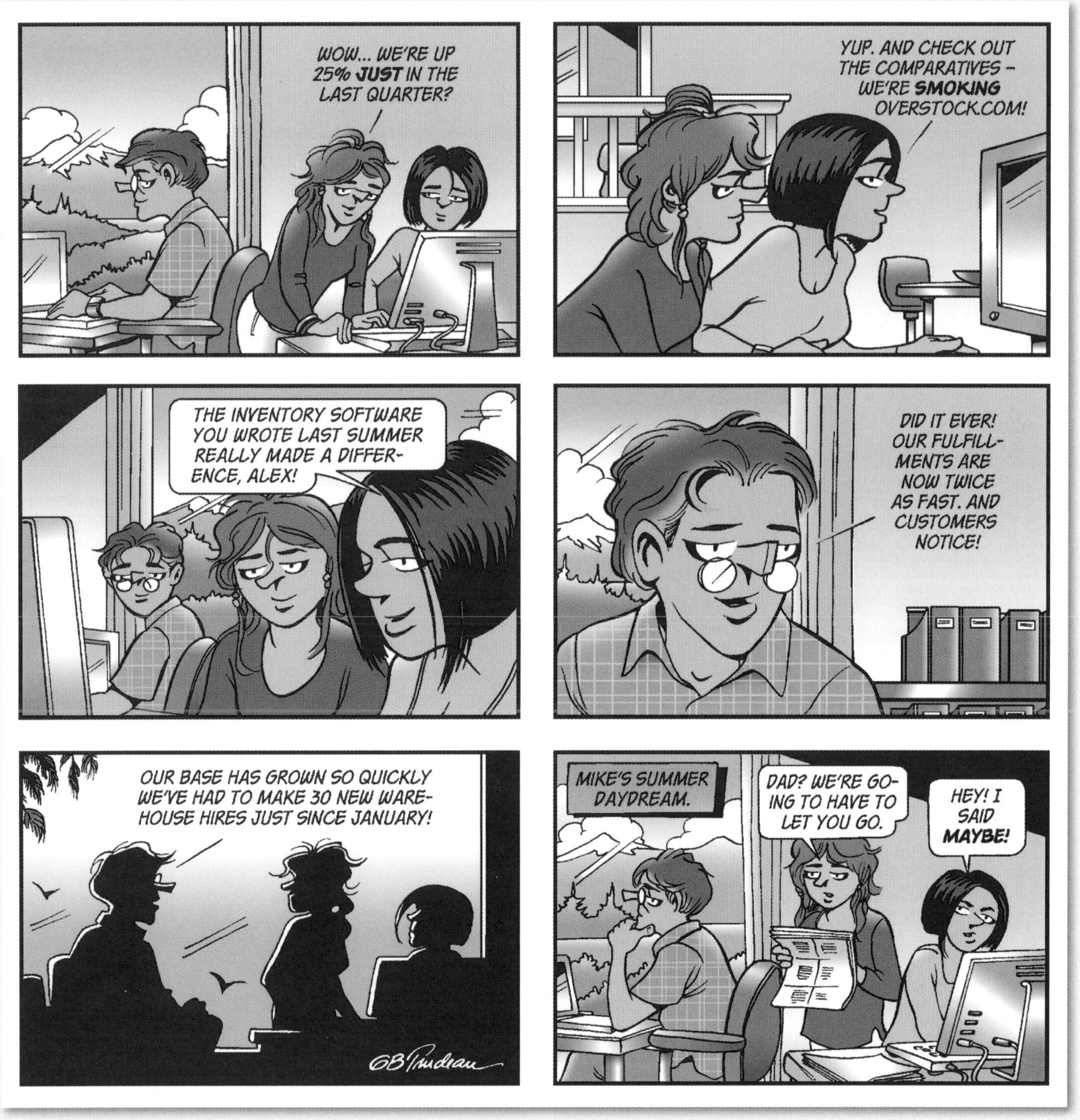
WOW... WE'RE UP 25% JUST IN THE LAST QUARTER?
YUP. AND CHECK OUT THE COMPARATIVES – WE'RE SMOKING OVERSTOCK.COM!
THE INVENTORY SOFTWARE YOU WROTE LAST SUMMER REALLY MADE A DIFFERENCE, ALEX!
DID IT EVER! OUR FULFILLMENTS ARE NOW TWICE AS FAST. AND CUSTOMERS NOTICE!
OUR BASE HAS GROWN SO QUICKLY WE'VE HAD TO MAKE 30 NEW WAREHOUSE HIRES JUST SINCE JANUARY!
GB Trudeau
MIKE'S SUMMER DAYDREAM.
DAD? WE'RE GOING TO HAVE TO LET YOU GO.
HEY! I SAID MAYBE!

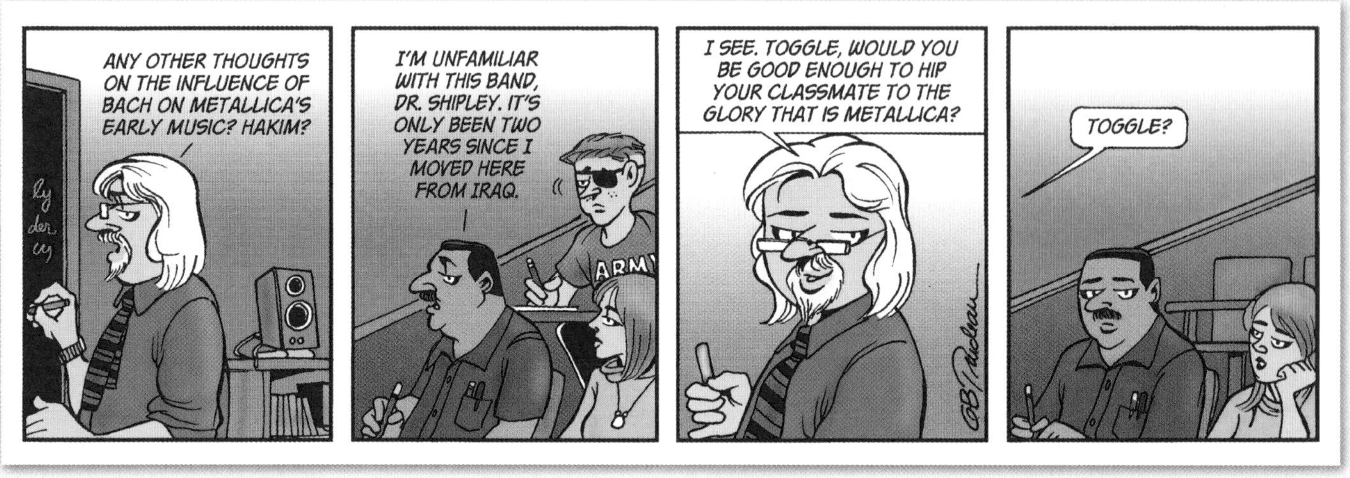
ANY OTHER THOUGHTS ON THE INFLUENCE OF BACH ON METALLICA'S EARLY MUSIC? HAKIM?
I'M UNFAMILIAR WITH THIS BAND, DR. SHIPLEY. IT'S ONLY BEEN TWO YEARS SINCE I MOVED HERE FROM IRAQ.
ARMY
I SEE. TOGGLE, WOULD YOU BE GOOD ENOUGH TO HIP YOUR CLASSMATE TO THE GLORY THAT IS METALLICA?
TOGGLE?

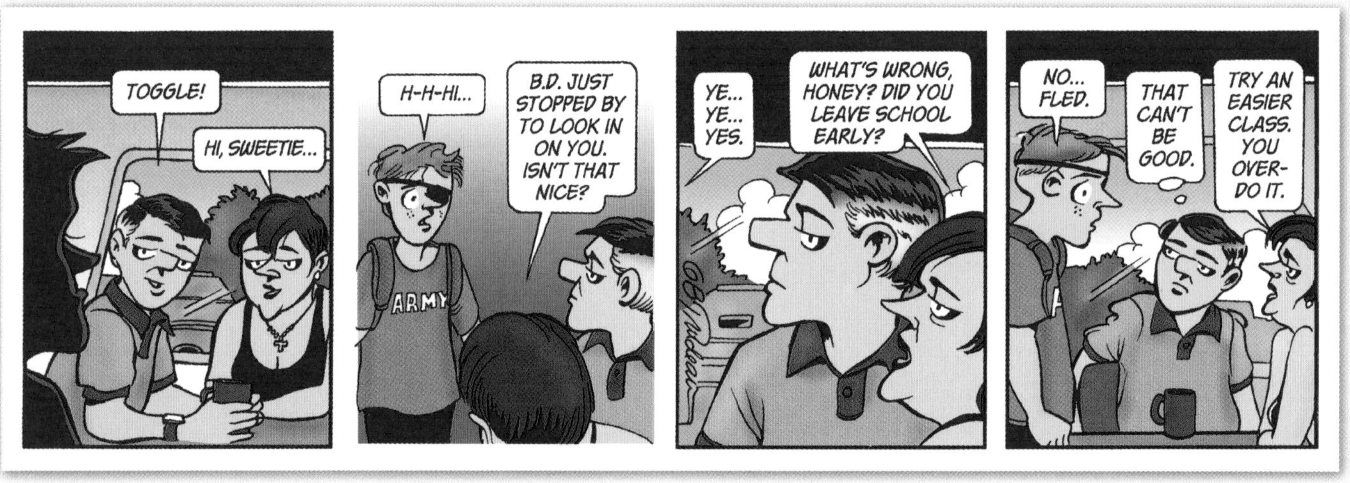
TOGGLE!
HI, SWEETIE...
H-H-HI...
B.D. JUST STOPPED BY TO LOOK IN ON YOU. ISN'T THAT NICE?
ARMY
YE... YE... YES.
WHAT'S WRONG, HONEY? DID YOU LEAVE SCHOOL EARLY?
NO... FLED.
THAT CAN'T BE GOOD.
TRY AN EASIER CLASS. YOU OVER-DO IT.

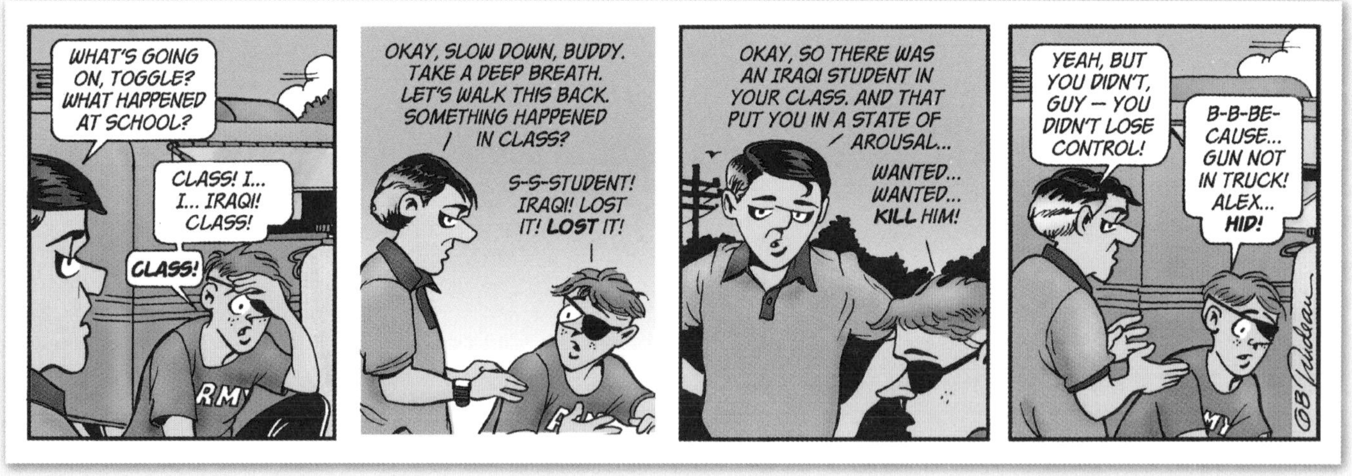
WHAT'S GOING ON, TOGGLE? WHAT HAPPENED AT SCHOOL?
CLASS! I... I... IRAQI! CLASS!
CLASS!
ARMY
OKAY, SLOW DOWN, BUDDY. TAKE A DEEP BREATH. LET'S WALK THIS BACK. SOMETHING HAPPENED IN CLASS?
S-S-STUDENT! IRAQI! LOST IT! **LOST** IT!
OKAY, SO THERE WAS AN IRAQI STUDENT IN YOUR CLASS. AND THAT PUT YOU IN A STATE OF AROUSAL...
WANTED... WANTED... **KILL** HIM!
YEAH, BUT YOU DIDN'T, GUY — YOU DIDN'T LOSE CONTROL!
B-B-BE-CAUSE... GUN NOT IN TRUCK! ALEX... **HID!**

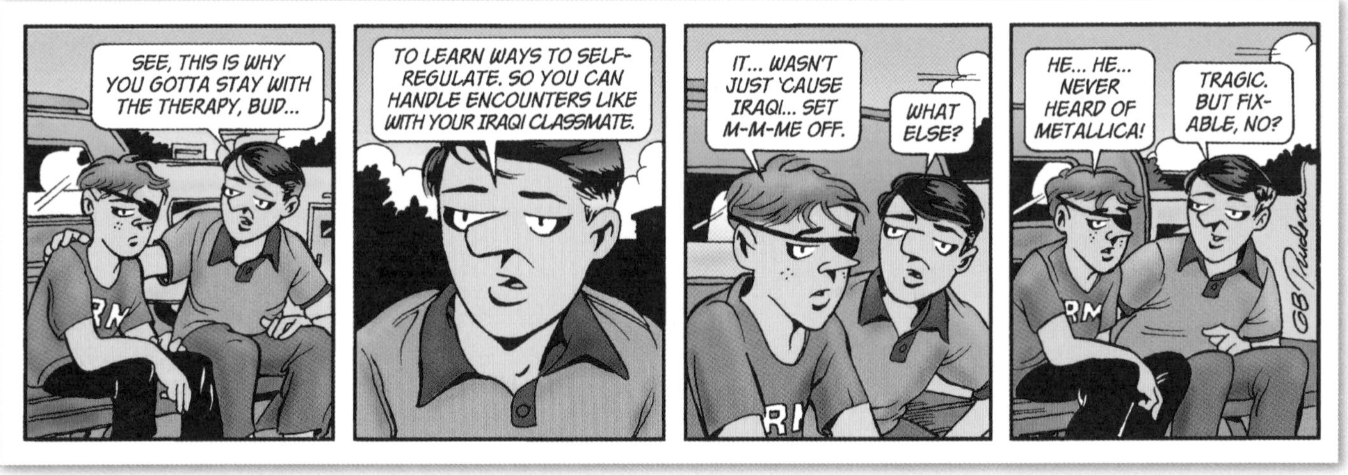
SEE, THIS IS WHY YOU GOTTA STAY WITH THE THERAPY, BUD...
TO LEARN WAYS TO SELF-REGULATE. SO YOU CAN HANDLE ENCOUNTERS LIKE WITH YOUR IRAQI CLASSMATE.
IT... WASN'T JUST 'CAUSE IRAQI... SET M-M-ME OFF.
WHAT ELSE?
HE... HE... NEVER HEARD OF METALLICA!
TRAGIC. BUT FIX-ABLE, NO?

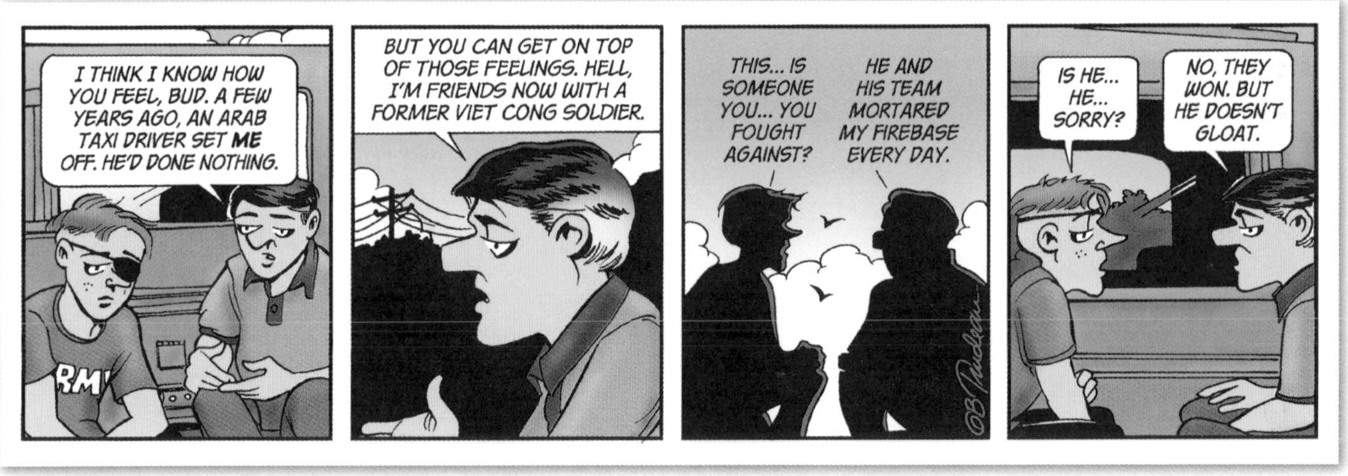
I THINK I KNOW HOW YOU FEEL, BUD. A FEW YEARS AGO, AN ARAB TAXI DRIVER SET **ME** OFF. HE'D DONE NOTHING.
BUT YOU CAN GET ON TOP OF THOSE FEELINGS. HELL, I'M FRIENDS NOW WITH A FORMER VIET CONG SOLDIER.
THIS... IS SOMEONE YOU... YOU FOUGHT AGAINST?
HE AND HIS TEAM MORTARED MY FIREBASE EVERY DAY.
IS HE... HE... SORRY?
NO, THEY WON. BUT HE DOESN'T GLOAT.

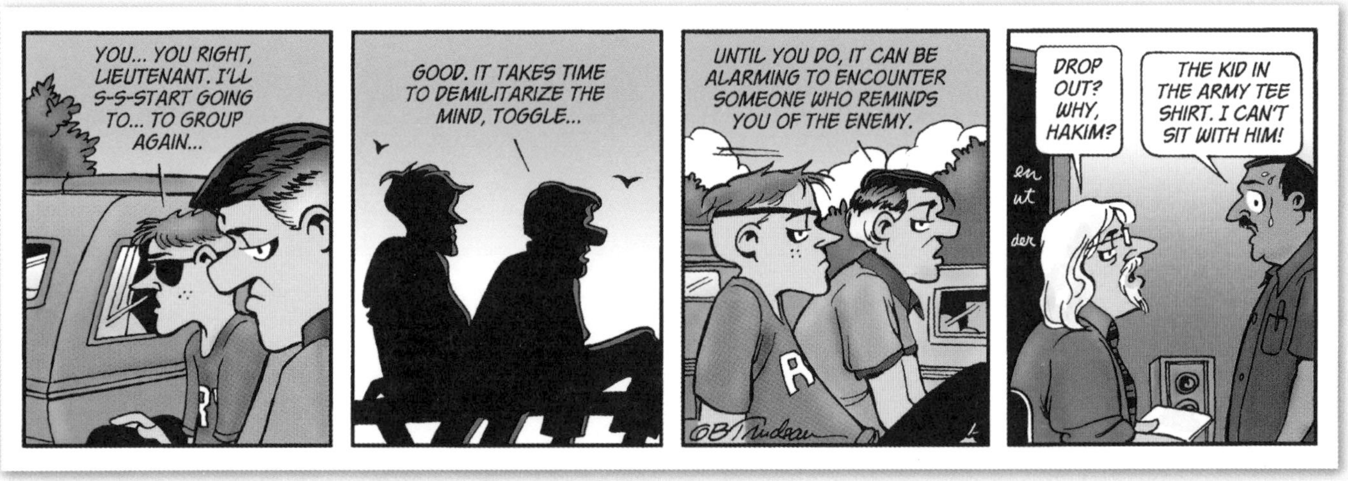
YOU... YOU RIGHT, LIEUTENANT. I'LL S-S-START GOING TO... TO GROUP AGAIN...
GOOD. IT TAKES TIME TO DEMILITARIZE THE MIND, TOGGLE...
UNTIL YOU DO, IT CAN BE ALARMING TO ENCOUNTER SOMEONE WHO REMINDS YOU OF THE ENEMY.
DROP OUT? WHY, HAKIM?
THE KID IN THE ARMY TEE SHIRT. I CAN'T SIT WITH HIM!

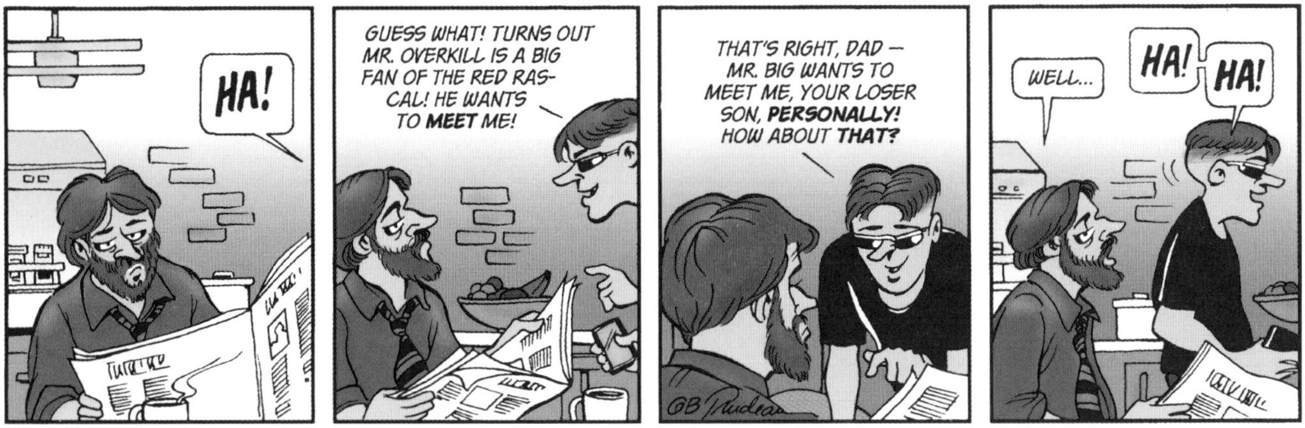
HA!
GUESS WHAT! TURNS OUT MR. OVERKILL IS A BIG FAN OF THE RED RASCAL! HE WANTS TO MEET ME!
THAT'S RIGHT, DAD — MR. BIG WANTS TO MEET ME, YOUR LOSER SON, PERSONALLY! HOW ABOUT THAT?
WELL...
HA!
HA!

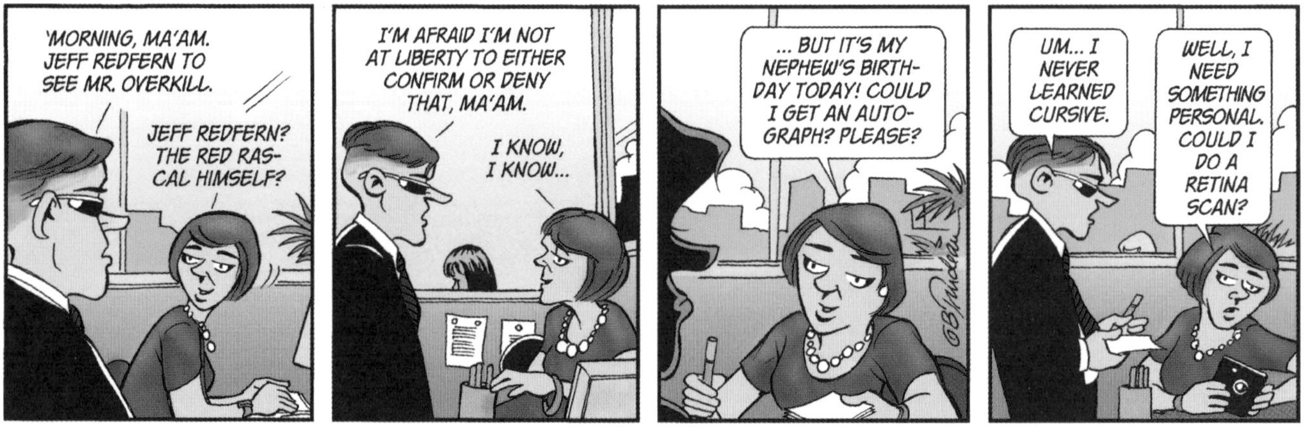
'MORNING, MA'AM. JEFF REDFERN TO SEE MR. OVERKILL.
JEFF REDFERN? THE RED RASCAL HIMSELF?
I'M AFRAID I'M NOT AT LIBERTY TO EITHER CONFIRM OR DENY THAT, MA'AM.
I KNOW, I KNOW...
... BUT IT'S MY NEPHEW'S BIRTHDAY TODAY! COULD I GET AN AUTOGRAPH? PLEASE?
UM... I NEVER LEARNED CURSIVE.
WELL, I NEED SOMETHING PERSONAL. COULD I DO A RETINA SCAN?

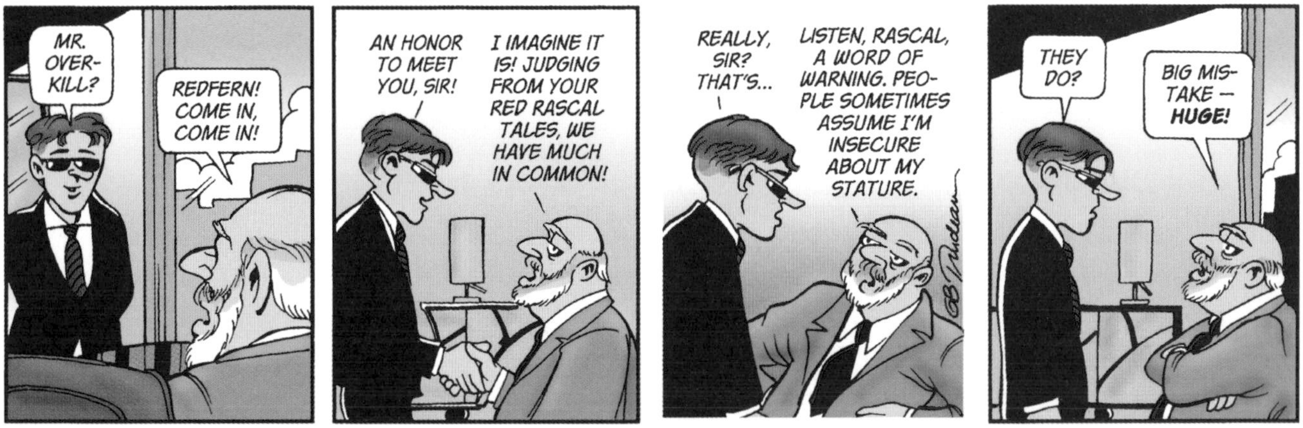
MR. OVERKILL?
REDFERN! COME IN, COME IN!
AN HONOR TO MEET YOU, SIR!
I IMAGINE IT IS! JUDGING FROM YOUR RED RASCAL TALES, WE HAVE MUCH IN COMMON!
REALLY, SIR? THAT'S...
LISTEN, RASCAL, A WORD OF WARNING. PEOPLE SOMETIMES ASSUME I'M INSECURE ABOUT MY STATURE.
THEY DO?
BIG MISTAKE — HUGE!

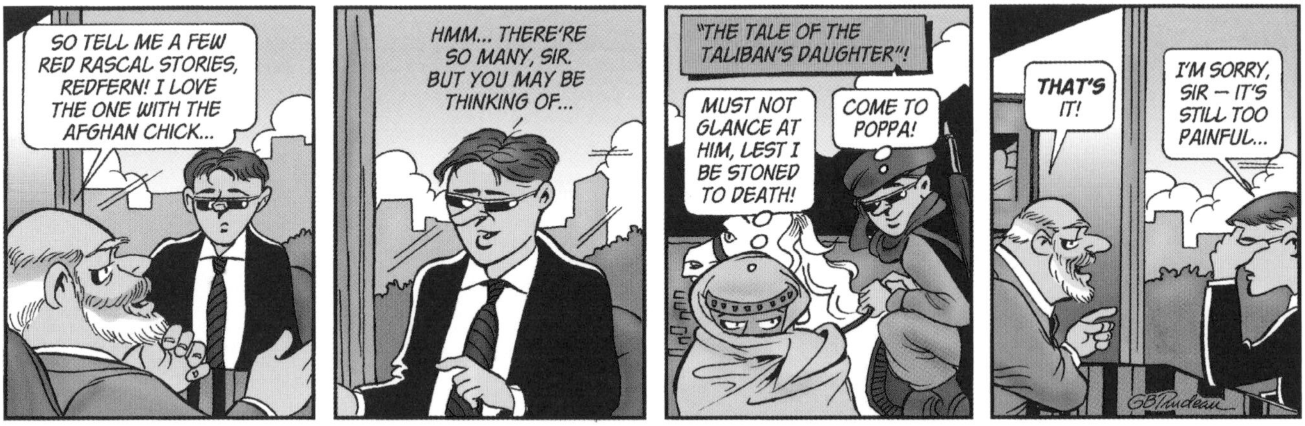
SO TELL ME A FEW RED RASCAL STORIES, REDFERN! I LOVE THE ONE WITH THE AFGHAN CHICK...
HMM... THERE'RE SO MANY, SIR. BUT YOU MAY BE THINKING OF...
"THE TALE OF THE TALIBAN'S DAUGHTER"!
MUST NOT GLANCE AT HIM, LEST I BE STONED TO DEATH!
COME TO POPPA!
THAT'S IT!
I'M SORRY, SIR — IT'S STILL TOO PAINFUL...
GBTrudeau

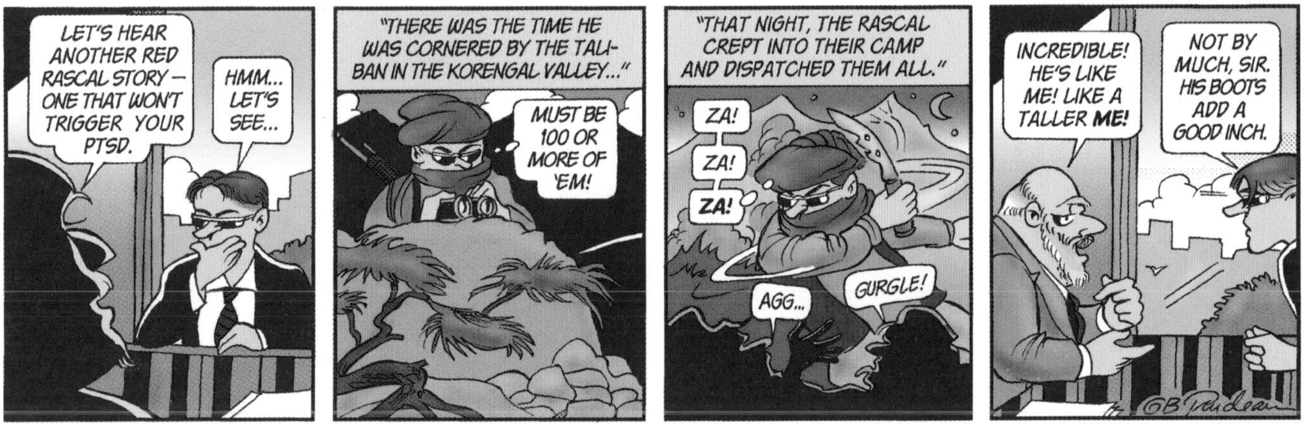
LET'S HEAR ANOTHER RED RASCAL STORY — ONE THAT WON'T TRIGGER YOUR PTSD.
HMM... LET'S SEE...
"THERE WAS THE TIME HE WAS CORNERED BY THE TALIBAN IN THE KORENGAL VALLEY..."
MUST BE 100 OR MORE OF 'EM!
"THAT NIGHT, THE RASCAL CREPT INTO THEIR CAMP AND DISPATCHED THEM ALL."
ZA!
ZA!
ZA!
AGG...
GURGLE!
INCREDIBLE! HE'S LIKE ME! LIKE A TALLER **ME!**
NOT BY MUCH, SIR. HIS BOOTS ADD A GOOD INCH.
GBTrudeau

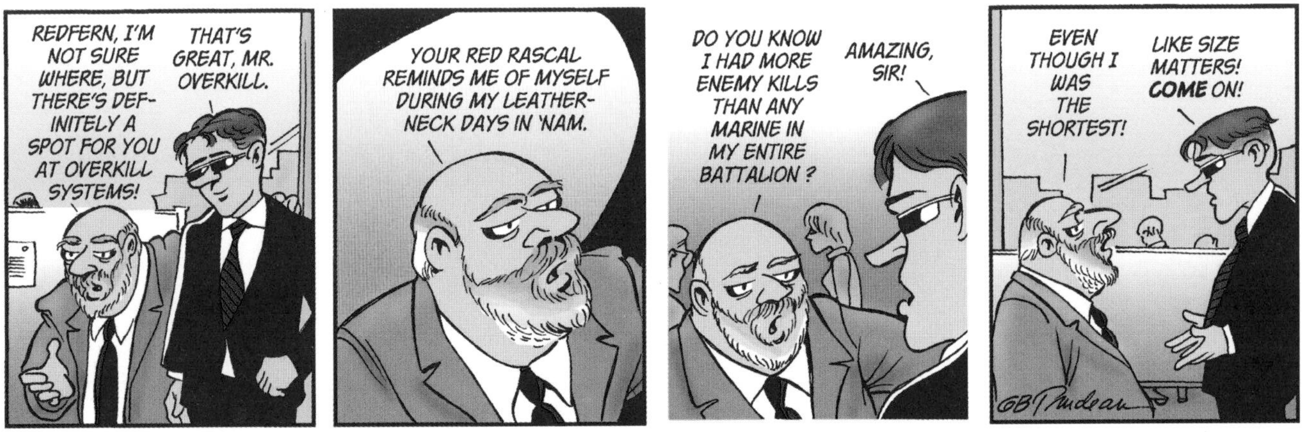
REDFERN, I'M NOT SURE WHERE, BUT THERE'S DEFINITELY A SPOT FOR YOU AT OVERKILL SYSTEMS!
THAT'S GREAT, MR. OVERKILL.
YOUR RED RASCAL REMINDS ME OF MYSELF DURING MY LEATHERNECK DAYS IN 'NAM.
DO YOU KNOW I HAD MORE ENEMY KILLS THAN ANY MARINE IN MY ENTIRE BATTALION ?
AMAZING, SIR!
EVEN THOUGH I WAS THE SHORTEST!
LIKE SIZE MATTERS! **COME** ON!
GBTrudeau

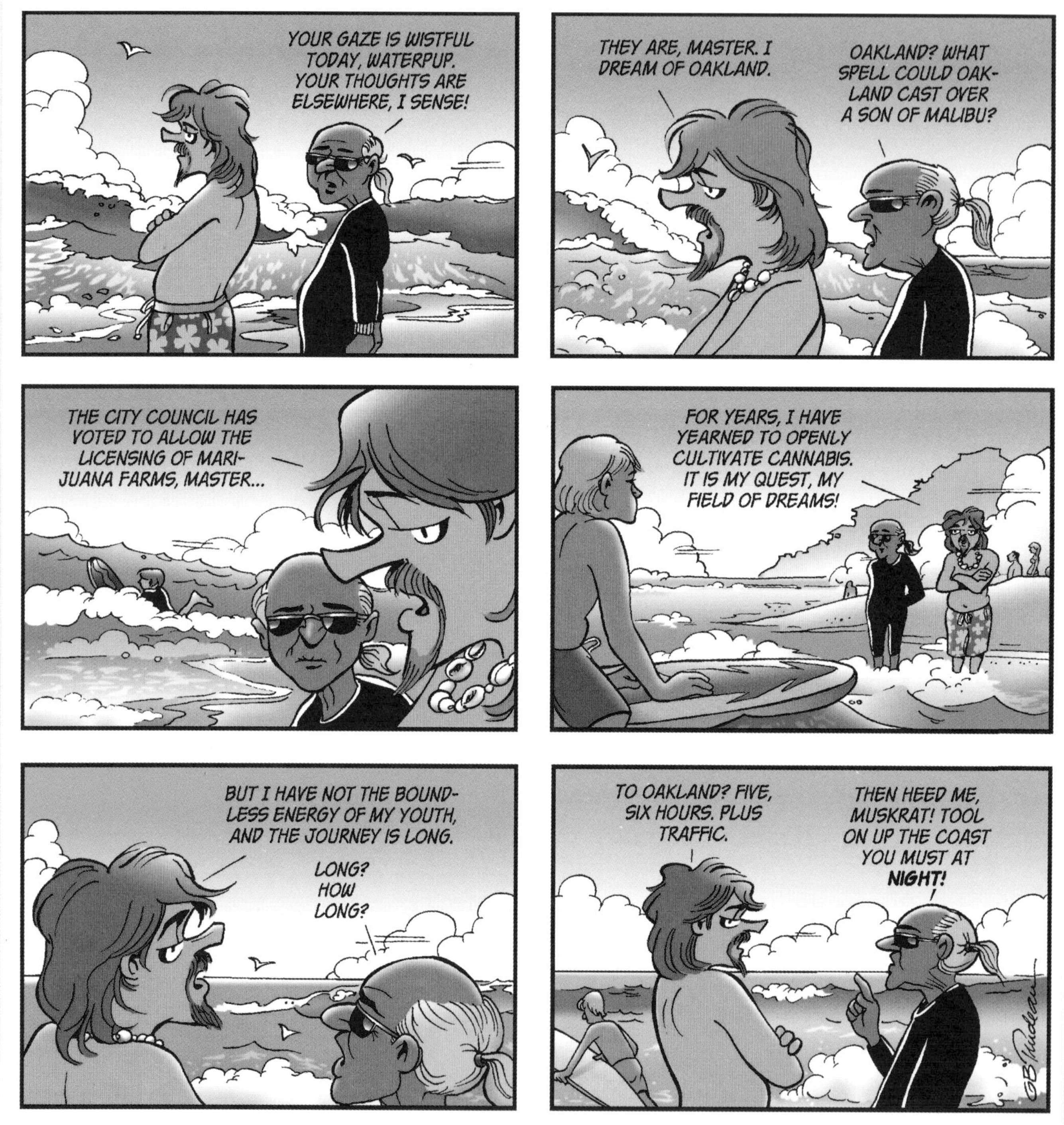
YOUR GAZE IS WISTFUL TODAY, WATERPUP. YOUR THOUGHTS ARE ELSEWHERE, I SENSE!
THEY ARE, MASTER. I DREAM OF OAKLAND.
OAKLAND? WHAT SPELL COULD OAK-LAND CAST OVER A SON OF MALIBU?
THE CITY COUNCIL HAS VOTED TO ALLOW THE LICENSING OF MARI-JUANA FARMS, MASTER...
FOR YEARS, I HAVE YEARNED TO OPENLY CULTIVATE CANNABIS. IT IS MY QUEST, MY FIELD OF DREAMS!
BUT I HAVE NOT THE BOUND-LESS ENERGY OF MY YOUTH, AND THE JOURNEY IS LONG.
LONG? HOW LONG?
TO OAKLAND? FIVE, SIX HOURS. PLUS TRAFFIC.
THEN HEED ME, MUSKRAT! TOOL ON UP THE COAST YOU MUST AT **NIGHT!**
GBTrudeau

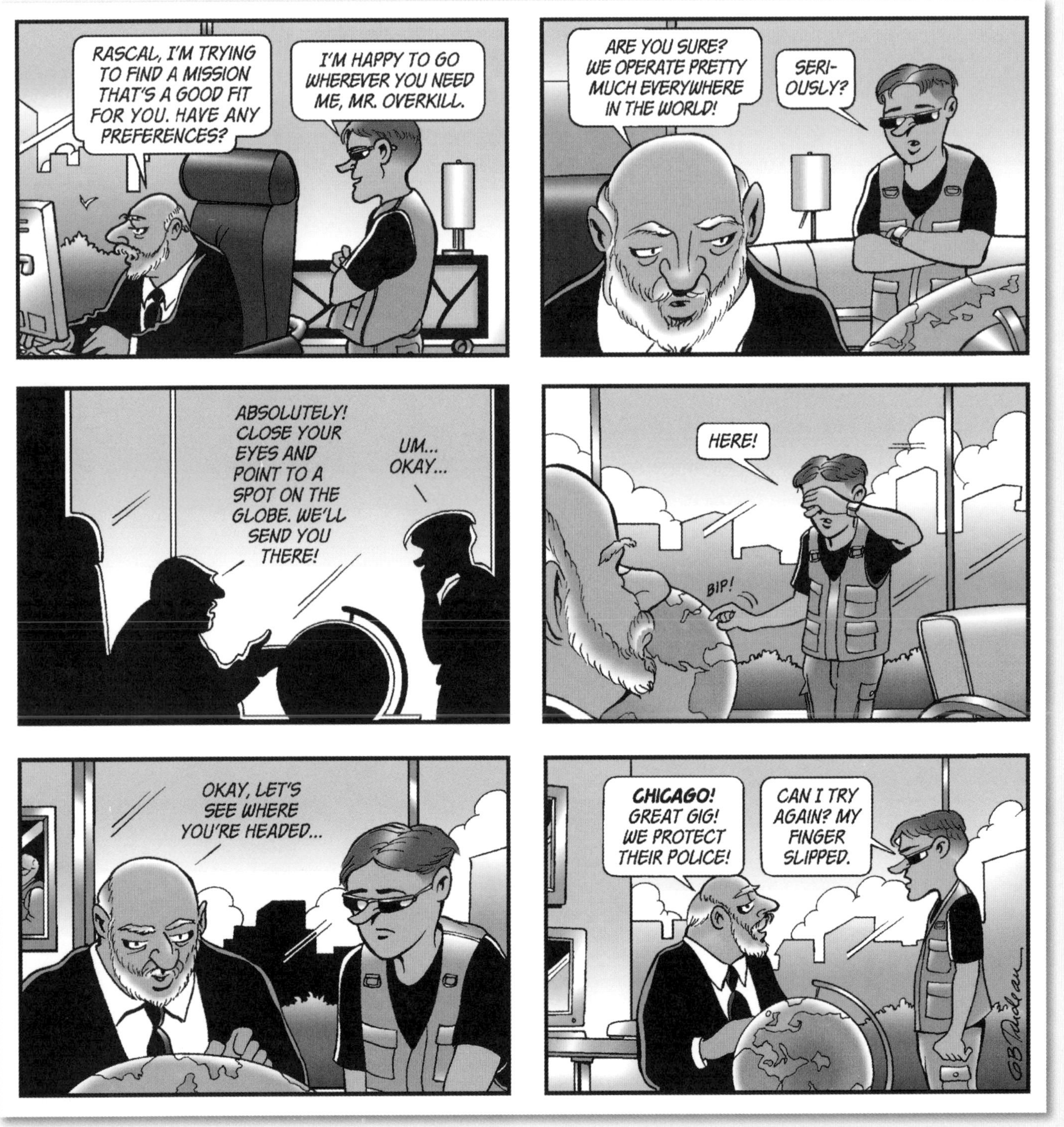
RASCAL, I'M TRYING TO FIND A MISSION THAT'S A GOOD FIT FOR YOU. HAVE ANY PREFERENCES?
I'M HAPPY TO GO WHEREVER YOU NEED ME, MR. OVERKILL.
ARE YOU SURE? WE OPERATE PRETTY MUCH EVERYWHERE IN THE WORLD!
SERI-OUSLY?
ABSOLUTELY! CLOSE YOUR EYES AND POINT TO A SPOT ON THE GLOBE. WE'LL SEND YOU THERE!
UM... OKAY...
HERE!
BIP!
OKAY, LET'S SEE WHERE YOU'RE HEADED...
CHICAGO! GREAT GIG! WE PROTECT THEIR POLICE!
CAN I TRY AGAIN? MY FINGER SLIPPED.
GB Trudeau

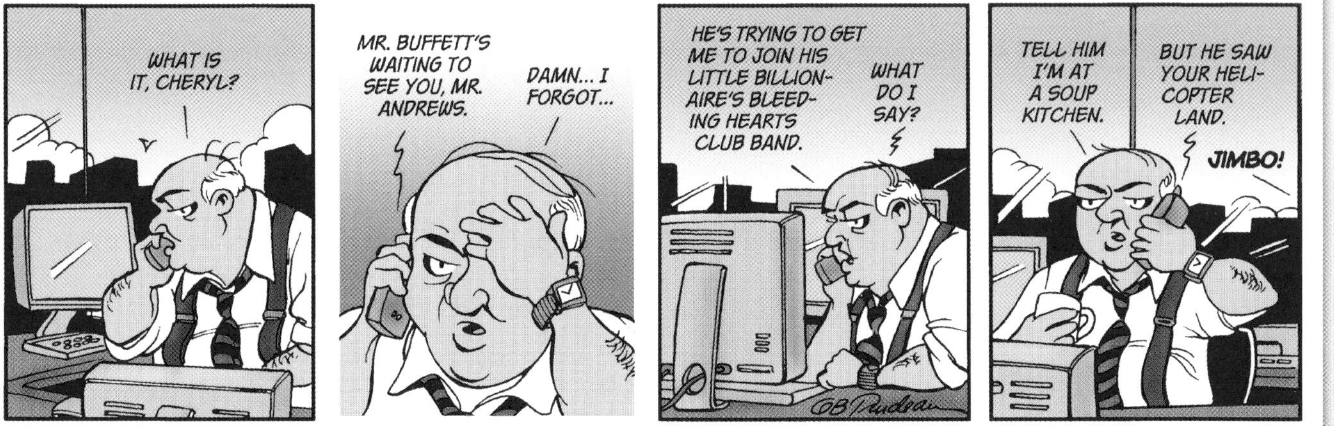
WHAT IS IT, CHERYL?
MR. BUFFETT'S WAITING TO SEE YOU, MR. ANDREWS.
DAMN... I FORGOT...
HE'S TRYING TO GET ME TO JOIN HIS LITTLE BILLIONAIRE'S BLEEDING HEARTS CLUB BAND.
WHAT DO I SAY?
TELL HIM I'M AT A SOUP KITCHEN.
BUT HE SAW YOUR HELICOPTER LAND.
JIMBO!
©B Trudeau

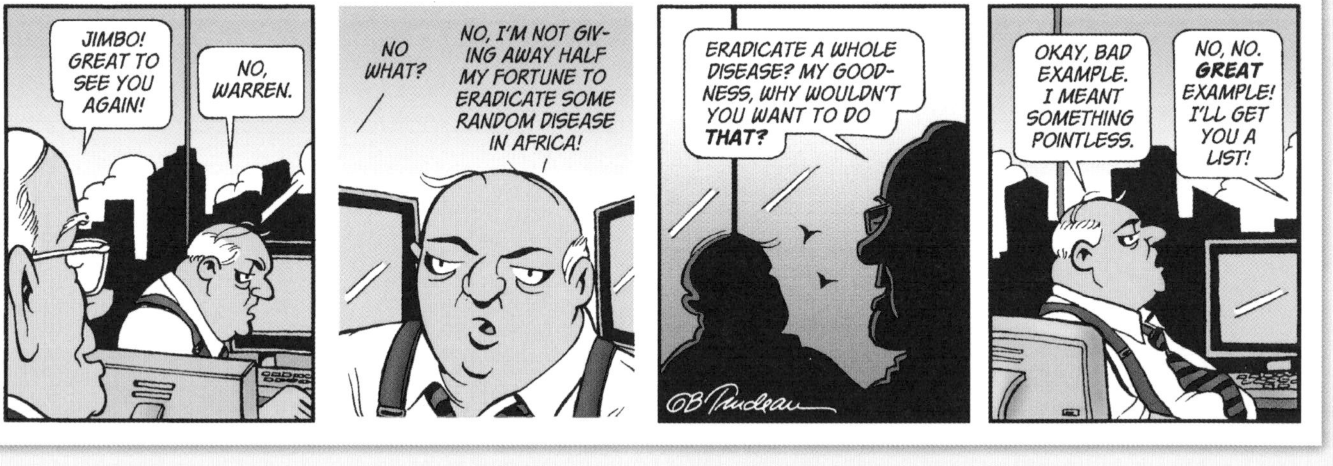
JIMBO! GREAT TO SEE YOU AGAIN!
NO, WARREN.
NO WHAT?
NO, I'M NOT GIVING AWAY HALF MY FORTUNE TO ERADICATE SOME RANDOM DISEASE IN AFRICA!
ERADICATE A WHOLE DISEASE? MY GOODNESS, WHY WOULDN'T YOU WANT TO DO THAT?
OKAY, BAD EXAMPLE. I MEANT SOMETHING POINTLESS.
NO, NO. GREAT EXAMPLE! I'LL GET YOU A LIST!
©B Trudeau

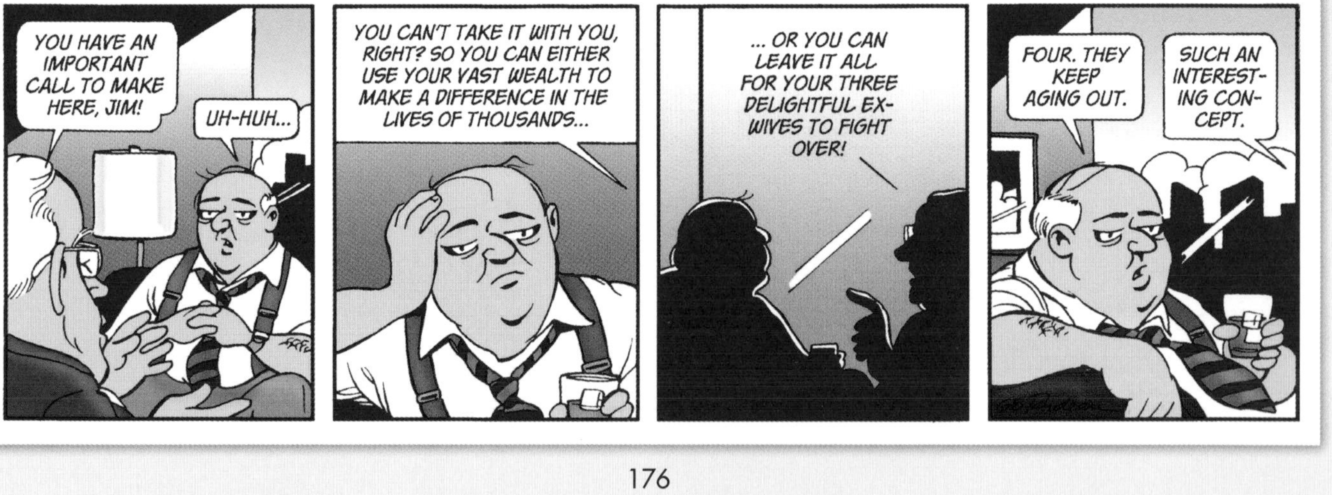
YOU HAVE AN IMPORTANT CALL TO MAKE HERE, JIM!
UH-HUH...
YOU CAN'T TAKE IT WITH YOU, RIGHT? SO YOU CAN EITHER USE YOUR VAST WEALTH TO MAKE A DIFFERENCE IN THE LIVES OF THOUSANDS...
... OR YOU CAN LEAVE IT ALL FOR YOUR THREE DELIGHTFUL EX-WIVES TO FIGHT OVER!
FOUR. THEY KEEP AGING OUT.
SUCH AN INTERESTING CONCEPT.

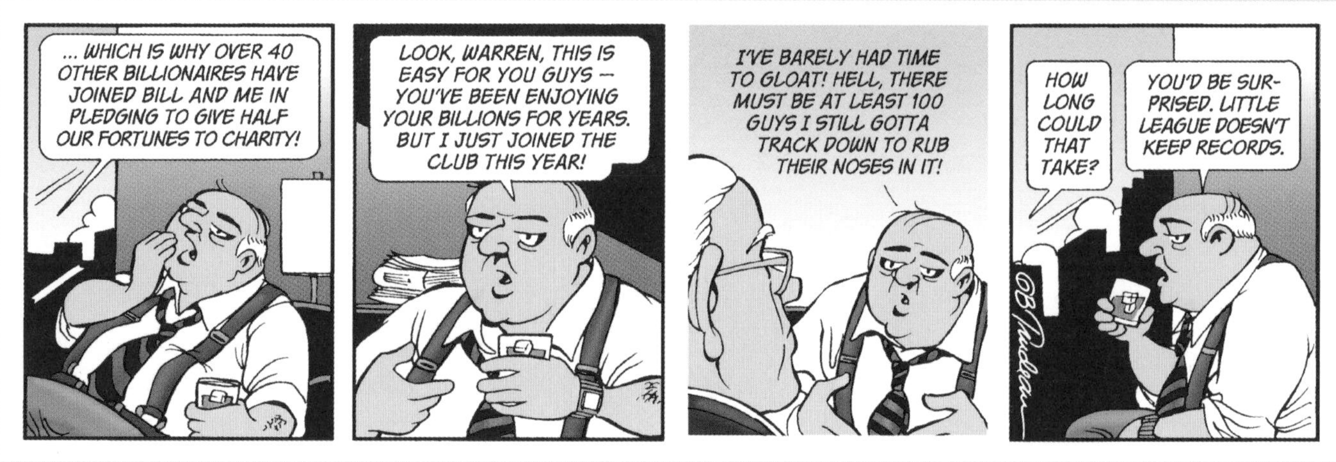
... WHICH IS WHY OVER 40 OTHER BILLIONAIRES HAVE JOINED BILL AND ME IN PLEDGING TO GIVE HALF OUR FORTUNES TO CHARITY!
LOOK, WARREN, THIS IS EASY FOR YOU GUYS — YOU'VE BEEN ENJOYING YOUR BILLIONS FOR YEARS. BUT I JUST JOINED THE CLUB THIS YEAR!
I'VE BARELY HAD TIME TO GLOAT! HELL, THERE MUST BE AT LEAST 100 GUYS I STILL GOTTA TRACK DOWN TO RUB THEIR NOSES IN IT!
HOW LONG COULD THAT TAKE?
YOU'D BE SURPRISED. LITTLE LEAGUE DOESN'T KEEP RECORDS.
GB Trudeau

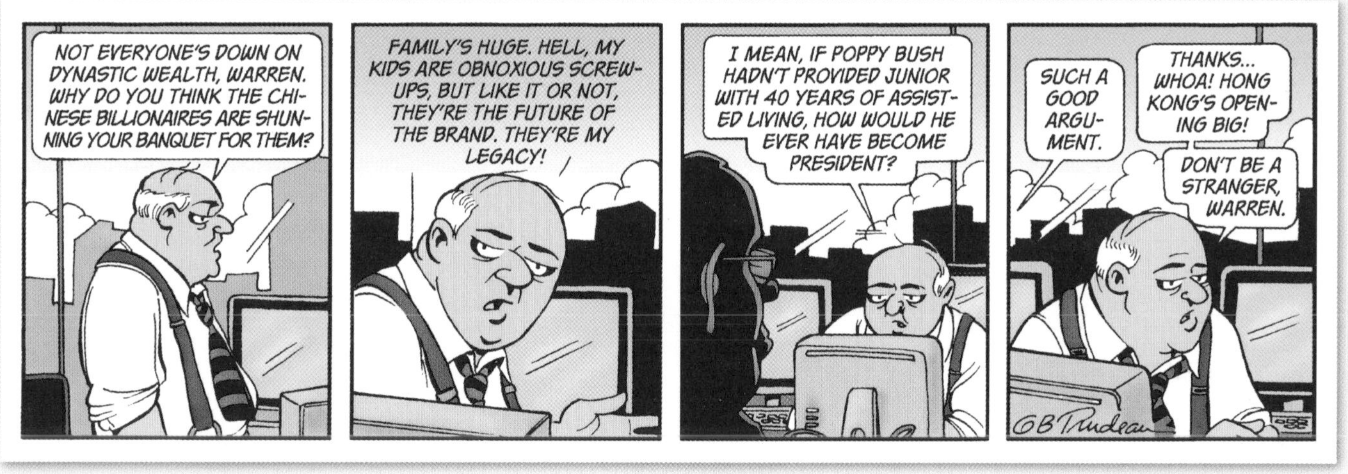
NOT EVERYONE'S DOWN ON DYNASTIC WEALTH, WARREN. WHY DO YOU THINK THE CHINESE BILLIONAIRES ARE SHUNNING YOUR BANQUET FOR THEM?
FAMILY'S HUGE. HELL, MY KIDS ARE OBNOXIOUS SCREW-UPS, BUT LIKE IT OR NOT, THEY'RE THE FUTURE OF THE BRAND. THEY'RE MY LEGACY!
I MEAN, IF POPPY BUSH HADN'T PROVIDED JUNIOR WITH 40 YEARS OF ASSISTED LIVING, HOW WOULD HE EVER HAVE BECOME PRESIDENT?
SUCH A GOOD ARGUMENT.
THANKS... WHOA! HONG KONG'S OPENING BIG!
DON'T BE A STRANGER, WARREN.
GB Trudeau

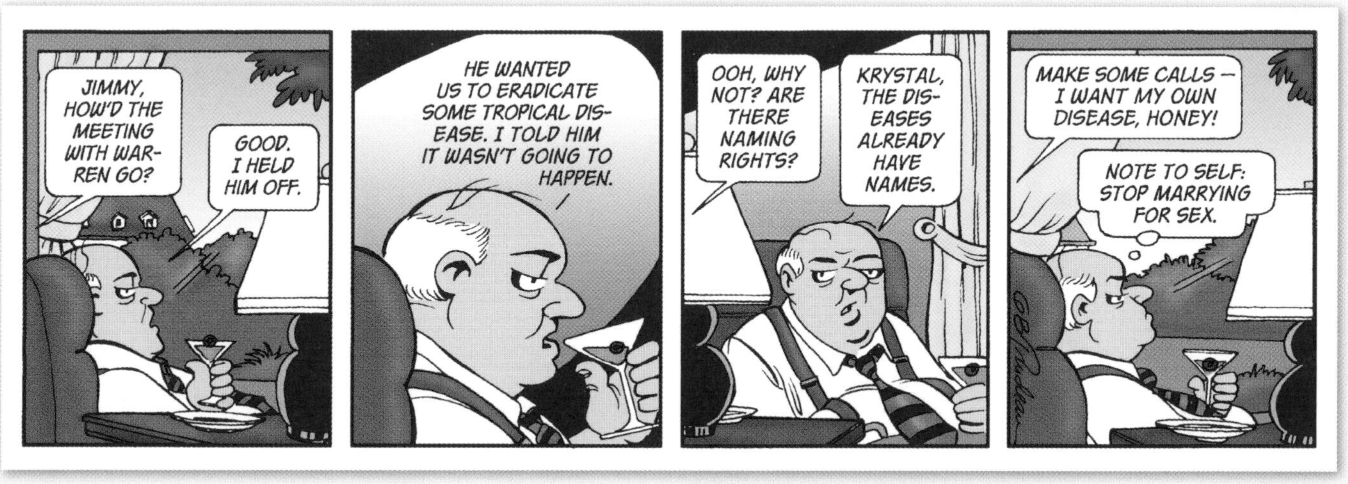
JIMMY, HOW'D THE MEETING WITH WARREN GO?
GOOD. I HELD HIM OFF.
HE WANTED US TO ERADICATE SOME TROPICAL DISEASE. I TOLD HIM IT WASN'T GOING TO HAPPEN.
OOH, WHY NOT? ARE THERE NAMING RIGHTS?
KRYSTAL, THE DISEASES ALREADY HAVE NAMES.
MAKE SOME CALLS — I WANT MY OWN DISEASE, HONEY!
NOTE TO SELF: STOP MARRYING FOR SEX.
GB Trudeau

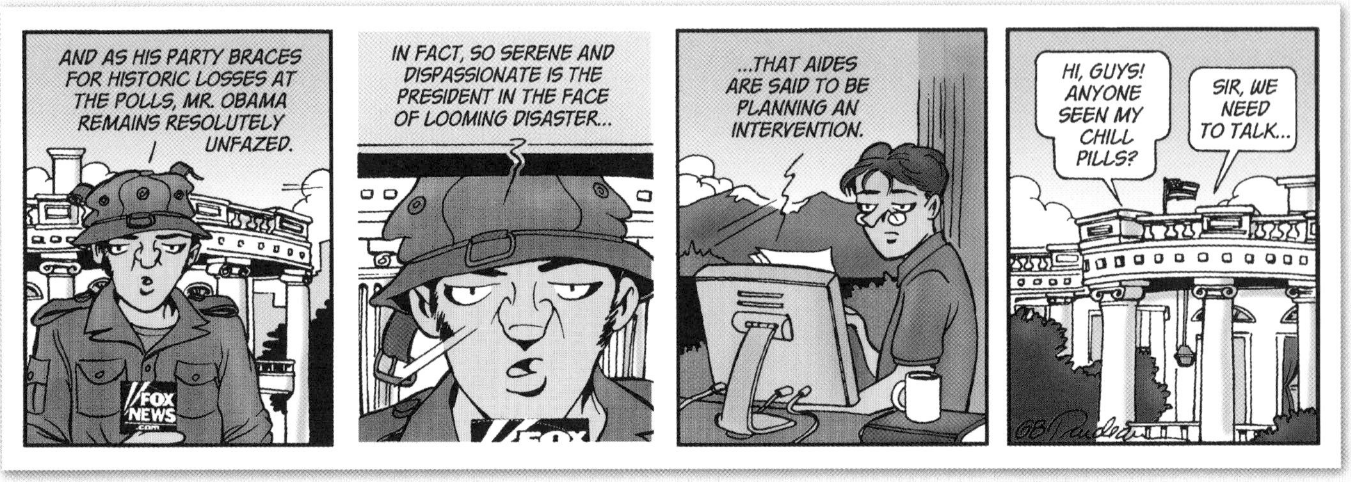
AND AS HIS PARTY BRACES FOR HISTORIC LOSSES AT THE POLLS, MR. OBAMA REMAINS RESOLUTELY UNFAZED.
FOX NEWS .com
IN FACT, SO SERENE AND DISPASSIONATE IS THE PRESIDENT IN THE FACE OF LOOMING DISASTER...
...THAT AIDES ARE SAID TO BE PLANNING AN INTERVENTION.
HI, GUYS! ANYONE SEEN MY CHILL PILLS?
SIR, WE NEED TO TALK...

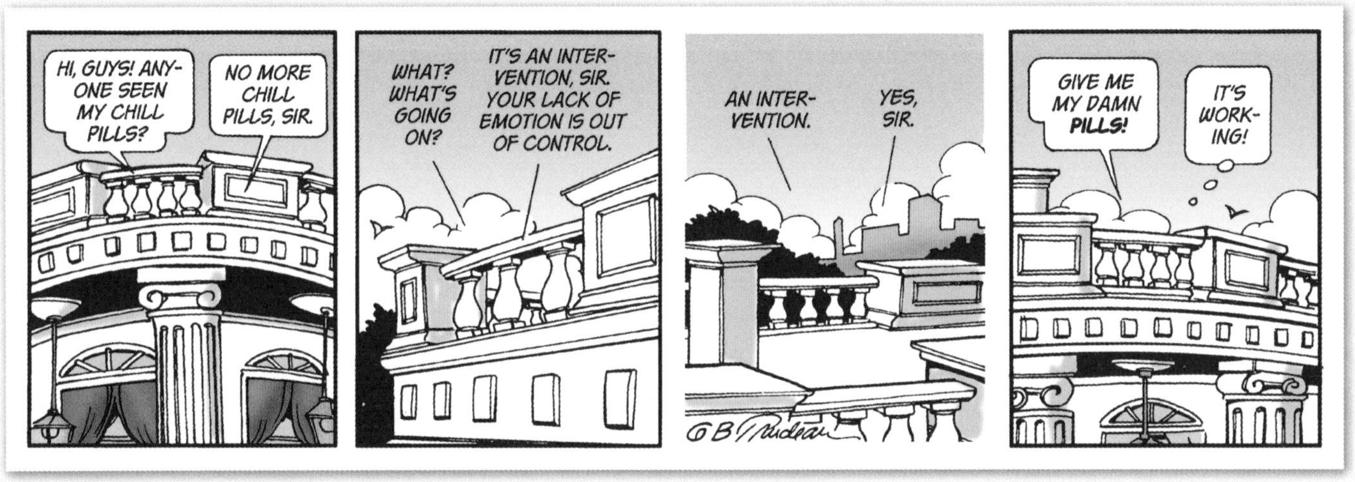
HI, GUYS! ANYONE SEEN MY CHILL PILLS?
NO MORE CHILL PILLS, SIR.
WHAT? WHAT'S GOING ON?
IT'S AN INTERVENTION, SIR. YOUR LACK OF EMOTION IS OUT OF CONTROL.
AN INTERVENTION.
YES, SIR.
GIVE ME MY DAMN **PILLS!**
IT'S WORKING!

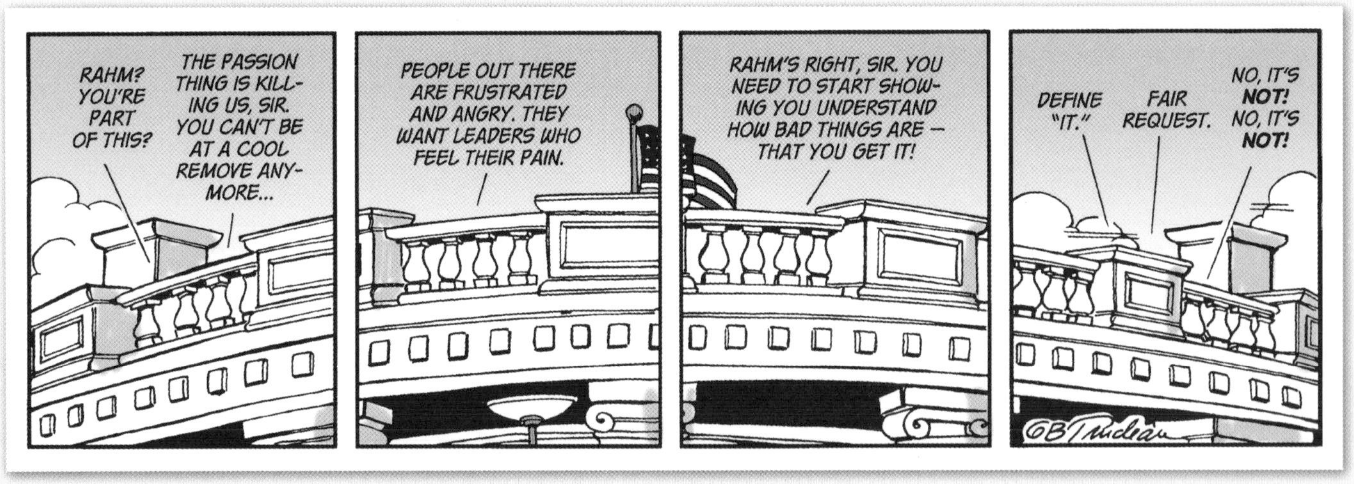
RAHM? YOU'RE PART OF THIS?
THE PASSION THING IS KILLING US, SIR. YOU CAN'T BE AT A COOL REMOVE ANYMORE...
PEOPLE OUT THERE ARE FRUSTRATED AND ANGRY. THEY WANT LEADERS WHO FEEL THEIR PAIN.
RAHM'S RIGHT, SIR. YOU NEED TO START SHOWING YOU UNDERSTAND HOW BAD THINGS ARE — THAT YOU GET IT!
DEFINE "IT."
FAIR REQUEST.
NO, IT'S **NOT!** NO, IT'S **NOT!**

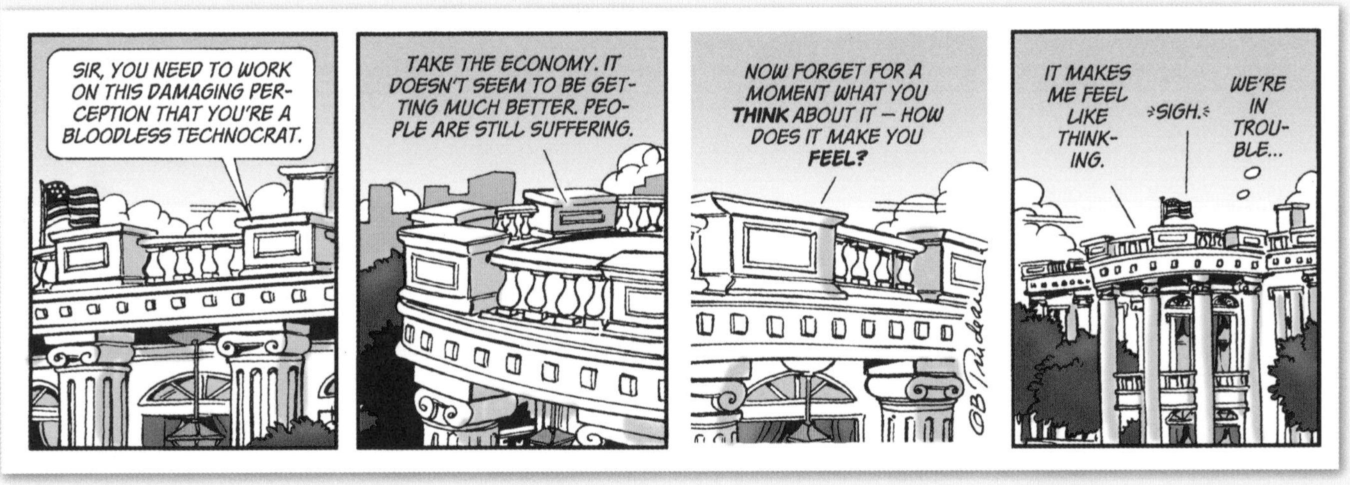
SIR, YOU NEED TO WORK ON THIS DAMAGING PERCEPTION THAT YOU'RE A BLOODLESS TECHNOCRAT.
TAKE THE ECONOMY. IT DOESN'T SEEM TO BE GETTING MUCH BETTER. PEOPLE ARE STILL SUFFERING.
NOW FORGET FOR A MOMENT WHAT YOU **THINK** ABOUT IT — HOW DOES IT MAKE YOU **FEEL?**
IT MAKES ME FEEL LIKE THINKING.
SIGH.
WE'RE IN TROUBLE...

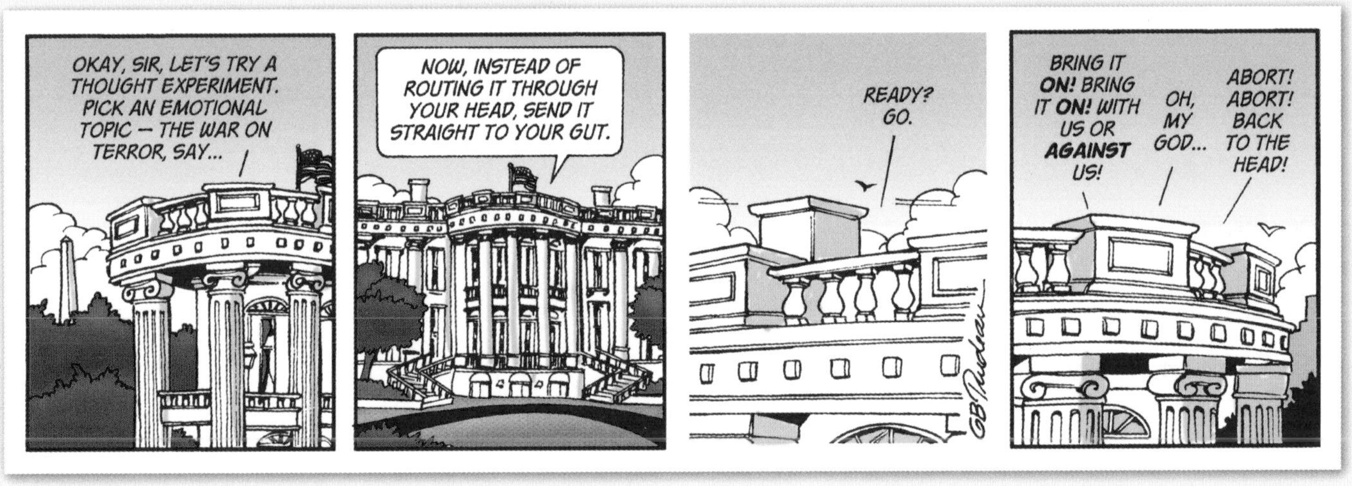
OKAY, SIR, LET'S TRY A THOUGHT EXPERIMENT. PICK AN EMOTIONAL TOPIC — THE WAR ON TERROR, SAY...
NOW, INSTEAD OF ROUTING IT THROUGH YOUR HEAD, SEND IT STRAIGHT TO YOUR GUT.
READY? GO.
BRING IT **ON!** BRING IT **ON!** WITH US OR **AGAINST** US!
OH, MY GOD...
ABORT! ABORT! BACK TO THE HEAD!

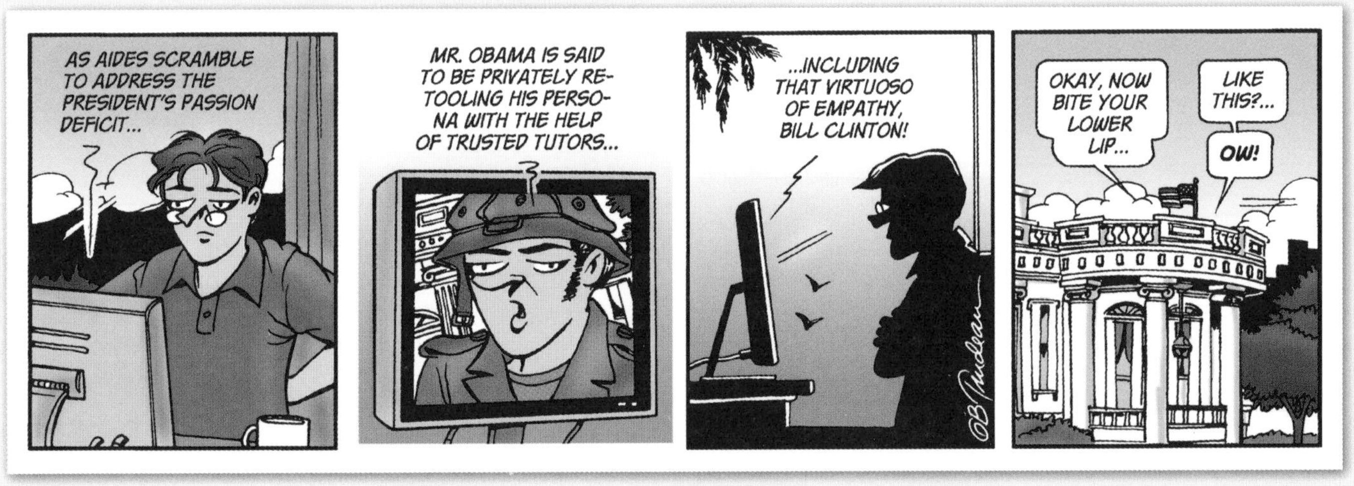
AS AIDES SCRAMBLE TO ADDRESS THE PRESIDENT'S PASSION DEFICIT...
MR. OBAMA IS SAID TO BE PRIVATELY RETOOLING HIS PERSONA WITH THE HELP OF TRUSTED TUTORS...
...INCLUDING THAT VIRTUOSO OF EMPATHY, BILL CLINTON!
OKAY, NOW BITE YOUR LOWER LIP...
LIKE THIS?...
OW!

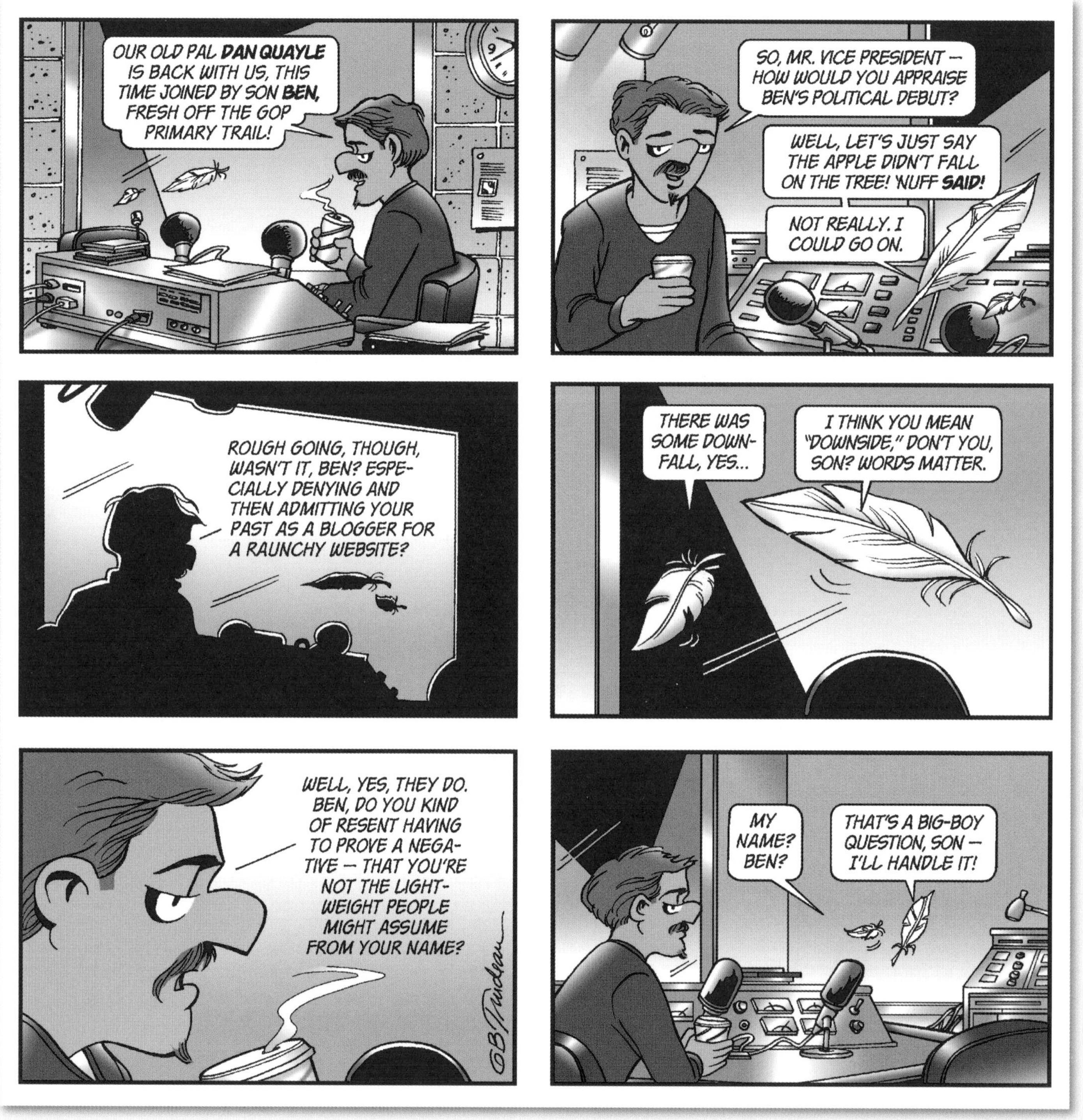
OUR OLD PAL DAN QUAYLE IS BACK WITH US, THIS TIME JOINED BY SON BEN, FRESH OFF THE GOP PRIMARY TRAIL!
SO, MR. VICE PRESIDENT — HOW WOULD YOU APPRAISE BEN'S POLITICAL DEBUT?
WELL, LET'S JUST SAY THE APPLE DIDN'T FALL ON THE TREE! 'NUFF SAID!
NOT REALLY. I COULD GO ON.
ROUGH GOING, THOUGH, WASN'T IT, BEN? ESPECIALLY DENYING AND THEN ADMITTING YOUR PAST AS A BLOGGER FOR A RAUNCHY WEBSITE?
THERE WAS SOME DOWNFALL, YES...
I THINK YOU MEAN "DOWNSIDE," DON'T YOU, SON? WORDS MATTER.
WELL, YES, THEY DO. BEN, DO YOU KIND OF RESENT HAVING TO PROVE A NEGATIVE — THAT YOU'RE NOT THE LIGHTWEIGHT PEOPLE MIGHT ASSUME FROM YOUR NAME?
GBTrudeau
MY NAME? BEN?
THAT'S A BIG-BOY QUESTION, SON — I'LL HANDLE IT!

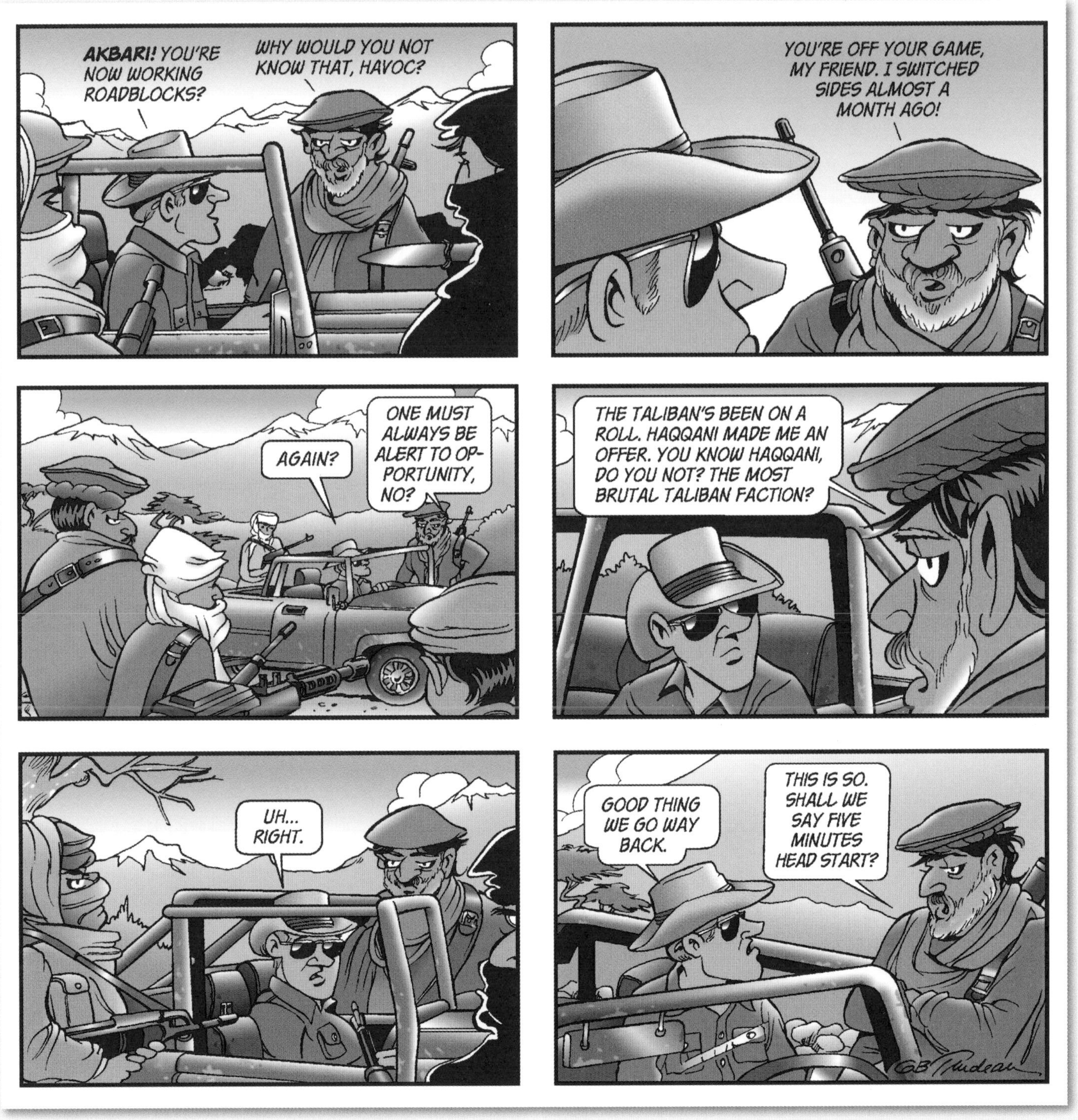
AKBARI! YOU'RE NOW WORKING ROADBLOCKS?
WHY WOULD YOU NOT KNOW THAT, HAVOC?
YOU'RE OFF YOUR GAME, MY FRIEND. I SWITCHED SIDES ALMOST A MONTH AGO!
AGAIN?
ONE MUST ALWAYS BE ALERT TO OP-PORTUNITY, NO?
THE TALIBAN'S BEEN ON A ROLL. HAQQANI MADE ME AN OFFER. YOU KNOW HAQQANI, DO YOU NOT? THE MOST BRUTAL TALIBAN FACTION?
UH... RIGHT.
GOOD THING WE GO WAY BACK.
THIS IS SO. SHALL WE SAY FIVE MINUTES HEAD START?
GB Trudeau

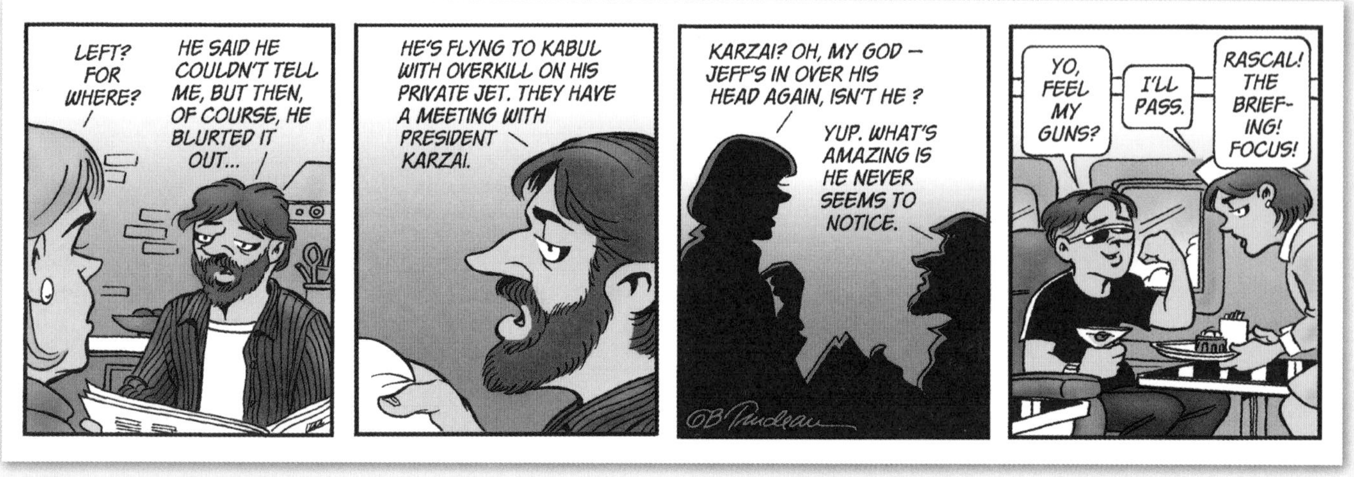
LEFT? FOR WHERE?
HE SAID HE COULDN'T TELL ME, BUT THEN, OF COURSE, HE BLURTED IT OUT...
HE'S FLYNG TO KABUL WITH OVERKILL ON HIS PRIVATE JET. THEY HAVE A MEETING WITH PRESIDENT KARZAI.
KARZAI? OH, MY GOD — JEFF'S IN OVER HIS HEAD AGAIN, ISN'T HE ?
YUP. WHAT'S AMAZING IS HE NEVER SEEMS TO NOTICE.
YO, FEEL MY GUNS?
I'LL PASS.
RASCAL! THE BRIEF-ING! FOCUS!

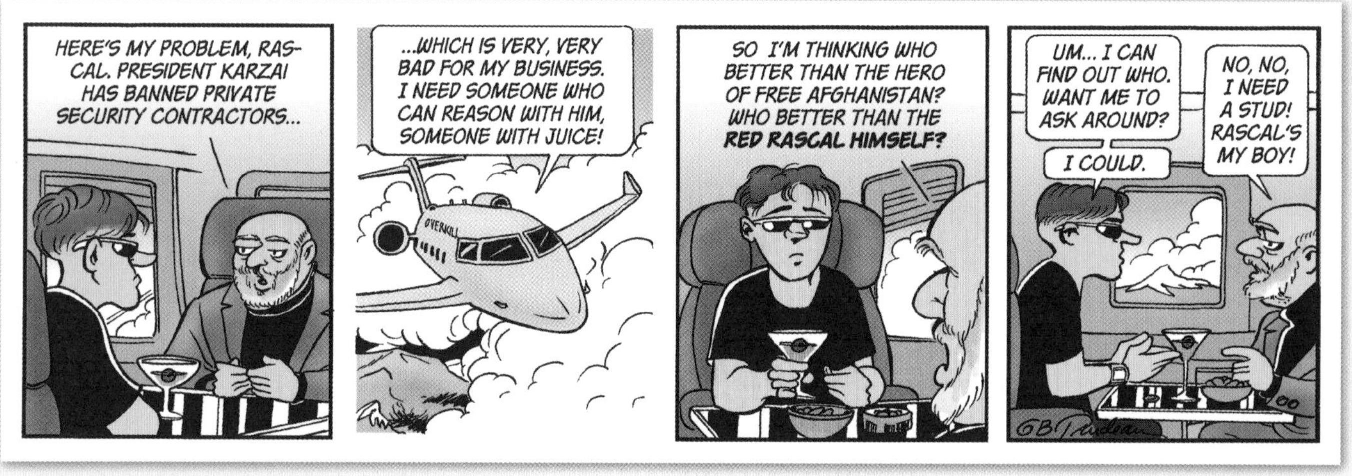
HERE'S MY PROBLEM, RAS-CAL. PRESIDENT KARZAI HAS BANNED PRIVATE SECURITY CONTRACTORS...
...WHICH IS VERY, VERY BAD FOR MY BUSINESS. I NEED SOMEONE WHO CAN REASON WITH HIM, SOMEONE WITH JUICE!
OVERKILL
SO I'M THINKING WHO BETTER THAN THE HERO OF FREE AFGHANISTAN? WHO BETTER THAN THE **RED RASCAL HIMSELF?**
UM... I CAN FIND OUT WHO. WANT ME TO ASK AROUND?
I COULD.
NO, NO, I NEED A STUD! RASCAL'S MY BOY!

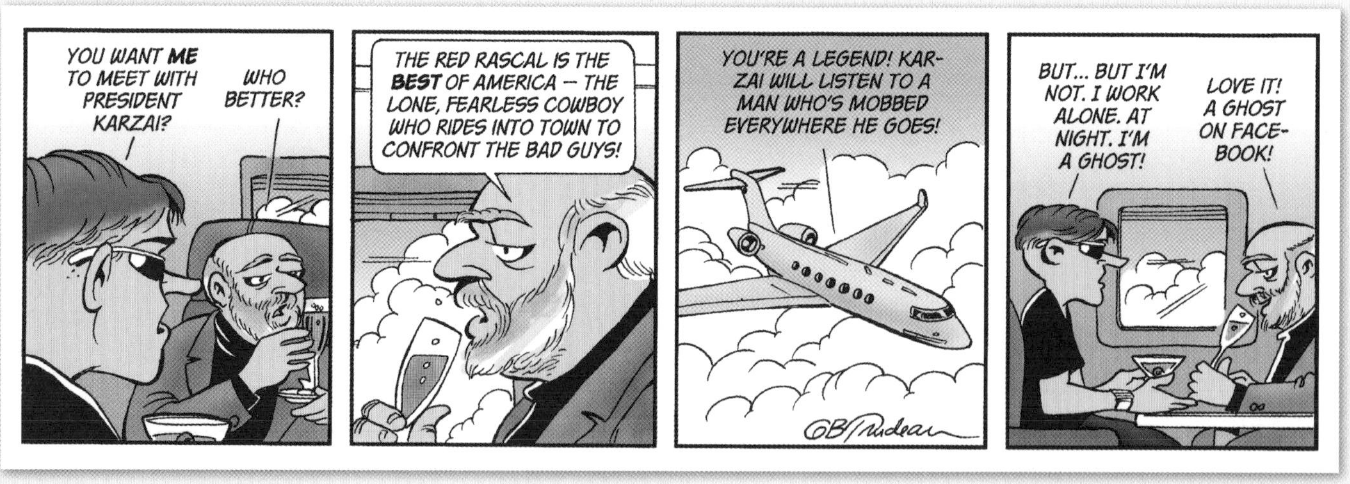
YOU WANT **ME** TO MEET WITH PRESIDENT KARZAI?
WHO BETTER?
THE RED RASCAL IS THE **BEST** OF AMERICA — THE LONE, FEARLESS COWBOY WHO RIDES INTO TOWN TO CONFRONT THE BAD GUYS!
YOU'RE A LEGEND! KAR-ZAI WILL LISTEN TO A MAN WHO'S MOBBED EVERYWHERE HE GOES!
BUT... BUT I'M NOT. I WORK ALONE. AT NIGHT. I'M A GHOST!
LOVE IT! A GHOST ON FACE-BOOK!

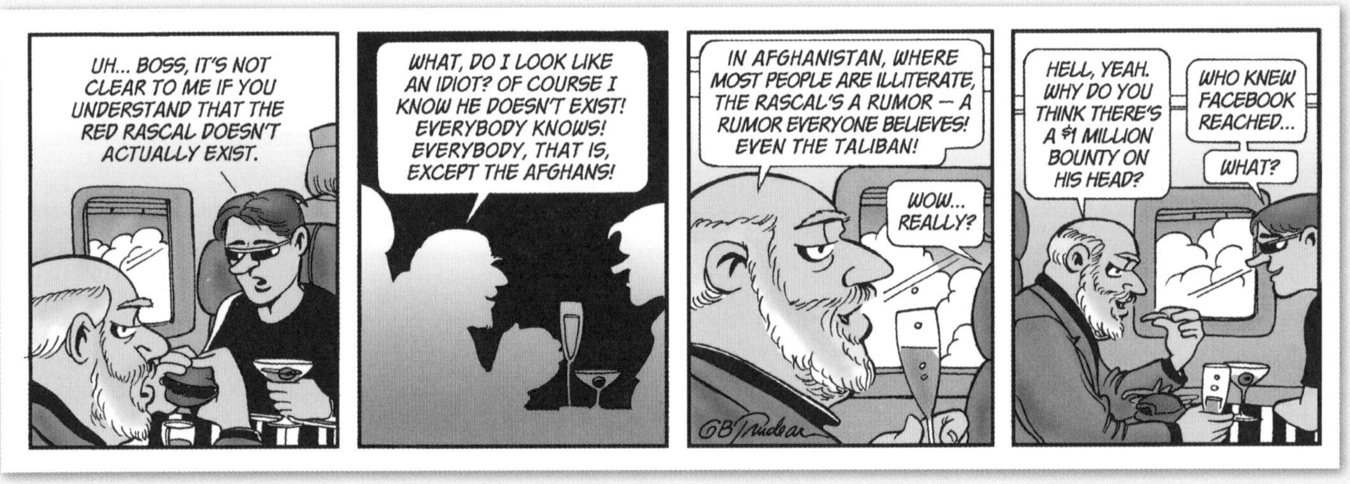
UH... BOSS, IT'S NOT CLEAR TO ME IF YOU UNDERSTAND THAT THE RED RASCAL DOESN'T ACTUALLY EXIST.
WHAT, DO I LOOK LIKE AN IDIOT? OF COURSE I KNOW HE DOESN'T EXIST! EVERYBODY KNOWS! EVERYBODY, THAT IS, EXCEPT THE AFGHANS!
IN AFGHANISTAN, WHERE MOST PEOPLE ARE ILLITERATE, THE RASCAL'S A RUMOR — A RUMOR EVERYONE BELIEVES! EVEN THE TALIBAN!
WOW... REALLY?
HELL, YEAH. WHY DO YOU THINK THERE'S A $1 MILLION BOUNTY ON HIS HEAD?
WHO KNEW FACEBOOK REACHED...
WHAT?

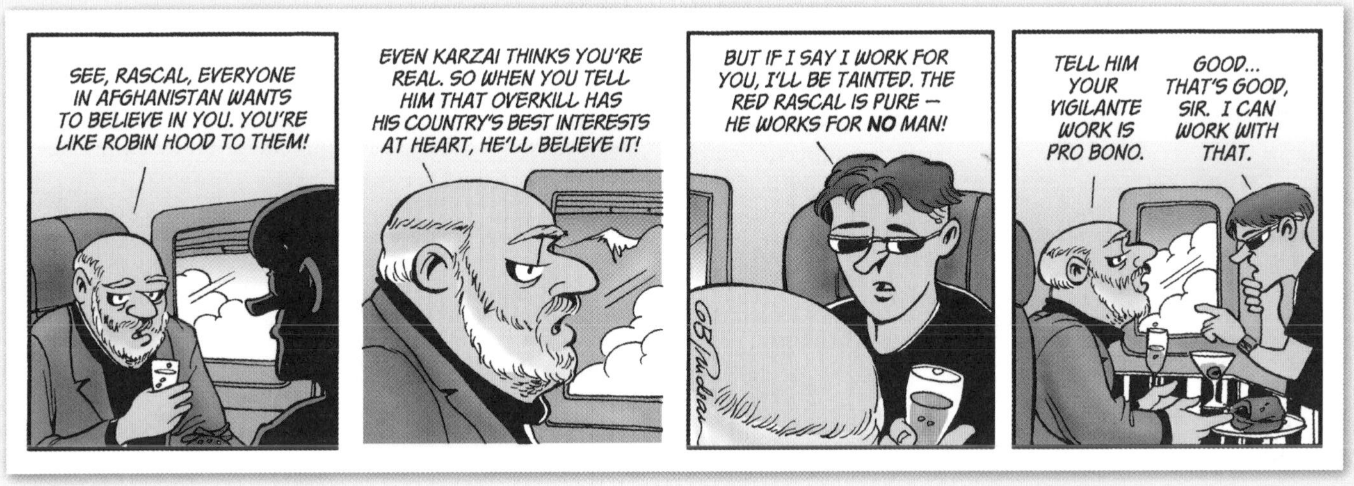
SEE, RASCAL, EVERYONE IN AFGHANISTAN WANTS TO BELIEVE IN YOU. YOU'RE LIKE ROBIN HOOD TO THEM!
EVEN KARZAI THINKS YOU'RE REAL. SO WHEN YOU TELL HIM THAT OVERKILL HAS HIS COUNTRY'S BEST INTERESTS AT HEART, HE'LL BELIEVE IT!
BUT IF I SAY I WORK FOR YOU, I'LL BE TAINTED. THE RED RASCAL IS PURE — HE WORKS FOR NO MAN!
TELL HIM YOUR VIGILANTE WORK IS PRO BONO.
GOOD... THAT'S GOOD, SIR. I CAN WORK WITH THAT.

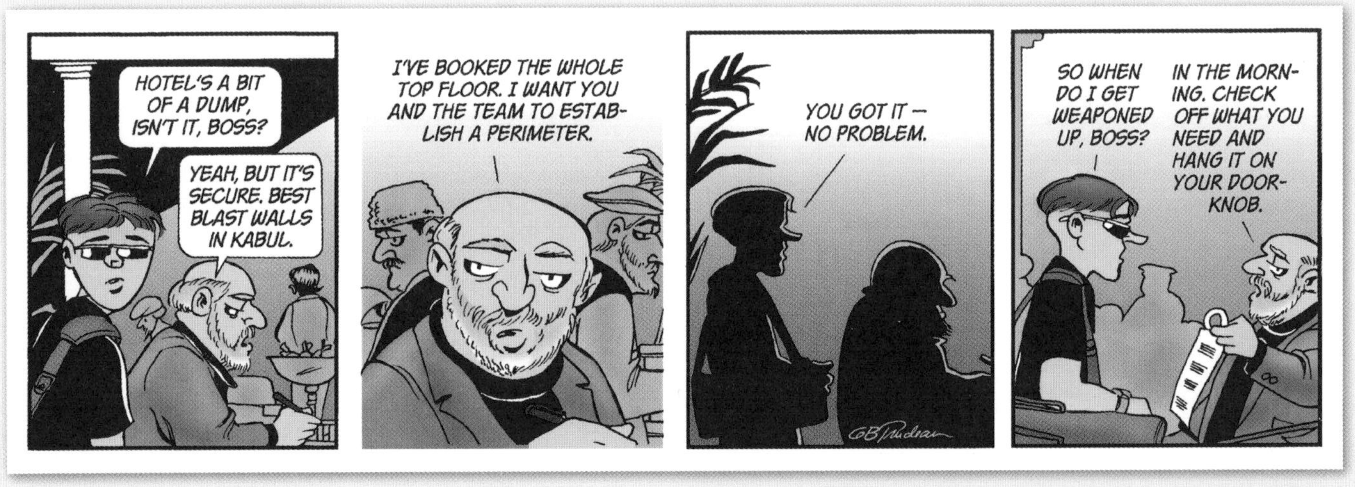
HOTEL'S A BIT OF A DUMP, ISN'T IT, BOSS?
YEAH, BUT IT'S SECURE. BEST BLAST WALLS IN KABUL.
I'VE BOOKED THE WHOLE TOP FLOOR. I WANT YOU AND THE TEAM TO ESTABLISH A PERIMETER.
YOU GOT IT — NO PROBLEM.
SO WHEN DO I GET WEAPONED UP, BOSS?
IN THE MORNING. CHECK OFF WHAT YOU NEED AND HANG IT ON YOUR DOORKNOB.

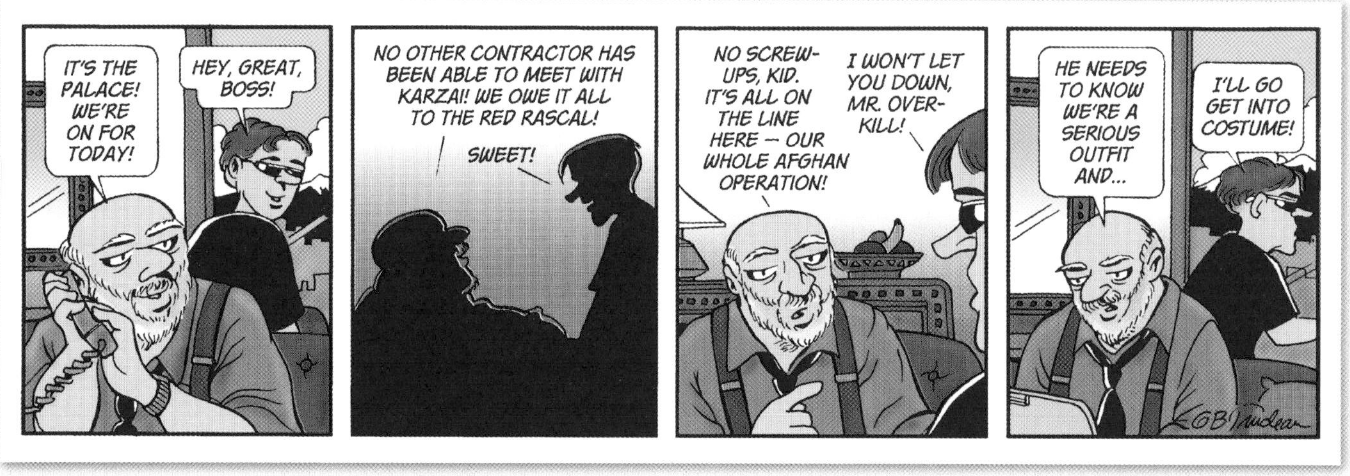
IT'S THE PALACE! WE'RE ON FOR TODAY!
HEY, GREAT, BOSS!
NO OTHER CONTRACTOR HAS BEEN ABLE TO MEET WITH KARZAI! WE OWE IT ALL TO THE RED RASCAL!
SWEET!
NO SCREW-UPS, KID. IT'S ALL ON THE LINE HERE — OUR WHOLE AFGHAN OPERATION!
I WON'T LET YOU DOWN, MR. OVERKILL!
HE NEEDS TO KNOW WE'RE A SERIOUS OUTFIT AND...
I'LL GO GET INTO COSTUME!

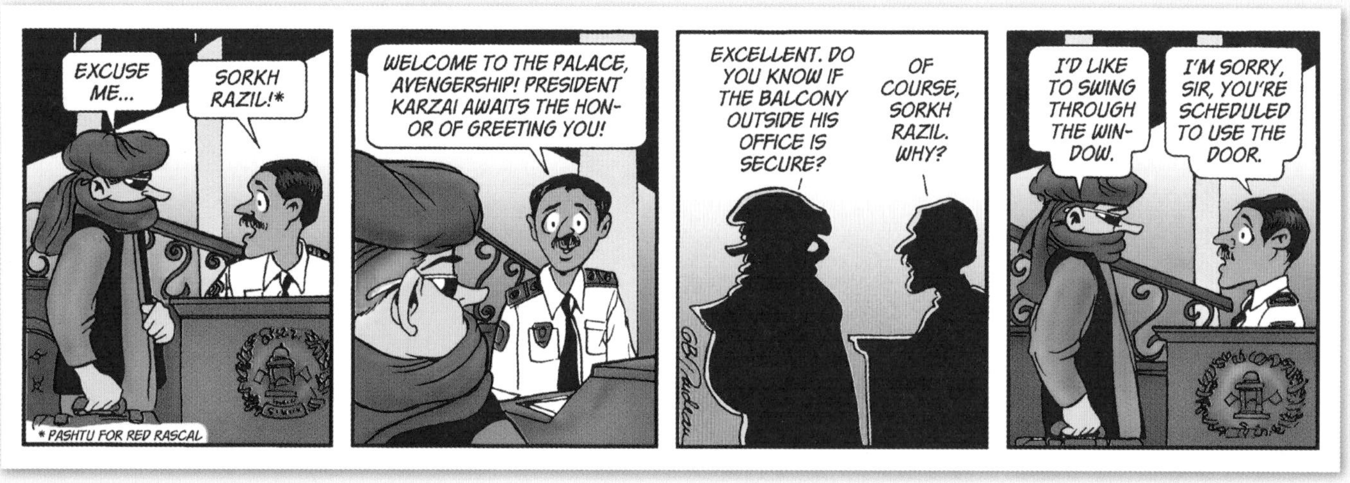
EXCUSE ME...
SORKH RAZIL!*
* PASHTU FOR RED RASCAL
WELCOME TO THE PALACE, AVENGERSHIP! PRESIDENT KARZAI AWAITS THE HONOR OF GREETING YOU!
EXCELLENT. DO YOU KNOW IF THE BALCONY OUTSIDE HIS OFFICE IS SECURE?
OF COURSE, SORKH RAZIL. WHY?
I'D LIKE TO SWING THROUGH THE WINDOW.
I'M SORRY, SIR, YOU'RE SCHEDULED TO USE THE DOOR.

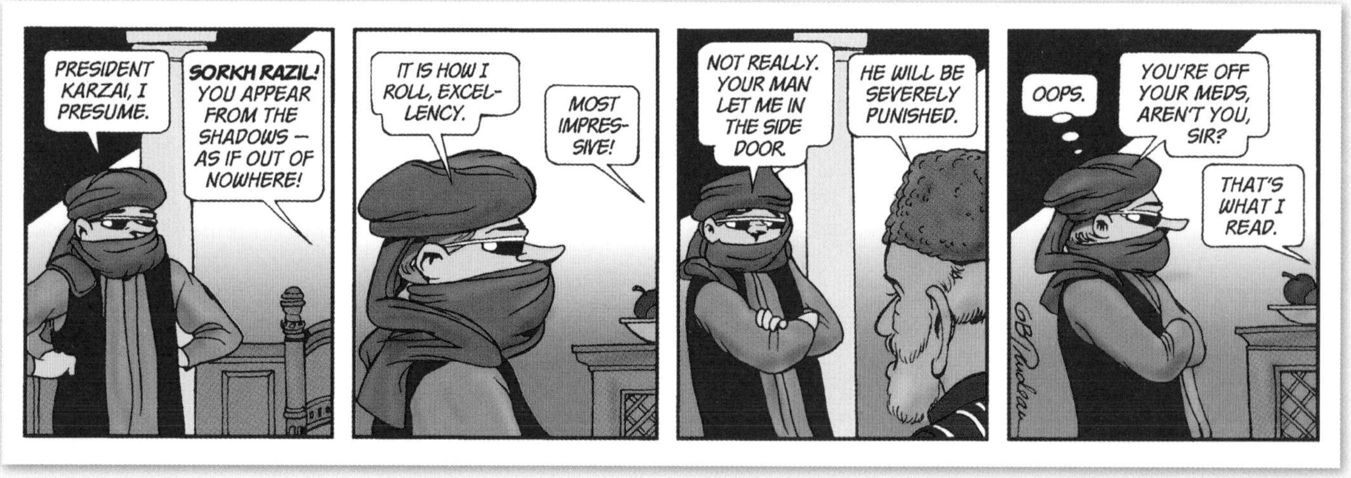
PRESIDENT KARZAI, I PRESUME.
SORKH RAZIL! YOU APPEAR FROM THE SHADOWS — AS IF OUT OF NOWHERE!
IT IS HOW I ROLL, EXCELLENCY.
MOST IMPRESSIVE!
NOT REALLY. YOUR MAN LET ME IN THE SIDE DOOR.
HE WILL BE SEVERELY PUNISHED.
OOPS.
YOU'RE OFF YOUR MEDS, AREN'T YOU, SIR?
THAT'S WHAT I READ.

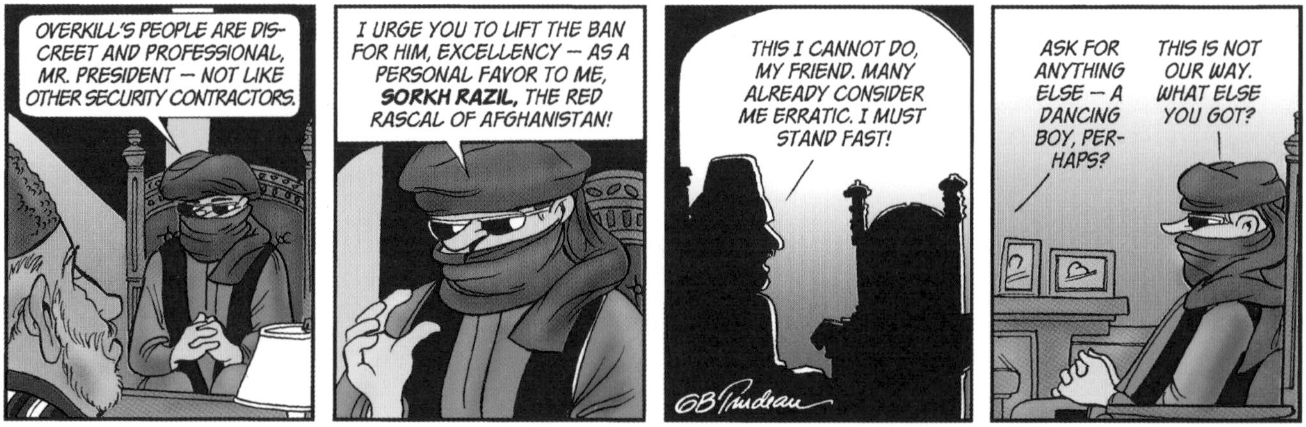
OVERKILL'S PEOPLE ARE DISCREET AND PROFESSIONAL, MR. PRESIDENT — NOT LIKE OTHER SECURITY CONTRACTORS.
I URGE YOU TO LIFT THE BAN FOR HIM, EXCELLENCY — AS A PERSONAL FAVOR TO ME, **SORKH RAZIL,** THE RED RASCAL OF AFGHANISTAN!
THIS I CANNOT DO, MY FRIEND. MANY ALREADY CONSIDER ME ERRATIC. I MUST STAND FAST!
GB Trudeau
ASK FOR ANYTHING ELSE — A DANCING BOY, PERHAPS?
THIS IS NOT OUR WAY. WHAT ELSE YOU GOT?

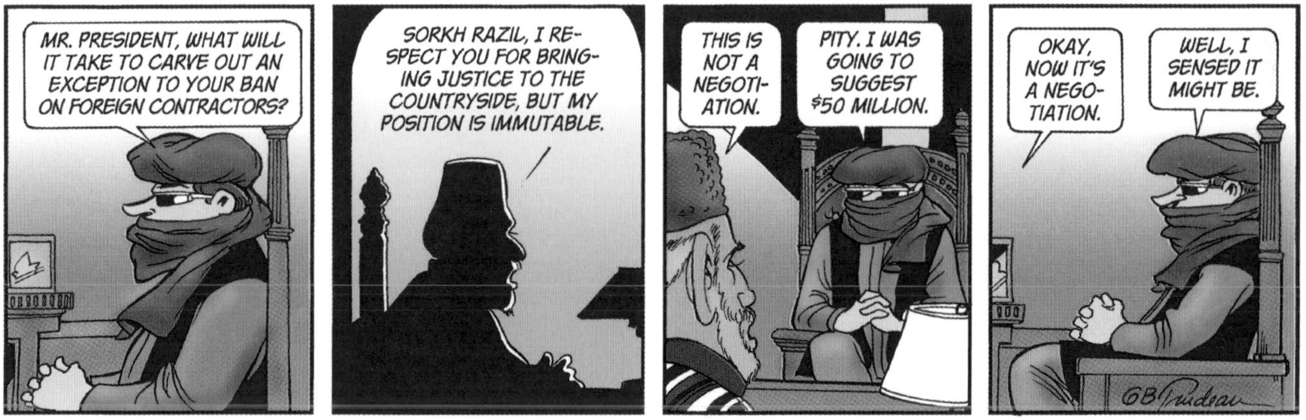
MR. PRESIDENT, WHAT WILL IT TAKE TO CARVE OUT AN EXCEPTION TO YOUR BAN ON FOREIGN CONTRACTORS?
SORKH RAZIL, I RESPECT YOU FOR BRINGING JUSTICE TO THE COUNTRYSIDE, BUT MY POSITION IS IMMUTABLE.
THIS IS NOT A NEGOTIATION.
PITY. I WAS GOING TO SUGGEST $50 MILLION.
OKAY, NOW IT'S A NEGOTIATION.
WELL, I SENSED IT MIGHT BE.
GB Trudeau

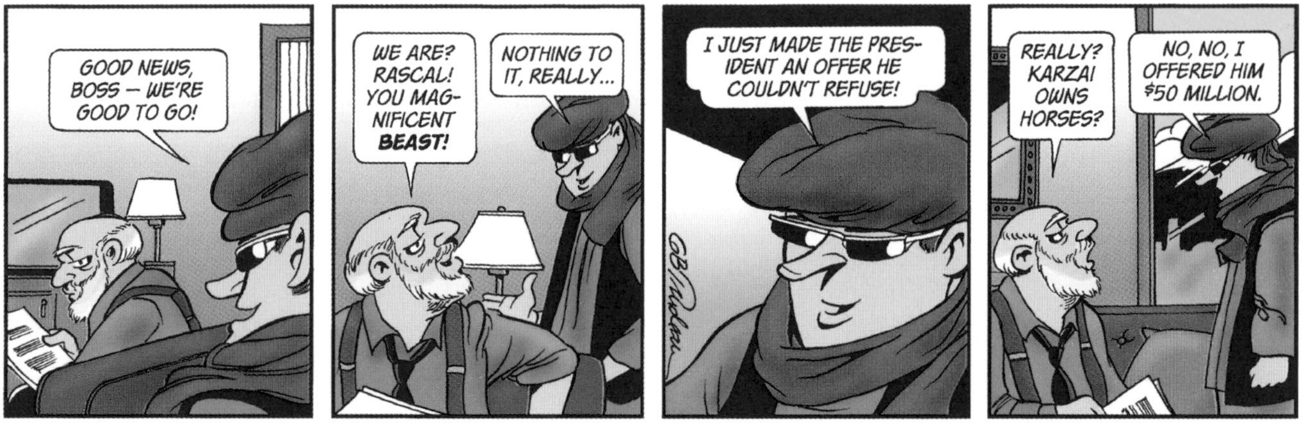
GOOD NEWS, BOSS — WE'RE GOOD TO GO!
WE ARE? RASCAL! YOU MAGNIFICENT **BEAST!**
NOTHING TO IT, REALLY...
I JUST MADE THE PRESIDENT AN OFFER HE COULDN'T REFUSE!
GB Trudeau
REALLY? KARZAI OWNS HORSES?
NO, NO, I OFFERED HIM $50 MILLION.

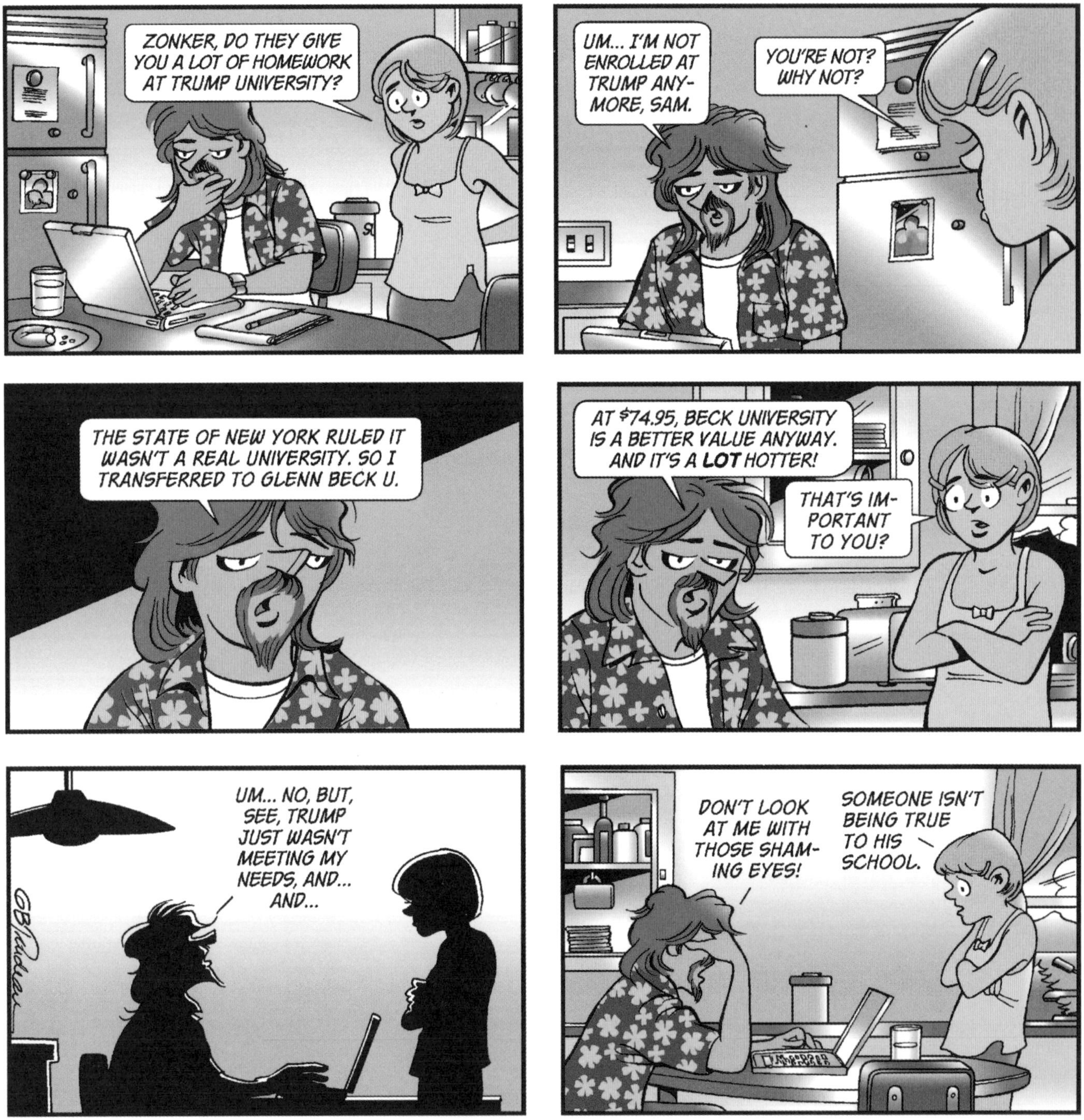
ZONKER, DO THEY GIVE YOU A LOT OF HOMEWORK AT TRUMP UNIVERSITY?
UM... I'M NOT ENROLLED AT TRUMP ANYMORE, SAM.
YOU'RE NOT? WHY NOT?
THE STATE OF NEW YORK RULED IT WASN'T A REAL UNIVERSITY. SO I TRANSFERRED TO GLENN BECK U.
AT $74.95, BECK UNIVERSITY IS A BETTER VALUE ANYWAY. AND IT'S A LOT HOTTER!
THAT'S IMPORTANT TO YOU?
UM... NO, BUT, SEE, TRUMP JUST WASN'T MEETING MY NEEDS, AND... AND...
DON'T LOOK AT ME WITH THOSE SHAMING EYES!
SOMEONE ISN'T BEING TRUE TO HIS SCHOOL.

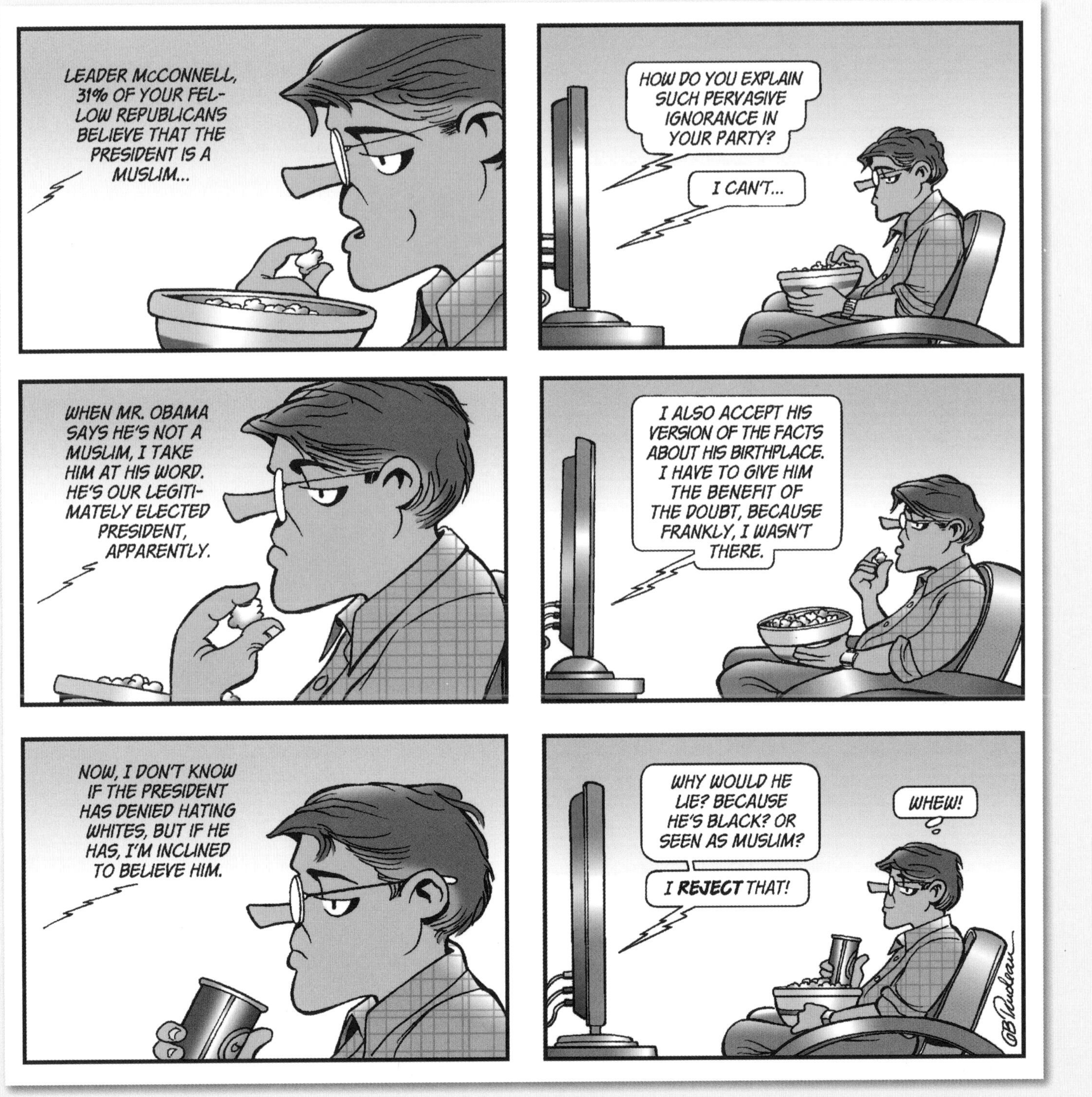
LEADER McCONNELL, 31% OF YOUR FEL-LOW REPUBLICANS BELIEVE THAT THE PRESIDENT IS A MUSLIM...
HOW DO YOU EXPLAIN SUCH PERVASIVE IGNORANCE IN YOUR PARTY?
I CAN'T...
WHEN MR. OBAMA SAYS HE'S NOT A MUSLIM, I TAKE HIM AT HIS WORD. HE'S OUR LEGITI-MATELY ELECTED PRESIDENT, APPARENTLY.
I ALSO ACCEPT HIS VERSION OF THE FACTS ABOUT HIS BIRTHPLACE. I HAVE TO GIVE HIM THE BENEFIT OF THE DOUBT, BECAUSE FRANKLY, I WASN'T THERE.
NOW, I DON'T KNOW IF THE PRESIDENT HAS DENIED HATING WHITES, BUT IF HE HAS, I'M INCLINED TO BELIEVE HIM.
WHY WOULD HE LIE? BECAUSE HE'S BLACK? OR SEEN AS MUSLIM?
I **REJECT** THAT!
WHEW!

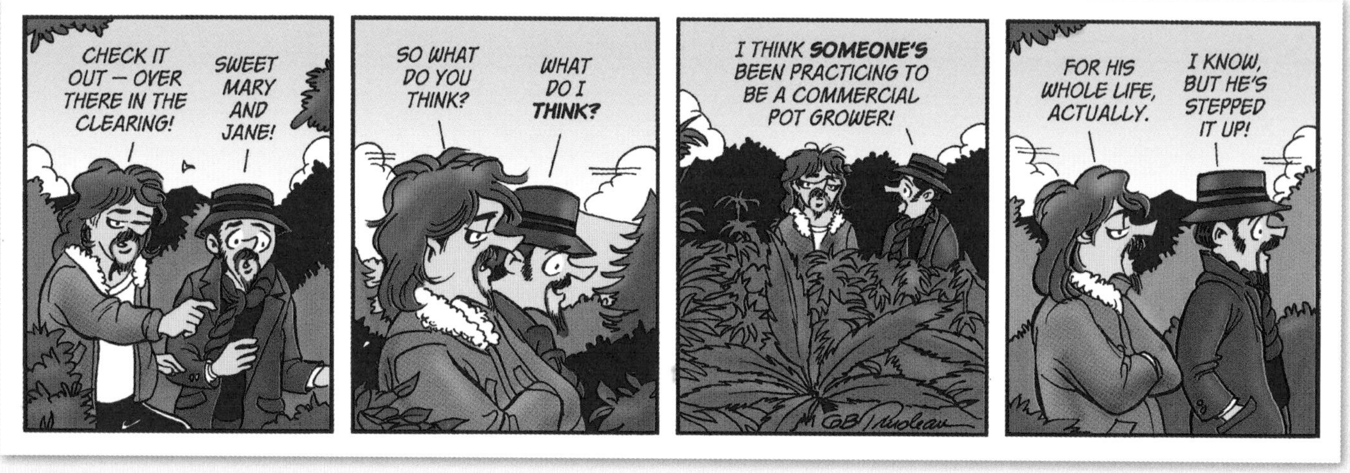
CHECK IT OUT — OVER THERE IN THE CLEARING!
SWEET MARY AND JANE!
SO WHAT DO YOU THINK?
WHAT DO I **THINK?**
I THINK **SOMEONE'S** BEEN PRACTICING TO BE A COMMERCIAL POT GROWER!
FOR HIS WHOLE LIFE, ACTUALLY.
I KNOW, BUT HE'S STEPPED IT UP!

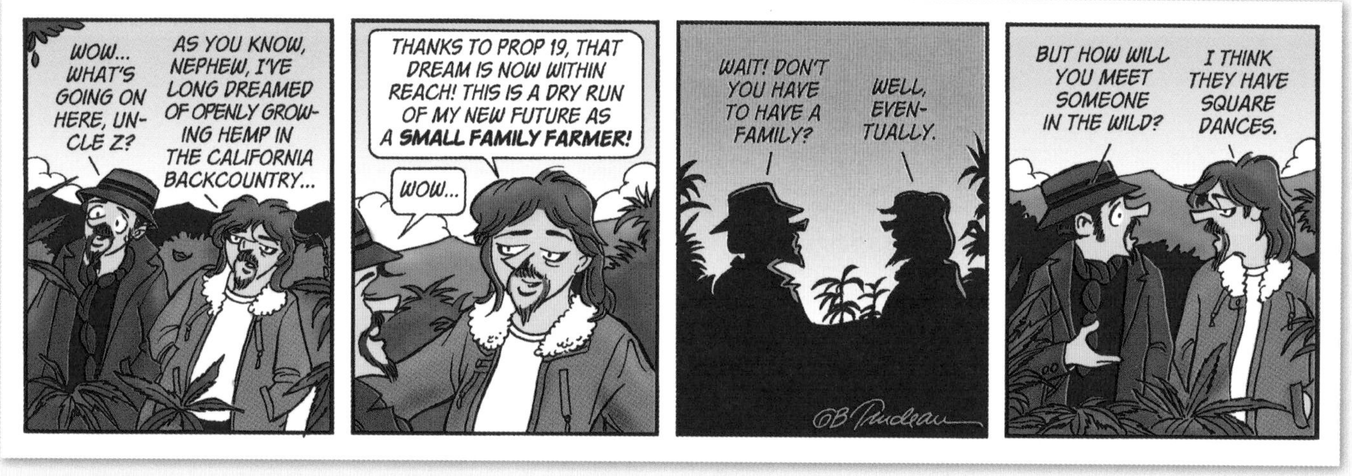
WOW... WHAT'S GOING ON HERE, UNCLE Z?
AS YOU KNOW, NEPHEW, I'VE LONG DREAMED OF OPENLY GROWING HEMP IN THE CALIFORNIA BACKCOUNTRY...
THANKS TO PROP 19, THAT DREAM IS NOW WITHIN REACH! THIS IS A DRY RUN OF MY NEW FUTURE AS A **SMALL FAMILY FARMER!**
WOW...
WAIT! DON'T YOU HAVE TO HAVE A FAMILY?
WELL, EVENTUALLY.
BUT HOW WILL YOU MEET SOMEONE IN THE WILD?
I THINK THEY HAVE SQUARE DANCES.

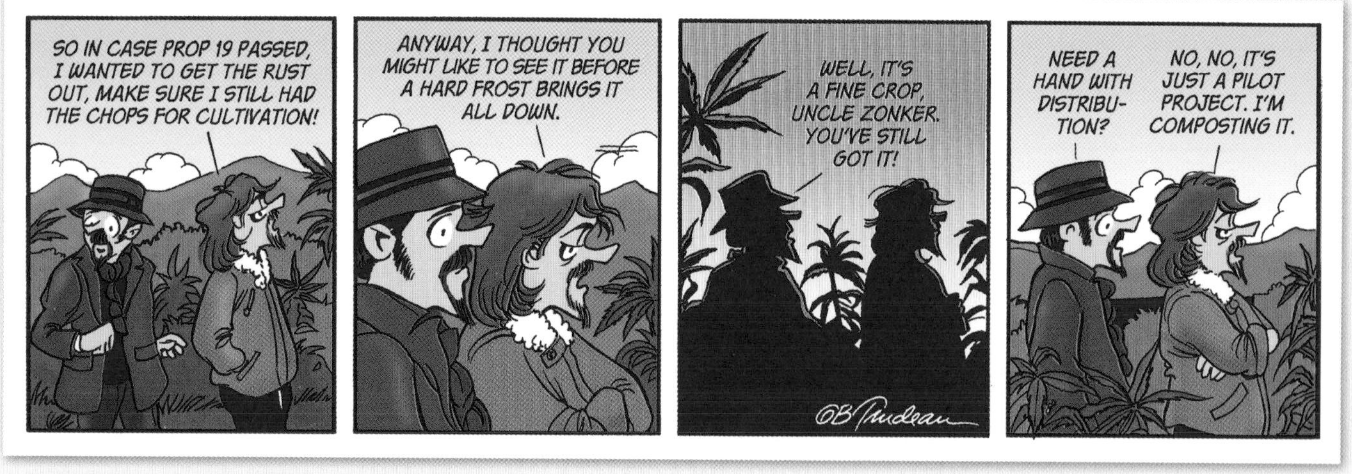
SO IN CASE PROP 19 PASSED, I WANTED TO GET THE RUST OUT, MAKE SURE I STILL HAD THE CHOPS FOR CULTIVATION!
ANYWAY, I THOUGHT YOU MIGHT LIKE TO SEE IT BEFORE A HARD FROST BRINGS IT ALL DOWN.
WELL, IT'S A FINE CROP, UNCLE ZONKER. YOU'VE STILL GOT IT!
NEED A HAND WITH DISTRIBUTION?
NO, NO, IT'S JUST A PILOT PROJECT. I'M COMPOSTING IT.

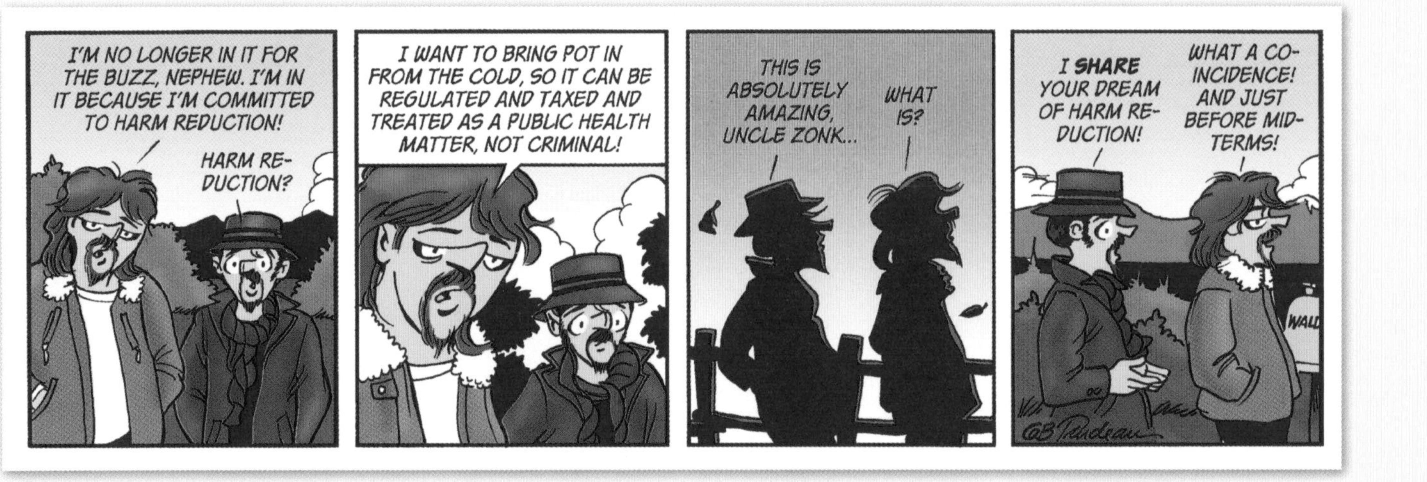
I'M NO LONGER IN IT FOR THE BUZZ, NEPHEW. I'M IN IT BECAUSE I'M COMMITTED TO HARM REDUCTION!
HARM REDUCTION?
I WANT TO BRING POT IN FROM THE COLD, SO IT CAN BE REGULATED AND TAXED AND TREATED AS A PUBLIC HEALTH MATTER, NOT CRIMINAL!
THIS IS ABSOLUTELY AMAZING, UNCLE ZONK...
WHAT IS?
I **SHARE** YOUR DREAM OF HARM REDUCTION!
WHAT A COINCIDENCE! AND JUST BEFORE MIDTERMS!
©B Trudeau

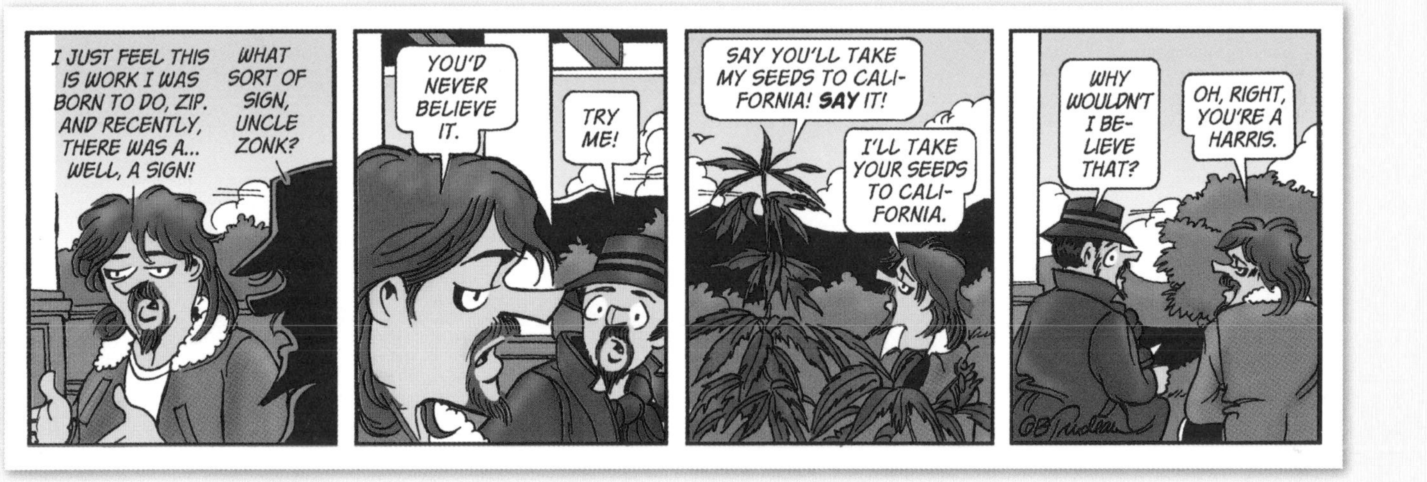
I JUST FEEL THIS IS WORK I WAS BORN TO DO, ZIP. AND RECENTLY, THERE WAS A... WELL, A SIGN!
WHAT SORT OF SIGN, UNCLE ZONK?
YOU'D NEVER BELIEVE IT.
TRY ME!
SAY YOU'LL TAKE MY SEEDS TO CALIFORNIA! **SAY** IT!
I'LL TAKE YOUR SEEDS TO CALIFORNIA.
WHY WOULDN'T I BELIEVE THAT?
OH, RIGHT, YOU'RE A HARRIS.
©B Trudeau

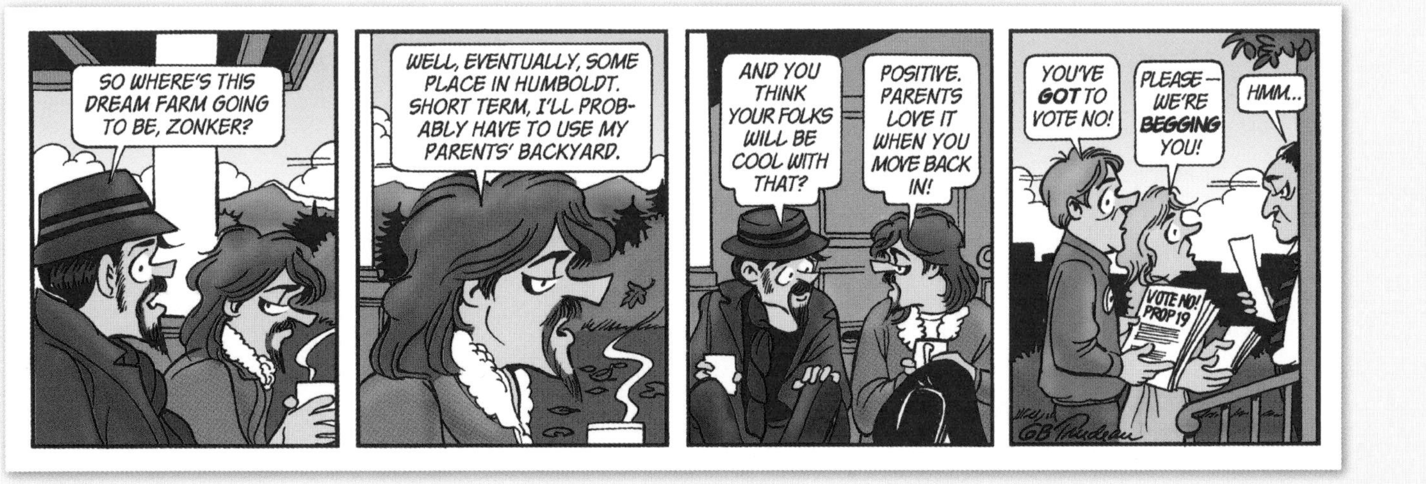
SO WHERE'S THIS DREAM FARM GOING TO BE, ZONKER?
WELL, EVENTUALLY, SOME PLACE IN HUMBOLDT. SHORT TERM, I'LL PROBABLY HAVE TO USE MY PARENTS' BACKYARD.
AND YOU THINK YOUR FOLKS WILL BE COOL WITH THAT?
POSITIVE. PARENTS LOVE IT WHEN YOU MOVE BACK IN!
YOU'VE **GOT** TO VOTE NO!
PLEASE— WE'RE **BEGGING** YOU!
HMM...
VOTE NO! PROP 19
©B Trudeau

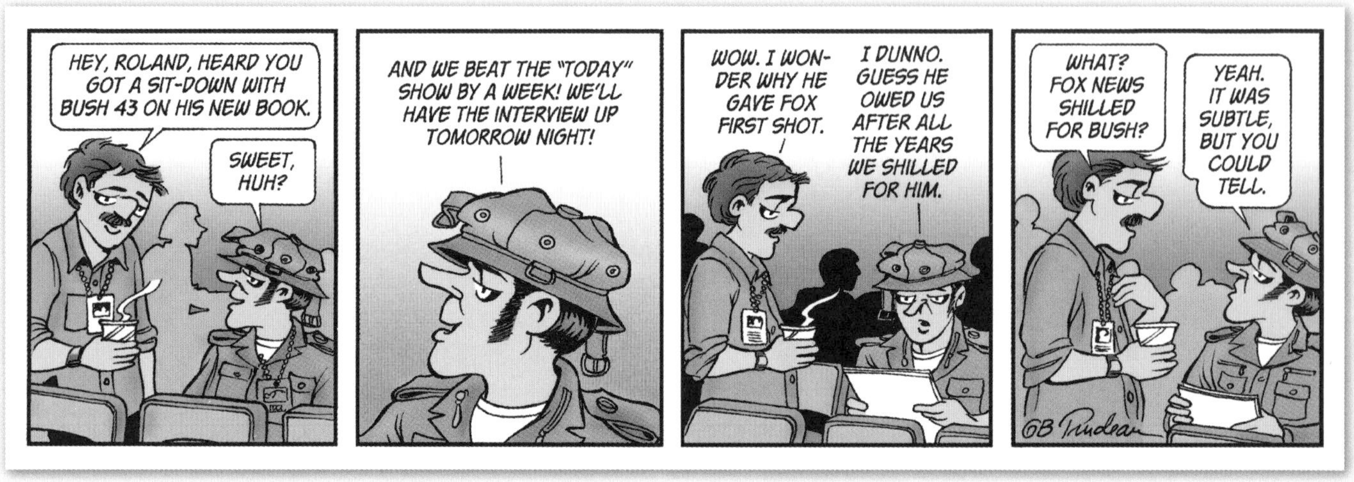
HEY, ROLAND, HEARD YOU GOT A SIT-DOWN WITH BUSH 43 ON HIS NEW BOOK.
SWEET, HUH?
AND WE BEAT THE "TODAY" SHOW BY A WEEK! WE'LL HAVE THE INTERVIEW UP TOMORROW NIGHT!
WOW. I WONDER WHY HE GAVE FOX FIRST SHOT.
I DUNNO. GUESS HE OWED US AFTER ALL THE YEARS WE SHILLED FOR HIM.
WHAT? FOX NEWS SHILLED FOR BUSH?
YEAH. IT WAS SUBTLE, BUT YOU COULD TELL.

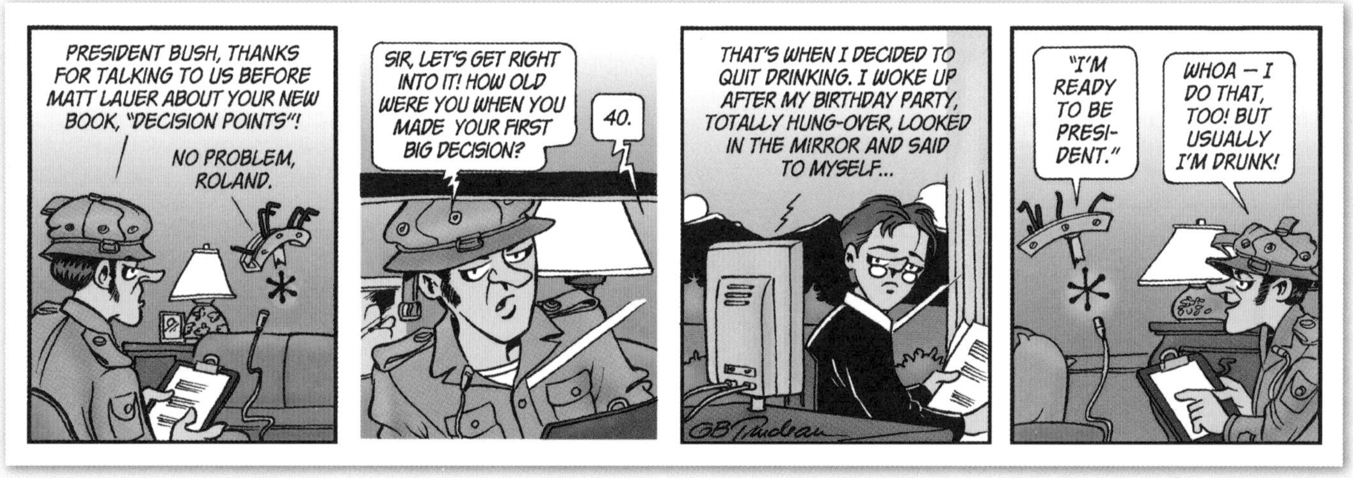
PRESIDENT BUSH, THANKS FOR TALKING TO US BEFORE MATT LAUER ABOUT YOUR NEW BOOK, "DECISION POINTS"!
NO PROBLEM, ROLAND.
SIR, LET'S GET RIGHT INTO IT! HOW OLD WERE YOU WHEN YOU MADE YOUR FIRST BIG DECISION?
40.
THAT'S WHEN I DECIDED TO QUIT DRINKING. I WOKE UP AFTER MY BIRTHDAY PARTY, TOTALLY HUNG-OVER, LOOKED IN THE MIRROR AND SAID TO MYSELF...
"I'M READY TO BE PRESIDENT."
WHOA — I DO THAT, TOO! BUT USUALLY I'M DRUNK!

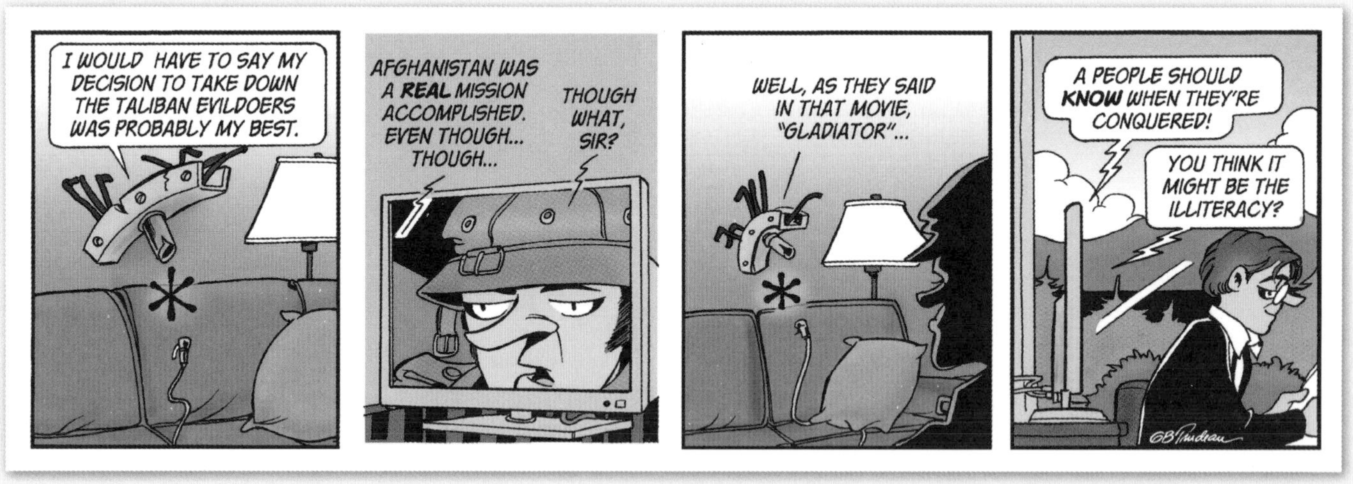
I WOULD HAVE TO SAY MY DECISION TO TAKE DOWN THE TALIBAN EVILDOERS WAS PROBABLY MY BEST.
AFGHANISTAN WAS A **REAL** MISSION ACCOMPLISHED. EVEN THOUGH... THOUGH...
THOUGH WHAT, SIR?
WELL, AS THEY SAID IN THAT MOVIE, "GLADIATOR"...
A PEOPLE SHOULD **KNOW** WHEN THEY'RE CONQUERED!
YOU THINK IT MIGHT BE THE ILLITERACY?

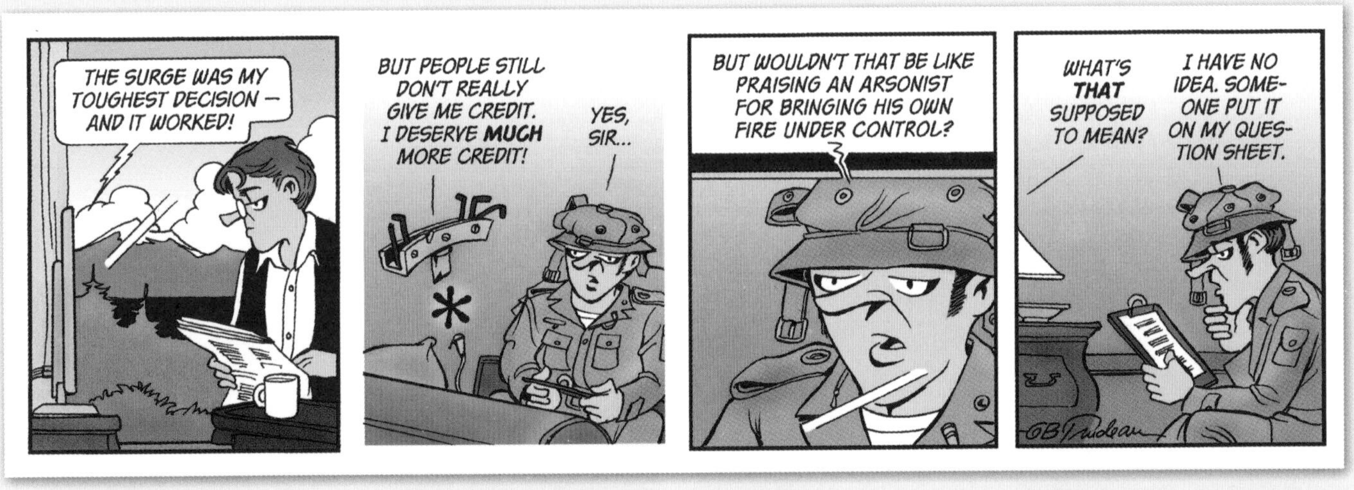
THE SURGE WAS MY TOUGHEST DECISION — AND IT WORKED!
BUT PEOPLE STILL DON'T REALLY GIVE ME CREDIT. I DESERVE MUCH MORE CREDIT!
YES, SIR...
BUT WOULDN'T THAT BE LIKE PRAISING AN ARSONIST FOR BRINGING HIS OWN FIRE UNDER CONTROL?
WHAT'S THAT SUPPOSED TO MEAN?
I HAVE NO IDEA. SOMEONE PUT IT ON MY QUESTION SHEET.

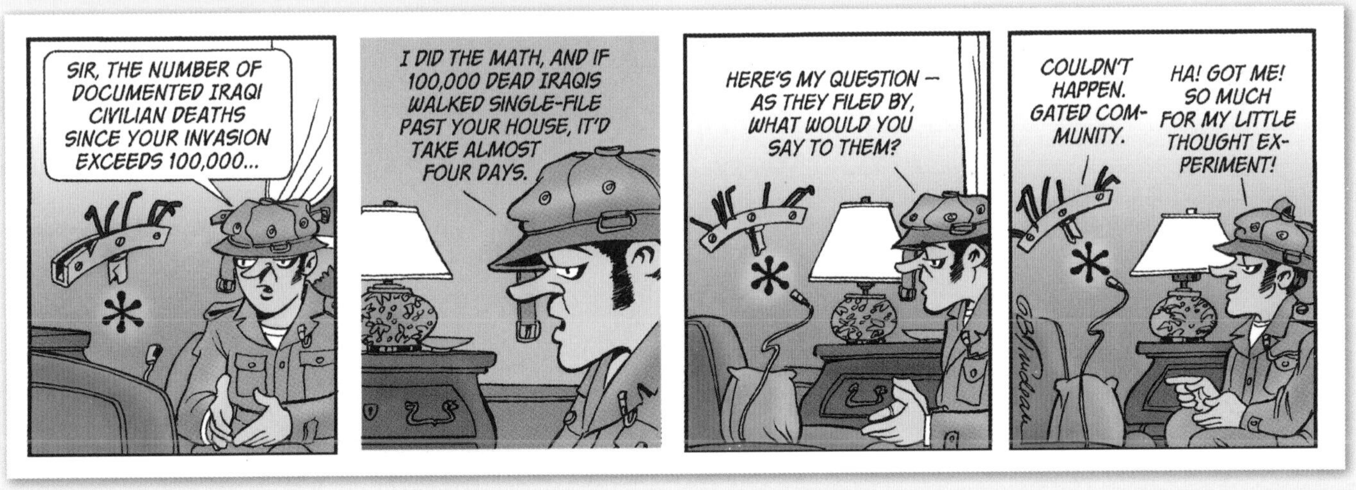
SIR, THE NUMBER OF DOCUMENTED IRAQI CIVILIAN DEATHS SINCE YOUR INVASION EXCEEDS 100,000...
I DID THE MATH, AND IF 100,000 DEAD IRAQIS WALKED SINGLE-FILE PAST YOUR HOUSE, IT'D TAKE ALMOST FOUR DAYS.
HERE'S MY QUESTION — AS THEY FILED BY, WHAT WOULD YOU SAY TO THEM?
COULDN'T HAPPEN. GATED COMMUNITY.
HA! GOT ME! SO MUCH FOR MY LITTLE THOUGHT EXPERIMENT!

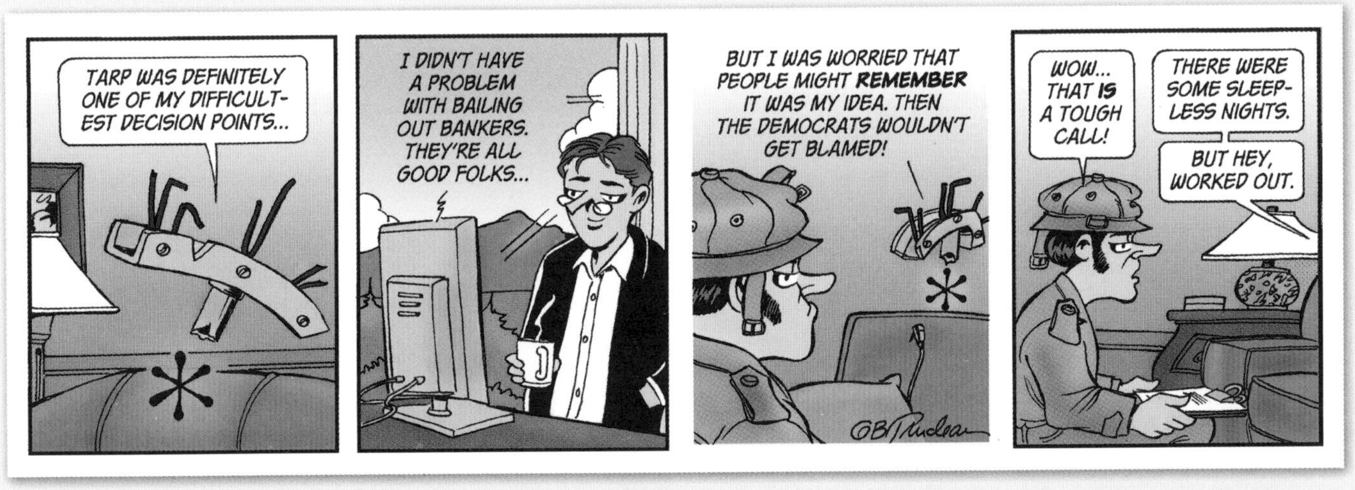
TARP WAS DEFINITELY ONE OF MY DIFFICULTEST DECISION POINTS...
I DIDN'T HAVE A PROBLEM WITH BAILING OUT BANKERS. THEY'RE ALL GOOD FOLKS...
BUT I WAS WORRIED THAT PEOPLE MIGHT REMEMBER IT WAS MY IDEA. THEN THE DEMOCRATS WOULDN'T GET BLAMED!
WOW... THAT IS A TOUGH CALL!
THERE WERE SOME SLEEPLESS NIGHTS.
BUT HEY, WORKED OUT.

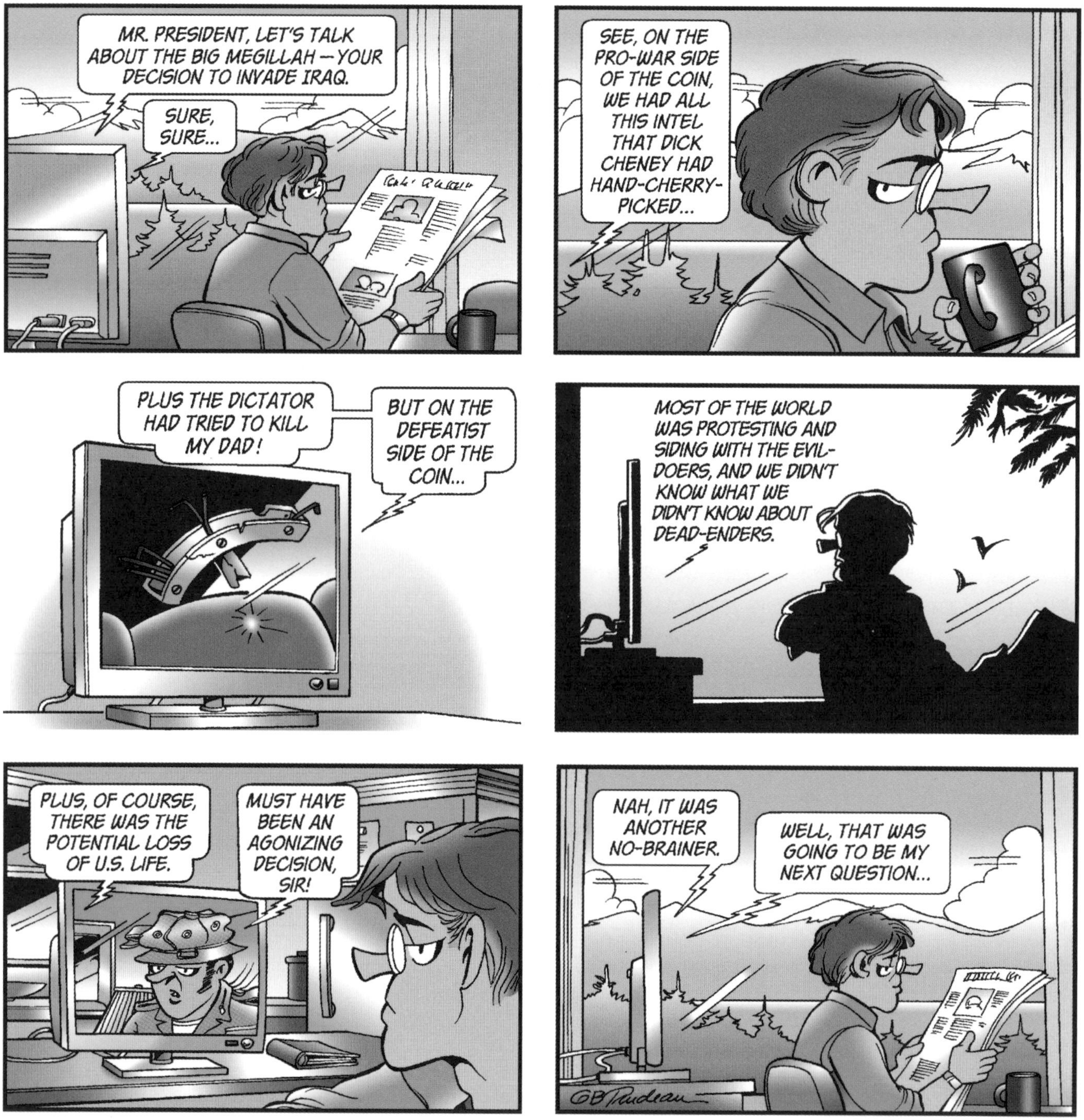
MR. PRESIDENT, LET'S TALK ABOUT THE BIG MEGILLAH — YOUR DECISION TO INVADE IRAQ.
SURE, SURE...
SEE, ON THE PRO-WAR SIDE OF THE COIN, WE HAD ALL THIS INTEL THAT DICK CHENEY HAD HAND-CHERRY-PICKED...
PLUS THE DICTATOR HAD TRIED TO KILL MY DAD!
BUT ON THE DEFEATIST SIDE OF THE COIN...
MOST OF THE WORLD WAS PROTESTING AND SIDING WITH THE EVIL-DOERS, AND WE DIDN'T KNOW WHAT WE DIDN'T KNOW ABOUT DEAD-ENDERS.
PLUS, OF COURSE, THERE WAS THE POTENTIAL LOSS OF U.S. LIFE.
MUST HAVE BEEN AN AGONIZING DECISION, SIR!
NAH, IT WAS ANOTHER NO-BRAINER.
WELL, THAT WAS GOING TO BE MY NEXT QUESTION...
GBTrudeau

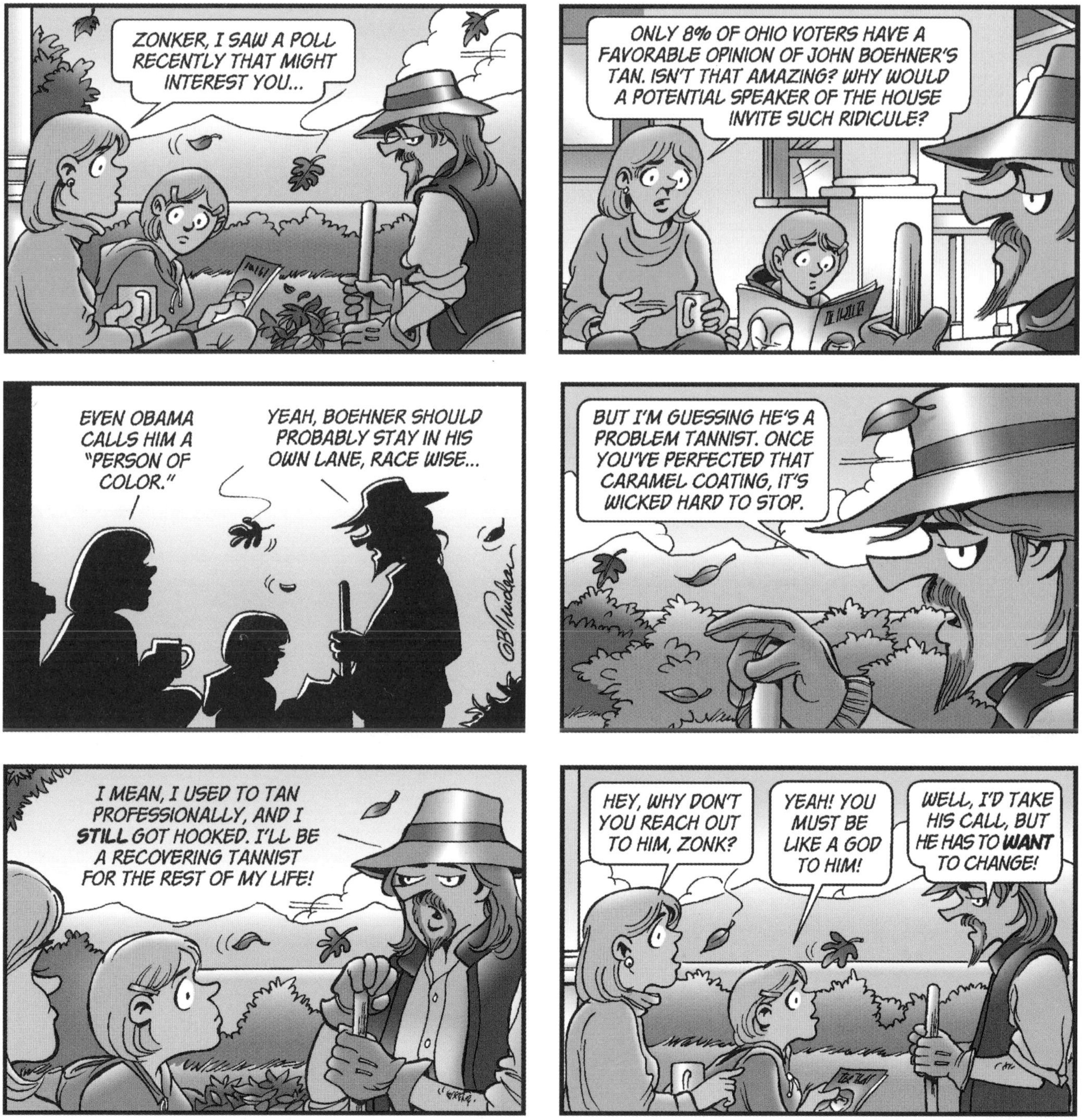
ZONKER, I SAW A POLL RECENTLY THAT MIGHT INTEREST YOU...
ONLY 8% OF OHIO VOTERS HAVE A FAVORABLE OPINION OF JOHN BOEHNER'S TAN. ISN'T THAT AMAZING? WHY WOULD A POTENTIAL SPEAKER OF THE HOUSE INVITE SUCH RIDICULE?
EVEN OBAMA CALLS HIM A "PERSON OF COLOR."
YEAH, BOEHNER SHOULD PROBABLY STAY IN HIS OWN LANE, RACE WISE...
BUT I'M GUESSING HE'S A PROBLEM TANNIST. ONCE YOU'VE PERFECTED THAT CARAMEL COATING, IT'S WICKED HARD TO STOP.
I MEAN, I USED TO TAN PROFESSIONALLY, AND I **STILL** GOT HOOKED. I'LL BE A RECOVERING TANNIST FOR THE REST OF MY LIFE!
HEY, WHY DON'T YOU REACH OUT TO HIM, ZONK?
YEAH! YOU MUST BE LIKE A GOD TO HIM!
WELL, I'D TAKE HIS CALL, BUT HE HAS TO **WANT** TO CHANGE!

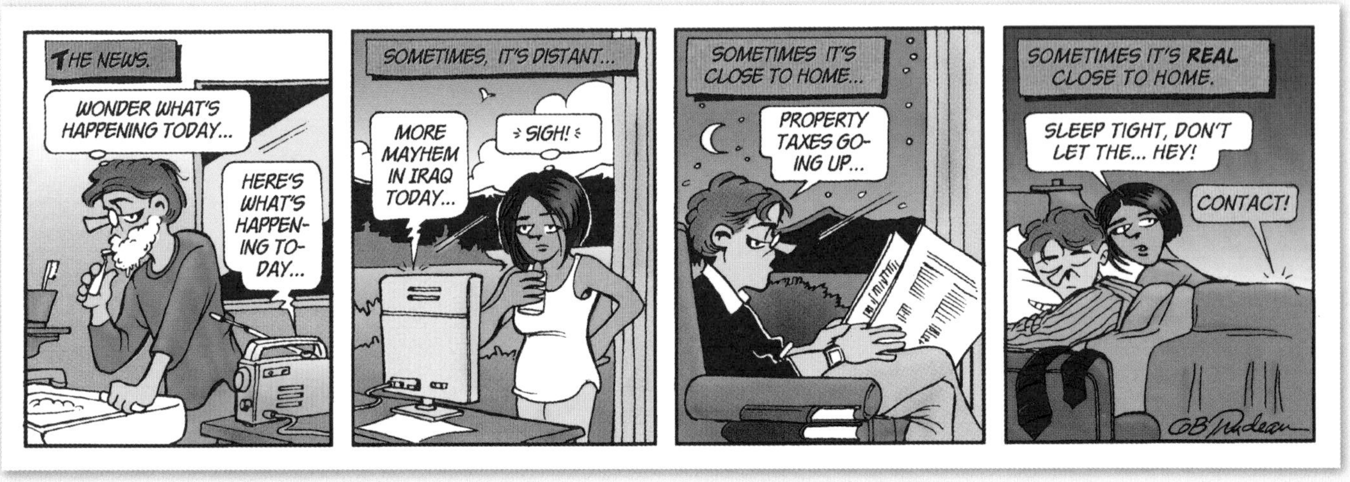
THE NEWS.
WONDER WHAT'S HAPPENING TODAY...
HERE'S WHAT'S HAPPENING TODAY...
SOMETIMES, IT'S DISTANT...
MORE MAYHEM IN IRAQ TODAY...
SIGH!
SOMETIMES IT'S CLOSE TO HOME...
PROPERTY TAXES GOING UP...
SOMETIMES IT'S REAL CLOSE TO HOME.
SLEEP TIGHT, DON'T LET THE... HEY!
CONTACT!
GB Trudeau

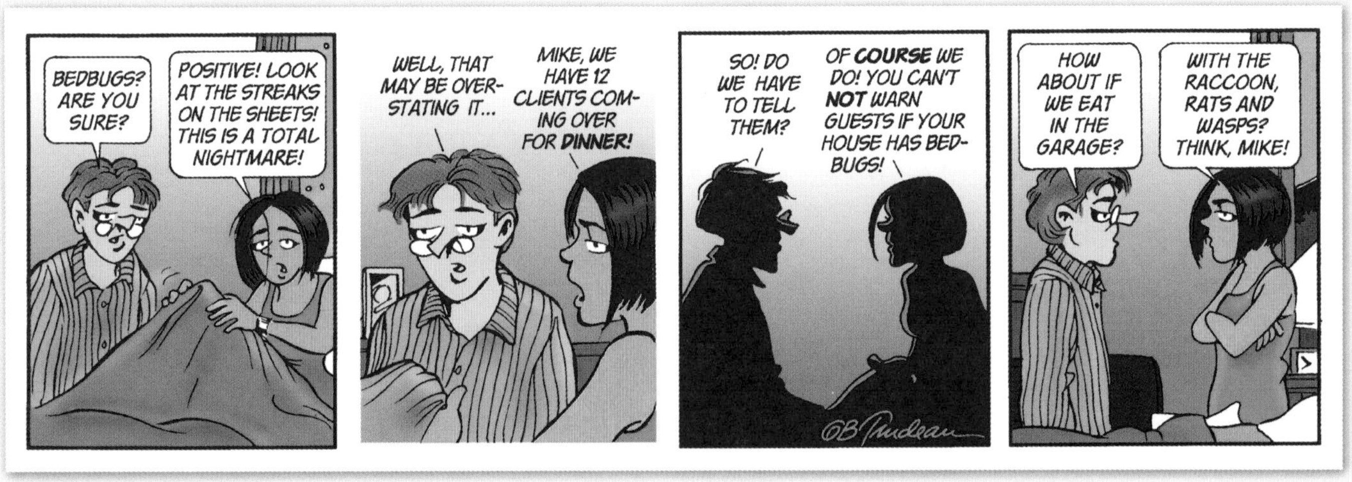
BEDBUGS? ARE YOU SURE?
POSITIVE! LOOK AT THE STREAKS ON THE SHEETS! THIS IS A TOTAL NIGHTMARE!
WELL, THAT MAY BE OVERSTATING IT...
MIKE, WE HAVE 12 CLIENTS COMING OVER FOR DINNER!
SO! DO WE HAVE TO TELL THEM?
OF COURSE WE DO! YOU CAN'T NOT WARN GUESTS IF YOUR HOUSE HAS BEDBUGS!
GB Trudeau
HOW ABOUT IF WE EAT IN THE GARAGE?
WITH THE RACCOON, RATS AND WASPS? THINK, MIKE!

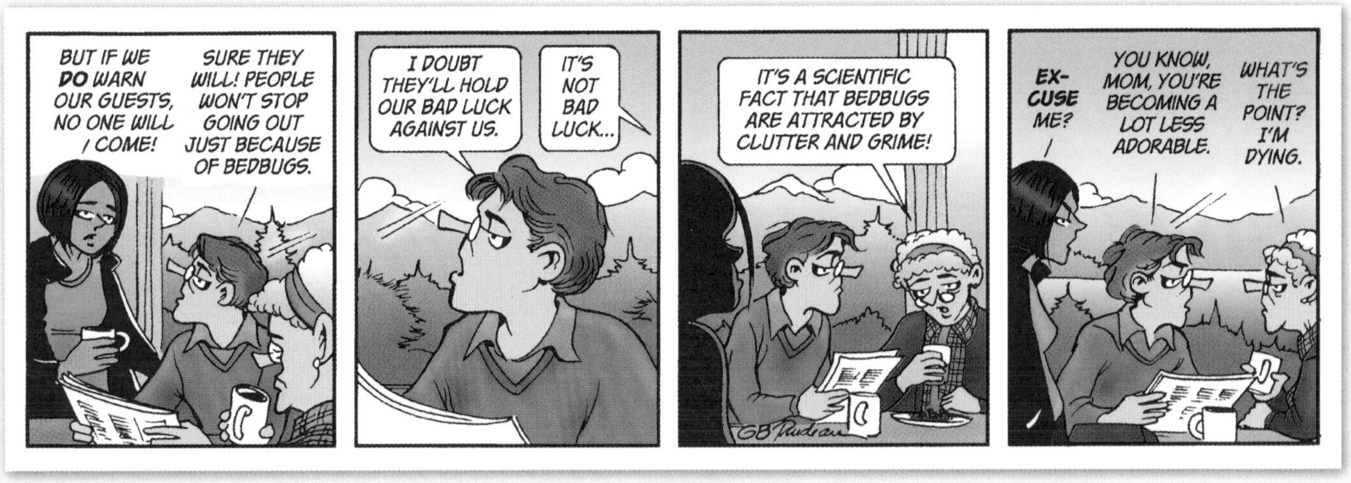
BUT IF WE DO WARN OUR GUESTS, NO ONE WILL COME!
SURE THEY WILL! PEOPLE WON'T STOP GOING OUT JUST BECAUSE OF BEDBUGS.
I DOUBT THEY'LL HOLD OUR BAD LUCK AGAINST US.
IT'S NOT BAD LUCK...
IT'S A SCIENTIFIC FACT THAT BEDBUGS ARE ATTRACTED BY CLUTTER AND GRIME!
GB Trudeau
EXCUSE ME?
YOU KNOW, MOM, YOU'RE BECOMING A LOT LESS ADORABLE.
WHAT'S THE POINT? I'M DYING.

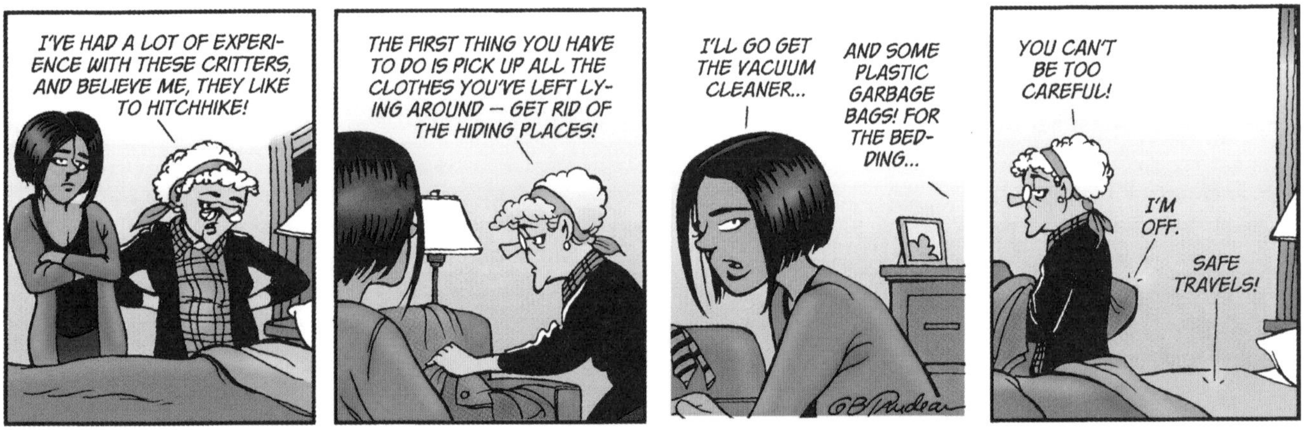
I'VE HAD A LOT OF EXPERIENCE WITH THESE CRITTERS, AND BELIEVE ME, THEY LIKE TO HITCHHIKE!
THE FIRST THING YOU HAVE TO DO IS PICK UP ALL THE CLOTHES YOU'VE LEFT LYING AROUND — GET RID OF THE HIDING PLACES!
I'LL GO GET THE VACUUM CLEANER...
AND SOME PLASTIC GARBAGE BAGS! FOR THE BEDDING...
YOU CAN'T BE TOO CAREFUL!
I'M OFF.
SAFE TRAVELS!

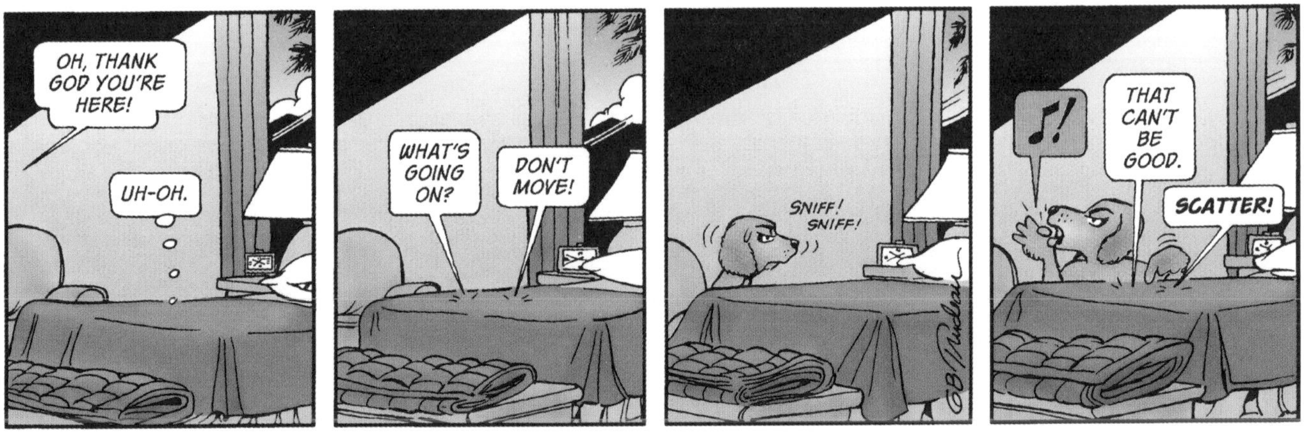
OH, THANK GOD YOU'RE HERE!
UH-OH.
WHAT'S GOING ON?
DON'T MOVE!
SNIFF! SNIFF!
♪!
THAT CAN'T BE GOOD.
SCATTER!

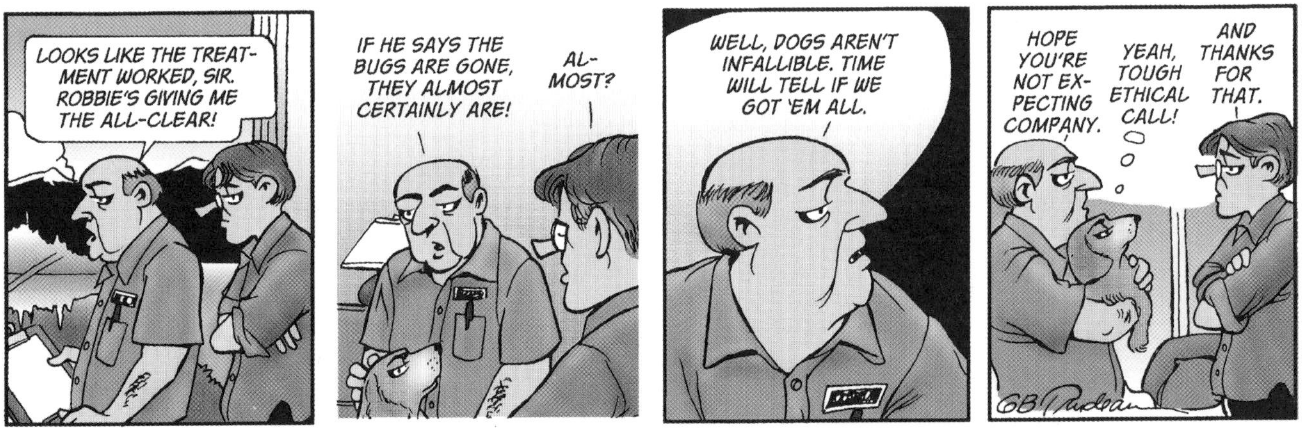
LOOKS LIKE THE TREATMENT WORKED, SIR. ROBBIE'S GIVING ME THE ALL-CLEAR!
IF HE SAYS THE BUGS ARE GONE, THEY ALMOST CERTAINLY ARE!
ALMOST?
WELL, DOGS AREN'T INFALLIBLE. TIME WILL TELL IF WE GOT 'EM ALL.
HOPE YOU'RE NOT EXPECTING COMPANY.
YEAH, TOUGH ETHICAL CALL!
AND THANKS FOR THAT.

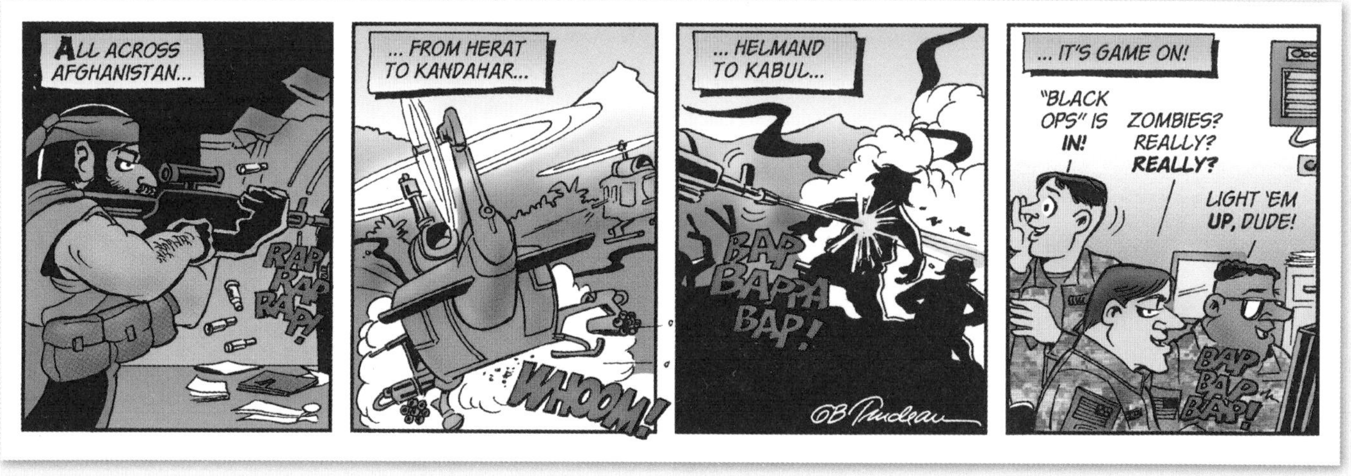
ALL ACROSS AFGHANISTAN...
RAP RAP RAP!
... FROM HERAT TO KANDAHAR...
WHOOM!
... HELMAND TO KABUL...
BAP BAPPA BAP!
... IT'S GAME ON!
"BLACK OPS" IS IN!
ZOMBIES? REALLY? REALLY?
LIGHT 'EM UP, DUDE!
BAP BAP BAP!

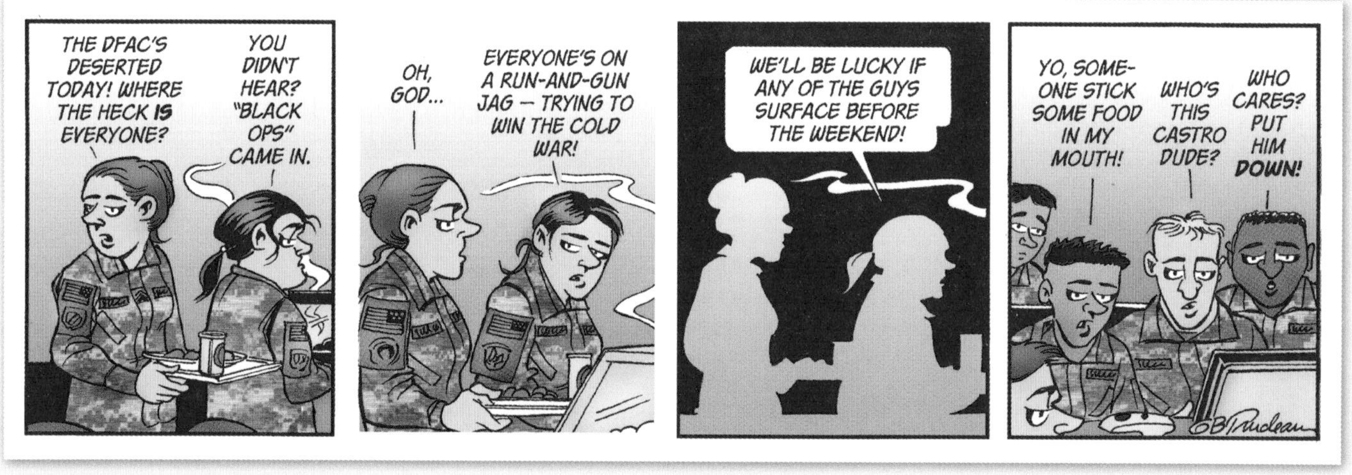
THE DFAC'S DESERTED TODAY! WHERE THE HECK IS EVERYONE?
YOU DIDN'T HEAR? "BLACK OPS" CAME IN.
OH, GOD...
EVERYONE'S ON A RUN-AND-GUN JAG — TRYING TO WIN THE COLD WAR!
WE'LL BE LUCKY IF ANY OF THE GUYS SURFACE BEFORE THE WEEKEND!
YO, SOME-ONE STICK SOME FOOD IN MY MOUTH!
WHO'S THIS CASTRO DUDE?
WHO CARES? PUT HIM DOWN!

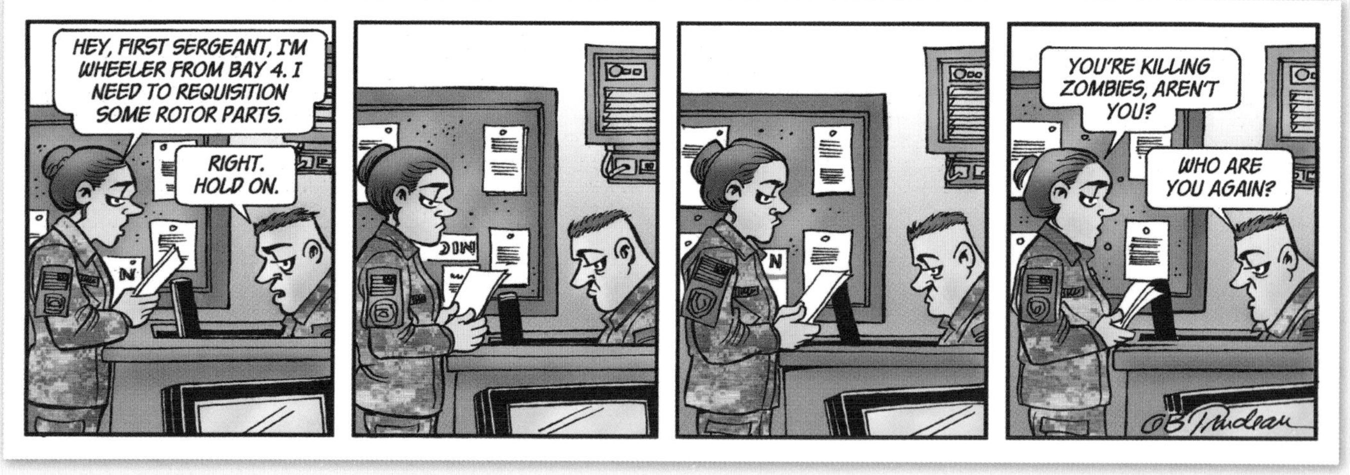
HEY, FIRST SERGEANT, I'M WHEELER FROM BAY 4. I NEED TO REQUISITION SOME ROTOR PARTS.
RIGHT. HOLD ON.
YOU'RE KILLING ZOMBIES, AREN'T YOU?
WHO ARE YOU AGAIN?

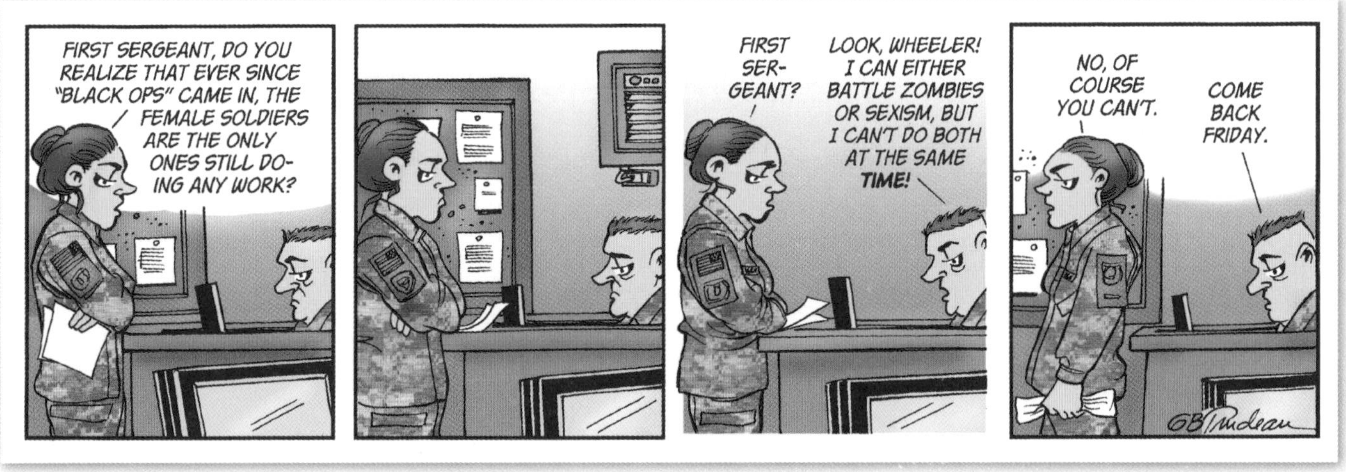
FIRST SERGEANT, DO YOU REALIZE THAT EVER SINCE "BLACK OPS" CAME IN, THE FEMALE SOLDIERS ARE THE ONLY ONES STILL DOING ANY WORK?
FIRST SERGEANT?
LOOK, WHEELER! I CAN EITHER BATTLE ZOMBIES OR SEXISM, BUT I CAN'T DO BOTH AT THE SAME **TIME!**
NO, OF COURSE YOU CAN'T.
COME BACK FRIDAY.

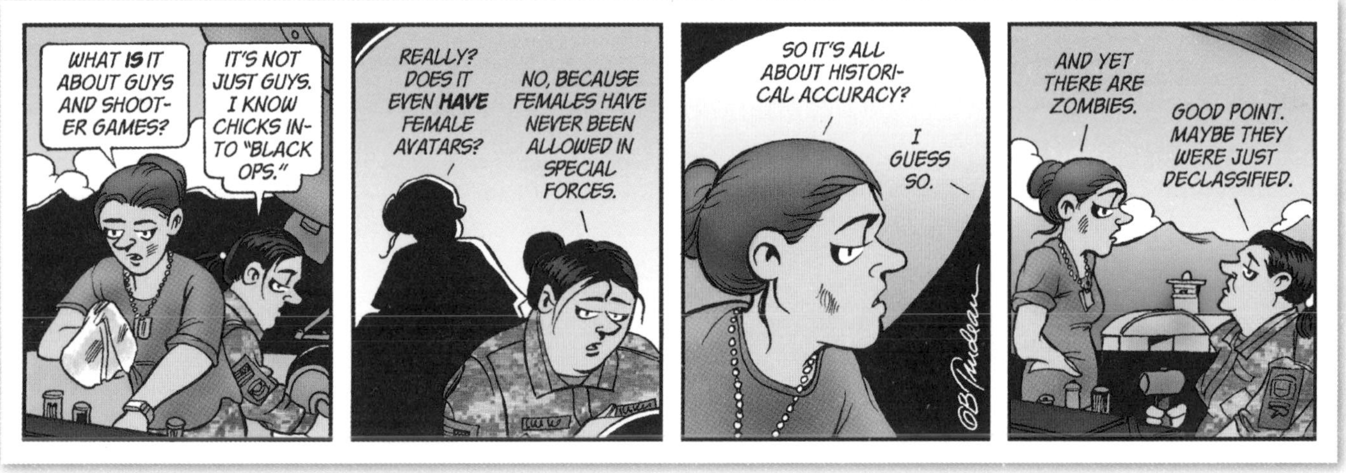
WHAT **IS** IT ABOUT GUYS AND SHOOTER GAMES?
IT'S NOT JUST GUYS. I KNOW CHICKS INTO "BLACK OPS."
REALLY? DOES IT EVEN **HAVE** FEMALE AVATARS?
NO, BECAUSE FEMALES HAVE NEVER BEEN ALLOWED IN SPECIAL FORCES.
SO IT'S ALL ABOUT HISTORICAL ACCURACY?
I GUESS SO.
AND YET THERE ARE ZOMBIES.
GOOD POINT. MAYBE THEY WERE JUST DECLASSIFIED.

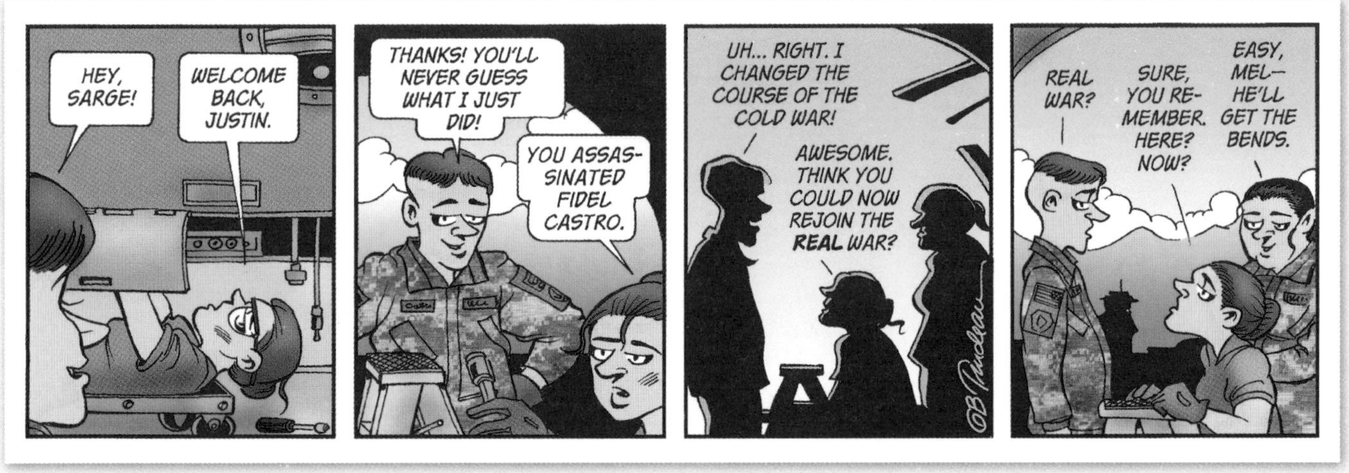
HEY, SARGE!
WELCOME BACK, JUSTIN.
THANKS! YOU'LL NEVER GUESS WHAT I JUST DID!
YOU ASSASSINATED FIDEL CASTRO.
UH... RIGHT. I CHANGED THE COURSE OF THE COLD WAR!
AWESOME. THINK YOU COULD NOW REJOIN THE **REAL** WAR?
REAL WAR?
SURE, YOU REMEMBER. HERE? NOW?
EASY, MEL— HE'LL GET THE BENDS.

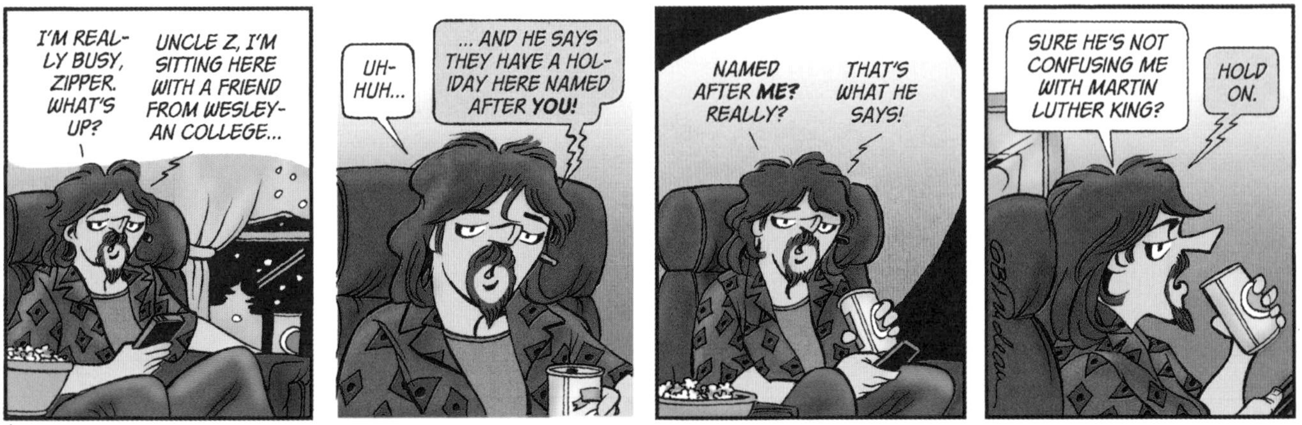
I'M REALLY BUSY, ZIPPER. WHAT'S UP?
UNCLE Z, I'M SITTING HERE WITH A FRIEND FROM WESLEYAN COLLEGE...
UH-HUH...
... AND HE SAYS THEY HAVE A HOLIDAY HERE NAMED AFTER **YOU!**
NAMED AFTER **ME?** REALLY?
THAT'S WHAT HE SAYS!
SURE HE'S NOT CONFUSING ME WITH MARTIN LUTHER KING?
HOLD ON.
GBTrudeau

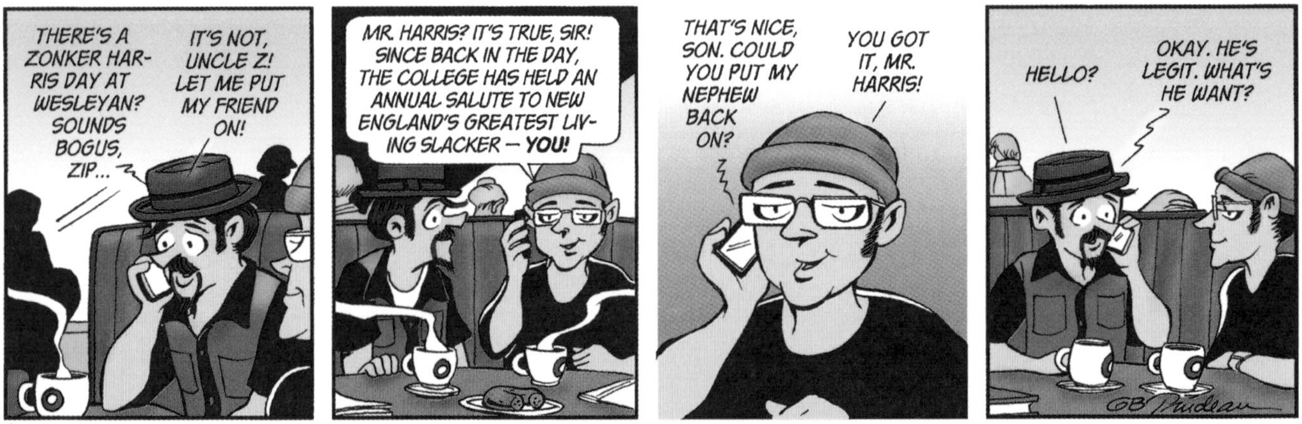
THERE'S A ZONKER HARRIS DAY AT WESLEYAN? SOUNDS BOGUS, ZIP...
IT'S NOT, UNCLE Z! LET ME PUT MY FRIEND ON!
MR. HARRIS? IT'S TRUE, SIR! SINCE BACK IN THE DAY, THE COLLEGE HAS HELD AN ANNUAL SALUTE TO NEW ENGLAND'S GREATEST LIVING SLACKER — **YOU!**
THAT'S NICE, SON. COULD YOU PUT MY NEPHEW BACK ON?
YOU GOT IT, MR. HARRIS!
HELLO?
OKAY. HE'S LEGIT. WHAT'S HE WANT?
GBTrudeau

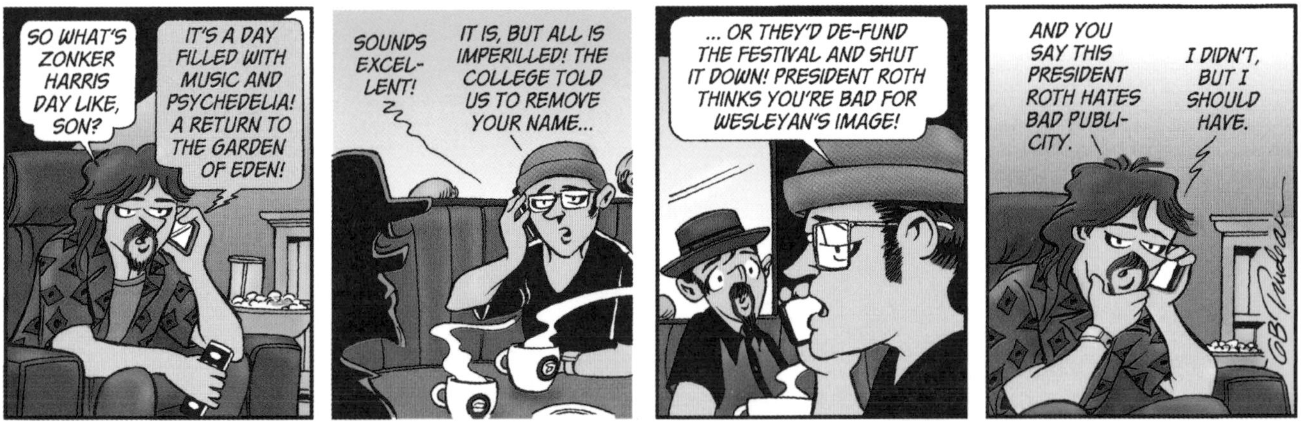
SO WHAT'S ZONKER HARRIS DAY LIKE, SON?
IT'S A DAY FILLED WITH MUSIC AND PSYCHEDELIA! A RETURN TO THE GARDEN OF EDEN!
SOUNDS EXCELLENT!
IT IS, BUT ALL IS IMPERILLED! THE COLLEGE TOLD US TO REMOVE YOUR NAME...
... OR THEY'D DE-FUND THE FESTIVAL AND SHUT IT DOWN! PRESIDENT ROTH THINKS YOU'RE BAD FOR WESLEYAN'S IMAGE!
AND YOU SAY THIS PRESIDENT ROTH HATES BAD PUBLICITY.
I DIDN'T, BUT I SHOULD HAVE.
GBTrudeau

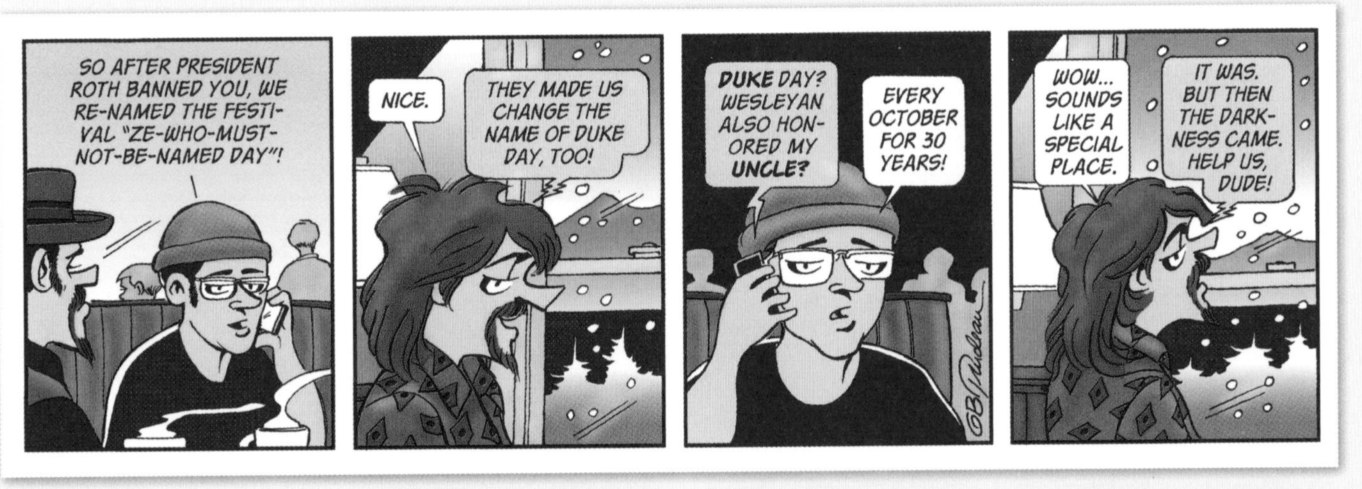
SO AFTER PRESIDENT ROTH BANNED YOU, WE RE-NAMED THE FESTIVAL "ZE-WHO-MUST-NOT-BE-NAMED DAY"!
NICE.
THEY MADE US CHANGE THE NAME OF DUKE DAY, TOO!
DUKE DAY? WESLEYAN ALSO HONORED MY UNCLE?
EVERY OCTOBER FOR 30 YEARS!
WOW... SOUNDS LIKE A SPECIAL PLACE.
IT WAS. BUT THEN THE DARKNESS CAME. HELP US, DUDE!

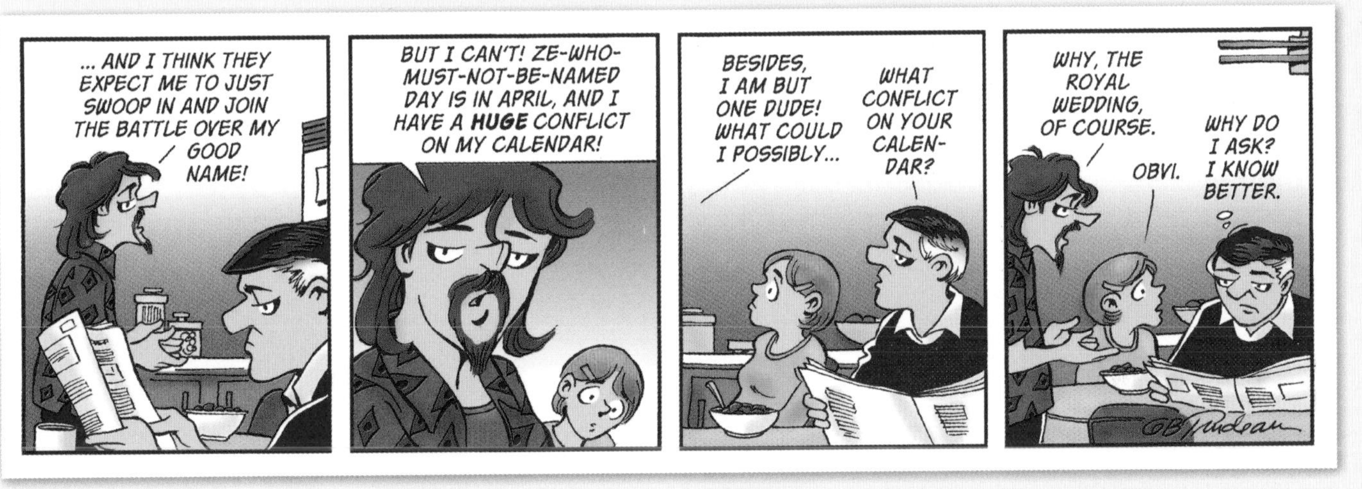
... AND I THINK THEY EXPECT ME TO JUST SWOOP IN AND JOIN THE BATTLE OVER MY GOOD NAME!
BUT I CAN'T! ZE-WHO-MUST-NOT-BE-NAMED DAY IS IN APRIL, AND I HAVE A HUGE CONFLICT ON MY CALENDAR!
BESIDES, I AM BUT ONE DUDE! WHAT COULD I POSSIBLY...
WHAT CONFLICT ON YOUR CALENDAR?
WHY, THE ROYAL WEDDING, OF COURSE.
OBVI.
WHY DO I ASK? I KNOW BETTER.

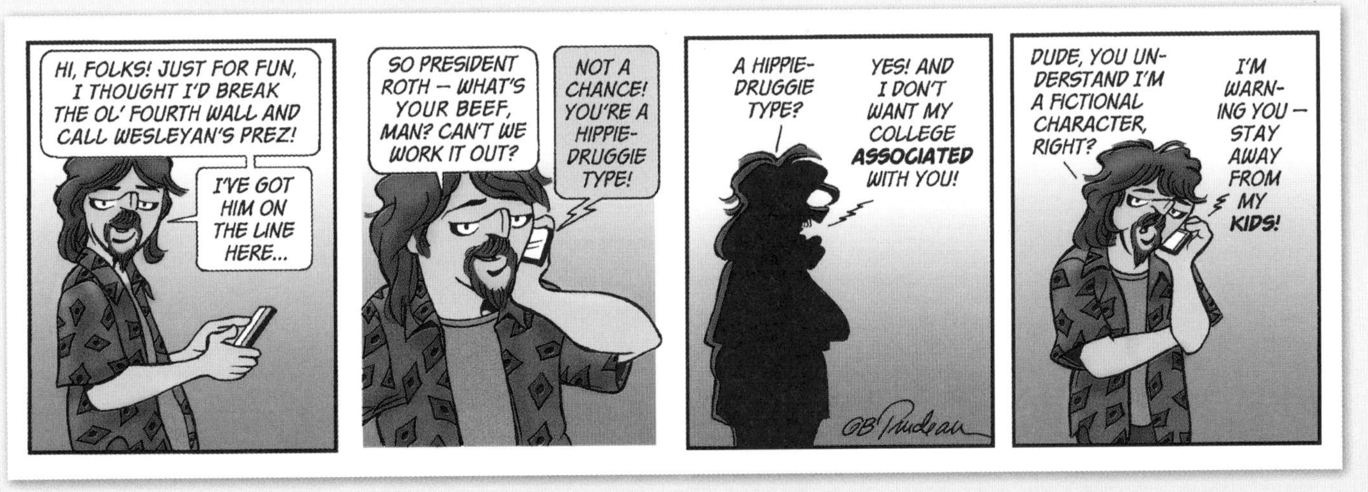
HI, FOLKS! JUST FOR FUN, I THOUGHT I'D BREAK THE OL' FOURTH WALL AND CALL WESLEYAN'S PREZ!
I'VE GOT HIM ON THE LINE HERE...
SO PRESIDENT ROTH — WHAT'S YOUR BEEF, MAN? CAN'T WE WORK IT OUT?
NOT A CHANCE! YOU'RE A HIPPIE-DRUGGIE TYPE!
A HIPPIE-DRUGGIE TYPE?
YES! AND I DON'T WANT MY COLLEGE ASSOCIATED WITH YOU!
DUDE, YOU UNDERSTAND I'M A FICTIONAL CHARACTER, RIGHT?
I'M WARNING YOU — STAY AWAY FROM MY KIDS!

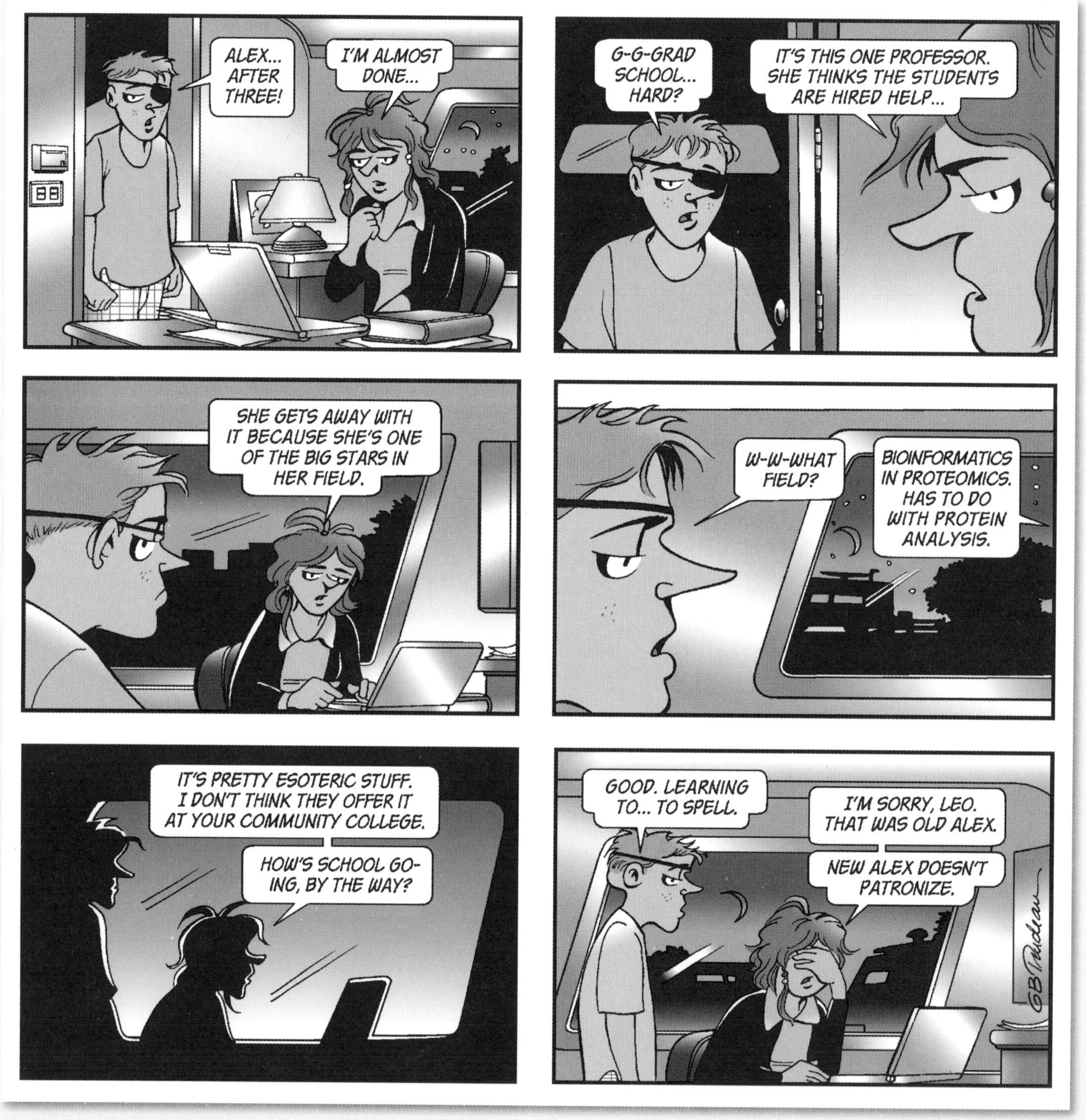
ALEX... AFTER THREE!
I'M ALMOST DONE...
G-G-GRAD SCHOOL... HARD?
IT'S THIS ONE PROFESSOR. SHE THINKS THE STUDENTS ARE HIRED HELP...
SHE GETS AWAY WITH IT BECAUSE SHE'S ONE OF THE BIG STARS IN HER FIELD.
W-W-WHAT FIELD?
BIOINFORMATICS IN PROTEOMICS. HAS TO DO WITH PROTEIN ANALYSIS.
IT'S PRETTY ESOTERIC STUFF. I DON'T THINK THEY OFFER IT AT YOUR COMMUNITY COLLEGE.
HOW'S SCHOOL GOING, BY THE WAY?
GOOD. LEARNING TO... TO SPELL.
I'M SORRY, LEO. THAT WAS OLD ALEX.
NEW ALEX DOESN'T PATRONIZE.
GB Trudeau

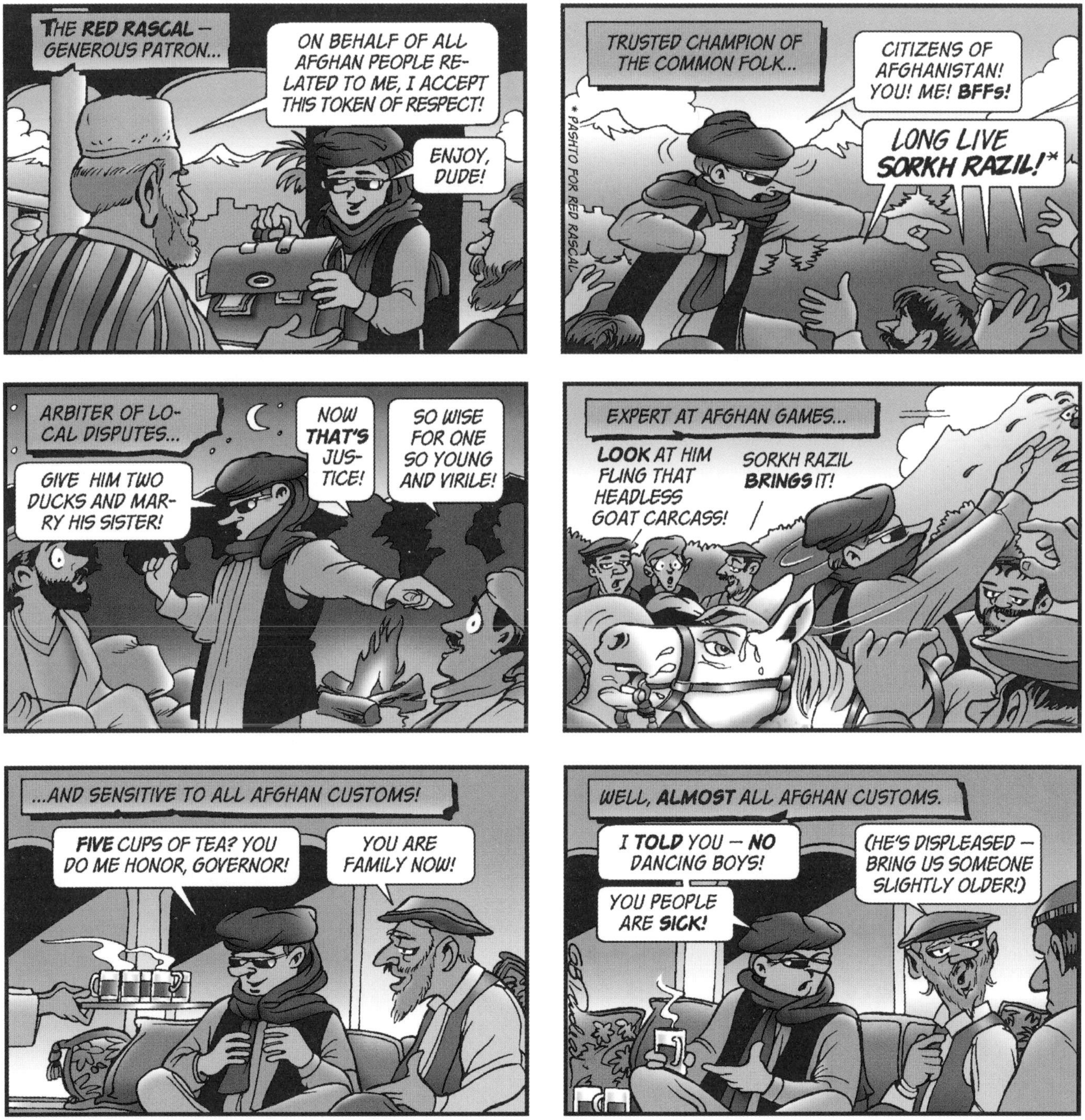
THE RED RASCAL — GENEROUS PATRON...
ON BEHALF OF ALL AFGHAN PEOPLE RELATED TO ME, I ACCEPT THIS TOKEN OF RESPECT!
ENJOY, DUDE!
TRUSTED CHAMPION OF THE COMMON FOLK...
CITIZENS OF AFGHANISTAN! YOU! ME! BFFs!
LONG LIVE SORKH RAZIL!*
* PASHTO FOR RED RASCAL
ARBITER OF LOCAL DISPUTES...
GIVE HIM TWO DUCKS AND MARRY HIS SISTER!
NOW THAT'S JUSTICE!
SO WISE FOR ONE SO YOUNG AND VIRILE!
EXPERT AT AFGHAN GAMES...
LOOK AT HIM FLING THAT HEADLESS GOAT CARCASS!
SORKH RAZIL BRINGS IT!
...AND SENSITIVE TO ALL AFGHAN CUSTOMS!
FIVE CUPS OF TEA? YOU DO ME HONOR, GOVERNOR!
YOU ARE FAMILY NOW!
WELL, ALMOST ALL AFGHAN CUSTOMS.
I TOLD YOU — NO DANCING BOYS!
YOU PEOPLE ARE SICK!
(HE'S DISPLEASED — BRING US SOMEONE SLIGHTLY OLDER!)

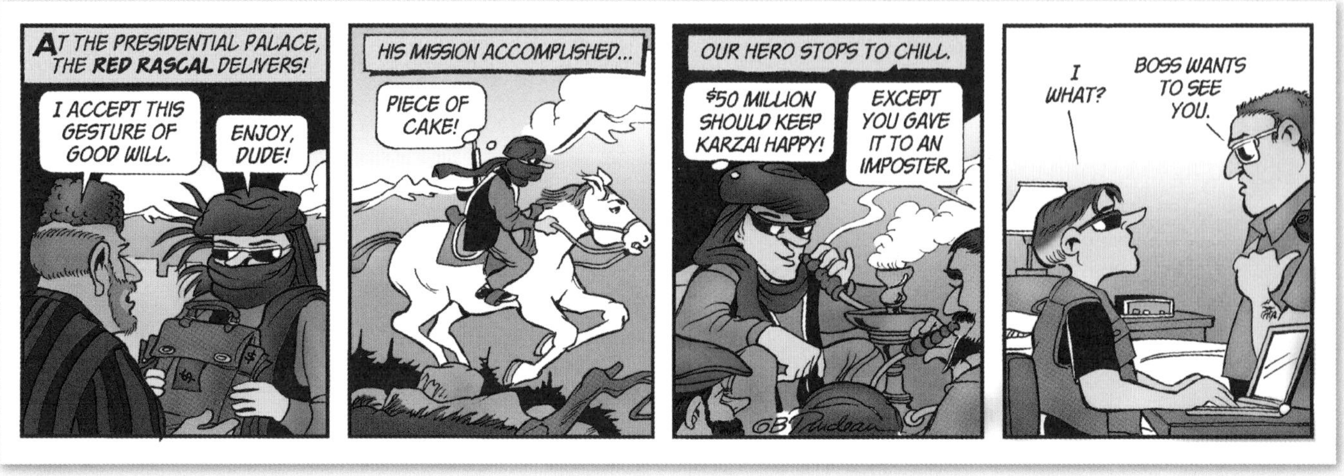
AT THE PRESIDENTIAL PALACE, THE **RED RASCAL** DELIVERS!
I ACCEPT THIS GESTURE OF GOOD WILL.
ENJOY, DUDE!
HIS MISSION ACCOMPLISHED...
PIECE OF CAKE!
OUR HERO STOPS TO CHILL.
$50 MILLION SHOULD KEEP KARZAI HAPPY!
EXCEPT YOU GAVE IT TO AN IMPOSTER.
BOSS WANTS TO SEE YOU.
I WHAT?

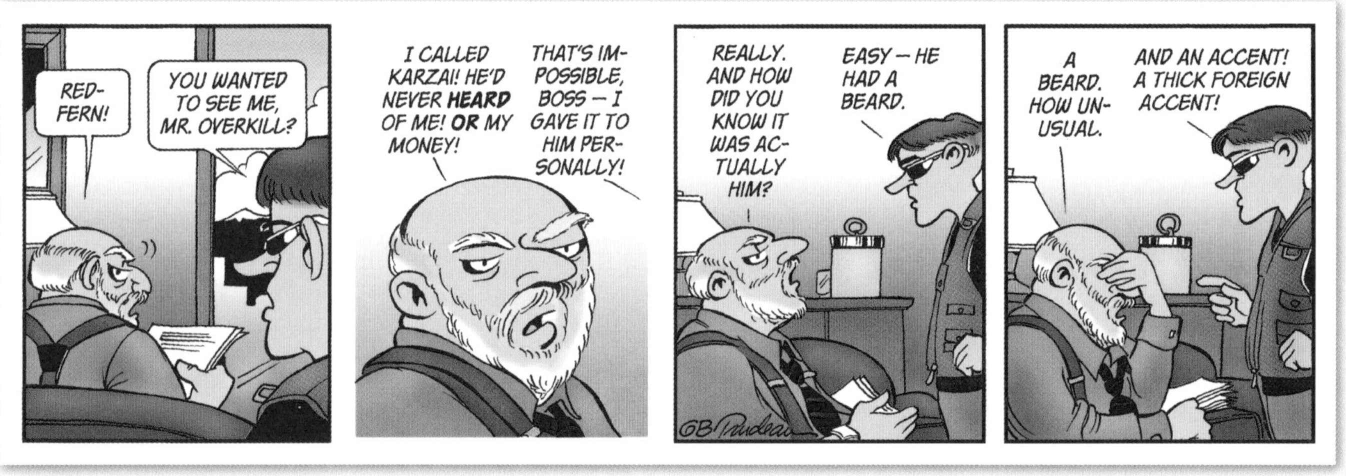
RED-FERN!
YOU WANTED TO SEE ME, MR. OVERKILL?
I CALLED KARZAI! HE'D NEVER **HEARD** OF ME! **OR** MY MONEY!
THAT'S IMPOSSIBLE, BOSS — I GAVE IT TO HIM PERSONALLY!
REALLY. AND HOW DID YOU KNOW IT WAS ACTUALLY HIM?
EASY — HE HAD A BEARD.
A BEARD. HOW UNUSUAL.
AND AN ACCENT! A THICK FOREIGN ACCENT!

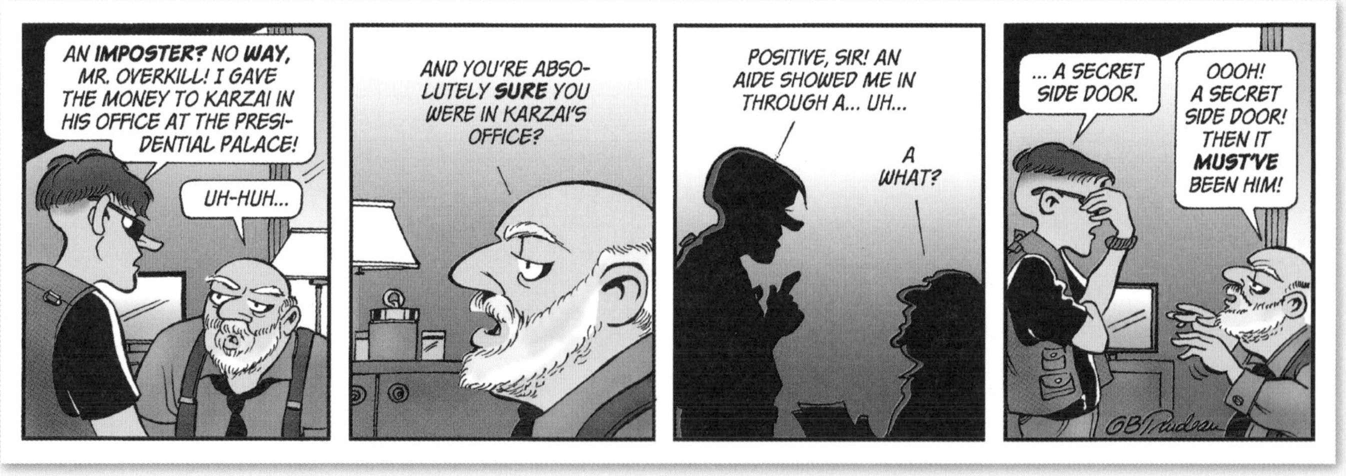
AN **IMPOSTER?** NO **WAY,** MR. OVERKILL! I GAVE THE MONEY TO KARZAI IN HIS OFFICE AT THE PRESIDENTIAL PALACE!
UH-HUH...
AND YOU'RE ABSOLUTELY **SURE** YOU WERE IN KARZAI'S OFFICE?
POSITIVE, SIR! AN AIDE SHOWED ME IN THROUGH A... UH...
A WHAT?
... A SECRET SIDE DOOR.
OOOH! A SECRET SIDE DOOR! THEN IT **MUST'VE** BEEN HIM!

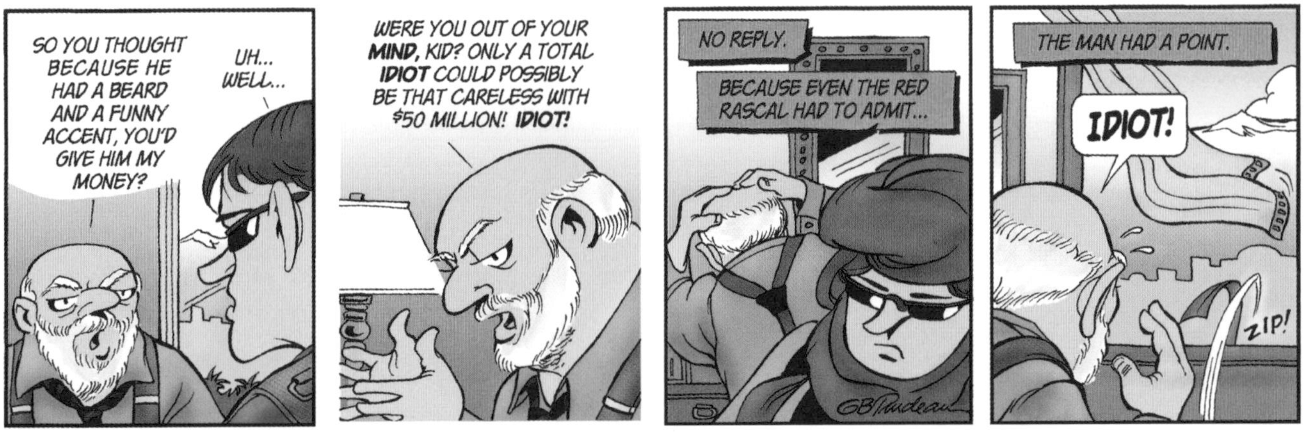
SO YOU THOUGHT BECAUSE HE HAD A BEARD AND A FUNNY ACCENT, YOU'D GIVE HIM MY MONEY?
UH... WELL...
WERE YOU OUT OF YOUR **MIND**, KID? ONLY A TOTAL **IDIOT** COULD POSSIBLY BE THAT CARELESS WITH $50 MILLION! **IDIOT!**
NO REPLY.
BECAUSE EVEN THE RED RASCAL HAD TO ADMIT...
THE MAN HAD A POINT.
IDIOT!
ZIP!

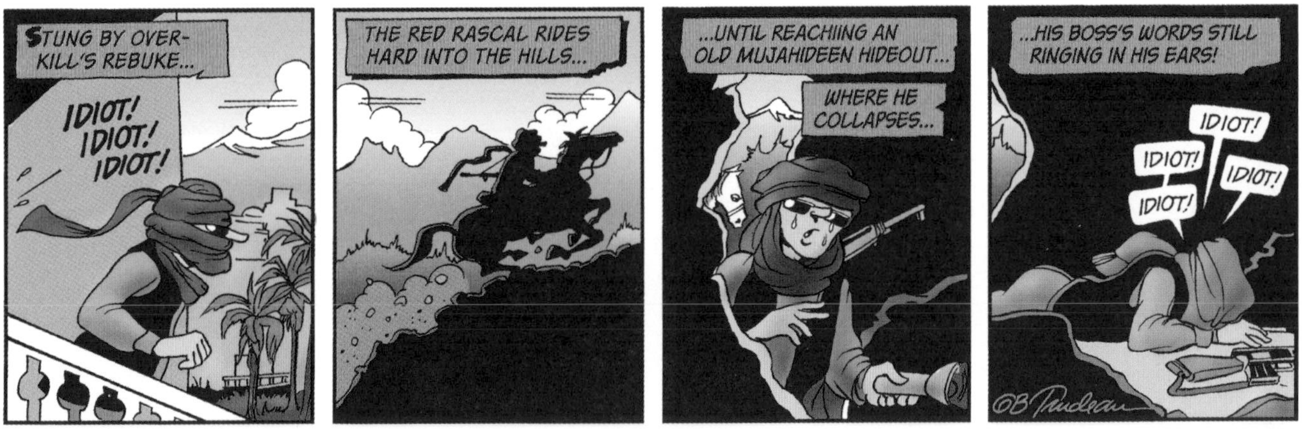
STUNG BY OVER-KILL'S REBUKE...
IDIOT! IDIOT! IDIOT!
THE RED RASCAL RIDES HARD INTO THE HILLS...
...UNTIL REACHIING AN OLD MUJAHIDEEN HIDEOUT...
WHERE HE COLLAPSES...
...HIS BOSS'S WORDS STILL RINGING IN HIS EARS!
IDIOT!
IDIOT!
IDIOT!
IDIOT!

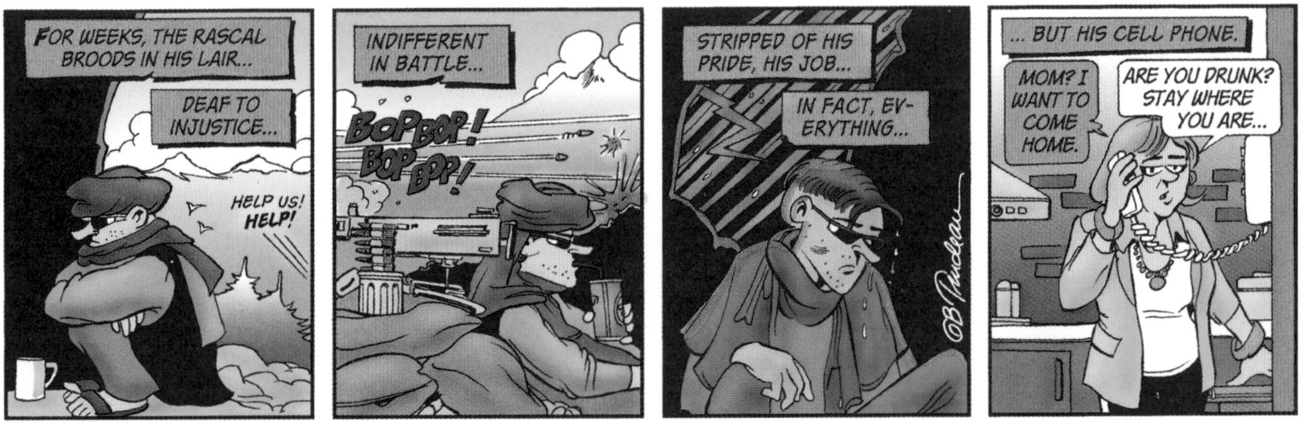
FOR WEEKS, THE RASCAL BROODS IN HIS LAIR...
DEAF TO INJUSTICE...
HELP US! HELP!
INDIFFERENT IN BATTLE...
STRIPPED OF HIS PRIDE, HIS JOB...
IN FACT, EV-ERYTHING...
... BUT HIS CELL PHONE.
MOM? I WANT TO COME HOME.
ARE YOU DRUNK? STAY WHERE YOU ARE...

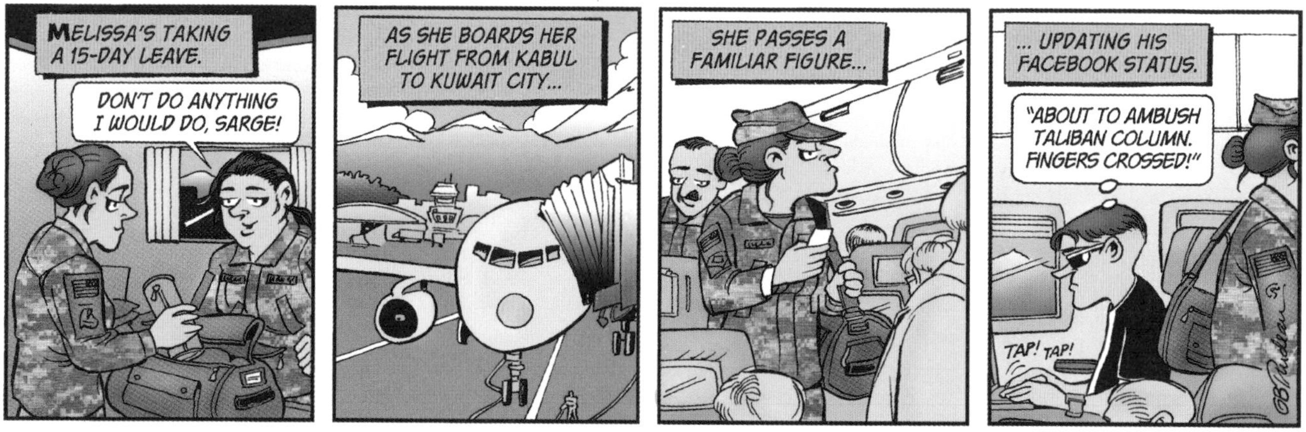
MELISSA'S TAKING A 15-DAY LEAVE.
DON'T DO ANYTHING I WOULD DO, SARGE!
AS SHE BOARDS HER FLIGHT FROM KABUL TO KUWAIT CITY...
SHE PASSES A FAMILIAR FIGURE...
... UPDATING HIS FACEBOOK STATUS.
"ABOUT TO AMBUSH TALIBAN COLUMN. FINGERS CROSSED!"
TAP! TAP!

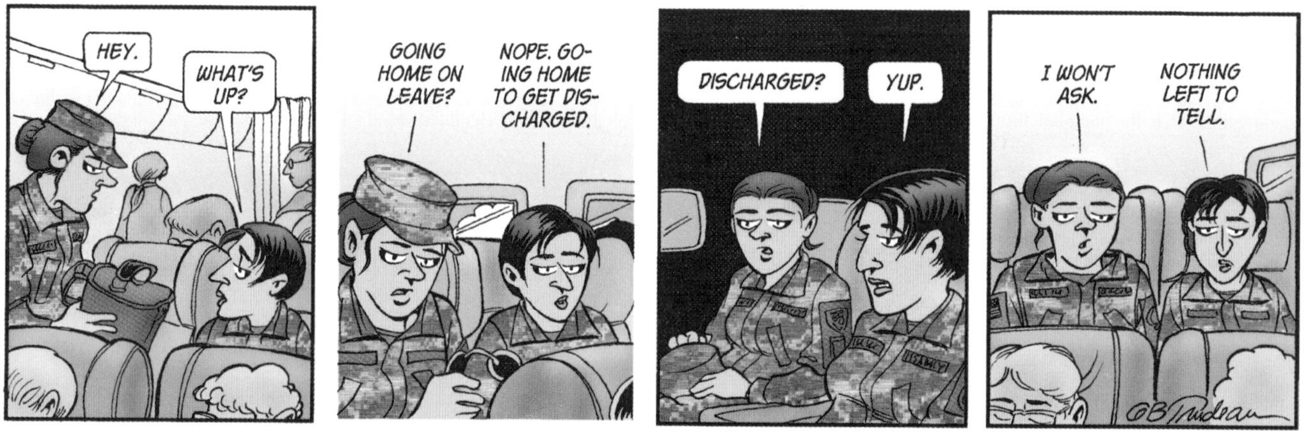
HEY.
WHAT'S UP?
GOING HOME ON LEAVE?
NOPE. GO-ING HOME TO GET DIS-CHARGED.
DISCHARGED?
YUP.
I WON'T ASK.
NOTHING LEFT TO TELL.

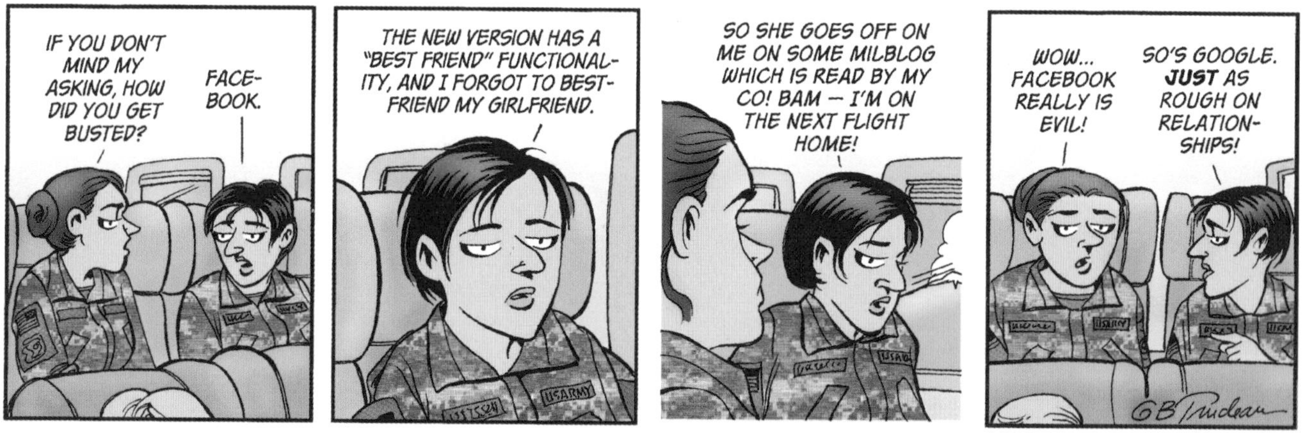
IF YOU DON'T MIND MY ASKING, HOW DID YOU GET BUSTED?
FACE-BOOK.
THE NEW VERSION HAS A "BEST FRIEND" FUNCTIONAL-ITY, AND I FORGOT TO BEST-FRIEND MY GIRLFRIEND.
SO SHE GOES OFF ON ME ON SOME MILBLOG WHICH IS READ BY MY CO! BAM — I'M ON THE NEXT FLIGHT HOME!
WOW... FACEBOOK REALLY IS EVIL!
SO'S GOOGLE. JUST AS ROUGH ON RELATION-SHIPS!

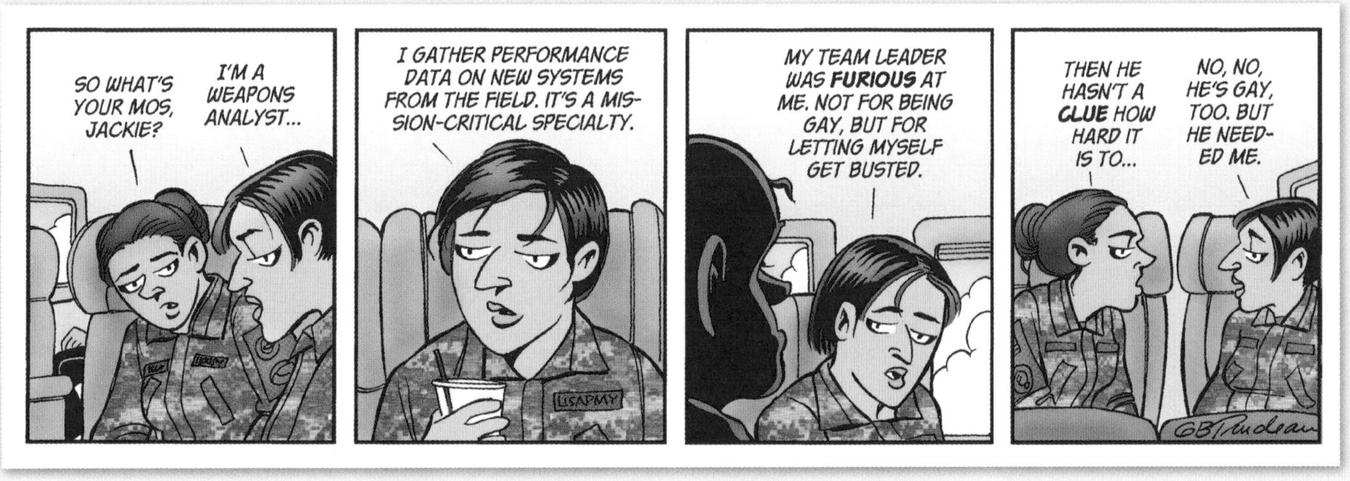
SO WHAT'S YOUR MOS, JACKIE?
I'M A WEAPONS ANALYST...
I GATHER PERFORMANCE DATA ON NEW SYSTEMS FROM THE FIELD. IT'S A MISSION-CRITICAL SPECIALTY.
MY TEAM LEADER WAS **FURIOUS** AT ME. NOT FOR BEING GAY, BUT FOR LETTING MYSELF GET BUSTED.
THEN HE HASN'T A **CLUE** HOW HARD IT IS TO...
NO, NO, HE'S GAY, TOO. BUT HE NEEDED ME.
GBTrudeau

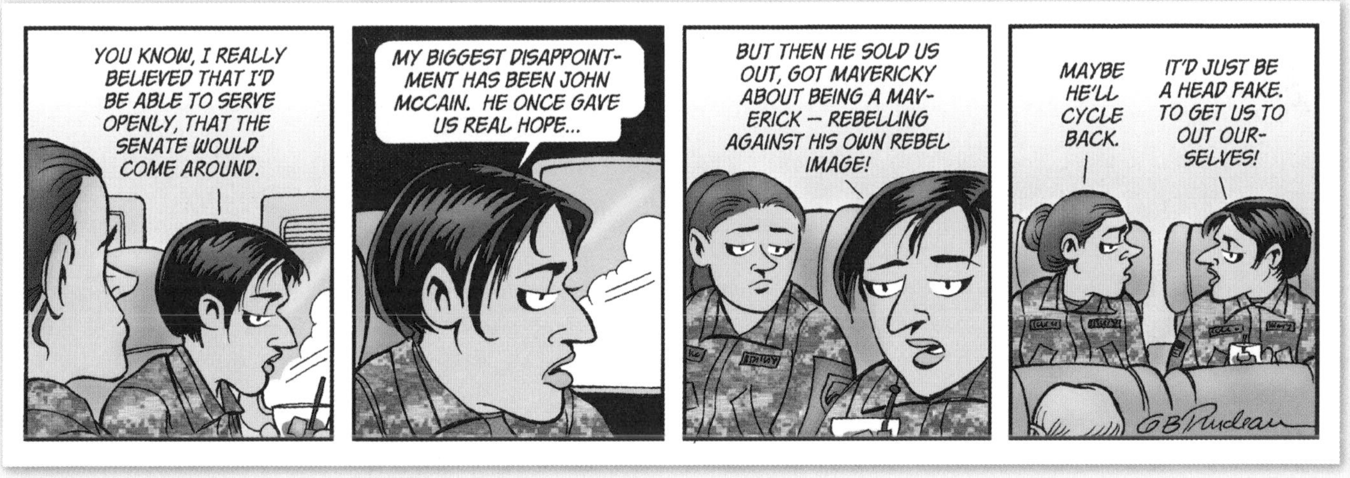
YOU KNOW, I REALLY BELIEVED THAT I'D BE ABLE TO SERVE OPENLY, THAT THE SENATE WOULD COME AROUND.
MY BIGGEST DISAPPOINTMENT HAS BEEN JOHN McCAIN. HE ONCE GAVE US REAL HOPE...
BUT THEN HE SOLD US OUT, GOT MAVERICKY ABOUT BEING A MAVERICK — REBELLING AGAINST HIS OWN REBEL IMAGE!
MAYBE HE'LL CYCLE BACK.
IT'D JUST BE A HEAD FAKE. TO GET US TO OUT OURSELVES!
GBTrudeau

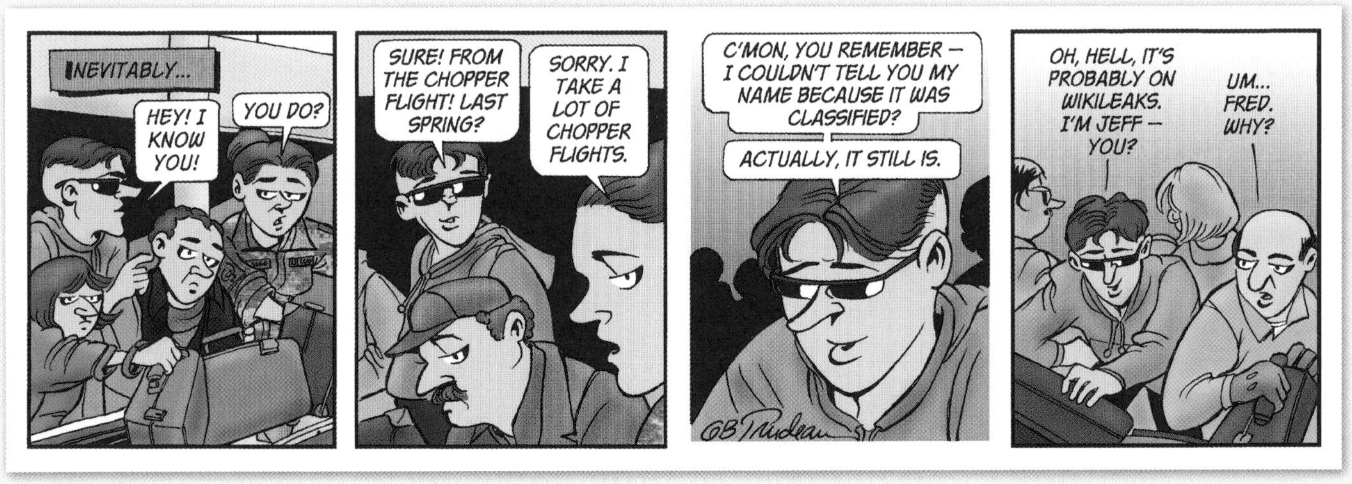
INEVITABLY...
HEY! I KNOW YOU!
YOU DO?
SURE! FROM THE CHOPPER FLIGHT! LAST SPRING?
SORRY. I TAKE A LOT OF CHOPPER FLIGHTS.
C'MON, YOU REMEMBER — I COULDN'T TELL YOU MY NAME BECAUSE IT WAS CLASSIFIED?
ACTUALLY, IT STILL IS.
GBTrudeau
OH, HELL, IT'S PROBABLY ON WIKILEAKS. I'M JEFF — YOU?
UM... FRED. WHY?

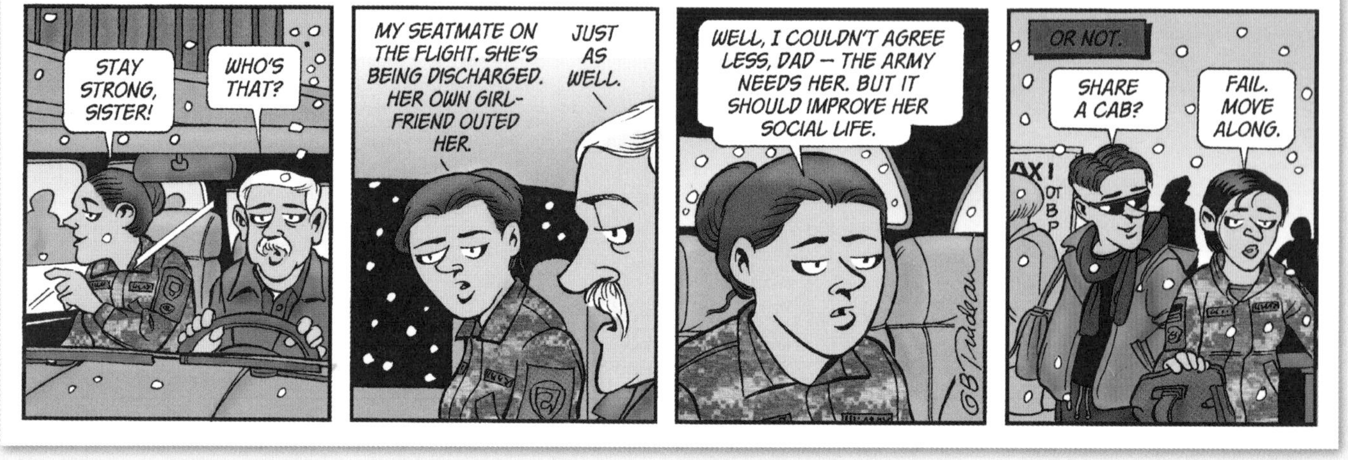
STAY STRONG, SISTER!
WHO'S THAT?
MY SEATMATE ON THE FLIGHT. SHE'S BEING DISCHARGED. HER OWN GIRL-FRIEND OUTED HER.
JUST AS WELL.
WELL, I COULDN'T AGREE LESS, DAD — THE ARMY NEEDS HER. BUT IT SHOULD IMPROVE HER SOCIAL LIFE.
GB Trudeau
OR NOT.
SHARE A CAB?
FAIL. MOVE ALONG.

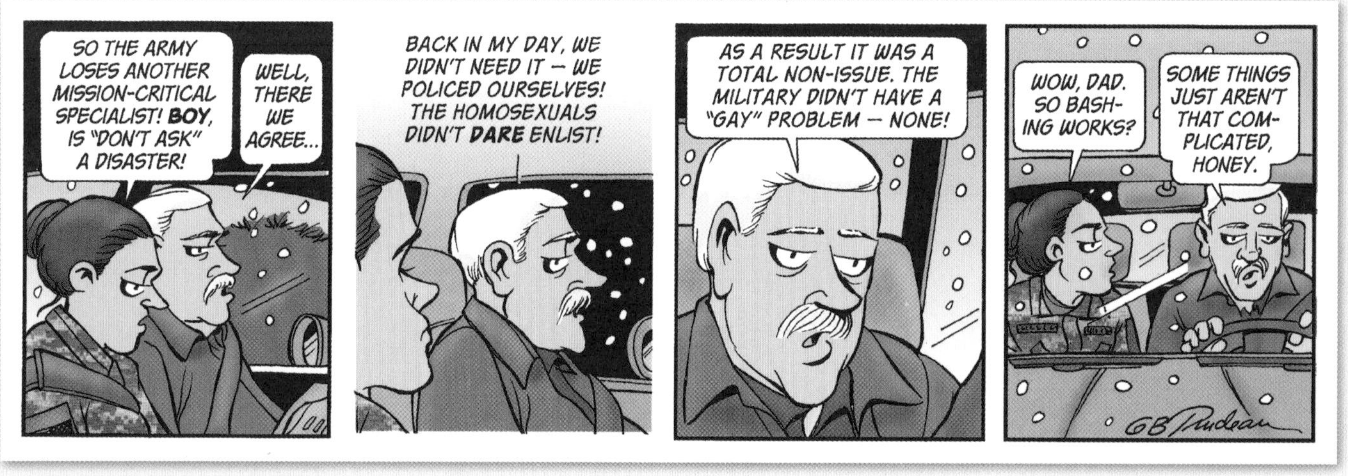
SO THE ARMY LOSES ANOTHER MISSION-CRITICAL SPECIALIST! **BOY**, IS "DON'T ASK" A DISASTER!
WELL, THERE WE AGREE...
BACK IN MY DAY, WE DIDN'T NEED IT — WE POLICED OURSELVES! THE HOMOSEXUALS DIDN'T **DARE** ENLIST!
AS A RESULT IT WAS A TOTAL NON-ISSUE. THE MILITARY DIDN'T HAVE A "GAY" PROBLEM — NONE!
WOW, DAD. SO BASH-ING WORKS?
SOME THINGS JUST AREN'T THAT COM-PLICATED, HONEY.
GB Trudeau

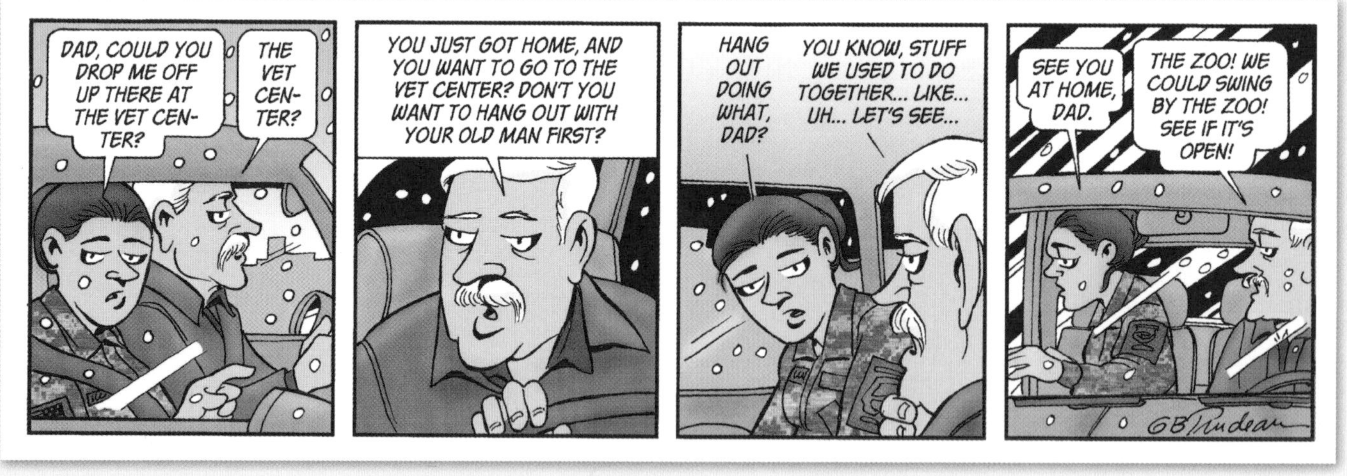
DAD, COULD YOU DROP ME OFF UP THERE AT THE VET CEN-TER?
THE VET CEN-TER?
YOU JUST GOT HOME, AND YOU WANT TO GO TO THE VET CENTER? DON'T YOU WANT TO HANG OUT WITH YOUR OLD MAN FIRST?
HANG OUT DOING WHAT, DAD?
YOU KNOW, STUFF WE USED TO DO TOGETHER... LIKE... UH... LET'S SEE...
SEE YOU AT HOME, DAD.
THE ZOO! WE COULD SWING BY THE ZOO! SEE IF IT'S OPEN!
GB Trudeau

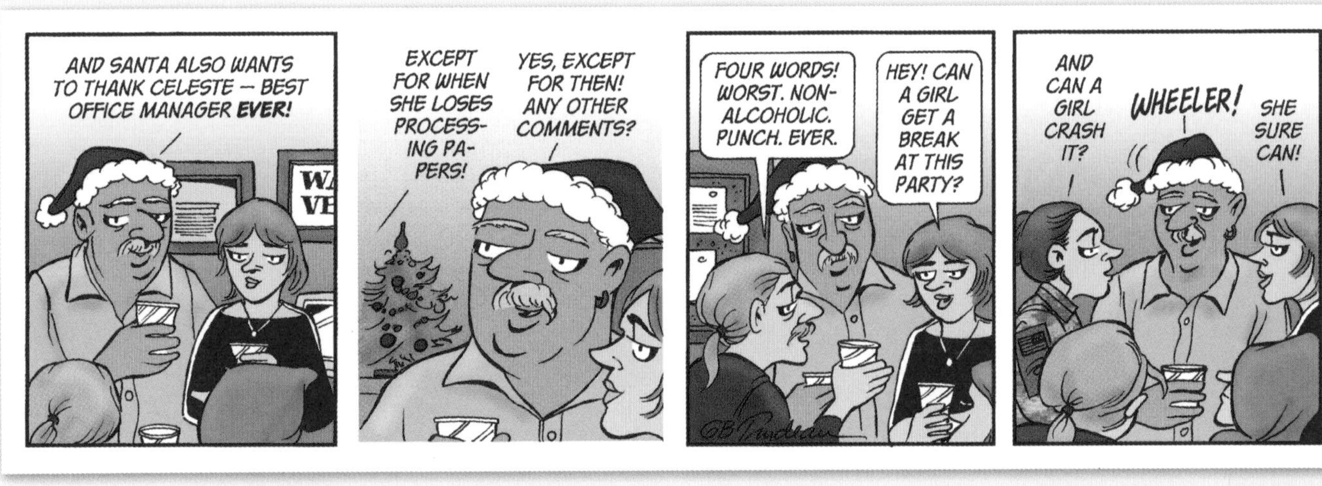
AND SANTA ALSO WANTS TO THANK CELESTE — BEST OFFICE MANAGER **EVER!**
EXCEPT FOR WHEN SHE LOSES PROCESSING PAPERS!
YES, EXCEPT FOR THEN! ANY OTHER COMMENTS?
FOUR WORDS! WORST. NON-ALCOHOLIC. PUNCH. EVER.
HEY! CAN A GIRL GET A BREAK AT THIS PARTY?
AND CAN A GIRL CRASH IT?
WHEELER!
SHE SURE CAN!
GB Trudeau

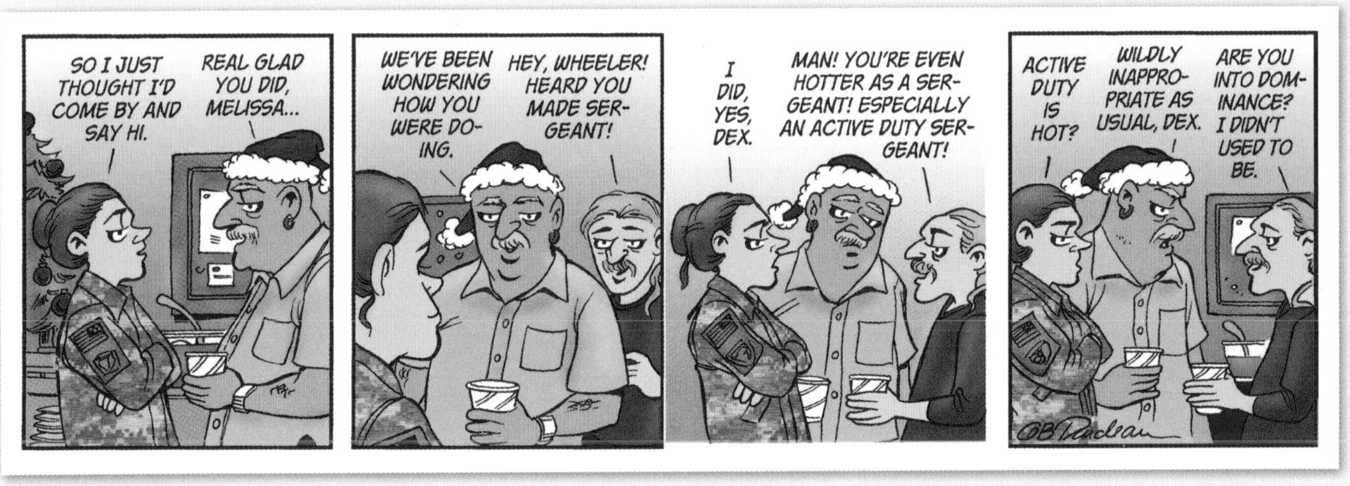
SO I JUST THOUGHT I'D COME BY AND SAY HI.
REAL GLAD YOU DID, MELISSA...
WE'VE BEEN WONDERING HOW YOU WERE DOING.
HEY, WHEELER! HEARD YOU MADE SERGEANT!
I DID, YES, DEX.
MAN! YOU'RE EVEN HOTTER AS A SERGEANT! ESPECIALLY AN ACTIVE DUTY SERGEANT!
ACTIVE DUTY IS HOT?
WILDLY INAPPROPRIATE AS USUAL, DEX.
ARE YOU INTO DOMINANCE? I DIDN'T USED TO BE.
GB Trudeau

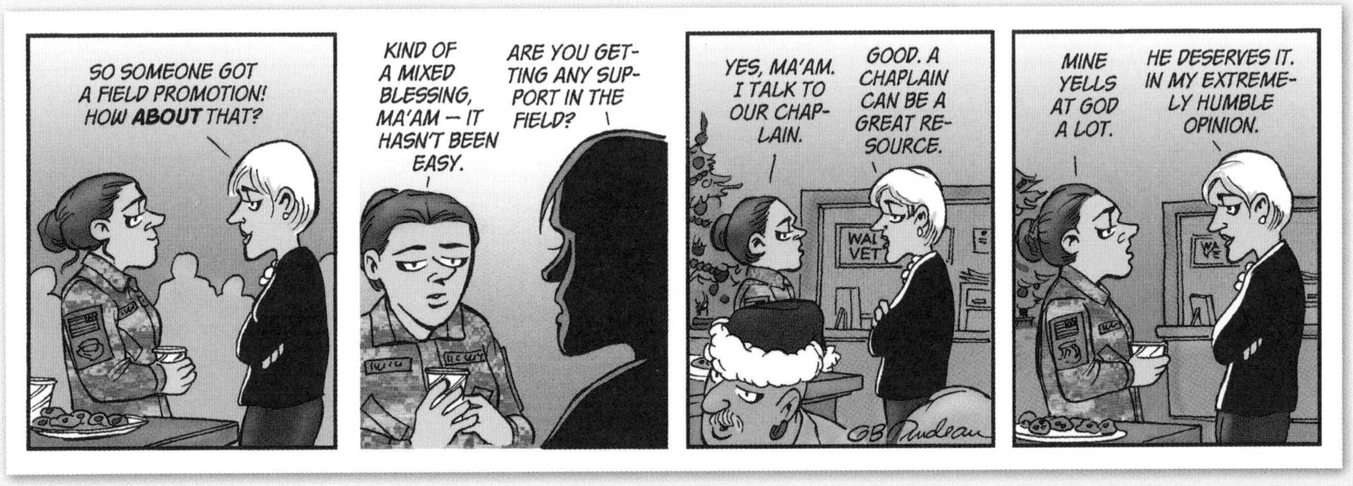
SO SOMEONE GOT A FIELD PROMOTION! HOW **ABOUT** THAT?
KIND OF A MIXED BLESSING, MA'AM — IT HASN'T BEEN EASY.
ARE YOU GETTING ANY SUPPORT IN THE FIELD?
YES, MA'AM. I TALK TO OUR CHAPLAIN.
GOOD. A CHAPLAIN CAN BE A GREAT RESOURCE.
MINE YELLS AT GOD A LOT.
HE DESERVES IT. IN MY EXTREMELY HUMBLE OPINION.
GB Trudeau

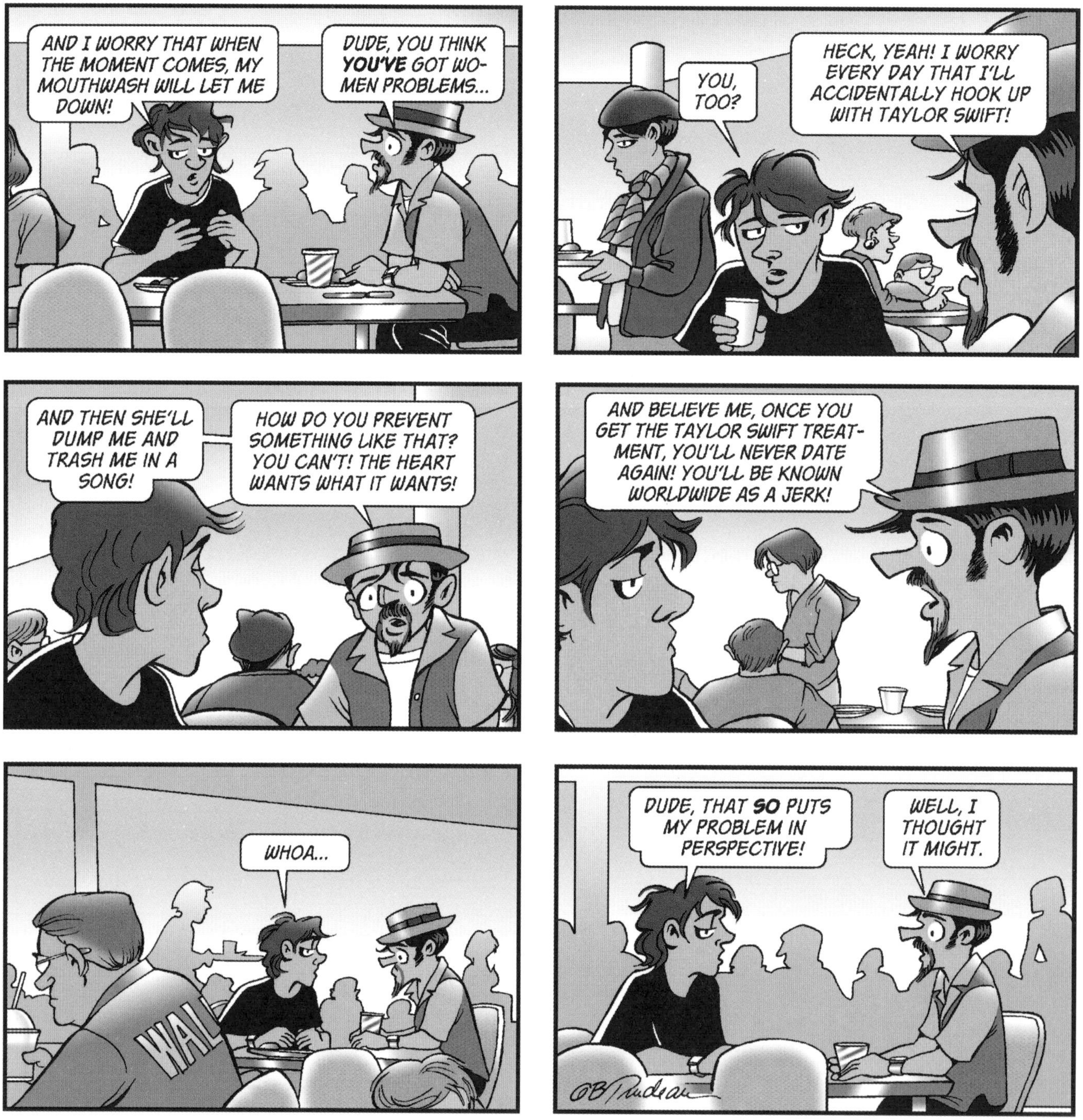
AND I WORRY THAT WHEN THE MOMENT COMES, MY MOUTHWASH WILL LET ME DOWN!
DUDE, YOU THINK **YOU'VE** GOT WOMEN PROBLEMS...
YOU, TOO?
HECK, YEAH! I WORRY EVERY DAY THAT I'LL ACCIDENTALLY HOOK UP WITH TAYLOR SWIFT!
AND THEN SHE'LL DUMP ME AND TRASH ME IN A SONG!
HOW DO YOU PREVENT SOMETHING LIKE THAT? YOU CAN'T! THE HEART WANTS WHAT IT WANTS!
AND BELIEVE ME, ONCE YOU GET THE TAYLOR SWIFT TREATMENT, YOU'LL NEVER DATE AGAIN! YOU'LL BE KNOWN WORLDWIDE AS A JERK!
WHOA...
WAL
DUDE, THAT **SO** PUTS MY PROBLEM IN PERSPECTIVE!
WELL, I THOUGHT IT MIGHT.
GBTrudeau

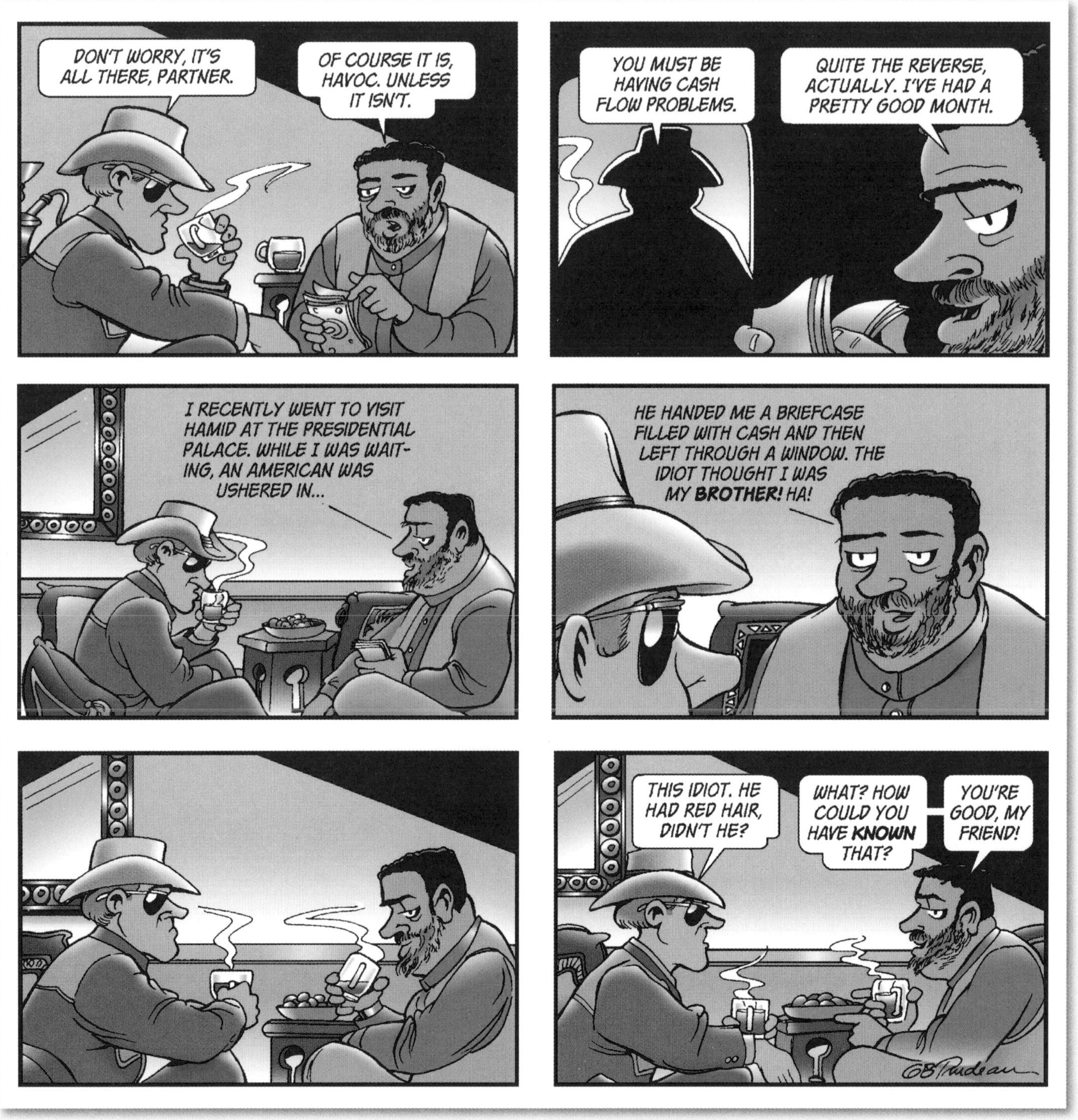
DON'T WORRY, IT'S ALL THERE, PARTNER.
OF COURSE IT IS, HAVOC. UNLESS IT ISN'T.
YOU MUST BE HAVING CASH FLOW PROBLEMS.
QUITE THE REVERSE, ACTUALLY. I'VE HAD A PRETTY GOOD MONTH.
I RECENTLY WENT TO VISIT HAMID AT THE PRESIDENTIAL PALACE. WHILE I WAS WAITING, AN AMERICAN WAS USHERED IN...
HE HANDED ME A BRIEFCASE FILLED WITH CASH AND THEN LEFT THROUGH A WINDOW. THE IDIOT THOUGHT I WAS MY **BROTHER!** HA!
THIS IDIOT. HE HAD RED HAIR, DIDN'T HE?
WHAT? HOW COULD YOU HAVE **KNOWN** THAT?
YOU'RE GOOD, MY FRIEND!
GB Trudeau

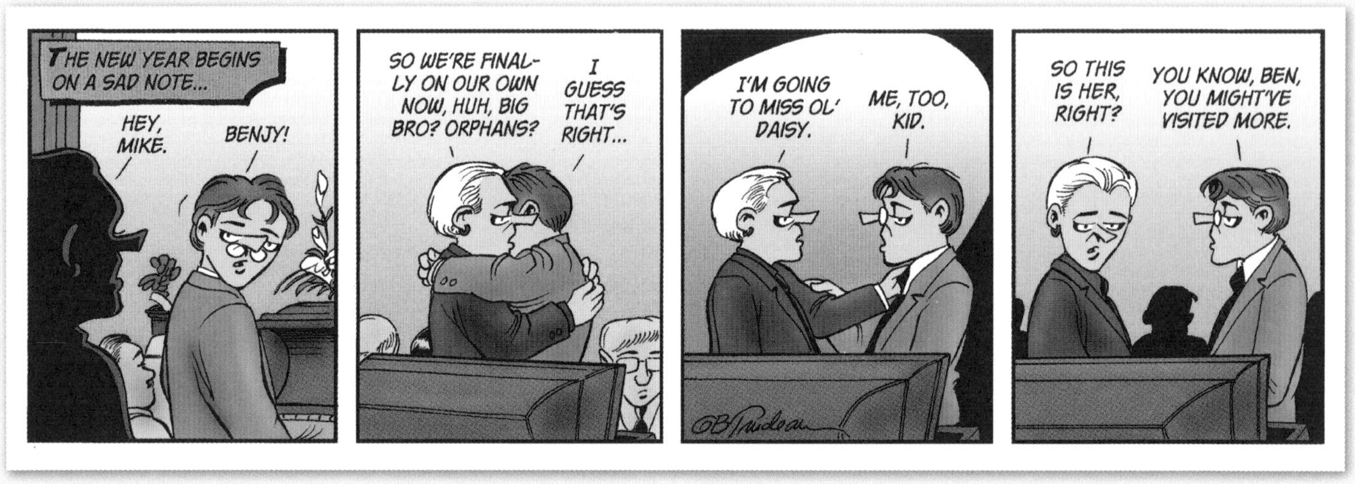
THE NEW YEAR BEGINS ON A SAD NOTE...
HEY, MIKE.
BENJY!
SO WE'RE FINALLY ON OUR OWN NOW, HUH, BIG BRO? ORPHANS?
I GUESS THAT'S RIGHT...
I'M GOING TO MISS OL' DAISY.
ME, TOO, KID.
SO THIS IS HER, RIGHT?
YOU KNOW, BEN, YOU MIGHT'VE VISITED MORE.

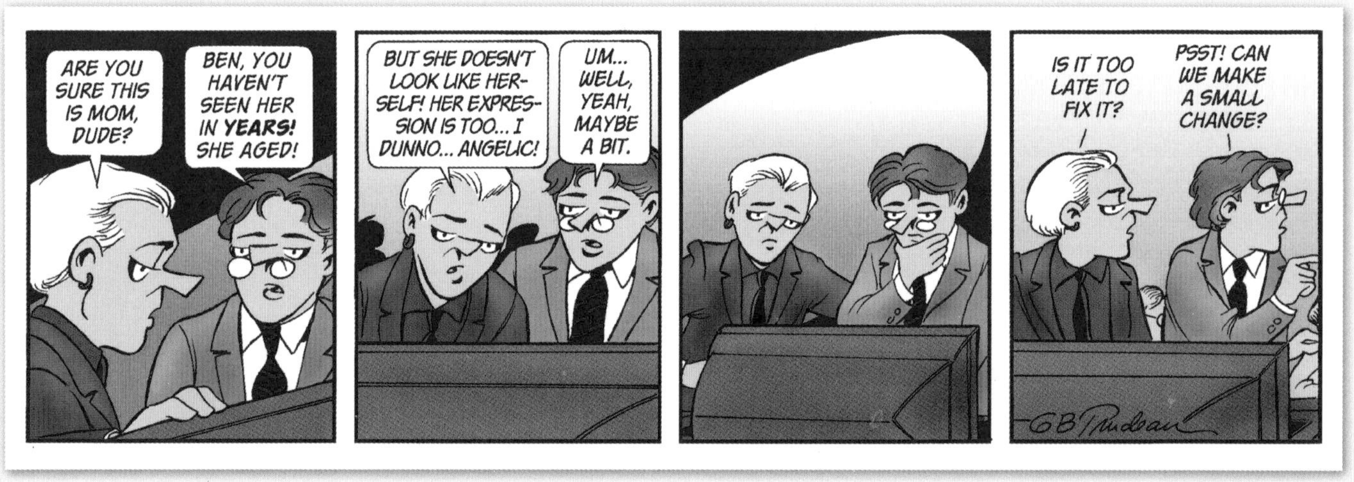
ARE YOU SURE THIS IS MOM, DUDE?
BEN, YOU HAVEN'T SEEN HER IN **YEARS!** SHE AGED!
BUT SHE DOESN'T LOOK LIKE HERSELF! HER EXPRESSION IS TOO... I DUNNO... ANGELIC!
UM... WELL, YEAH, MAYBE A BIT.
IS IT TOO LATE TO FIX IT?
PSST! CAN WE MAKE A SMALL CHANGE?

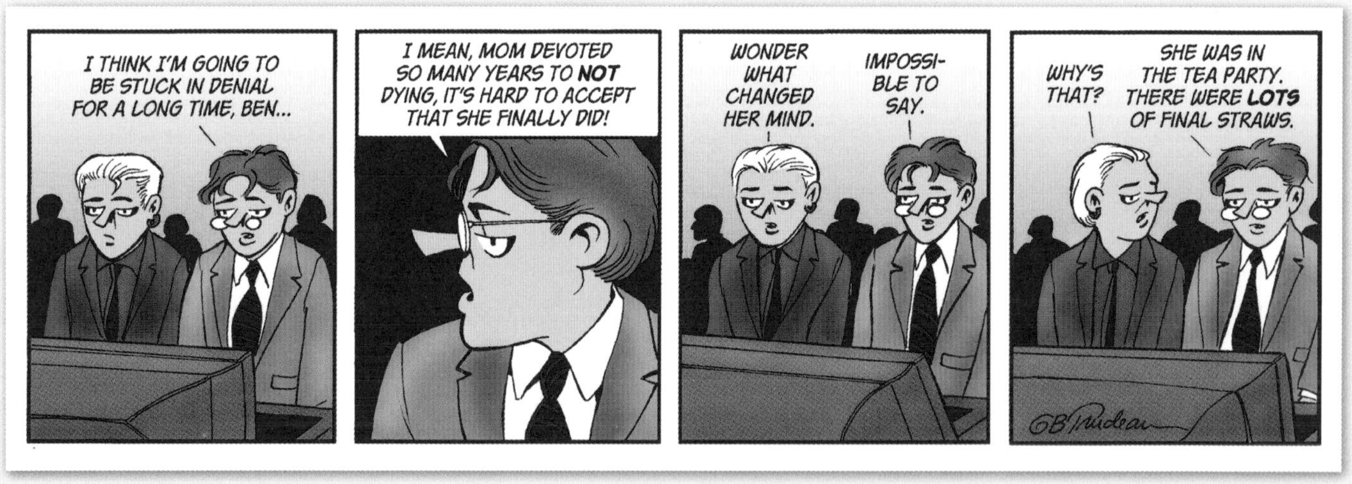
I THINK I'M GOING TO BE STUCK IN DENIAL FOR A LONG TIME, BEN...
I MEAN, MOM DEVOTED SO MANY YEARS TO **NOT** DYING, IT'S HARD TO ACCEPT THAT SHE FINALLY DID!
WONDER WHAT CHANGED HER MIND.
IMPOSSIBLE TO SAY.
WHY'S THAT?
SHE WAS IN THE TEA PARTY. THERE WERE **LOTS** OF FINAL STRAWS.

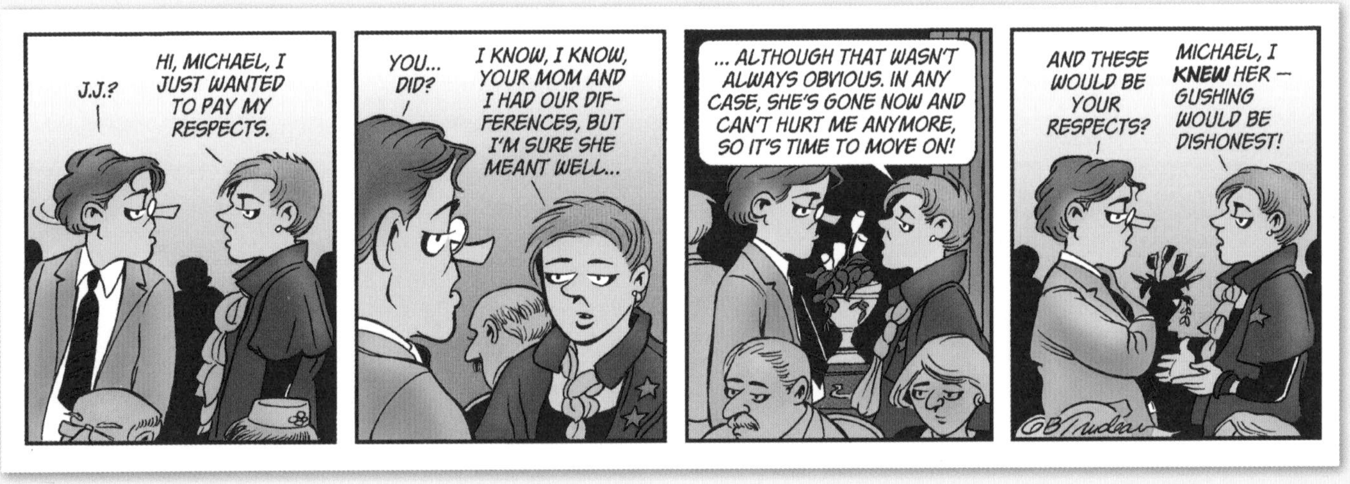
J.J.?
HI, MICHAEL, I JUST WANTED TO PAY MY RESPECTS.
YOU... DID?
I KNOW, I KNOW, YOUR MOM AND I HAD OUR DIFFERENCES, BUT I'M SURE SHE MEANT WELL...
... ALTHOUGH THAT WASN'T ALWAYS OBVIOUS. IN ANY CASE, SHE'S GONE NOW AND CAN'T HURT ME ANYMORE, SO IT'S TIME TO MOVE ON!
AND THESE WOULD BE YOUR RESPECTS?
MICHAEL, I **KNEW** HER — GUSHING WOULD BE DISHONEST!
GB Trudeau

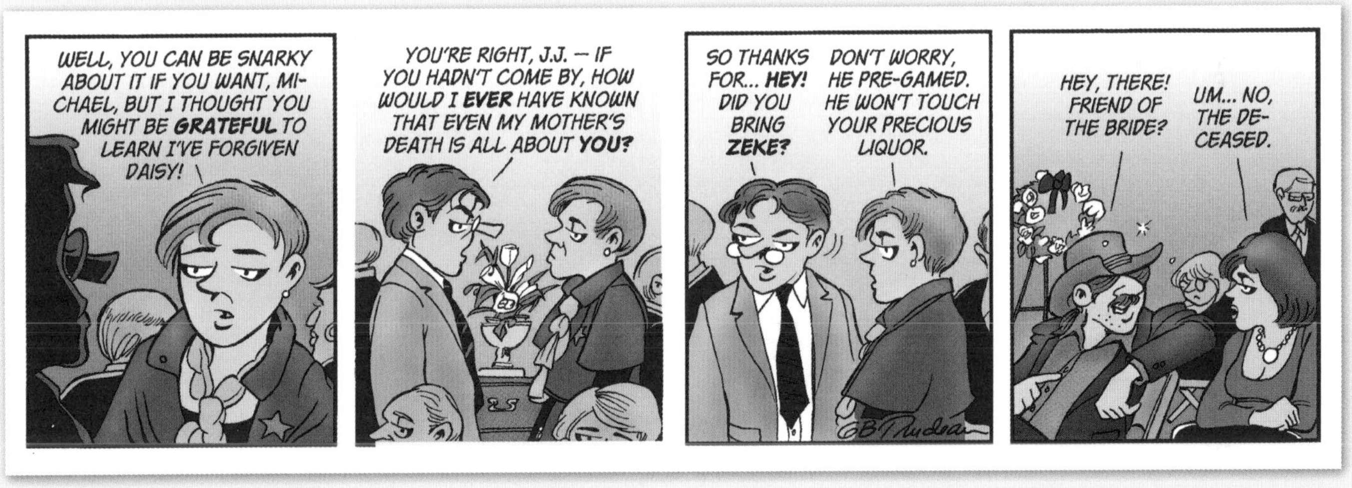
WELL, YOU CAN BE SNARKY ABOUT IT IF YOU WANT, MICHAEL, BUT I THOUGHT YOU MIGHT BE **GRATEFUL** TO LEARN I'VE FORGIVEN DAISY!
YOU'RE RIGHT, J.J. — IF YOU HADN'T COME BY, HOW WOULD I **EVER** HAVE KNOWN THAT EVEN MY MOTHER'S DEATH IS ALL ABOUT **YOU?**
SO THANKS FOR... **HEY!** DID YOU BRING **ZEKE?**
DON'T WORRY, HE PRE-GAMED. HE WON'T TOUCH YOUR PRECIOUS LIQUOR.
HEY, THERE! FRIEND OF THE BRIDE?
UM... NO, THE DECEASED.
GB Trudeau

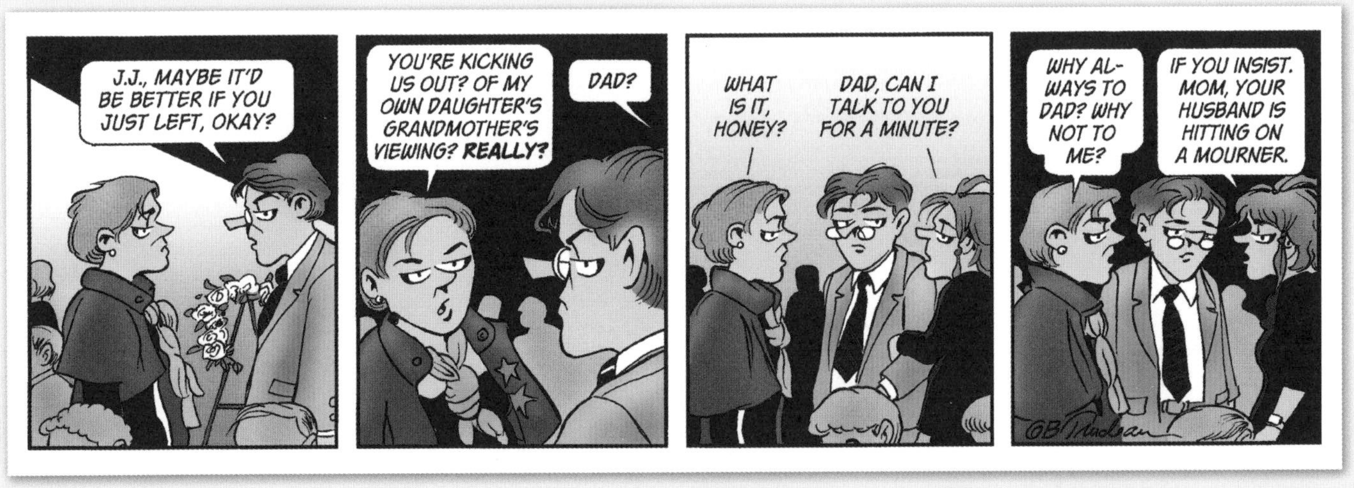
J.J., MAYBE IT'D BE BETTER IF YOU JUST LEFT, OKAY?
YOU'RE KICKING US OUT? OF MY OWN DAUGHTER'S GRANDMOTHER'S VIEWING? **REALLY?**
DAD?
WHAT IS IT, HONEY?
DAD, CAN I TALK TO YOU FOR A MINUTE?
WHY ALWAYS TO DAD? WHY NOT TO ME?
IF YOU INSIST. MOM, YOUR HUSBAND IS HITTING ON A MOURNER.
GB Trudeau

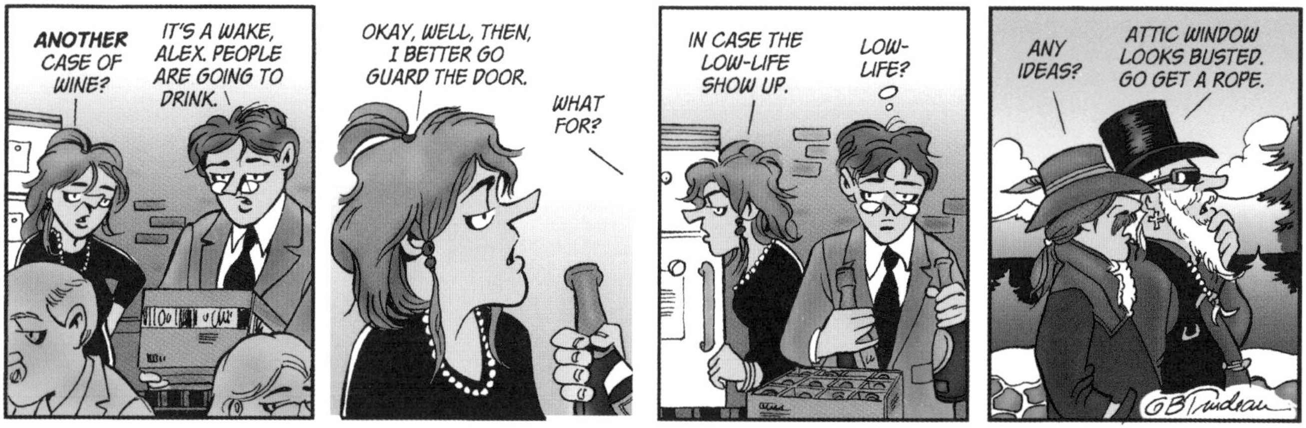
ANOTHER CASE OF WINE?
IT'S A WAKE, ALEX. PEOPLE ARE GOING TO DRINK.
OKAY, WELL, THEN, I BETTER GO GUARD THE DOOR.
WHAT FOR?
IN CASE THE LOW-LIFE SHOW UP.
LOW-LIFE?
ANY IDEAS?
ATTIC WINDOW LOOKS BUSTED. GO GET A ROPE.

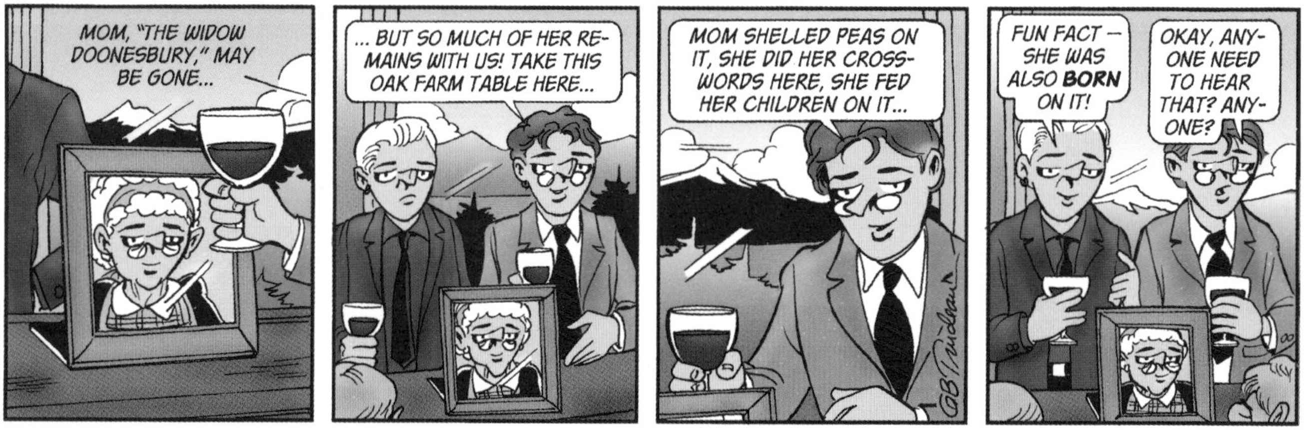
MOM, "THE WIDOW DOONESBURY," MAY BE GONE...
... BUT SO MUCH OF HER REMAINS WITH US! TAKE THIS OAK FARM TABLE HERE...
MOM SHELLED PEAS ON IT, SHE DID HER CROSSWORDS HERE, SHE FED HER CHILDREN ON IT...
FUN FACT — SHE WAS ALSO BORN ON IT!
OKAY, ANYONE NEED TO HEAR THAT? ANYONE?

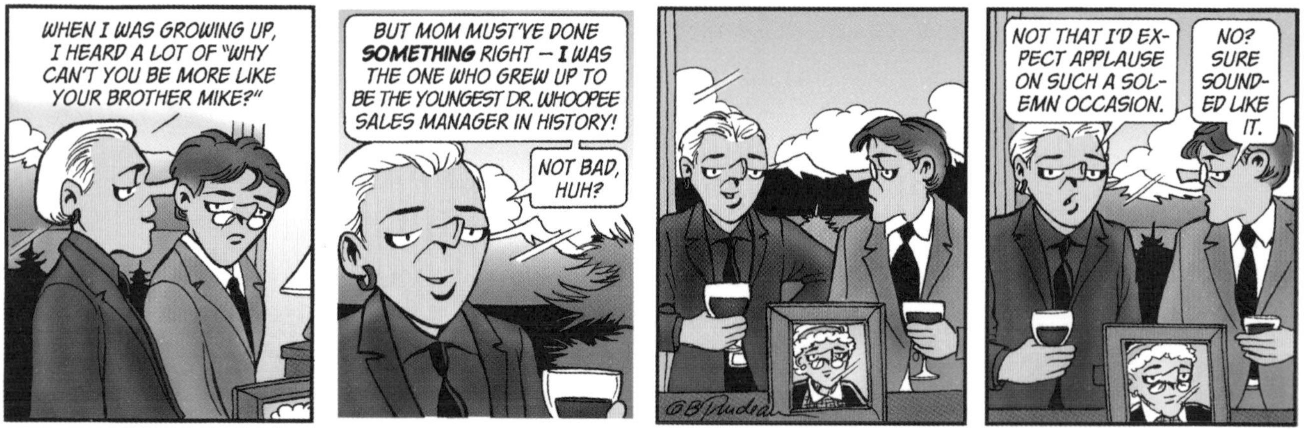
WHEN I WAS GROWING UP, I HEARD A LOT OF "WHY CAN'T YOU BE MORE LIKE YOUR BROTHER MIKE?"
BUT MOM MUST'VE DONE SOMETHING RIGHT — I WAS THE ONE WHO GREW UP TO BE THE YOUNGEST DR. WHOOPEE SALES MANAGER IN HISTORY!
NOT BAD, HUH?
NOT THAT I'D EXPECT APPLAUSE ON SUCH A SOLEMN OCCASION.
NO? SURE SOUNDED LIKE IT.

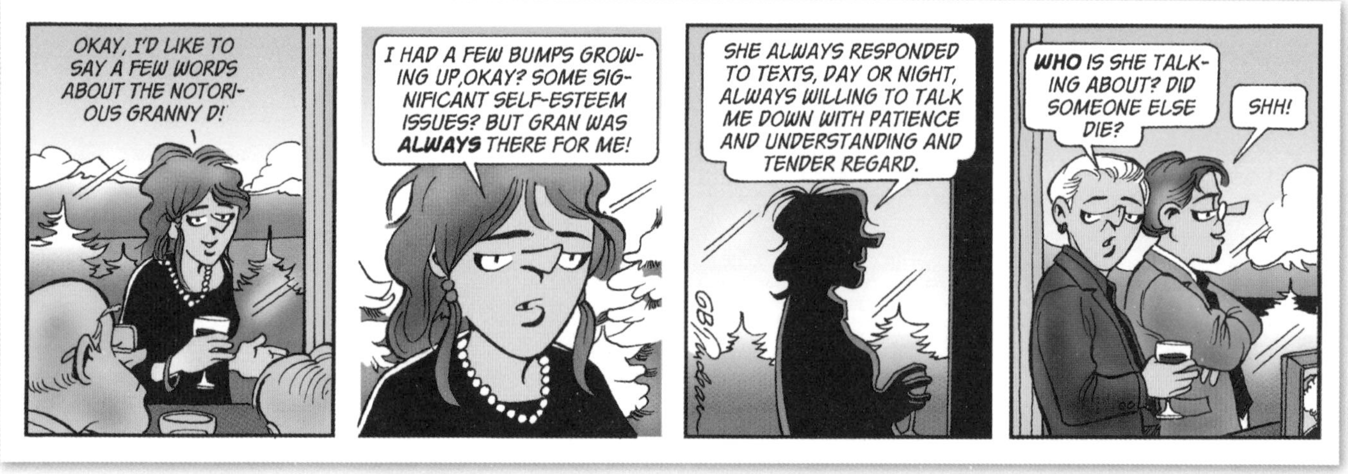
OKAY, I'D LIKE TO SAY A FEW WORDS ABOUT THE NOTORIOUS GRANNY D!
I HAD A FEW BUMPS GROWING UP, OKAY? SOME SIGNIFICANT SELF-ESTEEM ISSUES? BUT GRAN WAS **ALWAYS** THERE FOR ME!
SHE ALWAYS RESPONDED TO TEXTS, DAY OR NIGHT, ALWAYS WILLING TO TALK ME DOWN WITH PATIENCE AND UNDERSTANDING AND TENDER REGARD.
WHO IS SHE TALKING ABOUT? DID SOMEONE ELSE DIE?
SHH!

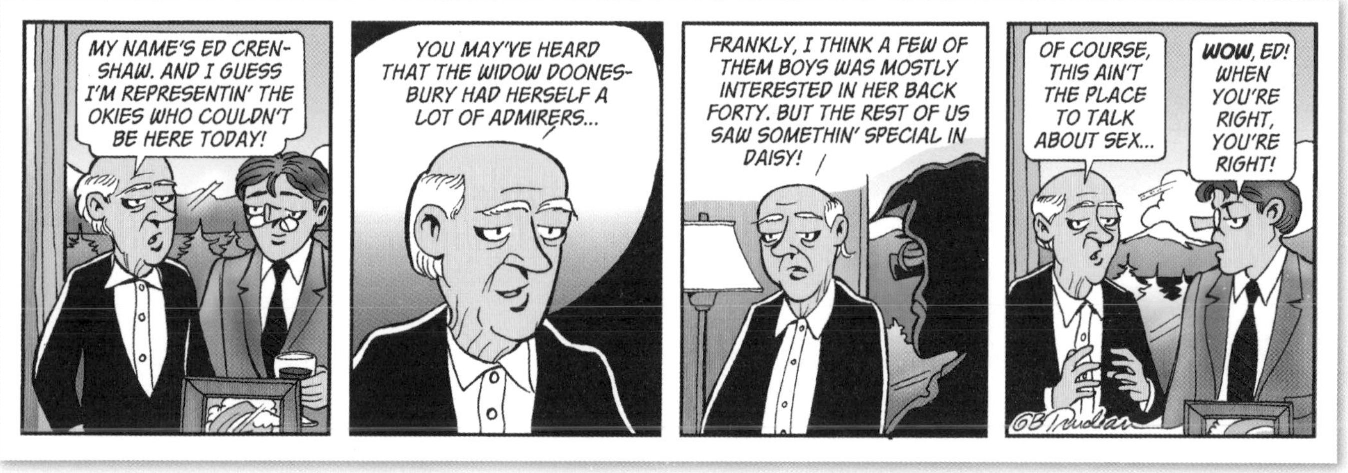
MY NAME'S ED CRENSHAW. AND I GUESS I'M REPRESENTIN' THE OKIES WHO COULDN'T BE HERE TODAY!
YOU MAY'VE HEARD THAT THE WIDOW DOONESBURY HAD HERSELF A LOT OF ADMIRERS...
FRANKLY, I THINK A FEW OF THEM BOYS WAS MOSTLY INTERESTED IN HER BACK FORTY. BUT THE REST OF US SAW SOMETHIN' SPECIAL IN DAISY!
OF COURSE, THIS AIN'T THE PLACE TO TALK ABOUT SEX...
WOW, ED! WHEN YOU'RE RIGHT, YOU'RE RIGHT!

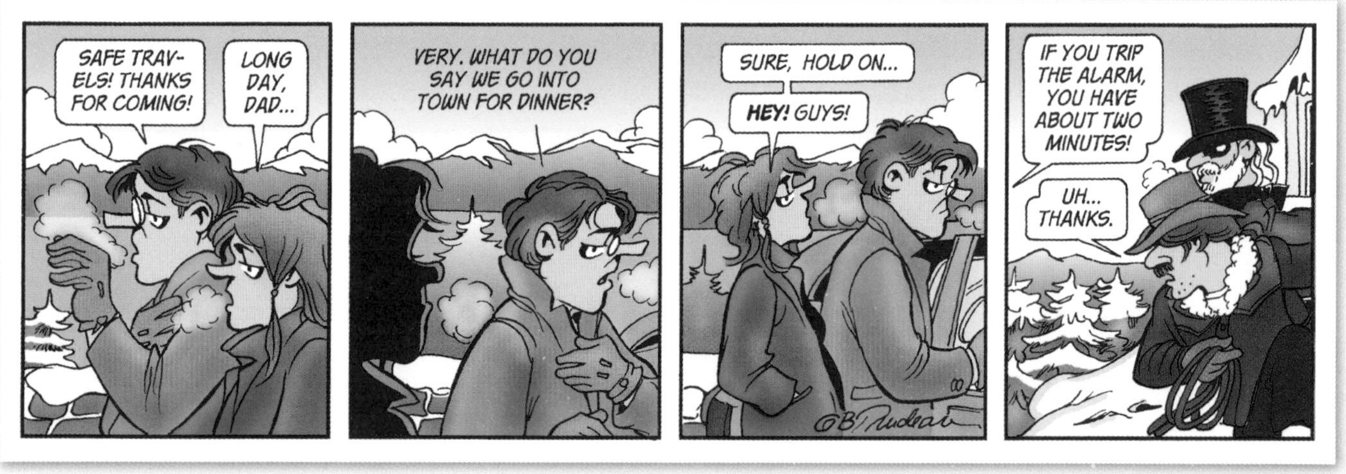
SAFE TRAVELS! THANKS FOR COMING!
LONG DAY, DAD...
VERY. WHAT DO YOU SAY WE GO INTO TOWN FOR DINNER?
SURE, HOLD ON...
HEY! GUYS!
IF YOU TRIP THE ALARM, YOU HAVE ABOUT TWO MINUTES!
UH... THANKS.

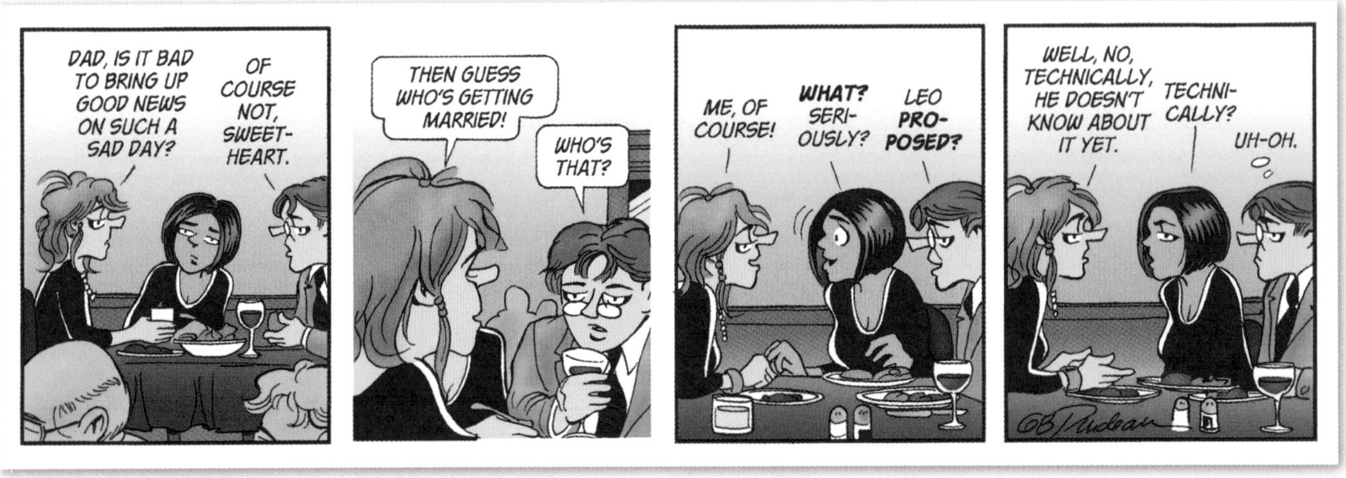
DAD, IS IT BAD TO BRING UP GOOD NEWS ON SUCH A SAD DAY?
OF COURSE NOT, SWEET-HEART.
THEN GUESS WHO'S GETTING MARRIED!
WHO'S THAT?
ME, OF COURSE!
WHAT? SERI-OUSLY?
LEO PRO-POSED?
WELL, NO, TECHNICALLY, HE DOESN'T KNOW ABOUT IT YET.
TECHNI-CALLY?
UH-OH.

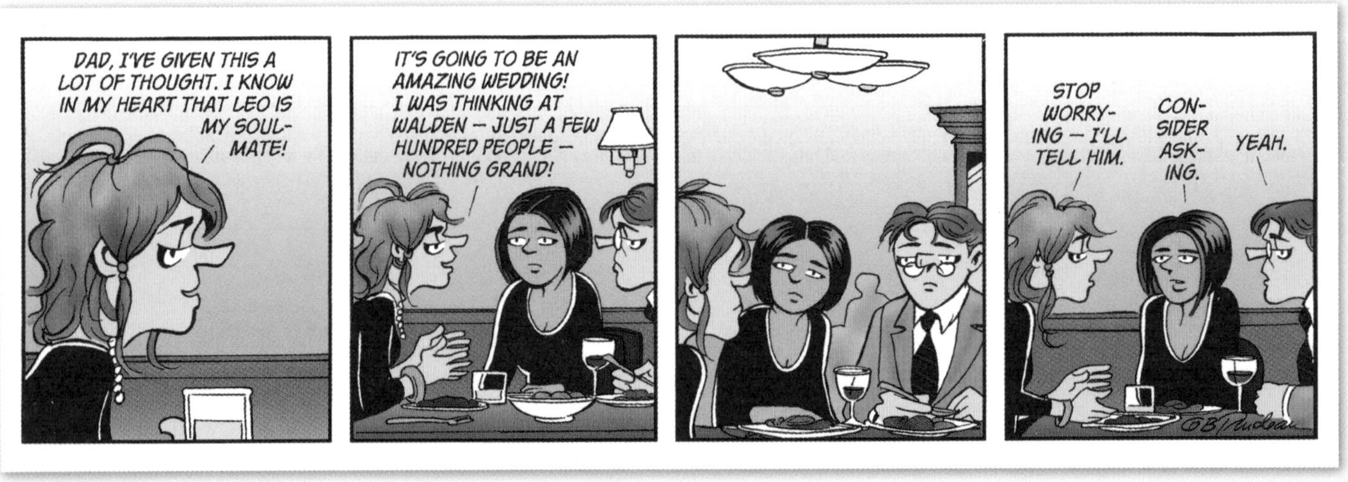
DAD, I'VE GIVEN THIS A LOT OF THOUGHT. I KNOW IN MY HEART THAT LEO IS MY SOUL-MATE!
IT'S GOING TO BE AN AMAZING WEDDING! I WAS THINKING AT WALDEN — JUST A FEW HUNDRED PEOPLE — NOTHING GRAND!
STOP WORRY-ING — I'LL TELL HIM.
CON-SIDER ASK-ING.
YEAH.

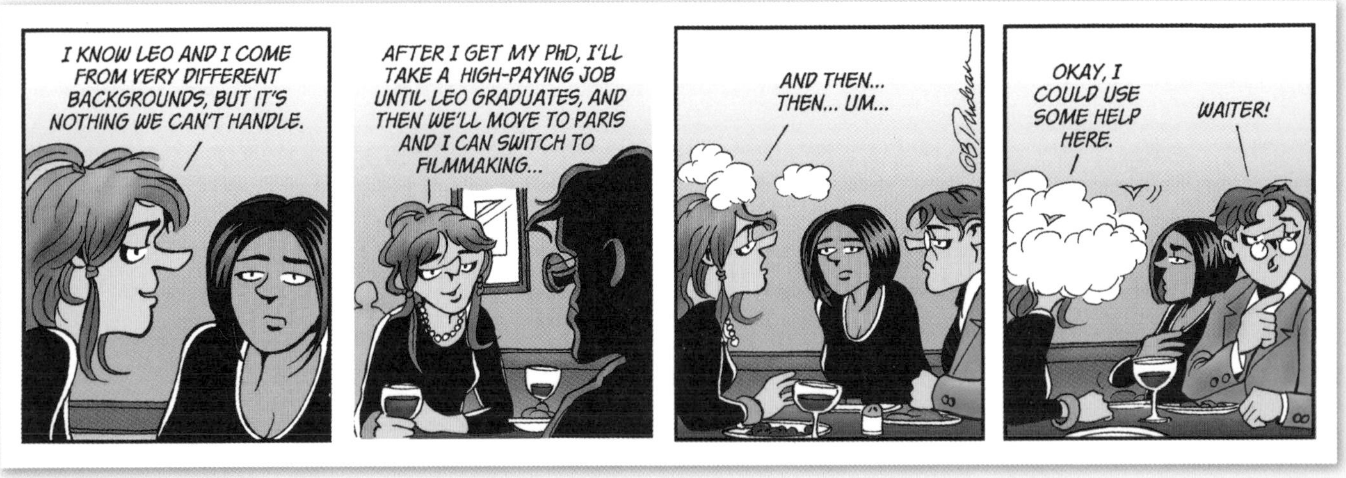
I KNOW LEO AND I COME FROM VERY DIFFERENT BACKGROUNDS, BUT IT'S NOTHING WE CAN'T HANDLE.
AFTER I GET MY PhD, I'LL TAKE A HIGH-PAYING JOB UNTIL LEO GRADUATES, AND THEN WE'LL MOVE TO PARIS AND I CAN SWITCH TO FILMMAKING...
AND THEN... THEN... UM...
OKAY, I COULD USE SOME HELP HERE.
WAITER!

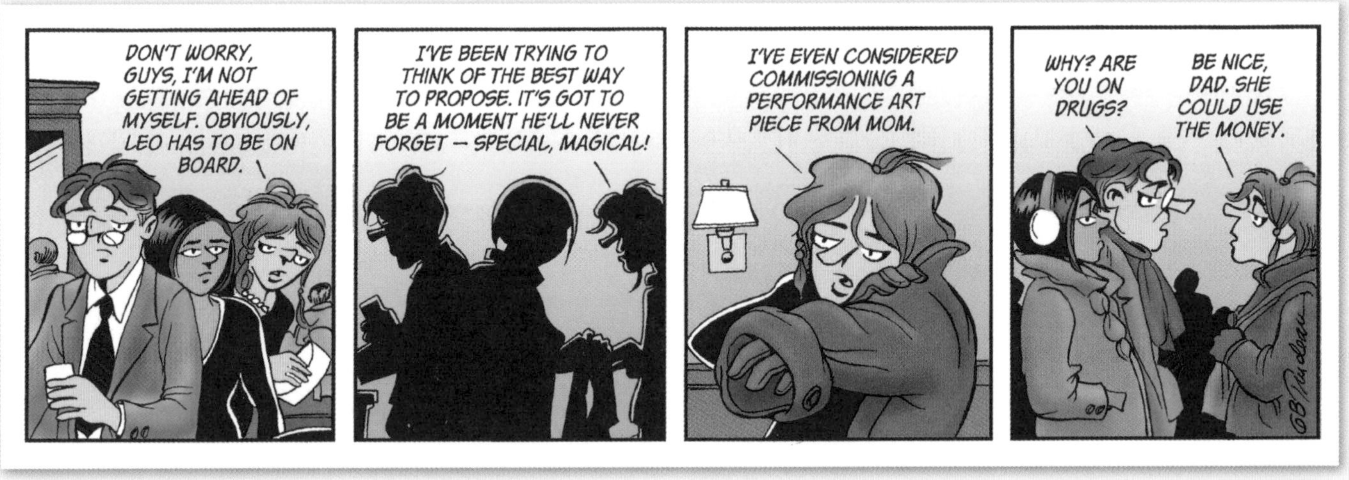
DON'T WORRY, GUYS, I'M NOT GETTING AHEAD OF MYSELF. OBVIOUSLY, LEO HAS TO BE ON BOARD.
I'VE BEEN TRYING TO THINK OF THE BEST WAY TO PROPOSE. IT'S GOT TO BE A MOMENT HE'LL NEVER FORGET — SPECIAL, MAGICAL!
I'VE EVEN CONSIDERED COMMISSIONING A PERFORMANCE ART PIECE FROM MOM.
WHY? ARE YOU ON DRUGS?
BE NICE, DAD. SHE COULD USE THE MONEY.

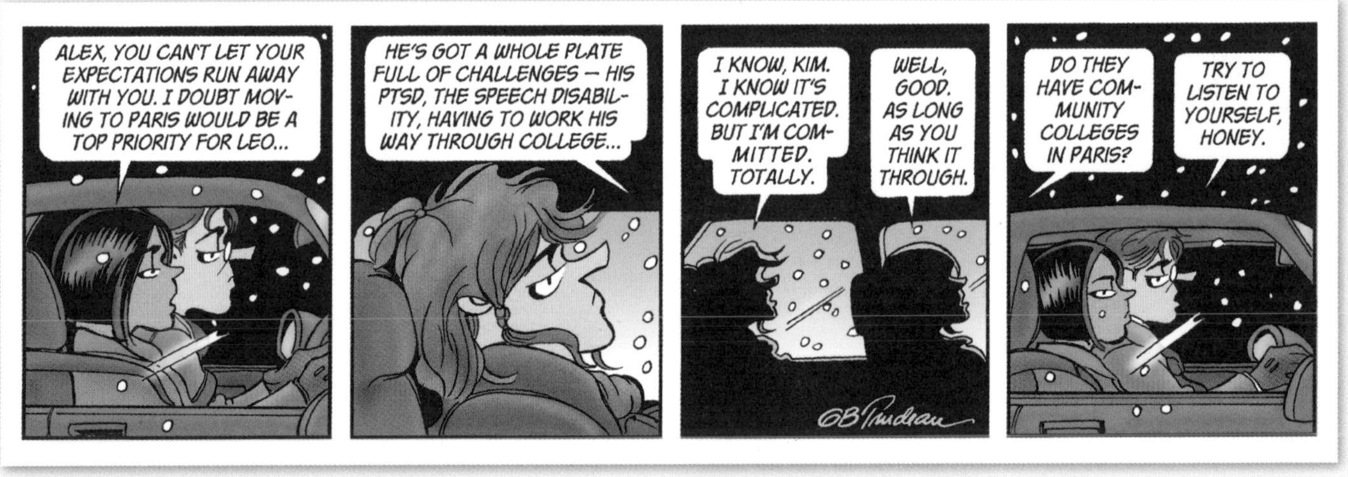
ALEX, YOU CAN'T LET YOUR EXPECTATIONS RUN AWAY WITH YOU. I DOUBT MOVING TO PARIS WOULD BE A TOP PRIORITY FOR LEO...
HE'S GOT A WHOLE PLATE FULL OF CHALLENGES — HIS PTSD, THE SPEECH DISABILITY, HAVING TO WORK HIS WAY THROUGH COLLEGE...
I KNOW, KIM. I KNOW IT'S COMPLICATED. BUT I'M COMMITTED. TOTALLY.
WELL, GOOD. AS LONG AS YOU THINK IT THROUGH.
DO THEY HAVE COMMUNITY COLLEGES IN PARIS?
TRY TO LISTEN TO YOURSELF, HONEY.

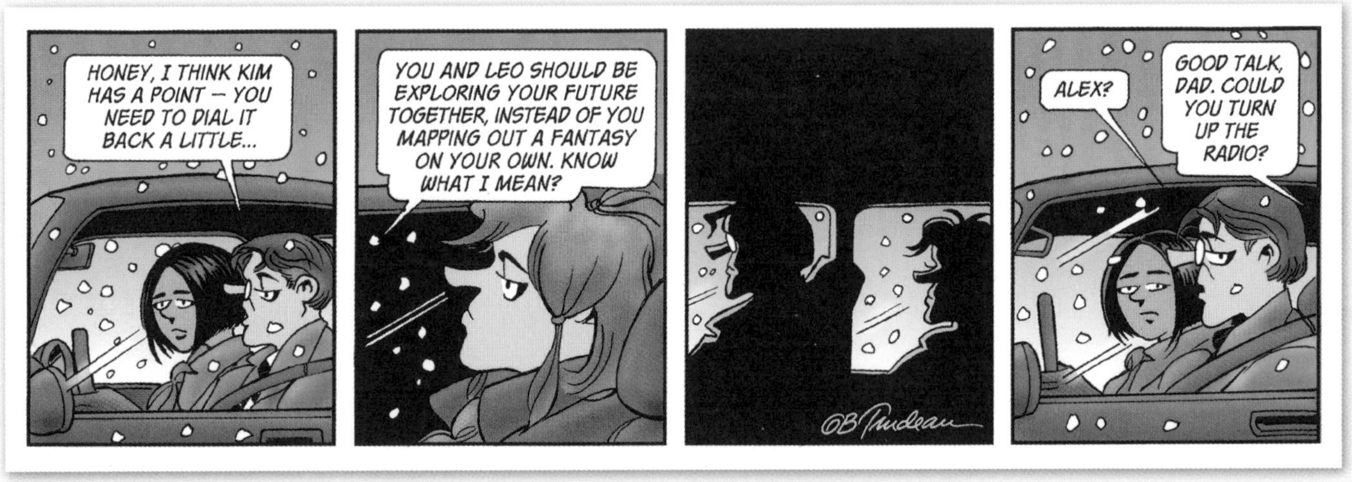
HONEY, I THINK KIM HAS A POINT — YOU NEED TO DIAL IT BACK A LITTLE...
YOU AND LEO SHOULD BE EXPLORING YOUR FUTURE TOGETHER, INSTEAD OF YOU MAPPING OUT A FANTASY ON YOUR OWN. KNOW WHAT I MEAN?
ALEX?
GOOD TALK, DAD. COULD YOU TURN UP THE RADIO?

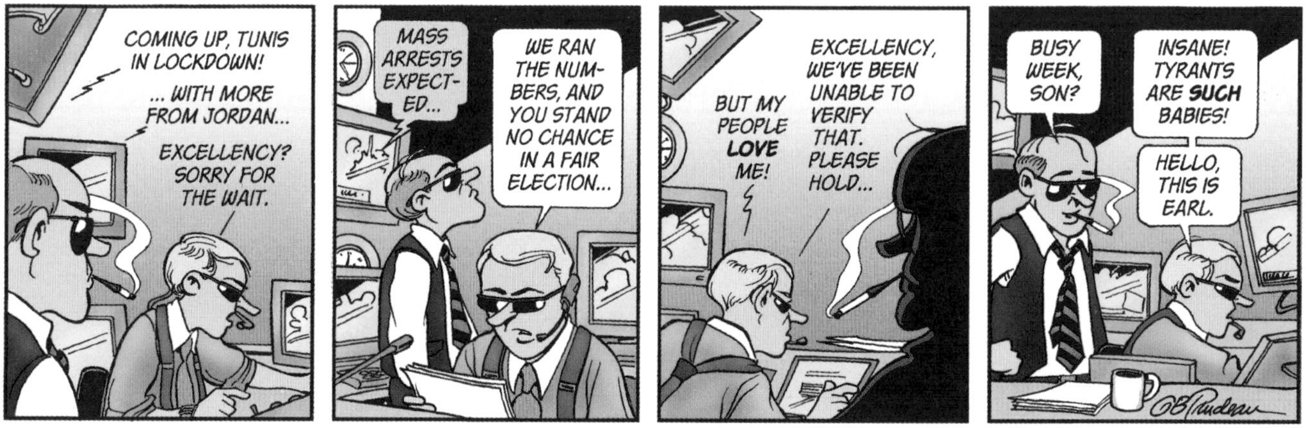
COMING UP, TUNIS IN LOCKDOWN!
... WITH MORE FROM JORDAN...
EXCELLENCY? SORRY FOR THE WAIT.
MASS ARRESTS EXPECT-ED...
WE RAN THE NUM-BERS, AND YOU STAND NO CHANCE IN A FAIR ELECTION...
BUT MY PEOPLE **LOVE** ME!
EXCELLENCY, WE'VE BEEN UNABLE TO VERIFY THAT. PLEASE HOLD...
BUSY WEEK, SON?
INSANE! TYRANTS ARE **SUCH** BABIES!
HELLO, THIS IS EARL.
GBTrudeau

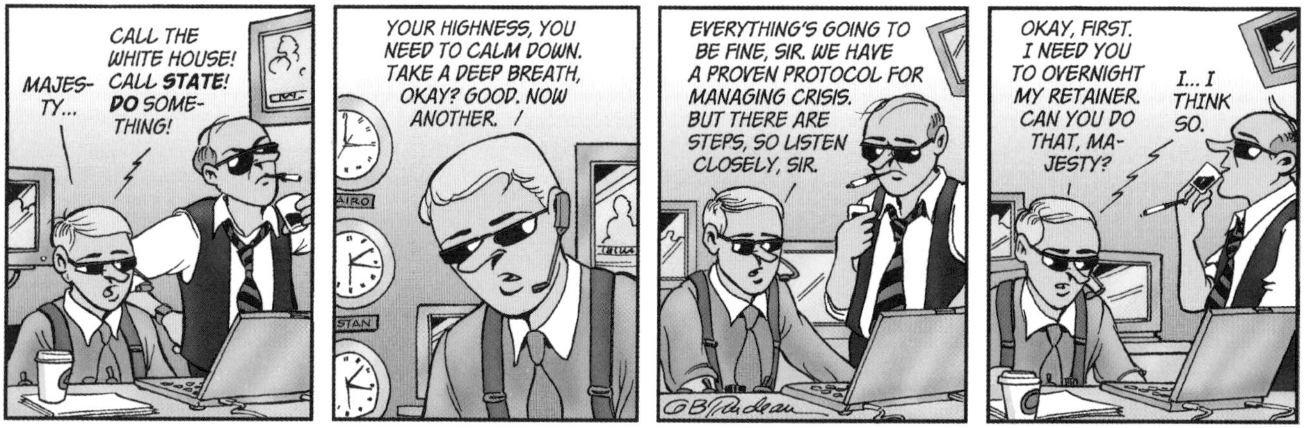
MAJES-TY...
CALL THE WHITE HOUSE! CALL **STATE**! **DO** SOME-THING!
YOUR HIGHNESS, YOU NEED TO CALM DOWN. TAKE A DEEP BREATH, OKAY? GOOD. NOW ANOTHER.
EVERYTHING'S GOING TO BE FINE, SIR. WE HAVE A PROVEN PROTOCOL FOR MANAGING CRISIS. BUT THERE ARE STEPS, SO LISTEN CLOSELY, SIR.
OKAY, FIRST. I NEED YOU TO OVERNIGHT MY RETAINER. CAN YOU DO THAT, MA-JESTY?
I... I THINK SO.
GBTrudeau

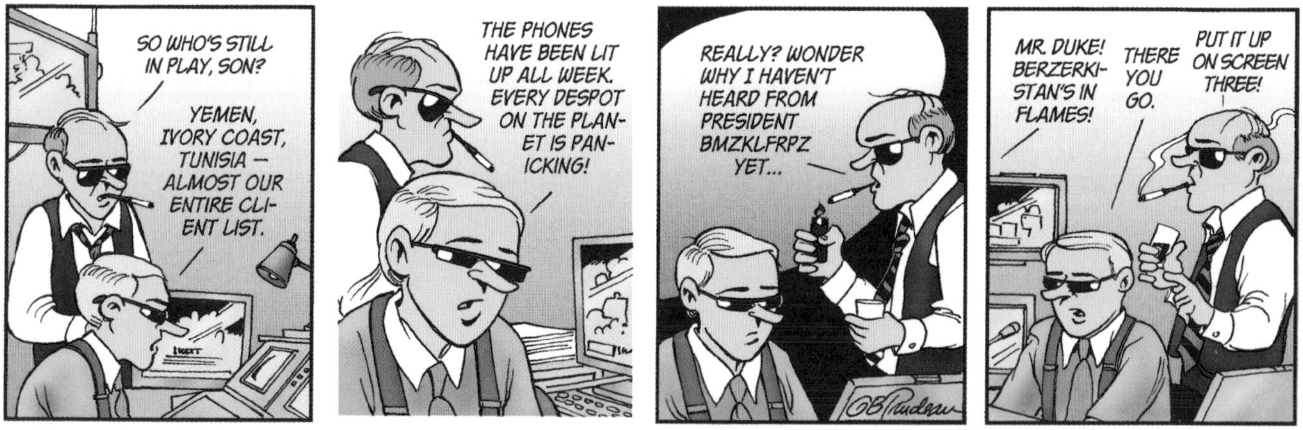
SO WHO'S STILL IN PLAY, SON?
YEMEN, IVORY COAST, TUNISIA — ALMOST OUR ENTIRE CLI-ENT LIST.
THE PHONES HAVE BEEN LIT UP ALL WEEK. EVERY DESPOT ON THE PLAN-ET IS PAN-ICKING!
REALLY? WONDER WHY I HAVEN'T HEARD FROM PRESIDENT BMZKLFRPZ YET...
MR. DUKE! BERZERKI-STAN'S IN FLAMES!
THERE YOU GO.
PUT IT UP ON SCREEN THREE!
GBTrudeau

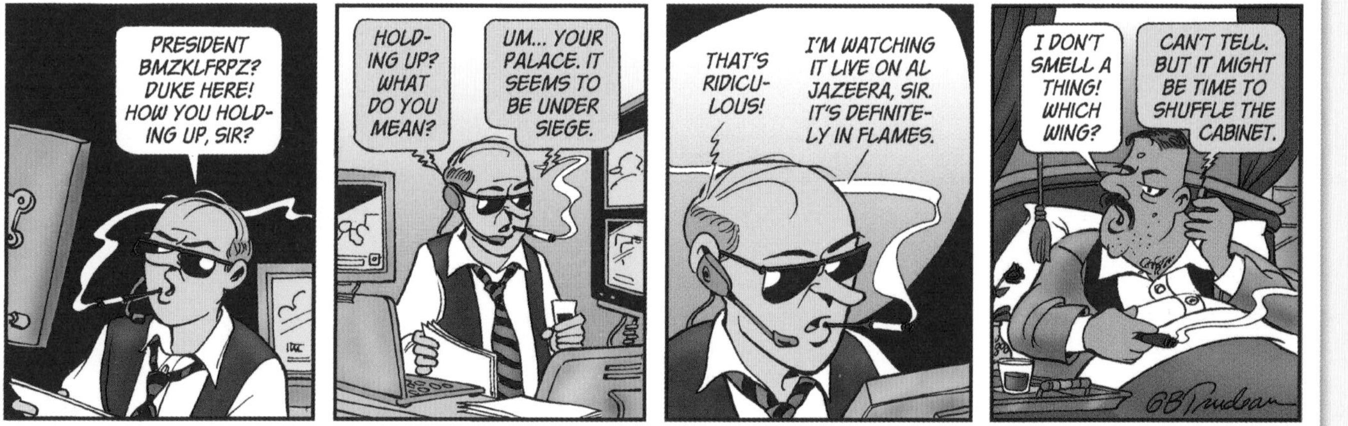
PRESIDENT BMZKLFRPZ? DUKE HERE! HOW YOU HOLDING UP, SIR?
HOLDING UP? WHAT DO YOU MEAN?
UM... YOUR PALACE. IT SEEMS TO BE UNDER SIEGE.
THAT'S RIDICULOUS!
I'M WATCHING IT LIVE ON AL JAZEERA, SIR. IT'S DEFINITELY IN FLAMES.
I DON'T SMELL A THING! WHICH WING?
CAN'T TELL. BUT IT MIGHT BE TIME TO SHUFFLE THE CABINET.
GBTrudeau

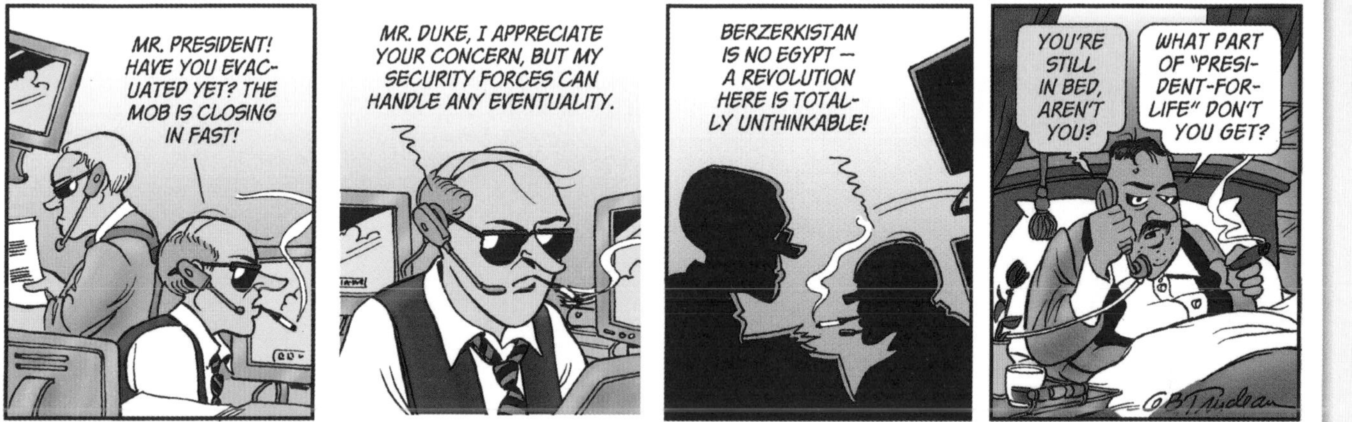
MR. PRESIDENT! HAVE YOU EVACUATED YET? THE MOB IS CLOSING IN FAST!
MR. DUKE, I APPRECIATE YOUR CONCERN, BUT MY SECURITY FORCES CAN HANDLE ANY EVENTUALITY.
BERZERKISTAN IS NO EGYPT — A REVOLUTION HERE IS TOTALLY UNTHINKABLE!
YOU'RE STILL IN BED, AREN'T YOU?
WHAT PART OF "PRESIDENT-FOR-LIFE" DON'T YOU GET?
GBTrudeau

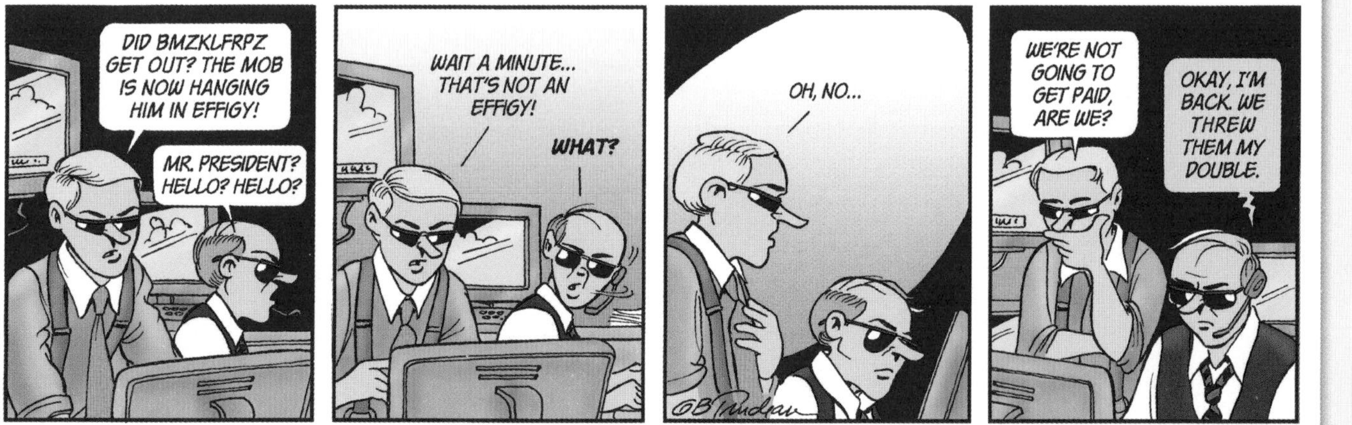
DID BMZKLFRPZ GET OUT? THE MOB IS NOW HANGING HIM IN EFFIGY!
MR. PRESIDENT? HELLO? HELLO?
WAIT A MINUTE... THAT'S NOT AN EFFIGY!
WHAT?
OH, NO...
GBTrudeau
WE'RE NOT GOING TO GET PAID, ARE WE?
OKAY, I'M BACK. WE THREW THEM MY DOUBLE.

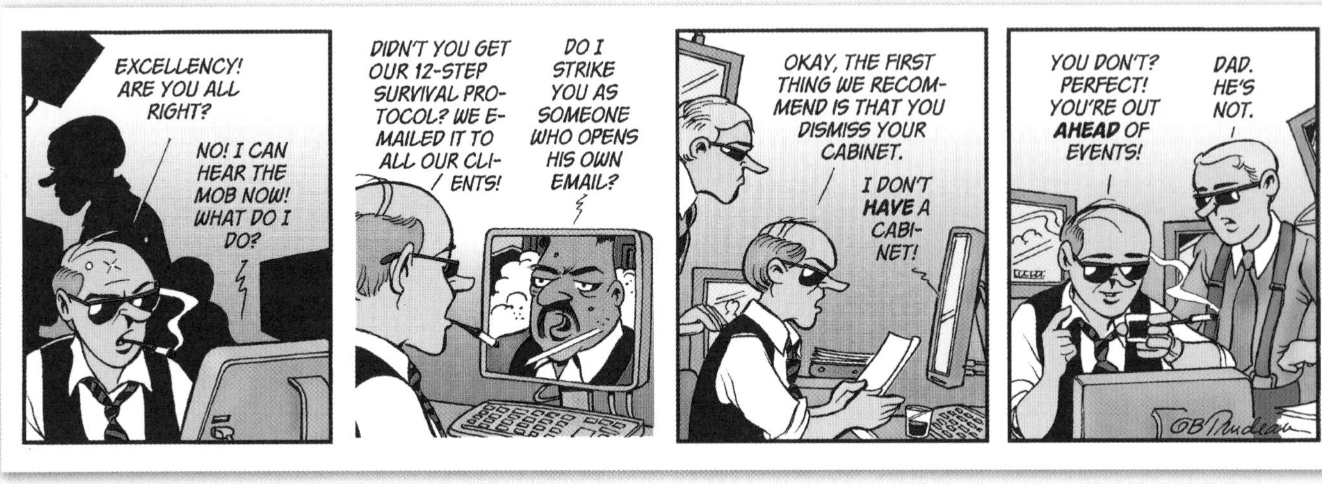
EXCELLENCY! ARE YOU ALL RIGHT?
NO! I CAN HEAR THE MOB NOW! WHAT DO I DO?
DIDN'T YOU GET OUR 12-STEP SURVIVAL PROTOCOL? WE E-MAILED IT TO ALL OUR CLIENTS!
DO I STRIKE YOU AS SOMEONE WHO OPENS HIS OWN EMAIL?
OKAY, THE FIRST THING WE RECOMMEND IS THAT YOU DISMISS YOUR CABINET.
I DON'T **HAVE** A CABINET!
YOU DON'T? PERFECT! YOU'RE OUT **AHEAD** OF EVENTS!
DAD. HE'S NOT.
GB Trudeau

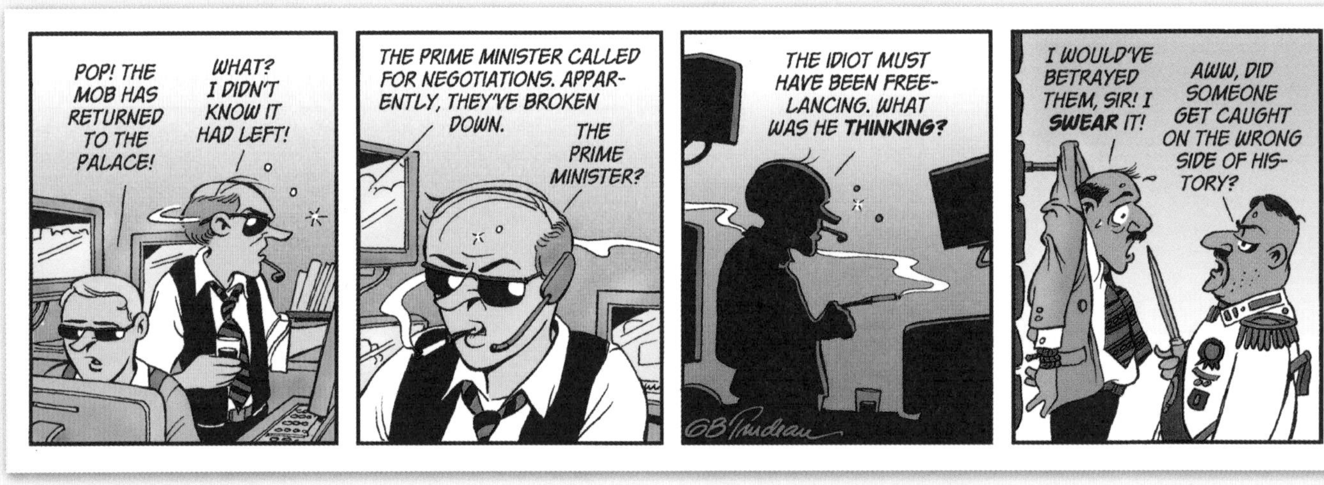
POP! THE MOB HAS RETURNED TO THE PALACE!
WHAT? I DIDN'T KNOW IT HAD LEFT!
THE PRIME MINISTER CALLED FOR NEGOTIATIONS. APPARENTLY, THEY'VE BROKEN DOWN.
THE PRIME MINISTER?
THE IDIOT MUST HAVE BEEN FREELANCING. WHAT WAS HE **THINKING?**
GB Trudeau
I WOULD'VE BETRAYED THEM, SIR! I **SWEAR** IT!
AWW, DID SOMEONE GET CAUGHT ON THE WRONG SIDE OF HISTORY?

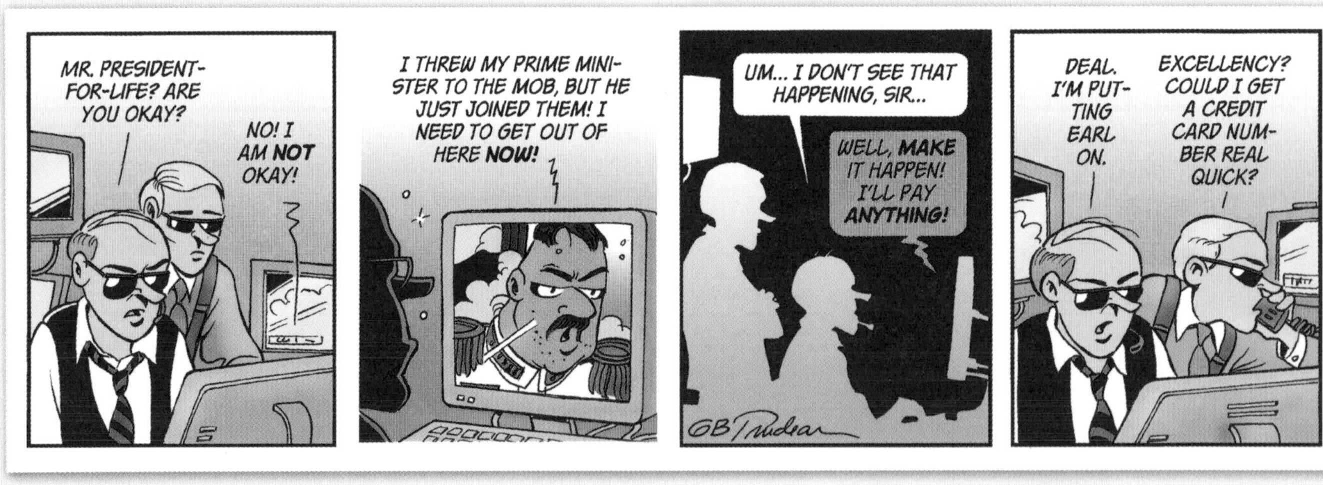
MR. PRESIDENT-FOR-LIFE? ARE YOU OKAY?
NO! I AM **NOT** OKAY!
I THREW MY PRIME MINISTER TO THE MOB, BUT HE JUST JOINED THEM! I NEED TO GET OUT OF HERE **NOW!**
UM... I DON'T SEE THAT HAPPENING, SIR...
WELL, **MAKE** IT HAPPEN! I'LL PAY **ANYTHING!**
GB Trudeau
DEAL. I'M PUTTING EARL ON.
EXCELLENCY? COULD I GET A CREDIT CARD NUMBER REAL QUICK?

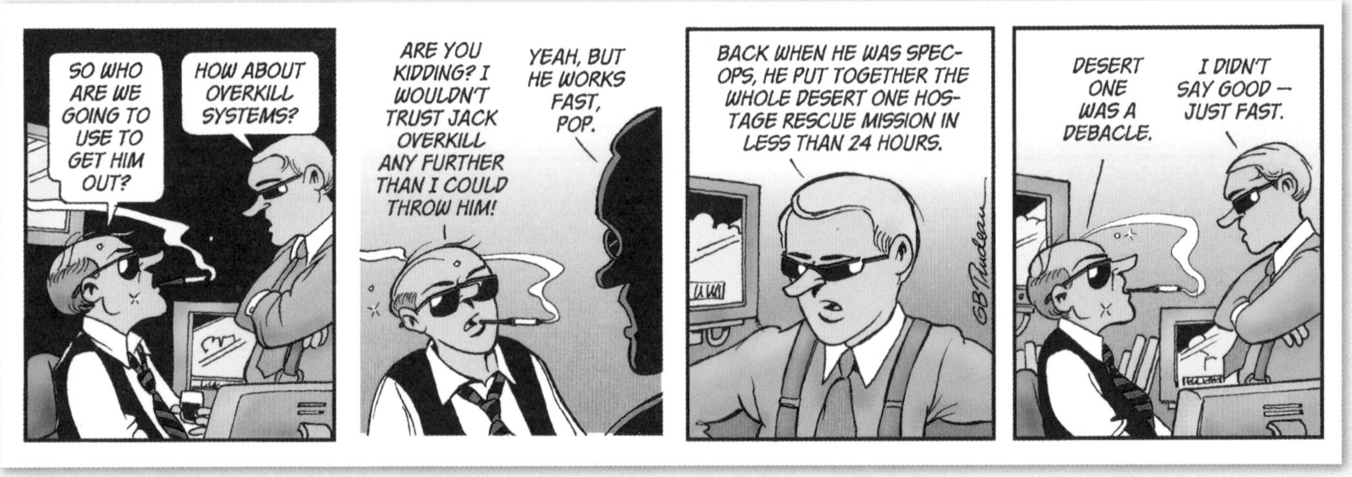
SO WHO ARE WE GOING TO USE TO GET HIM OUT?
HOW ABOUT OVERKILL SYSTEMS?
ARE YOU KIDDING? I WOULDN'T TRUST JACK OVERKILL ANY FURTHER THAN I COULD THROW HIM!
YEAH, BUT HE WORKS FAST, POP.
BACK WHEN HE WAS SPEC-OPS, HE PUT TOGETHER THE WHOLE DESERT ONE HOSTAGE RESCUE MISSION IN LESS THAN 24 HOURS.
DESERT ONE WAS A DEBACLE.
I DIDN'T SAY GOOD — JUST FAST.
GB Trudeau

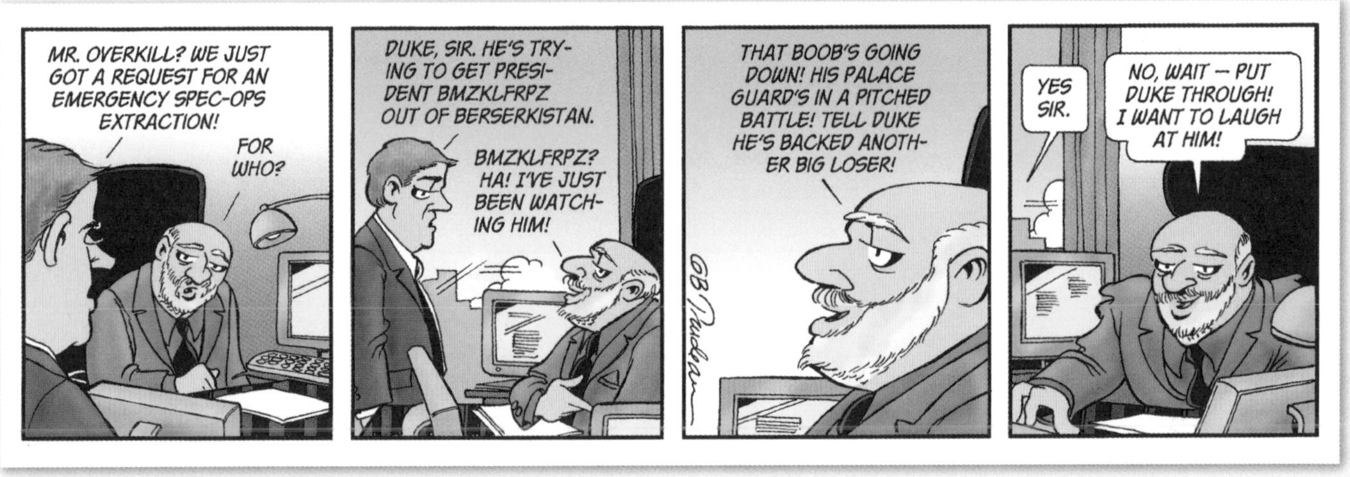
MR. OVERKILL? WE JUST GOT A REQUEST FOR AN EMERGENCY SPEC-OPS EXTRACTION!
FOR WHO?
DUKE, SIR. HE'S TRYING TO GET PRESIDENT BMZKLFRPZ OUT OF BERSERKISTAN.
BMZKLFRPZ? HA! I'VE JUST BEEN WATCHING HIM!
THAT BOOB'S GOING DOWN! HIS PALACE GUARD'S IN A PITCHED BATTLE! TELL DUKE HE'S BACKED ANOTHER BIG LOSER!
GB Trudeau
YES SIR.
NO, WAIT — PUT DUKE THROUGH! I WANT TO LAUGH AT HIM!

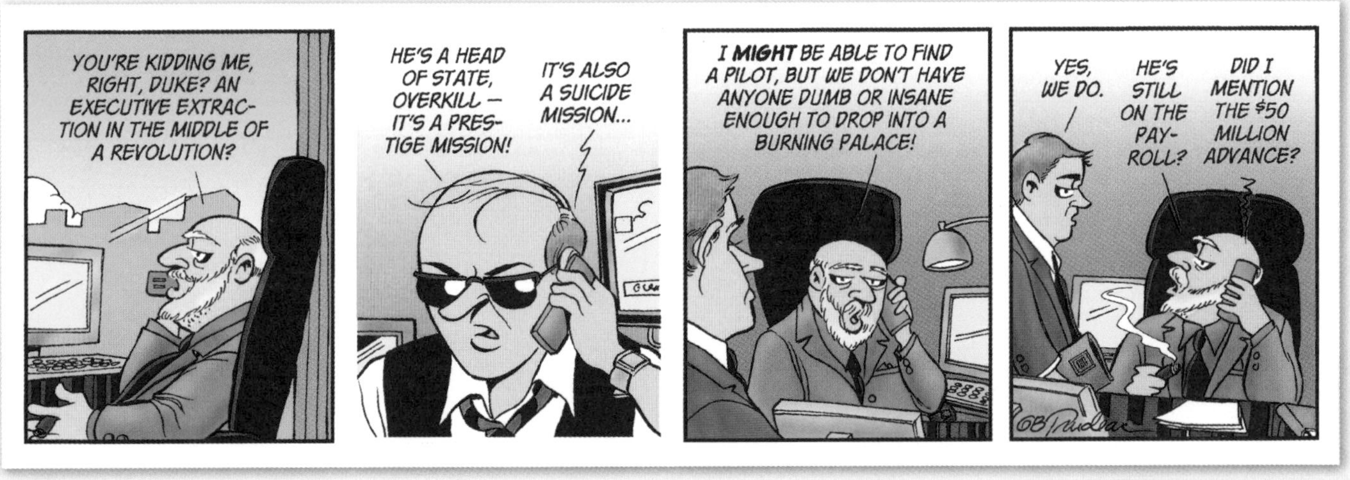
YOU'RE KIDDING ME, RIGHT, DUKE? AN EXECUTIVE EXTRACTION IN THE MIDDLE OF A REVOLUTION?
HE'S A HEAD OF STATE, OVERKILL — IT'S A PRESTIGE MISSION!
IT'S ALSO A SUICIDE MISSION...
I **MIGHT** BE ABLE TO FIND A PILOT, BUT WE DON'T HAVE ANYONE DUMB OR INSANE ENOUGH TO DROP INTO A BURNING PALACE!
YES, WE DO.
HE'S STILL ON THE PAYROLL?
DID I MENTION THE $50 MILLION ADVANCE?
GB Trudeau

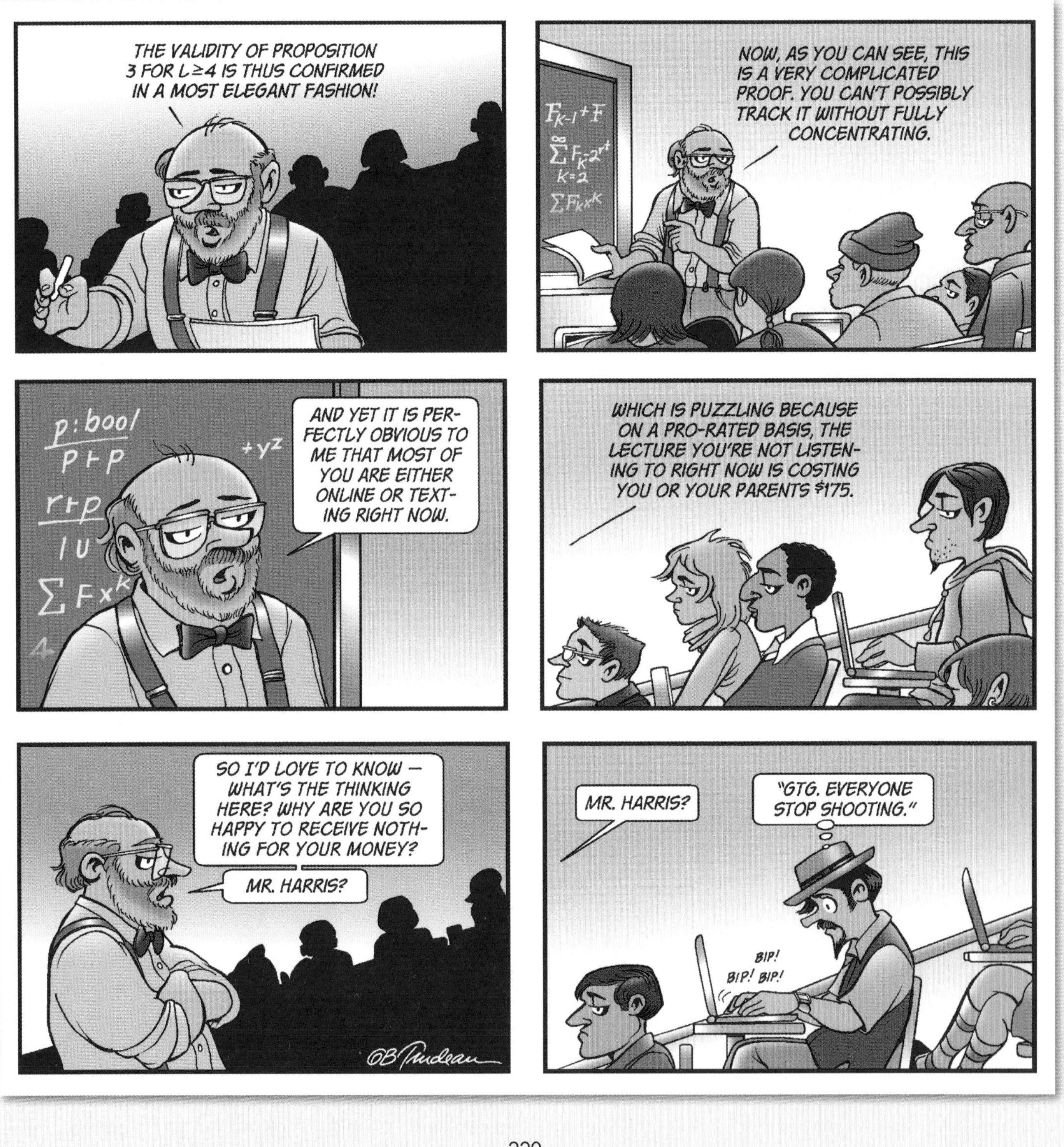
THE VALIDITY OF PROPOSITION 3 FOR L≥4 IS THUS CONFIRMED IN A MOST ELEGANT FASHION!
NOW, AS YOU CAN SEE, THIS IS A VERY COMPLICATED PROOF. YOU CAN'T POSSIBLY TRACK IT WITHOUT FULLY CONCENTRATING.
AND YET IT IS PERFECTLY OBVIOUS TO ME THAT MOST OF YOU ARE EITHER ONLINE OR TEXTING RIGHT NOW.
WHICH IS PUZZLING BECAUSE ON A PRO-RATED BASIS, THE LECTURE YOU'RE NOT LISTENING TO RIGHT NOW IS COSTING YOU OR YOUR PARENTS $175.
SO I'D LOVE TO KNOW — WHAT'S THE THINKING HERE? WHY ARE YOU SO HAPPY TO RECEIVE NOTHING FOR YOUR MONEY?
MR. HARRIS?
MR. HARRIS?
"GTG. EVERYONE STOP SHOOTING."
BIP! BIP! BIP!

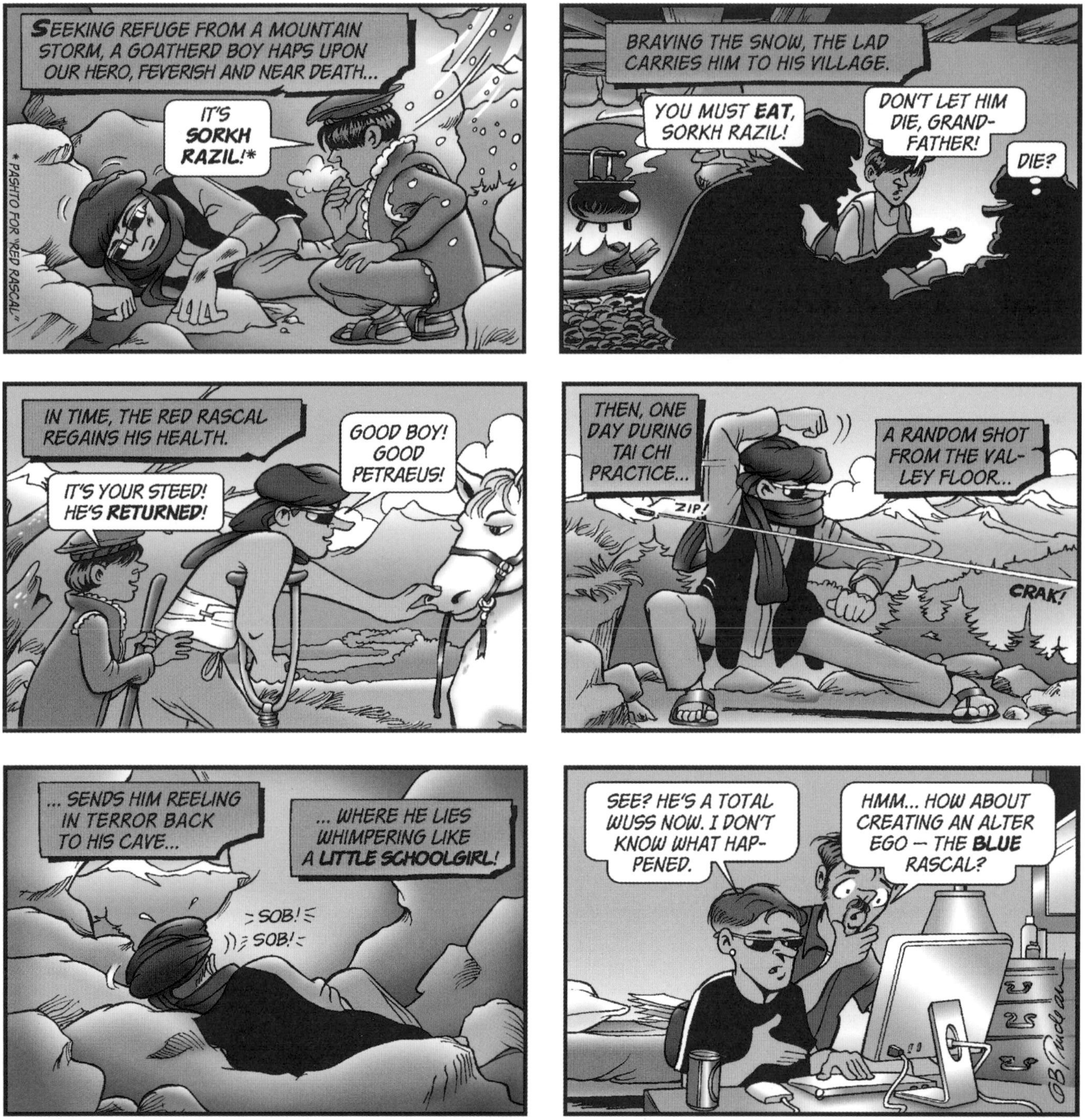
SEEKING REFUGE FROM A MOUNTAIN STORM, A GOATHERD BOY HAPS UPON OUR HERO, FEVERISH AND NEAR DEATH...
IT'S SORKH RAZIL!*
* PASHTO FOR "RED RASCAL"
BRAVING THE SNOW, THE LAD CARRIES HIM TO HIS VILLAGE.
YOU MUST EAT, SORKH RAZIL!
DON'T LET HIM DIE, GRANDFATHER!
DIE?
IN TIME, THE RED RASCAL REGAINS HIS HEALTH.
IT'S YOUR STEED! HE'S RETURNED!
GOOD BOY! GOOD PETRAEUS!
THEN, ONE DAY DURING TAI CHI PRACTICE...
A RANDOM SHOT FROM THE VALLEY FLOOR...
ZIP!
CRAK!
... SENDS HIM REELING IN TERROR BACK TO HIS CAVE...
... WHERE HE LIES WHIMPERING LIKE A LITTLE SCHOOLGIRL!
SOB!
SOB!
SEE? HE'S A TOTAL WUSS NOW. I DON'T KNOW WHAT HAPPENED.
HMM... HOW ABOUT CREATING AN ALTER EGO — THE BLUE RASCAL?
GB Trudeau

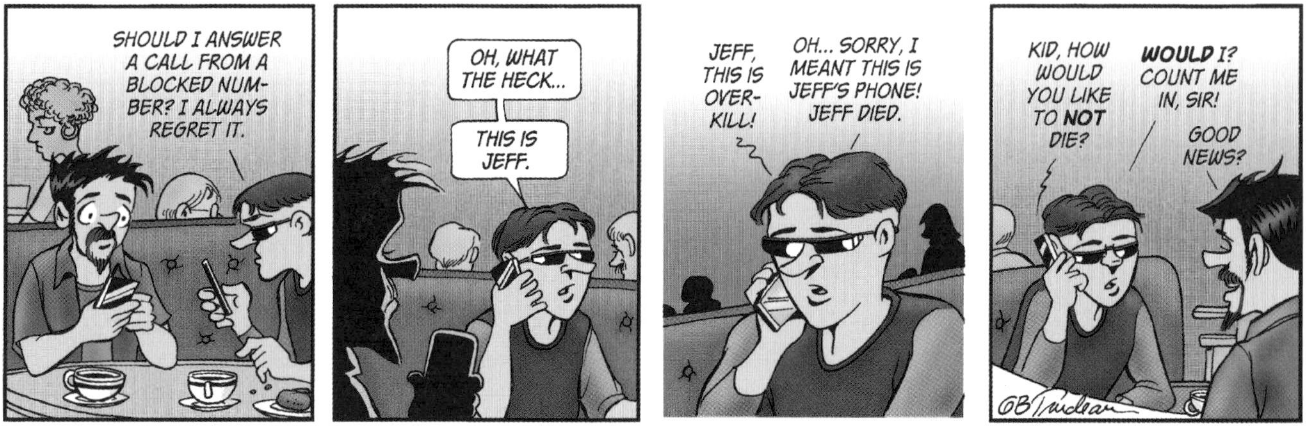
SHOULD I ANSWER A CALL FROM A BLOCKED NUMBER? I ALWAYS REGRET IT.
OH, WHAT THE HECK...
THIS IS JEFF.
JEFF, THIS IS OVERKILL!
OH... SORRY, I MEANT THIS IS JEFF'S PHONE! JEFF DIED.
KID, HOW WOULD YOU LIKE TO **NOT** DIE?
WOULD I? COUNT ME IN, SIR!
GOOD NEWS?

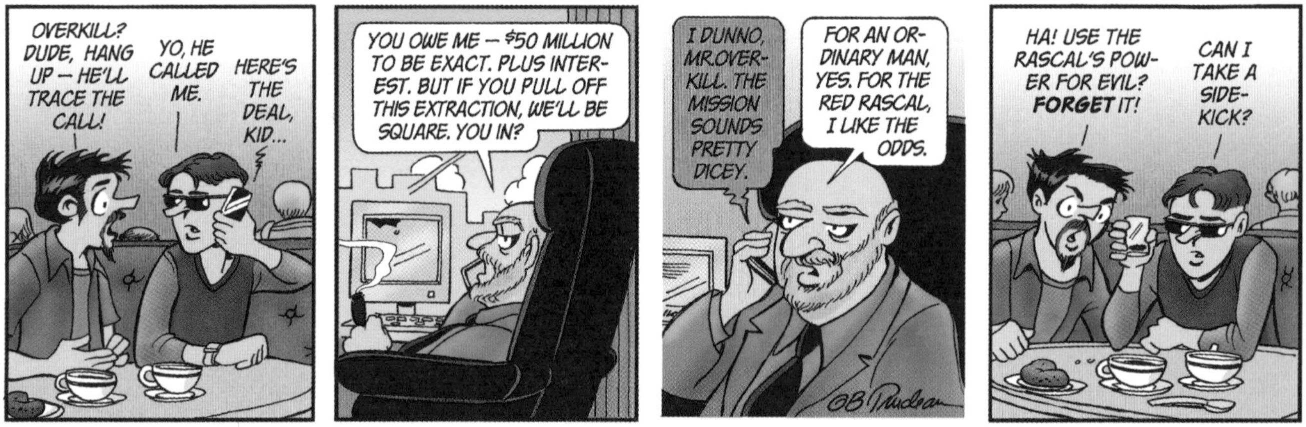
OVERKILL? DUDE, HANG UP — HE'LL TRACE THE CALL!
YO, HE CALLED ME.
HERE'S THE DEAL, KID...
YOU OWE ME — $50 MILLION TO BE EXACT. PLUS INTEREST. BUT IF YOU PULL OFF THIS EXTRACTION, WE'LL BE SQUARE. YOU IN?
I DUNNO, MR. OVERKILL. THE MISSION SOUNDS PRETTY DICEY.
FOR AN ORDINARY MAN, YES. FOR THE RED RASCAL, I LIKE THE ODDS.
HA! USE THE RASCAL'S POWER FOR EVIL? **FORGET** IT!
CAN I TAKE A SIDEKICK?

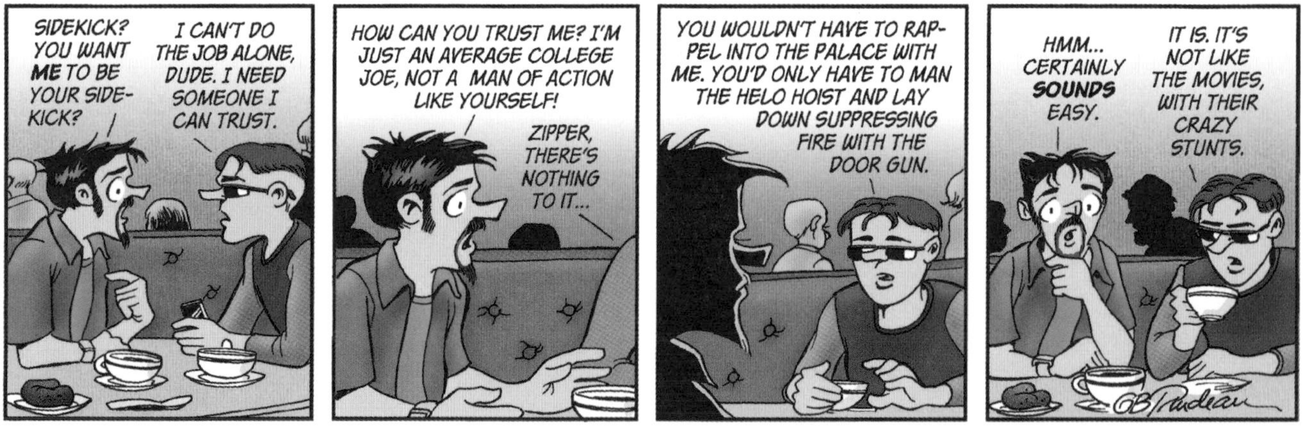
SIDEKICK? YOU WANT **ME** TO BE YOUR SIDEKICK?
I CAN'T DO THE JOB ALONE, DUDE. I NEED SOMEONE I CAN TRUST.
HOW CAN YOU TRUST ME? I'M JUST AN AVERAGE COLLEGE JOE, NOT A MAN OF ACTION LIKE YOURSELF!
ZIPPER, THERE'S NOTHING TO IT...
YOU WOULDN'T HAVE TO RAPPEL INTO THE PALACE WITH ME. YOU'D ONLY HAVE TO MAN THE HELO HOIST AND LAY DOWN SUPPRESSING FIRE WITH THE DOOR GUN.
HMM... CERTAINLY **SOUNDS** EASY.
IT IS. IT'S NOT LIKE THE MOVIES, WITH THEIR CRAZY STUNTS.

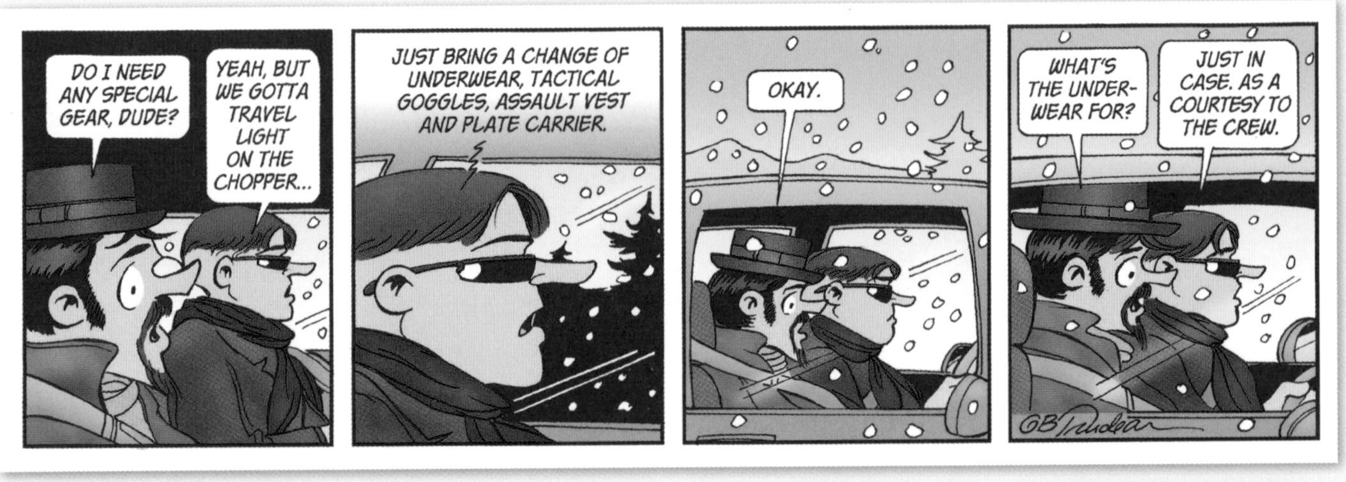
DO I NEED ANY SPECIAL GEAR, DUDE?
YEAH, BUT WE GOTTA TRAVEL LIGHT ON THE CHOPPER...
JUST BRING A CHANGE OF UNDERWEAR, TACTICAL GOGGLES, ASSAULT VEST AND PLATE CARRIER.
OKAY.
WHAT'S THE UNDER-WEAR FOR?
JUST IN CASE. AS A COURTESY TO THE CREW.
GBTrudeau

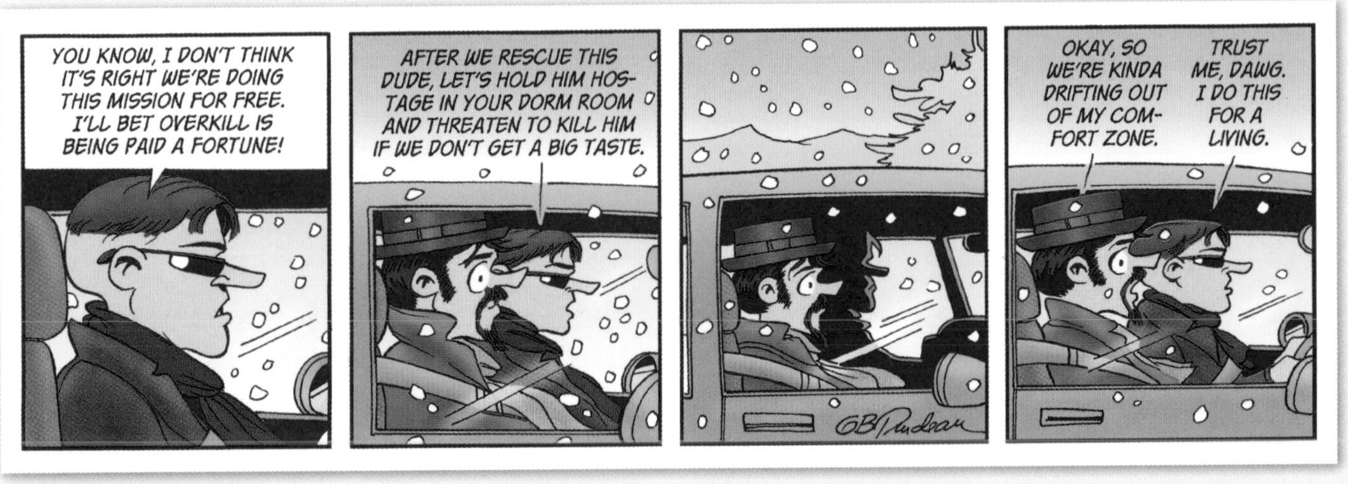
YOU KNOW, I DON'T THINK IT'S RIGHT WE'RE DOING THIS MISSION FOR FREE. I'LL BET OVERKILL IS BEING PAID A FORTUNE!
AFTER WE RESCUE THIS DUDE, LET'S HOLD HIM HOS-TAGE IN YOUR DORM ROOM AND THREATEN TO KILL HIM IF WE DON'T GET A BIG TASTE.
OKAY, SO WE'RE KINDA DRIFTING OUT OF MY COM-FORT ZONE.
TRUST ME, DAWG. I DO THIS FOR A LIVING.
GBTrudeau

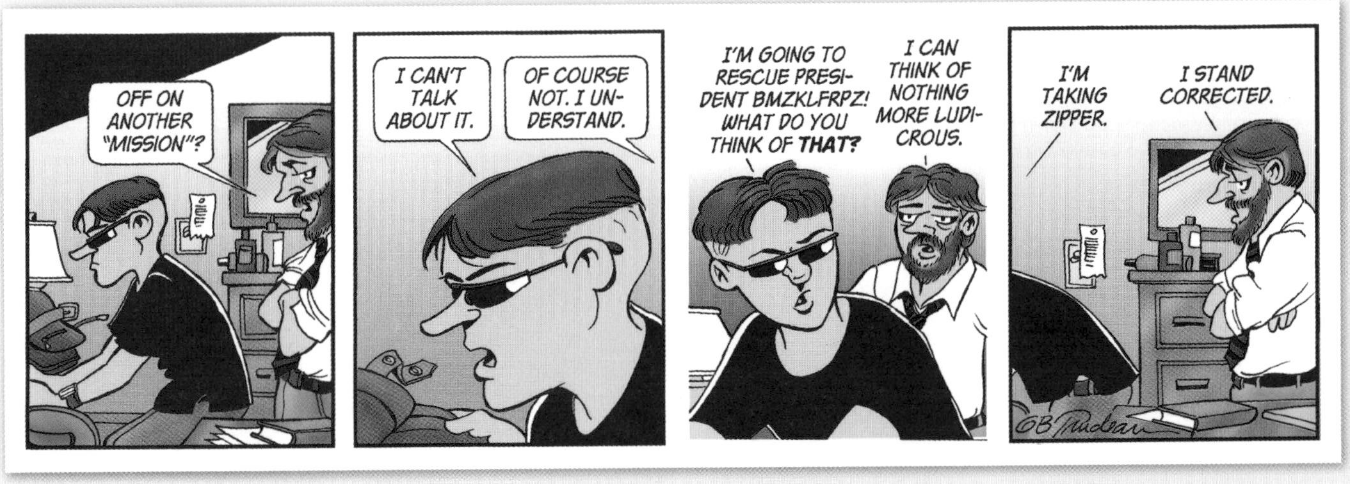
OFF ON ANOTHER "MISSION"?
I CAN'T TALK ABOUT IT.
OF COURSE NOT. I UN-DERSTAND.
I'M GOING TO RESCUE PRESI-DENT BMZKLFRPZ! WHAT DO YOU THINK OF **THAT?**
I CAN THINK OF NOTHING MORE LUDI-CROUS.
I'M TAKING ZIPPER.
I STAND CORRECTED.
GBTrudeau

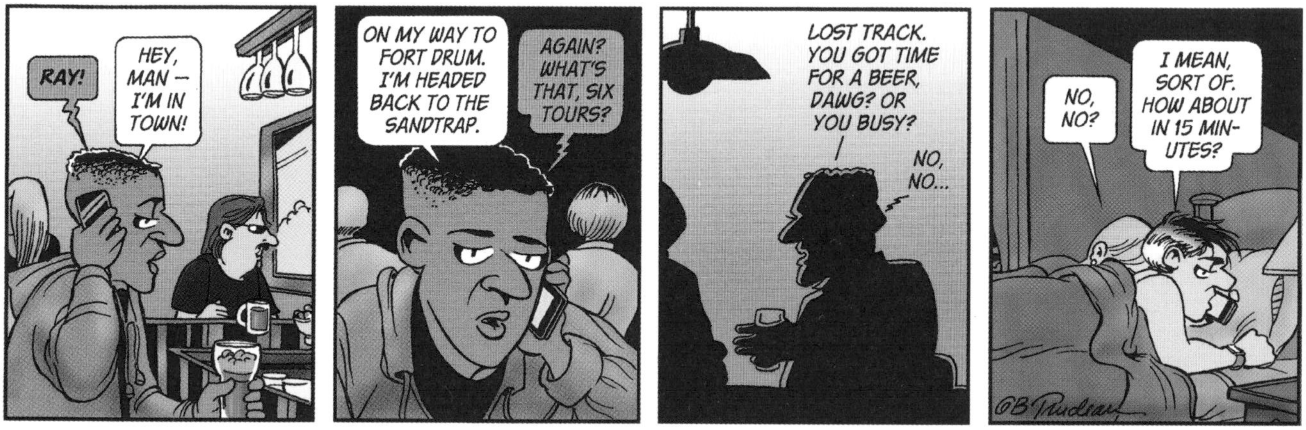
RAY!
HEY, MAN — I'M IN TOWN!
ON MY WAY TO FORT DRUM. I'M HEADED BACK TO THE SANDTRAP.
AGAIN? WHAT'S THAT, SIX TOURS?
LOST TRACK. YOU GOT TIME FOR A BEER, DAWG? OR YOU BUSY?
NO, NO...
NO, NO?
I MEAN, SORT OF. HOW ABOUT IN 15 MIN-UTES?

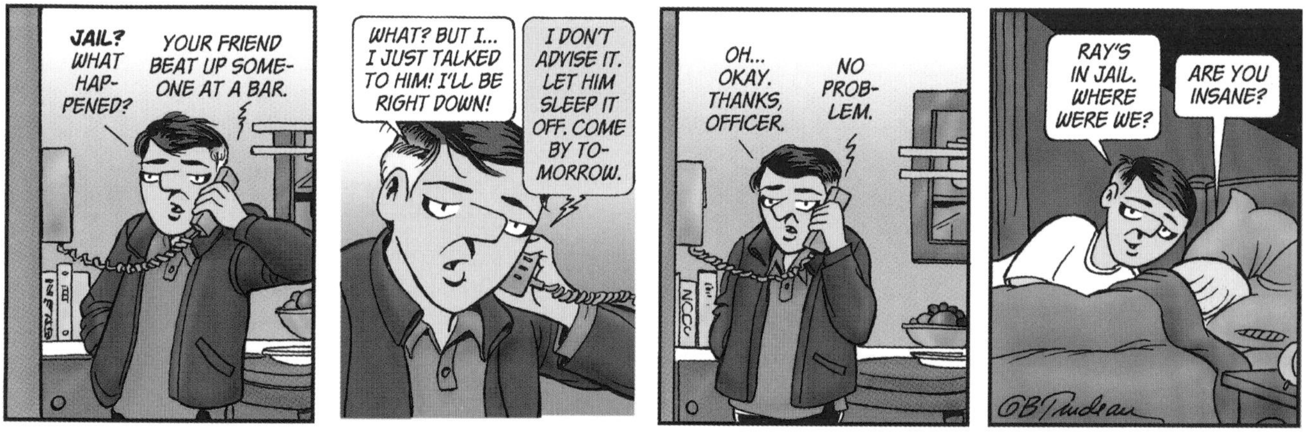
JAIL? WHAT HAP-PENED?
YOUR FRIEND BEAT UP SOME-ONE AT A BAR.
WHAT? BUT I... I JUST TALKED TO HIM! I'LL BE RIGHT DOWN!
I DON'T ADVISE IT. LET HIM SLEEP IT OFF. COME BY TO-MORROW.
OH... OKAY. THANKS, OFFICER.
NO PROB-LEM.
RAY'S IN JAIL. WHERE WERE WE?
ARE YOU INSANE?

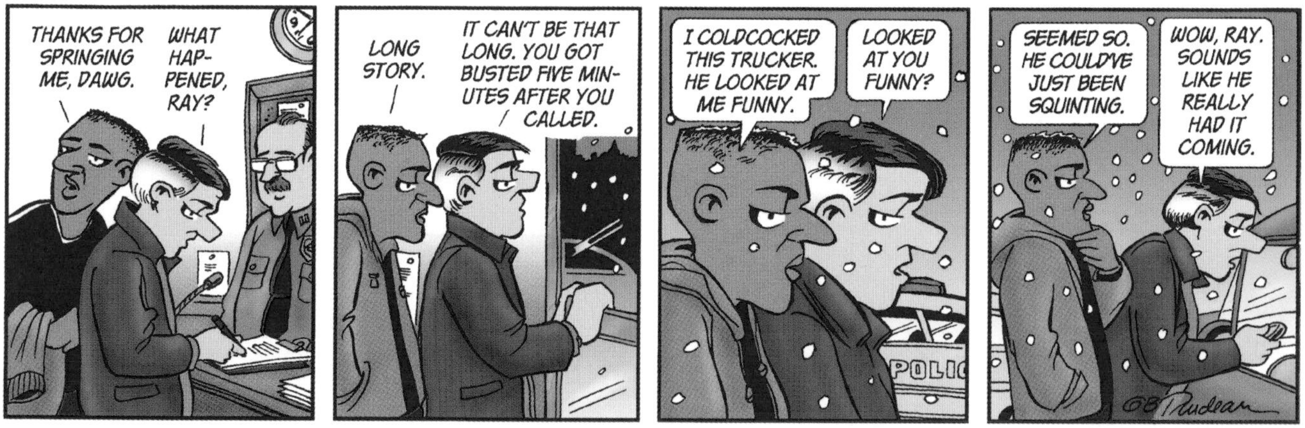
THANKS FOR SPRINGING ME, DAWG.
WHAT HAP-PENED, RAY?
LONG STORY.
IT CAN'T BE THAT LONG. YOU GOT BUSTED FIVE MIN-UTES AFTER YOU CALLED.
I COLDCOCKED THIS TRUCKER. HE LOOKED AT ME FUNNY.
LOOKED AT YOU FUNNY?
SEEMED SO. HE COULD'VE JUST BEEN SQUINTING.
WOW, RAY. SOUNDS LIKE HE REALLY HAD IT COMING.

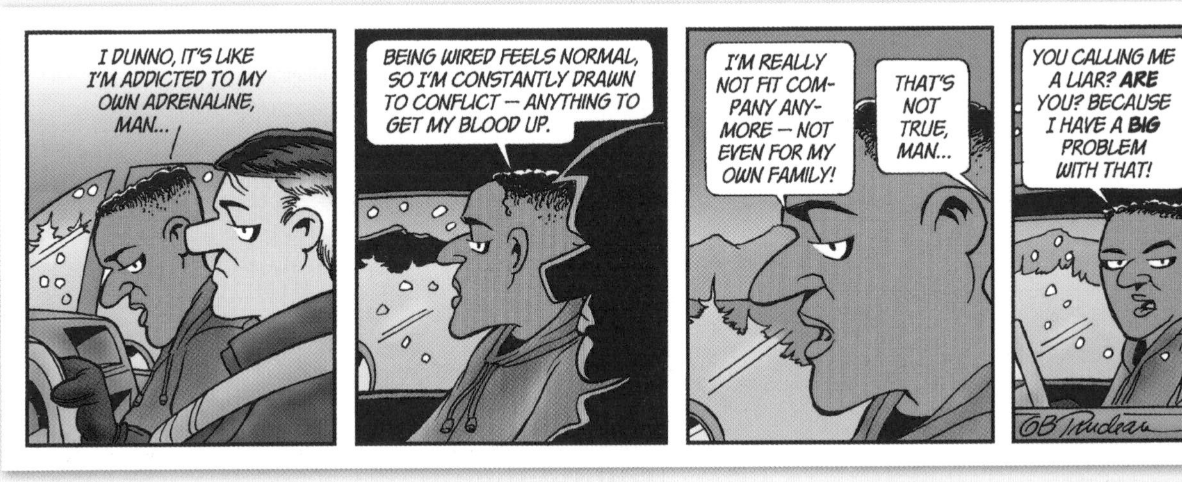
I DUNNO, IT'S LIKE I'M ADDICTED TO MY OWN ADRENALINE, MAN...
BEING WIRED FEELS NORMAL, SO I'M CONSTANTLY DRAWN TO CONFLICT -- ANYTHING TO GET MY BLOOD UP.
I'M REALLY NOT FIT COMPANY ANYMORE -- NOT EVEN FOR MY OWN FAMILY!
THAT'S NOT TRUE, MAN...
YOU CALLING ME A LIAR? ARE YOU? BECAUSE I HAVE A BIG PROBLEM WITH THAT!
OKAY, LET'S WALK THAT ONE BACK...
GB Trudeau

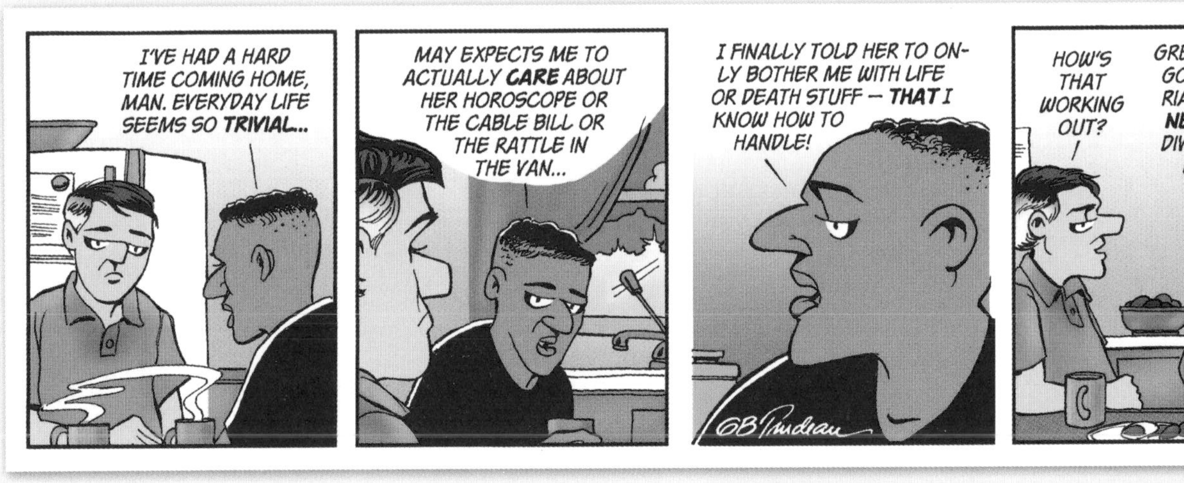
I'VE HAD A HARD TIME COMING HOME, MAN. EVERYDAY LIFE SEEMS SO TRIVIAL...
MAY EXPECTS ME TO ACTUALLY CARE ABOUT HER HOROSCOPE OR THE CABLE BILL OR THE RATTLE IN THE VAN...
I FINALLY TOLD HER TO ONLY BOTHER ME WITH LIFE OR DEATH STUFF -- THAT I KNOW HOW TO HANDLE!
GB Trudeau
HOW'S THAT WORKING OUT?
GREAT -- IN A GOOD MARRIAGE, YOU NEED THAT DIVISION OF LABOR.

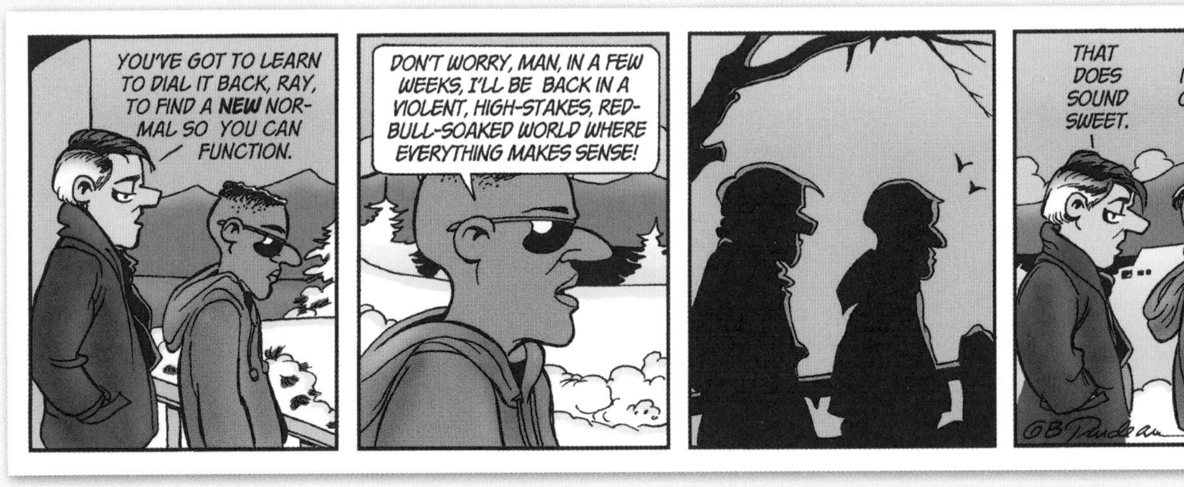
YOU'VE GOT TO LEARN TO DIAL IT BACK, RAY, TO FIND A NEW NORMAL SO YOU CAN FUNCTION.
DON'T WORRY, MAN, IN A FEW WEEKS, I'LL BE BACK IN A VIOLENT, HIGH-STAKES, RED-BULL-SOAKED WORLD WHERE EVERYTHING MAKES SENSE!
THAT DOES SOUND SWEET.
OF COURSE IT DOES. OUR OLD NORMAL ROCKS.
GB Trudeau

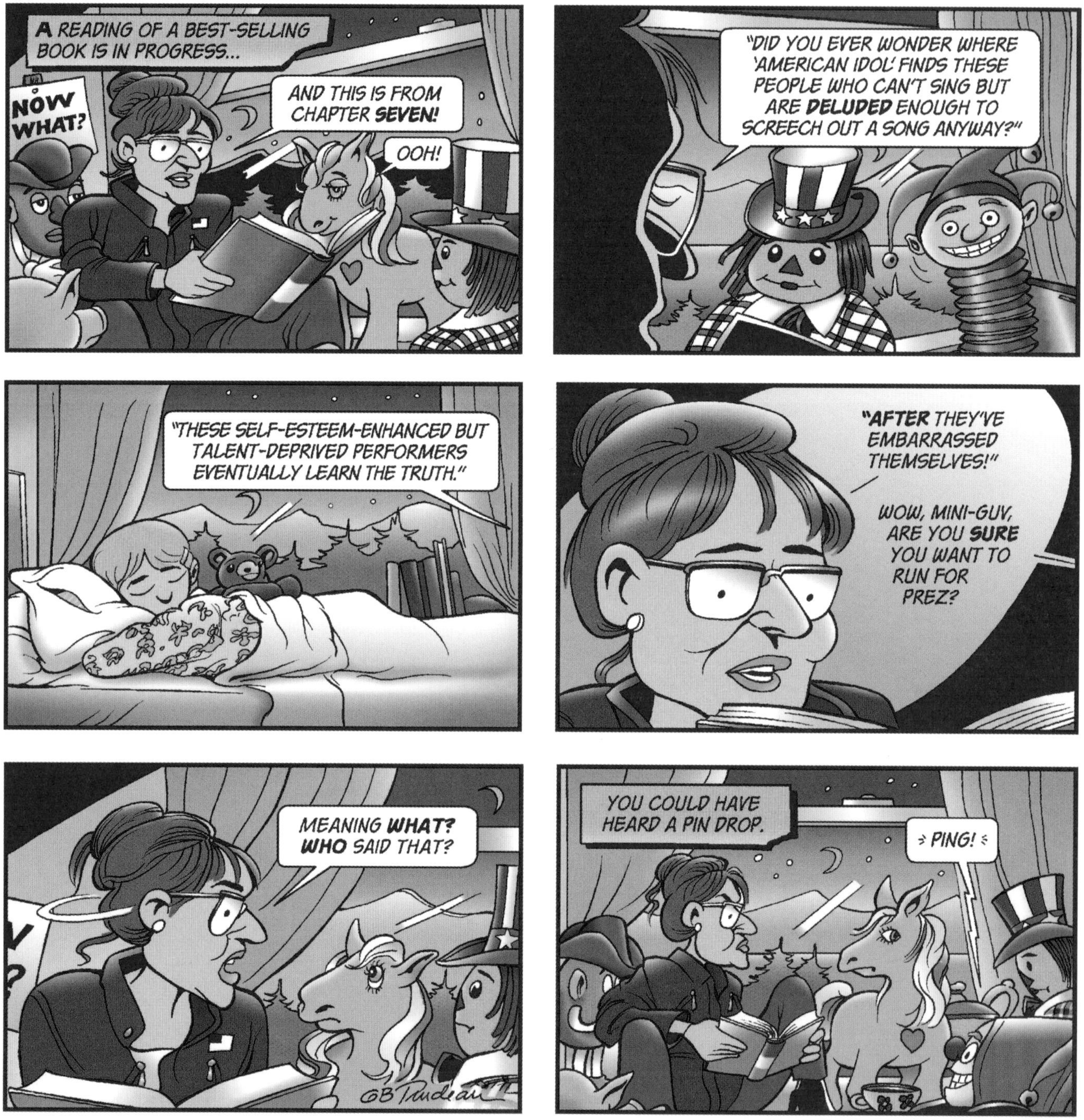
A READING OF A BEST-SELLING BOOK IS IN PROGRESS...
NOW WHAT?
AND THIS IS FROM CHAPTER SEVEN!
OOH!
"DID YOU EVER WONDER WHERE 'AMERICAN IDOL' FINDS THESE PEOPLE WHO CAN'T SING BUT ARE DELUDED ENOUGH TO SCREECH OUT A SONG ANYWAY?"
"THESE SELF-ESTEEM-ENHANCED BUT TALENT-DEPRIVED PERFORMERS EVENTUALLY LEARN THE TRUTH."
"AFTER THEY'VE EMBARRASSED THEMSELVES!"
WOW, MINI-GUV, ARE YOU SURE YOU WANT TO RUN FOR PREZ?
MEANING WHAT? WHO SAID THAT?
GB Trudeau
YOU COULD HAVE HEARD A PIN DROP.
PING!

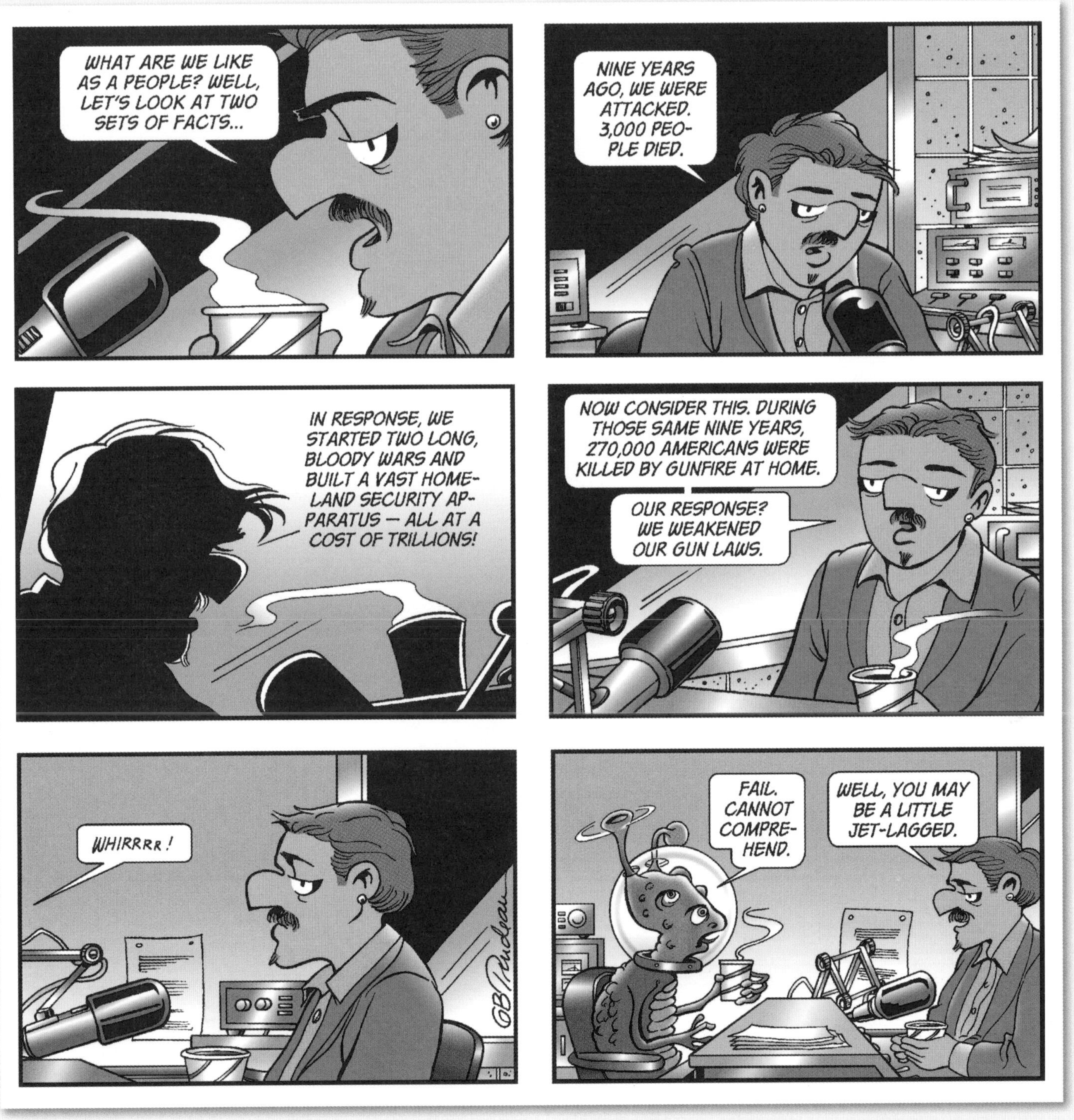
WHAT ARE WE LIKE AS A PEOPLE? WELL, LET'S LOOK AT TWO SETS OF FACTS...
NINE YEARS AGO, WE WERE ATTACKED. 3,000 PEO-PLE DIED.
IN RESPONSE, WE STARTED TWO LONG, BLOODY WARS AND BUILT A VAST HOME-LAND SECURITY AP-PARATUS — ALL AT A COST OF TRILLIONS!
NOW CONSIDER THIS. DURING THOSE SAME NINE YEARS, 270,000 AMERICANS WERE KILLED BY GUNFIRE AT HOME.
OUR RESPONSE? WE WEAKENED OUR GUN LAWS.
WHIRRRR!
GB Trudeau
FAIL. CANNOT COMPRE-HEND.
WELL, YOU MAY BE A LITTLE JET-LAGGED.

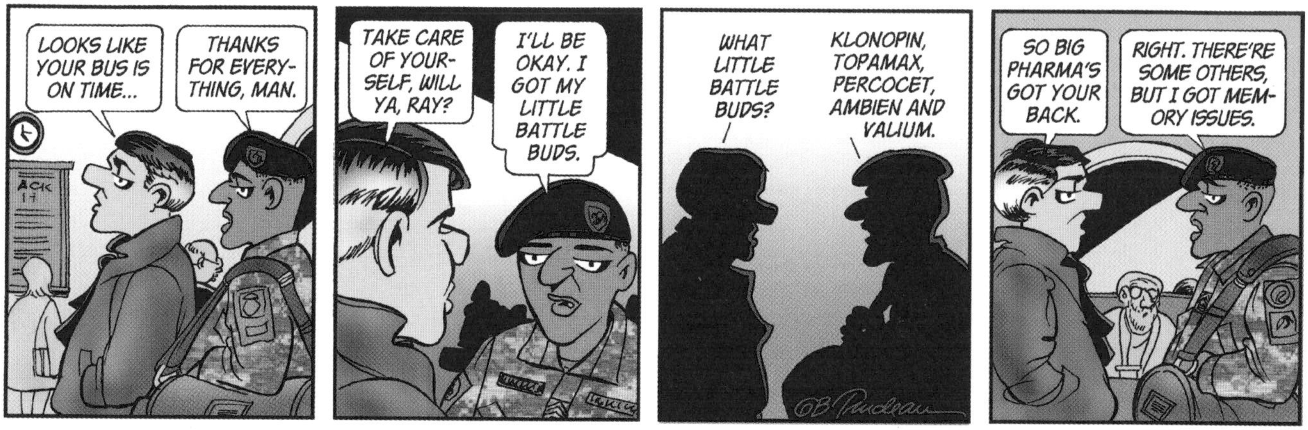
LOOKS LIKE YOUR BUS IS ON TIME...
THANKS FOR EVERY-THING, MAN.
TAKE CARE OF YOUR-SELF, WILL YA, RAY?
I'LL BE OKAY. I GOT MY LITTLE BATTLE BUDS.
WHAT LITTLE BATTLE BUDS?
KLONOPIN, TOPAMAX, PERCOCET, AMBIEN AND VALIUM.
SO BIG PHARMA'S GOT YOUR BACK.
RIGHT. THERE'RE SOME OTHERS, BUT I GOT MEM-ORY ISSUES.

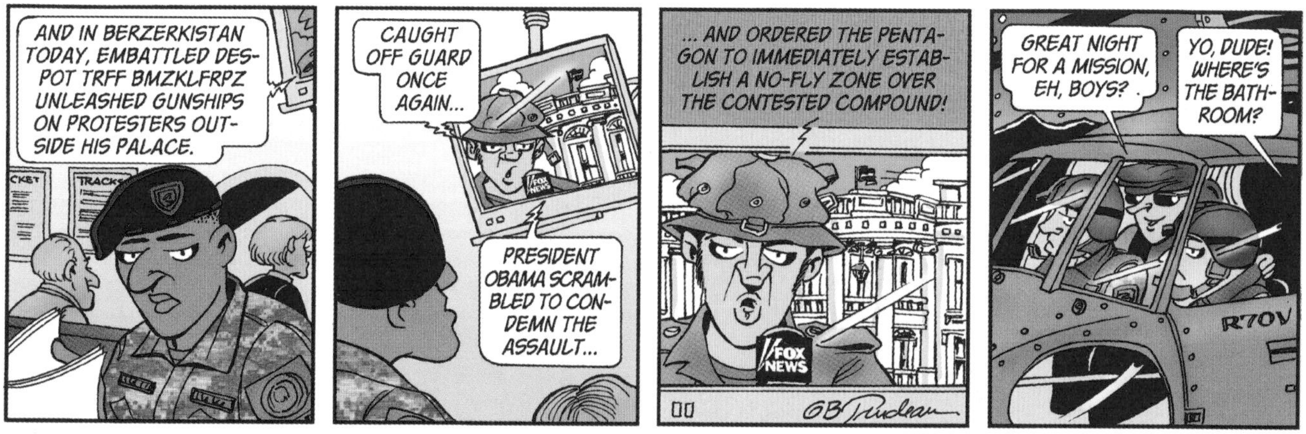
AND IN BERZERKISTAN TODAY, EMBATTLED DES-POT TRFF BMZKLFRPZ UNLEASHED GUNSHIPS ON PROTESTERS OUT-SIDE HIS PALACE.
CAUGHT OFF GUARD ONCE AGAIN...
PRESIDENT OBAMA SCRAM-BLED TO CON-DEMN THE ASSAULT...
... AND ORDERED THE PENTA-GON TO IMMEDIATELY ESTAB-LISH A NO-FLY ZONE OVER THE CONTESTED COMPOUND!
FOX NEWS
GREAT NIGHT FOR A MISSION, EH, BOYS?
YO, DUDE! WHERE'S THE BATH-ROOM?
R70V

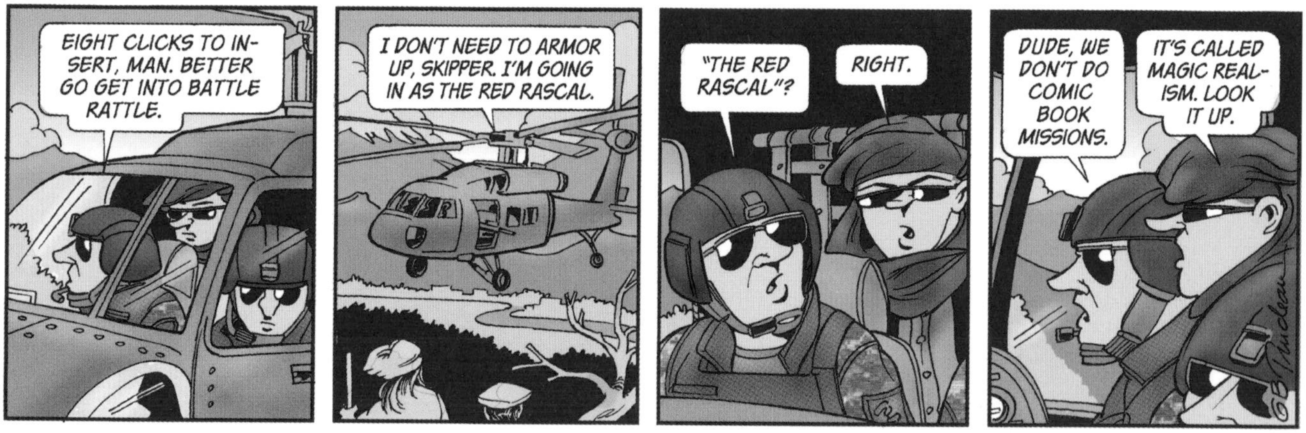
EIGHT CLICKS TO IN-SERT, MAN. BETTER GO GET INTO BATTLE RATTLE.
I DON'T NEED TO ARMOR UP, SKIPPER. I'M GOING IN AS THE RED RASCAL.
"THE RED RASCAL"?
RIGHT.
DUDE, WE DON'T DO COMIC BOOK MISSIONS.
IT'S CALLED MAGIC REAL-ISM. LOOK IT UP.

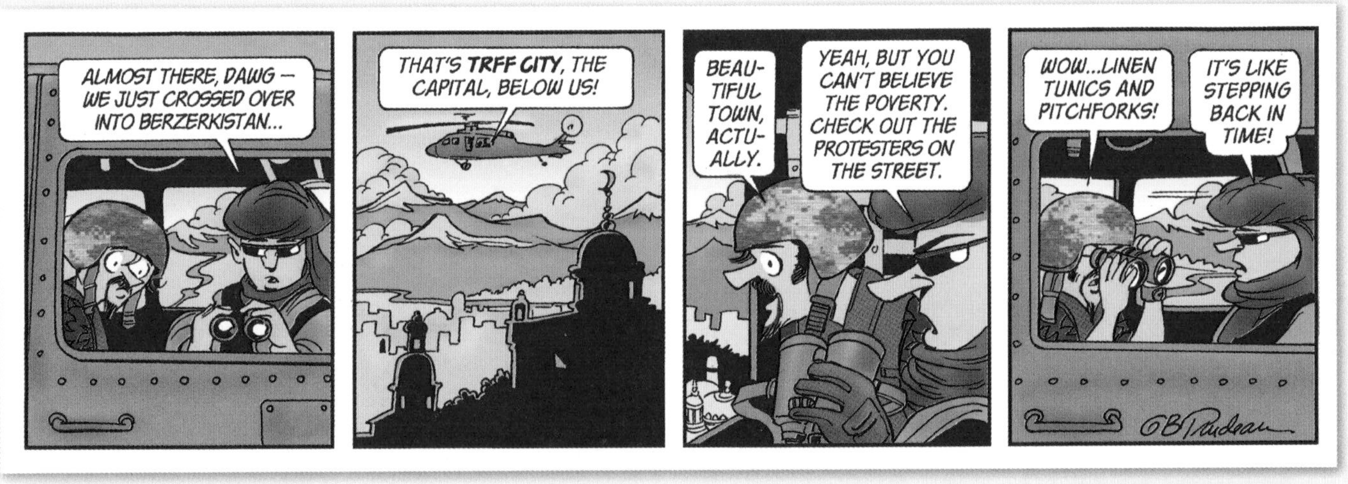
ALMOST THERE, DAWG — WE JUST CROSSED OVER INTO BERZERKISTAN...
THAT'S **TRFF CITY**, THE CAPITAL, BELOW US!
BEAU-TIFUL TOWN, ACTU-ALLY.
YEAH, BUT YOU CAN'T BELIEVE THE POVERTY. CHECK OUT THE PROTESTERS ON THE STREET.
WOW...LINEN TUNICS AND PITCHFORKS!
IT'S LIKE STEPPING BACK IN TIME!
©B Trudeau

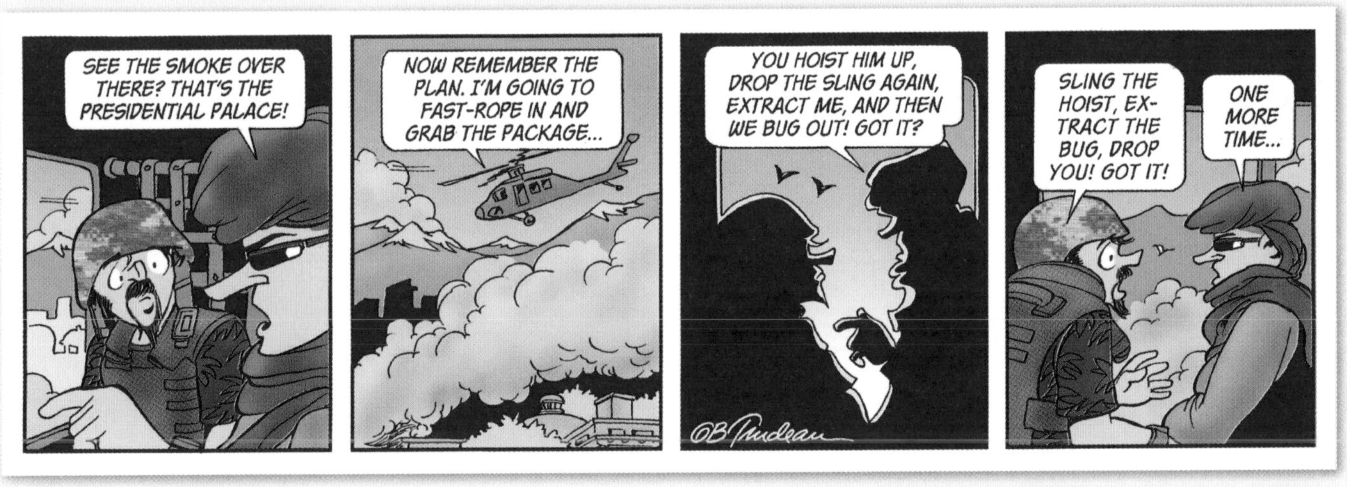
SEE THE SMOKE OVER THERE? THAT'S THE PRESIDENTIAL PALACE!
NOW REMEMBER THE PLAN. I'M GOING TO FAST-ROPE IN AND GRAB THE PACKAGE...
YOU HOIST HIM UP, DROP THE SLING AGAIN, EXTRACT ME, AND THEN WE BUG OUT! GOT IT?
©B Trudeau
SLING THE HOIST, EX-TRACT THE BUG, DROP YOU! GOT IT!
ONE MORE TIME...

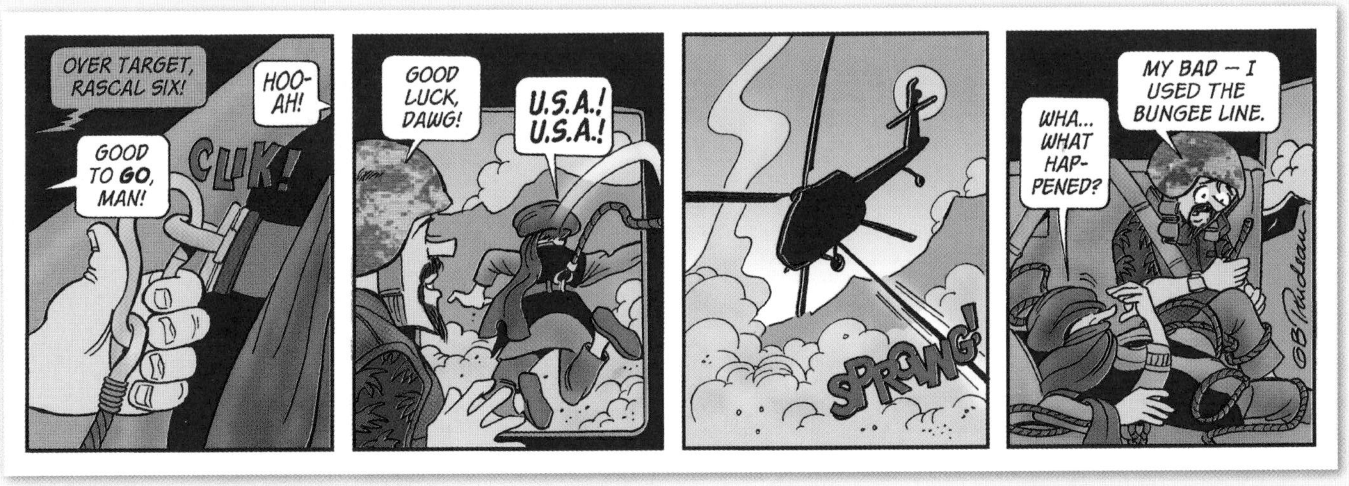
OVER TARGET, RASCAL SIX!
HOO-AH!
GOOD TO **GO**, MAN!
CLIK!
GOOD LUCK, DAWG!
U.S.A.! U.S.A.!
SPROING!
MY BAD — I USED THE BUNGEE LINE.
WHA... WHAT HAP-PENED?
©B Trudeau

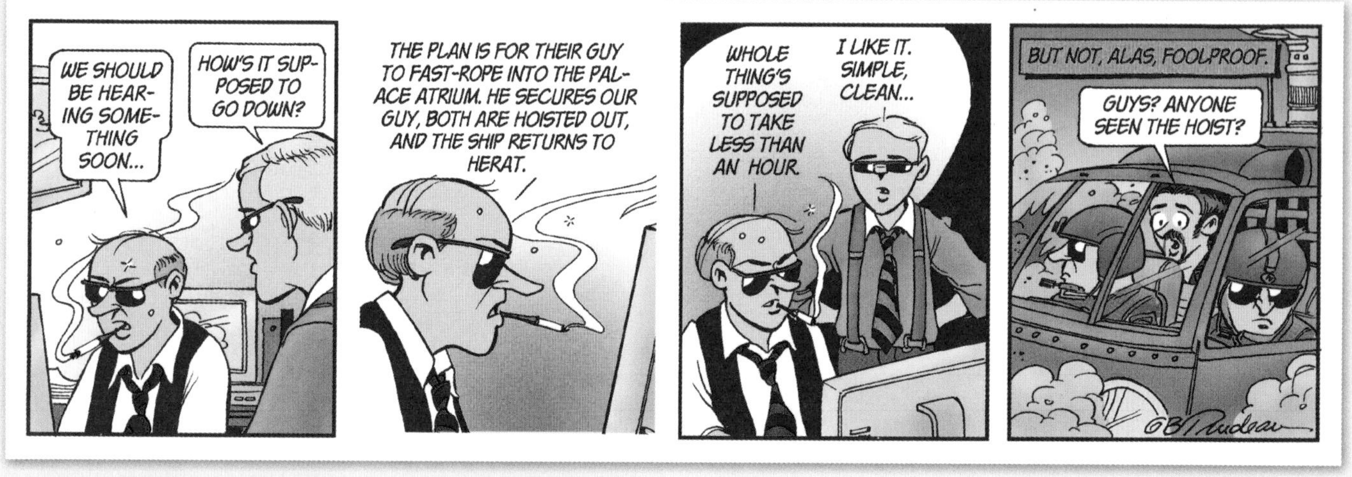
WE SHOULD BE HEARING SOMETHING SOON...
HOW'S IT SUPPOSED TO GO DOWN?
THE PLAN IS FOR THEIR GUY TO FAST-ROPE INTO THE PALACE ATRIUM. HE SECURES OUR GUY, BOTH ARE HOISTED OUT, AND THE SHIP RETURNS TO HERAT.
WHOLE THING'S SUPPOSED TO TAKE LESS THAN AN HOUR.
I LIKE IT. SIMPLE, CLEAN...
BUT NOT, ALAS, FOOLPROOF.
GUYS? ANYONE SEEN THE HOIST?
GBTrudeau

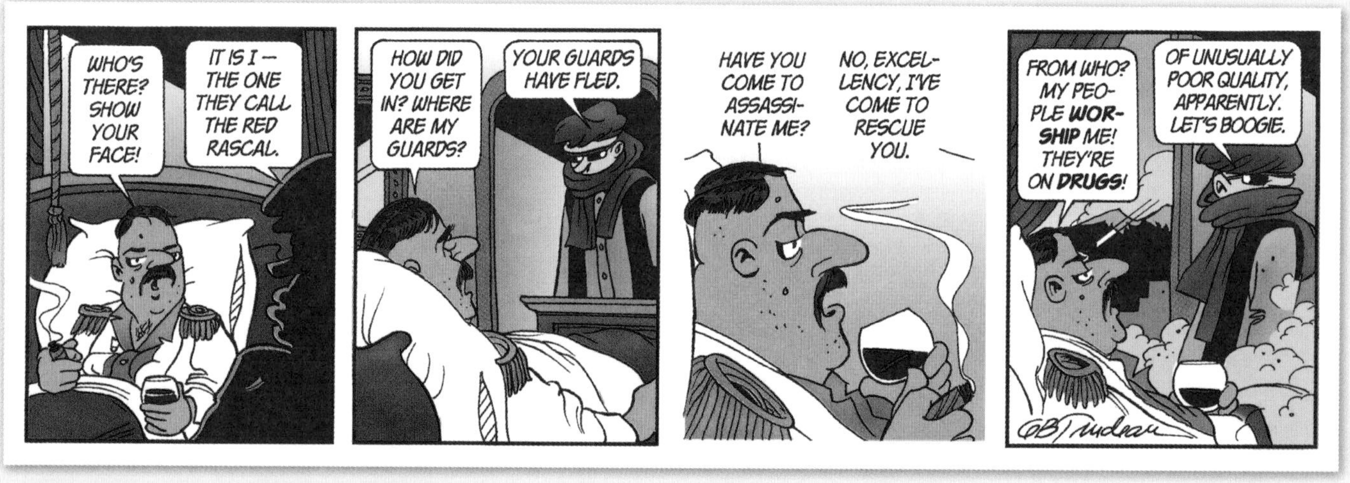
WHO'S THERE? SHOW YOUR FACE!
IT IS I — THE ONE THEY CALL THE RED RASCAL.
HOW DID YOU GET IN? WHERE ARE MY GUARDS?
YOUR GUARDS HAVE FLED.
HAVE YOU COME TO ASSASSINATE ME?
NO, EXCELLENCY, I'VE COME TO RESCUE YOU.
FROM WHO? MY PEOPLE WORSHIP ME! THEY'RE ON DRUGS!
OF UNUSUALLY POOR QUALITY, APPARENTLY. LET'S BOOGIE.
GBTrudeau

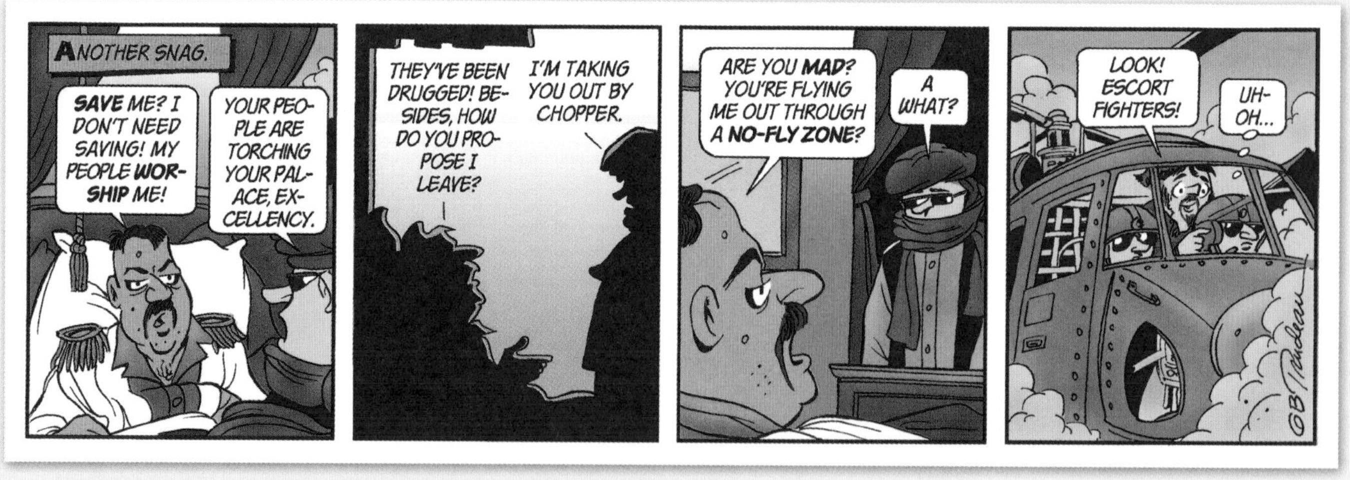
ANOTHER SNAG.
SAVE ME? I DON'T NEED SAVING! MY PEOPLE WORSHIP ME!
YOUR PEOPLE ARE TORCHING YOUR PALACE, EXCELLENCY.
THEY'VE BEEN DRUGGED! BESIDES, HOW DO YOU PROPOSE I LEAVE?
I'M TAKING YOU OUT BY CHOPPER.
ARE YOU MAD? YOU'RE FLYING ME OUT THROUGH A NO-FLY ZONE?
A WHAT?
LOOK! ESCORT FIGHTERS!
UH-OH...
GBTrudeau

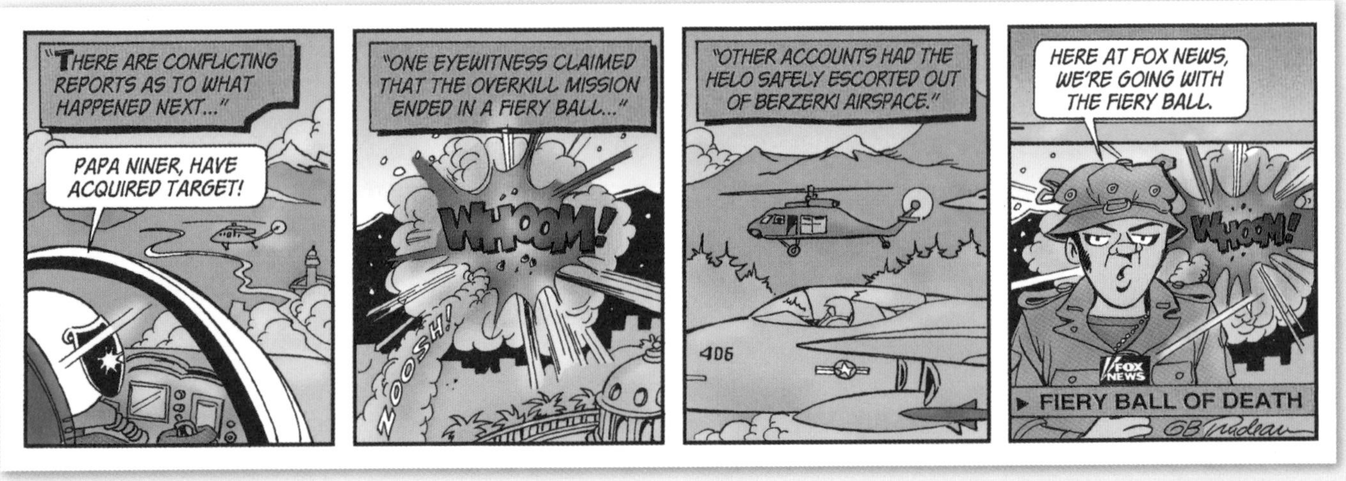
"THERE ARE CONFLICTING REPORTS AS TO WHAT HAPPENED NEXT..."
PAPA NINER, HAVE ACQUIRED TARGET!
"ONE EYEWITNESS CLAIMED THAT THE OVERKILL MISSION ENDED IN A FIERY BALL..."
WHOOM!
ZOOSH!
"OTHER ACCOUNTS HAD THE HELO SAFELY ESCORTED OUT OF BERZERKI AIRSPACE."
406
HERE AT FOX NEWS, WE'RE GOING WITH THE FIERY BALL.
WHOOM!
FOX NEWS
FIERY BALL OF DEATH
GB Trudeau

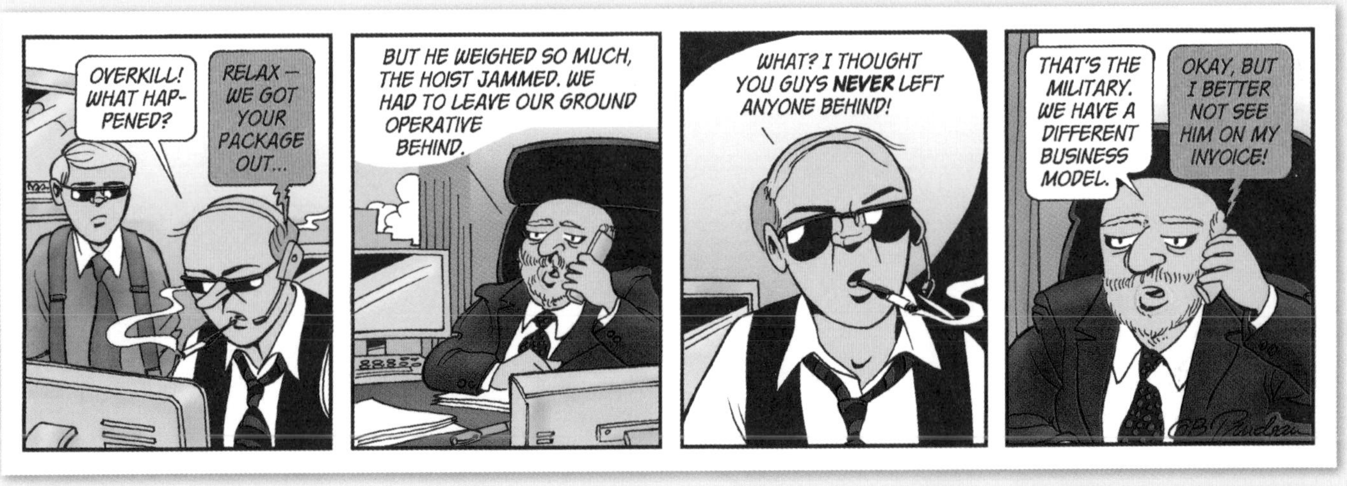
OVERKILL! WHAT HAP-PENED?
RELAX — WE GOT YOUR PACKAGE OUT...
BUT HE WEIGHED SO MUCH, THE HOIST JAMMED. WE HAD TO LEAVE OUR GROUND OPERATIVE BEHIND.
WHAT? I THOUGHT YOU GUYS NEVER LEFT ANYONE BEHIND!
THAT'S THE MILITARY. WE HAVE A DIFFERENT BUSINESS MODEL.
OKAY, BUT I BETTER NOT SEE HIM ON MY INVOICE!
GB Trudeau

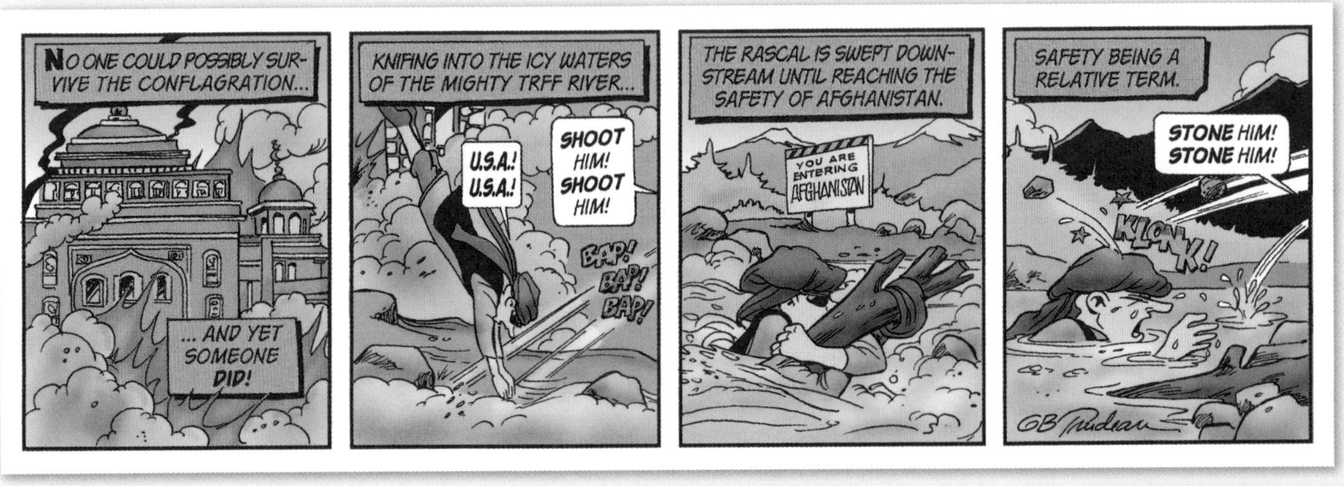
NO ONE COULD POSSIBLY SURVIVE THE CONFLAGRATION...
... AND YET SOMEONE DID!
KNIFING INTO THE ICY WATERS OF THE MIGHTY TRFF RIVER...
U.S.A.! U.S.A.!
SHOOT HIM! SHOOT HIM!
BAP! BAP! BAP!
THE RASCAL IS SWEPT DOWNSTREAM UNTIL REACHING THE SAFETY OF AFGHANISTAN.
YOU ARE ENTERING AFGHANISTAN
SAFETY BEING A RELATIVE TERM.
STONE HIM! STONE HIM!
KLONK!
GB Trudeau

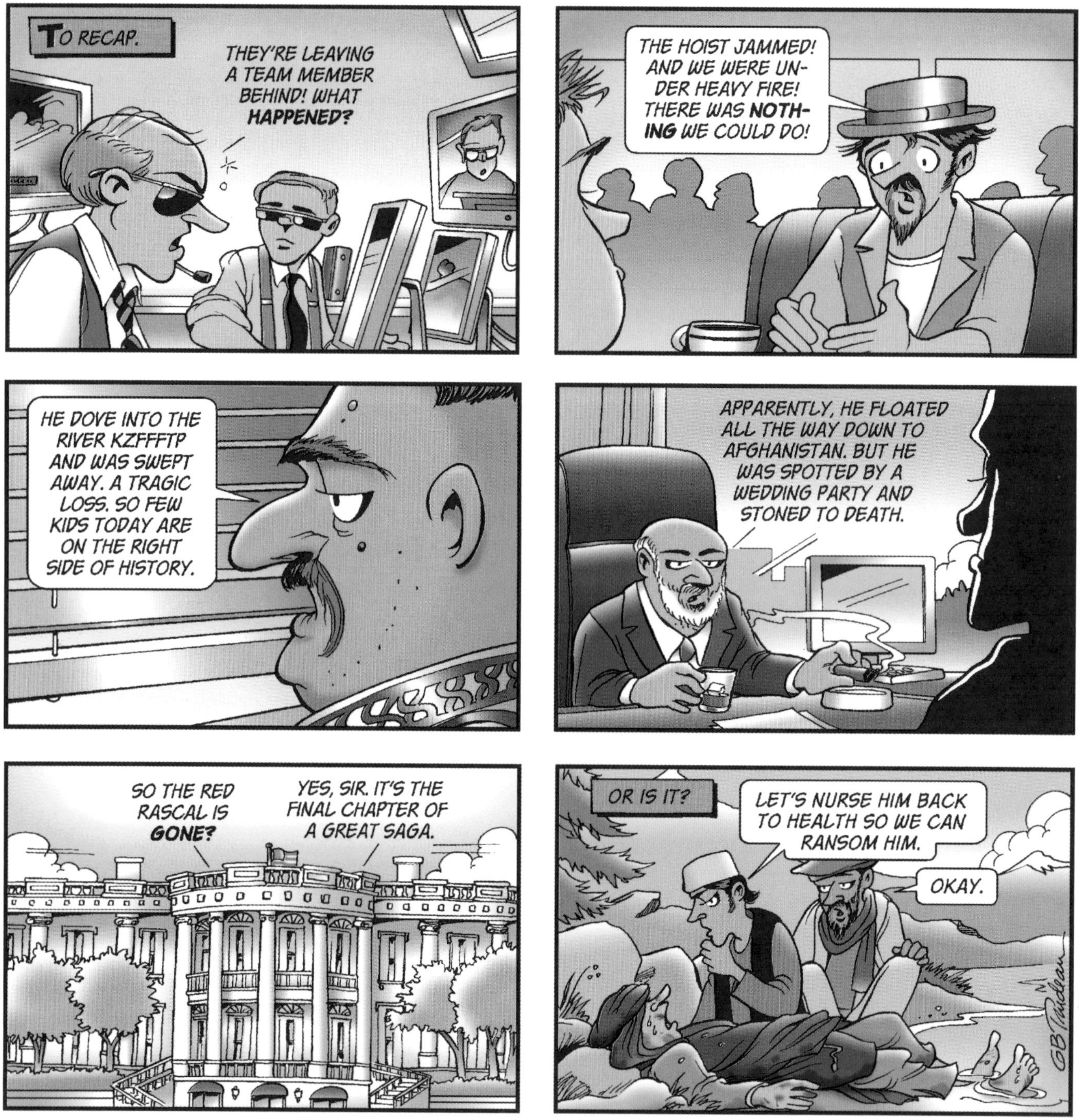
TO RECAP.
THEY'RE LEAVING A TEAM MEMBER BEHIND! WHAT HAPPENED?
THE HOIST JAMMED! AND WE WERE UNDER HEAVY FIRE! THERE WAS NOTHING WE COULD DO!
HE DOVE INTO THE RIVER KZFFFTP AND WAS SWEPT AWAY. A TRAGIC LOSS. SO FEW KIDS TODAY ARE ON THE RIGHT SIDE OF HISTORY.
APPARENTLY, HE FLOATED ALL THE WAY DOWN TO AFGHANISTAN. BUT HE WAS SPOTTED BY A WEDDING PARTY AND STONED TO DEATH.
SO THE RED RASCAL IS GONE?
YES, SIR. IT'S THE FINAL CHAPTER OF A GREAT SAGA.
OR IS IT?
LET'S NURSE HIM BACK TO HEALTH SO WE CAN RANSOM HIM.
OKAY.
GB Trudeau

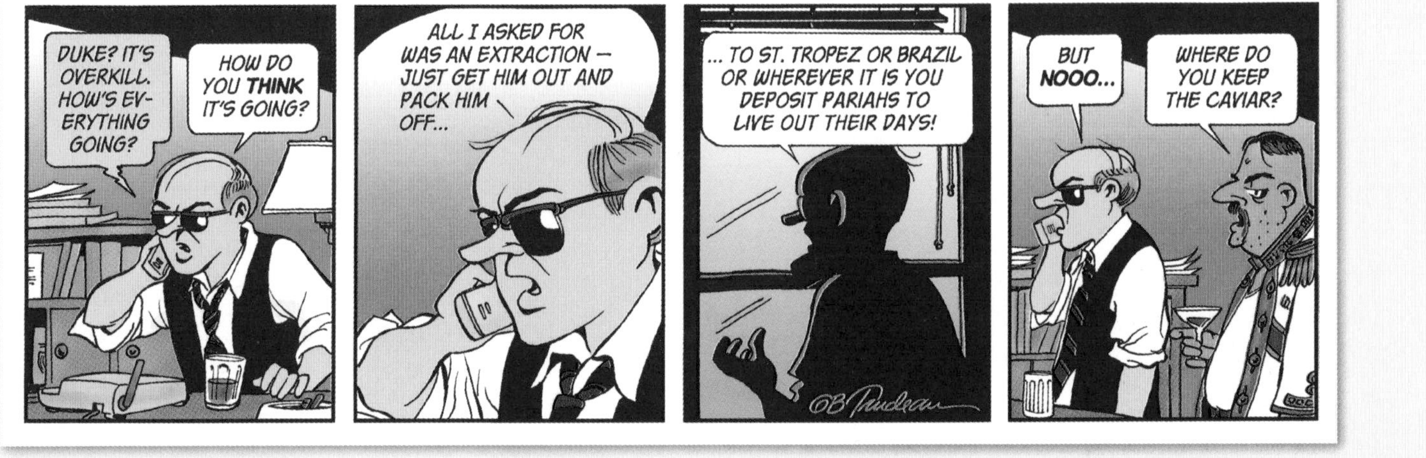
DUKE? IT'S OVERKILL. HOW'S EVERYTHING GOING?
HOW DO YOU THINK IT'S GOING?
ALL I ASKED FOR WAS AN EXTRACTION — JUST GET HIM OUT AND PACK HIM OFF...
... TO ST. TROPEZ OR BRAZIL OR WHEREVER IT IS YOU DEPOSIT PARIAHS TO LIVE OUT THEIR DAYS!
BUT NOOO...
WHERE DO YOU KEEP THE CAVIAR?

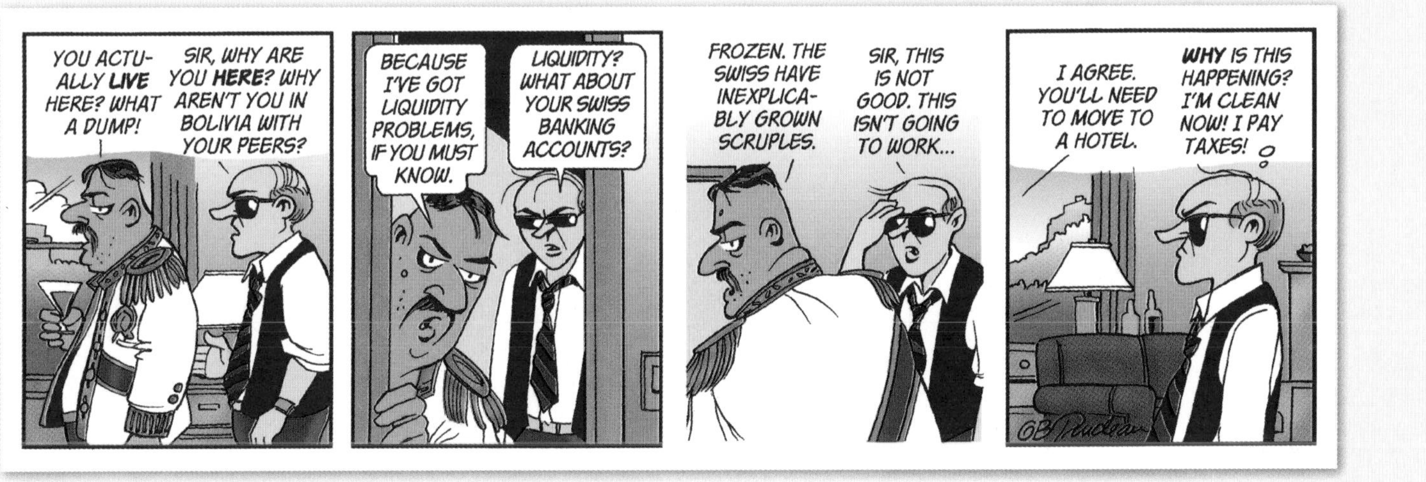
YOU ACTUALLY LIVE HERE? WHAT A DUMP!
SIR, WHY ARE YOU HERE? WHY AREN'T YOU IN BOLIVIA WITH YOUR PEERS?
BECAUSE I'VE GOT LIQUIDITY PROBLEMS, IF YOU MUST KNOW.
LIQUIDITY? WHAT ABOUT YOUR SWISS BANKING ACCOUNTS?
FROZEN. THE SWISS HAVE INEXPLICABLY GROWN SCRUPLES.
SIR, THIS IS NOT GOOD. THIS ISN'T GOING TO WORK...
I AGREE. YOU'LL NEED TO MOVE TO A HOTEL.
WHY IS THIS HAPPENING? I'M CLEAN NOW! I PAY TAXES!

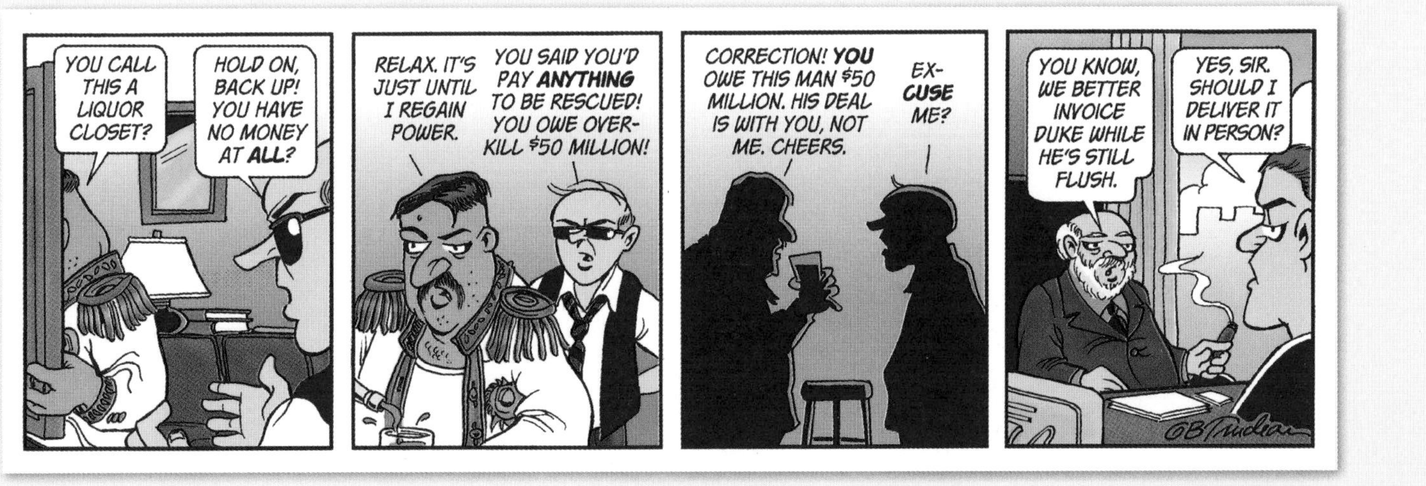
YOU CALL THIS A LIQUOR CLOSET?
HOLD ON, BACK UP! YOU HAVE NO MONEY AT ALL?
RELAX. IT'S JUST UNTIL I REGAIN POWER.
YOU SAID YOU'D PAY ANYTHING TO BE RESCUED! YOU OWE OVERKILL $50 MILLION!
CORRECTION! YOU OWE THIS MAN $50 MILLION. HIS DEAL IS WITH YOU, NOT ME. CHEERS.
EXCUSE ME?
YOU KNOW, WE BETTER INVOICE DUKE WHILE HE'S STILL FLUSH.
YES, SIR. SHOULD I DELIVER IT IN PERSON?

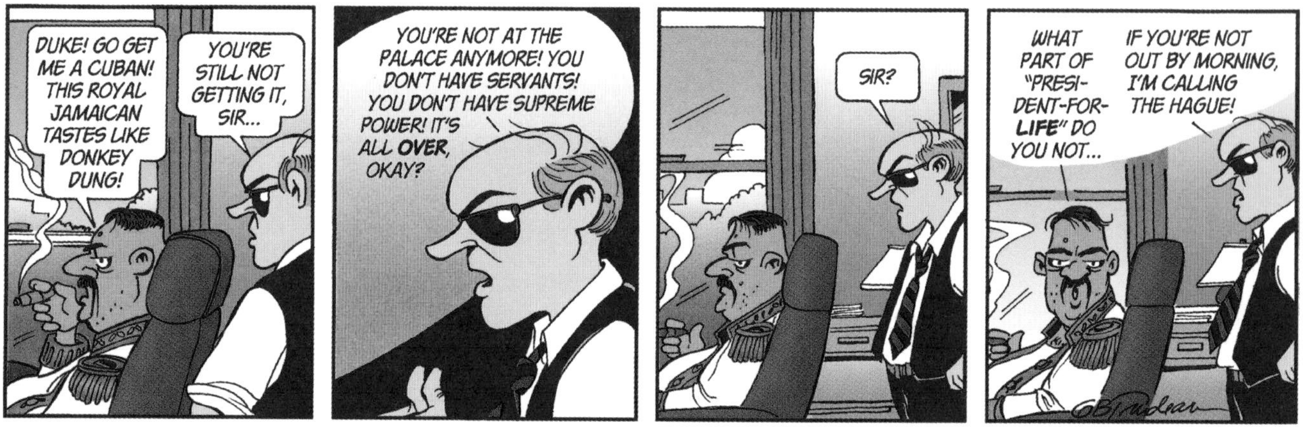
DUKE! GO GET ME A CUBAN! THIS ROYAL JAMAICAN TASTES LIKE DONKEY DUNG!
YOU'RE STILL NOT GETTING IT, SIR...
YOU'RE NOT AT THE PALACE ANYMORE! YOU DON'T HAVE SERVANTS! YOU DON'T HAVE SUPREME POWER! IT'S ALL OVER, OKAY?
SIR?
WHAT PART OF "PRESI-DENT-FOR-LIFE" DO YOU NOT...
IF YOU'RE NOT OUT BY MORNING, I'M CALLING THE HAGUE!

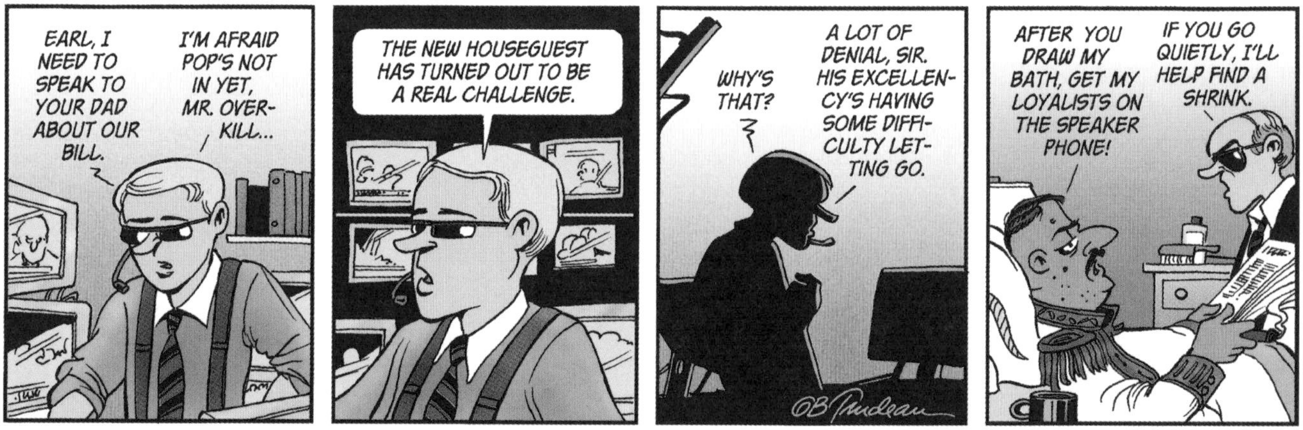
EARL, I NEED TO SPEAK TO YOUR DAD ABOUT OUR BILL.
I'M AFRAID POP'S NOT IN YET, MR. OVER-KILL...
THE NEW HOUSEGUEST HAS TURNED OUT TO BE A REAL CHALLENGE.
WHY'S THAT?
A LOT OF DENIAL, SIR. HIS EXCELLEN-CY'S HAVING SOME DIFFI-CULTY LET-TING GO.
AFTER YOU DRAW MY BATH, GET MY LOYALISTS ON THE SPEAKER PHONE!
IF YOU GO QUIETLY, I'LL HELP FIND A SHRINK.

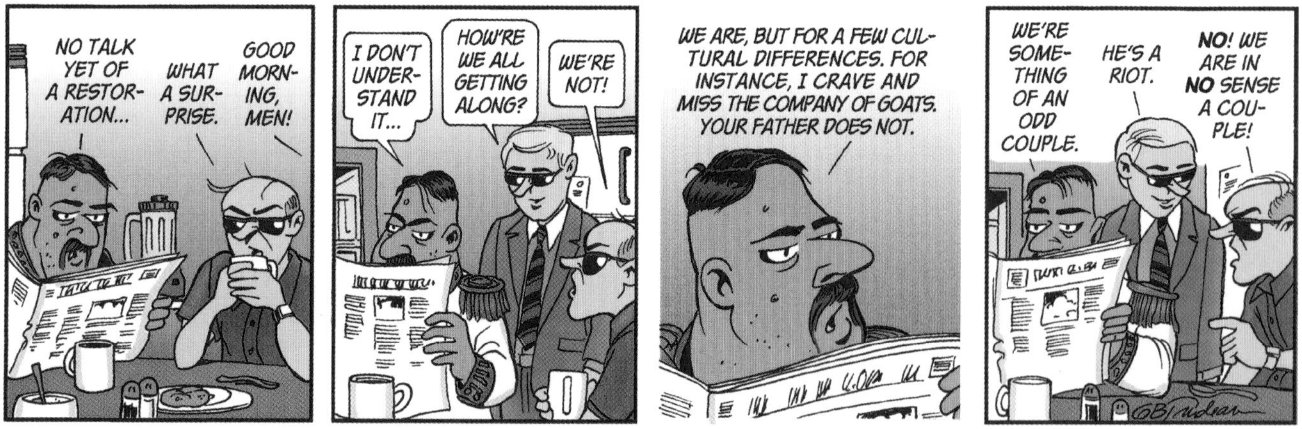
NO TALK YET OF A RESTOR-ATION...
WHAT A SUR-PRISE.
GOOD MORN-ING, MEN!
I DON'T UNDER-STAND IT...
HOW'RE WE ALL GETTING ALONG?
WE'RE NOT!
WE ARE, BUT FOR A FEW CUL-TURAL DIFFERENCES. FOR INSTANCE, I CRAVE AND MISS THE COMPANY OF GOATS. YOUR FATHER DOES NOT.
WE'RE SOME-THING OF AN ODD COUPLE.
HE'S A RIOT.
NO! WE ARE IN NO SENSE A COU-PLE!

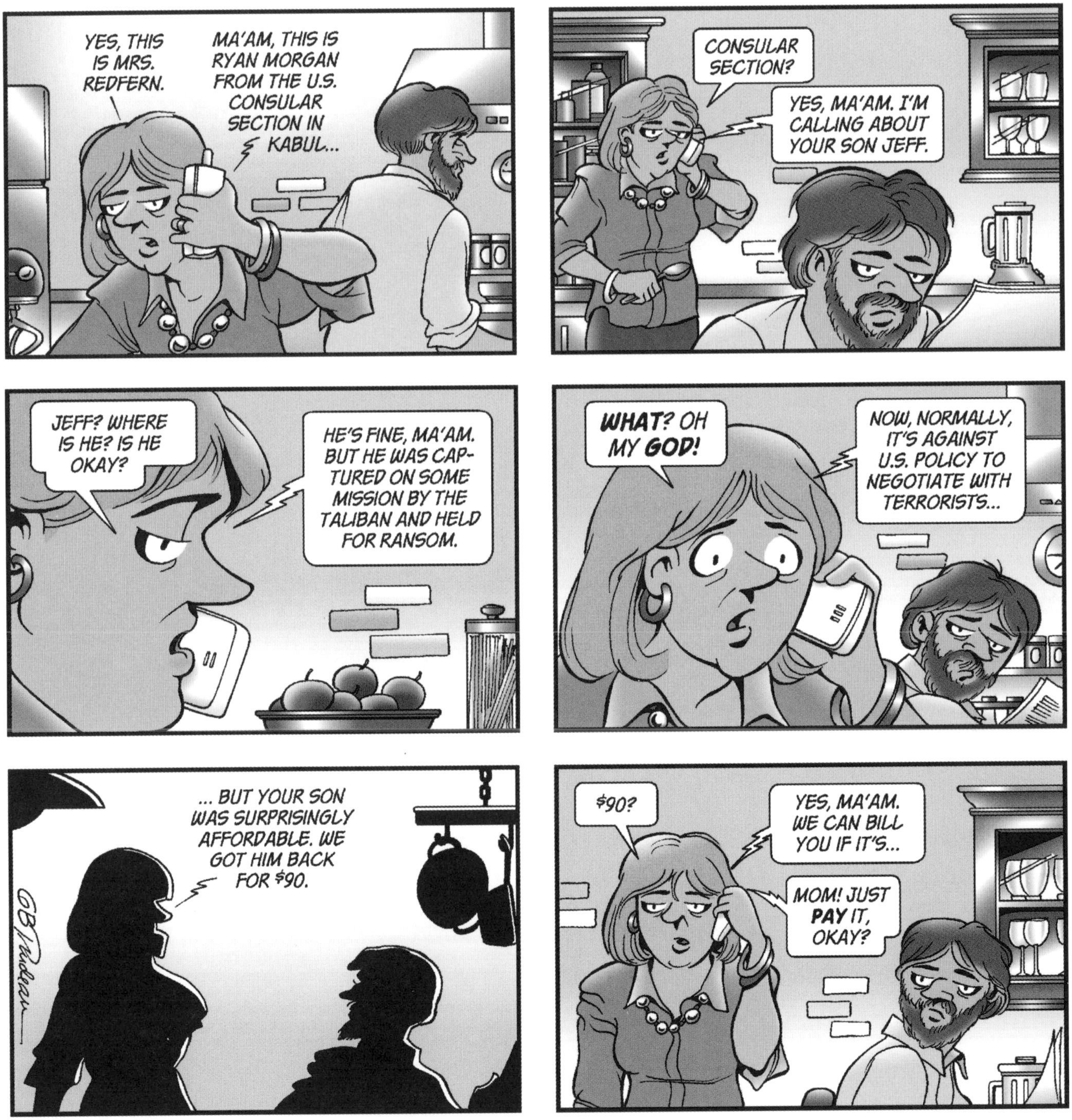
YES, THIS IS MRS. REDFERN.
MA'AM, THIS IS RYAN MORGAN FROM THE U.S. CONSULAR SECTION IN KABUL...
CONSULAR SECTION?
YES, MA'AM. I'M CALLING ABOUT YOUR SON JEFF.
JEFF? WHERE IS HE? IS HE OKAY?
HE'S FINE, MA'AM. BUT HE WAS CAPTURED ON SOME MISSION BY THE TALIBAN AND HELD FOR RANSOM.
WHAT? OH MY GOD!
NOW, NORMALLY, IT'S AGAINST U.S. POLICY TO NEGOTIATE WITH TERRORISTS...
... BUT YOUR SON WAS SURPRISINGLY AFFORDABLE. WE GOT HIM BACK FOR $90.
GB Trudeau
$90?
YES, MA'AM. WE CAN BILL YOU IF IT'S...
MOM! JUST PAY IT, OKAY?

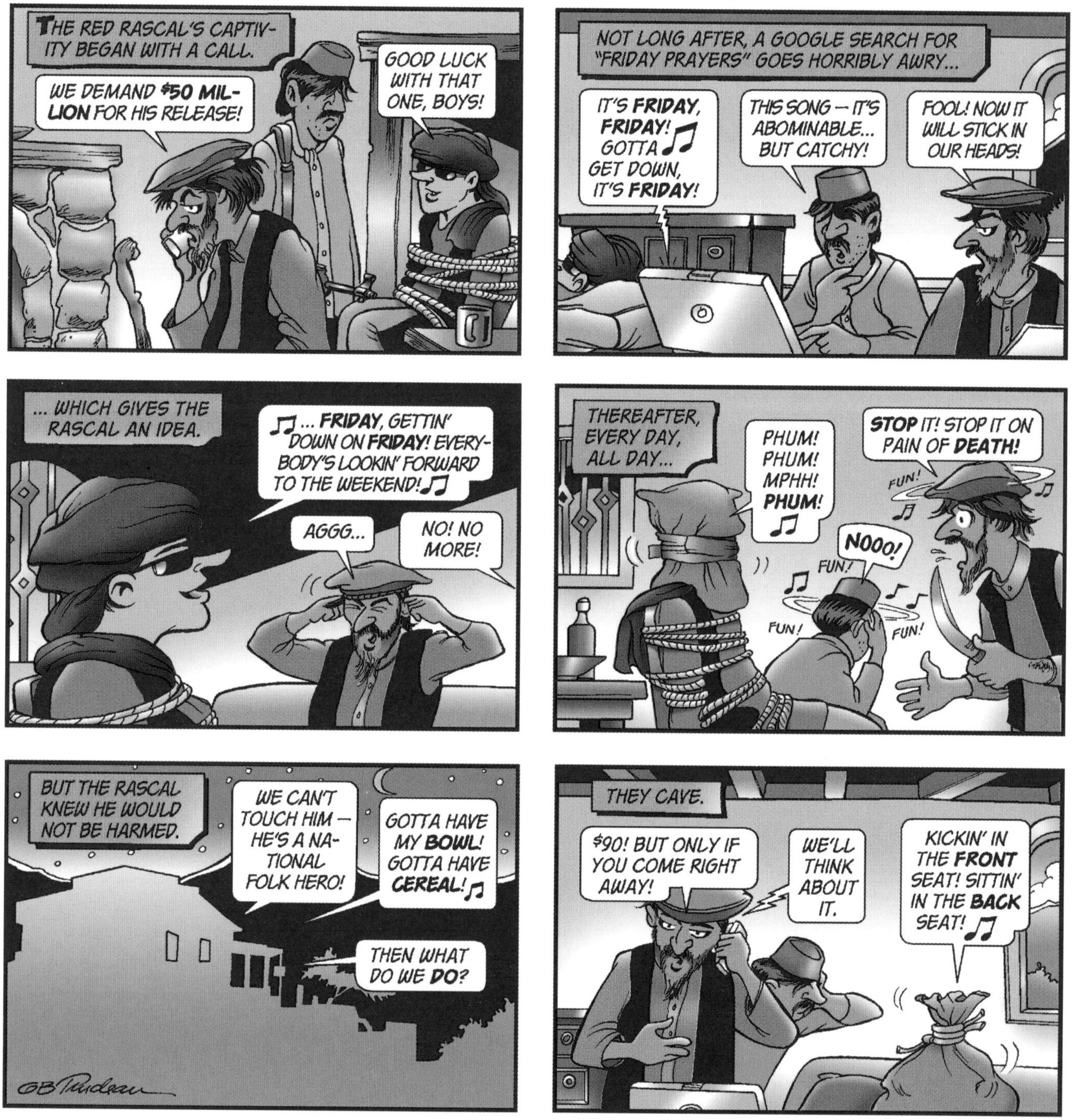
THE RED RASCAL'S CAPTIVITY BEGAN WITH A CALL.
WE DEMAND $50 MILLION FOR HIS RELEASE!
GOOD LUCK WITH THAT ONE, BOYS!
NOT LONG AFTER, A GOOGLE SEARCH FOR "FRIDAY PRAYERS" GOES HORRIBLY AWRY...
IT'S FRIDAY, FRIDAY! GOTTA GET DOWN, IT'S FRIDAY!
THIS SONG — IT'S ABOMINABLE... BUT CATCHY!
FOOL! NOW IT WILL STICK IN OUR HEADS!
... WHICH GIVES THE RASCAL AN IDEA.
... FRIDAY, GETTIN' DOWN ON FRIDAY! EVERYBODY'S LOOKIN' FORWARD TO THE WEEKEND!
AGGG...
NO! NO MORE!
THEREAFTER, EVERY DAY, ALL DAY...
PHUM! PHUM! MPHH! PHUM!
STOP IT! STOP IT ON PAIN OF DEATH!
FUN!
NOOO!
FUN!
FUN!
FUN!
BUT THE RASCAL KNEW HE WOULD NOT BE HARMED.
WE CAN'T TOUCH HIM — HE'S A NATIONAL FOLK HERO!
GOTTA HAVE MY BOWL! GOTTA HAVE CEREAL!
THEN WHAT DO WE DO?
GB Trudeau
THEY CAVE.
$90! BUT ONLY IF YOU COME RIGHT AWAY!
WE'LL THINK ABOUT IT.
KICKIN' IN THE FRONT SEAT! SITTIN' IN THE BACK SEAT!

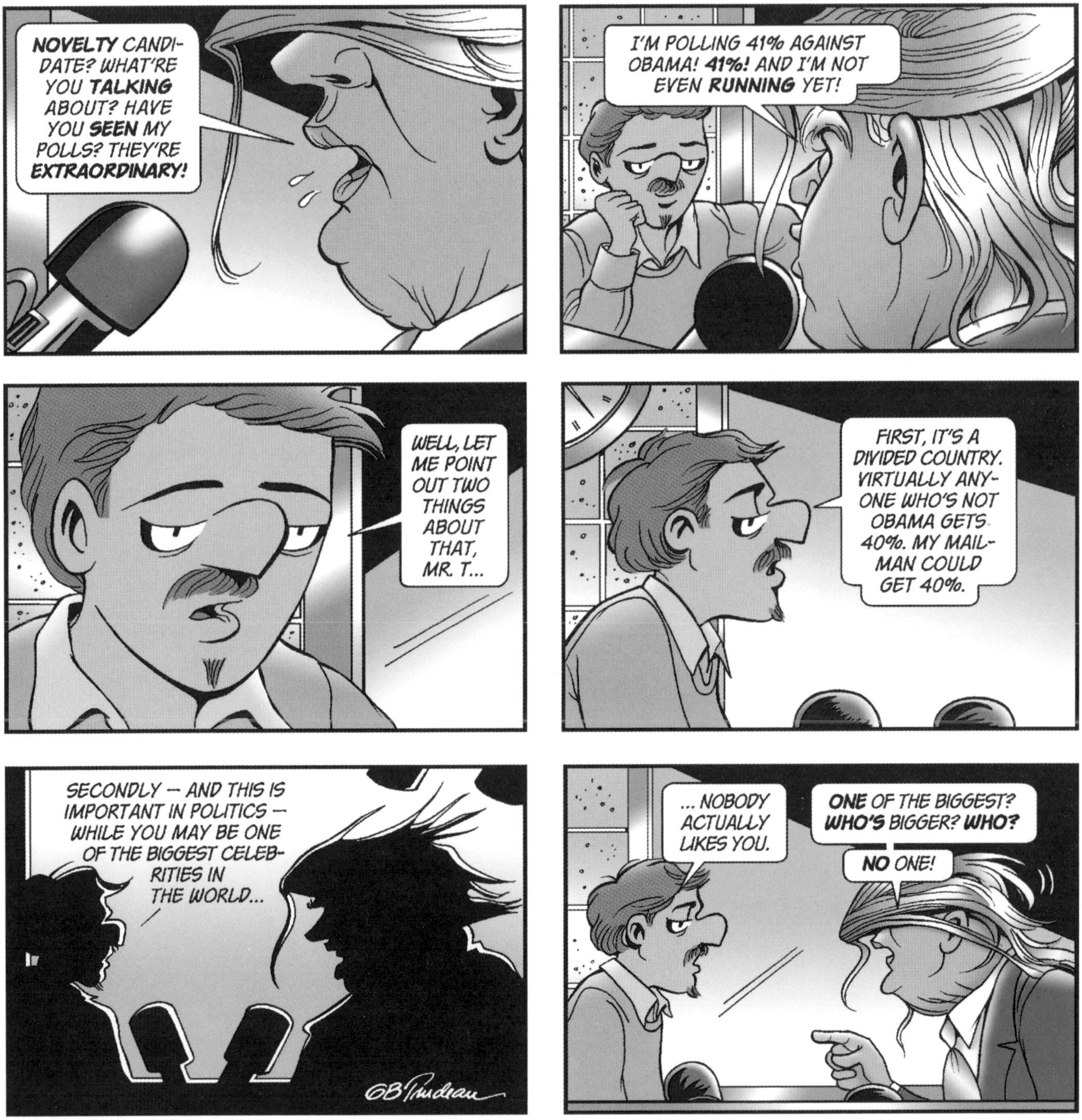
NOVELTY CANDIDATE? WHAT'RE YOU TALKING ABOUT? HAVE YOU SEEN MY POLLS? THEY'RE EXTRAORDINARY!
I'M POLLING 41% AGAINST OBAMA! 41%! AND I'M NOT EVEN RUNNING YET!
WELL, LET ME POINT OUT TWO THINGS ABOUT THAT, MR. T...
FIRST, IT'S A DIVIDED COUNTRY. VIRTUALLY ANYONE WHO'S NOT OBAMA GETS 40%. MY MAILMAN COULD GET 40%.
SECONDLY — AND THIS IS IMPORTANT IN POLITICS — WHILE YOU MAY BE ONE OF THE BIGGEST CELEBRITIES IN THE WORLD...
GB Trudeau
... NOBODY ACTUALLY LIKES YOU.
ONE OF THE BIGGEST? WHO'S BIGGER? WHO?
NO ONE!

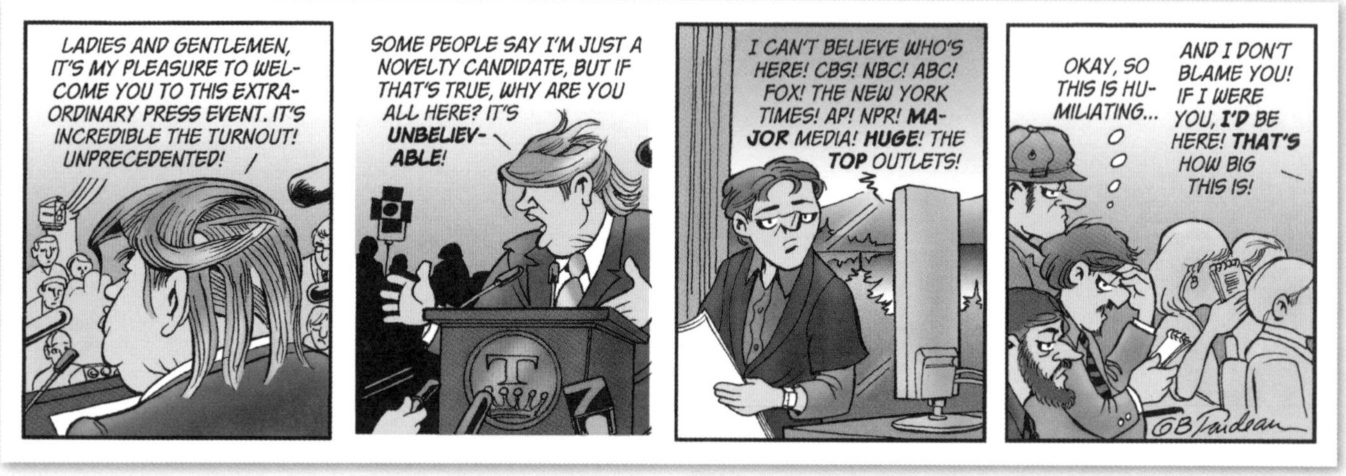
LADIES AND GENTLEMEN, IT'S MY PLEASURE TO WELCOME YOU TO THIS EXTRAORDINARY PRESS EVENT. IT'S INCREDIBLE THE TURNOUT! UNPRECEDENTED!
SOME PEOPLE SAY I'M JUST A NOVELTY CANDIDATE, BUT IF THAT'S TRUE, WHY ARE YOU ALL HERE? IT'S UNBELIEVABLE!
I CAN'T BELIEVE WHO'S HERE! CBS! NBC! ABC! FOX! THE NEW YORK TIMES! AP! NPR! MAJOR MEDIA! HUGE! THE TOP OUTLETS!
OKAY, SO THIS IS HUMILIATING...
AND I DON'T BLAME YOU! IF I WERE YOU, I'D BE HERE! THAT'S HOW BIG THIS IS!
©B Trudeau

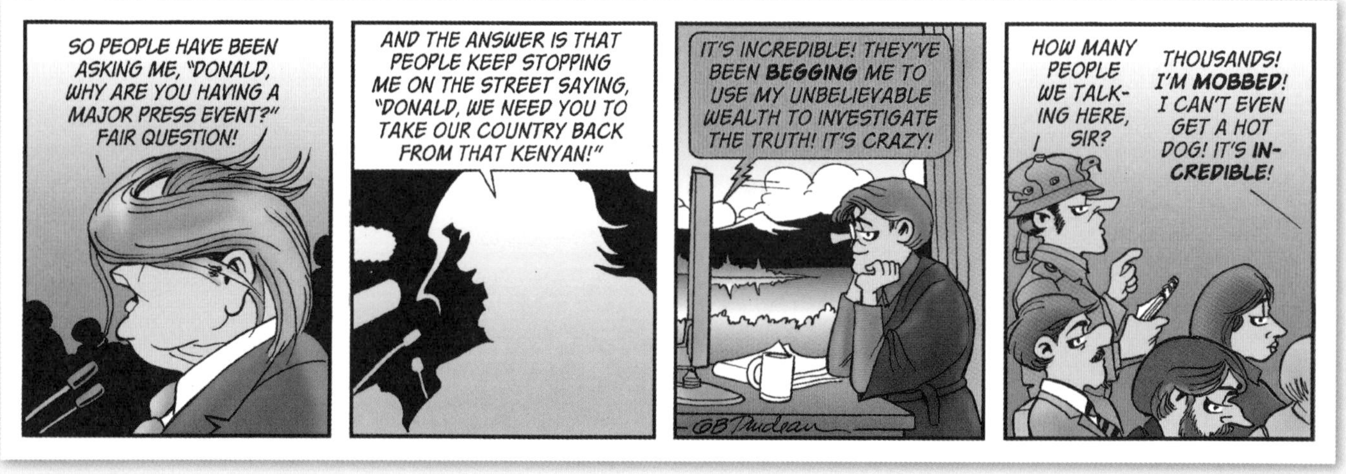
SO PEOPLE HAVE BEEN ASKING ME, "DONALD, WHY ARE YOU HAVING A MAJOR PRESS EVENT?" FAIR QUESTION!
AND THE ANSWER IS THAT PEOPLE KEEP STOPPING ME ON THE STREET SAYING, "DONALD, WE NEED YOU TO TAKE OUR COUNTRY BACK FROM THAT KENYAN!"
IT'S INCREDIBLE! THEY'VE BEEN BEGGING ME TO USE MY UNBELIEVABLE WEALTH TO INVESTIGATE THE TRUTH! IT'S CRAZY!
©B Trudeau
HOW MANY PEOPLE WE TALKING HERE, SIR?
THOUSANDS! I'M MOBBED! I CAN'T EVEN GET A HOT DOG! IT'S INCREDIBLE!

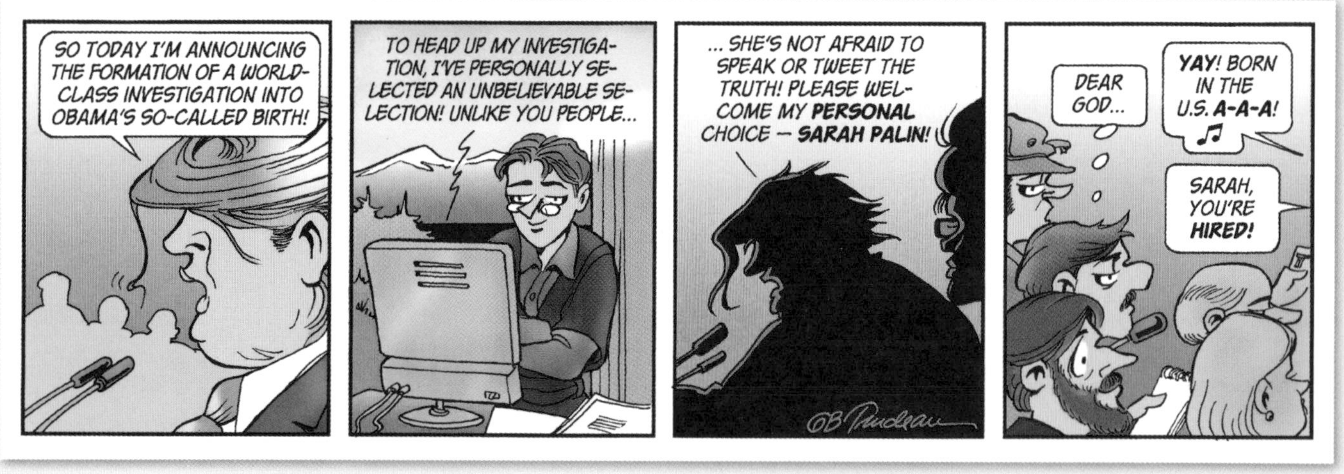
SO TODAY I'M ANNOUNCING THE FORMATION OF A WORLD-CLASS INVESTIGATION INTO OBAMA'S SO-CALLED BIRTH!
TO HEAD UP MY INVESTIGATION, I'VE PERSONALLY SELECTED AN UNBELIEVABLE SELECTION! UNLIKE YOU PEOPLE...
... SHE'S NOT AFRAID TO SPEAK OR TWEET THE TRUTH! PLEASE WELCOME MY PERSONAL CHOICE — SARAH PALIN!
©B Trudeau
DEAR GOD...
YAY! BORN IN THE U.S. A-A-A! ♫
SARAH, YOU'RE HIRED!

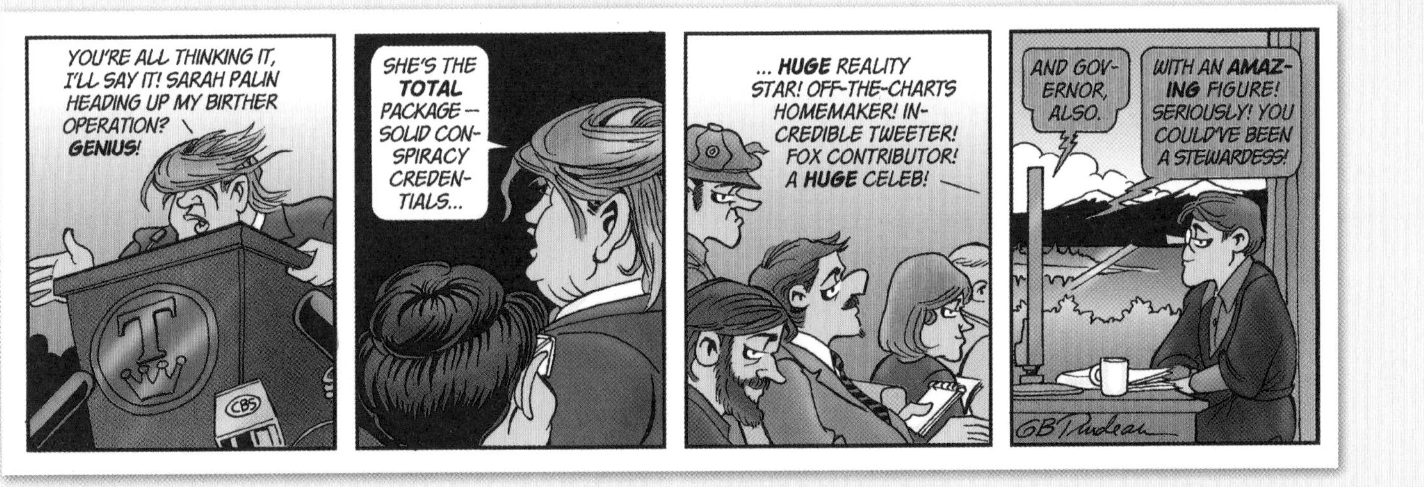
YOU'RE ALL THINKING IT, I'LL SAY IT! SARAH PALIN HEADING UP MY BIRTHER OPERATION? GENIUS!
SHE'S THE TOTAL PACKAGE -- SOLID CONSPIRACY CREDENTIALS...
... HUGE REALITY STAR! OFF-THE-CHARTS HOMEMAKER! INCREDIBLE TWEETER! FOX CONTRIBUTOR! A HUGE CELEB!
AND GOVERNOR, ALSO.
WITH AN AMAZING FIGURE! SERIOUSLY! YOU COULD'VE BEEN A STEWARDESS!
CBS
GBTrudeau

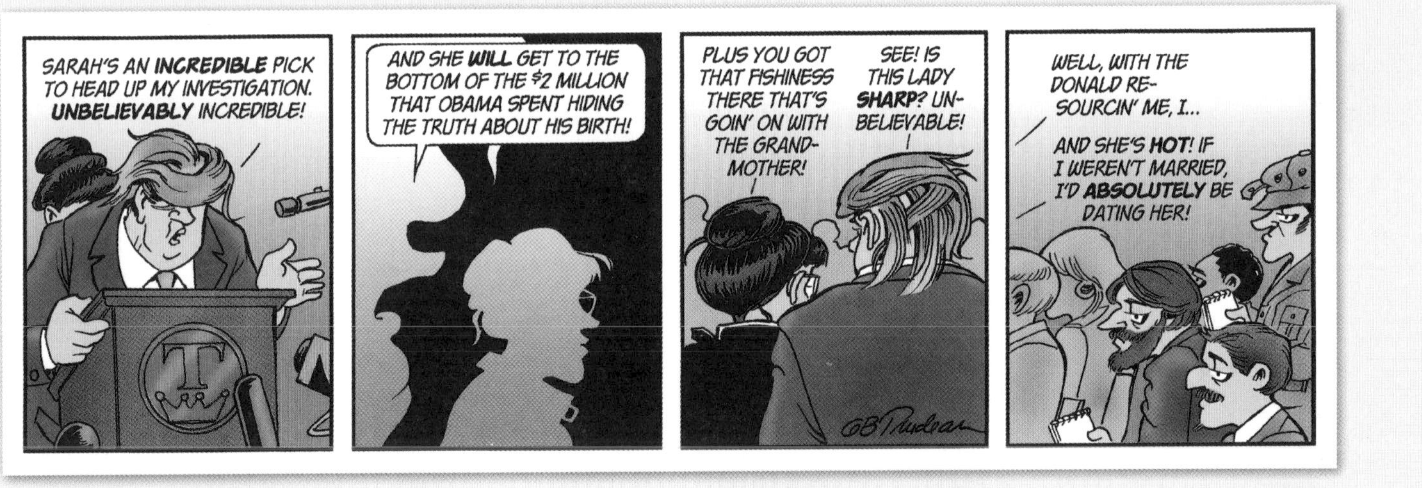
SARAH'S AN INCREDIBLE PICK TO HEAD UP MY INVESTIGATION. UNBELIEVABLY INCREDIBLE!
AND SHE WILL GET TO THE BOTTOM OF THE $2 MILLION THAT OBAMA SPENT HIDING THE TRUTH ABOUT HIS BIRTH!
PLUS YOU GOT THAT FISHINESS THERE THAT'S GOIN' ON WITH THE GRANDMOTHER!
SEE! IS THIS LADY SHARP? UNBELIEVABLE!
WELL, WITH THE DONALD RESOURCIN' ME, I...
AND SHE'S HOT! IF I WEREN'T MARRIED, I'D ABSOLUTELY BE DATING HER!
GBTrudeau

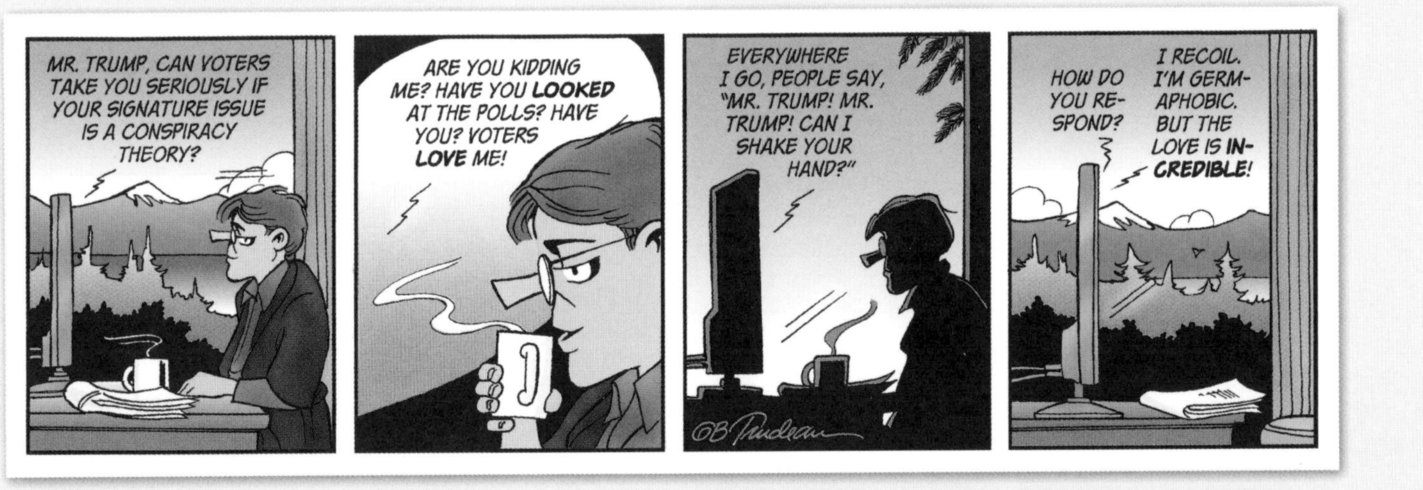
MR. TRUMP, CAN VOTERS TAKE YOU SERIOUSLY IF YOUR SIGNATURE ISSUE IS A CONSPIRACY THEORY?
ARE YOU KIDDING ME? HAVE YOU LOOKED AT THE POLLS? HAVE YOU? VOTERS LOVE ME!
EVERYWHERE I GO, PEOPLE SAY, "MR. TRUMP! MR. TRUMP! CAN I SHAKE YOUR HAND?"
HOW DO YOU RESPOND?
I RECOIL. I'M GERMAPHOBIC. BUT THE LOVE IS INCREDIBLE!
GBTrudeau

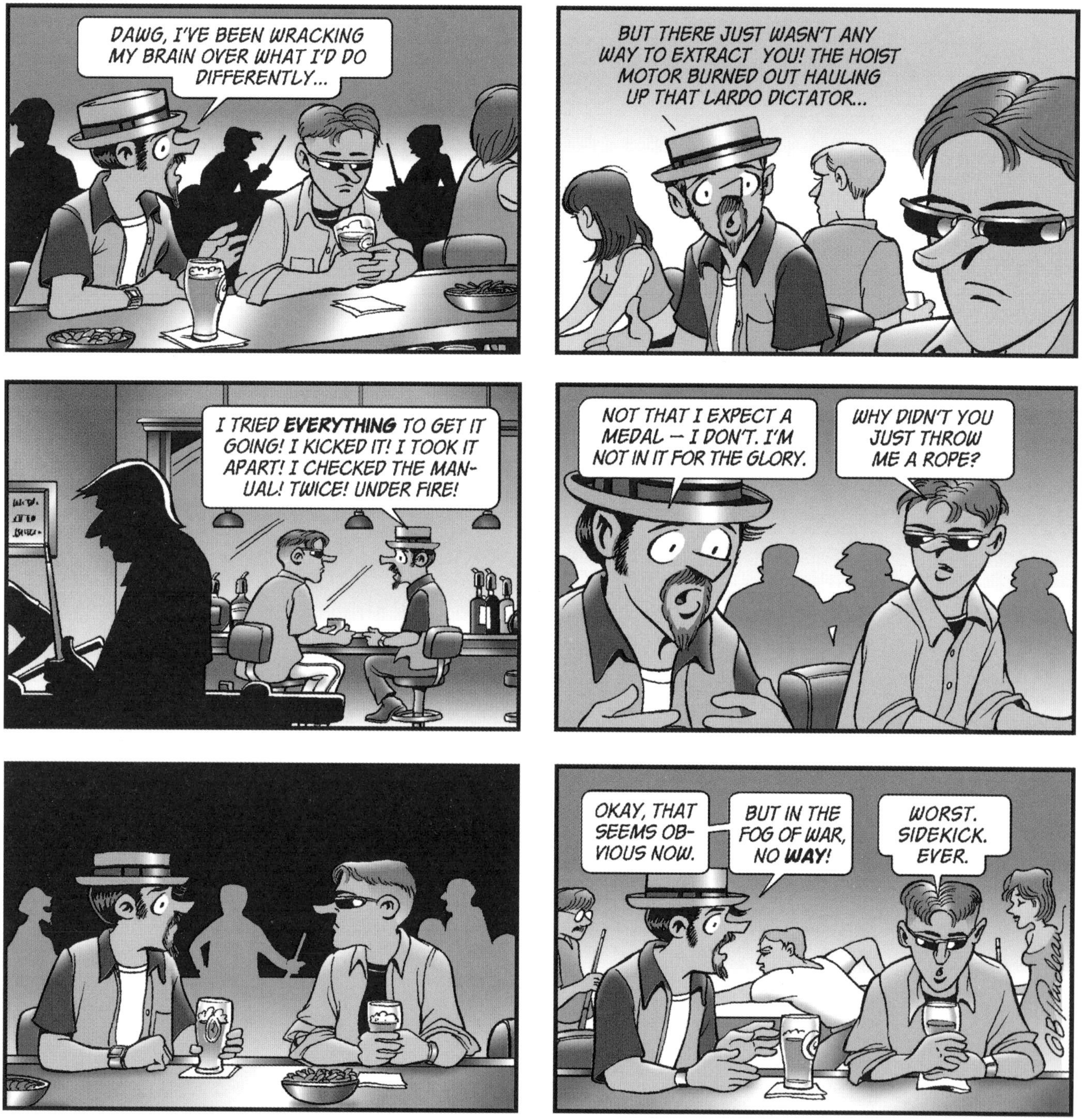
DAWG, I'VE BEEN WRACKING MY BRAIN OVER WHAT I'D DO DIFFERENTLY...
BUT THERE JUST WASN'T ANY WAY TO EXTRACT YOU! THE HOIST MOTOR BURNED OUT HAULING UP THAT LARDO DICTATOR...
I TRIED **EVERYTHING** TO GET IT GOING! I KICKED IT! I TOOK IT APART! I CHECKED THE MANUAL! TWICE! UNDER FIRE!
NOT THAT I EXPECT A MEDAL — I DON'T. I'M NOT IN IT FOR THE GLORY.
WHY DIDN'T YOU JUST THROW ME A ROPE?
OKAY, THAT SEEMS OBVIOUS NOW.
BUT IN THE FOG OF WAR, NO **WAY**!
WORST. SIDEKICK. EVER.
GBTrudeau